P9-CKK-280

Praise for *The Lucifer Effect*:

'Philip Zimbardo's anatomy of human psychology and contemporary culture is as scholarly as it is scary. His books take us where angels fear to treat, uncovering the "Lucifer" that sits incubating in each individual and every human institution . . .This timely study screams out at us to be on the alert, to be ever mindful and ever ready lest we fall into this heart of darkness. We should be grateful for his insight and heed his warning . . . at out peril.' Brian Keenan, author of *An Evil Cradling*

'Detailed and absorbing . . . masterly and honest . . . Zimbardo has written not just another book of applied moral philosophy. On the contrary, he has thrown light on the nature of morality itself, and on the nature of human beings ' Mary Warnock, *Times Higher Education Supplement*

'a formidable piece of research into the nature of evil and the systems and situations that foster it . . . told with precision, in detail and with narrative skill' *Observer*

'*The Lucifer Effect* is an important book; if enough people absorbed its argument, we might find ourselves in a better polity' *Sunday Times*

'Professor Zimbardo deserves heartfelt thanks for disclosing and illuminating the dark, hidden corners of the human soul' Václav Havel, former president of the Czech Republic.

'an absorbing work, packed with insight into human behaviour and streetwise observations' *Literary Review*

'Zimbardo has a well-earned reputation for tackling large and complex problems. In this book, he takes on nothing less than the psychology of evil itself . . . This important book should be required reading not only for social scientists, but also for politicians, decision makers, educators and just about anyone else disturbed by the self-destructive directions in which the United States and the rest of the world seem to be moving' Robert Levine, *American Scientist*

'This is a book for our times, a multilayered classic. What is truly remarkable is its blending of sensitive personal exploration, brilliant social-psychological analysis, and sustained ethical passion' Robert Jay Lifton, author of *The Nazi Doctors* and *Superpower Syndrome*

'If there has been a more important and compelling book written in the last twenty-five years, I've not encountered it. Phil Zimbardo's engaging and beautifully written tour de force uncovers the sources of evil – big and small. *The Lucifer Effect* accomplishes more than simply making the darkness visible; it also helps to make lightness possible. It is crucial reading for everyone' Jon D. Hanson, Professor of Law, Harvard Law School

'Philip Zimbardo is one of the most distinguished social scientists of our age . . . if you have any interest in the nature of evil you will read this book . . . Zimbardo is not merely recording academic accounts, he is specifically challenging us to look at our behaviour' *Catholic Herald*

'The most disturbing portraits in [*The Lucifer Effect*] are not of our rulers, but of the rest of us. As prisoners in an alien jail, Zimbardo suggests, most of us would be craven. As guards, we would be vicious to our captives, or would stand by and watch as others hurt them' *Telegraph*

'This important book is very readable and I recommend it' Stuart Wheeler, *Spectator* magazine

'As one of the Senior Criminal Investigation Division agents who saw conditions at Abu Ghraib first hand, it is clear to me that Phil Zimbardo truly understands all the factors that come into play here. His book is a must read for military leaders, mental health professionals and law enforcement officers' CW4 Marcia Drewry, Retired USA CIDC Special Agent

'Only Zimbardo, with his personal responsibility and experience of the Stanford Prison Experiment, could have written this important, multi-layered book, a tour de force which is absorbing, stimulating, instructive, brimful of evidence and information' *Human Givens* Journal

About the Author

PHILIP ZIMBARDO is professor emeritus of psychology at Stanford University and has also taught at Yale, New York University, and Columbia. He is the co-author of the classic psychology texts *Psychology and Life* and *Shyness,* which together have sold more than 2.5 million copies. Zimbardo has been president of the American Psychological Association and is now director of the Stanford Center on Interdisciplinary Policy, Education, and Research on Terrorism. He also narrated the award-winning PBS series *Discovering Psychology,* which he helped create. In 2004, he acted as an expert witness in the court-martial hearings of one of the U.S. Army reservists accused of criminal behavior in the Abu Ghraib Prison in Iraq. His informative website www.prisonexperiment.org is visited by millions every year. Visit the author's personal website at www.zimbardo.com. Also visit this book's website at www.LuciferEffect.com.

Also by Philip Zimbardo

Shyness: What It Is, What to Do About It

The Shy Child (co-author)

Psychology and Life (co-author)

Psychology: Core Concepts (co-author)

*The Psychology of Attitude
Change and Social Influence* (co-author)

THE
LUCIFER
EFFECT

How Good People Turn Evil

Philip Zimbardo

RIDER

LONDON · SYDNEY · AUCKLAND · JOHANNESBURG

1 3 5 7 9 10 8 6 4 2

First published in the UK in 2007 by Rider, an imprint of Ebury Publishing
This paperback edition published by Rider in 2009
First published in the USA by Random House, Inc., in 2007

Ebury Publishing is a Random House Group company

Copyright © Philip G. Zimbardo 2007

Philip G. Zimbardo has asserted his right to be identified as the author of this Work in
accordance with the Copyright, Designs and Patents Act 1988.

All rights reserved. No part of this publication may be reproduced, stored in a retrieval system,
or transmitted in any form or by any means, electronic, mechanical, photocopying, recording
or otherwise, without the prior permission of the copyright owner.

The Random House Group Limited Reg. No. 954009

Addresses for companies within the Random House Group can be found at
www.rbooks.co.uk

A CIP catalogue record for this book is available from the British Library

The Random House Group Limited supports The Forest Stewardship
Council (FSC), the leading international forest certification organisation. All our
titles that are printed on Greenpeace approved FSC certified paper carry the FSC logo. Our paper
procurement policy can be found at
www.rbooks.co.uk/environment

Printed in the UK by CPI Cox & Wyman, Reading, RG1 8EX

ISBN 9781846041037

Copies are available at special rates for bulk orders. Contact the sales development team on 020
7840 8487 or visit www.booksforpromotions.co.uk for more information.

To buy books by your favourite authors and register for offers, visit www.rbooks.co.uk

Dedicated to the serene heroine of my life,

Christina Maslach Zimbardo

Preface

I wish I could say that writing this book was a labor of love; it was not that for a single moment of the two years it took to complete. First of all, it was emotionally painful to review all of the videotapes from the Stanford Prison Experiment (SPE) and to read over and over the typescripts prepared from them. Time had dimmed my memory of the extent of creative evil in which many of the guards engaged, the extent of the suffering of many of the prisoners, and the extent of my passivity in allowing the abuses to continue for as long as I did—an evil of inaction.

I had also forgotten that the first part of this book was actually begun thirty years ago under contract from a different publisher. However, I quit shortly after beginning to write because I was not ready to relive the experience while I was still so close to it. I am glad that I did not hang in and force myself to continue writing then because this is the right time. Now I am wiser and able to bring a more mature perspective to this complex task. Further, the parallels between the abuses at Abu Ghraib and the events in the SPE have given our Stanford prison experience added validity, which in turn sheds light on the psychological dynamics that contributed to creating horrific abuses in that real prison.

A second emotionally draining obstacle to writing was becoming personally and intensely involved in fully researching the Abu Ghraib abuses and tortures. As an expert witness for one of the MP prison guards, I became more like an investigative reporter than a social psychologist. I worked at uncovering everything I could about this young man, from intensive interviews with him and conversations and correspondence with his family members to checking on his background in corrections and in the military, as well as with other military personnel who had served in that dungeon. I came to feel what it was like to walk in his boots on the Tier 1A night shift from 4 P.M. to 4 A.M. every single night for forty nights without a break.

As an expert witness testifying at his trial to the situational forces that contributed to the specific abuses he had perpetrated, I was given access to all of the many hundreds of digitally documented images of depravity. That was an ugly and unwelcomed task. In addition, I was provided with all of the then-available reports from various military and civilian investigating committees. Because I was told that I would not be allowed to bring detailed notes to the trial, I had to memorize as many of their critical features and conclusions as I could. That cognitive challenge added to the terrific emotional strain that arose after Sergeant Ivan "Chip" Frederick was given a harsh sentence and I became an informal psychological counselor for him and his wife, Martha. Over time, I became, for them, "Uncle Phil."

I was doubly frustrated and angry, first by the military's unwillingness to accept any of the many mitigating circumstances I had detailed that had directly contributed to his abusive behavior and should have reduced his harsh prison sentence. The prosecutor and judge refused to consider any idea that situational forces could influence individual behavior. Theirs was the standard individualism conception that is shared by most people in our culture. It is the idea that the fault was entirely "dispositional," the consequence of Sergeant Chip Frederick's freely chosen rational decision to engage in evil. Added to my distress was the realization that many of the "independent" investigative reports clearly laid the blame for the abuses at the feet of senior officers and on their dysfunctional or "absentee landlord" leadership. These reports, chaired by generals and former high-ranking government officials, made evident that the military and civilian chain of command had built a "bad barrel" in which a bunch of good soldiers became transformed into "bad apples."

Had I written this book shortly after the end of the Stanford Prison Experiment, I would have been content to detail the ways in which situational forces are more powerful than we think, or that we acknowledge, in shaping our behavior in many contexts. However, I would have missed the big picture, the bigger power for creating evil out of good—that of the System, the complex of powerful forces that create the Situation. A large body of evidence in social psychology supports the concept that situational power triumphs over individual power in given contexts. I refer to that evidence in several chapters. However, most psychologists have been insensitive to the deeper sources of power that inhere in the political, economic, religious, historic, and cultural matrix that defines situations and gives them legitimate or illegitimate existence. A full understanding of the dynamics of human behavior requires that we recognize the extent and limits of personal power, situational power, and systemic power.

Changing or preventing undesirable behavior of individuals or groups requires an understanding of what strengths, virtues, and vulnerabilities they bring into a given situation. Then, we need to recognize more fully the complex of situational forces that are operative in given behavioral settings. Modifying them, or learning to avoid them, can have a greater impact on reducing undesirable individual reactions than remedial actions directed only at changing the people in the situation. That means adopting a public health approach in place of the standard medical model approach to curing individual ills and wrongs. However, unless we become sensitive to the real power of the System, which is invariably hidden behind a veil of secrecy, and fully understand its own set of rules and regulations, behavioral change will be transient and situational change illusory. Throughout this book, I repeat the mantra that attempting to understand the situational and systemic contributions to any individual's behavior does not excuse the person or absolve him or her from responsibility in engaging in immoral, illegal, or evil deeds.

In reflecting on the reasons that I have spent much of my professional career studying the psychology of evil—of violence, anonymity, aggression, vandalism, torture, and terrorism—I must also consider the situational formative force acting upon me. Growing up in poverty in the South Bronx, New York City, ghetto shaped much of my outlook on life and my priorities. Urban ghetto life is all about surviving by developing useful "street-smart" strategies. That means figuring out who has power that can be used against you or to help you, whom to avoid, and with whom you should ingratiate yourself. It means deciphering subtle situational cues for when to bet and when to fold, creating reciprocal obligations, and determining what it takes to make the transition from follower to leader.

In those days, before heroin and cocaine hit the Bronx, ghetto life was about people without possessions, about kids whose most precious resource in the absence of toys and technologies was other kids to play with. Some of these kids became victims or perpetrators of violence; some kids I thought were good ended up doing some really bad things. Sometimes it was apparent what the catalyst was. For instance, consider Donny's father, who punished him for any perceived wrongdoing by stripping him naked and making him kneel on rice kernels in the bathtub. This "father as torturer" was at other times charming, especially around the ladies who lived in the tenement. As a young teenager, Donny, broken by that experience, ended up in prison. Another kid took out his frustrations by skinning cats alive. As part of the gang initiation process we all had to steal, fight against another kid, do some daring deeds, and intimidate girls and Jewish kids going to synagogue. None of this was ever considered evil or even bad; it was merely obeying the group leader and conforming to the norms of the gang.

For us kids systemic power resided in the big bad janitors who kicked you off their stoops and the heartless landlords who could evict whole families by getting the authorities to cart their belongings onto the street for failure to pay the rent. I still feel for their public shame. But our worst enemy was the police, who would swoop down on us as we played stickball in the streets (with a broomstick bat and Spalding rubber ball). Without offering any reason, they would confiscate our stickball bats and force us to stop playing in the street. Since there was not a playground within a mile of where we lived, streets were all we had, and there was little danger posed to citizens by our pink rubber ball. I recall a time when we hid the bats as the police approached, but the cops singled me out to spill the beans as to their location. When I refused, one cop said he would arrest me and as he pushed me into his squad car my head smashed against the door. After that, I never trusted grown-ups in uniform until proven otherwise.

With such rearing, all in the absence of any parental oversight—because in those days kids and parents never mixed on the streets—it is obvious where my curiosity about human nature came from, especially its darker side. Thus, *The Lucifer Effect* has been incubating in me for many years, from my ghetto sandbox days through my formal training in psychological science, and has led me to ask big questions and answer them with empirical evidence.

The structure of this book is somewhat unusual. It starts off with an opening chapter that outlines the theme of the transformation of human character, of good people and angels turning to do bad things, even evil, devilish things. It raises the fundamental question of how well we really know ourselves, how confident we can be in predicting what we would or would not do in situations we have never before encountered. Could we, like God's favorite angel, Lucifer, ever be led into the temptation to do the unthinkable to others?

The segment of chapters on the Stanford Prison Experiment unfolds in great detail as our extended case study of the transformation of individual college students as they play the randomly assigned roles of prisoner or guard in a mock prison—that became all too real. The chapter-by-chapter chronology is presented in a cinematic format, as a personal narrative told in the present tense with minimal psychological interpretation. Only after that study concludes—it had to be terminated prematurely—do we consider what we learned from it, describe and explain the evidence gathered from it, and elaborate upon the psychological processes that were involved in it.

One of the dominant conclusions of the Stanford Prison Experiment is that the pervasive yet subtle power of a host of situational variables can dominate an individual's will to resist. That conclusion is given greater depth in a series of chapters detailing this phenomenon across a body of social science research. We see how a range of research participants—other college student subjects and average citizen volunteers alike—have come to conform, comply, obey, and be readily seduced into doing things they could not imagine doing when they were outside those situational force fields. A set of dynamic psychological processes is outlined that can induce good people to do evil, among them deindividuation, obedience to authority, passivity in the face of threats, self-justification, and rationalization. Dehumanization is one of the central processes in the transformation of ordinary, normal people into indifferent or even wanton perpetrators of evil. Dehumanization is like a cortical cataract that clouds one's thinking and fosters the perception that other people are less than human. It makes some people come to see those others as enemies deserving of torment, torture, and annihilation.

With this set of analytical tools at our disposal, we turn to reflect upon the causes of the horrendous abuses and torture of prisoners at Iraq's Abu Ghraib Prison by the U.S. Military Police guarding them. The allegation that these immoral deeds were the sadistic work of a few rogue soldiers, so-called bad apples, is challenged by examining the parallels that exist in the situational forces and psychological processes that operated in that prison with those in our Stanford prison. We examine in depth, the Place, the Person, and the Situation to draw conclusions about the causative forces involved in creating the abusive behaviors that are depicted in the revolting set of "trophy photos" taken by the soldiers in the process of tormenting their prisoners.

However, it is then time to go up the explanatory chain from person to situation to system. Relying on a half dozen of the investigative reports into these abuses and other evidence from a variety of human rights and legal sources, I adopt a prosecutorial stance to put the System on trial. Using the limits of our legal system, which demands that individuals and not situations or systems be tried for wrongdoing, I bring charges against a quartet of senior military officers and then extend the argument for command complicity to the civilian command structure within the Bush administration. The reader, as juror, will decide if the evidence supports the finding of guilty as charged for each of the accused.

This rather grim journey into the heart and mind of darkness is turned around in the final chapter. It is time for some good news about human nature, about what we as individuals can do to challenge situational and systemic power. In all the research cited and in our real-world examples, there were always some individuals who resisted, who did not yield to temptation. What delivered them from evil was not some inherent magical goodness but rather, more likely, an understanding, however intuitive, of mental and social tactics of resistance. I outline a set of such strategies and tactics to help anyone be more able to resist unwanted social influence. This advice is based on a combination of my own experiences and the wisdom of my social psychological colleagues who are experts in the domains of influence and persuasion. (It is supplemented and expanded upon in a module available on the website for this book, www.lucifereffect.com).

Finally, when most give in and few rebel, the rebels can be considered heroes for resisting the powerful forces toward compliance, conformity, and obedience. We have come to think of our heroes as special, set apart from us ordinary mortals by their daring deeds or lifelong sacrifices. Here we recognize that such special individuals do exist, but that they are the exception among the ranks of heroes, the few who make such sacrifices. They are a special breed who organize their lives around a humanitarian cause, for example. By contrast, most others we recognize as heroes are heroes of the moment, of the situation, who act decisively when the call to service is sounded. So, *The Lucifer Effect* journey ends on a positive note by celebrating the ordinary hero who lives within each of us. In contrast to the "banality of evil," which posits that ordinary people can be responsible for the most despicable acts of cruelty and degradation of their fellows, I posit the "banality of heroism," which unfurls the banner of the heroic Everyman and Everywoman who heed the call to service to humanity when their time comes to act. When that bell rings, they will know that it rings for them. It sounds a call to uphold what is best in human nature that rises above the powerful pressures of Situation and System as the profound assertion of human dignity opposing evil.

Acknowledgments

This book would not have been possible without a great deal of help at every stage along the long journey from conception to its realization in this final form.

EMPIRICAL RESEARCH

It all began with the planning, execution, and analysis of the experiment we did at Stanford University back in August 1971. The immediate impetus for this research came out of an undergraduate class project on the psychology of imprisonment, headed by David Jaffe, who later became the warden in our Stanford Prison Experiment. In preparation for conducting this experiment, and to better understand the mentality of prisoners and correctional staff, as well as to explore what were the critical features in the psychological nature of any prison experience, I taught a summer school course at Stanford University covering these topics. My co-instructor was Andrew Carlo Prescott, who had recently been paroled from a series of long confinements in California prisons. Carlo came to serve as an invaluable consultant and dynamic head of our "Adult Authority Parole Board." Two graduate students, William Curtis Banks and Craig Haney, were fully engaged at every stage in the production of this unusual research project. Craig has used this experience as a springboard into a most successful career in psychology and law, becoming a leading advocate for prisoner rights and authoring a number of articles and chapters with me on various topics related to the institution of prisons. I thank them each for their contribution to that study and its intellectual and practical aftermath. In addition, my appreciation goes to each of those college students who volunteered for an experience that, decades later, some of them still cannot forget. As I also say in the text, I apologize to them again for any suffering they endured during and following this research.

SECONDARY RESEARCH

The task of assembling the archival prison experiment videos into DVD formats from which transcripts could be prepared fell to Sean Bruich and Scott Thompson, two exceptional Stanford students. In addition to highlighting significant episodes in these materials, Sean and Scott also helped pull together a wide array of background materials that we had gathered on various aspects of the study.

Tanya Zimbardo and Marissa Allen assisted with the next task of helping to organize and assemble extensive background materials from media clippings, my notes, and assorted articles. A team of other Stanford students, notably Kieran O'Connor and Matt Estrada, expertly conducted reference checking. Matt also transferred my audiotaped interview with Sergeant Chip Frederick into an understandable typescript.

I value the feedback that I received on various chapters in first and second drafts from colleagues and students alike, among them Adam Breckenridge, Stephen Behnke, Tom Blass, Rose McDermott, and Jason Weaver. Anthony Pratkanis and Cindy Wang earn special thanks for their assistance with the section of the final chapter that deals with resisting unwanted influence, as does Zeno Franco for his contributions to the new views on the psychology of heroism.

My understanding of the military situation at Abu Ghraib and other theaters of the war benefited from the wisdom of Warrant Officer Marci Drewry and of Colonel Larry James, also a military psychologist. Doug Bracewell has continually supplied me with useful online sources of information about a host of topics related to issues I deal with in the two chapters of the book on Abu Ghraib. Gary Myers, the legal counsel for Sergeant Frederick, not only served on this case for an extended period without remuneration but also provided me with all the source materials and information that I needed to make sense of that complex setting. Adam Zimbardo offered a perceptive analysis of the sexual nature of the "trophy photos" that emerged from the "fun and games" on Tier 1 A's night shift.

In partitioning my acknowledgments, a major share goes to Bob Johnson (my psychologist co-author buddy on our introductory psychology textbook, *Core Concepts*). Bob read the entire manuscript and offered endlessly valuable suggestions on ways to improve it, as did Sasha Lubomirsky, who helped to coordinate Bob's input with that of Rose Zimbardo. Rose is a Distinguished Professor of English Literature who made sure that every sentence of this book functioned as it should to convey my message to general readers. Thanks to each of them for handling this chore with such grace and good sense.

Thanks also to my Random House editor, Will Murphy, for his meticulous editing, a lost art among many editors, and his valiant attempt to pare it down to essential themes. Lynn Anderson performed admirably and astutely as copy editor, who, along with Vincent La Scala, added consistency and clarity to my messages. John Brockman has been the guardian angel agent for this book and its promotion.

Finally, having written for a dozen or so hours on end, day in and night out, my aching body was prepped for the next round by my massage therapist, Gerry Huber, of Healing Winds Massage in San Francisco, and by Ann Hollingsworth of the Gualala Sea Spa, whenever I worked at my Sea Ranch hideout.

To each of these helpers, family, friends, colleagues, and students, who enabled me to transform thoughts into words into a manuscript and into this book, please accept my sincerest thanks.

Ciao,
Phil Zimbardo

Contents

List of Illustrations

THE
LUCIFER
EFFECT

M. C. Escher's "Circle Limit IV" © 2006 The M. C. Escher Company-Holland.
All rights reserved. www.mcescher.com.

CHAPTER ONE

The Psychology of Evil:
Situated Character Transformations

The mind is its own place, and in itself can make a heaven of hell, a hell of heaven.

—John Milton, *Paradise Lost*

Look at this remarkable image for a moment. Now close your eyes and conjure it in your memory.

Does your mind's eye see the many white angels dancing about the dark heavens? Or do you see the many black demons, horned devils inhabiting the bright white space of Hell? In this illusion by the artist M. C. Escher, both perspectives are equally possible. Once aware of the congruence between good and evil, you cannot see only one and not the other. In what follows, I will not allow you to drift back to the comfortable separation of Your Good and Faultless Side from Their Evil and Wicked Side. "Am I capable of evil?" is the question that I want you to consider over and over again as we journey together to alien environments.

Three psychological truths emerge from Escher's image. First, the world is filled with both good and evil—was, is, will always be. Second, the barrier between good and evil is permeable and nebulous. And third, it is possible for angels to become devils and, perhaps more difficult to conceive, for devils to become angels.

Perhaps this image reminds you of the ultimate transformation of good into evil, the metamorphosis of Lucifer into Satan. Lucifer, the "light bearer," was God's favorite angel until he challenged God's authority and was cast into Hell along with his band of fallen angels. "Better to reign in Hell than serve in Heaven," boasts Satan, the "adversary of God" in Milton's *Paradise Lost*. In Hell, Lucifer-Satan becomes a liar, an empty imposter who uses boasts, spears, trumpets, and banners, as some national leaders do today. At the Demonic Conference in Hell of all the major demons, Satan is assured that he cannot regain Heaven in any direct confrontation.[1] However, Satan's statesman, Beelzebub, comes up with the most evil of solutions in proposing to avenge themselves against God by corrupting God's greatest creation, humankind. Though Satan succeeds in tempting Adam and Eve to disobey God and be led into evil, God decrees that they will in time be saved. However, for the rest of time, Satan will be allowed to slither around that injunction, enlisting witches to tempt people to evil. Satan's intermediaries would thereafter become the target of zealous inquisitors who want to rid the world of evil, but their horrific methods would breed a new form of systemic evil the world had never before known.

Lucifer's sin is what thinkers in the Middle Ages called "cupiditas."* For Dante, the sins that spring from that root are the most extreme "sins of the wolf," the spiritual condition of having an inner black hole so deep within oneself that no amount of power or money can ever fill it. For those suffering the mortal malady called cupiditas, whatever exists outside of one's self has worth only as it can be exploited by, or taken into one's self. In Dante's Hell those guilty of that sin are in the ninth circle, frozen in the Lake of Ice. Having cared for nothing but self in life, they are encased in icy Self for eternity. By making people focus only on oneself in this way, Satan and his followers turn their eyes away from the harmony of love that unites all living creatures.

The sins of the wolf cause a human being to turn away from grace and to make self his only good—and also his prison. In the ninth circle of the Inferno, the sinners, possessed of the spirit of the insatiable wolf, are frozen in a self-imposed prison where prisoner and guard are fused in an egocentric reality.

In her scholarly search for the origins of Satan, the historian Elaine Pagels offers a provocative thesis on the psychological significance of Satan as humanity's mirror:

> What fascinates us about Satan is the way he expresses qualities that go beyond what we ordinarily recognize as human. Satan evokes more than the greed, envy, lust, and anger we identify with our own worst impulses, and more than what we call brutality, which imputes to human beings a resemblance to animals ("brutes"). . . . Evil, then, at its worst, seems to involve the supernatural—what we recognize, with a shudder, as the diabolic inverse of Martin Buber's characterization of God as "wholly other."[2]

We fear evil, but are fascinated by it. We create myths of evil conspiracies and come to believe them enough to mobilize forces against them. We reject the "Other" as different and dangerous because it's unknown, yet we are thrilled by

---

Cupiditas, in English, is cupidity, which means avarice, greed, the strong desire for wealth or power over another. What *cupiditas* means is the desire to turn into oneself or take into oneself everything that is "other" than self. For instance, lust and rape are forms of cupiditas, because they entail using another person as a thing to gratify one's own desire; murder for profit is also cupiditas. It is the opposite of the concept of *caritas,* which means envisioning oneself as part of a ring of love in which each individual self has worth in itself but also as it relates to every other self. "Do unto others as you would have them do unto you" is a weak expression of caritas. The Latin *"Caritas et amor, Deus ibi est"* is probably the best expression of the concept "wherever caritas and love are, God is."

contemplating sexual excess and violations of moral codes by those who are not our kind. Professor of religious studies David Frankfurter concludes his search for Evil Incarnate by focusing on the social construction of this evil other.

> [T]he construction of the *social* Other as cannibal-savage, demon, sorcerer, vampire, or an amalgam of them all, draws upon a consistent repertoire of symbols of inversion. The stories we tell about people out on the periphery play with their savagery, libertine customs, and monstrosity. At the same time, the combined horror and pleasure we derive from contemplating this Otherness—sentiments that influenced the brutality of colonists, missionaries, and armies entering the lands of those Others—certainly affect us at the level of individual fantasy, as well.[3]

TRANSFORMATIONS: ANGELS, DEVILS, AND THE REST OF US MERE MORTALS

The Lucifer Effect is my attempt to understand the processes of transformation at work when good or ordinary people do bad or evil things. We will deal with the fundamental question "What makes people go wrong?" But instead of resorting to a traditional religious dualism of good versus evil, of wholesome nature versus corrupting nurture, we will look at real people engaged in life's daily tasks, enmeshed in doing their jobs, surviving within an often turbulent crucible of human nature. We will seek to understand the nature of their character transformations when they are faced with powerful situational forces.

Let's begin with a definition of evil. Mine is a simple, psychologically based one: *Evil consists in intentionally behaving in ways that harm, abuse, demean, dehumanize, or destroy innocent others—or using one's authority and systemic power to encourage or permit others to do so on your behalf.* In short, it is "knowing better but doing worse."[4]

What makes human behavior work? What determines human thought and action? What makes some of us lead moral, righteous lives, while others seem to slip easily into immorality and crime? Is what we think about human nature based on the assumption that *inner determinants* guide us up the good paths or down the bad ones? Do we give insufficient attention to the *outer determinants* of our thoughts, feelings, and actions? To what extent are we creatures of the situation, of the moment, of the mob? And is there anything that anyone has ever done that you are absolutely certain you could never be compelled to do?

Most of us hide behind egocentric biases that generate the illusion that we are special. These self-serving protective shields allow us to believe that each of us is above average on any test of self-integrity. Too often we look to the stars through the thick lens of personal invulnerability when we should also look down to the slippery slope beneath our feet. Such egocentric biases are more commonly found in societies that foster independent orientations, such as Euro-

American cultures, and less so in collectivist-oriented societies, such as in Asia, Africa, and the Middle East.[5]

In the course of our voyage through good and evil, I will ask you to reflect upon three issues: How well do you really know yourself, your strengths and weaknesses? Does your self-knowledge come from reviewing your behavior in familiar situations or from being exposed to totally new settings where your old habits are challenged? In the same vein, how well do you really know the people with whom you interact daily: your family, friends, co-workers, and lover? One thesis of this book is that most of us know ourselves only from our limited experiences in familiar situations that involve rules, laws, policies, and pressures that constrain us. We go to school, to work, on vacation, to parties; we pay the bills and the taxes, day in and year out. But what happens when we are exposed to totally new and unfamiliar settings where our habits don't suffice? You start a new job, go on your first computer-matched date, join a fraternity, get arrested, enlist in the military, join a cult, or volunteer for an experiment. The old you might not work as expected when the ground rules change.

Throughout our journey I would like you to continually ask the "Me also?" question as we encounter various forms of evil. We will examine genocide in Rwanda, the mass suicide and murder of Peoples Temple followers in the jungles of Guyana, the My Lai massacre in Vietnam, the horrors of Nazi concentration camps, the torture by military and civilian police around the world, and the sexual abuse of parishioners by Catholic priests, and search for lines of continuity between the scandalous, fraudulent behavior of executives at Enron and World-Com corporations. Finally, we will see how some common threads in all these evils run through the recently uncovered abuses of civilian prisoners at Abu Ghraib Prison in Iraq. One especially significant thread tying these atrocities together will come out of a body of research in experimental social psychology, particularly a study that has come to be known as the Stanford Prison Experiment.

Evil: Fixed and Within or Mutable and Without?

The idea that an unbridgeable chasm separates good people from bad people is a source of comfort for at least two reasons. First, it creates a binary logic, in which Evil is *essentialized*. Most of us perceive Evil as an entity, a quality that is inherent in some people and not in others. Bad seeds ultimately produce bad fruits as their destinies unfold. We define evil by pointing to the really bad tyrants in our era, such as Hitler, Stalin, Pol Pot, Idi Amin, Saddam Hussein, and other political leaders who have orchestrated mass murders. We must also acknowledge the more ordinary, lesser evils of drug dealers, rapists, sex-trade traffickers, perpetrators of fraudulent scams on the elderly, and those whose bullying destroys the well-being of our children.

Upholding a Good–Evil dichotomy also takes "good people" off the responsibility hook. They are freed from even considering their possible role in creating,

sustaining, perpetuating, or conceding to the conditions that contribute to delinquency, crime, vandalism, teasing, bullying, rape, torture, terror, and violence.
"It's the way of the world, and there's not much that can be done to change it, certainly not by me."

An alternative conception treats evil in *incrementalist* terms, as something of
which we are all capable, depending on circumstances. People may at any time
possess a particular attribute (say intelligence, pride, honesty, or evil) to a greater
or lesser degree. Our nature can be changed, whether toward the good or the bad
side of human nature. The incrementalist view implies an acquisition of qualities
through experience or concentrated practice, or by means of an external intervention, such as being offered a special opportunity. In short, we can learn to become good or evil regardless of our genetic inheritance, personality, or family
legacy.[6]

Alternative Understandings: Dispositional, Situational, and Systemic

Running parallel to this pairing of essentialist and incremental conceptions is the
contrast between *dispositional* and *situational* causes of behavior. When faced with
some unusual behavior, some unexpected event, some anomaly that doesn't
make sense, how do we go about trying to understand it? The traditional approach has been to identify inherent personal qualities that lead to the action: genetic makeup, personality traits, character, free will, and other dispositions. Given
violent behavior, one searches for sadistic personality traits. Given heroic deeds,
the search is on for genes that predispose toward altruism.

In the United States, a rash of shootings in which high school students murder and wound scores of other students and teachers rocks suburban communities.[7] In England, a pair of ten-year-old boys kidnap two-year-old Jamie Bulger
from a shopping center and brutally murder him in cold blood. In Palestine and
Iraq, young men and women become suicide bombers. In most European countries during World War II, many people protected Jews from capture by the Nazis
even though they knew that if they were caught, they and their families would be
killed. In many countries "whistle-blowers" risk personal loss by exposing injustice and immoral actions of superiors. Why?

The traditional view (among those who come from cultures that emphasize
individualism) is to look within for answers—for pathology or heroism. Modern
psychiatry is dispositionally oriented. So are clinical psychology and personality
and assessment psychology. Most of our institutions are founded on such a perspective, including law, medicine, and religion. Culpability, illness, and sin, they
assume, are to be found within the guilty party, the sick person, and the sinner.
They begin their quest for understanding with the "Who questions": *Who* is responsible? *Who* caused it? *Who* gets the blame? and *Who* gets the credit?

Social psychologists (such as myself) tend to avoid this rush to dispositional
judgment when trying to understand the causes of unusual behaviors. They pre-

fer to begin their search for meaning by asking the "What questions": *What* conditions could be contributing to certain reactions? *What* circumstances might be involved in generating behavior? *What* was the situation like from the perspective of the actors? Social psychologists ask: To what extent can an individual's actions be traced to factors outside the actor, to situational variables and environmental processes unique to a given setting?

The dispositional approach is to the situational as a medical model of health is to a public health model. A medical model tries to find the source of the illness, disease, or disability within the affected person. By contrast, public health researchers assume that the vectors of disease transmission come from the environment, creating conditions that foster illness. Sometimes the sick person is the end product of environmental pathogens, which unless counteracted will affect others, regardless of attempts to improve the health of the individual. For example, in the dispositional approach a child who exhibits a learning disability may be given a variety of medical and behavioral treatments to overcome that handicap. But in many cases, especially among the poor, the problem is caused by ingesting lead in paint that flakes off the walls of tenement apartments and is worsened by conditions of poverty—the situational approach. These alternative perspectives are not just abstract variations in conceptual analyses but lead to very different ways of dealing with personal and societal problems.

The significance of such analyses extends to all of us who, as intuitive psychologists, go about our daily lives trying to figure out why people do what they do and how they may be changed to do better. But it is the rare person in an individualist culture who is not infected with a dispositional bias, always looking first to motives, traits, genes, and personal pathologies. Most of us have a tendency both to overestimate the importance of dispositional qualities and to underestimate the importance of situational qualities when trying to understand the causes of other people's behavior.

In the following chapters I will offer a substantial body of evidence that counterbalances the dispositional view of the world and will expand the focus to consider how people's character may be transformed by their being immersed in situations that unleash powerful situational forces. People and situations are usually in a state of dynamic interaction. Although you probably think of yourself as having a consistent personality across time and space, that is likely not to be true. You are not the same person working alone as you are in a group; in a romantic setting versus an educational one; when you are with close friends or in an anonymous crowd; or when you are traveling abroad as when at home base.

The *Malleus Maleficarum* and the Inquisition's WID Program

One of the first documented sources of the widespread use of the dispositional view to understand evil and rid the world of its pernicious influence is found in a text that became the bible of the Inquisition, the *Malleus Maleficarum*, or "The

Witches' Hammer."[8] It was required reading for the Inquisition judges. It begins with a conundrum to be solved: How can evil continue to exist in a world governed by an all-good, all-powerful God? One answer: God allows it as a test of men's souls. Yield to its temptations, go to Hell; resist its temptations, and be invited into Heaven. However, God restricted the Devil's direct influence over people because of his earlier corruption of Adam and Eve. The Devil's solution was to have intermediaries do his evil bidding by using witches as his indirect link to people they would corrupt.

To reduce the spread of evil in Catholic countries, the proposed solution was to find and eliminate witches. What was required was a means to identify witches, get them to confess to heresy, and then destroy them. The mechanism for witch identification and destruction (which in our times might be known as the WID program) was simple and direct: find out through spies who among the population were witches, test their witchly natures by getting confessions using various torture techniques, and kill those who failed the test. Although I have made light of what amounted to a carefully designed system of mass terror, torture, and extermination of untold thousands of people, this kind of simplistic reduction of the complex issues regarding evil fueled the fires of the Inquisition. Making "witches" the despised dispositional category provided a ready solution to the problem of societal evil by simply destroying as many agents of evil as could be identified, tortured, and boiled in oil or burned at the stake.

Given that the Church and its State alliances were run by men, it is no wonder that women were more likely than men to be labeled as witches. The suspects were usually marginalized or threatening in some way: widowed, poor, ugly, deformed, or in some cases considered too proud and powerful. The terrible paradox of the Inquisition is that the ardent and often sincere desire to combat evil generated evil on a grander scale than the world had ever seen before. It ushered in the use by State and Church of torture devices and tactics that were the ultimate perversion of any ideal of human perfection. The exquisite nature of the human mind, which can create great works of art, science, and philosophy, was perverted to engage in acts of "creative cruelty" that were designed to break the will. The tools of the trade of the Inquisition are still on display in prisons around the world, in military and civilian interrogation centers, where torture is standard operating procedure (as we shall see later in our visit to Abu Ghraib Prison).[9]

Power Systems Exert Pervasive Top-Down Dominance

My appreciation of the power residing in systems started with an awareness of how institutions create mechanisms that translate ideology—say, the causes of evil—into operating procedures, such as the Inquisition's witch hunts. In other words, my focus has widened considerably through a fuller appreciation of the ways in which situational conditions are created and shaped by higher-order factors—*systems* of power. Systems, not just dispositions and situations, must be taken into account in order to understand complex behavior patterns.

Aberrant, illegal, or immoral behavior by individuals in service professions, such as policemen, corrections officers, and soldiers, is typically labeled the misdeeds of "a few bad apples." The implication is that they are a rare exception and must be set on one side of the impermeable line between evil and good, with the majority of good apples set on the other side. But who is making the distinction? Usually it is the guardians of the system, who want to isolate the problem in order to deflect attention and blame away from those at the top who may be responsible for creating untenable working conditions or for a lack of oversight or supervision. Again the bad apple–dispositional view ignores the apple barrel and its potentially corrupting situational impact on those within it. A systems analysis focuses on the barrel makers, on those with the power to design the barrel.

It is the "power elite," the barrel makers, often working behind the scenes, who arrange many of the conditions of life for the rest of us, who must spend time in the variety of institutional settings they have constructed. The sociologist C. Wright Mills has illuminated this black hole of power:

> The power elite is composed of men whose positions enable them to transcend the ordinary environments of ordinary men and women; they are in positions to make decisions having major consequences. Whether they do or do not make such decisions is less important than the fact that they do occupy such pivotal positions: their failure to act, their failure to make decisions, is itself an act that is often of greater significance than the decisions they do make. For they are in command of the major hierarchies and organizations of modern society. They rule the big corporations. They run the machinery of state and claim its prerogatives. They direct the military establishment. They occupy strategic command posts of the social structure, in which are now centered the effective means of power and the wealth and celebrity which they enjoy.[10]

As the interests of these diverse power brokers coalesce, they come to define our reality in ways that George Orwell prophesied in 1984. The military-corporate-religious complex is the ultimate megasystem controlling much of the resources and quality of life of many Americans today.

> It is when power is wedded to chronic fear that it becomes
> formidable.
>
> —Eric Hoffer, *The Passionate State of Mind*

The Power to Create "The Enemy"

The powerful don't usually do the dirtiest work themselves, just as Mafia dons leave the "whackings" to underlings. Systems create hierarchies of dominance with influence and communication going down—rarely up—the line. When a power elite wants to destroy an enemy nation, it turns to propaganda experts to fashion a program of hate. What does it take for the citizens of one society to hate the citizens of another society to the degree that they want to segregate them, torment them, even kill them? It requires a "hostile imagination," a psychological construction embedded deeply in their minds by propaganda that transforms those others into "The Enemy." That image is a soldier's most powerful motive, one that loads his rifle with ammunition of hate and fear. The image of a dreaded enemy threatening one's personal well-being and the society's national security emboldens mothers and fathers to send sons to war and empowers governments to rearrange priorities to turn plowshares into swords of destruction.

It is all done with words and images. To modify an old adage: Sticks and stones may break your bones, but names can sometimes kill you. The process begins with creating stereotyped conceptions of the other, dehumanized perceptions of the other, the other as worthless, the other as all-powerful, the other as demonic, the other as an abstract monster, the other as a fundamental threat to our cherished values and beliefs. With public fear notched up and the enemy threat imminent, reasonable people act irrationally, independent people act in mindless conformity, and peaceful people act as warriors. Dramatic visual images of the enemy on posters, television, magazine covers, movies, and the Internet imprint on the recesses of the limbic system, the primitive brain, with the powerful emotions of fear and hate.

The social philosopher Sam Keen brilliantly depicts how this hostile imagination is created by virtually every nation's propaganda on its path to war and reveals the transformative powers on the human psyche of these "images of the enemy."[11] Justifications for the desire to destroy these threats are really afterthoughts, proposed explanations intended for the official record but not for critical analysis of the damage to be done or being done.

The most extreme instance of this hostile imagination at work is of course when it leads to genocide, the plan of one people to eliminate from existence all those who are conceptualized as their enemy. We are aware of some of the ways in which Hitler's propaganda machine transformed Jewish neighbors, co-workers, even friends into despised enemies of the State who deserved the "final solution." This process was seeded in elementary school textbooks by means of images and texts that rendered all Jews contemptible and not worthy of human compassion. Here I would like to consider briefly a recent example of attempted genocide along with the use of rape as a weapon against humanity. Then I will show how one aspect of this complex psychological process, the dehumanization component, can be studied in controlled experimental research that isolates its critical features for systematic analysis.

CRIMES AGAINST HUMANITY: GENOCIDE, RAPE, AND TERROR

Literature has taught us for at least three thousand years that no person or state is incapable of evil. In Homer's account of the Trojan War, Agamemnon, commander of the Greek forces, tells his men before they engage their enemy, "We are not going to leave a single one of [the Trojans] alive, down to the babies in their mothers' wombs—not even they must live. The whole people must be wiped out of existence . . ." These vile words come from a noble citizen of one of the most civilized nation-states of its time, the home of philosophy, jurisprudence, and classical drama.

We live in the "mass murder century." More than 50 million people have been systematically murdered by government decrees, enacted by soldiers and civilian forces willing to carry out the kill orders. Beginning in 1915, Ottoman Turks slaughtered 1.5 million Armenians. The mid-twentieth century saw the Nazis liquidate at least 6 million Jews, 3 million Soviet POWs, 2 million Poles, and hundreds of thousands of "undesirable" peoples. As Stalin's Soviet empire murdered 20 million Russians, Mao Zedong's government policies resulted in an even greater number of deaths, up to 30 million of the country's own citizens. The Communist Khmer Rouge regime killed off 1.7 million people of its own nation in Cambodia. Saddam Hussein's Ba'ath Party is accused of killing 100,000 Kurds in Iraq. In 2006, genocide has erupted in Sudan's Darfur region, which most of the world has conveniently ignored.[12]

Note that almost exactly the same words that Agamemnon used three millennia ago were also spoken in our own time, in the African nation of Rwanda, as the ruling Hutus were in the process of wiping out their former neighbors, the Tutsi minority. One victim recalls what one of her tormentors told her: "We're going to kill all the Tutsi, and one day Hutu children will have to ask what a Tutsi child looked like."

The Rape of Rwanda

The peaceful Tutsi people of Rwanda in Central Africa learned that a weapon of mass destruction could be a simple machete, used against them with lethal efficiency. The systematic slaughter of Tutsis by their former neighbors, the Hutus, spread throughout the country in a few months during the spring of 1994 as death squads killed thousands of innocent men, women, and children with machetes and nail-studded clubs. A report by the United Nations estimates that between 800,000 and a million Rwandans were murdered in about three months' time, making the massacre the most ferocious in recorded history. Three quarters of the entire Tutsi population were exterminated.

Hutu neighbors were slaughtering former friends and next-door neighbors—on command. A Hutu murderer said in an interview a decade later that "The worst thing about the massacre was killing my neighbor; we used to drink together, his cattle would graze on my land. He was like a relative." A Hutu mother described how she had beaten to death the children next door, who looked at her with wide-eyed amazement because they had been friends and neighbors all their lives. She reported that someone from the government had told her that the Tutsi were their enemies and had given her a club and her husband a machete to use against this threat. She justified the slaughter as doing "a favor" to those children, who would have become helpless orphans given that their parents had already been murdered.

Until recently, there was little recognition of the systematic use of rape of these Rwandan women as a tactic of terror and spiritual annihilation. By some accounts it began when a Hutu leader, Mayor Silvester Cacumbibi, raped the daughter of his former friend and then had other men also rape her. She later reported that he had told her, "We won't waste bullets on you; we will rape you, and that will be worse for you."

Unlike the rapes of Chinese women by Japanese soldiers in Nanking (to be described subsequently), where the details of the nightmare were blurred by failures in early reporting and the reluctance of the Chinese to relive that experience by sharing it with outsiders, much is known about the psychological dynamics of the rape of Rwandan women.[13]

When the citizens of the village of Butare defended its borders against the onslaught of the Hutus, the interim government dispatched a special person to deal with what it considered a revolt. She was the national minister of family and women's affairs and Butare's favorite daughter, having grown up in the area. Pauline Nyiramasuhuko, a Tutsi and former social worker who lectured on women's empowerment, was the only hope of this village. That hope was instantly shattered. Pauline supervised a terrible trap, promising the people that the Red Cross would provide food and shelter in the local stadium; in reality, armed Hutu thugs (the Interahamwe) were awaiting their arrival, eventually murdering most of the innocent sanctuary seekers. They were machine-gunned, grenades were thrown into the unsuspecting throngs, and survivors were sliced apart with machetes.

Pauline gave the order that "Before you kill the women, you need to rape them." She ordered another group of these thugs to burn alive a group of seventy women and girls they were guarding and provided them with gasoline from her car to do so. Again she invited the men to rape their victims before killing them. One of the young men told a translator that they couldn't rape them because "we had been killing all day and we were tired. We just put the gasoline in bottles and scattered it among the women, then started burning."

A young woman, Rose, was raped by Pauline's son, Shalom, who announced that he had "permission" from his mother to rape Tutsi women. She was the only Tutsi allowed to live so she could deliver a progress report to God as the witness of the genocide. She was then forced to watch her mother being raped and twenty of her relatives slaughtered.

A U.N. report estimated that at least 200,000 women were raped during this brief period of horror, many of them killed afterward. "Some were penetrated with spears, gun barrels, bottles or the stamens of banana trees. Sexual organs were mutilated with machetes, boiling water and acid; women's breasts were cut off" (p. 85). "Making the matter worse, the rapes, most of them committed by many men in succession, were frequently accompanied by other forms of physical torture and often staged as public performances to multiply the terror and degradation" (p. 89). They were also used as a public way of promoting social bonding among the Hutu murderers. This shared emergent camaraderie is often a by-product of male group rape.

The extent of the inhumanity knew no boundaries. "A 45-year old Rwandan woman was raped by her 12-year-old son—with Interahamwe holding a hatchet to his throat—in front of her husband, while their five other young children were forced to hold open her thighs" (p. 116). The spread of AIDS among the living rape victims continues to wreak havoc in Rwanda. "By using a disease, a plague, as an apocalyptic terror, as biological warfare, you're annihilating the procreators, perpetuating death unto generations," according to Charles Strozier, professor of history at the John Jay College of Criminal Justice in New York (p. 116).

How do we even begin to understand the forces that were operating to make Pauline a new kind of criminal: one woman against enemy women? A combination of history and social psychology can provide a framework based on power and status differentials. First, she was moved by the widespread sense of the lower status of the Hutu women compared with the beauty and arrogance of Tutsi women. They were taller and lighter-skinned and had more Caucasian features, which made them appear more desirable to men than Hutu women were.

A racial distinction had arbitrarily been created by Belgian and German colonialists around the turn of the twentieth century to distinguish between people who for centuries had intermarried, spoke the same language, and shared the same religion. They forced all Rwandans to carry identification cards that declared them to be in either the majority Hutu or the minority Tutsi, with the benefits of higher education and administrative posts going to the Tutsi. That became another source of Pauline's pent-up desire for revenge. It was also true that she was a political opportunist in a male-dominated administration, needing to prove her loyalty, obedience, and patriotic zeal to her superiors by orchestrating crimes never before perpetrated by a woman against an enemy. It also became easier to encourage the mass murders and rapes of Tutsis by being able to view them as abstractions and also by calling them by the dehumanizing term "cockroaches," which needed to be "exterminated." Here is a living documentary of the hostile imagination that paints the faces of the enemy in hateful hues and then destroys the canvas.

As unimaginable as it may be to any of us for someone to intentionally inspire such monstrous crimes, Nicole Bergevin, Pauline's lawyer in her genocide trial, reminds us, "When you do murder trials, you realize that we are all susceptible, and you wouldn't even dream you would ever commit this act. But you come to understand that everyone is [susceptible]. It could happen to me, it could happen to my daughter. It could happen to you" (p. 130).

Highlighting even more clearly one of the main theses of this book is the considered opinion of Alison Des Forges of Human Rights Watch, who has investigated many such barbarous crimes. She forces us to see our reflection mirrored in these atrocities:

> This behavior lies just under the surface of any of us. The simplified accounts of genocide allow distance between us and the perpetrators of genocide. They are so evil we couldn't ever see ourselves doing the same thing. But if you consider the terrible pressure under which people were operating, then you automatically reassert their humanity—and that becomes alarming. You are forced to look at the situation and say, "What would I have done? Sometimes the answer is not encouraging." (p. 132)

The French journalist Jean Hatzfeld interviewed ten of the Hutu militia members now in prison for having macheted to death thousands of Tutsi civilians.[14] The testimonies of these ordinary men—mostly farmers, active churchgoers, and a former teacher—are chilling in their matter-of-fact, remorseless depiction of unimaginable cruelty. Their words force us to confront the unthinkable again and again: that human beings are capable of totally abandoning their humanity for a mindless ideology, to follow and then exceed the orders of charismatic authorities to destroy everyone they label as "The Enemy." Let's reflect on a few of these accounts, which make Truman Capote's *In Cold Blood* pale in comparison.

> "Since I was killing often, I began to feel it did not mean anything to me. I want to make clear that from the first gentleman I killed to the last, I was not sorry about a single one."

> "We were doing a job to order. We were lining up behind everyone's enthusiasm. We gathered into teams on the soccer field and went out hunting as kindred spirits."

> "Anyone who hesitated to kill because of feelings of sadness absolutely had to watch his mouth, to say nothing about the reason for his reticence, for fear of being accused of complicity."

> "We killed everyone we tracked down [hiding] in the papyrus. We had no reason to choose, to expect or fear anyone in particular. We were cutters of acquaintances, cutters of neighbors, just plan cutters."

> "Our Tutsi neighbors, we knew they were not guilty of no misdoing, but we thought all Tutsis at fault for our constant troubles. We no longer looked

at them one by one, we no longer stopped to recognize them as they had been, not even as colleagues. They had become a threat greater than all we had experienced together, more important than our way of seeing things in the community. That's how we reasoned and how we killed at the same time."

"We no longer saw a human being when we turned up a Tutsi in the swamps. I mean a person like us, sharing similar thoughts and feelings. The hunt was savage, the hunters were savage, the prey was savage—savagery took over the mind."

A particularly moving reaction to these brutal murders and rapes, which expresses a theme we will revisit, comes from one of the surviving Tutsi women, Berthe:

"Before, I knew that a man could kill another man, because it happens all the time. Now I know that even the person with whom you've shared food, or with whom you've slept, even he can kill you with no trouble. The closest neighbor can kill you with his teeth: that is what I have learned since the genocide, and my eyes no longer gaze the same on the face of the world."

Lieutenant General Roméo Dallaire has authored a powerful testimony about his experiences as the force commander for the U.N. Assistance Mission to Rwanda in *Shake Hands with the Devil*.[15] Although he was able to save thousands of people by his heroic ingenuity, this top military commander was left devastated by his inability to summon more aid from the United Nations to prevent many more atrocities. He ended up with severe post-traumatic stress disorder as a psychological casualty of this massacre.[16]

The Rape of Nanking, China

So graphically horrifying—yet so easily visualized—is the concept of rape that we use the term metaphorically to describe other, almost unimaginable atrocities of war. Japanese soldiers butchered between 260,000 and 350,000 Chinese civilians in just a few bloody months of 1937. Those figures represent more deaths than the total annihilation caused by the atomic bombing of Japan and all the civilian deaths in most European countries during all of World War II.

Beyond the sheer number of Chinese slaughtered, it is important for us to recognize the "creatively evil" ways devised by their tormentors to make even death desirable. The author Iris Chang's investigation of that horror revealed that Chinese men were used for bayonet practice and in decapitation contests. An estimated 20,000 to 80,000 women were raped. Many soldiers went beyond rape to disembowel women, slice off their breasts, and nail them to walls alive. Fathers were forced to rape their daughters and sons their mothers as other family members watched.[17]

War engenders cruelty and barbaric behavior against anyone considered the Enemy, as the dehumanized, demonic Other. The Rape of Nanking is notorious for the graphic detail of the horrific extremes soldiers went to to degrade and destroy innocent civilian "enemy non-combatants." However, were it a singular incident and not just another part of the historical tapestry of such inhumanities against civilians we might think it an anomaly. British troops executed and raped civilians during the U.S. Revolutionary War. Soviet Red Army soldiers raped an estimated 100,000 Berlin women toward the end of Word War II and between 1945 and 1948. In addition to the rapes and murders of more than 500 civilians at the My Lai massacre in 1968, recently released secret Pentagon evidence describes 320 incidents of American atrocities against Vietnamese and Cambodian civilians.[18]

Dehumanization and Moral Disengagement in the Laboratory

We can assume that most people, most of the time, are moral creatures. But imagine that this morality is like a gearshift that at times gets pushed into neutral. When that happens, morality is disengaged. If the car happens to be on an incline, car and driver move precipitously downhill. It is then the nature of the circumstances that determines outcomes, not the driver's skills or intentions. This simple analogy, I think, captures one of the central themes in the theory of moral disengagement developed by my Stanford colleague Albert Bandura. In a later chapter, we will review his theory, which will help explain why some otherwise good people can be led to do bad things. At this point, I want to turn to the experimental research that Bandura and his assistants conducted, which illustrates the ease with which morality can be disengaged by the tactic of dehumanizing a potential victim.[19] In an elegant demonstration that shows the power of dehumanization, one single word is shown to increase aggression toward a target. Let's see how the experiment worked.

Imagine you are a college student who has volunteered for a study of group problem solving as part of a three-person team from your school. Your task is to help students from another college improve their group problem-solving performance by punishing their errors. That punishment takes the form of administering electric shocks that can be increased in severity over successive trials. After taking your names and those of the other team, the assistant leaves to tell the experimenter that the study can begin. There will be ten trials during each of which you can decide the shock level to administer to the other student group in the next room.

You don't realize that it is part of the experimental script, but you "accidentally" overhear the assistant complaining over the intercom to the experimenter that the other students "seem like animals." You don't know it, but in two other conditions to which other students like you have been randomly assigned, the assistant describes the other students as "nice guys" or does not label them at all.

Do these simple labels have any effect? It doesn't seem so initially. On the first trial all the groups respond in the same way by administering low levels of shock, around level 2. But soon it begins to matter what each group has heard about these anonymous others. If you know nothing about them, you give a steady average of about a level 5. If you have come to think of them as "nice guys," you treat them in a more humane fashion, giving them significantly less shock, about a level 3. However, imagining them as "animals" switches off any sense of compassion you might have for them, and when they commit errors, you begin to shock them with ever-increasing levels of intensity, significantly more than in the other conditions, as you steadily move up toward the high level 8.

Think carefully for a moment about the psychological processes that a simple label has tripped off in your mind. You overheard a person, whom you do not know personally, tell some authority, whom you have never seen, that other college students like you seem like "animals." That single descriptive term changes your mental construction of these others. It distances you from images of friendly college kids who must be more similar to you than different. That new mental set has a powerful impact on your behavior. The post hoc rationalizations the experimental students generated to explain why they needed to give so much shock to the "animal-house" students in the process of "teaching them a good lesson" were equally fascinating. This example of using controlled experimental research to investigate the underlying psychological processes that occur in significant real-world cases of violence will be extended in chapters 12 and 13 when we consider how behavioral scientists have investigated various aspects of the psychology of evil.

> Our ability to selectively engage and disengage our moral
> standards . . . helps explain how people can be barbarically
> cruel in one moment and compassionate the next.

—Albert Bandura[20]

Horrific Images of Abuse at Abu Ghraib Prison

The driving force behind this book was the need to better understand the how and why of the physical and psychological abuses perpetrated on prisoners by American Military Police at the Abu Ghraib Prison in Iraq. As the photographic evidence of these abuses rocketed around the world in May 2004, we all saw for the first time in recorded history vivid images of young American men and women engaged in unimaginable forms of torture against civilians they were supposed to be guarding. The tormentors and the tormented were captured in an extensive display of digitally documented depravity that the soldiers themselves had made during their violent escapades.

Why did they create photographic evidence of such illegal acts, which if found would surely get them into trouble? In these "trophy photos," like the proud displays by big-game hunters of yesteryear with the beasts they have killed, we saw smiling men and women in the act of abusing their lowly animal creatures. The images are of punching, slapping, and kicking detainees; jumping on their feet; forcibly arranging naked, hooded prisoners in piles and pyramids; forcing naked prisoners to wear women's underwear over their heads; forcing male prisoners to masturbate or simulate fellatio while being photographed or videotaped with female soldiers smiling or encouraging it; hanging prisoners from cell rafters for extended time periods; dragging a prisoner around with a leash tied to his neck; and using unmuzzled attack dogs to frighten prisoners.

The iconic image that ricocheted from that dungeon to the streets of Iraq and every corner of the globe was that of the "triangle man": a hooded detainee is standing on a box in a stress position with his outstretched arms protruding from under a garment blanket revealing electrical wires attached to his fingers. He was told that he would be electrocuted if he fell off the box when his strength gave out. It did not matter that the wires went nowhere; it mattered that he believed the lie and must have experienced considerable stress. There were even more shocking photographs that the U.S. government chose not to release to the public because of the greater damage they would surely have done to the credibility and moral image of the U.S. military and President Bush's administrative command. I have seen hundreds of these images, and they are indeed horrifying.

I was deeply distressed at the sight of such suffering, of such displays of arrogance, of such indifference to the humiliation being inflicted upon helpless prisoners. I was also amazed to learn that one of the abusers, a female soldier who had just turned twenty-one, described the abuse as "just fun and games."

I was shocked, but I was not surprised. The media and the "person in the street" around the globe asked how such evil deeds could be perpetrated by these seven men and women, whom military leaders had labeled as "rogue soldiers" and "a few bad apples." Instead, I wondered what circumstances in that prison cell block could have tipped the balance and led even good soldiers to do such bad things. To be sure, advancing a situational analysis for such crimes does not excuse them or make them morally acceptable. Rather, I needed to find the meaning in this madness. I wanted to understand how it was possible for the characters of these young people to be so transformed in such a short time that they could do these unthinkable deeds.

Parallel Universes in Abu Ghraib and Stanford's Prison

The reason that I was shocked but not surprised by the images and stories of prisoner abuse in the Abu Ghraib "Little Shop of Horrors" was that I had seen something similar before. Three decades earlier, I had witnessed eerily similar scenes as they unfolded in a project that I directed, of my own design: naked, shackled prisoners with bags over their heads, guards stepping on prisoners' backs as they did push-ups, guards sexually humiliating prisoners, and prisoners suffering from extreme stress. Some of the visual images from my experiment are practically interchangeable with those of the guards and prisoners in that remote prison in Iraq, the notorious Abu Ghraib.

The college students role-playing guards and prisoners in a mock prison experiment conducted at Stanford University in the summer of 1971 were mirrored in the real guards and real prison in the Iraq of 2003. Not only had I seen such events, I had been responsible for creating the conditions that allowed such abuses to flourish. As the project's principal investigator, I designed the experiment that randomly assigned normal, healthy, intelligent college students to enact the roles of either guards or prisoners in a realistically simulated prison setting where they were to live and work for several weeks. My student research associates, Craig Haney, Curt Banks, and David Jaffe, and I wanted to understand some of the dynamics operating in the psychology of imprisonment.

How do ordinary people adapt to such an institutional setting? How do the power differentials between guards and prisoners play out in their daily interactions? If you put good people in a bad place, do the people triumph or does the place corrupt them? Would the violence that is endemic to most real prisons be absent in a prison filled with good middle-class boys? These were some of the exploratory issues to be investigated in what started out as a simple study of prison life.

EXPLORING THE DARK SIDE OF HUMAN NATURE

Our journey together will be one that the poet Milton might say leads into "darkness visible." It will take us to places where evil, by any definition of the word, has flourished. We will meet a host of people who have done very bad things to others, often out of a sense of high purpose, the best ideology, and moral imperative. You are alerted to watch for demons along the path, but you may be disappointed by their banality and their similarity to your next-door neighbor. With your permission, as your adventure guide, I will invite you to walk in their shoes and see through their eyes in order to give you an insider's perspective upon evil, up close and personal. At times, the view will be downright ugly, but only by examining and understanding the causes of such evil might we be able to change it, to contain it, to transform it through wise decisions and innovative communal action.

The basement of Stanford University's Jordan Hall is the backdrop I will use to help you understand what it was like to be a prisoner, a guard, or a prison superintendent at that time in that special place. Although the research is widely known from media sound bites and some of our research publications, the full story has never before been told. I will narrate the events as they unfold in first person, present tense, re-creating the highlights of each day and night in chronological sequence. After we consider the implications of the Stanford Prison Experiment—ethical, theoretical, and practical—we will expand the bases of the psychological study of evil by exploring a range of experimental and field research by psychologists that illustrates the power of situational forces over individual behavior. We will examine in some detail research on conformity, obedience, deindividuation, dehumanization, moral disengagement, and the evil of inaction.

"Men are not prisoners of fate, but only prisoners of their own minds," said President Franklin Roosevelt. Prisons are metaphors for constraints on freedom, both literal and symbolic. The Stanford Prison Experiment went from initially being a symbolic prison to becoming an all-too-real one in the minds of its prisoners and guards. What are other self-imposed prisons that limit our basic freedoms? Neurotic disorders, low self-esteem, shyness, prejudice, shame, and excessive fear of terrorism are just some of the chimeras that limit our potentiality for freedom and happiness, blinding our full appreciation of the world around us.[21]

With that knowledge in mind, Abu Ghraib returns to capture our attention. But now let us go beyond the headlines and TV images to appreciate more fully what it was like to be a prison guard or a prisoner in that horrid prison at the time of those abuses. Torture forces its way into our investigation in the new forms that it has taken since the Inquisition. I will take you into the court-martial of one of those military policemen, and we will witness some of the negative fallout of the soldiers' actions. Throughout, we will bring to bear all we know about the triadic components of our social psychological understanding, focusing on acting people in particular situations, created and maintained by systemic forces. We will put on trial the command structure of the U.S. military, CIA officials, and top government leaders for their combined complicity in creating a dysfunctional system that spawned the torture and abuses of Abu Ghraib.

The first part of our final chapter will offer some guidelines on how to resist unwanted social influence, how to build resistance to the seductive lures of influence professionals. We want to know how to combat mind control tactics used to compromise our freedom of choice to the tyranny of conformity, compliance, obedience, and self-doubting fears. Although I preach the power of the situation, I also endorse the power of people to act mindfully and critically as informed agents directing their behavior in purposeful ways. By understanding how social influence operates and by realizing that any of us can be vulnerable to its subtle and pervasive powers, we can become wise and wily consumers instead of being easily influenced by authorities, group dynamics, persuasive appeals, and compliance strategies.

I want to end by reversing the question with which we started. Instead of considering whether you are capable of evil, I want you to consider whether you are capable of becoming a hero. My final argument introduces the concept of the "banality of heroism." I believe that any one of us is a potential hero, waiting for the right situational moment to make the decision to act to help others despite personal risk and sacrifice. But we have far to travel before we get to that happy conclusion, so *andiamo!*

> Power said to the world,
> "You are mine."
> The world kept it prisoner on her throne.
> Love said to the world, "I am thine."
> The world gave it the freedom of her house.
>
> —Rabindranath Tagore, *Stray Birds*[22]

CHAPTER TWO

Sunday's Surprise Arrests

Little did this band of young strangers realize that Palo Alto's church bells were tolling for them, that their lives would soon be transformed in totally unexpected ways.

It is Sunday, August 14, 1971, 9:55 A.M. The temperature is in the seventies, the humidity is low, as usual, the visibility is unlimited; there is a cloudless azure blue sky above. Another postcard-perfect summer day begins in Palo Alto, California. The Chamber of Commerce would not have it otherwise. Imperfection and irregularity are as little tolerated in this western paradise as is litter in the streets or weeds in a neighbor's garden. It feels good to be alive on a day like this, in a place like this.

This is the Eden where the American dream plays out, the end of the frontier. Palo Alto's population is closing in on 60,000 citizens, but its main distinction derives from the 11,000 students living and studying about a mile away down Palm Drive with its hundreds of palm trees lining the entrance to Stanford University. Stanford is like a sprawling mini-city covering more than eight thousand acres, with its own police and fire departments and post office. Just an hour's drive north is San Francisco. Palo Alto, by contrast, is safer, cleaner, quieter, and whiter. Most blacks live across the Highway 101 tracks at the east end of town, in East Palo Alto. In comparison to the run-down, multistory tenement buildings I was used to, East Palo Alto's single- and two-family houses more nearly resemble a suburb where my high school teacher might have dreamed of living if he could have saved enough money by moonlighting as a cab driver.

Yet, all around this oasis, trouble has begun brewing of late. Over in Oakland, the Black Panther Party is promoting black pride, backed by black power, to resist racist practices "by all means necessary." Prisons are becoming centers for recruiting a new breed of political prisoners, inspired by George Jackson, who is about to go on trial with his "Soledad Brothers" for the alleged murder of a prison guard. The women's liberation movement is picking up steam, dedicated to ending women's secondary citizenship and fostering new opportunities for them. The unpopular war in Vietnam drags on as body counts soar daily. That tragedy worsens as the Nixon-Kissinger administration reacts to antiwar activists with evergreater bombings in reaction to the mass demonstrations against the war. The "military-industrial complex" is the enemy of this new generation of people, who openly question its aggressive-commercial-exploitation values. For anyone who likes to live in a truly dynamic era, this Zeitgeist is unlike any in recent history.

COMMUNAL EVIL, COMMUNAL GOOD

Intrigued by the contrasts between the sense of ambient anonymity I lived with in New York City and this sense of community and personal identity that I felt in Palo Alto, I decided to conduct a simple field experiment to test the validity of this difference. I had become interested in the antisocial effects that anonymity induced when people felt no one could identify them when they were in a setting that encouraged aggression. Based on the *Lord of the Flies* conception of masks liberating hostile impulses, I had conducted research showing that research participants who were "deindividuated" more readily inflicted pain on others than did those who felt more individuated.[1] Now I wanted to see what the good citizens of Palo Alto would do in response to the temptation offered by an invitation to vandalism. I designed a *Candid Camera*–type field study that involved abandoning automobiles in Palo Alto and, as a comparison, three thousand miles away in the Bronx. Good-looking cars were placed across the street from the campuses of New York University's Bronx campus and Stanford University, with their hoods raised and license plates removed—sure "releaser" signals to lure citizens into becoming vandals. From concealed vantage points, my research team watched and photographed the action in the Bronx and videotaped the Palo Alto scene.[2]

We had not yet set up our recording equipment in the Bronx when the first vandals appeared and began stripping the car—Dad barking orders for Mom to empty the trunk and the son to check out the glove compartment while he removed the battery. Passersby, walking and driving, stopped to strip our helpless car of any and all items of value before the demolition derby began. This episode was followed by a parade of vandals who systematically stripped and then demolished that vulnerable New York City car.

Time magazine carried this sad tale of urban anonymity at work under the heading "Diary of an Abandoned Automobile."[3] In a matter of days, we recorded twenty-three separate destructive incidents on that hapless Oldsmobile in the Bronx. The vandals turned out to be just ordinary citizens. They were all white, well-dressed adults who, under other circumstances, might demand more police protection and less coddling of criminals and would "very definitely agree" with the opinion poll item about the necessity for more law and order. Contrary to expectation, only one of these acts was performed by kids simply delighting in the joys of destruction. Even more surprising, all this destruction took place in broad daylight, so we had no need for our infrared film. Internalized anonymity needs no darkness for its expression.

But what was the fate of our abandoned Palo Alto car, which had also been made to look obviously vulnerable to assault? After a full week, there was not a single act of vandalism against it! People passed by, drove by, looked at it, but no one even touched it. Well, not exactly. It rained one day, and a kindly gentleman shut the hood. (God forbid the engine should get wet!) When I drove the car away, back to the Stanford campus, three neighbors called the police to report a possible theft of an abandoned car.[4] That is my operational definition of "community," people caring enough to take action in the face of an unusual or possibly illegal event on their turf. I believe such prosocial behavior comes from the assumption of reciprocal altruism, others would do the same to protect their property or person.

The message of this little demonstration is that conditions that make us feel anonymous, when we think that others do not know us or care to, can foster anti-social, self-interested behaviors. My earlier research highlighted the power of masking one's identity to unleash aggressive acts against other people in situations that gave permission to violate the usual taboos against interpersonal violence. This abandoned car demonstration extended that notion to include ambient anonymity as a precursor to violations of the social contract.

Curiously, this demonstration has become the only bit of empirical evidence used to support the "Broken Windows Theory" of crime, which posits *public disorder* as a situational stimulus to crime, along with the presence of criminals.[5] Any setting that cloaks people in anonymity reduces their sense of personal accountability and civic responsibility for their actions. We see this in many institutional settings, such as our schools and jobs, the military, and prisons. Broken Windows advocates argue that alleviating physical disorder—removing abandoned cars from the streets, wiping out graffiti, and fixing broken windows—can reduce crime and disarray in city streets. There is evidence that such proactive measures work well in some cities, such as New York, but not as well in other cities.

Community spirit thrives in a quiet, orderly way in places such as Palo Alto where people care about the physical and social quality of their lives and have the resources to work at improving both. Here there is a sense of fairness and trust that contrasts with the nagging tugs of inequity and cynicism that drag down folks in some other places. Here, for example, people have faith in their police department to control crime and contain evil—justifiably so, because the police are well educated, well trained, friendly, and honest. The police go "by the book," which makes them act fairly, even if, on rare occasions, people forget that police are just blue-collar workers who happen to wear blue uniforms and can get laid off when the city budget is in the red. At rare times, however, even the best of them can let authority rule over their humanity. That doesn't happen often in a place like Palo Alto, but it did in a curious way that forms the back story of how the Stanford Prison Experiment started off with a big bang.

TOWN–GOWN CONFRONTATIONS AT
STANFORD AND BEYOND

The only blemish on the otherwise excellent service and citizenship record of Palo Alto's finest was their loss of composure during a confrontation with Stanford student radicals during the 1970 strike against the United States involvement in Indochina. When these students started "trashing" campus buildings, I helped organize several thousand other students in constructive antiwar activities to show that violence and vandalism got only negative media attention and had no impact on the conduct of the war, while our pro-peace tactics might.[6] Unfortunately, the new university president, Kenneth Pitzer, panicked and called in the cops, and, as in many such confrontations happening all over America, too many cops lost their professional composure and beat up the kids they had previously felt it was their duty to protect. There were even more violent police–campus confrontations—at the University of Wisconsin (October 1967), Kent State University in Ohio (May 1970), and Jackson State University in Mississippi (also May 1970). College students were shot at, wounded, and killed by local police and National Guardsmen, who in other times are counted on as their protectors. (See Notes for details.)[7]

From *The New York Times*, May 2, 1970 (pp. 1, 9):

> The resurgence of campus antiwar sentiment—with Cambodian developments as its central issue—took a variety of forms yesterday and included the following incidents:
>
> Two National Guard units were put on alert by Gov. Marvin Mandel of Maryland after students at the University of Maryland clashed with the state police following a rally and a hit-and-run attack on the R.O.T.C. headquarters on the College Park Campus.
>
> About 2,300 Princeton University Students and faculty members voted to strike until at least Monday afternoon, when a mass meeting is scheduled: this will conclude a boycott of all social functions. . . . A student strike at Stanford University developed into a rock-throwing melee on the California campus: police used tear gas to disperse the demonstrators.

A Stanford report described a level of violence that had never before been seen on this bucolic campus. Police were called to campus at least thirteen times and made more than forty arrests. The most serious demonstrations occurred on April 29 and 30, 1970, following news of the U.S. invasion in Cambodia. Police from as far away as San Francisco were summoned, rocks were thrown, and tear gas was first used on campus during these two nights, which President Pitzer described as "tragic." Approximately sixty-five people, including many police officers, were hurt.

Hard feelings arose between the Stanford college community, on the one side, and the Palo Alto police and hard-line, "hawk" townies, on the other. This was a strange conflict because there had never been the same kind of love–hate, town–gown relationship that existed between the townies in New Haven and Yale University students that I had experienced as a graduate student .

The new chief of police, Captain James Zurcher, who had taken charge of the department in February 1971, was eager to dissolve any lingering animosity from the riot-torn days of his predecessor and was thus receptive to my request to collaborate in a program of city police—Stanford student "depolarization."[8] Young, articulate officers conducted student tours of the Police Department's sparkling new facility, while students reciprocated by inviting police to share dormitory meals with them and sit in on classes. I suggested further that interested police rookies might even participate in some of our research. It was another sign that reasonable people could work out reasonable solutions to what seemed like insoluble social problems. However, it was in this context that I naively helped to create a new pocket of evil in Palo Alto.

Chief Zurcher agreed that it would be interesting to study how men become socialized into the role of police officers and what went into transforming a rookie into a "good cop." Great idea, I replied, but that would require a big grant that I didn't have. But I did have a small grant to study what went into the making of a prison guard, since that was a role narrower in function as well as in territory. How about creating a prison in which rookie cops and college students would be both mock guards and mock prisoners? That sounded like a good idea to the chief. In addition to whatever I might learn, the chief felt that it would be a good personal training experience for some of his men. So he agreed to assign several of his rookies to be in this mock prison experience. I was delighted, knowing that with that foot in the door, I could then ask to have his officers conduct mock arrests of the students who were soon to become our prisoners.

Shortly before we were ready to begin, the chief reneged on his promise to use his own men as mock prisoners or guards, saying they could not be spared for the next two weeks. Nevertheless, the spirit of détente was maintained, and he volunteered to assist in my prison study in whatever other way feasible.

I suggested that the ideal way to start the study most realistically and with dramatic flair would be for his officers to stage arrests of the would-be mock prisoners. It would take only a few hours on an off-time Sunday morning, and it would surely make a big difference in the success of the research if the prisoners-to-be had their freedom suddenly stripped away as they would in real arrests, rather than coming to Stanford voluntarily to surrender their freedom as research subjects. The chief acquiesced halfheartedly and promised that the duty sergeant would assign one squad car for this purpose on Sunday morning.

DISASTER: MISSION ABOUT TO ABORT BEFORE TAKEOFF

My mistake was not getting this confirmation in writing. Reality checks demand written documents (when an agreement is not filmed or taped). When I realized this truth on Saturday and called the station for a confirmation, Chief Zurcher was already away for the weekend. Bad omen.

As I expected, on Sunday the duty sergeant had no intention of committing the Palo Alto Police Department to a surprise mass arrest of a band of college students for alleged penal code violations, certainly not without written authorization from his chief. No way this old-timer was going to get involved in any experiment conducted by someone like me, whom his vice president, Spiro Agnew, had dismissed as an "effete intellectual snob." There were obviously more important things for his officers to do than to play cops and robbers as part of some lamebrained experiment. In his view, psychology experiments meant meddling into other people's affairs and finding out things better left private. He must have thought psychologists could read people's minds if they looked into their eyes, so he avoided looking at me when he said, "Sorry about that, Professor. I'd like to help you out, but rules are rules. Can't reassign the men to a new duty post without formal authorization."

Before he could say, "Come back on Monday, when the chief's here," I had a flash of this well-planned study going aground before even being launched. All systems were go: our mock prison had been carefully constructed in the basement of Stanford's Psychology Department; the guards had selected their uniforms and were eagerly waiting to receive their first prisoners; the first day's food had already been bought; the prisoners' uniforms had been all hand sewn by my secretary's daughter; videotaping facilities and taped bugging of the prisoner cells had been readied, the university Health Department, the Legal Department, the Fire Department, and the campus police had all been alerted; and arrangements for renting beds and linens were complete. Much more had been done to accommodate the daunting logistics of dealing with at least two dozen volunteers for two weeks, half living in our prison day and night, the others working eight-hour shifts. I had never before conducted an experiment that lasted more than one hour per subject per session. All this, and with one simple "No"; it might all crash and burn.

Having learned that precaution is the better part of scientific wisdom and that an ace in the hole is the best attribute of a Bronx wiseguy, I had anticipated this scenario as soon as I learned that Captain Zurcher had split from the scene. Therefore, I had persuaded a San Francisco TV director at station KRON to film the exciting surprise police arrests as a special feature for its evening news program. I counted on the power of the media to soften institutional resistance and even more on the lure of showbiz to get the arresting officers on my side—in front of the camera.

"Sure is a shame, Sergeant, that we can't proceed today as the chief expected we would. We have a TV cameraman right here from Channel 4 all ready to film the arrests for tonight's evening news. It would have been good public relations for the department, but maybe the chief won't be too upset that you decided not to permit us to go ahead as planned."

"Look, I didn't say I was against it, it's only that I'm not sure any of our men would be willing to do it. We can't just pull them off their duty, you know."

Vanity, Thy Name Is TV News Time

"Why don't we leave it up to the two officers here? If they don't mind being filmed for TV while they go through a few routine police arrests, then maybe we could go ahead as the chief agreed we should."

"No big thing, Sarge," said the younger officer, Joe Sparaco, combing his wavy black hair as he looked at the cameraman with his big camera resting snugly on his shoulder. "It's a slow Sunday morning, and this seems like it might be sort of interesting."

"All right, the chief must know what he's doing; I don't want to make any trouble if everything's all set up already. But hear me, you better be ready to answer any calls and cut the experiment short if I need you."

I chimed in, "Officers, would you spell your names for the TV man so that he can pronounce them right when the news report is shown tonight?" I needed to ensure their cooperation no matter what came up in Palo Alto before all of our prisoners had been arrested and gone through the formal booking process down here at headquarters.

"Must be a pretty important experiment to have TV coverage and all, huh, Professor?" Officer Bob asked, straightening his tie and automatically fingering the handle of his gun.

"I guess the TV people think so," I said, with full awareness of the precariousness of my perch, "what with surprise arrests by the police and all. It is a rather unusual experiment that might have some interesting effects; probably that's the reason the chief gave us the go-ahead. Here is a list of the names and addresses of each of the nine suspects to be arrested. I will be driving with Craig Haney, my graduate research assistant, behind your squad car. Drive slowly, so the cameraman can film your movements. Arrest one at a time using your standard operating procedure, read them their Miranda rights, search them, and handcuff them, as you would any dangerous suspect. The charge is burglary for the first five suspects, a 459 Penal Code violation, and make it armed robbery for the next four arrests, a Section 211 Code. Return each one to headquarters for booking, fingerprinting, filling out criminal identification cards, and whatever you usually do.

"Then put each one in a detention cell while you pick up the next suspect on the list. We will transfer the prisoner from your holding cell to our jail. The only irregular thing we'd like you to do is to blindfold the prisoner when you put him into the holding cell, with one of these blindfolds. When we transfer him out, we don't want him to see us or know exactly where he is headed. Craig, with my other assistant, Curt Banks, and one of our guards, Vandy, will do the transport."

"Sounds fine, Professor, Bob and I can handle it just fine, no problem."

NOW COMES THE MAIN STORY LINE[9]

We leave the sergeant's front office to go downstairs to check out the booking room—Joe and Bob, Craig, the cameraman, Bill, and I. Everything is spanking new; this unit was just constructed within the main Palo Alto City office center, a short distance but a far cry from the old jail, which had become run down, not from overuse but just old age. I wanted the officers and the cameraman to stay involved in the proceedings from the first arrest to the last to keep the arrests as standardized as possible. I had debriefed the TV man earlier about the purpose of the study but done so in a cursory manner because my concern had been winning over the anticipated resistance of the duty sergeant. It occurred to me that I should lay out for all of them some of the procedural details of the study as well as some of the reasons for doing this kind of experiment. It would help create a team feeling and also show that I cared enough to take the time to answer their questions.

"Do these kids know they are going to be arrested? Do we tell them it's part of an experiment or what?"

"Joe, they have all volunteered for a study of prison life. They answered an ad we put in the newspapers calling for college students who want to earn fifteen dollars a day to participate in a two-week experiment on the psychology of imprisonment, and—"

"You mean to say these kids are getting paid fifteen bucks a day to do nothin' but sit in a jail cell for two weeks? Maybe Joe and I could volunteer. Sounds like easy money."

"Maybe. Maybe it's easy money, and maybe if anything interesting turns up, we will do the study again, using some police officers as prisoners and guards, as I had told your chief."

"Well, you can count on us if you do."

"As I was saying, the nine students you are about to arrest were part of a large group of about a hundred men who answered our ads in the *Palo Alto Times* and *The Stanford Daily*. We screened out the obvious weirdos, the ones with prior arrests of any kind, and any with medical or mental problems. After an hourlong psychological assessment and in-depth interviews by my assistants, Craig Haney and Curt Banks, we selected twenty-four of these volunteers to be our research subjects."

"Twenty-four times fifteen bucks times fourteen days is a lot of money you're gonna hafta pay out. It's not outta your pocket, is it, Doc?"

"It comes to $5,040, but the research is supported by a government grant from the Office of Naval Research to study antisocial behavior, so I don't have to pay the salaries myself."

"Did all the students want to be prison guards?"

"Well, no, in fact no one wanted to be a guard; they all preferred to take the prisoner's role."

"How come? Seems like being a guard would be more fun and less hassle than being a prisoner, at least to me it does. Another thing is that fifteen bucks for twenty-four hours' work as a prisoner is peanuts. It's better pay for the guards if they only work usual shifts."

"That's right, the guards are planning to work eight-hour shifts, with three crews of three guards around the clock covering the nine prisoners. But the reason why these students preferred being in the prisoner role is that they might at some time become a prisoner, for draft evasion or DUI charges, for example, or arrested in some protest for civil rights or against the war. Most of them said they could never imagine ever being a prison guard—they didn't go to college in the hope of becoming a prison guard. So although they are all participating primarily for the money, some of them also expect to learn something about how they will handle themselves in this novel prison situation."

"How did you choose your guards? Bet you picked the biggest guys?"

"No, Joe, we randomly assigned all the volunteers to each of the two conditions, like tossing a coin. If it came up heads, the volunteer was assigned to be a guard; if it was tails, a prisoner. The guards were told yesterday that they had come up heads. They came to our little jail in the basement of Stanford's Psychology Department to help us put the finishing touches on it, so that they would feel like it was their place. Each of them picked out a uniform at the local Army surplus store, and they are waiting now for the action to begin."

"Did they get any training to be guards?"

"Wish I had the time to do that, but all we did was give them a brief orientation yesterday; no specific training in how to act their new role. The main thing is for them to maintain law and order, no violence against prisoners, and not allow any escapes. I also tried to convey to them the kind of psychological mind-set of prisoners being powerless that we want to create in this prison.

"The kids you are going to arrest were simply told to wait at home, in a dormitory, or at some designated house if they lived too far away, and they would be hearing from us this morning."

"And so they soon will, huh, Joe? We'll give 'em the real thing."

"I'm a little confused about a couple of things."

"Sure, fire away, Joe. You too, Bill, if there is something you want to know to help share later with your producer for tonight's show."

"My question is this, Doc: What's the point of going through all the trouble to set up a prison of your own down at Stanford, arresting these college students, paying out all that money, when we already have prisons enough and criminals enough? Why not just observe what goes on in the county jail or the action over at San Quentin? Wouldn't that tell you what you want to know about guards and prisoners in real prisons?"

Joe had hit the nail right on the head. Instantly I was into my college professor role, eager to profess to curious listeners: "I'm interested in discovering what it means psychologically to be a prisoner or a prison guard. What changes does a person undergo in the process of adapting to that new role? Is it possible in the short time of only a few weeks to take on a new identity that is different from one's usual self?

"There have been studies of actual prison life by sociologists and criminologists, but they suffer from some serious drawbacks. Those researchers are never free to observe all phases of prison life. Their observations are usually limited in scope, without much direct access to prisoners and even less to the guards. Since there are only two classes of people that populate prisons, staff and inmates, all researchers are outsiders viewed with suspicion, if not distrust, by all the system's insiders. They can see only what they are allowed to see on guided tours that rarely get beneath the surface of prison life. We'd like to better understand the deeper structure of the prisoner/guard relationship by re-creating the *psychological* environment of a prison, and then to be in a position to observe, record, and document the entire process of becoming indoctrinated into the mental set of prisoner and guard."

"Yes, I guess it makes sense the way you put it," Bill chimes in, "but the big difference between your Stanford jail and real ones is the type of prisoners and guards you're starting out with. In a real prison, we're dealing with criminal types, violent guys who think nothing about breaking the law or attacking guards. And you gotta have tough guards to keep them in line, ready to break heads if necessary. Your sweet little Stanford kids aren't mean or violent or tough like real guards and prisoners are."

"Let me throw in a zinger," says Bob. "How can you expect these college kids who know they're getting fifteen bucks a day for doing nothing will not just cool it for two weeks and have some fun and games at your expense, Doc?"

"First, I should mention that our subjects are not all Stanford students, only a few are. The others come from all over the country and even from Canada. As you know, a lot of young people come to the Bay Area in the summer, and we've recruited a cross section of them who were just finishing summer school at Stanford or at Berkeley. But you're right in saying that the Stanford County Jail will not be populated with the usual prison types. We went out of our way to select young men who seemed to be normal, healthy, and average on all the psychological dimensions we measured. Along with Craig, here, and another advanced graduate student, Curt Banks, I carefully selected our final sample from among all those we interviewed."

Craig, who had been waiting patiently for this sign of recognition from his mentor to get a word in edgewise, was ready to add to the thesis being laid down: "In a real prison, when we observe some event—for example, prisoners stabbing each other or a guard smashing an inmate—we can't determine the extent to which the particular person *or* the particular situation is responsible. There are indeed some prisoners who are violent sociopaths, and there are some guards who are sadistic. But do their personalities account for all or even most of what goes on in prison? I doubt it. We have to take the situation into account."

I beamed at Craig's eloquent argument. I also shared the same dispositional doubt but felt reassured to have Craig put it so well to the police officers. I continued, warming into my best minilecture style:

"The rationale is this: our research will attempt to differentiate between what people bring into a prison situation from what the situation brings out in the people who are there. By preselection, our subjects are generally representative of middle-class, educated youth. They are a homogeneous group of students who are quite similar to each other in many ways. By randomly assigning them to the two different roles, we begin with 'guards' and 'prisoners' who are comparable—indeed, are interchangeable. The prisoners are not more violent, hostile, or rebellious than the guards, and the guards aren't more power-seeking authoritarians. At this moment 'prisoner' and 'guard' are one and alike. No one wanted to be a guard; no one really committed any crime that would justify imprisonment and punishment. In two weeks, will these youngsters still be so indistinguishable? Will their roles change their personalities? Will we see any transformations of their character? That's what we plan to discover."

Craig added, "Another way of looking at it is, you're putting good people in an evil situation to see who or what wins."

"Thanks, Craig, I like that," gushed Cameraman Bill. "My director will want to use that tonight as a tease. The station didn't have a communicaster available this morning, so I have to both shoot and also come up with some angles to hook the arrest footage on. Say, Professor, time is running. I'm ready, can we get started now?"

"Of course, Bill. But, Joe, I never did answer your first question about the experiment."

"Which was?"

"Whether the prisoners knew they would be arrested as part of the experiment. The answer is no. They were merely told to be available for participation in the experiment this morning. They may assume that the arrest is part of the research since they know they did not commit the crimes for which they will be charged. If they ask you about the experiment, be vague, neither say it is or isn't. Just go about doing your duty as if it were a real arrest; ignore any of their questions or protests."

Craig couldn't resist adding, "In a sense, the arrest, like everything else they will be experiencing, should merge reality and illusion, role-playing and identity."

A bit flowery, I thought, but certainly worth saying. Just before Joe started the siren on his all-white squad car, he put on his silver reflecting sunglasses, the kind the guard wore in the movie *Cool Hand Luke*, the kind that prevents anyone from seeing your eyes. I grinned, as did Craig, knowing that all our guards would also be donning the same anonymity-inducing goggles as part of our attempt to create a sense of deindividuation. Art, life, and research were beginning to merge.

"THERE'S A COP KNOCKING ON THE DOOR"[10]

"Momma, Momma, there's a policeman at the door and he's going to arrest Hubbie!" screeched the youngest Whittlow girl.

Mrs. Dexter Whittlow didn't quite hear the message, but from the sound of Nina's screech there was some sort of trouble that Father should attend to.

"Please ask your father to see to it." Mrs. Whittlow was involved in examining her conscience because she had many misgivings about the changes that had been taking place in the church services from which she had just returned. She had also been thinking a lot about Hubbie recently, preparing herself for a life of twice-a-year visits from her beautiful fuzzy-blond, blue-eyed charmer. One blessing of his going away to college that she secretly prayed for was the "out of sight, out of mind" effect that would cool the all-too-obvious passion between Hubbie and his girlfriend from Palo Alto High School. For men, a good career had to come before hasty marriage plans, she told him often.

The only fault she could find in this lovable child was that he sometimes got carried away when he was with his friends, like last month, when they had painted the tile rooftops on the high school for pranks, or when they went about reversing and "ripping off" street signs. "It's plain silly and immature, Hubbie, and you could get in trouble for it!"

"Momma, Dad's not home, he's over at the golf course with Mr. Marsden, and Hubbie's downstairs being arrested by a policeman!"

"Hubbie Whittlow, you're wanted on a violation of Penal Code number 459, residential burglary. I'm going to take you to police headquarters for booking. Be-

fore I search and handcuff you, I must warn you of your rights as a citizen."
(Mindful of the TV camera grinding away, recording for posterity this classic arrest, Joe was all Super Cop in stance and all *Dragnet*'s cool Joe Friday in delivery.)
"Let me make some facts clear: You have the right to remain silent and are not required to answer any questions. Anything you say can and will be used against
you in a court of law. You have the right to consult an attorney before you answer
any questions, and an attorney may be present during the questioning. And if you
have no funds to hire an attorney, the public defender will provide you with one to
represent you at all stages of the proceedings. Do you understand your rights?
Good. Having these rights in mind, I am taking you to Central Station for booking
on the crime you are charged with. Now come peacefully over to the squad car."

Mrs. Whittlow was stunned to see her son being body searched, handcuffed,
and spread-eagled against the police car like a common criminal one sees on the
TV news. Gathering her composure, she demanded courteously: "What is this all
about, Officer?"

"Ma'am, I have instructions to arrest Hubbie Whittlow on charges of burglary, he—"

"I know, Officer, I told him not to take those street signs, that he shouldn't be
influenced by those Jennings boys."

"Momma, you don't understand, this is part of—"

"Officer, Hubbie is a good boy. His father and I will be glad to pay for the costs
of replacing anything that was taken. You see it was just a prank, nothing serious
intended."

By now a small crowd of neighbors was gathering at a respectable distance,
lured by the treat of a threat to someone's security or safety. Mrs. Whittlow made
a special effort not to notice them so as not to be distracted from the task at hand,
ingratiating herself with the police officer so he would be nicer to her son. "If only
George were here, he'd know how to handle the situation," she thought. "This is
what happens when golf comes before God on Sunday."

"Okay, let's move along, we've got a busy schedule; there's a lot more arrests
to be made this morning," Joe said as he moved the suspect into the squad car.

"Momma, Dad knows all about it, ask him, he signed the release, it's all right,
don't worry, it's just part of—"

The wailing siren of the squad car and its flashing lights brought out even
more curious neighbors to console poor Mrs. Whittlow, whose son seemed like
such a nice boy.

Hubbie felt uneasy for the first time, seeing his mother's distress and feeling
guilty sitting there alone in the backseat of a cop car, handcuffed behind the cop's
protective mesh screen. "So this is how it feels to be a criminal," he was thinking
when his pink cheeks suddenly flushed with embarrassment as Neighbor Palmer
pointed at him and exclaimed to his daughter, "What is this world coming to?
Now it's the Whittlow boy who's committed a crime!"

At the station, the booking procedure was dispatched with customary efficiency, given the cooperativeness of the suspect. Officer Bob took charge of Hubbie while Joe discussed with us how this first arrest had gone. I thought it had taken a little too long, considering that there were eight more to go. However, the cameraman wanted it to move more slowly so he could get positioned better since he had to shoot only a few good arrest sequences to convey the story. We agreed that the next arrest could be deliberate in its filmed sequences, but after that—good TV shots or not—the experiment would come first and the arrests would have to be sped up. Whittlow alone had already taken thirty minutes; at that rate it would take most of the day to complete the arrests.

I was mindful that the police's cooperation was not independent of the power of the media, so I worried that once the filming was completed they might be reluctant to follow through with all the remaining arrests on the list. Interesting as this part of the study was to observe, I knew that its success was not under my control. So many things could go wrong, most of which I had anticipated and tried to counteract, but there was always the unexpected event that could wipe out even the best-laid plans. There are too many uncontrolled variables in the real world, or the "field," as social scientists call it. That's the comfort of laboratory research: The experimenter is in charge. The action is all under exquisite control. The subject is on the researcher's turf. It's as the police interrogation manuals caution: "Never interrogate suspects or witnesses in their homes; bring them to the station, where you can capitalize on the unfamiliarity, seize on the lack of social supports, and in addition, you need not worry about unplanned interruptions."

I tried gently to urge the policeman to move a bit faster, but Bill kept intruding with requests for one more shot, one more angle. Joe was blindfolding Hubbie. Form C11-6, Bureau of Criminal Identification and Investigation, had been completed with the required information and full set of fingerprints, with only the mug shot remaining. We would do that with our Polaroid camera at our jail to save time, shooting after all prisoners were in their new uniforms. Hubbie had navigated through the booking process without comment or emotion after his first and only attempt at a joke had been rebuffed by Joe: "What are you, a wise guy or somethin'?" Now he was sitting in a small detention cell at Central Station, blindfolded, alone, and helpless, wondering why he had ever gotten himself into this mess and asking himself whether it was worth it. But he took solace in knowing that if things got too tough to handle, his father and his cousin, the public defender, could be counted on to arrive and get him out of the contract.

"OINK, OINK, THE PIGS ARE HERE"

The next arrest scenario played itself out in a small Palo Alto apartment.

"Doug, wake up, damn it, it's the police. One minute, please, he's coming. Get your pants on, will you."

"What d'ya mean, the police? What do they want with us? Look, Suzy, don't get uptight, act cool, we haven't done anything they can prove. Let me do the talking to the pigs. I know my rights. The fascists can't push us around."

Sensing a troublemaker at hand, Officer Bob used his friendly persuasion approach.

"Are you Mr. Doug Karlson?"

"Yeah, what of it?"

"I'm sorry, but you are suspected of Penal Code violation number 459, burglary, and I am taking you downtown to the station for booking. You have the right to remain silent, you have—"

"Cut it, I know my rights, I'm not a college graduate for nothing. Where's the warrant for my arrest?"

As Bob was thinking about how to handle this problem tactfully, Doug heard the nearby church bells tolling. "It's Sunday!" He had forgotten it was Sunday!

He said to himself, "Prisoner, huh, so that's the game? I prefer it, didn't go to college to become a pig, but I might get ripped off by the police someday, like I almost did at last year's antiwar riots at Cal. As I told the interviewer—Haney, I think it was—I don't want this for the money and not the experience because the whole idea sounds ridiculous, and I don't think it will work, but I'd like to see how I deal with being oppressed as a political prisoner.

"I have to laugh when I think of their silly question 'Estimate the likelihood of your remaining in the prison experiment for the full two weeks, on a 0 to 100 percent scale.' For me, 100 percent, with no sweat. It's not a real prison, only a simulated prison. If I don't dig it, I quit, just walk away. And I wonder how they reacted to my answer to 'What would you like to be doing ten years from now?' 'My ideal occupation, which I hope would entail an active part in the world's future—the revolution.' "

"Who am I? What is unique about me? How's my straight-from-the-shoulder answer: 'From a religious perspective, I'm an atheist. From a "conventional" perspective, I'm a fanatic. From a political perspective, I'm a socialist. From a mental health perspective, I'm healthy. From an existential-social perspective, I'm split, dehumanized, and detached—and I don't cry much.' "

Doug was reflecting on the oppression of the poor and the need to seize power back from the capitalist-military rulers of this country as he sat defiantly in the rear of the squad car on its swift journey to the station house. "It's good to be a prisoner," he thought. "All the exciting revolutionary ideas have come out of the prison experience." He felt a kinship with Soledad Brother George Jackson, liked his letters, and knew that in the solidarity of all oppressed people lies the strength to win the revolution. Maybe this little experiment would be the first step in training his mind and body for the eventual struggle against the fascists ruling America.

The booking officer ignored Doug's flippant comments as his height, weight, and fingerprints were efficiently recorded. He was all business. Joe easily rolled each finger to get a clear set of fingerprints even when Doug tried to make his hand rigid. Doug was a bit surprised at how strong the pig was, or maybe he was just a little weak from hunger since he hadn't had any breakfast yet. Out of somber proceedings evolved a slightly paranoid thought: "Hey, maybe those rat finks at Stanford really turned me in to the cops. What a fool I was, giving them so much personal background that they might use against me."

"Hey, Copper," Doug called out in his high-pitched voice, "tell me again, what am I charged with?"

"Burglary. On a first conviction, you could be paroled in a couple of years."

"I AM PREPARED TO BE ARRESTED, SIR"

The next scenario occurs at the designated pickup place for Tom Thompson, the porch of my secretary, Rosanne. Tom was built like a baby bull, five feet, eight inches tall, 170 pounds of solid muscle under his crew cut. If there were ever a no-nonsense person, it was this eighteen-year-old soldier boy. When we had asked him in our interview, "What would you like to be doing ten years from now?" his reply was surprising: "Where and what are unimportant—the kind of work would involve organization and efficiency producing in unorganized and inefficient areas of our government."

Marital plans: "I plan to marry only after I am solid financially."

Any therapy, drugs, tranquilizers, or criminal experience? "I have never committed a criminal act. I still remember the experience when I was five or six of seeing my father take a piece of candy to eat in a store while shopping. I was ashamed of his act."

In order to save on rent money, Tom Thompson had been sleeping in the backseat of his car, accommodations that were neither comfortable nor well suited to studying. Recently he had had to "fight off a spider that bit me twice, once on the eye and once on the lip." Nevertheless, he had just completed a full summer school course load in order to advance his credit standing. He was also working forty-five hours a week at assorted jobs and eating leftover food at the student food service to save up for next fall's tuition. As a result of his tenacity and frugality, Tom planned to graduate six months early. He was also bulking up by exercising seriously in his spare time, which apparently he had a lot of given his total absence of dates or close friends.

To be a paid participant in the prison study was the ideal job for Tom since his studies and summer jobs were now over and he needed the money. Three square meals a day, a real bed, and maybe a hot shower were like winning the lottery. However, more than anything else—or anyone else—he envisioned the next two weeks as a paid vacation.

He had not been doing squats for long on the porch at 450 Kingsley Street, where he was waiting to start his stint in our experiment, before the squad car pulled up behind his '65 Chevy. At a distance was Haney's Fiat with the undaunted cameraman filming what was to be the last outside arrest. After this, he'd get more interior footage in the station, then over at our mock prison. Bill was eager to get back to KRON with some hot video for what is usually a tame Sunday-evening news show.

"I'm Tom Thompson, sir. I am prepared to be arrested without any resistance."

Bob was leery of this one; he might be some kind of nut who wanted to prove something with his karate lessons. The handcuffs were slapped on right away, even before Miranda rights were read. And his search for concealed weapons was more thorough than it had been with the others because he had a funny feeling about guys who showed this particular kind of nonresistance. It was too cocky, too self-assured for someone facing an arrest; usually it meant a trap of some kind: the dude was packing a gun, a false-arrest charge was in the making, or there was something else out of the ordinary. "I'm no psychologist," Joe told me later, "but there is something off the wall about that guy Thompson, he's like a military drill officer—a sergeant in the enemy."

Fortunately, there were no crimes that Sunday in Palo Alto, or cats stranded up trees, to summon Bob and Joe away from finishing their ever-more-efficient arrest procedures. By early afternoon all of our prisoners had been booked and taken down to our jail, to the eager waiting arms of our guards-in-the-making. These young men would be leaving this sunny Palo Alto paradise, going down a short concrete staircase into the transformed basement of the Psychology Department in Jordan Hall, on Serra Street. For some it would become a descent into Hell.

CHAPTER THREE

Let Sunday's Degradation
Rituals Begin

As each of the blindfolded prisoners is escorted down the flight of steps in front of Jordan Hall into our little jail, our guards order them to strip and remain standing naked with their arms outstretched against the wall and legs spread apart. They hold that uncomfortable position for a long time as the guards ignore them because they are busy with last-minute chores, like packing away the prisoners' belongings for safekeeping, fixing up their guards quarters, and arranging beds in the three cells. Before being given his uniform, each prisoner is sprayed with powder, alleged to be a delouser, to rid him of lice that might be brought in to contaminate our jail. Without any staff encouragement, some guards begin to make fun of the prisoners' genitals, remarking on their small penis size or laughing at their unevenly hanging testicles. Such a guy thing!

Still blindfolded, each prisoner is then given his uniform, nothing fancy, just a smock, like a tan muslin dress, with numbers on front and back for identification. The numbers have been sewn on from sets we bought from a Boy Scout supply store. A woman's nylon stocking serves as a cap covering the long hair of many of these prisoners. It is a substitute for the head shaving that is part of the newcomer ritual in the military and some prisons. Covering the head is also a method of erasing one of the markers of individuality and promoting greater anonymity among the prisoner caste. Next, each prisoner dons a pair of rubber clogs, and a locked chain is attached to one ankle—a constant reminder of imprisonment. Even when he is asleep, the prisoner will be reminded of his status when the chain hits his foot as he turns in his sleep. The prisoners are allowed no underwear, so when they bend over their behinds show.

When the prisoners have been fully outfitted, the guards remove the blindfolds so that the prisoners can reflect on their new look in the full-length mirror propped against the wall. A Polaroid photo documents each prisoner's identity on an official booking form, where an ID number replaces "Name" on the form. The humiliation of being a prisoner has begun, much as it does in many institutions from military boot camps to prisons, hospitals, and low-level jobs.

"Don't move your head; don't move your mouth; don't move your hands; don't move your feet; and don't move anything. Now shut up, and stay where you are," barks Guard Arnett in his first show of authority.[1] He and the other day shift guards, J. Landry and Markus, are already starting to wield their police billy clubs in menacing positions as they undress and outfit the prisoners. The first four prisoners are lined up and told some of the basic rules, which the guards and the warden had formulated during the guard orientation on the previous day. "I don't like the warden to correct my work," says Arnett, "so I will make it desirable for you *not* to have to correct me. Listen carefully to these rules. You must address prisoners by number and by number only. Address guards as 'Mr. Correctional Officer.' "

As more prisoners are brought into the Yard, they are similarly deloused, outfitted, and made to join their fellows standing against the wall for indoctrination. The guards are trying to be very serious. "Some of you prisoners already know the rules, but others of you have shown you don't know how to act, so you need to learn them." Each rule is read slowly, seriously, and authoritatively. The

prisoners are slouching, shuffling, gazing around this strange new world. "Stand up straight, number 7258. Hands at your sides, prisoners."

Arnett begins to quiz the prisoners on the rules. He is demanding and critical, working hard to set a serious tone in official military manner. His style seems to say that he is just doing his job, nothing personal intended. But the prisoners are having none of that; they are giggling, laughing, not taking him seriously. They are hardly into playing their role as prisoners—yet.

"No laughing!" orders Guard J. Landry. Stocky, with long, shaggy blond hair, Landry is about six inches shorter than Arnett, who is a tall, slim fellow with aquiline features, dark brown curly hair, and tightly pursed lips.

Suddenly, Warden David Jaffe enters the jail. "Stand at attention against this wall for the full rule reading," says Arnett. Jaffe, who is actually one of my undergraduate Stanford students, is a little guy, maybe five feet five, but he seems to be taller than usual, standing very erect, shoulders back, head held high. He is already into his role as the warden.

I am watching the proceedings from a small scrim-covered window behind a partition that conceals our videocamera, Ampex taping system, and a tiny viewing space at the south end of the Yard. Behind the scrim, Curt Banks and others on our research team will record a series of special events throughout the next two weeks, such as meals, prisoner count-offs, visits by parents, friends, and a prison chaplain, and any disturbances. We don't have sufficient funds to record continuously, so we do so judiciously. This is also the site where we experimenters and other observers can look in on the action without disturbing it and without anyone being aware of when we are taping or watching. We can observe and tape-record only that action taking place directly in front of us in the Yard.

Although we cannot see into the cells, we can listen. The cells are bugged with audio devices that enable us to eavesdrop on some of the prisoners' talk. The prisoners are not aware of the hidden microphones concealed behind the indirect lighting panels. This information will be used to let us know what they are thinking and feeling when in private, and what kinds of things they share with one another. It may also be useful in identifying prisoners who need special attention because they are becoming overly stressed.

I am amazed at Warden Jaffe's pontificating and surprised at seeing him all dressed up for the first time in a sports jacket and tie. His clothing is rare for students in these hippie days. Nervously, he twirls his big Sonny Bono mustache, as he gets into his new role. I have told Jaffe that this is the time for him to introduce himself to this new group of prisoners as their warden. He is a bit reluctant because he is not a demonstrative kind of guy; he is lower-key, quietly intense. Because he was out of town, he did not take part in our extensive setup plans but arrived just yesterday, in time for the guard orientation. Jaffe felt a little out of the loop, especially since Craig and Curt were graduate students, while he was only an undergraduate. Perhaps he also felt uneasy because he was the littlest one among our otherwise all six-foot-plus-tall staff. But he stiffens his spine and comes on as strong and serious.

"As you probably already know, I am your warden. All of you have shown that you are unable to function outside in the real world for one reason or another. Somehow, you lack the sense of responsibility of good citizens of this great country. We in this prison, your correctional staff, are going to help you to learn what your responsibility as citizens of this country is. You heard the rules. Sometime in the very near future there will be a copy of the rules posted in each cell. We expect you to know them and be able to recite them by number. If you follow all of these rules, keep your hands clean, repent for your misdeeds, and show a proper attitude of penitence, then you and I will get along just fine. Hopefully I won't have to be seeing you too often."

It was an amazing improvisation, followed by an order from Guard Markus, talking up for the first time: "Now you thank the warden for his fine speech to you." In unison, the nine prisoners shout their thanks to the warden but without much sincerity.

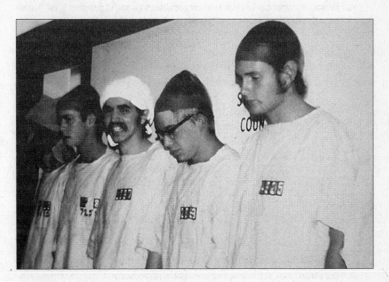

THESE ARE THE RULES YOU WILL LIVE BY

The time has come to impose some formality on the situation by exposing to the new prisoners the set of rules that will govern their behavior for the next few weeks. With all the guards giving some input, Jaffe worked out these rules in an intense session yesterday at the end of the guard orientation.[2]

Guard Arnett talks it over with Warden Jaffe, and they decide that Arnett will read the full set of the rules aloud—his first step in dominating the day shift. He begins slowly and with precise articulation. The seventeen rules are:

1. Prisoners must remain silent during rest periods, after lights out, during meals, and whenever they are outside the prison yard.
2. Prisoners must eat at mealtimes and only at mealtimes.
3. Prisoners must participate in all prison activities.
4. Prisoners must keep their cell clean at all times. Beds must be made and personal effects must be neat and orderly. Floors must be spotless.
5. Prisoners must not move, tamper with, deface, or damage walls, ceilings, windows, doors, or any prison property.
6. Prisoners must never operate cell lighting.
7. Prisoners must address each other by number only.
8. Prisoners must always address the guards as "Mr. Correctional Officer" and the Warden as "Mr. Chief Correctional Officer."
9. Prisoners must never refer to their condition as an "experiment" or "simulation." They are imprisoned until paroled.

"We are halfway there. I hope you are paying close attention, because you will commit each and every one of these rules to memory, and we will test at random intervals," the guard forewarns his new charges.

10. Prisoners will be allowed 5 minutes in the lavatory. No prisoner will be allowed to return to the lavatory within 1 hour after a scheduled lavatory period. Lavatory visitations are controlled by the guards.
11. Smoking is a privilege. Smoking will be allowed after meals or at the discretion of the guard. Prisoners must never smoke in the cells. Abuse of the smoking privilege will result in permanent revocation of the smoking privilege.
12. Mail is a privilege. All mail flowing in and out of the prison will be inspected and censored.
13. Visitors are a privilege. Prisoners who are allowed a visitor must meet him or her at the door to the yard. The visit will be supervised by a guard, and the guard may terminate the visit at his discretion.
14. All prisoners in each cell will stand whenever the warden, the prison superintendent, or any other visitors arrive on the premises. Prisoners will wait on orders to be seated or to resume activities.
15. Prisoners must obey all orders issued by guards at all times. A guard's order supersedes any written order. A warden's order supersedes both the guard's orders and the written rules. Orders of the superintendent of the prison are supreme.
16. Prisoners must report all rule violations to the guards.

"Last, but the most important, rule for you to remember at all times is number seventeen," adds Guard Arnett in an ominous warning:

17.   Failure to obey any of the above rules may result in punishment.

Later on in the shift, Guard J. Landry decides that he wants some of the action and rereads the rules, adding his personal embellishment: "Prisoners are a part of a correctional community. In order to keep the community running smoothly, you prisoners must obey the following rules."

Jaffe nods in agreement; he already likes to think of this as a prison community, in which reasonable people giving and following rules can live harmoniously.

The First Count in This Strange Place

According to the plan developed by the guards at their orientation meeting the day before, Guard J. Landry continues the process of establishing the guards' authority by giving instructions for the count. "Okay, to familiarize yourselves with your numbers, we are going to have you count them off from left to right, and fast." The prisoners shout out their numbers, which are arbitrary four- or three-digit numbers on the front of their smocks. "That was pretty good, but I'd like to see them at attention." The prisoners reluctantly stand erect at attention. "You were too slow in standing tall. Give me ten push-ups." (Push-ups soon become a staple in the guards' control and punishment tactics.) "Was that a smile?" Jaffe asks. "I can see that smile from down here. This is not funny, this is serious business that you have gotten yourselves into." Jaffe soon leaves the Yard to come around back to confer with us on how he did in his opening scene. Almost in unison, Craig, Curt, and I give him a pat on the ego: "Right on, Dave, way to go!"

Initially the purpose of counts, as in all prisons, is an administrative necessity to ensure that all prisoners are present and accounted for, that none has escaped or is still in his cell sick or needing attention. In this case, the secondary purpose of the counts is for prisoners to familiarize themselves with their new numbered identity. We want them to begin thinking of themselves, and the others, as prisoners with numbers, not people with names. What is fascinating is how the nature of the counts is transformed over time from routine memorizing and reciting of IDs to an open forum for guards to display their total authority over the prisoners. As both groups of student research participants, who are initially interchangeable, get into their roles, the counts provide public demonstration of the transformation of characters into guards and prisoners.

The prisoners are finally sent into their cells to memorize the rules and get acquainted with their new cellmates. The cells, designed to emphasize the ambient anonymity of prison living conditions, are actually reconstructed small offices, ten by twelve feet in size. For the office furniture we substituted three cots, pushed together side by side. The cells are totally barren of any other furniture, except for

Cell 3, which has a sink and faucet, which we have turned off but which the guards can turn back on at will to reward designated good prisoners put into that special cell. The office doors were replaced with specially made black doors fitted with a row of iron bars down a central window, with each of the three cell numbers prominently displayed on the door.

The cells run the length of the wall down the right side of the Yard, as it appears from our vantage point behind the one-way observation screen. The Yard is a long, narrow corridor, nine feet wide and thirty-eight feet long. There are no windows, simply indirect neon lighting. The only entrance and exit is at the far north end of the corridor, opposite our observation wall. Because there is only a single exit, we have several fire extinguishers handy in case of a fire, by order of the Stanford University Human Subjects Research Committee, which reviewed and approved our research. (However, fire extinguishers can also become weapons.)

Yesterday, the guards posted signs on the walls of the Yard, designating this "The Stanford County Jail." Another sign forbade smoking without permission, and a third indicated, ominously, the location of solitary confinement, "the Hole." Solitary consisted of a small closet in the wall opposite the cells. It had been used for storage, and its file boxes took up all but about a square yard of open space. That is where unruly prisoners would spend time as punishment for various offenses. In this small space, prisoners would stand, squat, or sit on the floor in total darkness for the length of time ordered by a guard. They would be able to hear the goings-on outside on the Yard and hear all too well anyone banging on the doors of the Hole.

The prisoners are sent to their arbitrarily assigned cells: Cell 1 is for 3401, 5704, and 7258; Cell 2 is for 819, 1037, and 8612; while Cell 3 houses 2093, 4325, and 5486. In one sense, this is like a prisoner-of-war situation wherein a number of the enemy are captured and imprisoned as a unit, rather than like a civilian prison, where there is a preexistent prisoner community into which each new inmate is socialized and into which prisoners are always entering and being paroled out of.

All in all, our prison was a much more humane facility than most POW camps—and certainly more commodious, clean, and orderly than the hard site at Abu Ghraib Prison (which, by the way, Saddam Hussein made notorious for torture and murder long before American soldiers did more recently). Yet, despite its relative "comfort," this Stanford prison would become the scene of abuses that eerily foreshadowed the abuses of Abu Ghraib by Army Reserve Military Police years later.

Role Adjustments

It takes a while for the guards to get into their roles. From the Guard Shift Reports, made at the end of each of the three different shifts, we learn that Guard Vandy feels uneasy, not sure what it takes to be a good guard, wishes he had been given some training, but thinks it is a mistake to be too nice to the prisoners. Guard Geoff Landry, kid brother of J. Landry, reports feeling guilty during the humiliating degradation rituals in which the prisoners had to stand naked for a long time in uncomfortable positions. He is sorry that he did not try to stop some things of which he did not approve. Instead of raising an objection, he just left the Yard as often as possible rather than continue to experience these unpleasant interactions. Guard Arnett, a graduate student in sociology, who is a few years older than the others, doubts that the prisoner induction is having its desired effect. He thinks that the security on his shift is bad and the other guards are being too polite. Even after this first day's brief encounters, Arnett is able to single out those prisoners who are troublemakers and those who are "acceptable." He also points out something that we missed in our observations but Officer Joe had remarked about during the arrest of Tom Thompson—a concern about Prisoner 2093.

Arnett doesn't like the fact that Tom-2093 is "too good" in his "rigid adherence to all orders and regulations."[3] (Indeed, 2093 will later be disparagingly nicknamed "Sarge" by the other prisoners precisely because of his militaristic style of obediently following orders. He has brought some strong values into our situation that may come into conflict with those of the guards, something to notice as we go along. Recall that it was something also noticed about Tom by the arresting police officer.)

In contrast, Prisoner 819 considers the whole situation quite "amusing."[4] He found the first counts rather enjoyable, "just a joke," and he felt that some of the guards did as well. Prisoner 1037 had watched as all the others were processed in the same humiliating fashion as he was. However, he refused to take any of it seriously. He was more concerned with how hungry he had become, having eaten only a small breakfast and expecting to be fed lunch, which never came. He assumed that the failure to provide lunch was another arbitrary punishment inflicted by the guards, despite the fact that most prisoners had been well behaved. In truth, we had simply forgotten to pick up lunch because the arrests had taken so long and there was so much for us to deal with, which included a last-minute cancellation by one of the students assigned to the guard role. Fortunately, we got a replacement from the original pool of screened applicants for the night shift, Guard Burdan.

The Night Shift Takes Over

The night shift guards arrive before their starting time at 6 P.M. to don their new uniforms, try on the sleek silver reflecting sunglasses, and equip themselves with whistles, handcuffs, and billy clubs. They report to the Guards' Office, located down a few steps from the entrance to the Yard, in a corridor that also houses the offices of the warden and the superintendent, each with his own sign printed on the door. There the day shift guards greet their new buddies, tell them that everything is under control and everything is in place, but add that some prisoners are not yet fully with the program. They deserve watching, and pressure should be applied to get them into line. "We're gonna do that just fine, you'll see a *straight line* when you come back tomorrow," boasts one of the newcomer guards.

The first meal is finally served at seven o'clock. It's a simple one, offered cafeteria style on a table set out in the Yard.[5] There is room for only six inmates at the table, so when they finish the remaining three come to eat what is left. Right off, Prisoner 8612 tries to talk the others into going on a sit-down strike to protest these "unacceptable" prison conditions, but they are all too hungry and tired to go along right now. 8612 is wise guy Doug Karlson, the anarchist who gave the arresting cops some lip.

Back in their cells, the prisoners are ordered to remain silent, but 819 and 8612 disobey, talk loudly and laugh, and get away with it—for now. Prisoner 5704, the tallest of the lot, has been silent until now, but his tobacco addiction has gotten to him, and he demands that his cigarettes be returned to him. He's told that he has to *earn* the right to smoke by being a good prisoner. 5704 challenges this principle, saying it is breaking the rules, but to no avail. According to the rules of the experiment, any participant could leave at any time, but this seems to have been forgotten by the disgruntled prisoners. They could have used the threat to quit as a tactic to improve their conditions or reduce the mindless hassling they endured, but they did not as they slowly slipped more deeply into their roles.

Warden Jaffe's final official task of this first day is to inform the prisoners about Visiting Nights, which are coming up soon. Any prisoners who have friends or relatives in the vicinity should write to them about coming to visit. He describes the letter-writing procedures and gives each one who asks for it a pen, Stanford County Jail stationery, and a stamped envelope. They are to complete their letters and return these materials by the end of the brief "writing period." He makes it clear that the guards have discretion to decide whether anyone will not be allowed to write a letter, because he has failed to follow the rules, did not know his prisoner ID number, or for any other reason a guard may have. Once the letters are written and handed to the guards, the prisoners are ordered back out of their cells for the first count on the night shift. Of course, the staff reads each letter for security purposes, also making copies for our files before mailing them out. The lure of Visiting Night and the mail, then, become tools that the guards use instinctively and effectively to tighten their control on the prisoners.

The New Meaning of Counts

Officially, as far as I was concerned, the counts were supposed to serve two functions: to familiarize the prisoners with their ID numbers and to establish that all prisoners were accounted for at the start of each guard shift. In many prisons, the counts also serve as a means of disciplining the prisoners. Though the first count started out innocently enough, our nightly counts and their early-morning counterparts would eventually escalate into tormenting experiences.

"Okay, boys, now we are going to have a little count! Going to be a lot of fun,"

Guard Hellmann tells them with a big grin. Guard Geoff Landry quickly adds, "The better you do it, the shorter it'll be." As the weary prisoners file out into the yard, they are silent and sullen, not looking at one another. It has already been a long day, and who knows what's in store before they can finally get a good night's sleep.

Geoff Landry takes command: "Turn around, hands against the wall. No talking! You want this to last all night? We're going to do this until you get it right. Start by counting off in ones." Hellmann adds his two cents: "I want you to do it fast, and I want you to do it loud." The prisoners obey. "I didn't hear it very well, we'll have to do it again. Guys, that was awful slow, so once again." "That's right," Landry chimes in, "we'll have to do it again." As soon as a few numbers are called out, Hellmann yells, "Stop! Is that loud? Maybe you didn't hear me right, I said loud, and I said clear." "Let's see if they can count backwards. Now try it from the other end," Landry says playfully. "Hey! I don't want anybody laughing!" Hellmann says gruffly. "We'll be here all night until we get it right."

Some of the prisoners are becoming aware that a struggle for dominance is going on between these two guards, Hellmann and the younger Landry. Prisoner 819, who has not been taking any of this seriously, begins to laugh aloud as Landry and Hellmann one-up each other at the prisoners' expense. "Hey, did I say that you could laugh, 819? Maybe you didn't hear me right." Hellmann is getting angry for the first time. He gets right up in the prisoner's face, leans on him, and pushes him back with his billy club. Now Landry pushes his fellow guard aside and commands 819 to do twenty push-ups, which he does without comment.

Hellmann moves back to center stage: "This time, *sing it*." As the prisoners start to count off again, he interrupts. "Didn't I say that you had to sing? Maybe you gentlemen have those stocking caps too tight around your head and you can't hear me too well." He is becoming more creative in control techniques and dialogue. He turns on Prisoner 1037 for singing his number off key and demands twenty jumping jacks. After he finishes, Hellmann adds, "Would you do ten more for me? And don't make that thing rattle so much this time." Because there is no way to do jumping jacks without the ankle chain making noise, the commands are becoming arbitrary, but the guards are beginning to take pleasure in giving commands and forcing the prisoners to execute them.

Even though it is funny to have the prisoners singing numbers, the two guards alternate in saying "There's nothing funny about it" and complaining "Oh, that's terrible, really bad." "Now once more," Hellmann tells them. "I'd like you to sing, I want it to sound *sweet*." Prisoner after prisoner is ordered to do more push-ups for being too slow or too sour.

When the replacement guard, Burdan, appears with the warden, the dynamic duo of Hellmann and Landry immediately switches to having the prisoners count off by their prison ID numbers and not just their lineup numbers from one to nine, as they had been doing, which of course, made no official sense. Now Hellmann insists that they can't look at their numbers when they count since by now they should have memorized them. If anyone of the prisoners gets his number wrong, the punishment is a dozen push-ups for everyone. Still competing with Landry for dominance in the guards' pecking order, Hellmann becomes ever more arbitrary: "I don't like the way you count when you're going *down*. I want you to count when you're going *up*. Do ten more push-ups for me, will you, 5486." The prisoners are clearly complying with orders more and more quickly. But that just reinforces the guards' desire to demand more of them. Hellmann: "Well, that's just great. Why don't you sing it this time? You men don't sing very well, it just doesn't sound too sweet to me." Landry: "I don't think they're keeping very good time. Make it nice and sweet, make it a pleasure to the ear." 819 and 5486 continue to mock the process but, oddly, comply with the guards' demands to perform many jumping jacks as their punishment.

The new guard, Burdan, gets into the act even more quickly than did the other guards, but he has had on-the-job training watching his two role models strut their stuff. "Oh, that was pretty! Now, that's the way I want you to do it. 3401, come out here and do a solo, tell us what your number is!" Burdan goes beyond what his fellow guards have been doing by physically pulling prisoners out of line to sing their solos in front of the others.

Prisoner Stew-819 has become marked. He has been made to sing a solo tune, again and again, but his song is deemed never "sweet enough." The guards banter back and forth: "He sure doesn't sound sweet!" "No, he doesn't sound sweet to me at all." "Ten more." Hellmann appreciates Burdan's beginning to act like a guard, but he is not ready to relinquish control to him or to Landry. He asks the prisoners to recite the number of the prisoner next down in line to them. When they don't know it, as most do not, ever more push-ups.

"5486, you sound real tired. Can't you do any better? Let's have five more." Hellmann has come up with a creative new plan to teach Jerry-5486 his number in an unforgettable way: "First do *five* push-ups, then *four* jumping jacks, then *eight* push-ups and *six* jumping jacks, just so you will remember exactly what that number is, 5486." He is becoming more cleverly inventive in designing punishments, the first signs of creative evil.

Landry has withdrawn to the far side of the Yard, apparently ceding dominance to Hellmann. As he does, Burdan moves in to fill the space, but instead of competing with Hellmann, he supports him, typically either adding to his commands or elaborating upon them. But Landry is not out of it yet. He moves back in and demands another number count. Not really satisfied with the last one, he tells the nine tired prisoners to count off now by twos, then by threes, and up and up. He is obviously not as creative as Hellmann but competitive nevertheless. 5486 is confused and made to do more and more push-ups. Hellmann interrupts, "I'd have you do it by 7s, but I know you're not that smart, so come over and get your blankets." Landry tries to continue: "Wait, wait, hold it. Hands against the wall." But Hellmann will have none of that and, in a most authoritative fashion, ignores Landry's last order and dismisses the prisoners to get sheets and blankets, make their beds, and stay in their cells until further notice. Hellmann, who has taken charge of the keys, locks them in.

THE FIRST SIGN OF REBELLION BREWING

At the end of his shift, as he is leaving the Yard, Hellmann yells out to the prisoners, "All right, gentlemen, did you enjoy our counts?" "No sir!" "Who said that?" Prisoner 8612 owns up to that remark, saying he was raised not to tell a lie. All three guards rush into Cell 2 and grab 8612, who is giving the clenched-fist salute of dissident radicals as he shouts, "All power to the people!" He is dumped into the Hole—with the distinction of being its first occupant. The guards show that they are united about one principle: they will not tolerate any dissent. Landry now follows up on Hellmann's previous question to the prisoners. "All right, did you enjoy your count?" "Yes sir." "Yes sir, what?" "Yes sir, Mr. Correctional Officer." "That's more like it." Since no one else is willing to openly challenge their authority, the three caballeros walk down the hall in formation, as though in a military parade. Before going off to the guards' quarters, Hellmann peers into Cell 2 to remind its occupants that "I want these beds in real apple pie order." Prisoner 5486 later reported feeling depressed when 8612 was put into the Hole. He also felt guilty for not having done anything to intervene. But he rationalized his behavior in not wanting to sacrifice his comfort or get thrown into solitary as well by reminding himself that "it's only an experiment."[6]

Before lights out at 10 P.M. sharp, prisoners are allowed their last toilet privilege of the night. To do so requires permission, and one by one, or two by two, they are blindfolded and led to the toilet—out the entrance to the prison and around the corridor by a circuitous route through a noisy boiler room to confuse them about both its location and their own. Later, this inefficient procedure will be streamlined as all prisoners tread this toilet route ensemble, and it might include an elevator ride for further confusion.

At first, Prisoner Tom-2093 says he needs more than the brief time allocated because he can't urinate since he is so tense. The guards refuse, but the other prisoners unify in their insistence that he be allowed sufficient time. "It was a matter of establishing that there were certain things that we wanted," 5486 later defiantly reported.[7] Small events like this one are what can combine to give a new collective identity to prisoners as something more than a collection of individuals trying to survive on their own. Rebel Doug-8612 feels that the guards are obviously role-playing, that their behavior is just a joke, but that they are "going overboard." He will continue his efforts to organize the other prisoners so they will have more power. In contrast, our fair-haired-boy prisoner, Hubbie-7258, reports that "As the day goes on, I wish I was a guard."[8] Not surprisingly, none of the guards wishes to be a prisoner.

Another rebellious prisoner, 819, showed his stuff in his letter to his family, asking them to come to Visiting Night. He signed it, "All power to the oppressed brothers, victory is inevitable. No kidding, I am as happy here as a prisoner can be!"[9] While playing cards in their quarters, the night shift guards and the warden decide on a plan for the first count of the morning shift that will distress the prisoners. Shortly after the start of their shift, the guards will stand close to the cell doors and awaken their charges with loud, shrieking whistles. This will also quickly get the new guard shift energized into their roles and disturb the sleep of the prisoners at the same time. Landry, Burdan, and Hellmann all like that plan and as they continue playing discuss how they can be better guards the following night. Hellmann thinks it is all "fun and games." He has decided to act like "hot shit" from now on, "to play a more domineering role," as in a fraternity hazing or in movies about prisons, like *Cool Hand Luke*.[10]

Burdan is in a critical position as swingman, as the guard in the middle, on this night shift. Geoff Landry started out strong but, as the night wore on, deferred to Hellmann's creative inventions and finally gave in to his powerful style. Later, Landry will move into the role of a "good guard"—friendly toward the inmates and doing nothing to degrade them. If Burdan sides with Landry, then together they might dim Hellmann's bright lights. But if Burdan sides with the tough guy, Landry will be odd man out and the shift will move in a sinister direction. In his retrospective diary, Burdan writes that he felt anxious when he was suddenly called at 6 P.M. that night to be on duty ASAP.

Putting on a military-style uniform made him feel silly, given the overflowing black hair on his face and head, a contrast that he worried might make prisoners laugh at him. He consciously decided not to look them in the eyes, nor smile, nor treat the scenario as a game. Compared with Hellmann and Landry, who look self-assured in the new roles, he is not. He thinks of them as "the regulars" even though they were at their jobs only a few hours before his arrival. What he enjoys most about his costume is carrying the big billy club, which conveys a sense of power and security as he wields it, rattling it against the bars of the cell doors, banging it on the Hole door, or just pounding into his hand, which becomes his routine gesture. The rap session at the end of his shift with his new buddies has made him more like his old self, less like a power-drunk guard. He does, however, give Landry a pep talk about the necessity for all of them to work as a team in order to keep the prisoners in line and not to tolerate any rebelliousness.

Shrieking Whistles at 2:30 A.M.

The morning shift comes on in the middle of the night, 2 A.M., and quits at 10 A.M. This shift consists of Andre Ceros, another long-haired, bearded young man, who is joined by Karl Vandy. Remember that Vandy had helped the day shift to transport prisoners from the County Jail to our jail, so he starts out rather tired. Like Burdan, he sports a full head of long, sleek hair. The third guard, Mike Varnish, is built like an offensive lineman, sturdy and muscular but shorter than the other two. When the warden tells them that there will be a surprise wake-up notice to announce that their shift is at work, all three are delighted to start off with such a big bang.

The prisoners are sound asleep. Some are snoring in their dark, cramped cells. Suddenly the silence is shattered. Loud whistles shriek, voices yell, "Up and at 'em." "Wake up and get out here for the count!" "Okay, you sleeping beauties, it's time to see if you learned how to count." Dazed prisoners line up against the wall and count off mindlessly as the three guards alternate in coming up with new variations on count themes. The count and its attendant push-ups and jumping jacks for failures continue on and on for nearly a weary hour. Finally, the prisoners are ordered back to sleep—until reveille a few hours later. Some prisoners report that they felt the first signs of time distortion, feeling surprised, exhausted, and angry. Some later admit that they considered quitting at this point.

Guard Ceros, at first uncomfortable in his uniform, now likes the effect of wearing silver reflecting glasses. They make him feel "safely authoritative." But the loud whistles echoing through the dark chamber scare him a bit. He feels he is too soft to be a good guard, so he tries to turn his urge to laugh into a "sadistic smile."[11] He goes out of his way to compliment the warden on his constant suggestions for sadistic ways to enhance the count. Varnish later reported that he knew it would be tough for him to be a strong guard, and therefore he looked to the others for clues about how to behave in this unusual setting, as most of us do when we find ourselves in an alien situation. He felt that the main task of the guards was to help create an environment in which the prisoners would lose their old identities and take on new ones.

Some Initial Observations and Concerns

My notes at this time raise the following questions on which to focus our attention over the coming days and nights: Will the arbitrary cruelty of the guards continue to increase, or will it reach some equilibrium point? When they go home and reflect on what they did here, can we expect them to repent, feel somewhat ashamed of their excesses, and act more kindly? Is it possible that the verbal aggression will escalate and even turn to more physical force? Already, the boredom of tedious eight-hour guard shifts has driven the guards to entertain themselves by using the prisoners as playthings. How will they deal with this boredom as the experiment goes forward? For the prisoners, how will they deal with the boredom of living as prisoners around the clock? Will the prisoners be able to maintain some measure of dignity or rights for themselves by unifying in their opposition, or will they allow themselves to become completely subject to the guards' demands? How long will it be before the first prisoner decides he has had too much and quits the experiment, and will that cascade into others following suit? We've seen very different styles between the day shift and the night shift. What will the morning shift's style be like?

It is evident that it has taken a while for these students to take on their new roles, and with considerable hesitation and some awkwardness. There is still a clear sense that it is an experiment on prison life and not really much like an actual prison. They may never transcend that psychological barrier of feeling as though one were imprisoned in a place in which he had lost his freedom to leave at will. How could we expect that outcome in something that was so obviously an experiment, despite the mundane reality of the police arrests? In my orientation of the guards on Saturday, I had tried to initiate them into thinking of this place as a prison in its imitation of the psychological functionality of real prisons. I had described the kinds of mental sets that characterize the guard–prisoner experiences that take place in prisons, which I had learned from my contacts with our prison consultant, the formerly incarcerated Carlo Prescott, and from the summer school course we had just completed on the psychology of imprisonment. I worried that I might have given too much direction to them, which would demand behavior that they were simply following rather than gradually internalizing their new roles through their on-the-job-experiences. So far, it seemed as if the guards were rather varied in their behavior and not acting from a preplanned script. Let's review what transpired in that earlier guard orientation.

SATURDAY'S GUARD ORIENTATION

In preparation for the experiment, our staff met with the dozen guards to discuss the purpose of the experiment, give them their assignments, and suggest means of keeping the prisoners under control without using physical punishment. Nine of the guards had been randomly assigned to the three shifts, with the other three as backup, or relief, guards, available for emergency duty. After I provided an overview of why we were interested in a study of prison life, Warden David Jaffe described some of the procedures and duties of the guards, while Craig Haney and Curt Banks, in the role of psychological counselors, gave detailed information about Sunday's arrest features and the induction of the new prisoners into our jail.

In reviewing the purpose of the experiment, I told them that I believe all prisons to be physical metaphors for the loss of freedom that all of us feel in different ways for different reasons. As social psychologists, we want to understand the psychological barriers that prisons create between people. Of course, there were limits to what could be accomplished in an experiment using only a "mock prison." The prisoners knew they were being imprisoned for only the relatively short time of two weeks, unlike the long years most real inmates serve. They also knew that there were limits to what we could do to them in an experimental setting, unlike real prisons, where prisoners can be beaten, electrically shocked, gang-raped, and sometimes even killed. I made it clear that we couldn't physically abuse the "prisoners" in any way.

I also made it evident that, despite these constraints, we wanted to create a psychological atmosphere that would capture some of the essential features characteristic of many prisons I had learned about recently.

"We cannot physically abuse or torture them," I said. "We can create boredom. We can create a sense of frustration. We can create fear in them, to some degree. We can create a notion of the arbitrariness that governs their lives, which are totally controlled by us, by the system, by you, me, Jaffe. They'll have no privacy at all, there will be constant surveillance—nothing they do will go unobserved. They will have no freedom of action. They will be able to do nothing and say nothing that we don't permit. We're going to take away their individuality in various ways. They're going to be wearing uniforms, and at no time will anybody call them by name; they will have numbers and be called only by their numbers. In general, what all this should create in them is a sense of powerlessness. We have total power in the situation. They have none. The research question is, What will they do to try to gain power, to regain some degree of individuality, to gain some freedom, to gain some privacy? Will the prisoners essentially work against us to regain some of what they now have as they freely move outside the prison?"[12]

I indicated to these neophyte guards that the prisoners were likely to think of this all as "fun and games" but it was up to all of us as prison staff to produce the required psychological state in the prisoners for as long as the study lasted. We would have to make them feel as though they were in prison; we should never mention this as a study or an experiment. After answering various questions from these guards-in-the-making, I outlined the way in which the three shifts would be chosen by their preferences so as to have three of them on each shift. I then made it clear that the seemingly least desirable night shift was likely to be the easiest because the prisoners would be sleeping at least half the time. "There'll be relatively little for you to do, although you can't sleep. You have to be there in case they plan something." Despite my assumption that there would be little work for the night shift, that shift ended up doing the most work—and carrying out the most abusive treatment of the prisoners.

I should mention again that my initial interest was more in the prisoners and their adjustment to this prisonlike situation than it was in the guards. The guards were merely ensemble players who would help create a mind-set in the prisoners of the feeling of being imprisoned. I think that perspective came from my lower-class background, which made me identify more with prisoners than guards. It surely was shaped by my extensive personal contact with Prescott and the other former inmates I had recently gotten to know. So my orientation speech was designed to get the guards "into the mood of the joint" by outlining some of the key situational and psychological processes at work in typical prisons. Over time, it became evident to us that the behavior of the guards was as interesting as, or sometimes even more interesting than, that of the prisoners. Would we have gotten the same outcome without this orientation, had we allowed only the behavioral context and role-playing to operate? As you will see, despite this biasing guidance, the guards initially did little to enact the attitudes and behaviors that were needed to create such negative mind-sets in the prisoners. It took time for their new roles and the situational forces to operate upon them in ways that would gradually transform them into perpetrators of abuse against the prisoners—the evil that I was ultimately responsible for creating in this Stanford County Jail.

Looked at another way, these guards had no formal training in becoming guards, were told primarily to maintain law and order, not to allow prisoners to escape, and never to use physical force against the prisoners, and were given a general orientation about the negative aspects of the psychology of imprisonment. The procedure is much like many systems of inducting guards into correctional service with limited training, only that they are allowed to use whatever force is necessary under threatening circumstances. The set of rules given by the warden and the guards to the prisoners and my orientation instructions to the guards represent the contributions of the System in creating a set of initial situational conditions that would challenge the values, attitudes, and personality dispositions that these experimental participants brought into this unique setting. We will soon see how the conflict between the power of the situation and the power of the person was resolved.

Guards	Prisoners
Day Shift: 10 A.M.–6 P.M.	*Cell #1*
Arnett, Markus,	3401—Glenn
Landry (John)	5704—Paul
Night Shift: 6 P.M.–2 A.M.	7258—Hubbie
Hellmann, Burdan	*Cell #2*
Landry (Geoff)	819—Stewart
Morning Shift: 2 A.M.–10 A.M.	1037—Rich
Vandy, Ceros	8612—Doug
Varnish	*Cell #3*
Back-up Guards	2093—Tom "Sarge"
Morismo, Peters	4325—Jim
	5486—Jerry

CHAPTER FOUR

Monday's Prisoner Rebellion

Monday, Monday, dreary and weary for all of us after a much too long first day and a seemingly endless night. But there go the shrill whistles again, rousing the prisoners from sleep promptly at 6 A.M. They drift out of their cells bleary-eyed, adjusting their stocking caps and smocks, untangling their ankle chains. They are a sullen lot. 5704 later told us that it was depressing to face this new day knowing he would have to go through "all the same shit again, and maybe worse."[1]

Guard Ceros is lifting up the droopy heads—especially that of 1037, who looks as though he is sleepwalking. He pushes their shoulders back to more erect positions while physically adjusting the posture of slouching inmates. He's like a mother preparing her sleepy children for their first day at school, only a bit rougher. It is time for more rule learning and morning exercise before breakfast can be served. Vandy takes command: "Okay, we're going to teach you these rules until you have all of them memorized."[2] His energy is contagious, stimulating Ceros to walk up and down the line of prisoners, brandishing his billy club. Quickly losing patience, Ceros yells, "Come on, come on!" when the prisoners do not repeat the rules fast enough. Ceros smacks his club against his open palm, making the *wap, wap* sound of restrained aggression.

Vandy goes through toilet instructions for several minutes and repeats them many times until the prisoners meet his standards, repeating what he has told them about how they will use the facilities, for how long, and in silence. "819 thinks it's funny. Maybe we'll have something special for 819." Guard Varnish stands off to the side, not doing much at all. Ceros and Vandy switch roles. Prisoner 819 continues to smile and even laugh at the absurdity of it all. "It's not funny, 819."

Throughout, Guard Markus alternates with Ceros in reading the rules. Ceros: "Louder on that one! Prisoners must report all rule violations to the guards." Prisoners are made to sing the rules, and after so many repetitions they have obviously learned all of them. Next come instructions regarding proper military style upkeep of their cots. "From now on your towels will be rolled up and placed neatly at the foot of your beds. Neatly, not thrown around, got that?" says Vandy.

Prisoner 819 starts acting up. He quits the exercises and refuses to continue. The others also stop until their buddy rejoins them. The guard asks him to continue, which he does—for the sake of his comrades.

"Nice touch, 819, now take a seat in the Hole," orders Vandy. 819 goes into solitary but with a defiant swagger.

As he methodically paces up and down the corridor in front of the prisoners, the tall guard Karl Vandy is beginning to like the feeling of dominance.

"Okay, what kind of day is this?" Mumbled responses.

"Louder. Are you all happy?"

"Yes, Mr. Correctional Officer."

Varnish, trying to get into the act and be cool, asks, "Are we all happy? I didn't hear the two of you."

"Yes, Mr. Correctional Officer."

"4325, what kind of day is this?"

"It's a good day, Mr. Correctional Offic—"

"No. It's a *wonderful* day!"

"Yes sir, Mr. Correctional Officer."

They begin to chant, "It's a wonderful day, Mr. Correctional Officer."

"4325, what kind of day is it?"

"It's a good day."

Vandy: "Wrong. It's a *wonderful* day!"

"Yes sir. It's a wonderful day."

"And you, 1037?"

1037 gives his response a peppy, sarcastic intonation: "It's a *wonderful* day."

Vandy: "I think you'll do. Okay, return to your cells and have them neat and orderly in three minutes. Then stand by the foot of your bed." He gives instructions to Varnish about how to inspect the cells. Three minutes later, the guards enter the individual cells while the prisoners stand by their beds in military inspection style.

REBELLION BEGINS BREWING

There's no question that the prisoners are getting frustrated by having to deal with what the guards are doing to them. Moreover, they are hungry and still tired from lack of a sound night's rest. However, they are going along with the show and are doing a pretty good job of making their beds, but not good enough for Vandy.

"You call that neat, 8612? It's a mess, remake it right." With that, he rips off the blanket and sheets and throws them on the floor. 8612 reflexively lunges at him, screaming, "You can't do that, I just made it!"

Caught off guard, Vandy pushes the prisoner off and hits him in the chest with his fist as he yells out for reinforcements, "Guards, emergency in Cell 2!"

All the guards surround 8612 and roughly throw him into the Hole, where he joins 819, who has been sitting there quietly. Our rebels begin to plot a revolution in the dark, tight confines. But they miss the chance to go to the toilet, to which the others are escorted in pairs. It soon becomes painful to hold in the urge to urinate, so they decide not to make trouble just yet, but soon. Interestingly, Guard Ceros later told us that it was difficult to maintain the guard persona when he was alone with a prisoner going to, in, or from the toilet, because there were not the external physical props of the prison setting on which to rely. He and most of the other guards reported that they acted tougher and were more demanding on those prisoner toilet runs in order to counter their tendency to ease up when off site. It was just harder to act the tough-guard role when alone with a solitary prisoner one on one. There was also a sense of shame in grown-ups like them being reduced to toilet patrol.[3]

The rebel duo occupying the Hole also misses breakfast, which is served promptly at 8 A.M. al fresco in the open Yard. Some eat sitting on the floor, while others stand. They violate the "no talking rule," by talking and discussing a hunger strike to show prisoner solidarity. They also agree that they should start to demand a lot of things to test their power, like getting their eyeglasses, meds, and books back and not doing the exercises. Previously silent prisoners, including 3401, our only Asian-American participant, now become energized in their open support.

After breakfast, 7258 and 5486 test the plan by refusing orders to return to their cells. This forces the three guards to push them into their respective cells. Ordinarily, such disobedience would have earned them Hole time, but the Hole is already overcrowded, two people being its physical limit. In the rising cacophony, I am amazed to hear prisoners from Cell 3 volunteer to clean the dishes. This gesture is in line with the generally cooperative stance of cellmate Tom-2093, but is at odds with their buddies, who are in the process of planning rebellion. Maybe they were hoping to cool the mark, to ease the rising tensions.

With the curious exception of those in Cell 3, the prisoners are careening out of control. The morning shift guard trio decides that the prisoners must consider the guards too lax, which is encouraging this mischief. They decide it is time to stiffen up. First, they institute a morning work period, which today means scrubbing down the walls and floors. Then, in the first stroke of their collective creative revenge, they take the blankets off the prisoners' beds in Cells 1 and 2, carry them outside the building, and drag them through the underbrush until the blankets are covered with stickers or burrs. Unless prisoners don't mind being stuck by these sharp pins, they must spend an hour or more picking out each of them if they want to use their blankets. Prisoner 5704 goes ballistic, screaming at the senseless stupidity of this chore. But that is exactly the point. Senseless, mindless arbitrary tasks are the necessary components of guard power. The guards want to punish the rebels and also to induce unquestioning conformity. After initially refusing, 5704 reconsiders when he thinks it will get him on the good side of Guard Ceros and gain him a cigarette, so he starts picking and picking out the hundreds of stickers in his blanket. The chore was all about order, control, and power—who had it and who wanted it.

Guard Ceros asks, "Nothing but the best in this prison, wouldn't you all agree?"

Prisoners mutter various sounds of approval.

"Really fine, Mr. Correctional Officer," replies someone in Cell 3.

Nevertheless, 8612, just released from solitary back to Cell 2, has a somewhat different answer: "Oh, *fuck you*, Mr. Correctional Officer." 8612 is ordered to shut his filthy mouth.

I realize that this is the first obscenity that has been uttered in this setting. I had expected the guards to curse a lot as part of establishing the macho role, but they have not yet done so. However, Doug-8612 does not hesitate to fling obscenities around.

Guard Ceros: "It was weird to be in command. I felt like shouting that everyone was the same. Instead, I made prisoners shout at each other, 'You guys are a bunch of assholes!' I was in disbelief when they recited it over and over upon my command."[4]

Vandy added, "I found myself taking on the guard role. I didn't apologize for it; in fact, I became quite a bit bossier. The prisoners were getting quite rebellious, and I wanted to punish them for breaking up our system."[5]

The next sign of rebellion comes from a small group of prisoners, Stew-819 and Paul-5704, and, for the first time, 7258, the previously docile Hubbie. Tearing the ID numbers from the front of their uniforms, they protest loudly against the unacceptable living conditions. The guards immediately retaliate by stripping each of them stark naked until their numbers are replaced. The guards retreat to their quarters with an uneasy sense of superiority, but an eerie silence falls over the Yard as they eagerly await the end of their much too long first shift on this job.

Welcome to the Rebellion, Day Shift

When the day shift arrives and suits up before their 10 A.M. duty, they discover that all is not as under control as it was when they left yesterday. The prisoners in Cell 1 have barricaded themselves in. They refuse to come out. Guard Arnett immediately takes over and requests the morning shift to stay on until this matter is resolved. His tone implies that they are somehow responsible for letting things get out of hand.

The ringleader of the revolt is Paul-5704, who got his buddies in Cell 1, Hubbie-7258 and Glenn-3401, to agree that it was time to react against the violation of the original contract they made with the authorities (me). They push their beds against the cell door, cover the door opening with blankets, and shut off the lights. Unable to push the door open, the guards vent their anger on Cell 2, which is filled with the usual top-of-the-line troublemakers, Doug-8612, Stew-819, veterans of the Hole, and Rich-1037. In a surprise counterattack, the guards rush in, grab the three cots and haul them out into the yard, while 8612 struggles furiously to resist. There are pushing and shoving and shouting all around that cell, spilling out into the Yard.

"Up against the wall!"

"Give me the handcuffs!"

"Get everything, take everything!"

819 screams wildly, "No, no, no! This is an *experiment*! Leave me alone! Shit, let go of me, fucker! You're not going to take our fucking beds!"

8612: "A fucking simulation. It's a fucking simulated experiment. It's no prison. And fuck Dr. *Zimbargo*!"

Arnett, in a remarkably calm voice, intones, "When the prisoners in Cell 1 start behaving properly, your beds will be returned. You can use whatever influence you can on them to make them behave properly."

A calmer-sounding prisoner's voice importunes the guards, "These are *our beds*. You should not take them away."

In utter bewilderment, the naked prisoner 8612 says in a plaintive voice, "They took our clothes, and they took our beds! This is unbelievable! They took our clothes, and they took our beds." He adds, "They don't do that in *real* prisons." Curiously, another prisoner calls back, "They do."[6]

The guards burst into laughter. 8612 thrusts his hands between the cell door bars, open palms facing upward, in a pleading gesture, an unbelieving expression on his face and a new, strange tone to his voice. Guard J. Landry tells him to get his hands off the door, but Ceros is more direct and smacks his club against the bars. 8612 pulls his hands back just in time to avoid his fingers being smashed. The guards laugh.

Now the guards move toward Cell 3 as 8612 and 1037 call out to their Cell 3 comrades to barricade themselves in. "Get your beds in front of the door!" "One horizontal and one vertical! Don't let them in! They'll take your beds!" "They've taken our beds! Oh shit!"

1037 goes over the top with his call to violent resistance: "Fight them! Resist violently! The time has come for violent revolution!"

Guard Landry returns armed with a big fire extinguisher and shoots bursts of skin-chilling carbon dioxide into Cell 2, forcing the prisoners to flee backward. "Shut up and stay away from the door!" (Ironically, this is the same extinguisher that the Human Subjects Research Committee insisted we have available in case of an emergency!)

But as the beds are pulled from Cell 3 into the corridor, the rebels in Cell 2 feel betrayed.

"Cell 3, what's going on? We told you to barricade the doors!"

"What kind of solidarity is that? Was it the 'sergeant'? 'Sergeant' (2093), if it was your fault, that's all right because we all understand that you're impossible."

"But hey, Cell 1, keep your beds like that. Don't let them in."

The guards realize that six of them can subdue a prisoner rebellion this time, but in the future they will have to get by with only three guards against the nine prisoners, and that could add up to trouble. Never mind: Arnett formulates the divide-and-conquer psychological tactic of making Cell 3 the privileged cell and gives its members the special privileges of washing, brushing their teeth, beds and bedding returned, and water turned on in their cell.

Guard Arnett loudly announces that because Cell 3 has been behaving well, "their beds are not being torn up; they will be returned when order is restored in Cell 1."

The guards are trying to solicit the "good prisoners" to persuade the others to behave properly. "Well, if we knew what was wrong, we could tell them!" one of the "good prisoners" exclaims.

Vandy replies, "You don't need to know what's wrong. You can just tell them to straighten up."

8612 yells out, "Cell 1, we're with ya, all three of us." Then he makes a vague threat to the guards as they cart him off back to solitary wearing only a towel: "The unfortunate thing is, you guys think we've played all our cards."

That job done, the guards take a brief time-out for a smoke and to formulate a plan of action to deal with the Cell 1 barricade.

When Rich-1037 refuses to come out of Cell 2, three guards manhandle him, throw him to the ground, handcuff his ankles, and drag him by his feet out into the Yard. He and rebel 8612 yell back and forth from the Hole to the Yard about their condition, pleading with the full prisoner contingent to sustain the rebellion. Some guards are trying to make space in the hall closet for another place in an expanded Hole in which to deposit 1037. While they move boxes around to free up some more room, they drag him back into his cell along the floor with his feet still chained together.

Guards Arnett and Landry confer and agree on a simple way to bring some order to this bedlam: Start the count. The count confers order on chaos. Even with only four prisoners in line, all at attention, the guards begin by making the prisoners call out their numbers.

"My number is 4325, Mr. Correctional Officer."

"My number is 2093, Mr. Correctional Officer."

The count sounds out up and down the line, consisting of the three "goodies" from Cell 3 and 7258 naked with only a towel around his waist. Remarkably, 8612 calls out his number from the Hole, but in mocking fashion.

The guards now drag 1037 into solitary by the feet, putting him in a far corner of the hall closet that has become a makeshift second Hole. Meanwhile, 8612 continues yelling for the prison superintendent: "Hey, Zimbardo, get your ass over here!" I decide not to intervene at this point but to watch the confrontation and the attempts to restore law and order.

Some interesting comments are recorded in the retrospective diaries of the prisoners (completed after the study had ended).

Paul-5704 talks about the first effects of the time distortion that is beginning to alter everyone's thinking. "After we had barricaded ourselves in this morning, I fell asleep for a while, still exhausted from lack of a full sleep last night. When I awoke I thought it was the next morning, but it wasn't even lunch today yet!" He fell asleep again in the afternoon, thinking it was night when he awoke, but it was only 5 P.M. Time distortion also got to 3401, who felt starved and was angry that dinner had not been served, thinking it was 9 or 10 P.M. when it was not yet 5 P.M.

Although the guards eventually crushed the rebellion and used it as justification for escalating their dominance and control over these now potentially "dangerous prisoners," many of the prisoners felt good about having had the courage to challenge the system. 5486 remarked that his "spirits were good, guys together, ready to raise hell. We staged the 'Jock Strap Rebellion.' No more jokes, no jumping jacks, no playing with our heads." He added that he was limited by what his cellmates in the "good cell" would agree to back him up on. Had he been in Cell 1 or 2, he would have "done as they did" and rebelled more violently. Our smallest, most physically fragile prisoner, Glenn-3401, the Asian-American student, seemed to have had an epiphany during the rebellion: "I suggested moving the beds against the door to keep the guards out. Although I am usually quiet, I don't like to be pushed around like this. Having helped to organize and participate in our rebellion was important for me. I built my ego from there. I felt it was the best thing in my entire experience. Sort of asserting myself after the barricade made me more known to myself."[7]

After Lunch, Maybe an Escape

With Cell 1 still barricaded and some rebels in solitary, lunch is set for only a few. The guards have prepared a special lunch for "Good Cell 3," for them to eat in front of their less-well-behaved fellows. Surprising us again, they refuse the meal. The guards try to persuade them just to taste the delicious meal, but even though they are hungry after their minimal oatmeal breakfast and last night's slim dinner, the Cell 3 inmates cannot agree to act as such traitors, as "rat finks." A strange silence pervades the Yard for the next hour. However, these Cell 3 men are totally cooperative during the work period chores, some of which include taking more stickers out of their blankets. Prisoner Rich-1037 is offered a chance to leave solitary and join the work brigade but refuses. He is coming to prefer the relative quiet in the dark. The rules say only one hour max in the Hole, but that max is being stretched to two hours now for 1037, and also for occupant 8612.

Meanwhile in Cell 1, two prisoners are quietly executing the first stage of their new escape plan. Paul-5704 will use his long fingernails, strengthened from guitar picking, to loosen the screws in the faceplate of the power outlet. Once that is accomplished, they plan to use the edge of the plate as a screwdriver to unscrew the cell door lock. One will pretend to be sick and, when the guard is taking him to the toilet, will open the main entrance door down the hall. Signaled by a whistle, the other cellmate will burst out. They will knock the guard down and run away to freedom! As in real prisons, prisoners can show remarkable creativity in fashioning weapons out of virtually anything and hatching ingenious escape plans. Time and oppression are the fathers of rebellious invention.

But as bad luck would have it, Guard John Landry, making routine rounds, turns the door handle on Cell 1, and it falls out to the ground with a resounding thud. Panic ensues. "Help!" Landry screams out. "Escape!" Arnett and Markus rush in, block the door, and then get handcuffs to chain the would-be escapees together on the floor of their cell. Of course, 8612 was one of the troublemakers, so he gets his frequent-flyer trip back into the Hole.

A Nice Count to Calm the Restless Masses

Several anxious hours have passed since the day shift reported for work. It is time to soothe the savage beasts before further trouble erupts. "Good behavior is rewarded, and bad behavior is not rewarded." That calm, commanding voice is now clearly identified as Arnett's. He and Landry once again join forces to line up their charges for another count. Arnett takes charge. He has emerged as the leader of the day shift. "Hands against the wall, on this wall here. Now let's see how well everyone is learning his numbers. As before, sound your number, starting at this end."

Sarge starts it off, setting the tone of a fast, loud response, which the other prisoners pick up with some variations. 4325 and 7258 are fast and obedient. We have not heard much from Jim-4325, a big, robust six-footer who could be a lot to handle if he decided to get physical with the guards. In contrast, Glenn-3401 and Stew-819 are always slower, evidently reluctant to comply mindlessly. Not satisfied, and imposing his own brand of control, Arnett makes them count in creative ways. They do it by threes, backward, any way he can devise that will make it unnecessarily difficult. Arnett is also demonstrating his creativity to all onlookers, as does Guard Hellmann, but Arnett doesn't seem to take nearly as much personal pleasure in his performance as the other shift leader does. For him, this is more a job to be done efficiently.

Landry suggests having the prisoners sing their numbers; Arnett asks, "Was that popular last night? Did people like singing?" Landry: "I thought they liked it last night." But a few prisoners respond that they don't like to sing. Arnett: "Oh, well, you must learn to do things you don't like; it's part of reintegrating into regular society."

819 complains, "People out on the streets don't have numbers."

Arnett responds, "People out on the street don't have to have numbers! You have to have numbers because of your status here!"

Landry gives specific instructions about how to sing their scales: sing up a scale, like "do re mi." All of the prisoners conform and sing the ascending scale to the best of their ability, then the descending scale, except for 819, who doesn't attempt any scales. "819 can't sing for a damn; let's hear it again." 819 starts to explain why he can't sing. Arnett, however, clarifies the purpose of this exercise. "I didn't ask you *why* you couldn't sing, the object is for you to *learn* to sing." Arnett criticizes the prisoners for their poor singing, but the weary prisoners just giggle and laugh when they make mistakes.

In contrast to his shift mates, Guard John Markus seems listless. He rarely gets involved in the main activities in the Yard. Instead, he volunteers to do off-site chores, like picking up food at the college cafeteria. His body posture gives the impression that he is not enacting the macho guard image; he slouches, shoulders down, head drooping. I ask Warden Jaffe to talk to him about being more responsive to the job for which he is getting paid. The warden takes him off the Yard into his office and chastises him.

"The guards have to know that every guard has to be what we call a 'tough guard.' The success of this experiment rides on the behavior of the guards to make it seem as realistic as possible." Markus challenges him, "Real-life experience has taught me that tough, aggressive behavior is counterproductive." Jaffe gets defensive. He starts saying that the purpose of the experiment is not to reform prisoners but to understand how prisons change people when they are faced with the situation of guards being all-powerful.

"But *we* are also being affected by this situation. Just putting on this guard uniform is a pretty heavy thing for me." Jaffe becomes more reassuring; "I understand where you are coming from. We need you to act in a certain way. For the time being, we need you to play the role of 'tough guard.' We need you to react as you imagine the 'pigs' would. We're trying to set up the stereotype guard—your individual style has been a little too soft."

"Okay, I will try to adjust somewhat."

"Good, I knew we could count on you."[8]

Meanwhile, 8612 and 1037 remain in solitary. However, now they are yelling out complaints about violations of the rules. No one is paying attention. Each of them separately says he needs to see a doctor. 8612 says he is feeling ill, feeling strange. He mentions a weird sensation of his stocking cap still being on his head when he knows it is not there. His demand to see the warden will be granted later in the day.

At four o'clock, beds are returned to good Cell 3, as the guards' attention focuses on the prisoners in the still rebellious Cell 1. The night shift guards are asked to come in early, and together with the day shift they storm the cell, shooting the fire extinguisher at the door opening to keep the prisoners at bay. They strip the three prisoners naked, take away their beds, and threaten to deprive them of dinner if they show any further disobedience. Already hungry from missing lunch, the prisoners melt into a sullen, quiet blob.

The Stanford County Jail Prisoners' Grievance Committee

Realizing that the situation is becoming volatile, I have the warden announce over the loudspeaker that prisoners should elect three members to the newly formed "Stanford County Jail Prisoners' Grievance Committee," who will meet with Superintendent Zimbardo as soon as they agree on what grievances they want to have addressed and rectified. We later learn from a letter that Paul-5704 sent to his girlfriend that he was proud to be nominated by his comrades to head this committee. This is a remarkable statement, showing how the prisoners had lost their broad time perspectives and were living "in the moment."

The Grievance Committee, consisting of elected members, Paul-5704, Jim-4325, and Rich-1037, tell me that their contract has been violated in many ways. Their prepared list includes that: the guards are being both physically and verbally abusive; there is an unnecessary level of harassment; the food is not adequate; they want to have their books, glasses, and various pills and meds returned; they want more than one Visiting Night; and some of them want religious services. They argue that all of these conditions justified their need to rebel openly as they had all day long.

Behind my silver reflecting sunglasses, I slip into the superintendent role automatically. I start out by saying I am sure we can resolve any disagreements amicably, to our mutual satisfaction. I note that this Grievance Committee is a fine first step in that direction. I am willing to work directly with them as long as they represent the will of all the others. "But you have to understand that a lot of the guards' hassling and physical actions have been induced by your bad behavior. You have brought it upon yourselves by disrupting our planned schedules and by creating panic among the guards, who are new to this line of work. They took away many of your privileges rather than becoming more physically abusive to the rebellious prisoners." The Grievance Committee members nod knowingly. "I promise to take this grievance list to my staff tonight and to change as many negative conditions as possible, and to institute some of the positive things you have suggested. I will bring a prison chaplain down tomorrow and have a second Visiting Night this week, for starters."

"That's great, thanks," says the head prisoner, Paul-5704, and the others nod in agreement that progress is being made toward a more civil prison.

We stand and shake hands, and they leave pacified. I hope that they will tell their buddies to cool it from now on, so we can avoid such confrontations.

PRISONER 8612 BEGINS A MELTDOWN

Doug-8612 is not in a cooperative mood. He is not buying the goodwill message of the grievance guys. More insubordination earns him more Hole time, with his hands cuffed continuously. He says he is feeling sick and demands to see the warden. A while later, Warden Jaffe meets with him in his office and listens to the prisoner complain about the arbitrary and "sadistic" behavior of the guards. Jaffe tells him that *his* behavior is triggering the guards' reactions. If he would be more cooperative, Jaffe would see to it that the guards would lighten up on him. 8612 says that unless that happens soon, he wants out. Jaffe is also concerned about his medical complaints and asks if he wants to see a doctor, to which 8612 demurs for now. The prisoner is escorted back to his cell, from which he yells back and forth to comrade Rich-1037, who is still sitting in solitary complaining about the intolerable conditions and also wanting to see a doctor.

Although seemingly comforted by his exchange with the warden, Prisoner 8612 goes off screaming in rage, insisting on seeing "the fucking Dr. Zimbardo, Superintendent." I agree to see him immediately.

Our Prison Consultant Mocks the Mock Prisoner

That afternoon, I had arranged for the first visit to the prison of my consultant Carlo Prescott, who had helped me design many of the features in the experiment to simulate a functional equivalent of imprisonment in a real jail. Carlo had recently been paroled from San Quentin State Prison after serving seventeen years there, as well as time served at Folsom and Vacaville Prisons, mostly for convictions on armed robbery felonies. I had met him a few months before during one of the course projects that my social psychology students organized around the theme of individuals in institutional settings. Carlo had been invited by one of the students to give the class an insider's view of the realities of prison life.

Carlo was only four months out of prison and filled with anger at the injustice of the prison system. He railed against American capitalism, racism, black Uncle Toms who do the Man's work against Brothers, warmongers, and much more. But he was remarkably perceptive and insightful about social interactions, as well as exceptionally eloquent, with a resonant baritone voice and seamless, nonstop delivery. I was intrigued by this man's views, especially since we were about the same age—me thirty-eight, him forty—and both of us had grown up in an East or West coast ghetto. But while I was going to college, Carlo was going to jail. We became fast friends. I became his confidant, patient listener to his extended monologues, psychological counselor, and "booking agent" for jobs and lectures. His first job was to co-teach with me a new summer school course at Stanford University on the psychology of imprisonment. Carlo not only told the class intimate details of his personal prison experiences, he arranged for other formerly incarcerated men and women to share theirs. We added prison guards, prison lawyers, and others knowledgeable about the American prison system. That experience and intense mentoring by Carlo helped to infuse our little experiment with a kind of situational savvy never before seen in any comparable social science research.

It is about 7 P.M. when Carlo and I watch one of the counts on the TV monitor that is recording the day's special events. Then we retreat to my superintendent's office to discuss how things are going and how I should handle tomorrow's Visiting Night. Suddenly, Warden Jaffe bursts in to report that 8612 is really distraught, wants out, and insists on seeing me. Jaffe can't tell whether 8612 is just faking it to get released and then to make some trouble for us, or if he is genuinely feeling ill. He insists that it is my call and not his to make.

"Sure, bring him in so I can assess the problem," I say.

A sullen, defiant, angry, and confused young man enters the office. "What seems to be the trouble, young man?"

"I can't take it anymore, the guards are hassling me, they are picking on me, putting me in the Hole all the time, and—"

"Well, from what I have seen, and I have seen it all, you have brought this all on yourself; you are the most rebellious, insubordinate prisoner in the whole prison."

"I don't care, you have all violated the contract, I didn't expect to get treated like this, you—"[9]

"Stop right there, punk!" Carlo lashes out against 8612 with a vengeance. "You can't take what? Push-ups, jumping' jacks, guards calling you names and yelling at you? Is that what you mean by 'hassling'? Don't interrupt me. And you're crying about being put in that closet for a few hours? Let me straighten you out, white boy. You would not last a day at San Quentin. We would all smell your fear and weakness. The guards would be banging you upside your head, and before they put you in their real solitary concrete barren pit that I endured for weeks at a time, they'd throw you to us. Snuffy, or some other bad gang boss, would've bought you for two, maybe three packs of cigarettes, and your ass would be bleeding bright red, white, and blue. And that would be just the beginning of turning you into a sissy."

8612 is frozen by the fury of Carlo's harangue. I need to rescue him because I can sense that Carlo is about to explode. Seeing our prisonlike setting has brought to his mind years of torment from which Carlo is but a few months away.

"Carlo, thanks for providing this reality check. But I need to know some things from this prisoner before we can proceed properly. 8612, you realize that I have the power to get the guards not to hassle you, if you choose to stay and cooperate. Do you need the money—the rest of which you will forfeit by quitting early?"

"Yeah, sure, but—"

"Okay, then here's the deal, no more guards hassling you, you stay and earn your money, and in return all you have to do is cooperate from time to time, sharing a little information with me from time to time that might be helpful to me in running this prison."

"I don't know about that . . ."

"Look, think over my offer, and if, later on, after a good dinner, you still want to leave, then that will be fine, and you will be paid for time you have served. However, if you choose to continue, make all the money, not be hassled, and cooperate with me, then we can put the first day's problems behind us and start over. Agreed?"

"Maybe, but—"

"No need to decide either way right now, reflect on my offer and decide later tonight, okay?"

As 8612 quietly utters, "Well, all right," I escort him out to the warden's next-door office to be returned to the Yard. I tell Jaffe that he is still deciding about staying and will make his decision later on.

I had thought up the Faustian bargain on the spot. I had acted like an evil prison administrator, not the good-hearted professor I like to think I am. As superintendent, I do not want 8612 to leave, because it might have a negative impact on the other inmates and because I think we might be able to get him to be more cooperative if we have guards back off their abusive behaviors toward him. But I have invited 8612, the rebel leader, to be a "snitch," an informer, sharing information with me in return for special privileges. In the Prisoner Code, a snitch is the lowest form of animal life and is often kept in solitary by the authorities because if his informer role became known, he would be murdered. Later, Carlo and I retreat to Ricky's restaurant, where I try to put this ugly image behind me for a short time while enjoying Carlo's new stories over a plate of lasagna.

The Prisoner Tells Everyone That No One Can Quit

Back in the Yard, Guards Arnett and J. Landry have the prisoners lined up against the wall doing yet another count before the end of their extended day shift. Once more, Stew-819 is being ridiculed by the guards for being so listless in joining his peers, who are calling out in unison, "Thank you, Mr. Correctional Officer, for a fine day!"

The prison entrance door squeaks as it opens. The line of prisoners all look down the hall to see 8612 returning from his meeting with the prison authorities. He announced to them before seeing me that it was his *bon voyage* meeting. He was quitting, and there was nothing they could do to make him stay any longer. Doug-8612 now pushes his way through the line of his friends into Cell 2, throwing himself on his cot.

"8612, out here against the wall," Arnett orders.

"Fuck you," he replies defiantly.

"Against the wall, 8612."

"Fuck you!" replies 8612.

Arnett: "Somebody help him!"

J. Landry asks Arnett, "Do you have the key to the handcuffs, sir?"

Still in his cell, 8612 yells out, "If I gotta be in here, I'm not going to put up with any of your shit." As he saunters out into the Yard, with half the prisoners lined up on either side of Cell 2, Doug-8612 offers them a new terrible reality: "I mean, you know, really. I mean, *I couldn't get out!* I spent all this time talking to doctors and lawyers and . . ."

His voice trails off, and it is not clear what this means. The other prisoners are giggling at him. Standing in front of the other prisoners, defying orders to stand against the wall, 8612 delivers an uppercut to his buddies. He continues to rant in his high-pitched, whiny voice: *"I couldn't get out! They wouldn't let me out! You can't get out of here!"*

The inmates' initial giggles are replaced by nervous laughter. The guards ignore 8612 as they continue trying to discover where the keys to the handcuffs are, assuming they will handcuff 8612 and stuff him back in the Hole if he keeps this up.

One prisoner asks 8612, "You mean you couldn't break the contract?"

Another prisoner inquires desperately, but not of anyone in particular, "Can I cancel my contract?"

Arnett toughens up: "No talking on the line. 8612 will be around later for you all to talk with."

This revelation from one of their respected leaders is a powerful blow to the prisoners' resolve and defiance. Glenn-3401 reported on the impact of 8612's assertion: "He said you can't get out. You felt like you were really a prisoner. Maybe you were a prisoner in Zimbardo's experiment and maybe you were getting paid for it, but damn it, you were a prisoner. You were really a prisoner."[10]

He begins to fantasize some worst-case scenarios: "The thought that we had signed our lives away for two weeks, body and soul, was exceptionally frightening. The actual belief that 'we are really prisoners' was real—one couldn't escape without truly drastic action followed by a series of unknown consequences. Would the Palo Alto Police try to pick us up again? Would we get paid? How do I get my wallet back?"[11]

Rich-1037, who had been a problem for the guards all day long, was also stunned by this new realization. He later reported, "I was told that I couldn't quit. At that point, I felt it was really a prison. There's no way I can describe how I felt at that moment. I felt totally helpless. More helpless than I have ever felt before."[12]

It was evident to me that 8612 had trapped himself in multiple dilemmas. He was caught between wanting to be the tough-guy rebel leader but not wanting to deal with the guards' hassling, wanting to stay and earn the money he needed but not wanting to be my informer. He was probably planning to become a double agent, lying to me or misleading me about prisoner activities, but not sure of his ability to carry off that deception. He should have immediately refused my offer to trade up for some comfort by becoming the official "snitch," but he did not. At that moment, if he had insisted on being released, I would have had to allow him that option. Again, maybe he was too shamed by Carlo's taunting him to yield readily in front of him. All of these were possible mind games that he resolved by insisting to the others that it was our official decision not to release him, putting the blame on the system.

Nothing could have had a more transformative impact on the prisoners than the sudden news that in this experiment they had lost their liberty to quit on demand, lost their power to walk out at will. At that moment, the Stanford Prison Experiment was changed into the Stanford Prison, not by any top-down formal declarations by the staff but by this bottom-up declaration from one of the prisoners themselves. Just as the prisoner rebellion changed the way the guards began to think about the prisoners as dangerous, this prisoner's assertion about no one being allowed to quit changed the way all the mock prisoners felt about their new status as helpless prisoners.

WE'RE BACK, IT'S NIGHT SHIFT TIME

As if things were not bad enough for the prisoners, it is now night shift time, once again. Hellmann and Burdan have been pacing the Yard waiting for the day shift to move out. They are wielding their billy clubs, yelling something into Cell 2, threatening 8612, insisting that a prisoner get back from the door, and pointing the fire extinguisher at the cell, shouting to ask whether they want more of this cool carbon dioxide spray in their faces.

A prisoner asks Guard Geoff Landry: "Mr. Correctional Officer, I have a request. It's somebody's birthday tonight. Can we sing 'Happy Birthday'?"

Before Landry can answer, Hellmann replies from the background, "We'll sing 'Happy Birthday' at lineup. Now it is dinner time, three at a time." The prisoners now sit around a table laid out in the middle of the yard to eat their skimpy dinner. No talking allowed.

Reviewing the tapes of this shift, I see a prisoner being brought in through the main doors by Burdan. The prisoner, who had just attempted to escape, stands at attention in the center of the hallway just beyond the dinner table. He is blindfolded. Landry asks the prisoner how he removed the lock on the door. He refuses to spill the beans. When the blindfold is taken off the escapee, Geoff warns menacingly, "If we see your hands near that lock, 8612, we'll have something really good for you." It was Doug-8612 who tried the escape plan! Landry pushes him back into his cell, where 8612 begins to scream obscenities again, louder than before, and a stream of 'Fuck yous' floods the Yard. Hellmann says wearily into Cell 2, "8612, your game is getting very old. Very old. It's not even amusing anymore."

The guards rush to the dinner table to stop 5486 from conferring with his Cell mates, who have been forbidden to communicate. Geoff Landry shouts at 5486, "Hey, hey! We can't deprive you of a meal, but we can take the rest of it away. You've had something. The warden says we can't deprive you of meals, but you've already had a meal, at least part of it. So we can take the rest away." He then makes a general pronouncement to everyone: "You guys seem to have forgotten about all of the privileges we can give you." He reminds them of the visiting hours tomorrow, which, of course, could be canceled if there is a lockdown. Some prisoners who are still eating say that they have not forgotten about Tuesday's seven o'clock visiting hours and are looking forward to them.

Geoff Landry insists that 8612 put back on his stocking cap, which he had taken off during dinner. "We wouldn't want you dropping anything out of your hair into your meal and getting sick on it."

8612 responds strangely, as though he is losing contact with reality: "I can't put it on my head, it's too tight. I'll get a headache. What? I know that's really weird. That's why I'm trying to get out of here . . . they keep saying 'No, you won't get a headache,' but I know I will get a headache."

Now it becomes Rich-1037's turn to be despondent and detached. He is looking glassy-eyed, speaking only in a slow monotone. Lying on the floor of his cell, he keeps coughing, insists on seeing the superintendent. (I see him when I return from my dinner, give him some cough drops, and tell him that he can leave if he feels he can't take it anymore but that things will go better if he does not spend so much time and energy rebelling. He reports feeling better and promises to try his best.)

The guards next turn their attention on Paul-5704, who is now being more assertive, as if to stand in for former rebel leader Doug-8612. "You don't look too happy, 5704," Landry says, as Hellmann starts running his club against the bars of the cell door, making a loud clanging sound. Burdan adds, "You think they'd like that [the loud bar clanging] after lights out, maybe tonight?"

5704 attempts a joke, but the guards are not laughing, although some of the prisoners are. Landry says, "Oh, that's good, that's real good. Keep it up, really. We're really getting entertained now. I haven't heard this type of kid stuff in about ten years."

The guards, standing tall, all in a row, stare at 8612, who is eating slowly and by himself. With one hand on their hips and the other swinging their billy clubs menacingly, the guards display a united front. "We have a bunch of resisters, revolutionaries, here!" exclaims Geoff Landry.

8612 then bolts up from the dinner table and races across to the rear wall, where he rips down the black scrim covering the video camera. The guards grab him and drag him back into the Hole yet again. He says sarcastically, "Sorry, guys!"

One of them responds, "You're sorry, huh. We'll have something for you later that you will be sorry for."

When Hellmann and Burdan both start banging on the door of the Hole with their billy clubs, 8612 starts screaming that it is deafening and is making his headache worse.

Doug-8612 yells out, "Fuckin' don't do that man, it hurts my ears!"

Burdan: "Maybe you'll think about that before you want to do something that gets you into the Hole next time, 8612."

8612 answers, "Nah, you can just fuck off, buddy! Next time the doors go down, I mean it!" (He is threatening to tear down the door to his cell, the entrance door, and perhaps he means the wall where the observation camera is located.)

A prisoner asks if they'll be having a movie tonight, as they had expected to get when the original details of the prison were described to them. A guard replies, "I don't know if we'll *ever* have a movie!"

The guards openly discuss the consequences of damaging prison property, and Hellmann grabs a copy of the prison rules, reading off the rule about damaging prison property. As he leans against Cell 1's doorframe and twirls his billy club, he seems to be inhaling confidence and dominance moment by moment. Instead of movie time, he will give them either work or R&R time, Hellmann tells his buddies.

Hellmann: "Okay, let's have your attention, please. We have some fun lined up for everyone tonight. Cell 3, you're on rest and recreation, you can do what you please because you washed your dishes and did your chores well. Cell 2, you've still got a little bit of work to do. And Cell 1, we've got a great blanket for you to pick *all* the stickers out of. Okay, bring them on in here, Officer, let's let them see, they gonna do just fine for Cell 1 to work on tonight if they want to sleep on a blanket without stickers."

Landry hands Hellman some blankets coated with a new collection of stickers. "Oh, isn't that a beauty?" He continues his monologue: "Just look at that blanket, ladies and gentleman! Look at that blanket! Isn't that a masterpiece? I want you to take each and every one of those stickers out of that blanket, because that's what you're gonna have to sleep on." A prisoner tells him, "We'll just sleep on the floor," to which Landry replies simply, "Suit yourself, suit yourself."

It is interesting to see how Geoff Landry vacillates between the tough-guard and good-guard roles. He still has not relinquished control to Hellmann, to whose dominance he may aspire at some level, while feeling greater sympathy for the prisoners than Hellmann seems capable of. (In a later interview, the thoughtful prisoner Jim-4325 describes Hellmann as one of the bad guards, nicknaming him "John Wayne." He describes the Landry brothers as two of the "good guards," while most other prisoners agree that Geoff Landry was more often good than bad as a guard.)

A prisoner in Cell 3 asks whether it would be possible for them to get some books to read. Hellmann suggests giving them all "a couple of copies of the rules" as their bedtime reading material. Now it is time for another count. "Okay, there'll be no goofing off tonight, remember? Let's start at 2093, and let's count off, just so we can keep in practice," he says.

Burdan jumps on the bandwagon, walks right up in the prisoners' faces, and says, "We didn't teach you to count that way. Loud, clear, and fast! 5704, you are sure slow enough! You can start off with the jumping jacks."

The guards' punishment is becoming indiscriminate; they're no longer punishing prisoners for any specific reason. 5704 is having none of that: "I'm not gonna do it!"

Burdan forces him into it, so he goes down, but not far enough, apparently. "Down, man, down!" pushing him down by pressing on his back with his billy club.

"Don't push, man."

"What do you mean, 'Don't push'?" in a ridiculing tone.

"That's what I said, don't push!"

"Just go on now and do your push-ups," Burdan orders. "Now get back in line."

Burdan is decidedly much more vocal and involved than he was before, but Hellmann is still clearly the "alpha male." However, when Burdan and Hellmann become the dynamic duo, suddenly Geoff Landry recedes into the background or is not on the Yard scene at all.

Even 2093, the best prisoner, "Sarge," is forced to do push-ups and jumping jacks for no apparent reason. "Oh, that's nice! See how he does those? He's got a *lot* of energy tonight," says Hellmann. Then he turns on 3401: "Are *you* smiling? What are you smiling about?" His sidekick, Burdan, chimes in, "Are you smiling, 3401? You think this is funny? You wanna sleep tonight?"

"I don't want to see anyone smiling! This is no locker room here. If I see one person smile it's going to be jumping jacks for everyone for a long time!" Hellmann assures them.

Picking up on the prisoners' need to lighten their grim surroundings, Hellmann tells Burdan a joke for the benefit of the grim prisoners: "Officer, did you hear the one about the dog with *no* legs? Every night, his owner would take him out for a *drag.*" He and Burdan laugh but note that the prisoners do not laugh. Burdan chides him, "They don't like your joke, Officer."

"Did you like my joke, 5486?"

Jerry-5486 prisoner answers truthfully, "No."

"Come out here and do ten push-ups for not liking my joke. And do five more for smiling, Fifteen in all."

Hellmann is on a roll. He makes all the prisoners face the wall; then, when they turn around, he shows them the "one-armed pencil salesman." He puts one hand down his pants and puts his finger at his crotch, pushing out his pants as if he had an erection. The prisoners are told *not* to laugh. Some do laugh and are then forced do push-ups or sit-ups. 3401 says he didn't think it was funny, but he has to do push-ups for being honest. Next comes singing their numbers. Hellmann asks Sarge-2093 if that sounded like singing.

"It sounded like singing to me, Mr. Correctional Officer."

Hellmann makes him do push-ups for disagreeing with his judgment.

Unexpectedly, Sarge asks, "May I do *more*, sir?"

"You can do ten if you like."

Then Sarge challenges him in an even more dramatic way: "Shall I do them until I *drop?*"

"Sure, whatever." Hellmann and Burdan are unsure how to react to this taunt, but the prisoners look at one another in dismay, knowing that Sarge may set new criteria for self-inflicted punishment that will then be imposed on them. He is becoming a sick joke to them all.

When next the prisoners are asked to count off in a complicated order, Burdan adds mockingly, "That shouldn't be so hard for boys with so much *education!*" In a sense, he is picking up on the current conservative ridicule of educated college people as "effete intellectuals snobs," even though, of course, he is a college student himself.

The prisoners are asked if they need their blankets and beds. All say they do. "And what," Hellmann asks, "did you boys do to deserve beds and blankets?" "We took the foxtails out of our blankets," says one of them. He tells them to never say "foxtails." They should call them "stickers." Here is a simple instance of power determining language use, which, in turn, creates reality. Once the prisoner calls them "stickers," Burdan says that they should get their pillows and blankets. Hellmann comes back with blankets and pillows under his arms. He then hands them out to everyone except Prisoner 5704. He asks him why it took him so long to get to work. "Do you feel like having a pillow? Why should I give you a pillow if you didn't feel like working?" "Good karma," answers 5704, feeling a bit playful.

"I'll ask you again, why should I give you a pillow?"

"Because I'm asking you to, Mr. Correctional Officer."

"But you didn't get to work until ten minutes after everyone else did," says Hellmann. He adds, "See to it that in the future you do work when you are told." Despite this misbehavior, Hellmann finally relents and gives him the pillow.

Not to be totally upstaged by Hellmann, Burdan tells 5704, "Thank him real sweet."

"Thank you."

"Say it again. Say, 'Bless you, Mr. Correctional Officer.' " The sarcasm seeps through heavily.

Hellmann successfully isolates 5704 from his revolutionary comrades by making him beg for a pillow. Simple self-interest is starting to win out over prisoner solidarity.

Happy Birthday, Prisoner 5704

Prisoner Jerry-5486 reminds the guards of his request to sing "Happy Birthday" to 5704, which is a curious request at this point given that the prisoners are so tired and the guards are about to let them return to their cells and to sleep. Perhaps it is a measure of their connection with normal rituals in the outside world or a small way to normalize what is rapidly approaching Abnormal.

Burdan tells Hellmann, "We have a point of discussion from Prisoner 5486, Officer; he wants to do the 'Happy Birthday' song." Hellmann is upset when the birthday song is intended for 5704. "It's your birthday, and you didn't work!"

The prisoner replies that he shouldn't have to work on his birthday. The guards go down the line and ask each one to say aloud whether he does or does not want to sing the birthday song. Each agrees that it is right to sing the birthday song to 5704 tonight. Prisoner Hubbie-7258 is then ordered to lead the others in singing "Happy Birthday"—the only pleasant sound in this place all day and night. The first time through, there is a mixture of ways in which the recipient is addressed—some sing happy birthday to "comrade," others to "5704." As soon as this happens, Hellmann and Burdan both scream at them.

Burdan reminds them, "This gentleman's name is 5704. Now take it from the top."

Hellmann compliments 7258 for his singing: "You give them a swing tempo, and then you sing it straight." He says that about cut-time music, showing off a bit of his musical knowledge. But he then requests they sing the song again in a more familiar style, and they do. But their performance is not good enough, so again they are told, "Let's have a little enthusiasm! A boy's birthday only happens once a year." This prisoner-initiated break in routine to share some positive feelings among themselves is turned into another occasion of learning routinized dominance and submission.

The Final Breakdown and Release of 8612

After lights out, and after Doug-8612 is finally turned out of solitary for the nth time, he goes ballistic: "I mean, Jesus Christ, I'm burning up inside! Don't you know?"

The prisoner is screaming his angry confusion and torment to the warden during his second visit with Jaffe. "I want to get out! This is all fucked up inside! I can't stand another night! I just can't take it anymore! I gotta have a lawyer! Do I have a right to ask for a lawyer? Contact my mother!"

Trying to remind himself that this is just an experiment, he continues raving, "You're messing up my head, man, my head! This is an experiment; that contract is not serfdom! You have no right to fuck with my head!"

He threatens to do anything necessary to get out, even to slit his wrists! "I'll do anything to get out! I'll wreck your cameras, and I'll hurt the guards!"

The warden tries his best to comfort him, but 8612 is having none of it; he cries and screams louder and louder. Jaffe assures 8612 that as soon as he can contact one of the psychological counselors his request will be seriously considered.

A short while later, Craig Haney returns from his late dinner and, after listening to Jaffe's tape recording of this dramatic scene, he interviews 8612 to determine whether he should be released immediately based on such severe emotional distress. At the time, we were all uncertain about the legitimacy of 8612's reactions; he might be just playacting. A check of his background information revealed that he was also a leading antiwar activist at his university, just last year. How could he really be "breaking down" in only thirty-six hours?

8612 was indeed confused, as he revealed to us later: "I couldn't decide whether the prison experience had really freaked me out, or whether I had induced those reactions [purposefully]."

The conflict that Craig Haney was experiencing over being forced to make this decision on his own, while I was out having dinner, is vividly expressed in his later analysis:

> Although in retrospect it seems like an easy call, at the time it was a daunting one. I was a 2nd year graduate student, we had invested a great deal of time, effort, and money into this project, and I knew that the early release of a participant would compromise the experimental design we had carefully drawn up and implemented. As experimenters, none of us had predicted an event like this, and of course, we had devised no contingency plan to cover it. On the other hand, it was obvious that this young man was more disturbed by his brief experience in the Stanford Prison than any of us had expected any of the participants to be even by the end of 2 weeks. So I decided to release Prisoner 8612, going with the ethical/humanitarian decision over the experimental one.[13]

Craig contacted 8612's girlfriend, who quickly came by and collected him and his belongings. Craig reminded the two of them that if this distress continued, he could visit Student Health in the morning because we had arranged for some of its staff to help deal with any such reactions.

Fortunately, Craig made the right decision based on both humane considerations and legal ones. It was also the right decision considering the probable negative effect on the staff and inmates of keeping 8612 imprisoned in his state of emotional disarray. However, when Craig later informed Curt and me about his decision to release 8612, we were skeptical and thought that he had been taken in, conned by a good acting job. However, after a long discussion of all the evidence, we agreed that he had done the right thing. But then we had to explain why this extreme reaction had occurred so suddenly, almost at the very start of our two-week adventure. Even though personality tests had revealed no hint of mental instability, we persuaded ourselves that the emotional distress 8612 revealed was the product of his overly sensitive personality and his overreaction to our simulated prison conditions. Together Craig, Curt, and I engaged in a bit of "groupthink," advancing the rationalization that there must have been a flaw in our selection process that had allowed such a "damaged" person to slip by our screening—while ignoring the other possibility that the situational forces operating in this prison simulation had become overwhelming for him.

Consider, for a moment, the meaning of that judgment. Here we were in the midst of a study designed to demonstrate the power of situational forces over dispositional tendencies, yet we were making a dispositional attribution!

In retrospect, Craig expressed the fallacy in our thinking aptly: "It was only later that we appreciated this obvious irony, that we had 'dispositionally explained' the first truly unexpected and extraordinary demonstration of situational power in our study by resorting to precisely the kind of thinking we had designed the study to challenge and critique."[14]

Confusion remained about 8612's ulterior motives. On the one hand, we wondered, was he really out of control, suffering from an extreme stress reaction, and so of course had to be released? Alternatively, had he started out by pretending to be "crazy," knowing that if he did a good job, we would have to release him? It might be that, in spite of himself, he had ended up temporarily "crazed" by his over-the-top method acting. In a later report, 8612 complicates any simple understanding of his reactions: "I left when I should have stayed. That was very bad. The revolution isn't going to be fun, and I must see that. I should have stayed because it helps the fascists knowing that [revolutionary] leaders will desert when things get rough, that they are just manipulators. And I should have fought for what was right, and not thought of my interests."[15]

Shortly after 8612 was terminated, one of the guards overheard the prisoners in Cell 2 discussing a plot in which Doug would return the next day with a band of his buddies to trash our prison and liberate the prisoners. It sounded to me like a far-fetched rumor until a guard reported seeing 8612 sneaking around the hallways of the Psychology Department the next morning. I ordered the guards to capture him and return him to the prison since he had probably been released under false pretenses: not sick, just tricking us. Now I knew that I had to prepare for an all-out assault on my prison. How could we avert a major violent confrontation? What could we do to keep our prison functioning—and oh, yes, our experiment also continuing?

CHAPTER FIVE

Tuesday's Double Trouble:
Visitors and Rioters

Our prisoners are looking raggedy and bleary-eyed, and our little prison is beginning to smell like a men's toilet in a New York subway station. Seems that some guards have made toilet visits a privilege to be awarded infrequently and never after lights out. During the night, prisoners have to urinate and defecate in buckets in their cells, and some guards refuse to allow them to be emptied till morning. Complaints are coming fast and furiously from many of the prisoners. 8612's breakdown of last night seemed to create a ripple effect among the prisoners, who talked about not being able to take it anymore—according to what we were picking up from their bugged cells.

With that as our canvas, we had to paint a brighter picture for the parents, friends, and girlfriends of the prisoners who would be coming to visit tonight. As a parent, I surely would not let my son continue in such a place if I saw such exhaustion and obvious signs of stress after only three days. Contemplating ways to cope with that impending challenge had to take a backseat to the more urgent issue of the rumored break-in by rioters that 8612 could bring down upon us at any time. Perhaps it would come today, maybe even synchronized with visiting hours, when we would be most vulnerable.

The day is just beginning for the morning shift at 2 A.M. Apparently the night shift has hung around and all six guards are on the Yard at the same time after they have conferred in the guards' quarters about the need for stricter rules to control the prisoners and prevent more rebellions.

Seeing them all together makes clear that size does matter in deciding who will emerge as shift leader. The tallest guards are Hellmann, leader of the night shift; Vandy, moving into leadership of the morning shift; and Arnett, day shift majordomo. The shortest guards, Burdan and Ceros, have become henchmen of their shift leaders. Both are very bossy, quite aggressive vocally—shouting in the prisoners' faces—and decidedly more physical with the prisoners. They push

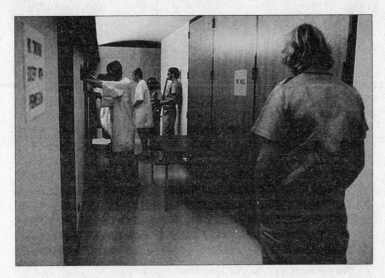

them around, poke them, pull them out of lineups, and are the ones who drag reluctant prisoners into solitary. We are getting reports that they sometimes trip prisoners down the stairs when walking them to the toilet or push them into the wall urinals when they are alone with them in the bathroom. It is evident that they love their nightsticks. They are constantly holding the billy clubs close to their chests, banging them against the bars and the doors or on the table to loudly make their presence known. Some analysts might claim that they are using their weapons to compensate for their smaller stature. But whatever the psychological dynamic involved, it is clear that they are becoming the meanest of the guards.

However, Markus and Varnish, who are also on the shorter side, have been relatively passive, much quieter, less vocal, and less active than the rest. I have asked the warden to make them more assertive. The Landry brothers are an interesting pair. Geoff Landry is a bit taller than Hellmann and has vied with him for dominance on the night shift, but he is no match for the creative exercises that our budding John Wayne continually concocted. Instead, he moves in to give orders and to exercise control, then drifts back and out of the scene over and over again in a kind of vacillation that's not seen in any other guard. Tonight he is not carrying his nightstick at all; later on he even removes his silver reflecting sunglasses—a big no-no, according to our experimental protocol. His shorter brother, John, has been tough on the prisoners, but he is nevertheless "going by the book." He is not aggressively excessive, as Arnett is, but he does usually back up the boss with firm, no-nonsense orders.

The prisoners are all about the same average height, about five-eight to five-ten, except for Glenn-3401, who is the shortest of all, around five-two, and tall Paul-5704, who is tallest at maybe six feet two. Interestingly, 5704 is moving into the leadership position among the prisoners. He appears more self-confident lately and assured in his rebelliousness. His mates have noticed this change in him, as was evidenced by their electing him spokesperson for the Stanford County Jail Prisoners' Grievance Committee, which had earlier negotiated with me for a series of concessions and rights.

NEW RULES, BUT OLD COUNTS CONTINUE

For yet another count at 2:30 A.M., the Yard is a bit crowded, with six guards present and seven prisoners lined up against the wall. Even though there is no reason for the night shift to hang around longer, they do so on their own. Maybe they want to check out how the morning shift handles their routine. 8612 is gone, and someone else is missing. Vandy drags the reluctant, sleepy Prisoner 819 out of Cell 2 to complete the lineup. The guards are berating some prisoners for not wearing their stocking caps, reminding them that they are an essential part of their prison uniform.

Vandy: "Here it is, time for count. How do you like that?"

One prisoner says, "Fine, Mr. Correctional Officer."

"How about the rest of you?"

Sarge: "Wonderful, Mr. Correctional Officer!"

"Let's hear it from all of you, come on. You can do it better than that! Louder!"

"Just fine, Mr. Correctional Officer."

"Louder!"

"What time is it?"

"Time for a count, Mr. Correctional Officer," one prisoner answers in a weak voice.[1] The prisoners are all lined up against the wall, hands against the wall, legs spread apart. They are clearly sluggish counting this early because they have slept only a few hours.

Even though his shift time is over, Burdan is still being very assertive, shouting orders as he stalks around, waving his big stick. He pulls someone out of line randomly.

"Okay, young man, you gonna do some push-ups for me!" he shouts.

Now Varnish speaks up for the first time: "Okay, let's have your numbers. Starting with the right. Now!" Maybe he feels more confident among a larger group of guards.

Then Geoff Landry gets into the act: "Wait a minute, this guy over here, 7258, doesn't even know his number backwards!" But why is Geoff still active on this next shift? He walks around with his hands in his pockets, more like an uninvolved tourist than a prison guard. In fact, why is the whole night shift continuing to hang around after a long, tedious night? They should be on their way to bed now. Their presence is causing confusion and uncertainty about who should be giving orders. The counts follow the same formerly clever routines that are now becoming tedious: by twos, by ID numbers, backward, and singsong variations. Hellmann, having decided that this is not his cup of tea, says nothing, watches for a while, and then quietly exits.

The old rules are repeated, and they too are to be sung. As the rule reading goes on, Vandy exhorts the inmates to be louder, faster, crisper. The weary prisoners comply, their voices blending in dissonant synchrony. It is time for some new rules. So the guards, on their own, add some:

"Prisoners must participate in all prison activities. That means counts!"

"Beds must be made and personal effects must be neat and orderly!"

"Floors must be spotless!"

"Prisoners must not move, tamper with, or deface walls, ceilings, windows, doors, or any other prison property!"

Varnish has set up this drill that the prisoners must understand perfectly well, in both substance and style. If they do a halfhearted job, he simply forces them to repeat the rules over and over again in mind-numbing variations.

Varnish: "Prisoners must never operate cell lighting!"

Prisoners: "Prisoners must never operate cell lighting."

Vandy: "When must prisoners operate cell lighting?"

Prisoners (now in perfect unison): *"Never."*

They all sound exhausted, but their responses are crisper and louder than they were last night. All of a sudden, Varnish has become a leader—he's leading the recitation of the rules, insisting upon perfection from the prisoners, exerting dominance over them, and patronizing them. A new rule is proclaimed that is obviously geared to taunt Paul-5704, our nicotine addict.

Varnish: "Smoking is a privilege!"

Prisoners: "Smoking is a privilege."

"What is smoking?"

"A privilege."

"What?"

"A privilege."

"Smoking will be allowed only after meals or at the discretion of the guard."

Varnish: "I don't like this monotone, let's go up the scale."

The prisoners comply, repeating the words in a higher register.

"I suggest you start a little lower, you can't go higher from your top note."

He wants the prisoners to ascend the scale as they're speaking. Vandy demonstrates.

Varnish: "That's lovely!"

Varnish is reading these new rules from a sheet held in one hand, while in the other he holds his club. The rest of the guards are also caressing their clubs, except for Geoff L., whose continued presence makes no sense at all. As Varnish leads the prisoners in reciting the rules, Vandy, Ceros, and Burdan move into and out of the cells, in and around the prisoners, looking for the missing handcuff keys, weapons, or anything suspicious.

Ceros forces Sarge out of line and forces him to stand with his hands against the opposite wall, legs spread, as he blindfolds him. He then handcuffs Sarge, orders him to collect the refuse bucket, and then leads him to dump it in the toilet outside the prison.

One after another each prisoner shouts out, "The superintendent's!" as the answer to the question posed by Varnish: "Whose orders are supreme?" It's my turn on our early-morning shift to tape-record the key events while Curt and Craig catch some shut-eye. Seems strange to hear this assertion that my orders are "supreme." In my other life, I make it a point never to give orders, only suggestions or hints about what I want or need.

Varnish eggs them on, forcing them to sing out "Punishment" as the last word in the rule about what happens if any of the other rules are not obeyed. They must sing the feared word at their highest pitch again and again to make them feel ridiculous and humiliated.

This has been going on for nearly forty minutes, and the prisoners are squirming; their legs are getting stiff, their backs are aching, but none of them is complaining. Burdan orders the prisoners to turn around and face front for a uniform inspection.

Then Vandy questions 1037 about why he doesn't have on his stocking cap.

"One of the guards took it away, sir."

Vandy: "I don't know of any correctional officer who took it. Are you saying that the correctional officers really don't know what's happening?"

"No, I'm not saying that, Mr. Correctional Officer."

Vandy: "So it was you who lost the cap."

1037: "Yes, I did, Mr. Correctional Officer."

Vandy: "Fifteen push-ups."

"Would you like me to count?"

Vandy makes it public that prisoner 3401 has been complaining of being sick.

Varnish responds, "We don't like sick prisoners. Why don't you do twenty sit-ups, right now, to make you feel better?" He then accuses 3401 of being a crybaby and takes away his pillow.

"Okay, everyone who has a stocking cap, go back to your room. Those who don't, stand there. You can *sit* on your beds but not lie down. Actually, make your beds—no wrinkles whatsoever."

Then Varnish orders synchronized group push-ups for the three bareheaded inmates. He jumps down off the table where he has been sitting as he bangs his billy club for emphasis. He stands over the prisoners, shouting "Down, up!" as they do their punishment ritual. Paul-5704 stops, protesting that he just can't do any more. Varnish relents and allows the prisoners to stand up against the wall.

"Okay, you all stand by your beds until you find three stocking caps. If you're unable to find your stocking cap, put a towel on your head.

"819, what kind of a day was it?"

"A wonderful day, Mr. Correctional Officer."

"Okay, make your beds, without any wrinkles whatsoever, then sit on them."

By this time, the other guards have left, and only the morning shift guards remain, including the backup guard, Morison, quietly observing all this authoritarian abuse. He tells the prisoners that they can lie down if they wish, and they immediately hit the sack and are in dreamland almost instantly.

An hour or so later, the warden stops by, looking very dapper in a tweedy jacket and tie. He seems to be growing a little each day, or maybe he is standing more erect than I can recall his standing in the past.

"Attention, attention," he intones. "When the prisoners are properly attired, they should line up in the yard for further inspection."

The guards go to Cells 2 and 3 and tell the prisoners to get up and go out into the Yard. Once again, their brief nap is disrupted.

Out come the occupants of Cells 2 and 3 once more. Stew-819 has found his stocking cap; Rich-1037 is wearing a towel turban style, while Paul-5704 wears his towel in Little Red Riding Hood style, draped over his long black locks.

Varnish inquires of Sarge: "How did you sleep?"

"Wonderful, Mr. Correctional Officer."

5704 won't go that far and simply says, "Good." Varnish turns him to face the wall as another guard calls out a primary rule:

"Prisoners must always address the guards as 'Mr. Correctional Officer.' "

5704 does push-ups for not having added that note of respect to his halfhearted lie, "Good."

The warden walks slowly down the file of prisoners, like a general reviewing his troops: "This prisoner seems to have a problem with his hair, and he also seems to have a problem with proper identification. Before any further activity, he needs to be properly identified." The warden moves down the line, evaluating the problem prisoners, and asks the guards to take necessary remedial action. "This prisoner's hair is sticking out underneath his towel." He insists that the ID numbers be sown back on or replaced by numbers inked on with a Sharpie pen.

"Tomorrow is Visitors' Day. That means that we want to show all our visitors what good-looking prisoners we have. Isn't that right? That means that Prisoner 819 has to learn how to wear his stocking cap. I would suggest that at some future time, Prisoners 3401 and 5704 be taught to wear their towels in the way that Prisoner 1037 is wearing it. Now back to your cells."

The prisoners go back to sleep until awakened for breakfast. It's time for a new day, and the day shift comes on duty. A new count is tried out, this time cheerleader style, each prisoner cheering his number:

"Gimme a 5, gimme a 7, gimme an O, gimme a 4. What does that spell? 5704!" Arnett and John Landry and Markus are back with this new torment. Up and down the line, each prisoner steps forward to give this cheerleader rendition of his number. And on and on and . . .

Identity and Role Boundaries Are Becoming Permeable

After less than three days into this bizarre situation, some of the students role-playing prison guards have moved far beyond mere playacting. They have internalized the hostility, negative affect, and mind-set characteristic of some real prison guards, as is evident from their shift reports, retrospective diaries, and personal reflections.

Ceros is proud of the way the guards "picked it up today," saying, "We were more orderly, received excellent results from the prisoners." Still, he is concerned about possible danger: "Worried that the quietness may be deceptive, may be plans for a breakout are afoot."[2]

Varnish reveals his initial reluctance to get into the guard role, which was so apparent that I had to get the warden to set him straight. "It wasn't till the second day that I decided I would have to force myself to really go about this thing in the right way. I had to intentionally shut off all feelings I had towards any of the prisoners, to lose sympathy and any respect for them. I began to treat them as coldly and harshly as possible verbally. I would not let show any feelings they might like to see, like anger or despair." His group identification has also become stronger: "I saw the guards as a group of pleasant guys charged with the necessity of maintaining order among a group of persons unworthy of trust or sympathy—the prisoners." He notes further that the toughness of the guards peaked at tonight's 2:30 counts, and he likes that.[3]

Vandy, who has begun to share the dominant role with Varnish on the morning shift, is not as active today as earlier because he is very tired, feeling subdued from his lack of sleep. But he is pleased to see the prisoners getting so totally into their roles: "They don't see it as an experiment. It is real and they are fighting to keep their dignity. But we are always there to show them who is boss."

He reports feeling increasingly bossy and forgetting that this is just an experiment. He finds himself just "wanting to punish those who did not obey so that they would show the rest of the prisoners the right way to behave."

The depersonalization of the prisoners and the spreading extent of dehumanization are beginning to affect him, too: "As I got angrier and angrier, I didn't question this behavior as much. I couldn't let it affect me, so I started hiding myself deeper behind my role. It was the only way of not hurting yourself. I was really lost on what was happening but didn't even think about quitting."

Blaming the victims for their sorry condition—created by our failure to provide adequate shower and sanitation facilities—became common among the staff. We see this victim blame in operation as Vandy complains, "I got tired of seeing the prisoners in rags, smelling bad, and the prison stink."[4]

SAFEGUARDING THE SECURITY OF MY INSTITUTION

In my role as prison superintendent, my mind has become focused on the most important issue facing the head of any institution: What must I do to ensure the safety and security of the institution in my charge? The threat to our prison by the rumored assault forced my other role as researcher into the background. How must I deal here and now with the impending break-in by 8612's party of raiders?

Our morning staff meeting reviewed many options and settled on transferring the experiment to the old city jail, which was abandoned when the new central police station was completed, the one where our prisoners had been booked on Sunday. I remembered that the sergeant had asked that morning why we did not want to use the old jail for our study since it was vacant and had large cells available. Had I thought of it before, I would have, but we had already put into place the recording equipment, arrangements with the university food service, and other logistical details that would be easier to handle from the Psychology Department's building. This new alternative was just what we needed.

While I am away making arrangements for new facilities, Curt Banks will handle the Prisoners' Grievance Committee's second meeting. Craig Haney will supervise the preparations for visiting times, and Dave Jaffe will oversee the day's usual activities of his correctional officers.

I am pleased that the sergeant can meet me on such short notice. We meet in the old jail downtown on Ramona Street. I explain my predicament as the need to avoid a physical force confrontation, like the kind that happened last year when the police and students clashed on campus. I urge his cooperation. Together we inspect the site, as though I were a prospective buyer. It is perfect for a transfer of the remainder of the study and it will add even more prison realism to this experience.

Back at police headquarters, I fill out a set of official forms and request that the jail be ready for our use by nine that night (right after visiting hours). I also promise that for the next ten days we will keep it spanking clean, the prisoners will work at it, and I will pay for any damages that might occur. We make sure to shake hands with the firm shake that separates sissies from real men. I thank him profusely for saving the day. What a relief; that was easier than I had imagined.

Relieved by this stroke of luck and proud of my quick thinking, I treat myself to a cup of espresso and a cannoli, soaking in some rays at the outdoor café on yet another balmy summer day. It is still paradise in Palo Alto. Nothing has changed since Sunday.

Shortly after my celebratory staff briefing about our transfer plans, a disheartening call comes in from the Police Department: No go! The city manager is worried about getting sued if someone gets hurt while they are on the city property. Issues of false imprisonment are also raised. I beg the sergeant to allow me to try to persuade the city manager that his fears were unwarranted. I urge institutional cooperation, reminding him of my connection with Chief Zurcher. I plead for his understanding that someone is more likely to get hurt if there were to be a break-in at our low-security facility. "Please, can't we work it out?" "Sorry, but the answer is no; I hate to let you down, but it is purely a matter of business." I have lost my smart move for this righteous prisoner transfer, and clearly I am also losing my perspective.

What must that police officer be thinking about a psychology professor who believes he is a prison superintendent, wildly fearful about some assault on "his prison?" "Nutcase," maybe? "Over the top," likely. "Psycho psychologist," probably.

You know what? I told myself, who cares what he's thinking? Gotta move on, time is pressing. Ditch that plan, move to another: First, put an informant into the prisoner mix to get better information about the impending riot. Then arrange to foil the rioters by pretending the study is over when they break in. We will disassemble the prison cells to make it look as though everyone has gone home, and I will tell them that we have decided to discontinue the research, so no heroics, just go back where you came from.

After they leave, we will have time to fortify the prison and generate better options. We had found a large storage room on the top floor of the building where we would house the inmates right after visiting hours—assuming that the break-in does not occur during that time. Then later that night we will return them and fix up the prison so it will be more resistant to assault. Our shop technician is already working on ways to fortify the entrance doors, put up an outside surveillance camera, and enhance prison security in other ways. Seems like a sensible backup plan, no?

Obviously, I was irrationally obsessed with the imagined assault on "my prison."

Planting an Informer

We need more precise information about the impending attack, so I decide to put an informer into the jail, a presumed replacement for the released prisoner. David G. is a student of mine who had the kind of analytical mind we needed. Surely, his big bushy beard and unkempt appearance will endear him to the prisoners as one of their own. He had helped out earlier with videotaping during the initial stages of the study, to relieve Curt, and so had a sense of the place and the action. David agrees to participate for a few days and to give us whatever information he could glean that might be helpful. We will then have him sent to one of the staff offices on some pretext so he can spill the beans.

Dave quickly discovers the guards' new doctrine, which one of them makes explicit: "Good prisoners will have no cares, troublemakers will have no peace." Most of the prisoners are in the process of deciding that it does not make sense to accept their prisoner role in its most contentious form by constantly opposing the guards. They are beginning to accept their fate and to cope day by day with whatever is done to them because "the prospect of two weeks of hassling over sleep, meals, beds, and blankets was too much." But Dave notes a new mood that had not been present earlier. "Paranoia strikes deep here," he later said about the rumors of escape.[5]

No one questions David's introduction into the study. Nonetheless, he feels that the guards know he is different from the others—but they aren't quite sure what he is doing there. They do not know his identity and simply treat him like all the others—badly. David is soon distressed over the bathroom routine:

"I had to shit in 5 minutes, to piss with a bag over my head while someone tells me where the urinal is. I couldn't do it, in fact, I couldn't even piss in the urinal, had to go to the john and close it and know that somebody's not going to jump on me!"[6]

He befriends Rich-1037, his Cell 2 mate; they quickly bond. But all too quickly. In a matter of hours, our trusted informer, David G., is transformed, wearing the old uniform of Doug-8612. Dave reports "feeling guilty being sent to rat on these great guys, and was relieved when there was really nothing to tell."[7] But was there really no information to share?

1037 tells David that the prisoners cannot quit at any time. He goes on to advise him not to be as rebellious as he was in his first counts. It is not the best thing for them to do at this time. The way to plan an escape, 1037 confides, is to make "the prisoners play along with the guards so that we can get them at their weak spot."

In fact, David told us later that 8612 had not organized any escape plot at all! However, we had already wasted a lot of time and energy in preparing to blunt the attack. "Sure a few of these guys sort of dreamed of their friends coming during visitors' hours and busting them out," he said, "or of slipping away during washroom breaks, but it was clear it was all a dream"—a scrap of hope to hold on to.[8]

We gradually realize that David has violated his verbal contract with us to enact the informer role in this emergency. Accordingly, when someone steals the keys to the police handcuffs later that day, David tells us that he has no idea where they are. He had lied, as we learned from his diary report at the end of the experiment: "I knew where the handcuff key was after a while, but didn't tell, at least not until it didn't matter anymore. I would have told, but I was not about to betray these guys right in front of them."

This rather sudden and amazing transformation into the prisoner mentality was even more evident in some of David's other feedback. He felt that during his two days in our jail, he was no different from the others, "with the exception that I had knowledge of when I would get out, but even that knowledge became less and less certain since I was depending on people on the outside to get me out. I already hated this situation." And at the end of his first day in the Stanford County Jail, David, the informer, tells us, "I fell asleep that night feeling dirty, guilty, scared."

Grievances Are Vented

The same committee of three prisoners that I met with earlier came armed with a long list of grievances that they had delivered to Curt Banks while I was away dealing with the city police. The same three-prisoner team, headed by 5704, along with 4325 and 1037, were elected by all the prisoners. Curt listened respectfully to their complaints. Among them: unsanitary conditions due to toilet restrictions; no clean water to wash hands before meals; no showers; fear of communicable disease; handcuffs and leg chain irons too tight, causing bruises and abrasions. They also wanted church services on Sundays. In addition, they requested the option of alternating the chain from one leg to the other, exercise opportunities, recreation time, clean uniforms, allowing prisoners to communicate between cells, overtime pay for Sunday work, and, in general, the opportunity to be doing something more valuable than just lying around.

Curt listened impassively, as he usually did, without any show of emotion. William Curtis Banks, a light-skinned African-American man in his late twenties, father of two children, a second-year graduate student proud to have made it into the world's top psychology department, was as hardworking and high achieving as any student I had ever worked with. He had no time for frivolity, excess, weaknesses, excuses, or fools. Curt kept his emotions to himself behind a stoic façade.

Jim-4325, who was also a reserved person, must have interpreted Curt's detached manner as his being displeased. He hastened to add that these were not really "grievances," rather "just suggestions." Curt thanked them politely for their suggestions and promised to share them with his superiors for their consideration. I wonder whether they noticed that he took no notes and that they had failed to give him their penciled list for the record. What was most important to our System was to provide the semblance of democracy in this authoritarian setting.

However, citizen dissent demands changes in the system. If taken wisely, such change prevents open disobedience and rebellion. But when dissent is co-opted by the system, disobedience is curtailed and rebellion shelved. In fact, without getting any assurances of reasonable attempts to address any of their complaints, these elected officials had little likelihood of achieving any of their goals. The Stanford County Jail Prisoners' Grievance Committee failed in its main mission to make a dent in the system armor. However, they left feeling good about having openly vented and having some authority, even a low-level one, listen to their complaints.

The Prisoners Make Contact with the Outside World

The prisoners' first letters were invitations to potential visitors, some of whom would be coming by tonight, on this, the third day of the experiment. The second round of letters could be to visitors invited for the next visitor night or to any friend or family member who was too far away to visit. After the prisoners composed them on our official stationery, the guards collected them for mailing, and of course, as duly noted in one of the rules, they were screened for security. The following samples give some sense of what the prisoners were feeling, and at least in one case came as a major surprise to us.

Handsome All-American Hubbie-7258 suggests to his girlfriend that she "bring some interesting pictures or posters to break the boredom of sitting on a bed and staring at blank walls."

Tough guy, Zapata-mustached Rich-1037 conveys his anger to a buddy: "It's not like a job anymore, I'm fucked because you can't get out of here."

Stew-819, whose complaints have been increasing, sends mixed messages to his friend: "The food here is as good and plentiful as the 3rd day of Ebenezer's second voyage to Thailand. Not much happens here of interest, basically I sleep, shout my number, and get hassled. It will be great to get out."

The diminutive Asian-American prisoner, Glenn-3401, makes clear his disdain for this place: "Having a miserable time. Please fire bomb Jordan Hall as a diversionary tactic. My buddies and I are damn frustrated. We intend to make a run for it as soon as possible, but first I've promised to crack a few craniums on the way out." Then he adds a puzzling P.S.: "Be careful not to let the nitwits know you're real . . ." Real?

The surprise came from a letter by nicotine-addicted Paul-5704, the new leader of the prisoners. In that letter, 5704 does a stupid thing for a self-styled revolutionary. He tips off his girlfriend—in an unsecured letter—that he plans to write a story about his experience for a local underground newspaper when he gets out. He has discovered that the Office of Naval Research, of the Department of Defense, is supporting my research.[9] Consequently, he has hatched a conspiracy theory arguing that we are trying to find out how best to imprison student protestors who are opposing the Vietnam War! Obviously he is not an experienced revolutionary, because it was not smart to discuss his subversive plans in a letter that we would be likely to screen.

Little did he know that I myself was a radical, activist professor, against the Vietnam War since 1966, when I had organized one of the nation's first all-night university "teach-ins" at New York University, organized a large-scale walk-out at NYU's graduation ceremony to protest the university's awarding an honorary degree to Secretary of Defense Robert McNamara, and in the last year, at Stanford, I had organized thousands of students into constructive challenges to the continuing war. I was a kindred political spirit but not a mindlessly kindred revolutionary.

His letter begins, "I have made arrangements with The Tribe and The Berkeley Barb [alternative free radical newspapers] to carry the story when I get out." 5704 then brags about his new status in our little prison community: "Today I have gotten together a grievance committee of which I am chairman. Tomorrow I am organizing a Credit Union for our collective wages." He goes on to describe

that he is benefiting from this experience: "I am learning a lot about revolutionary incarceration tactics. Guards accomplish nothing because you just can't keep
the old freak morale down. Most of us here are freaks and I don't really think anyone will crack before this thing is over. A few are starting to get servile, but they
exert no influence on the rest of us." In addition, he signs off with a big, bold
"Your prisoner, 5704."

I decide not to share this information with the guards, who might really
abuse him in retaliation. But it is upsetting to think that my research grant status
is being accused of being a tool of the administration's war machine, especially
since I have worked to encourage effective dissent by student activists. That grant
was originally given to fund empirical and conceptual research on the effects of
anonymity, of conditions of deindividuation, and on interpersonal aggression.
When the idea for the prison experiment occurred, I got the granting agency to
extend the funding to pay for this research as well, without any other additional
funding. I am angry that Paul and probably his Berkeley buddies are spreading
this falsehood.

Whether driven by his sporadic mood shifts, nicotine cravings, or his desire to
make exciting material for his journalistic exposé, 5704 has created a lot of difficulty for all of us today—a day when we already had too much to handle. With
the help of his cellmates, he also bent the bars on Cell 1's door, for which he got
Hole time. While in the Hole, he kicked down the partition between the two compartments, for which action he was denied lunch and also received extended solitary time. He continues to be noncooperative during dinner and obviously upset
that no one has come to visit him. Fortunately, following his meeting after dinner
with the warden, who sternly rebuked him, we notice that 5704's behavior has
changed for the better.

PREPPING FOR THE VISITORS:
THE HYPOCRITICAL MASQUERADE

I had hoped Carlo would be able to come from Oakland to work with me on how
best to prepare for the onslaught of parents. But, as usual, his old car has broken
down and is being repaired, hopefully in time for his scheduled appearance the
next day as head of our Parole Board. After a long phone conversation, the game
plan is set. We will do just what all prisons do when unwelcome visitors descend
on them, ready to document abuses and confront the system with demands for
improvement: prison officials cover the bloodstains with doilies, hide the bodies by
putting troublemakers out of sight, and make the scene pretty.

Carlo offers sage advice about what I might do in the short time available to
create the appearance to parents of a well-oiled, benevolent system that is taking
good care of their children while we are in charge of them. He makes it clear,
however, that we must convince these middle-class, white parents to believe in
the good we are doing with the study and, like their sons, make them comply with

the demands of the authorities. Carlo laughs as he says, "You white folks sure like to conform to the Man, so they know they are doing the right thing, just doing like everyone else is doing."

Turn on Action Central: Prisoners wash the floors and their cells, the Hole sign is removed, and a disinfectant with a fresh eucalyptus scent is sprayed all over to counter the urine odors. The prisoners are shaved, sponge-washed, and as well groomed as can be. Stocking caps and head towels are stashed away. Finally, the warden warns everyone that any complaints will result in premature termination of the visit. We ask the day shift to do overtime until 9 P.M. both to cope with the visitors and also to be ready to assist should the anticipated riot materialize. For good measure, I invite our entire group of backup guards to come in as well.

Next we feed our prisoners their best hot meal, chicken pot pie, with seconds and double desserts for the gourmands among them. Music gently infuses the Yard as the men eat. The day guards are serving the dinner, while the night guards are watching. Without the laughter or snickering that usually accompanies the meals, the atmosphere is strangely civil and rather ordinary.

Hellmann is sitting at the head of the table, leaning back but still showing his big club, prominently swinging it around: "2093, you never had it so good, did you?"

2093 replies: "No, I haven't, Mr. Correctional Officer."

"Your mother never gave you seconds, did she?"

"No, she didn't, Mr. Correctional Officer," Sarge replies obediently.

"You see how good you've got it here, 2093?"

"Yes, I do, Mr. Correctional Officer." Hellmann picks some food from Sarge's plate and walks away, sneering at him. Bad blood is developing between them.

Meanwhile, in the corridor outside the main prison door, we are making final preparations for the visitors, whose potential for making trouble is a realistic fear. Opposite the wall housing the three offices of the guards, the warden, and the superintendent are a dozen folding chairs for visitors while they await entry. As they come down into the basement, full of good humor at what seems a novel, fun experience, we deliberately and systematically bring their behavior under situational control, according to plan. They have to be taught that they are our guests, to whom we were granting the privilege of visiting their sons, brothers, friends, and lovers.

Susie Phillips, our attractive receptionist, welcomes the visitors warmly. She is seated behind a large desk with a dozen fragrant red roses at one side. Susie is another of my students, a psychology major and also a Stanford Dolly, chosen for the cheerleading team for her good looks and gymnastic abilities. She signs each visitor in, noting time of arrival, number in party, and name and number of the inmate he or she will visit. Susie informs them of the procedure that *must* be followed tonight. First, each visitor or group sees the warden for a briefing, after which they can go into the prison when their relative or friend has finished his dinner. On the way out, they are to meet with the superintendent to discuss any concerns they may have or to share their reactions. They agree to these terms and then sit and wait while they listen to music piped in over the intercom.

Susie apologizes for their having to wait so long, but it seems that the prisoners are taking a longer time than usual tonight because they are enjoying double desserts. That does not sit well with some visitors, who have other things to do and are getting impatient to see their prisoner and this unusual prison place.

After conferring with the warden, our receptionist informs the visitors that because the prisoners have taken so long to eat, we will have to limit the visiting time to ten minutes and admit only two visitors per inmate. The visitors grumble; they are upset with their kids and friends for being so inconsiderate. "Why just two of us?" they ask.

Susie replies that the space inside is very tight and there is a fire law about maximum occupancy. She adds, as an aside, "Didn't your child or friend tell you about the limit of two visitors when he invited you here?"

"Damn! No, he didn't!"

"I'm sorry, I guess it must have slipped his mind, but now you will know next time you visit."

The visitors try to make the best of it, chatting among themselves about this interesting study. Some complain about the arbitrary rules, but, remarkably, they meekly comply with them, as good guests do. We have set the stage for them to believe that what they are seeing in this lovely place is standard, and to distrust what they might hear from their irresponsible, selfish kids and buddies, who are likely to complain. And so they too become unwitting participants in the prison drama we are staging.

Up-Close and Impersonal Visits

Prisoner 819's parents are the first to enter the Yard, looking around curiously when they notice their son seated at the end of the long table in the middle of the corridor.

Father asks the guard, "Can I shake hands with him?"

"Sure, why not?" he answers, surprised by the request.

Then his mother also shakes hands with her son! Shakes hands? No automatic hugging of parents and their child?

(This kind of awkward exchange involving minimal body contact is what happens when one is visiting a real maximum-security prison, but we never made that a condition for visiting in our prison. It was our previsit manipulation of the visitors' expectations that worked to create confusion about what behaviors were appropriate in this strange place. When in doubt, do the minimal amount.)

Burdan is standing over the prisoner and his parents. Hellmann comes and goes at will, invading the privacy of 819's interaction with his folks. He looms over 819 as this little familial triad pretends to ignore him and carry on a normal conversation. However, 819 knows that he has no chance to say anything bad about the prison or he will suffer later. His parents cut their visit short to only five minutes so that 819's brother and sister can share some of the limited visiting. They shake hands again as they say their good-byes.

"Yeah, things are pretty good here," Stew-819 tells his siblings.

They and other friends of the prisoners act a lot differently from the uptight ways of the generally more intense parents. They are more casual, more amused, and not as intimidated by the situational constraints as the parents. But guards are hovering over everyone.

819 continues, "We have some pleasant conversations with the correctional officers." He describes the "Hole for punishment," and as he points toward it, Burdan interrupts: "No more talking about the Hole, 819."

The sister asks about the number on his smock and wants to know what they do all day. 819 answers her questions and also describes the impact of the police arrest. As soon as he begins to talk about problems he has with the night guard shift, Burdan again stops him cold.

819: "They get us up early in the morning . . . some guards are really good, top correctional officers. There's not really any physical abuse; they do have clubs, but . . ."

His brother asks him what he would do if he could get out. 819 answers, as a good prisoner should, "I can't be out there, I am in this wonderful place."

Burdan ends the visit after precisely five minutes. Ceros has been sitting at the table the entire time, with Varnish standing behind the table. The guards outnumber the guests! 819's face turns grim as his guests smilingly wave good-bye.

In come the mom and dad of Prisoner Rich-1037. Burdan immediately sits down on the table, glowering over them. (I notice for the first time that Burdan looks like a sinister Che Guevara.)

1037: "Yesterday was kinda strange. Today we washed all the walls in here and cleaned our cells in here . . . we don't have a sense of time. We haven't been out to see the sun."

His dad asks whether they will stay inside for the entire two weeks. Son is not sure but imagines that is the case. This visit seems to be going well, the conversation is animated, but Mom shows that she is worried about her son's appearance. John Landry saunters over to chat with Burdan as both stand within hearing of the visitors' conversation. 1037 does not mention that the guards have taken away his bed and so he is sleeping on the floor.

"Thanks for coming," 1037 says with feeling. "I'm glad I came . . . see you soon, day after tomorrow, for sure." Mom comes back when 1037 asks her to call someone on his behalf.

"Now, you be good and follow the rules," she urges her son.

Dad gently ushers her out the door, aware that they might be staying overtime in their visit and preventing others from the chance to enjoy visiting privileges.

The guards all perk up when they spy Hubbie-7258's attractive girlfriend enter the yard. She is carrying a box of cupcakes, which she wisely shares with

them. The guards eagerly munch them down, making hearty sounds for the benefit of their captives. 7258 is allowed to eat one cupcake while he and his girl get
into an animated conversation. They seem to be trying hard to be oblivious of the
guard's breathing down their necks; all the while Burdan hovers next to them,
rapping his club on the table in staccato.

The intercom background music is playing the Rolling Stones' hit "Time Is
on My Side." This irony is missed as visitors come and go for their all-too-brief encounter.

Mother Knows Best, but Dad and I Do Her In

I thank each of the visitors for taking time from their busy schedules to make this
visit. Like the warden, I try to be as accommodating and congenial as possible. I
add that I hope they appreciate what we are to do by studying prison life in as realistic a fashion as possible within the limits of an experiment. I answer their
questions about future visits, about sending gift boxes, and counter their personal
asides urging that I especially look after their son. It is all going like clockwork,
only a few more visitors to process before I can turn my full attention to dealing
with the expected danger to our dungeon. However, thinking ahead to the next
game, I am blindsided by 1037's mother. I am not prepared for the intensity of her
distress.

As soon as she and Dad enter my office, she says in a quavering voice, "I don't
mean to make trouble, sir, but I am worried about my son. I have never seen him
looking so tired."

Red alert! She could make trouble for our prison! And she is right, 1037 looks
terrible, not only physically exhausted but depressed. He is one of the most
raggedy-looking kids of the entire lot.

"What seems to be *your son's problem?*"

This reaction is immediate, automatic, and like that of every authority confronted by a challenge to the operating procedures of his system. Like all other
perpetrators of institutional abuse, I ascribe the problem of her son as dispositional, as his problem—as something wrong *in him.*

She is having none of that diversionary tactic. Mom continues on to say that
he looks so haggard, has not been sleeping through the night, and—

"Does he have a sleep disorder?"

"No, he says that the guards wake them up for something called 'counts.' "

"Yes, of course, the counts. When each new shift of guards comes on duty,
they must be sure the men are all present and accounted for, so they have them
count off their numbers."

"But in the middle of the night?"

"Our guards work eight-hour shifts, and since one group of them starts at
two A.M., they have to wake up the prisoners to be sure they are all there, that
none have escaped. Doesn't that make sense to you?"

"Yes, but I'm not sure that—"

She is still primed to make trouble, so I move on to another more potent tactic and engage Dad, who has been silent. Looking him straight in the eye, I put his masculine pride at risk.

"Excuse me, sir. Don't you think that *your son* can take it?"

"Sure, he can, he's a real leader, you know, captain of the . . . and . . ."

Only half listening to the words but understanding their tone and accompanying gestures, I bond with Dad. "I'm with you. Your son seems to have the right stuff to handle this tough situation." Turning back to Mom, I add to reassure her, "Rest assured that I will keep an eye on your boy. Thanks for coming; hope to see you again soon."

Dad grips my hand firmly in a manly shake, as I wink at him with the assurance of the boss who is on his side. We silently acknowledge that "We will tolerate 'the little lady's' overreaction." What swine we are, and we do it all on automatic masculine pilot!

As a postscript to this smarmy episode, I received a tender letter from Mrs. Y., written that same night. Her observations and intuition about our prison situation and her son's condition were completely accurate.

> My husband and I visited our son at the "Stanford County Prison." It seemed very real to me. I had not expected anything so severe nor had my son when he volunteered I am sure. It gave me a depressed feeling when I saw him. He looked very haggard, and his chief complaint seemed to be that he had not seen the sun for so long. I asked if he was sorry he volunteered and he answered that at first he had been. However, he had gone through several different moods and he was more resigned. This will be the hardest money he will ever earn in his life, I am sure.
>
> Mother of 1037.
>
> PS: We hope this project is a big success.

Although I am getting ahead of our story, I should add here that her son Rich-1037, one of the original band of tough rebels, had to be released from our prison in the next few days because he was suffering from acute stress reactions that were overwhelming him. His mother had sensed that change coming over him.

DISGUISED ABANDONMENT TO FOIL THE RIOTERS

Once the last visitor had left, we could all breath a collective sigh of relief that the rioters had not crashed into our party when we were most vulnerable. But the threat was not over! Now it was time to swing into counterinsurgency mode. Our plan was for some guards to dismantle the jail props, to give the appearance of disarray. Other guards would chain the prisoners' legs together, put bags over their heads, and escort them in the elevator from our basement to a rarely used, large fifth-floor storage room, safe from invasion. When the conspirators charged in to liberate the jail, I would be sitting there all alone and would tell them that the experiment was over. We had ended it early and sent everyone home, so they were too late to liberate anything. After they checked out the place and left, we'd bring the prisoners back down and have time to redouble the security of our prison. We even thought of ways to capture 8612 and imprison him again if he was among the conspirators because he had been released under false pretenses.

Picture this scene. I am sitting alone in a vacant corridor, formerly AKA "the Yard." The remnants of the Stanford County Jail are strewn about in disorder, prison cell doors off their hinges, signs down, the front door wide open. I am psyched to spring what we consider to be our ingenious Machiavellian counterplot. Instead of the rioters, who should appear but one of my psychology colleagues—an old friend, a very serious scholar, and my graduate school roommate. Gordon asks what's going on here. He and his wife saw the bunch of prisoners up on the fifth floor and felt sorry for them. They went out and bought the prisoners a box of doughnuts because they all looked so miserable.

I describe the research as simply and quickly as possible, all the while expecting the sudden intrusion of the invaders. This scholarly intruder then poses a simple question: "Say, what's the independent variable in your study?" I should have answered that it was the allocation of pretested volunteer subjects to the roles of prisoner or guard, which of course had been randomly assigned. Instead, I get angry.

Here I had an incipient prison riot on my hands. The security of my men and the stability of my prison were at stake, and I had to contend with this bleeding-heart, liberal, academic, effete professor whose only concern was a ridiculous thing like an independent variable! I thought to myself: The next thing he'd be asking was whether I had a rehabilitation program! The dummy. I adroitly dismiss him and get back to the business of waiting for the attack to unfold. I wait and wait.

Finally, I realize that it is all a rumor. No substance to it at all. We had spent many hours and expended a great deal of energy in planning to foil the rumored attack. I had foolishly gone begging to the police for their aid; we had cleaned out a filthy storage room upstairs, dismantled our prison, and moved the prisoners up and out. More important, we had wasted valuable time. And, our biggest sin, as researchers, is that we had not collected any systematic data the whole day. All this from someone who has a professional interest in rumor transmission and distortion and who regularly does class demonstrations of such phenomena. We mortals can be fools, especially when mortal emotions rule over cool reason.

We resurrected the prison props and then moved the prisoners back down from the hot, stuffy windowless storage room where they had been stored for three mindless hours. What humiliation I suffered. Craig, Curt, Dave, and I could barely make eye contact for the rest of that evening. We tacitly agreed to keep it all to ourselves and not declare it "Dr. Z's Folly."

We Played the Fools, but Who Will Pay the Piper?

Obviously we all reacted with considerable frustration. We also suffered the tension of cognitive dissonance for so readily and firmly believing a lie and committing ourselves to much needless action without sufficient justification.[10] We had also experienced "groupthink." Once I, as leader, believed the rumor to be valid, everyone else accepted it as true. No one played devil's advocate, a figure that every group needs to avoid foolish or even disastrous decisions like this. It was reminiscent of President John Kennedy's "disastrous" decision to invade Cuba in the Bay of Pigs fiasco.[11]

It should also have been apparent to me that we were losing the scientific detachment essential for conducting any research with unbiased objectivity. I was well on the way to becoming a prison superintendent rather than a principal investigator. It should have been obvious that this was so from my earlier encounter with Mrs. Y. and her husband, not to mention my tantrums with the police sergeant. However, even psychologists are people, subject to the same dynamic processes at a personal level that they study at a professional level.

Our general sense of frustration and embarrassment spread silently across the prison Yard. In retrospect, we should have just admitted our mistake and moved on, but that is one of the hardest things that anyone can ever do. Just say it: "I made a mistake. Sorry." Instead, we unconsciously looked for scapegoats to deflect blame from ourselves. And we did not have to look far. All around us were prisoners who were going to pay the price for our failure and embarrassment.

CHAPTER SIX

Wednesday Is Spiraling Out of Control

On this fourth day of the experiment, I am looking forward to a less frenetic time than Tuesday's endless troubles had created. Our daily schedule seems filled with enough interesting events to contain the volatility that has been bursting the seams of our prison. A priest who had been a prison chaplain is coming to visit this morning to give me a sense of how realistic our prison simulation is to provide a benchmark, the actual prison experience, against which to measure ourselves. He is reciprocating an earlier favor I did for him, providing some references for a paper he was writing on prisons for a summer school course. Although his visit was arranged prior to the start of our study, it will do double duty by also partially satisfying the Grievance Committee's demand for church services, sort of. Afterward there will be the first Parole Board hearing for prisoners requesting to be paroled. The Board is going to be headed by our prison consultant on this project, Carlo Prescott. It will be interesting to see how he deals with this total role inversion: from a former prisoner who had repeatedly requested parole and been rejected, to the head of a parole board.

The promise of another Visiting Night after dinner should help to contain the distress of some prisoners. I also plan to admit a replacement prisoner, in uniform number 416, to fill the vacancy of troublesome Doug-8612. A lot of action is on today's agenda, but it is all in a good day's work for the superintendent of the Stanford County Jail and his staff.

A PRIESTLY PUZZLE

Father McDermott is a big man, about six feet, two inches tall. He is slim and trim; looks as if he does regular gym time. His receding hairline gives his face more territory to show off his big smile, finely crafted nose, and ruddy complexion. He stands straight, sits erect, and has a good sense of humor. McDermott is an Irish Catholic priest in his late forties who has had experience as a pastoral counselor in an East Coast prison.[1] With his starched collar and neatly pressed black suit, he is the movie version of the jovial yet firm parish priest. I am amazed at the fluidity with which he slips into and out of his priestly role. Now he is the serious scholar, now the concerned priest, now someone making a professional contact, but always he returns to his leading role as "the Priest-Man."

In the Superintendent's Office, we go over the long list of references with annotations that I have prepared for him to help on a report he is doing on interpersonal violence. He is obviously impressed that I'm taking so much time with him and pleased by the reference list, so he asks, "What can I do to help you?"

I respond, "All I would like is for you to talk with as many of the student subjects in our experiment as possible in the time you have available and then, on the basis of what they tell you and what you observe, give me your honest evaluation of how realistic their prison experience seems to you."

"Sure, pleased to reciprocate. I will use as my comparison base the prisoners I worked with in a Washington, D.C., correctional facility I was assigned to for several years," the father tells me.

"Great—I very much appreciate your assistance."

Now it's time for me to switch hats: "The warden has invited any inmates who want to talk with a minister to register for that privilege. A number of them do want to talk with you, and some want to request that religious services be held here this weekend. Only one prisoner, number 819, is feeling sick and wants more sleep so he won't be talking with you."

"Okay, let's go, it should be interesting," says Father McDermott.

The warden has set a pair of chairs against the wall between Cells 2 and 3 for the priest and each inmate who comes to him. I bring over another for me to sit on next to the priest. Jaffe is at my side, looking very serious as he personally escorts each inmate from his cell to the interview. Jaffe is obviously relishing the mock reality of this scenario with a real priest enacting his pastoral role with our mock prisoners. He really gets into it. I am more concerned about the prisoners' likely complaints and what the good father is likely to do to correct them. I ask Jaffe to be sure that Curt Banks is getting this on video as close up as possible, but the low level quality of our video camera doesn't allow close-ups as tight as I would like.

Most interactions take the same form.

The priest introduces himself, "Father McDermott, Son, and you?"

The prisoner responds, "I'm 5486, sir," or "I'm 7258, father." Only a few respond with their names; the rest just give him their numbers instead of their names. Curiously, the priest does not flinch; I am very surprised. Socialization into the prisoner role is clearly taking effect.

"What are you charged with?"

"Burglary" or "armed robbery" or "breaking and entering" or "459 Code violation" are the usual replies.

Some add, "But I am innocent" or "I was charged with . . . but did not do it, sir."

The priest then says, "Good to see you, young man" or says the prisoner's first name. He inquires about where he lives, about his family, about visitors.

"Why is the chain on your leg?" asks Father McDermott of one prisoner.

"I think it's to prevent us from moving around that freely" is the response.

Some he asks about how they are being treated, how they are feeling, whether they have any complaints, and whether he can offer any assistance. Then our priest goes beyond any of my expectations with basic questions about the legal aspect of their confinement.

"Anybody post bond for you?" He asks one of them. Alternatively, of 4325 he seriously inquires, "How does your lawyer feel about your case?"

For variety's sake, he asks others, "Have you told your family about the charges against you?" or "Have you seen the public defender yet?"

Suddenly, we are all in the "Twilight Zone." Father McDermott himself has slipped deeply into the role of prison chaplain. Apparently, our mock prison has created a very realistic situation that has drawn the priest in, just as it has the prisoners and the guards and me.

"We weren't allowed to make a phone call, and we have not yet been brought to trial; no trial date has even been mentioned, sir."

The priest says, "Well, someone has got to take your case. I mean, you can fight it from here, but what good does it do to simply write the criminal court chief justice? It is going to be very slow to get a response. You want your family making this contact with a lawyer because you don't have much pull at all in your current state."

Prisoner Rich-1037 says that he plans to "be my own lawyer, because I will be a lawyer soon after I finish law school in a few years."

The priest smiles sardonically. "It is my general observation that a lawyer who tries his own case tends to be too emotionally involved. You know the old saying 'Anyone who represents himself has a fool for an attorney.' "

I tell 1037 that his time is up and motion to the warden to replace him with the next prisoner.

The priest is taken aback by Sarge's excessive formality and his refusal to consider getting legal counsel because "it is only fair that I serve the time I have coming for the crime I am alleged to have committed." "Are there others like him, or is he a special case?" McDermott asks. "He's our special case, Father." It is hard to like Sarge; even the priest treats him in a patronizing manner.

Prisoner Paul-5704 slickly exploits this opportunity to bum a cigarette from the priest, knowing that he is not allowed to smoke. As he lights up and takes a deep puff, he gives me a shit-eating grin and a big "victory" sign—his nonverbal

"Gotcha." The head of the Grievance Committee is making the most of this pleasant respite from the prison routine. I expect him next to ask for another smoke for later. However, I notice that Guard Arnett is duly taking note of this affront and know that he will make the prisoner pay dearly for the contraband cigarette and his wise-aleck smirk.

As the interviews proceed one after another in small talk, complaints about mistreatment, and violations of the rules, I am becoming ever more agitated and confused.

Only Prisoner 5486 refuses to be sucked into this scenario, namely to play-acting that this is a real prison and he is a real prisoner who needs a real priest's help to get his freedom back. He is the only one who describes the situation as an "experiment"—one that is getting out of control. Jerry-5486 is the most level-headed guy in the mix but the least demonstrative. I realize that he has been a shadow until now, not usually called upon by the guards on any shift for special action and rarely even noticeable in any count, the rebellion or disturbances so far. I will keep my eye on him from now on.

The next prisoner, by contrast, is eager to have the priest help get him legal assistance. However, he is stunned by the awareness that it costs big money. "Well, suppose your attorney wanted five hundred dollars as a retainer right now. Do you have five hundred dollars on you? If not, your parents are going to have to come up with that and more—right away."

Prisoner Hubbie-7258 accepts the priest's offer of assistance and gives him his mother's name and phone number so that she can arrange for legal help. He says that his cousin is in the local public defender's office and he might be available to bail him out. Father McDermott promises to follow through on this request, and Hubbie lights up as if he were Santa Claus giving him a new car.

The whole production is becoming ever more weird.

Before leaving, and after having talked in earnest with seven of our inmates, the priest, in best priestly fashion, asks about the one reluctant prisoner, who might need his help. I ask Guard Arnett to encourage 819 to take a few minutes to talk with the priest; it might help him feel better.

During a lull, while Prisoner 819 is being prepared for his meeting with the pastoral counselor, Father McDermott confides in me, "They are all the naive type of prisoner. They don't know anything about prison or what a prison's for. It's typical of the educated people that I see. These are the people you want to try to change the prison system—tomorrow's leaders and today's voters—and they are the ones who are going to shape community education. They just don't know enough about what prisons are and what they can do to a person. But what you are doing here is good, it'll teach them."

I take this as a vote of confidence, register his homily for the day, but am no less confused.

Prisoner Stew-819 is looking terrible, to say the least: dark circles under his eyes, uncombed hair going in every direction but down. This morning, Stew-819 did a bad thing: In a rage, he messed up his cell, tearing open the pillow and throwing the feathers everywhere. He was put in the Hole and his cellmates had to clean up the mess. He has been depressed following his parents' visit last night. One of his buddies told a guard that while his parents thought that they had had a great talk with him, he felt otherwise. They had not listened to his complaints, and they had not cared about his condition, which he had tried to explain to them, but they had just talked on and on about some damn play they had just seen.

Priest: "I wonder if you discussed the idea that your family might get a lawyer for you."

819: "They knew I was a prisoner. I told them what I was doing here, about the numbers, the regulations, the hassles."

Priest: "How do you feel now?"

819: "I have a bad headache; I need a doctor."

I intervene, trying to discover the basis of his headache. I ask him whether it was a typical migraine; or maybe had been caused by exhaustion, hunger, heat, stress, constipation, or vision problems.

819: "I just feel kind of drained. Nervous."

Then he breaks down and starts to cry. Big tears, big heaving sighs. The priest calmly gives him his handkerchief to wipe the tears away.

"Now there, it can't be all that bad. How long have you been in this place?"

"Only three days!"

"You're going to have to be less emotional."

I try to comfort 819, arranging for him to take a time-out in the restroom off the Yard, actually behind the partition where we are doing our tape recording. I tell him that he can rest comfortably and I will get him some good food. Then we'll see if the headache goes away by this afternoon. If not, I will take him to Student Health for a checkup. I end by getting him to promise not to try to escape, because I am taking him to a minimum-security area. I ask him whether he is really feeling so bad that he should be released now. He insists that he wants to continue and agrees not to try any funny business.

Priest to 819: "Maybe you are responding to the smell of this place. The air here is oppressive. There's an unpleasant smell, it takes time to get used to it. Nevertheless, it's there, it has sort of a toxic quality, maybe that's too strong, but the stench brings home the reality of prison. [McDermott is smelling the urine and feces odor now clinging to our prison, to which we are habituated and don't notice until it is called to our attention.] You have to get your balance, plenty of prisoners learn to handle it."

As we walk off the Yard, down the hall to my office, the priest tells me that the study is working like a real prison and specifically that he is seeing the typical "first-offender syndrome"—one filled with confusion, irritability, rage, depression, and overemotionalization. He assures me that such reactions change after a week or so because it does not aid a prisoner's survival to be so effeminate. He adds that he thinks this situation is more real for 819 than the boy is willing to admit. We agree that he needs counseling. I note that although 819's lips were trembling, hands shaking, and eyes tearing, he still could not admit that he cannot make it here, that he wants out. I think that he cannot accept the idea that he is chickening out, that his masculinity might be threatened, so he wants us—wants *me*—to insist that he leave as a way of saving face. "Maybe so. That is an interesting possibility," Father McDermott adds, reflecting on all that has just transpired.

While I bid him adieu, I add in passing that the good father is not really going to call the parents, right? "Of course I am, I must. It is my duty."

"Sure, how stupid of me, your duty, that's right." (Just what I need is parents and lawyers to deal with because a priest made a promise he is obligated to keep in his role as a real priest even though he knows this is not a real prison and they are not real prisoners, but what the hell, the play must go on.)

The priest's visit highlights the growing confusion here between reality and illusion, between role-playing and self-determined identity. He is a real priest in the real world with personal experience in real prisons, and although he is fully aware that ours is a mock prison, he so fully and deeply enacts his assumed role that he helps to transform our show into reality. He sits erect, holds his hands in a particular way, gestures just so, leans forward to give personal advice, nods knowingly, pats shoulders, scowls at prisoners' foolishness, and talks in tones and cadences that take me back to my childhood in Sunday school at Saint Anselm's Catholic Church. He could not present a more perfect image of a priest had he been sent from Central Casting. While he was doing his priestly thing, it was as though we were on a bizarre movie set, and I admired how well this actor performed his role. If anything, the priestly visit further transformed our simulated experiment into an ever-more-realistic prison. This was especially so for those prisoners who had been able to sustain the realization that this is all "just an experiment." The priest has made his message a new medium. Is our scenario now in the hands of Franz Kafka or Luigi Pirandello?

Just then, an eruption booms from the Yard. The prisoners are shouting. They are chanting loudly something about Prisoner 819.

Arnett: "Prisoner 819 did a bad thing. Say it ten times, loudly."

Prisoners: "Prisoner 819 did a bad thing" (Over and over many times.)

Arnett: "What is happening to Prisoner 819 for doing the bad thing he did, Prisoner 3401?"

3401: "Prisoner 819 is being punished."

Arnett: "What is happening to Prisoner 819, 1037?"

1037: "I'm not sure, Mr. Correctional Officer."

Arnett: "He's being punished. From the top, 3401."

3401 repeats the mantra, as 1037 adds even louder, "Prisoner 819 is being punished, Mr. Correctional Officer."

1037 and each of the other prisoners is asked the same question in turn, and each responds identically, individually and then collectively.

Arnett: "Let's hear it five times to make sure you remember it. Because of the bad things that Prisoner 819 did, your cells are a mess. Let's hear it ten times."

"Because of what Prisoner 819 did, my cell is a mess."

The prisoners chant the phrase repeatedly, but 1037, the one who plans to be a lawyer, is no longer joining in. Guard John Landry gestures menacingly at him with his billy club to get with the program. Arnett stops the chant to ask what is wrong; Landry informs him of 1037's disobedience.

Prisoner 1037 challenges Arnett: "I have a question, Mr. Correctional Officer. Are we supposed to never tell lies?"

Arnett, in his most formal, unflustered, totally authentic style, replies, "We're not interested in your questions now. The task has been assigned, now let's hear it. 'Because of what Prisoner 819 did, my cell is a mess' ten times."

Prisoners chant the phrase but lose track and do so eleven times.

Arnett: "How many times were you told to do that, Prisoner 3401?"

3401: "Ten times."

Arnett: "How many times did you do it, Mr. 3401."?

3401: "Ten times, Mr. Correctional Officer"

Arnett: "Wrong, you all did it eleven times. Do it over again, do it properly, do it ten times, as I have *commanded* you to do: 'Because of what Prisoner 819 did, my cell is a mess'—ten times."

They shout it out in precision exactly ten more times.

Arnett: "Everyone assume the position."

Without a moment's hesitation, everyone falls to the ground for push-ups. "Down, up, down, up. 5486, these aren't belly rolls, they are push-ups, keep that back straight. Down, up, down, up, down, and stay down. Roll over on your backs for leg lifts."

Arnett: "Six inches is the important feature of this, men. Everybody goes six inches, and everybody's leg will stay there until everybody's leg is six inches."

Guard J. Landry measures to determine whether each prisoner's legs are lifted exactly six inches above the ground.

Arnett: "All together, ten times, 'I will not make the mistake that 819 did, Mr. Correctional Officer.' "

Arnett: "Now at the absolute top of your lungs, 'I will not make any mistakes, Mr. Correctional Officer!' "

They all obey in perfect unison. Prisoner 1037 refuses to shout but goes along with the chanting nevertheless, while Sarge is delighting in the chance to shout out his obedience to this authority. Then all sing out very politely in response to the officer's final command: "Thank you very much for this nice count, Mr. Correctional Officer."

The precise unison of the prisoners would be the envy of any choirmaster or

Hitler Youth rally leader, I think to myself. Moreover, how far have they—or we—come since Sunday's giggling counts and the playful antics of the new prisoners?

YOU'RE NOT 819: IT'S TIME TO GO HOME, STEWART

When I realize that 819 might be hearing all of this in the R&R Room on the other side of thin partition, I rush to check on him. What I find is 819 hunched over into a quivering mass, hysterical. I put my arms around him trying to comfort him, assuring him that he will be all right once he has left and gone home. To my surprise, he refuses to leave with me to see a doctor and then go home. "No, I can't leave. I have to go back in there," he insists through his tears. He can't leave knowing that the other prisoners have labeled him a "bad prisoner," that messing up his cell has made all this harassment come down upon them. Even though he is clearly distressed, he is willing to go back into that prison to prove that he is not really a bad guy.

"Listen carefully to me, now, you're *not* 819. You are Stewart, and my name is Dr. Zimbardo. I am a psychologist, not a prison superintendent, and this is not a real prison. This is just an experiment, and those guys in there are just students, like you. So it's time to go home, Stewart. Come with me now. Let's go."

He stops sobbing, wipes away the tears, straightens up, and looks into my eyes. He looks like a small child awakening from a nightmare, assured by his parent that it is not a real monster and that everything will be fine once he fully accepts that truth. "Ok, Stew, let's go." (I have broken through his illusion, but mine is still clinging on.)

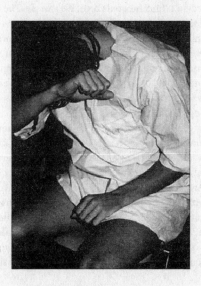

On the way to getting his civilian clothes and mustering Stew out of service, I recall that his day started out with a lot of trouble that set the stage for this emotional breakdown.

819 Messes Up Early On

The Warden's Log reports that 819 refused to get up at the 6:10 A.M. wake-up. He was put in the Hole and later given only half the time in the bathroom that the others got. All, including 819, were present for the fifteen-minute number count at 7:30, reciting it forward and in reverse repeatedly. However, during the exercise period, 819 refused. A guard came up with the social punishment of forcing the other prisoners to stand with their arms outstretched until 819 yielded.

819 would not yield, and the other prisoners' strength gave out as their arms dropped to their sides. 819 was put back in the Hole, where he ate his breakfast in the dark but refused to eat his egg. He was released for work duty to clean out the toilets with his bare hands and move boxes back and forth endlessly and mindlessly along with all the prisoners. When he returned to his cell, 819 locked himself in. He refused to clean off the stickers from a blanket thrown into his cell. His cellmates, 4325 and the replacement, 8612, were forced to do extra work until he complied. They moved boxes back and forth from one closet to the other. He did not relent but demanded to see a doctor. They were getting angry at his obstinence, for which they were suffering.

Ceros's Guard Shift Report notes, "A prisoner locked himself in his cell. We got our clubs and proceeded to get him out. He wouldn't come out. We made everyone stand up against the wall with their arms straight out. He lay back in his cell and laughed. I didn't think he would do it. We gave up. The rest of the prisoners hated us. I just smiled and did my job."

Guard Varnish in his report notes the psychological importance of this prisoner's behavior: "819's apparent indifference to the troubles of his fellow inmates upsets them." Varnish goes on to complain in his report about the lack of clear guidelines for what he could do to the prisoners. "I felt I was uncertain as to the amount of force we could in fact use, and this bothered me as I felt the limits on this case were not clearly defined."[2]

Vandy reports a different reaction: "I continued to become more involved than on the preceding day. I enjoyed harassing the prisoners at 2:30 A.M. It pleased my sadistic senses to cause bitterness between us." That is a rather remarkable statement, one that I am sure he would never have made four days earlier.

Stern Guard Arnett adds in his report: "The only time I felt I could not properly play my role was with 819 and 1037, when they were in such obvious difficulty on some occasions. At these times, I was not as tough as I should have been."[3]

"Basically the really oppressive thing about the prison experience is being totally at the mercy of other people who are trying to make things as difficult and unenjoyable for you as possible," Stew-819 later told me. "I simply can't stand being abused by other people. I developed a strong resentment of the fascist guards and a strong liking for the compassionate ones. I was pleased with the rebelliousness of some prisoners and angered at the complacency and total obedience of others. My sense of time was also affected, since each day's torturous moment seemed quite a bit longer than it would have been if one were enjoying oneself. The worst thing about this experience was the total depression that set in from being constantly hassled and the fact that there was no way of getting out. The best thing was finally being set free."[4]

Betrayal by Our Very Own Spy

Recall that David, who took over 8612's uniform, was brought into the prison as our spy. Unfortunately, for us, he was not providing any useful information because he had become sympathetic to the prisoners' cause and had transferred his allegiance to them in almost a heartbeat. I released him that morning in order to debrief him and get his assessment of what was going on. In his interview with the warden and me, our failed informer made clear his disdain for the guards and his frustration at not being able to mobilize the prisoners to disobey orders. He said that that morning, one guard had told him to fill the coffeepot with hot water in the bathroom but then another guard had dumped it out and made him fill it with cold water, admonishing him for disobeying orders. He hated this "chicken-shit" hazing. He also told us of the time distortion that expanded and contracted events and had confused him when he was awakened several times during the night for interminable counts. He reported a mental dullness like a fog surrounding everything.

"The arbitrariness and idiot work by the guards grates on you." In his new role as informer-turned-prisoner-revolutionary, he told us of his plan to energize his mates for action. "Today, I decided to be a shitty prisoner. I wanted to get some sort of spirit of resistance going among the prisoners. The punishment of making others do more if any prisoner refuses to work or to come out of his cell works only if the others are willing to do more. I tried to make them resist. But everyone was willing to do what they were told, even to the humiliating task of transferring the contents of one closet to the other and back again, or cleaning the toilet bowls with our bare hands."

David reported that nobody is angry with me or the warden, who is mostly just a crackling voice over the loudspeaker, but he and the others are pissed at the guards. He told one of them this morning, "Mr. Correctional Officer, do you think that when this job ends you're going to have enough time to become a human being again?" For which of course he got Hole time.

He was upset that he failed in this attempt to get the other prisoners to refuse to keep their arms lifted in collective punishment for 819's mess-up. Their arms dropped down eventually, but from fatigue, not disobedience. David's frustrations at not being an effective labor organizer are evident in his report to us:

Communication lines are severely limited when everybody's screaming so loudly, you can't stop it. But during silent periods I try to talk with my cell-mates, but 819 is always in the Hole, and the other guy, 4325 [Jim] is a drag and not much to talk to. And you know at meals, when it would be a good time to talk to all the guys about not giving in so easily to the guards, you can't talk. It's kind of like the energy stays within you and doesn't really ever get organized into action. I got depressed when one guy tells me, "I want to get paroled. Don't bug me. If you want to stick out your neck, that's cool, but I'm not gonna!"[5]

David did not give us "actionable intelligence," such as about escape plans or where the keys to the handcuffs were hidden. His personal reflections did, however, make evident that a powerful force was operating on the minds of the prisoners to suppress group action against their oppression. They had begun to focus inward to selfishly consider what they had to do singly to survive and maybe score an early parole.

WELCOME THE NEW PRISONER ON THE BLOCK

To replenish our depleted rank of prisoners, we admit a replacement, new prisoner number 416. This latecomer will soon play a remarkable role. We see him first on the video in the corner of the Yard. He has come into the prison wearing a shopping bag over his head; he is carefully stripped naked by Guard Arnett. He is really skinny, "all skin and bones," as my mother used to say: you could count each of his rib bones from a distance of ten feet. He is a rather pathetic sight, and he has not yet begun to realize what is in store for him.

Arnett sprays 416 slowly and systematically all over his body with the alleged delousing powder. On Day 1, this task was rushed because the guards had to process so many incoming prisoners. Now, given ample time, Arnett turns it into a special cleansing ritual. He pulls the number 416 smock over his head, chains his ankle, and tops him off with a new stocking cap. Voilà! The new prisoner is ready for action. Unlike the others, who were gradually acclimated to the daily escalations of arbitrary and hostile guard behavior, 416 is being thrust into this crucible of madness headfirst with no time for adjustment.

I was stunned by the arrest procedure. As a standby, I was never booked by the police, as the others had been. Called by a secretary to get my papers and report to the lobby of the Psychology Department before noon. I was really pleased to get the job, glad I had gotten a chance to do it. [Remember, these volunteers were being paid for two weeks on the job.] As I was waiting, a guard came out and after I told him my name, he immediately handcuffed me, put a paper bag over my head, brought me down a flight of stairs and I had to stand for a while with my hands on the wall, spread eagled. I had no idea what was going on. I think that I accepted being miserable, but it was much worse than I had expected. I didn't expect to come in and right off be stripped and deloused and struck on my legs with a baton. I decided that I would stay as mentally removed from the guards as I could while watching the other prisoners playing these social games. I said to myself, that I will do my best to keep out of that, but as time went on, I forgot my reasons for being here. I'd come in with reasons, like it'll make me money. Suddenly, 416 has been transformed into a prisoner—and one who is extremely dazed and upset.[6]

"Amazing Grace": In the Key of Irony

The new prisoner arrives just in time to hear Arnett dictating a letter that the prisoners must send to their prospective visitors for the next Visiting Night. As the guard reads out the text, they write it out on the prison stationery provided. Then he asks each of them to repeat parts of it aloud. One formula letter as dictated says:

Dear Mother,

I've been having a marvelous time. The food is great and there's always lots of fun and games. The officers have treated me very well. They are all swell guys. You would like them, Mother. No need to visit, it's seventh heaven. And put the name there that your mother gave you, whatever that may be.

Yours truly,
Your Loving Son

Guard Markus collects them all for later mailing—after, of course, first screening them for forbidden information or incendiary complaints. The prisoners put up with such nonsense because visits have become so important to them—after a relative few days without seeing family and friends. That link to the other world needs to be maintained as an assurance that this basement world is not all there is.

New trouble starts to percolate around a problem with the door lock in Cell 1. 5704, the wise guy who shamelessly bummed a cigarette from the priest earlier today, keeps opening the door to show that he is free to go in and out at any time. In silky smooth style, Guard Arnett gets a rope and ties it around the bars and across the wall to connect it to Cell 2. He does so methodically, as if it were for a Boy Scout merit badge for knot tying. He whistles the "Blue Danube Waltz" as he rings the rope around the bars of one cell and back to the other cell to prevent either from being opened from inside. Arnett whistles well. John Landry comes into view, using his billy club to twist the rope taut. The two guards smile approvingly at each other for a job well done. Now no one can go in to or out of those two cells until the guards have figured out how to fix that defective lock, which 5704 probably broke.

"No cigarettes for you, 5704, as long as the cell door is blockaded. You're going to be in solitary when you get out."

Rich-1037 yells out threateningly from Cell 2, "I have a weapon!"

Arnett challenges him: "You don't have a weapon. We can get that cell open anytime we want."

Someone calls out, "He has a needle!"

"That's not a very good thing for him to have. We will have to confiscate it and duly punish him." Landry pounds his club hard on the doors of all the cells to remind them of who is in charge. Arnett adds his slam on the bars of Cell 2, almost smashing the hands of one of the prisoners, who pulls back just in time. Then, as in the rebellion in the morning of Day 2, John Landry begins to spray the fire extinguisher with its skin-chilling carbon dioxide exhaust into Cell 2. Landry and Markus push their clubs into the cell bars to keep the inmates away from the barred opening, but a prisoner in Cell 2 steals one of their clubs away. They all start mocking the guards. New bedlam is about to break out now that the prisoners have a weapon.

Arnett maintains his cool demeanor, and, after some discussion, the guards arrange to take a lock from a vacant office and install it on Cell 1. "Actually, men, it's a one-way street in the last analysis, it's just a matter of how long it takes," he tells them patiently.

Eventually the guards triumph again; forcing their way into both cells and hauling big bad boy 5704 back into solitary. This time they are taking no chances. They tie him up hands and feet, using their cord taken off the cell doors, before dumping him into the Hole.

This uprising forfeits the privilege of lunch for all the prisoners. Too bad for 416, the new guy. He has had only a cup of coffee and a cookie for breakfast. He is hungry and has done nothing but look on in amazement as these bizarre events unfold around him. Would be nice to eat something warm, he thinks. Instead of lunch, the prisoners are all lined up against the wall. Paul-5704 is hauled out of solitary but remains bound up and helpless lying on the floor of the Yard. He is on display as a lesson against further thoughts of rebellion.

Guard Markus orders everyone to sing while doing jumping jacks, to the tune of "Row, Row, Row Your Boat."

"Since you guys are in such good voice, we're going to sing 'Amazing Grace,' " Arnett tells them. "We're just going to do one verse, I'm not going to strain God's credulity." As the rest of the prisoners assume the position on the floor for push-ups, 416 is singled out for his first public notice: "Here you go. You better memorize this, 416. 'Amazing Grace, How sweet the sound, to save a wretch like me, I once was blind, but now I see, in the first hour since God, I'm free.' "

Arnett resists the correction about "in the first hour since God" that Paul-

5704 offers him from the floor. "That's the way you're going to do it. That line might not be exactly it, but that's the way you're going to do it." Then he inexplicably changes the last line to "since the first hour I've seen God, I'm free."

Arnett, who obviously knows he is a good whistler, then whistles "Amazing Grace" once through, and whistles it all again in perfect tune. Prisoners applaud him in a nice, spontaneous gesture of appreciation for his talent, despite despising him for his attitude and assorted cruelty against them. As Guards Landry and Markus lounge back on the table, the prisoners sing the song, but clearly they are out of key and out of unison. Arnett is upset: "Did we scrape these people up from the Sixth Street ghetto in San Francisco, or something? Let's hear it again." Troublemaker 5704 makes another attempt to correct the inaccurate wording, but Arnett uses the opportunity to make his point loud and clear: "Of course there is a discrepancy here; you're to do the *prison version of 'Amazing Grace.'* It does not matter if it's wrong, because the guards are always right. 416, you stand up, everybody else in the push-up position. 416, while they do push-ups, you sing 'Amazing Grace,' as I have dictated it."

Only a few hours after being imprisoned, 416 is moved to center stage by Arnett, who isolates him from the other prisoners and forces him to perform a mindless task. The video captures this saddest of moments as the scrawny new prisoner sings in a high-pitched voice this song of spiritual freedom. His slackened shoulders and downward glance make evident his extreme discomfort, which worsens when he is corrected and has to repeat the song while the others are forced to keep pushing up and down and up and . . . the irony of being ordered to sing a song of freedom in this oppressive atmosphere where his song provides the cadence for mindless push-ups is not lost on 416. He vows not to be crushed by Arnett or any other guard.

It is not clear why Arnett has singled him out this way. Maybe it's just a tactic to get him into the pressure cooker faster. Alternatively, maybe there is something about 416's shabby and scrawny appearance that is offensive to a guard who tends to be meticulous and always well turned out.

"Now that you are in a singing mood, 416 will sing 'Row, Row, Row Your Boat' while everyone is on their back with legs up in the air. I want it loud enough so that 5704's loved one, Richard Nixon, can hear it, wherever the fuck he is. Legs up. Up! Up! Let's hear it a few more times, especially emphasizing that last line, 'Life is but a dream.'"

Prisoner Hubbie-7258, still hanging on to the ironic moment, asks if they can sing "*Prison* life is but a dream." The prisoners are literally screaming the song at this point, their chests heaving with each word. Life here is ever stranger.

Return of the TV Cameraman

Sometime this afternoon we had a visit from the TV cameraman from local San Francisco station KRON. He was sent down to do a brief follow-up on his Sunday shoot, which had sparked some interest at the station. I restricted him to shooting from behind our observation window and to talking only with the warden and me about the progress of the study. I did not want to have external interference upsetting the dynamic that was emerging between the prisoners and the guards. I wasn't able to see the TV coverage he made that night, because we were all enmeshed in too many more urgent matters that took our full attention—and then some.[7]

FAREWELL, DAY SHIFT, GOOD EVENING, NIGHT SHIFT

"Time to get ready for Sunday services," Arnett tells the prisoners, even though it is only Wednesday. "Everyone get in a circle and hold hands, like a religious ceremony. Say, 'Hi, 416, I'm your buddy, 5704.' Then each of you welcome your new comrade."

They continue these greetings around the circle in what amounts to a very tender ceremony. I am surprised that Arnett thought to include this sensitive communal activity. But then he goes and spoils it by having everyone skip around in a circle singing "Ring Around the Rosy," with 416 standing alone in the center of the sorry circle.

Before leaving for the day, Arnett throws in one more count, in which John Landry takes over dictating how it will be sung. It is 416's first count, and he shakes his head in disbelief at how the others follow every command in haunting unison. Arnett continues his dehumanizing treatment until the very last minute of his shift time.

"I've had enough of this, go back to your *cage*. Clean up your cells so when visitors come, they won't be nauseated by the sight of it." He leaves whistling 'Amazing Grace.' As a parting shot, he adds, "See ya, folks. See ya tomorrow, my fans."

Landry adds his two cents: "I want you to thank your correctional officers for the time they spent with you today." They give a reluctant "Thank you, Mr. Correctional Officers." John Landry is not buying that "shitty thank-you" and makes them shout it louder as he strides off the Yard along with Markus and Arnett. As they exit stage right, in comes the night shift, featuring John Wayne and his eager crew.

The new prisoner, 416, later told us about his fear of the guards:

I was terrified by each new shift of guards. I knew by the first evening that I had done something foolish to volunteer for this study. My first priority was to get out as soon as possible. That is what you did in prison if you had the vaguest possibility of it. And this was a real prison, run by psychologists and not by the State. I met this challenge by going on a hunger strike, to refuse to eat anything, to get sick and they would have to release 416. That is the plan that I stuck to no matter what the consequences.[8]

At dinner, although he was now very hungry, 416 followed his plan to refuse to eat anything.

Hellmann: "Hey guys, we got nice hot sausages for your dinner tonight."

416 (glibly): "Not for me, sir, I refuse to eat any food you give me."

Hellmann: "That is a rule violation, for which you will be punished accordingly."

416: "It does not matter, I will not eat your sausages."

As punishment, Hellmann puts 416 into the Hole, for his first of many visits there, and Burdan insists that he hold each of the sausages in his hands. After the others finish dinner, 416 has to sit and stare at his food, a plate of two cold sausages. This unexpected act of rebellion infuriates the night shift guards and especially Hellmann, who had thought that tonight everything was under strict control and would be flowing smoothly after last night's problems were resolved. Now this "pain in the ass" is making trouble and might incite the others to rebel, just when it seemed as if they were totally dominated and submissive.

Hellmann: "You don't want to eat two stinking sausages? You want me to take those and cram them up your ass? Is that what you want? Do you want me to take that and cram that up your ass?"

416 remains stoic, staring down expressionless at the plate of sausages.

Hellmann realizes that it is time to put the divide-and-conquer tactic into operation: "Now, listen here, 416, if you do not eat your sausages, that is an act of prisoner insubordination that will result in all prisoners being deprived of visitors tonight. Hear that?"

"I am sorry to hear that. My personal actions should have no consequences for the others," 416 replies in an imperious manner.

"They are not personal but prisoner reactions, and I will determine the consequences!" shouts Hellmann.

Burdan brings out Hubbie-7258 to persuade 416 to eat his sausages. 7258 says, "Just eat your sausages, okay?" Burdan adds, "Tell him why." 7258 continues, pleading that the prisoners won't get visiting hours if he doesn't eat the sausages.

"Don't you care about that? Just 'cause you don't got no friends. . . . Eat for the prisoners, not for the guards, okay?" Burdan throws in this uppercut, pitting 416 against the other prisoners.

Prisoner Hubbie-7258 continues talking to 416, gently trying to get him to eat the sausages because his girlfriend, MaryAnn, is about to visit him soon, and he would hate to be denied that privilege because of a few lousy sausages. Burdan continues to assume more of Hellmann's demeanor in his domineering style and substance:

"416, what's your problem? Answer me, *boy*! Yeah, what's your problem?"

416 begins to explain that he is on a hunger strike to protest the abusive treatment and contract violations.

"What the hell has that got to do with the sausages? Well, what?" Burdan is furious and slams his club down on the table with such a resounding thud that it echoes around the Yard walls in menacing reverberations.

"Answer my question, why don't you eat those sausages?"

In a barely audible voice, 416 continues to make a Gandhi nonviolent protest statement. Burdan never heard of Mahatma Gandhi and insists on a better reason. "You tell me the connection between those two things, I don't see it." Then 416 breaks the illusion, reminding those within earshot that the guards are violating the contract he signed when he volunteered for this *experiment*. (I am stunned that this reminder is ignored by them all. The guards are now totally absorbed in their illusory prison.)

"I don't give a damn about any contract!" Burdan yells. "You're in here because you deserve it, 416. That's how you got in here in the first place, you broke the law. This ain't no nursery school. I still don't understand why you don't eat those damn sausages. Did you expect this to be a nursery school, 416? Do you expect to go around breaking the law and wind up in a nursery school?" Burdan rants on about 416 not going to be a happy boy when his cellmate has to sleep without a bed on the floor tonight. However, just as it seems that Burdan is about to take a swing at 416, he turns away in a fury. Instead, he slaps his club into the palm of his hand and orders 416, "Get back into that Hole." 416 now knows the way.

Burdan bangs his fists against the door of the Hole, making a deafening sound that reverberates inside that dark closet. "Now each of you also thank 416 for his denying your visitors by banging on the Hole and saying 'Thank you.'"

Each prisoner does so, banging on the closet door "with relish," except for 5486, Jerry, who does so unwillingly. Hubbie-7258 is extremely angry by this unexpected twist of his fate.

To underscore the point, Hellmann pulls 416 out of the Hole, still gripping the two sausages. He then runs another tormenting count singlehandedly, not even giving Burdan a chance to participate. Good Guard Landry is nowhere in sight.

Here is Hellmann's chance to break any possibility of prisoner solidarity and to defuse 416's potential emergence as a rebellious hero. "Now you all are going to suffer because this prisoner refuses to do a simple thing like eat his dinner, for no good reason. It would be different if he was a vegetarian. Tell him to his face what you think about him." Some say, "Don't be so stupid"; others accuse him of being childish.

That was not good enough for "John Wayne": "Tell him that he is a 'pussy.'"

A few of them obey, but not Sarge. As a matter of principle, Sarge refuses to use any obscenity. Now, with two of them defying Hellmann at the same time, Hellman turns his wrath against Sarge, harassing him mercilessly, yelling at him that he is an "asshole" and, worse, insisting that he call 416 a "bastard."

The harsh count continues unabated for an hour, stopping only when visitors are at the door. I come on the Yard and make it clear to the guards that visiting hours must be honored. They are not pleased with this intrusion into their power domain but reluctantly acquiesce. There is always the post-visitor time for them to continue breaking down prisoner resistance.

Obedient Prisoners Get Visitors

Two of the more obedient prisoners, Hubbie-7258 and Sarge-2093, who have friends or relatives in the vicinity, are allowed to have them visit for a short time this evening. 7258 is deliriously happy when his pretty girlfriend arrives to see him. She is giving him news about their other friends, and he is listening intently, holding his head in his two hands. All the while, Burdan is sitting above them on the table, routinely banging his small white billy club. (We had to return the big dark ones we had borrowed from the local police department). Burdan is obviously taken with her beauty and breaks into their conversation frequently with questions and comments.

Hubbie tells MaryAnn that it is important to "Try to keep yourself up, it's not that bad in here if you just cooperate."

Girlfriend: "Are you cooperating?"

7258 (laughing): "Yes, they are making me."

Burdan intrudes: "Well, they had a little escape attempt."

Girlfriend: "I heard about that."

7258: "I didn't enjoy the rest of this day at all. We do not have anything; no bed, no nothing." He tells her about having to clean out stickers from dirty blankets and other nasty chores. Nevertheless, he remains upbeat and smiles and holds her hand for the full ten-minute visit. Burdan escorts her out as the prisoner returns to his lonely cell.

The other prisoner granted a visitor is Sarge, whose father comes by. Sarge is bragging about his total command of the rules. "There are seventeen rules . . . I have the rules memorized. The most basic rule is that you obey the guards."

Dad: "Can they tell you to do *anything*?"

Sarge: "Yes. Well, almost anything."

Dad: "And what right do they have to do that?" He rubs his forehead in seeming distress at his son's plight. He is the second visitor to be clearly upset. He is much like the mother of Prisoner Rich-1037—who was right to be concerned, given that he broke down the next day. Nevertheless, Sarge appears to be made of sterner stuff.

Sarge: "They're in charge of the running of the prison."

Dad asks about civil rights, and then Burdan jumps in—very harshly: "He has no civil rights."

Dad: *"Well, I think that they do, maybe . . ."* (We can't hear clearly his argument to Burdan, who is not afraid of this civilian.)

Burdan: "People in prison have no civil rights."

Dad (exasperated): "Anyway, how long do we have to talk here?"

"Only ten minutes," Burdan replies.

The father disputes the amount of time left. Burdan relents and gives them five more minutes. Dad would like more privacy. That is not permitted for visitors in this prison, replies Burdan. Dad gets even more upset, but remarkably, he too goes by the rules and accepts this infringement on his rights by a kid playacting being a guard!

Dad asks more about the rules, Sarge talks about counts, "exercising," chores, and lights-out.

Dad: "Is this what you expected it to be?"

Sarge: "I expected it to be worse."

In disbelief, Dad exclaims: "Worse? Why worse?"

Burdan interjects himself again. The father is now clearly annoyed by his unwanted presence. The guard tells him that there were originally nine prisoners but now there are only five. The father asks why.

Sarge: "Two have been paroled and two are in maximum security."[9]

Dad: "Maximum security where?"

He doesn't really know. Dad asks why they are in maximum security.

Sarge: "They were disciplinary problems. Very *dispositional.*"

Burdan responds at the same time: "Because they were bad."

Dad: "Do you feel like you're in a prison?"

Sarge (laughing, sidesteps a direct answer): "Well, I've never been in a prison *before.*" (Dad laughs.)

They are alone when Burdan runs off in response to a loud noise outside.

While he is gone, they talk about Sarge's coming up for parole, which he is sure he will get because he has been the most obedient prisoner to date. However, he still has a major concern: "I don't know what the criteria are for getting out on parole."

"Time's up," Geoff Landry announces. Father and son stand up, about to hug, but settle instead for a firm, manly handshake and a "See you soon."

Homophobia Rears Its Ugly Head

When I return from a quick dinner at the student cafeteria, I see troublemaker 5704 standing in the center of the Yard holding a chair on his head. A chair on his head! Hellmann is yelling at Sarge, and Burdan is chiming in. Good Prisoner Jerry-5486, who has been almost anonymous, is standing passively against the wall, while 7258 does push-ups. Apparently, 416 is back in solitary. Hellmann asks 5704 why he has that chair on his head—it was he who ordered him to wear it like a hat. The prisoner answers meekly that he is simply following orders. He looks dejected; all of the old spunk seems to have drained away from 5704. Burdan tells him not to look so stupid and to put the chair away. Then Burdan bangs on the Hole door with his club. "You having a good time in there, 416?"

It is time for Hellmann to take over as director of tonight's drama. He literally moves Burdan aside. (No sight of Good Guard Geoff Landry on the Yard following the visits.)

"While you got your hands in the air, 7258, why don't you play Franken-stein. 2093, you can be the Bride of Frankenstein, you stand right here."

"You go over there," he says to Sarge.

Sarge asks whether he should act it out.

"Of course you should act it out. You be the Bride of Frankenstein, 7258, you be Frankenstein. I want you to walk over here like Frankenstein walks, and say that you *love* 2093."

As 7258 starts to walk toward his bride, Burdan stops him in his tracks.

"That ain't no Frankenstein walk. We didn't ask you to walk like *you*."

Hellmann grabs Hubbie-7258 by the arm very aggressively, pulls him back, and makes him walk the proper Frankenstein walk.

7258: "I love you, 2093."

"Get up close! Get up close!" Shouts Burdan.

7258 is now inches away from Sarge. "I love you, 2093."

Hellmann pushes them together, his hands on each of their backs until their bodies are touching.

Again, Hubbie-Frankenstein-7258 says, "I love you, 2093." Hellmann be-rates Sarge for smiling. "Did I tell you that you could smile? This is not funny. You get down and do ten push-ups!"

With Prisoner 7258's arms still stretched out in front of him, back to the wall, his smock lifts, revealing part of his genitals. Sarge is told to tell the other prisoner, Jerry-5486, that he loves him; he complies reluctantly.

"Well, ain't that sweet? Ain't that sweet?" mocks Burdan.

Hellmann now gets up in the face of 5486.

"Are you smiling? Maybe you love him too. Would you go over there and tell him so?"

Jerry-5486 does so without hesitation but says quietly, "2093, I love you."

Hellmann is careening wildly from prisoner to prisoner with his verbal at-tacks.

"Put your arms down, 7258. That's why you stink so much."

"Now all of you stinking prisoners get down on the floor, you're gonna play leapfrog."

They start to play the game but are having difficulty because their shower clogs are falling off and their smocks are creeping up to expose their genitals as they jump over the bent bodies of their fellows. They can't do it right, and Burdan seems a bit uncomfortable with this game. Perhaps he finds the action too sexual or too gay for his tastes. Hellmann simplifies the game, directing only 2093 and 5704 to play together. They continue to try to leapfrog, as Burdan emits little groans.

The homoerotic game is having a perverse impact on Hellmann.

"That's the way dogs do it, isn't it? Isn't that the way dogs do it? He's all ready, ain't he, standing behind you, doggy style? Why don't you make like a dog?"

When tall Prisoner Paul-5704 had brought up complaints of guards hassling prisoners, I'll bet that the head of the Stanford County Jail Prisoners' Grievance Committee never imagined that the guards' insulting abuse would ever descend to this level. He is clearly upset, and he tells John Wayne that what he has been asked to do would be "a little obscene."

Hellmann takes that remark as a slap in the face: "I think your face is a little obscene too. Why don't you just play leapfrog and shut up."

Geoff Landry drifts onto the scene, standing directly behind 5704 and watching everything. He is obviously interested in this turn of events, but he keeps his hands in his pockets to maintain his neutrality and pose of indifference. He is not wearing his anonymity-enhancing sunglasses, even though the warden told him to do so.

"I'm sorry to offend the better nature of this sensitive prisoner," Hellmann says with derision.

Burdan succeeds in ending this game, which he has found distasteful from the beginning, "I'm tired of this game, this is ridiculous." They revert to their more traditional game, the count.

SARGE REVEALS A NEW MORAL IDENTITY

Hellmann is bored. He walks up and down the line of weary prisoners. Suddenly he whirls around and turns his wrath on Sarge: "Why are you such a ass-licker?"

"I don't know, sir."

"Why is it you try to be obedient so much?"

Sarge is not afraid of him and plays the game: "It's in my nature to be obedient, Mr. Correctional Officer."

"You are a liar. You are a stinkin' liar."

"If you say so, Mr. Correctional Officer."

Hellmann becomes ever more obscene, maybe aroused by the previous sexual games: "What if I told you to get down on that floor and *fuck* the floor, what would you do then?"

"I would tell you I didn't know how, Mr. Correctional Officer."

"What if I told you to come over here and hit your friend 5704 in the face as hard as you could?"

Sarge holds his ground: "I am afraid I would be unable to do that, Mr. Correctional Officer."

Hellmann scoffs and turns away, only to spin about and turn on a new victim. As he opens the door to the Hole, Hellmann, like a carnival pitchman, shouts, "I got something right here for everyone. Why don't you take a look at this man? 416, don't you go anywhere!"

416 blinks out of the darkness at the assembled prisoners and guards who are all looking at him. He is holding a sausage in each hand!

Burdan: "How come you holdin' on to your sausages, 416?"

"He hasn't ate no sausages yet," Hellmann says, his usually good grammar breaking down as he becomes more emotional. "And you know what that means for the rest of you?"

The prisoners respond knowingly in the negative, "No blanket tonight."

"That's right, it means no blankets tonight for all of you! Come over here one at a time and try to say something to 416 to get him to eat those sausages. Let's start with you, 5486."

The prisoner walks to the door, looks 416 in the eyes and tells him gently, "You eat those sausages if you want to, 416."

"That's sure a half-assed way to tell him to do something, 5486," Burdan admonishes. "I guess you don't want your blankets tonight. Next up, 7258, you tell him."

In sharp contrast to the first prisoner in line, 7258 yells at the rebel inmate, "Eat your sausages, 416, or I'll kick your ass!"

Hellmann is pleased at the expression of inmate enmity, and he grins from ear to ear. "Now, that's more like it! 5486, you come over here and do it again. Tell him you gonna kick his ass if he don't eat those sausages."

He now meekly complies. "2093, come over here and tell him you're gonna kick his ass."

Sarge makes a moving statement: "I am sorry, sir, I will not use a profane word toward another human being."

"Just what do you object to?"

"I object to the word that you used."

Hellmann tries to get him to say "ass," but his tricks don't work.

"Which word? 'Kick?' You don't wanna say 'kick,' is that what it is? Then what the hell are you talkin' about?"

Sarge tries to clarify himself, but Hellmann cuts him off: *"I gave you an order!"*

Hellmann is becoming frustrated by Sarge's refusal to follow his orders. For the first time, the seemingly mindless robot has shown he has backbone and soul.

"Now, you get over there and tell him what I told you to tell him."

Sarge continues to apologize but remains firm. "I am sorry, Mr. Correctional Officer. I am not capable of doing it."

"Well, you're not capable of having a bed tonight, is that what you want to say?"

Standing his ground, Sarge makes clear his values: "I would prefer to go without a bed than to say that, Mr. Correctional Officer."

Hellmann is steaming. He paces a few steps away and then turns back toward Sarge, as though he were going to whack him for his insubordination in front of this entire audience.

Good Guard Geoff Landry sensing the eruption, offers a compromise: "Go over and say you're gonna kick him in *the end*, then."

"Yes, Mr. Correctional Officer," says Sarge. He then walks over and says to 416, "Eat your sausages or I'll kick you in the *end.*"

Landry asks, "Do you mean it?"

"Yes . . . no, Mr. Correctional Officer. I'm sorry, I don't mean it."

Burdan asks why he's lying.

"I did what the correctional officer told me to say, sir."

Hellmann comes to the defense of his fellow officer: "He didn't tell you to lie."

Burdan realizes that Sarge is getting the upper hand by holding fast to his high moral ground and it could have an effect on the others. He deftly turns things around and down: "Nobody wants you to do any *lying* in here, 2093. So why don't you do some lying on the ground."

He makes Sarge lie on the floor facedown with his arms spread out.

"Now start giving us some push-ups from your position."

Hellmann joins in: "5704, you go over and sit on his back."

After more direction from Hellmann on how he should do push-ups from such a position, Sarge is strong enough to do so.

"And don't help him. Now do a push-up. 5486, you sit on his back too, facing the other way." He hesitates. "Let's go, on top of his back, now!" He complies.

Together the guards force Sarge to do a push-up with both prisoners 5486 and 5704 sitting on his back (they do so without any hesitation). Sarge struggles with all his might and pride to complete a push-up cycle.

He strains to raise himself from the floor but then collapses under the weight of this human burden. The devilish duo bursts into laugher, making fun of Sarge. They are not quite done humiliating Sarge, but 416's stubborn resistance against eating his sausages is of greater immediate consequence to these guards. Hellmann intones: "I just don't understand a thing like those sausages, 416. I don't understand how we can have so many counts and so many good times, we do it so nice, and tonight we just fuck it up. Why is that?"

While Hellmann seeks a simple answer, Burdan is quietly talking with 416 about the sausages, trying another soft-sell tactic: "How do they taste? Mmmm; I know you'd like 'em once you tasted 'em."

Hellmann repeats his question more loudly, in case any one has not heard it: "Why do we have so many good counts and then you try to *fuck up tonight*?"

As Hellmann goes down the line for explicit answers, 7258 responds, "I don't know; I guess we're just bastards, Mr. Correctional Officer."

Sarge answers, "I really wouldn't know, Mr. Correctional Officer."

Hellmann seizes upon another chance to get back at Sarge for his earlier victorious subordination: "Are *you* a bastard?"

"If you say so, Mr. Correctional Officer."

"If I say so? I want *you* to say it."

Sarge is steadfast: "I'm sorry sir, I object to the use of the language, Sir. I cannot say it."

Burdan jumps in: "You just said you couldn't say that stuff to other human beings, 2093. But this is a different question. You can't say it to yourself?"

Sarge counters, "I consider myself a human being, sir."

Burdan: "You consider yourself *another* human being?"

Sarge: "I made the statement that I could not say it to another human being."

Burdan: "And that includes *yourself*?"

Sarge replies in an even, measured, carefully phrased way, as though in a college debate, and in this situation, where he has been the target of such abuse, says, "The statement initially would not have included myself, sir. I would not think of saying it to myself. The reason is that because I would be . . ." He sighs and then trails off, mumbling, becoming emotionally battered.

Hellmann: "So that means *you* would be a bastard, wouldn't you?"

Sarge: "No, Mr.—"

Hellmann: "Yes, you would!"

Sarge: "Yes, if you say so, Mr. Correctional Officer."

Burdan: "You'd be saying very nasty things about your mother, that's what you'd be doing, 2093."

Burdan obviously wants a piece of the action, but Hellmann wants to run the game himself and does not appreciate his sidekick's intrusions.

Hellmann: "What would you be? What would you be? Would you be a *bastard*?"

Sarge: "Yes, Mr. Correctional Officer."

Hellmann: "Well, let me hear *you* say it."

Sarge: "I'm sorry, sir. I will not say it."

Hellmann: "Why the hell won't you say it?"

Sarge: "Because I do not use any profane language."

Hellmann: "Well, why did you apply it to yourself? What are you?"

Sarge: "I am whatever you wish me to be, Mr. Correctional Officer."

Hellmann: "Well, if you say it, if you say that you are a bastard—you wanna know something—then you just proved my point. That you was a bastard. You say so. Then why don't you say it?"

Sarge: "I'm sorry, sir, I will not say it."

Hellmann senses that he has lost another challenge, and he reverts to the divide-and-conquer tactic that has proven so effective before: "Now, boys, you wanna get a good night's sleep tonight, don't you?"

They all say, "Yes, sir!"

Hellmann: "Well, I think we gonna wait a little bit, to let 2093 think about just what a bastard he is. And then maybe he'll tell the rest of us that he thinks so."

(This is an unexpected power struggle between the most controlling, power-hungry guard and the prisoner who until now has been a totally obedient prisoner, so much so that he is ridiculed as "Sarge," whom most prisoners and guards dislike as they all have considered him to be nothing more than a military robot. He is proving that he has another admirable facet to his character; he is a man of principle.)

Sarge: "I think you are perfectly accurate in your condemnation of me, Mr. Correctional Officer."

Hellmann: "Oh, I know that."

Sarge: "But, I cannot say the word, Mr. Correctional Officer."

Hellmann: "Say what?"

Sarge: "I shall not say, with any meaning, the word 'bastard.' "

Bells, whistles, cannons, parade music sounds.

Burdan shouts out with unbridled joy: "He said it!"

Hellmann: "Well, *glory be!* Yes, indeed! Did he say that, 5704?"

5704: "Yes, he did, Mr. Correctional Officer."

Hellmann: "I believe we've got a winner."

Burdan: "These boys might even get to bed tonight, who knows?"

Not content to have won a partial victory, Hellmann has to demonstrate the arbitrary power he commands. "Just for swearing, 2093, you get down on the floor and do ten push-ups."

Sarge: "Thank you, Mr. Correctional Officer," he says as he executes perfect push-up form, despite his obvious exhaustion.

Burdan, upset that Sarge can still perform so well, derides even perfect push-ups: "2093, where do you think you are? Boot camp?"

Now laid-back Geoff Landry chimes in from the chair he has been lounging in for the past hour: "Do ten more." For the spectators he adds, "Do the rest of you think those are good push-ups?"

They answer, "Yes, they are." Big Landry shows an odd display of authority, perhaps to assure himself that he still has some in the eyes of the prisoners.

"Well you're wrong. 2093, do five more."

Sarge's account of this confrontation is framed in a curiously impersonal style:

> The guard ordered me to call another prisoner a 'bastard,' and call myself the same. The former I would never do, the latter of which would produce a logical paradox denying the validity of the former. He began as he always does before "punishments," alluding to the hint in his vocal intonation that the others would be punished for my actions. In order to avoid their punishment and avoid obeying that command, I produced a reaction that would solve both by saying, "I will not use the word bastard in any meaningful way"—giving both he and myself a way out.[10]

Sarge is emerging as a man of considerable principle, not the blindly obedient toady he initially seemed to be. Later, he tells us something interesting about the mind-set he adopted as a prisoner in this setting:

When I entered the prison I determined to be myself as closely as I know myself. My philosophy of prison was not to cause or add to the deterioration of character on the part of fellow prisoners or myself, and to avoid causing anyone punishments because of my actions.

THE POWER OF SAUSAGE SYMBOLISM

Why have those two shriveled, filthy sausages become so important? For 416, the sausages represent challenging an evil system by doing something that he can control and cannot be forced to do otherwise. In so doing, he foils the guards' dominance. For the guards, 416's refusal to eat the sausages represents a major violation of the rule that prisoners must eat at mealtimes and only at mealtimes. That rule was instituted so that prisoners would not be asking for or getting food at any time other than the three scheduled mealtimes. However, this rule has now been extended to cover the guards' power to force prisoners to eat food whenever it is served. Refusal to eat has become an act of disobedience that they will not tolerate, because such refusal could trigger further challenges to their authority from the others, who until now had traded rebellion for docility.

For the other prisoners, 416's refusal to knuckle under should have been seen as a heroic gesture. It might have rallied them around him to take a collective stand against their continuing and escalating abusive treatment by the guards. The strategic problem is that 416 did not first share his plan with the others to get them on his side by understanding the significance of his dissent. His decision to go on a hunger strike was private and thus did not engage his peers. Sensing 416's tenuous social position in the jail as the new guy who has not suffered as much as the others, the guards intuitively set about framing him into a "troublemaker" whose obstinance will only result in punishment or loss of privileges for them. They also characterize his hunger strike as a selfish act because he does not care that it can curtail prisoner-visiting privileges. However, the prisoners should see that it is the guards who are establishing this arbitrary illogicality between his eating sausages and their getting visitors.

Having dismissed Sarge's opposition, Hellmann turns back to his skinny nemesis, Prisoner 416. He orders him out of solitary to do fifteen push-ups, "Just for me, and real quick."

416 gets down on the floor and begins to do push-ups. However, he is so weak and so disoriented that they are hardly push-ups. He is mostly just raising his butt.

Hellmann can't believe what he is seeing. "What is he doing?" he shouts in an incredulous voice.

"Pushing his ass around," says Burdan.

Landry awakening from his dormant state adds, "We told him to do push-ups."

Hellmann is screaming: "Are those push-ups, 5486?"

The prisoner answers, "I guess so, Mr. Correctional Officer."

"No way. They are not push-ups."

Jerry-5486 agrees, "If you say so, they are not push-ups, Mr. Correctional Officer."

Burdan jumps in: "He's swishing his ass, isn't he, 2093?"

Sarge meekly acquiesces: "If you say so, Mr. Correctional Officer."

Burdan: "What's he doing?"

5486 complies: "He's swishin' his ass."

Hellmann makes Paul-5704 demonstrate the way to do good push-ups for 416's edification.

"See that, 416? He's not pushin' his ass. He's not fuckin' a hole in the ground. Now do it right!"

416 tries to imitate 5704, but he is unable to do so because he just does not have enough strength. Burdan adds his mean observation: "Can't you keep your body straight while you're doing this, 416? You look like you're on a roller coaster or something."

Hellmann rarely uses physical aggression. He prefers instead to dominate verbally, sarcastically, and with inventively sadistic games. He is always aware of the exact freedom allowed him by the margin of his role as guard—he may improvise but must not lose control of himself. However, this night's challenges have gotten to him. He stands beside 416, who is lying on the ground in a push-up position, and orders him to do slow push-ups. Hellmann then puts his foot on top of 416's back as he goes up and pushes down hard on the backstroke. The others all seem to be surprised at this physical abuse. After a couple of push-ups, the tough-guy guard lifts his foot off of the prisoner's back and orders him back into the Hole, slamming the door with a loud clang and locking it.

As I watch this, I recall prisoners' drawings of Nazi guards at Auschwitz doing the same thing, stepping on a prisoner's back as he does push-ups.

"A Self-Righteous, Pious Asshole"

Burdan yells to 416 through the door of his confinement, "You don't eat, you're not gonna have very much energy, 416." (I suspect Burdan is beginning to feel sorry for the plight of this puny little kid.)

Now it is time for Guard Hellmann's ascendancy. He delivers a minisermon: "I hope you boys are taking an example here. There is no reason for you to disobey orders. I haven't given you anything you can't obey. There's no reason why I should offend anybody. You're not in here for being upstanding citizens, you know. All this self-righteous drivel makes me puke. And you can knock it off right now."

He asks Sarge for an evaluation of his little speech, and Sarge answers, "I think you made a nice speech, Mr. Correctional Officer."

Getting close to his face, Hellmann goes back to attacking Sarge: "You think you're a self-righteous, pious asshole?"

Sarge replies: "If you wish to think so."

"Well, think about that. You are a self-righteous, pious asshole."

We are back on the not so merry-go-round, with Sarge replying "I will be one if you wish me to be, Mr. Correctional Officer."

"I don't wish you to be, you just are."

"As you say, Mr. Correctional Officer."

Hellmann again goes up and down the ranks desperate for approval, and each prisoner agrees with him.

"He's a self-righteous, pious asshole."

"A self-righteous, pious asshole, Mr. Correctional Officer."

"Yes, a self-righteous, pious asshole."

Delighted that at least this little world sees things his way, Hellmann tells Sarge, "I'm sorry, it's four to one. You lose."

Sarge responds that all that matters is what he thinks of himself.

"Well, if you think something else, then I think you're in very serious trouble. Because you're not really in touch with what is real, with reality. You live a life that's nothing but *mendacity*, that's what you doin'. I'm sick of you, 2093."

"I'm sorry, Mr. Correctional Officer."

"You such a self-righteous, pious bastard that I wanna puke."

"I'm sorry if I make you feel that way, Mr. Correctional Officer." Burdan makes Sarge bend over in a fixed position touching his toes, so that he doesn't have to look at his face again.

"Say, 'Thank You, 416!' "

The last thing that Hellmann must achieve in his battle against belligerents is to crush any sympathy that may be developing among the prisoners for the sad case of 416.

"It is unfortunate that we all have to suffer because some people just don't have their minds right. You've got a nice friend in here [as he bangs against the door of the Hole]. He's gonna see to it that you don't get blankets tonight."

Hellmann aligns his plight with that of the prisoners, against their *common* enemy, numero 416, who is about to harm them all by his foolish hunger strike.

Burdan and Hellmann line up the four prisoners and encourage them to say "Thanks" to their fellow Prisoner 416 sitting in the dark, cramped Hole. Each does so in turn.

"Why don't you all thank 416 for this?"

They all recite, "Thank you, 416."

Still even that is not sufficient for this devilish duo. Hellmann commands them, "Now go over there, next to the door. I want you to thank him with *your fists*, on the door."

They do so, one by one, banging on the door, as they recite, "Thank you, 416!" As they do, a loud, resonating noise booms through the Hole, to further terrify pitiable 416, alone in there.

Burdan: "That's the way, with real spirit."

(It's difficult to determine the extent to which the other prisoners are angry with 416 for causing them all this unnecessary grief, or are just following orders, or are indirectly working off some of their frustrations and rage against the guards' abuses.)

Hellmann shows them how to bang really hard against the door, several times for good measure. Sarge is last and surprisingly complies meekly and obediently. When he is finished, Burdan grabs Sarge by the shoulders and pushes him hard against the back wall. He then orders the prisoners back into their cells and says to his chief operating officer, Hellmann, "They're all ready for lights-out, Officer."

THE DIRTY BLANKET BARGAIN

Recall the classic southern prison movie *Cool Hand Luke*, from which I borrowed the idea that the guards and staff should wear silver reflecting sunglasses to create a sense of anonymity. Tonight Guard Hellmann would improvise a script that might rival the best that the scriptwriter could have created in shaping the nature of prison authority. He enacts a creatively evil scene that demonstrates that his power can create an arbitrary reality by providing the inmates with an illusion of choice to punish one of their fellows.

Lights dimmed, prisoners in their cells, 416 in solitary. An eerie quiet looms over the Yard. Hellmann slithers up on the table that is between the Hole and our observation post, behind which we are recording these events, allowing us to get a close look at the unfolding drama. As the chief night shift guard leans back against the wall, legs crossed in a Buddha-like lotus position, one arm hanging between his legs, the other resting on the table, Hellmann is the portrait of power in repose. He moves his head slowly from side to side. We notice his long sideburns, muttonchops, down to his chin. He licks his thick lips as he chooses his words carefully and articulates them with an accentuated southern drawl.

The Man has come up with a new Machiavellian plan. He lays out his terms for the release of 416 from solitary. It is not up to him to decide to keep the troublemaker in the Hole all night; rather, he is inviting all of them, the fellow prisoners, to make that decision: Should 416 be released now, or should he rot in the Hole all night?

Just then, Kindly Guard Geoff Landry saunters into the Yard. At six feet three and 185 pounds, he is the biggest of all the guards or prisoners. As usual, he holds a cigarette in one hand, the other hand in his pocket, sunglasses conspicuously absent. He walks to the center of the action, stops, looks distressed, frowns, seems about to intervene, and does nothing but passively observe John Wayne continue with showtime.

"Now, there are several ways to do this, depending on what *you* want to do. Now, if 416 does not want to eat his sausages, then you can give me your blankets and sleep on the bare mattress. Or you can keep your blankets and 416 will stay in there another day. Now what will it be?"

"I'll keep my blanket, Mr. Correctional Officer," 7258 calls out immediately. (Hubbie has no use for 416.)

"What will it be over here?"

"Keep my blanket," says Paul-5704, our former rebel leader.

"How about 5486?"

Refusing to yield to the social pressure, 5486 shows sympathy for the sad 416 by offering to give up his blanket so that 416 does not have to stay in solitary for another day.

Burdan yells at him, "We don't want your blanket!"

"Now, you boys are gonna have to come to some kind of decision here."

Burdan, who has been assuming the posture of a swaggering little authority figure with hands on hips, swinging his club as often as possible, walks up and down past each of the cells. He turns to Sarge in his cell and asks him, "What do you feel about it?"

Surprisingly, Sarge comes down from his high moral ground, which now seems limited only to not speaking obscenities, declares, "If the other two wish to keep their blankets, I'll keep my blanket." That proves to be the crucial swing vote.

Burdan exclaims, "We got three against one."

Hellmann repeats that message loud and clear, so that all can hear.

"We got three against one." As he slides off the table, the boss shouts into the Hole, "416, you're gonna be in there for a while, so just get used to it!"[11]

Hellmann struts off the Yard, with Burdan dutifully following and Landry taking up the reluctant rear. An apparent victory has been won in the endless struggle of guard power against organized prisoner resistance. Indeed, it has been a hard day's night for these guards, but they can now enjoy the sweet taste of victory in this battle of wills and wits.

CHAPTER SEVEN

The Power to Parole

Technically speaking, our Stanford Prison was more like a county jail filled with a group of adolescents who were being held in pretrial detention following their Sunday-morning mass arrests by the Palo Alto City Police. Obviously, no trial date had yet been set for any of these role-playing felons, and none of them had legal representation. Nevertheless, following the advice of the prison chaplain, Father McDermott, a mother of one of the prisoners was going about securing counsel for her son. After a full staff meeting with Warden David Jaffe and the "psychological counselors," the graduate assistants Craig Haney and Curt Banks, we decide to include a Parole Board hearing even though in fact that would not have occurred at this early stage in the criminal justice process.

This would provide an opportunity to observe each prisoner deal with an unexpected opportunity to be released from his imprisonment. Until now, each prisoner had appeared only as a single actor among an ensemble of players. By holding the hearing in a room outside the prison setting, the prisoners would get some respite from their oppressively narrow confines in the basement level. They might feel freer to express their attitudes and feelings in this new environment, which would include some personnel not directly connected with the prison staff. The procedure also added to the formality of our prison experience. The Parole Board hearing, like Visiting Nights, the prison chaplain's visit, and the anticipated visit by a public defender, lent credibility to the prison experience. Finally, I wanted to see how our prison consultant, Carlo Prescott, would enact his role as head of the Stanford County Jail Parole Board. As I said, Carlo had failed many parole board hearings in the past seventeen years and only recently had been granted lifetime parole for "good time served" on his armed robbery convictions. Would he be compassionate and side with the prisoners' requests, as someone who had been in their place pleading for parole?

The Parole Board hearings were held on the first floor of Stanford's Psy-

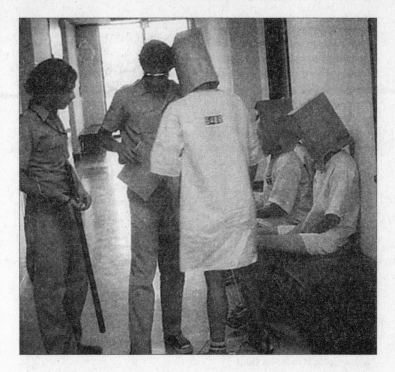

chology Department, in my laboratory, a carpeted, large room that included provisions for hidden videotaping and observation from behind a specially designed one-way window. The four members of the Board sat around a six-sided table. Carlo sat at the head place, next to Craig Haney, and on his other side sat a male graduate student and a female secretary, both of whom had little prior knowledge of our study and were helping us out as a favor. Curt Banks would serve as sergeant-at-arms to transfer each applicant from the guard command to the parole-hearing command. I would be videotaping the proceedings from the adjacent room.

Of the remaining eight prisoners on Wednesday morning, after 8612's release, four had been deemed potentially eligible for parole by the staff, based on generally good behavior. They had been given the opportunity to request a hearing of their case and had written formal requests explaining why they thought they deserved parole at this time. Some of the others would have a hearing another day. However, the guards insisted that Prisoner 416 not be granted such opportunity because of his persistent violation of Rule 2, "Prisoners must eat at mealtimes and only at mealtimes."

A CHANCE TO REGAIN FREEDOM

The day shift guards line up this band of four prisoners in the Yard, as was done routinely during each night's last toilet run. The chain upon one prisoner's leg is attached to that of the next, and large paper bags are put over their heads so they will not know how they got from the jail yard to the parole setting or where in the building it is located. They are seated on a bench in the hall outside the parole room. Their leg chains are removed, but they sit still handcuffed and bagged until Curt Banks comes out of the room to call each one by his number.

Curt, the sergeant-at-arms, reads the prisoner's parole statement, followed by the opposing statement of any of the guards to deny his parole. He escorts each to sit at the right-hand side of Carlo, who takes the lead from there. In order of appearance come Prisoner Jim-4325, Prisoner Glenn-3401, Prisoner Rich-1037, and finally Prisoner Hubbie-7258. After each has had his time before the Board, he is returned to the hallway bench, handcuffed, chained, and bagged until the session is completed and all the prisoners are returned to the prison basement.

Before the first prisoner appears, as I'm checking the video quality, the old-time pro, Carlo, begins to educate the Board neophytes on some basic Parole Board realities. (See Notes for his soliloquy.)[1] Curt Banks, sensing that Carlo is warming up to one of the long speeches he's heard too often during our summer school course, says authoritatively, "We've gotta move, time is running."

Prisoner 4325 Pleads Not Guilty

Prisoner Jim-4325 is escorted into the chamber; his handcuffs are removed, and he is offered a seat. He is a big, robust guy. Carlo challenges him right off with "Why are you in prison? How do you plead?" The prisoner responds, with all due seriousness, "Sir, I have been charged with assault with a deadly weapon. But I wish to plead not guilty to that charge."[2]

"Not guilty?" Carlo feigns total surprise. "So you're implying that the officers who arrested you didn't know what they were doing, that there's been some mistake, some confusion? That the people who were trained in law enforcement, and presumably have had a number of years of experience, are prone to pick *you* up out of the entire population of Palo Alto and that they don't know what they're talking about, that they have some confusion in their minds about what you've done? In other words, they're liars—are you saying that they're liars?"

4325: "I'm not saying they're liars, there must have been very good evidence and everything. I certainly respect their professional knowledge and everything. . . . I haven't seen any evidence, but I assume it must be pretty good for them to pick me up." (The prisoner is submitting to higher authority; his initial assertiveness is receding in the wake of Carlo's dominating demeanor.)

Carlo Prescott: "In that case, you've just verified that there must be something to what they say."

4325: "Well, obviously there must be something to what they say if they picked me up."

Prescott starts with questions that explore the prisoner's background and his future plans, but he is eager to know more about his crime: "What kinds of associations, what kinds of things do you do in your spare time that put you into a position to be arrested? That's a serious charge . . . you know you can kill someone when you assault them. What did you do? You shoot them or stab them or—?"

4325: "I'm not sure, sir. Officer Williams said—"

Prescott: "What did *you* do? Shoot them or stab them or bomb them? Did you use one of those rifles?"

Craig Haney and other members of the Board try to ease the tension by asking the prisoner about how he has been adjusting to prison life.

4325: "Well, by nature I'm something of an introvert . . . and I guess the first few days I thought about it, and I figured that the very best thing to do was to behave . . ."

Prescott takes over again: "Answer his question, we don't want a lot of intellectual bullshit. He asked you a direct question, now answer the question!"

Craig interrupts with a question about the rehabilitative aspects of the prison, to which the prisoner replies, "Well, yes, there's some merit to it, I've certainly learned to be obedient, and at points of stress I've been somewhat bitter, but the correctional officers are doing their job."

Prescott: "This Parole Board can't hold your hand outside. You say they've taught you a degree of obedience, taught you how to be cooperative, but you won't have anybody watching over you outside, you'll be on your own. What kind of a citizen do you think you can make, with these kinds of charges against you? I'm looking over your charges here. This is quite a list!" With total assurance and dominance, Carlo looks over a totally blank notepad as if it were the prisoner's "rap sheet," filled with his convictions, and remarks about his pattern of arrests and releases. He continues, "You know, you tell us that you can make it out there as a result of the discipline you learned in here. We can't hold your hand out there . . . what makes you think you can make it *now*?"

4325: "I've found something to look forward to. I am going to the University of California, to Berkeley, and going into a major. I want to try physics, I'm definitely looking forward to that experience."

Prescott cuts him short and switches to interrogate him about his religious beliefs and then about why he has not taken advantage of the prison's programs of group therapy or vocational therapy. The prisoner seems genuinely confused, saying he would have done so but he was never offered such opportunities. Carlo asks Curt Banks to check on the truth of that last assertion, which, he says, he personally doubts. (Of course, he knows that we have no such programs in this experiment, but it is what his parole board members have always asked him in the past.)

After a few more questions from other Board members, Prescott asks the correctional officer to take the inmate back to his cell. The prisoner stands and thanks the board. He then automatically extends his arms, palms facing each other, as the attending guard locks on the handcuffs. Jim-4325 is escorted out, rebagged, and made to sit in silence in the hallway while the next prisoner has his turn at the Board.

After the prisoner leaves, Prescott notes for the record, "Well, that guy's an awful smooth talker . . ."

My notes remind me that "Prisoner 4325 has appeared quite composed and generally in control of himself—he has been one of our 'model prisoners' so far. He seems confused by Prescott's aggressive interrogation about the crime for which he was arrested, and is easily pushed into admitting that he's probably guilty, despite the fact that his crime is completely fictional. Throughout the hearing, he is obedient and agreeable, which demeanor contributes to his relative success and probably longevity as a survivor in this prison setting."

A Shining Example Is Dimmed

Next, Curt announces that Prisoner 3401 is ready for our board hearing, and reads aloud his appeal:

> I want parole so that I may take my new life into this despairing world and show the lost souls that good behavior is rewarded with warm hearts; that the materialist pigs have no more than the impoverished poor; that the common criminal can be fully rehabilitated in less than a week, and that God, faith, and brotherhood are still strongly in us all. I deserve parole because I believe my conduct throughout my stay has been undoubtedly beyond reproach. I have enjoyed the comforts and find that it would be best to move on to higher and more sacred places. Also, being a cherished product of our environment, we all can be assured that my full rehabilitation is everlasting. God bless. Very truly yours, 3401. Remember me, please, as a shining example.

The guards' counter-recommendations present a stark contrast:

> 3401 has been a constant two-bit troublemaker. Not only that, he is a follower, finding no good within himself to develop. He meekly mimics bad things. I recommend no parole. Signed by Guard Arnett.

> I see no reason why 3401 deserves parole, nor can I even make the connection between the 3401 I know and the person described in this parole request. Signed by Guard Markus.

> 3401 doesn't deserve parole and his own sarcastic request indicates this. Signed by Guard John Landry.

Prisoner 3401 is then brought in with the paper bag still over his head, which Carlo wants removed so he can see the face of this "little punk." He and the other board members react with surprise when they discover that 3401, Glenn, is Asian American, the only non-Caucasian in the mix. Glenn is playing against type with his rebellious, flippant style. However, he fits the stereotype physically; a short five feet, two inches, slight but wiry build, cute face, and shiny jet black hair.

Craig starts by inquiring about the prisoner's role in the prisoner uprising that started when his cell created the barricade. What did he do to stop it?

3401 replies with surprising bluntness: "I did not stop it, I encouraged it!" After further inquiry into this situation by other board members, 3401 continues in a sarcastic tone, so different from Prisoner 4325's apparent humility, "I think the purpose of our institution is to rehabilitate the prisoners and not to antagonize them, and I felt that as a result of our actions—"

Warden Jaffe, seated along the side of the room and not at the Board table, cannot resist getting in his licks: "Perhaps you don't have the proper notion of what rehabilitation is. We're trying to teach you to be a productive member of society, not how to barricade yourself in the cell!"

Prescott has had enough of these diversions. He reasserts his role as head honcho: "At least two citizens have said that they observed you leaving the site of the crime." (He has invented this on the spot.) Carlo continues, " To challenge the vision of three people is to say that all of humanity is blind!" Now, did you write that 'God, faith, and brotherhood are still strong'? Is it brotherhood to take somebody else's property?"

Carlo then moves in to play the obvious race card: "Very few of you Oriental people are in the prisons . . . in fact, they're likely to be very good citizens. . . . You've been a constant troublemaker, you've mocked a prison situation here, you come in here and talk about rehabilitation as if you think you should be permitted to run a prison. You sit here at the table and you interrupt the warden by indicating that you think that what you're saying is much more important than anything that he could say. Frankly, I wouldn't parole you if you were the last man in the prison, I think you're the least likely prospect of parole we have, what do you think about that?"

"You're entitled to your opinion, sir," says 3401.

"*My opinion* means something in this particular place!" Carlo retorts angrily.

Prescott asks more questions, not allowing the prisoner a chance to answer them, and ends up denouncing and dismissing 3401: "I don't think we need to take any more time just now. I'm of the opinion that the record and his attitude in the boardroom indicate quite clearly what his attitude is . . . we've got a schedule, and I don't see any reason to even discuss this. What we have here is a recalcitrant who writes nice speeches."

Before leaving, the prisoner tells the Board that he has a skin rash that is going to break out and it is worrying him. Prescott asks whether he has seen a doctor, whether he has gone on sick call or done anything constructive to take care of his problem. When the prisoner says that he has not, Carlo reminds him that this is a parole board and not a medical board, and then dismisses his concern: "We try to find some reason to parole any man who comes in, and once you come into this particular prison it's up to you to maintain a record, a kind of demeanor which indicates to us that you can make an adjustment to society. . . . I want you to consider some of the things that you wrote at an intrinsic level; you're an intelligent man and know the language quite well, I think that you can probably change yourself, yes, you might have a chance to change yourself in the future."

Carlo turns to the guard and gestures to take the prisoner away. A now-contrite little boy slowly raises his arms outstretched as handcuffs are applied, and out he goes. He may be realizing that his flippant attitude has cost him dearly, that he was not prepared for this event to be so serious and the Parole Board so intense.

My notes indicate that Prisoner 3401 is more complex than he appears initially. He reveals an interesting mix of traits. He is usually quite serious and polite when he is dealing with the guards in the prison, but in this instance, he has written a sarcastic, humorous letter requesting parole, referencing a nonexistent rehabilitation, mentioning his spirituality, and claiming to be a model prisoner. The guards don't seem to like him, as is evident in their strong letters advising against parole. His bold parole request letter stands in striking contrast with his demeanor—the young man we see in this room, subdued, even cowed, by the experience. "No joking allowed here." The Board, especially Prescott, goes after him viciously, yet he doesn't cope with the attack effectively. As the hearing progresses, he becomes increasingly withdrawn and unresponsive. I wonder if he will survive the full two weeks.

A Rebel Relents

Next up is Prisoner 1037, Rich, whose mother was so worried about him last night when she visited and saw him looking so awful. He is the same one who blockaded himself in Cell 2 this morning. He is also a frequent occupant of the Hole. 1037's appeal is interesting but loses something when read quickly in a flat, unemotional tone by Curt Banks:

> I would like to be paroled so that I may spend the last moments of my teenage years with old friends. I will turn 20 on Monday. I believe that the correctional staff has convinced me of my many weaknesses. On Monday, I rebelled, thinking that I was being treated unjustly. However, that evening I finally realized that I was unworthy of better treatment. Since that time I have done my best to cooperate, and I now know that every member of the correctional staff is only interested in the well-being of myself and the other prisoners. Despite my horrible disrespect for them and their wishes, the prison staff has treated and is treating me well. I deeply respect their ability to turn the other cheek and I believe that because of

their own goodness I have been rehabilitated and transformed into a better human being. Sincerely, 1037.

Three guards have provided a collective recommendation, which Curt reads aloud:

While 1037 is improving since his rebellion phase, I believe he has a bit more to develop before being exposed to the public as one of our corrected products. I agree with the other officers' appraisal of 1037, and also with 1037, that he has gotten much better, but has not yet reached a perfectly acceptable level. 1037 has a way to go before parole, and is improving. I don't recommend parole.

When Rich-1037 enters the room, he reveals a strange blend of youthful energy and incipient depression. Immediately, he talks about his birthday, his only reason to request parole; it happens to be very important to him, and he forgot about it when he originally signed up. He is in full swing when the warden asks him a question that he can't answer without either getting into trouble or undoing his justification for leaving: "Don't you think our prison is capable of giving you a birthday party?"

Prescott seizes the opportunity: "You've been in society for a while, even at your age. You know the rules. You must recognize that prisons are for people who break rules, and you place that in jeopardy by doing exactly what you did. Son, I recognize that you're changing, it's indicated here, and I think seriously that you've improved. But here, in your own handwriting, 'despite my horrible disrespect for them and their wishes.' *Horrible disrespect!* You can't disrespect other people and their property. What would happen if everybody in this nation disrespected everybody else's property? You'll probably kill if you're apprehended."

As Carlo continues to seemingly review the prisoner's record on his still *blank* notepad, he stops at the point where he has discovered something vital: "I see here in your arrest reports that you were quite cantankerous, in fact you had to be repressed, and you could have inflicted hurt or worse on some of the arresting officers. I'm very impressed by your progress, and I think that you're beginning to recognize that your behavior has been immature and in many ways is entirely devoid of judgment and concern for other people. You turn people into sticks; you make them think that they are objects, for your use. You've manipulated people! All your life you seem to have manipulated people, all your reports talk about your indifference toward law and order. There are periods in which you don't seem to control your behavior. What makes you think that you could be a good parole prospect? What could you tell us? We're trying to help you."

Prisoner 1037 is not prepared for this personal attack on his character. He mumbles an incoherent explanation for being able to "walk away" from a situation that might tempt him to behave violently. He goes on to say that this prison experience has helped him: "Well, I've gotten to see a lot of people's different reactions to different situations, how they handled themselves with respect to other people, such as speaking with various cellmates, their reactions to the same situations. The three different shifts of guards, I've noticed the individual guards have small differences in the same situations."

1037 then curiously brings up his "weaknesses," namely his part as agitator in Monday's prisoner rebellion. He has become entirely submissive, blaming himself for defying the guards and never once criticizing them for their abusive behavior and nonstop hassling. (Before my eyes is a perfect example of mind control in action. The process exactly resembles American POWs in the Korean War confessing publicly to using germ warfare and other wrongdoings to their Chinese Communist captors.)

Unexpectedly, Prescott interrupts this discussion of the prisoner's weaknesses to ask assertively, "Do you use drugs?"

When 1037 replies "No," he is allowed to continue apologizing until interrupted again. Prescott notices a black-and-blue bruise on the inmate's arm and asks how he got that big bruise. Although it came from one or more of the scuffles between him and the guards, prisoner 1037 denies the guard's part in restraining him or dragging him into solitary, saying that the guards had been as gentle as they could. By continually disobeying their orders, he says, he brought the bruise on himself.

Carlo likes that mea culpa. "Keep up the good work, huh?"

1037 says that he would consider parole even if it meant forfeiting his salary. (That seems rather extreme, given how much he has been through to have nothing to show for it.) Throughout he answers the Board's questions competently, but his depression hovers over him, as Prescott notes in his comments after the hearing. His state of mind is something his mother detected immediately during her visit with him and in her complaints to me when she came to the Superintendent's Office. It is as though he were trying to hang on as long as possible in order to prove his manliness—perhaps to his dad? He provides some interesting answers to questions about what he has gained from his experience in the prison, but most of them sound like superficial lines made up simply for the benefit of the Board.

The Good-Looking Kid Gets Trashed

Last in line is the handsome young prisoner Hubbie-7258, whose appeal Curt reads with a bit of scorn:

> My first reason for parole is that my woman is going away on vacation very soon and I would like to see her a little bit more before she goes, seeing that when she gets back is just about the same time I leave for college. If I get back only after the full two weeks here, I will only see her for a total

time of one-half hour. Here we can't say good-bye and talk, with the correctional officer and the chaperone, the way we'd like to. Another reason is that I think that you have seen me and I know that I won't change. By change I mean breaking any of the rules set down for us, the prisoners, thus putting me out on parole would save my time and your expenditures. It is true that I did attempt an escape with former cellmate 8612, but ever since then, as I sat in my empty cell with no clothes on I knew that I shouldn't go against our correctional officers, so ever since then I have almost exactly followed all the rules. Also, you will note that I have the best cell in this prison.

Again, Guard Arnett's recommendations are at odds with the prisoner's statement: "7258 is a rebellious wise guy," is Guard Arnett's overall appraisal, which he follows up with this cynical condemnation: "He should stay here for the duration or until he rots, whichever comes later."

Guard Markus is more sanguine: "I like 7258 and he is an all-right prisoner, but I don't feel he is any more entitled to parole than any of the other prisoners, and I am confident that the prisoner experience will have a healthy effect on his rather unruly natural character."

"I also like 7258, almost as much as 8612 [David, our spy], but I don't think he should get parole. I won't go as far as Arnett does, but parole shouldn't be given," writes John Landry.

As soon as the prisoner is unbagged, he beams his usual big toothy smile, which irritates Carlo enough to spur his jumping all over him.

"As a matter of fact, this whole thing's funny to you. You're a 'rebellious wise guy,' as the guard's report accurately describes you. Are you the kind of person who doesn't care anything about your life?"

As soon as he starts to answer, Prescott changes course to ask about his education. "I plan to start college in the fall at Oregon State U." Prescott turns to other Board members. "Here's what I say. You know what, education is a waste on some people. Some people shouldn't be compelled to go to college. They'd probably be happier as a mechanic or a drugstore salesman," waving his hand disdainfully at the prisoner. "Okay, let's move on. What did you do to get in here?"

"Nothing, sir, but to sign up for *an experiment.*"

This reality check might otherwise threaten to unravel the proceedings, but not with skipper Prescott at the helm:

"So wise guy, you think this is just an *experiment?*" He takes back the steering wheel, pretending to examine the prisoner's dossier. Prescott notes matter-of-factly, "You were involved in a burglary."

Prescott turns to ask Curt Banks whether it was first- or second-degree burglary; Curt nods "first."

"First, huh, just as I thought." It is time to teach this Young Turk some of life's lessons, starting with reminding him of what happens to prisoners who are caught in an escape attempt. You're eighteen years old, and look what you've done with your life! You sit here in front of us and tell us that you'd even be willing to forfeit compensation to get out of prison. Everywhere I look in this report I see the same thing: 'wise guy,' 'smart aleck,' 'opposed to any sort of authority'! Where did you go wrong?"

After asking what his parents do, his religious background, and whether he goes to church regularly, Prescott is angered by the prisoner's statement that his religion is "nondenominational." He retorts, "You haven't even decided about something as important as that either."

The angered Prescott gets up and storms out of the room for a few minutes, as the other Board members ask some standard questions about how he plans to behave in the next week if his parole request is not granted.

Forfeiting Pay for Freedom

This break in the highly tense action gives me time to realize the importance of Prisoner 1037's assertion of willing to forfeit his pay for parole. We need to formalize that as a critical final question to be put to each of the prisoners. I tell Carlo to ask them, "Would you be willing to forfeit all the money you have earned as a prisoner if we were to parole you?"

At first, Carlo poses a more extreme form of the question: "How much would you be willing to pay us to get out of here?" Confused, Prisoner 7258 says he won't pay money to be released. Carlo reframes the question, asking whether the prisoner would forfeit the money he's made so far.

"Yes, indeed, sir, I would do that."

Prisoner 7258 doesn't come across as particularly bright or self-aware. He also doesn't seem to take his entire situation as seriously as some of the other prisoners do. He is the youngest, barely eighteen, and is quite immature in his attitudes and responses. Nevertheless, his detachment and sense of humor will serve him well in coping with most of what is in store for him and his peers in the week ahead.

Next, we have each of the prisoners return to the parole chamber to answer that same final question about forfeiting their pay in exchange for parole. Prisoner 1037, the rebellious birthday boy, says yes to forfeiting his money if paroled. The cooperative Prisoner 4325 answers in the affirmative as well. Only Prisoner 3401, the defiant Asian American, would not want parole if it involved forfeiting his money, since he really needs it.

In other words, three of these four young men want to be released so badly that they are willing to give up the hard-earned salary they have earned in their twenty-four-hour-a-day job as prisoners. What is remarkable to me is the power of the rhetorical frame in which this question is put. Recall that the primary motivation of virtually all the volunteers was financial, the chance to make fifteen dollars a day for up to two weeks at a time when they had no other source of income, just before school was to start in the fall. Now, despite all their suffering as prisoners, despite the physical and psychological abuse they have endured—the endless counts; the middle-of-the-night awakenings; the arbitrary, creative evil of some of the guards; the lack of privacy; the time spent in solitary; the nakedness; the chains; their bagged heads; the lousy food and minimal bedding—the majority of the prisoners are willing to leave without pay to get out of this place.

Perhaps even more remarkable is the fact that after saying that money was less important than their freedom, each prisoner passively submitted to the system, holding out his hands to be handcuffed, submitting to the bag being put back over his head, accepting the chain on his leg, and, like sheep, following the guard back down to that dreadful prison basement. During their Parole Board hearing, they were physically out of the prison, in the presence of some "civilians" who were not directly associated with their tormentors downstairs. Why did none of them say, "Since I do not want your money, I am free to quit this experiment and demand to be released now." We would have had to obey their request and terminate them at that moment.

Yet none did. Not one prisoner later told us that he had even considered that he could quit the experiment because virtually all of them had stopped thinking of their experience as just an experiment. They felt trapped in a prison being run by psychologists, not by the State, as 416 had told us. What they had agreed to do was forfeit money they had earned as prisoners—*if we chose to parole them.* The power to free or bind was with the Parole Board, not in their personal decision to stop being a prisoner. If they were prisoners, only the Parole Board had the power to release them, but if they were, as indeed they were, *experimental subjects*, each of the students always held the power to stay or quit at any time. It was apparent that a mental switch had been thrown in their minds, from "now I am a paid experimental volunteer with full civil rights" to "now I am a helpless prisoner at the mercy of an unjust authoritarian system."

During the postmortem, the Board discussed the individual cases and the overall reactions of this first set of prisoners. There was a clear consensus that all the prisoners seemed nervous, edgy, and totally consumed by their role as prisoners.

Prescott sensitively shares his real concerns for Prisoner 1037. He accurately detects a deep depression building in this once fearless rebel ringleader: "It's just a feeling that you get, living around people who jump over prison tiers to their deaths, or cut their wrists. Here's a guy who had himself together sufficiently to present himself to us, but there were lags between his answers. Then the last guy in, he's coherent, he knows what's happened, he still talks about 'an experiment,' but at the same time, he's willing to sit and talk about his father, he's willing to sit and talk about his feelings. He seemed unreal to me, and I'm basing that just on the feeling I had. The second guy, the Oriental [Asian-American] prisoner, he's a stone. To me, he was like a stone."

In summation, Prescott offers the following advice: "I join the rest of the group and propose letting a couple of prisoners out at different times, to try to get the prisoners trying to figure out what they have to begin to do in order to get out. Also, releasing a few prisoners soon would give some hope to the rest of them, and relieve some of their feelings of desperation."

The consensus seems to be to release the first prisoner soon, big Jim-4325, and then number three, Rich-1037, later on, perhaps replacing them with other standby prisoners. There are mixed feelings about whether 3401 or 7258 should be released next, or at all.

What Have We Witnessed Here?

Three general themes emerge from the first Parole Board hearings: the boundaries between simulation and reality have been blurred; the prisoners' subservience and seriousness has steadily increased in response to the guards' ever-greater domination, and there has been a dramatic character transformation in the performance of the Parole Board head, Carlo Prescott.

Blurring the Line Between the Prison Experiment and the Reality of Imprisonment

Impartial observers not knowing what had preceded this event might readily assume that they were witnessing an actual hearing of a local prison parole board in action. The strength and manifest reality of the dialectic at work between those imprisoned and society's appointed guardians of them was reflected in many ways, among them, the overall seriousness of the situation, the formality of the parole requests by inmates, the opposing challenges from their guards, the diverse composition of all the Parole Board members, the nature of the personal questions put to the inmates, and accusations made against them—in short, the intense affective quality of the entire proceeding. The basis of this interaction is obvious in the Board's questions and prisoners' answers regarding "past convictions," the rehabilitative activities of attending classes or participating in therapy or vocational training sessions, arranging for legal representation, the status of their trial, and their future plans for becoming good citizens.

It is as hard to realize that barely four days have passed in the lives of these student experimental volunteers as it is to imagine that their future as prisoners is little more than another week in the Stanford County Jail. Their captivity is not the many months or long years that the mock Parole Board seems to imply in its judgments. Role playing has become role internalization; the actors have assumed the characters and identities of their fictional roles.

The Prisoners' Subservience and Seriousness

By this point, for the most part, the prisoners have slipped reluctantly, but finally compliantly, into their highly structured roles in our prison. They refer to themselves by their identification numbers and answer immediately to questions put to their anonymous identities. They answer what should be ridiculous questions with full seriousness, for example inquiries into the nature of their crimes and their rehabilitation efforts. With few exceptions, they have become completely subservient to the authority of the Parole Board as well as to the domination of the correctional officers and the system in general. Only Prisoner 7258 had the temerity to refer to his reason for being here as volunteering for an "experiment," but he quickly backed away from that assertion under Prescott's verbal assaults.

The flippant style of some of their original parole requests, notably that of Prisoner 3401, the Asian-American student, withers under the negative judgment of the Board that such unacceptable behavior does not warrant release. Most of the prisoners seem to have completely accepted the premises of the situation. They no longer object to or rebel against anything they are told or commanded to do. They are like Method actors who continue to play their roles when offstage and off camera, and their role has come to consume their identity. It must be distressing to those who argue for innate human dignity to note the servility of the former prisoner rebels, the heroes of the uprisings, who have been reduced to beggars. No heroes are stepping out from this aggregation.

That feisty Asian-American prisoner, Glenn-3401, had to be released some hours after his stressful Parole Board experience, when he developed a full-body rash. Student Health Services provided the appropriate medication, and he was sent home to consult his own physician. The rash was his body's way of getting his release, as was Doug-8612's raging loss of emotional control.

The Dramatic Transformation of the Parole Board Head

I had known Carlo Prescott for more than three months before this event and had interacted with him almost daily in person and in frequent and long phone calls. As we co-taught a six-week-long course on the psychology of imprisonment, I had seen him in action as an eloquent, vehement critic of the prison system, which he judged to be a fascist tool designed to oppress people of color. He was remarkably perceptive in the ways in which prisons and all other authoritarian systems of control can change all those in their grip, both the imprisoned and their imprisoners. Indeed, during his Saturday-evening talk-show program on the local radio station KGO, Carlo frequently made his listeners aware of the failure of this antiquated, expensive institution that their tax dollars were wasted in continuing to support.

He had told me of the nightmares he would have anticipating the annual Parole Board hearings, in which an inmate has only a few minutes to present his appeal to several Board members, who do not seem to be paying any attention to him as they thumb through fat files while he pleads his case. Perhaps some of the files are not even his but are those of the next prisoner in line, and reading them now will save time. If you are asked questions about your conviction or anything negative in your rap sheet, you know immediately that parole will be delayed for at least another year because defending the past prevents you from envisioning anything positive in your future. Carlo's tales enlightened me about the kind of rage that such arbitrary indifference generates in the vast majority of prisoners who are denied parole year after year, as he was.[3]

However, what are the deeper lessons to be learned from such situations? Admire power, detest weakness. Dominate, don't negotiate. Hit first when they turn the other cheek. The golden rule is for them, not for us. Authority rules, rules are authority.

These are also some of the lessons learned by boys of abusive fathers, half of whom are transformed into abusive fathers themselves, abusing their children, spouses, and parents. Perhaps half of them identify with the aggressor and perpetuate his violence, while the others learn to identify with the abused and reject aggression for compassion. However, research does not help us to predict which abused kids will later become abusers and which will turn out to be compassionate adults.

Time Out for a Demonstration of Power Without Compassion

I am reminded of the classic demonstration by an elementary school teacher, Jane Elliott, who taught her students the nature of prejudice and discrimination by arbitrarily relating the eye color of children in her classroom to high or low status. When those with blue eyes were associated with privilege, they readily assumed a dominant role over their brown-eyed peers, even abusing them verbally and physically. Moreover, their newly acquired status spilled over to enhance their cognitive functioning. When they were on top, the blue-eyes improved their daily math and spelling performances (statistically significant, as I documented with Elliott's original class data). Just as dramatically, test performance of the "inferior" brown-eyed children deteriorated.

However, the most brilliant aspect of her classroom demonstration with these third-grade schoolchildren from Riceville, Iowa, was the status reversal the teacher generated the next day. Mrs. Elliott told the class she had erred. In fact, the opposite was true, she said; brown eyes were better than blue eyes! Here was the chance for the brown-eyed children, who had experienced the negative impact of being discriminated against, to show compassion now that they were on top of the heap. The new test scores reversed the superior performance of the haves and diminished the performance of the have-nots. But what about the lesson of compassion? Did the newly elevated brown-eyes understand the pain of the underdog, of those less fortunate, of those in a position of inferiority that they had personally experienced one brief day earlier?

There was no carryover at all! The brown-eyes gave what they got. They dominated, they discriminated, and they abused their former blue-eyed abusers.[4] Similarly, history is filled with accounts showing that many of those escaping religious persecution show intolerance of people of other religions once they are safe and secure in their new power domain.

Back to Brown-Eyed Carlo

This is a long side trip around the issue surrounding my colleague's dramatic transformation when he was put into the powerful position as head of the Parole Board. At first, he gave a truly outstanding improvisational performance, like a Charlie Parker solo. He improvised details of crimes, of the prisoners' past histories, on the spot, out of the blue. He did so without hesitation, with a fluid certainty. However, as time wore on, he seemed to embrace his new authority role with ever-increasing intensity and conviction. He was the head of the Stanford County Jail Parole Board, the authority whom inmates suddenly feared, to whom his peers deferred. Forgotten were the years of suffering he had endured as a brown-eyed inmate once he was granted the privileged position of seeing the world through the eyes of the all-powerful head of this Board. Carlo's statement to his colleagues at the end of this meeting showed the agony and disgust his transformation had instilled in him. He had become the oppressor. Later that night, over dinner, he confided that he had been sickened by what he had heard himself say and had felt when he was cloaked in his new role.

I wondered if his reflections would cause him to show the positive effects of his acquired self-knowledge when he headed the next Parole Board meeting on Thursday. Would he show greater consideration and compassion for the new set of prisoners who would be pleading to him for parole? Or would the role remake the man?

THURSDAY'S MEETING OF THE PAROLE AND DISCIPLINARY BOARD

The next day brings four more prisoners before a reconstituted Parole Board. Except for Carlo, all the other members of the Board are newcomers. Craig Haney, who had to leave town for urgent family business in Philadelphia, is replaced by another social psychologist, Christina Maslach, who quietly observes the proceedings with little apparent direct involvement—at this time. A secretary and two graduate students fill out the rest of this five-person Board. However, at the urging of the guards, in addition to considering parole requests, the Board also considers various disciplinary actions against the more serious troublemakers. Curt Banks continues in his role as sergeant-at-arms, and Warden David Jaffe also sits in to observe and comment when appropriate. Again I watch from behind the one-way viewing screen and record the proceedings for subsequent analysis on our Ampex video recorder. Another variation from yesterday is that we do not have the prisoners sit around the same table with the Board but separately in high chairs, on a pedestal, so to speak—all the better to observe them as in police detective interrogations.

A Hunger Striker Strikes Out

First up on the docket is Prisoner 416, recently admitted, who is still on a hunger strike. Curt Banks reads off the disciplinary charges that several guards have filed against him. Guard Arnett is especially angered at 416; he and the other guards are not sure what to make of him: "Here for such a short time, and he has been totally recalcitrant, disrupting all order and our routine."

The prisoner immediately agrees that they are right; he will not dispute any of the charges. He insists on securing legal representation before he consents to eat anything served him in this prison. Prescott goes after his demand for "legal aid," forcing a clarification.

Prisoner 416 replies in a strange fashion: "I'm in prison, for all practical purposes, because I signed a contract, which I'm not of legal age to sign." In other words, either we must get a lawyer to take his case and get him released, or he will continue with his hunger strike and get sick. Thus, he reasons, the prison authorities will be forced to release him.

This scrawny youngster presents much the same face to the Board that he does to the guards: he is intelligent, self-determined, and strong willed in his opinions. However, his justification for disputing his imprisonment—that he was not of legal age to sign the research informed consent contract—seems strangely legalistic and circumstantial for a person who has typically acted from ideological principles. Despite his disheveled, gaunt appearance, there is something about 416's demeanor that does not elicit sympathy from anyone who interacts with him—neither the guards, the other prisoners, nor this board. He looks like a homeless street person who makes passersby feel more guilty than sympathetic.

When Prescott asks on what charge 416 is in jail for, the prisoner responds, "There is no charge, I have not been charged. I was not arrested by the Palo Alto police."

Incensed, Prescott asks if 416 is in jail by mistake, then. "I was a standby, I—" Prescott is fuming now and confused. I realize that I had not briefed him on how 416 differed from all the others, as a newly admitted standby prisoner.

"What are you, anyway, a philosophy major?" Carlo takes time to light his cigarette and perhaps plan a new line of attack. "You been philosophizing since you've been in here."

When one of the secretaries on today's Board recommends exercise as a form of disciplinary action and 416 complains that he has been forced to undergo too much exercise, Prescott curtly replies, "He looks like a strong fellow, I think exercise would be ideal for him." He looks over at Curt and Jaffe to put that on their action list.

Finally, when asked the loaded question—Would he be willing to forfeit all the money he has earned as a prisoner if a parole were granted?—416 immediately and defiantly replies, "Yes, of course. Because I don't feel that the money is worth the time."

Carlo has had enough of him. "Take him away." 416 then does exactly what the others before him have done like automatons; without instruction he stands up, arms outstretched to be handcuffed, head bagged, and escorted away from these proceedings.

Curiously, he does not demand that the Board act now to terminate his role as a reluctant student research volunteer. He doesn't want any money, so why does he not simply say, "I quit this experiment. You must give me my clothes and belongings, and I am out of here!"

This prisoner's first name is Clay, but he will not be molded easily by anyone; he stands firmly by his principles and obstinately in the strategy he has advanced. Nevertheless, he has become too embedded in his prisoner identity to do the macroanalysis that should tell him he has now been given the keys to freedom by insisting to the Parole Board that he must be allowed to quit here and now while he is physically removed from the prison venue. However, he is now carrying that venue within his head.

Addicts Are Easy Game

Prisoner Paul-5704, next at bat, immediately complains about how he's missing the cigarette ration that he was promised for good behavior. His disciplinary charges by the guards include "Constantly and grossly insubordinate, with flares of violence and dark mood, and constantly tries to incite the other prisoners to insubordination and general uncooperativeness."

Prescott challenges his so-called good behavior, which will never get him another cigarette again. The prisoner answers in such a barely audible voice that Board members have to ask him to speak louder. When he is told that he acts badly even when he knows it will mean punishment for other prisoners, he again mumbles, staring toward the center of the table.

"We've discussed that . . . well, if something happens, we're just going to follow through with it . . . if someone else was doing something, I'd go through punishment for them." A Board member interrupts, "Have you gone through punishment for any of the other prisoners?" Paul-5704 responds yes, he has suffered for his comrades.

Prescott loudly and mockingly declares, "You're a martyr, then, huh?"

"Well, I guess we all are . . . ," 5704 says, again barely audible.

"What have you got to say for yourself?" Prescott demands. 5704 responds, but again it is unintelligible.

Recall that 5704, the tallest prisoner, had challenged many of the guards openly and been the insider in various escape attempts, rumors, and barricades. He was also the one who had written to his girlfriend expressing his pride at being elected head of the Stanford County Jail Prisoners' Grievance Committee. Further, it was this same 5704 who had volunteered for this experiment under false pretenses. He signed up with the intention of being a spy who was going to expose this research in articles he planned to write for several alternative, liberal, "underground" newspapers, on the assumption that this experiment was no more than a government-supported project for learning how to deal with political dissidents. Where had all that former bravado gone? Why had he suddenly become incoherent?

Before us in this room sits a subdued, depressed young man. Prisoner 5704 simply stares downward, nodding answers to the questions posed by the Parole Board, never making direct eye contact.

"Yes, I would be willing to give up any pay I've earned to get paroled now, sir," he answers as loudly as he can muster strength to do. (The tally is now yes from five of the six prisoners.)

I wonder how that dynamic, passionate, revolutionary spirit, so admirable in this young man, could have vanished so totally in such a short time?

As an aside, we later learned that it was Paul-5704 who had gotten so deeply into his prisoner role that as the first part of his escape plan he had used his long, hard, guitar-player fingernails to unscrew one of the electrical power plates from the wall. He then used that plate to help remove the doorknob on his cell. He also used those tough nails to mark on the wall of his cell the passage of days of his confinement with notches next to M/ T /W/ Th/, so far.

A Puzzling, Powerful Prisoner

The next parole request comes from Prisoner Jerry-5486. He is even more puzzling than those who appeared earlier. He shows an upbeat style, a sense of being able to cope quietly with whatever is coming his way. His physical robustness is in stark contrast to that of Prisoner 416 or some of the other slim prisoners, like Glenn-3401. Surely there is the sense that he will endure the full two weeks without complaint. However, there is insincerity in his statements, and he has shown little overt support for any of his comrades in distress. In a few minutes here, 5486 manages to antagonize Prescott as much as any other prisoner has. He answers immediately that he would not be willing to give up the pay he's earned so far in exchange for parole.

The guards report that 5486 does not deserve parole consideration because "he made a joke out of letter writing, and for his general non-cooperation." When asked to explain his action, Prisoner 5486 responds that "I knew it wasn't a legitimate letter . . . it didn't seem to be . . ."

Guard Arnett, who has been standing aside silently observing the proceedings, can't help but interrupt: "Did the correctional officers ask you to write the letter?" 5486 responds affirmatively, as Guard Arnett continues, "And you're saying that the correctional officers asked you to write a letter that was not legitimate?"

5486 backtracks: "Well, maybe I chose the wrong word . . ."

But Arnett does not let up. He reads his report to the Board: "5486 has been on a gradual downhill slide . . . he has become something of a jokester and minor cutup."

"You find that funny?" Carlo challenges him.

"Everybody [in the room] was smiling. I wasn't smiling till they smiled," 5486 replies defensively.

Carlo ominously interjects, "Everyone else can afford a smile—we're going *home* tonight." Still, he attempts to be less confrontational than the day before, and he asks a series of provocative questions: "If you were in my place, with the evidence I have, along with the report from staff, what would you do? How would you act? What would you do? What do you think is right for yourself?"

The prisoner answers evasively but never fully addresses those difficult questions. After a few more questions from the other members of the Board, an exasperated Prescott dismisses him: "I think we've seen enough, I think we know what we need to do. I don't see any reason to waste our time."

The prisoner is surprised at being dismissed so abruptly. It is apparent to him that he has created a bad impression on those he should have persuaded to support his cause—if not for this parole, then for the next time the Board meets. He has not acted in his best interests at this time. Curt has the guard handcuff him, place the bag over his head, and sit him on the bench in the hallway, awaiting the disposition of the next and final case before the prisoners are hauled back downstairs to resume their prison life.

Sarge's Surface Tension

The final inmate for the Board to evaluate is "Sarge," Prisoner 2093, who, true to type, sits upright in the high chair, chest out, head back, chin tucked in—a perfect military posture if I have ever seen one. He requests parole so that he can put his time "to more productive use," and he notes further that he has "followed all rules from Day One." Unlike most of his peers, 2093 would not give up the pay in exchange for parole.

"Were I to give up the pay I have earned thus far, it would be an even greater loss of five days of my life than it would have been otherwise." He adds that the relatively small pay hardly compensates for the time he has served.

Prescott goes after him for not sounding "genuine," for having thought everything out in advance, for not being spontaneous, for using words to disguise his feelings. Sarge apologizes for giving that impression because he always means what he says and tries hard to articulate clearly what he means. That softens Carlo, who assures Sarge that he and the Board will consider his case very seriously and then commends him for his good work in the prison.

Before ending the interview, Carlo asks Sarge why he didn't request parole the first time it was offered to all prisoners. Sarge explains, "I would have requested parole the first time only if not enough other prisoners requested it." He felt that other prisoners were having a harder time in the prison than he was, and he didn't want his request to be placed above another's. Carlo gently rebukes him for this show of shining nobility, which he thinks is a crass attempt to influence the Board's judgment. Sarge's show of surprise makes it evident that he meant what he said and was not attempting to impress the Board or anyone else.

This apparently intrigues Carlo, and he aims to learn about the young man's private life. Carlo asks about Sarge's family, his girlfriend, what kind of movies he likes, whether he takes time to buy an ice cream cone—all the little things that, taken together, give someone a unique identity.

Sarge replies matter-of-factly that he doesn't have a girlfriend, seldom goes to movies, and that he likes ice cream but has not been able to afford to buy a cone recently. "All I can say is that after having gone to summer quarter at Stanford and living in the back of my car, I had a little difficulty sleeping the first night because the bed was too soft here in prison, and also that I have been eating better in prison than I had for the past two months, and that I had more time to relax than I had the last two months. Thank you, sir."

Wow! What a violation of expectation this young man offers us. His sense of personal pride and stocky build belie his having gone hungry all summer and not having had a bed to sleep in while he attended summer school. That the horrid living conditions in our prison could be a better lifestyle for any college student comes as a shocker to us all.

In one sense, Sarge seems to be the most one-dimensional, mindlessly obedient prisoner of all, yet he is the most logical, thoughtful, and morally consistent prisoner of the group. It occurs to me that one problem this young man might have stems from his commitment to living by abstract principles and not knowing how to live effectively with other people or how to ask others for the support he needs, financial, personal, and emotional. He seems so tightly strung by this inner resolve and his outer military posturing that no one can really get access to his feelings. He may end up having a harder life than the rest of his fellows.

Contrition Doesn't Cut the Mustard

Just as the Board is preparing to end this session, Curt announces that Prisoner 5486, the flippant one, wants to make an additional statement to the Board. Carlo nods okay.

5486 contritely says that he didn't express what he really wanted to say, because he hadn't had a chance to think about it fully. He's experienced a personal decline while in this prison, because at first he expected to go to a trial and now he's given up on his hope for justice.

Guard Arnett, sitting behind him, relates a conversation they had during lunch today. in which 5486 said that his decline must have been because "he's fallen in with bad company."

Carlo Prescott and the Board are obviously confused by this transaction. How does this statement promote his cause?

Prescott is clearly upset at this display. He tells 5486 that if the Board were going to make any recommendations, "I would see to it personally that you were here until the last day. Nothing against you personally, but we're here to protect society. And I don't think that you can go out and do a constructive job, do the kinds of things that will make you an addition to the community. You went outside that door and you realized that you had talked to us like we were a couple of idiots, and you were dealing with cops or authority figures. You don't get along well with authority figures, do you? How do you get along with your folks? But what I'm trying to say is that you went outside the door and had a little time to think; now you're back in here trying to con us into looking at you with a different view. What real social consciousness do you have? What do you think you really owe society? I want to hear something real from you." (Carlo is back in Day 1 form!)

The prisoner is taken aback by this frontal assault on his character, and he scurries to make amends: "I have a new teaching job. It's a worthwhile job, I feel."

Prescott is not buying his story: "That may even make you more suspect. I don't think I'd want you to teach any of my youngsters. Not with your attitude, your gross immaturity, your indifference to responsibility. You can't even handle four days of prison without making yourself a nuisance. Then you tell me that you want to do a teaching job, do something that's really a privilege. It's a privilege to come into contact with decent people and have something to say to them. I don't know, you haven't convinced me. I just read your record for the first time, and you haven't showed me anything. Officer, take him away."

Chained, bagged, and carted back down to the basement prison, the prisoner will have to put on a better show at the next parole hearing—assuming he is granted the privilege again.

When a Paroled Prisoner Becomes the Chairman of the Parole Board

Before we return to what has been happening down below on the Yard in our absence during these two Parole Board time-aways, it is instructive to note the effect that this role-playing has had on our tough chairman of this "Adult Authority Hearing." A month later, Carlo Prescott offered a tender personal declaration of the impact this experience had on him:

"Whenever I came into the experiment, I invariably left with a feeling of depression—that's exactly how authentic it was. The experiment stopped being an experiment when people began to react to various kinds of things that happened during the course of the experiment. I noted in prison, for example, that people who considered themselves guards *had* to conduct themselves in a certain way. They had to put across certain impressions, certain attitudes. Prisoners in other ways had their certain attitudes, certain impressions that they acted out—the same thing occurred here.

"I can't begin to believe that an experiment permitted *me*, playing a board member, the chairman of the board—the Adult Authority Board—to say to one of the prisoners, 'How is it'—in the face of his arrogance and his defiant attitude—'how is it that Orientals seldom come to prison, seldom find themselves in this kind of a situation? What did you do?'

"It was at that particular point in the study that his whole orientation changed. He begin to react to me as an individual, he began to talk to me about his personal feelings. One man was so completely involved that he came back into the room as if he thought a second journey into the room to speak to the Adult Authority Board could result in his being paroled sooner."

Carlo continues with this self-disclosure: "Well, as a former prisoner, I must admit that each time I came here, the frictions, suspicion, the antagonism expressed as the men got into the roles . . . made me recognize the kind of deflated impression which came about as a result of the confinement. That's exactly what it was that induced in me a deep feeling of depression, as if I were back in a prison atmosphere. The whole thing was authentic, not make-believe at all.

"[The prisoners] were reacting as human beings to a situation, however improvisational, that had become part of what they were experiencing at that particular time. I imagine that as such, it reflected the kind of metamorphosis that takes place in a prisoner's thinking. After all, he is completely aware of the things that are going on in the external world—the bridge building, the birth of children—they have absolutely nothing to do with him. For the first time he is totally alienated from the rest of society—from humanity, for that matter.

"His fellows, in their funk and stink and their bitterness, become his comrades, and all other things except for an occasional period when he can, as a result of a visit, as a result of something happening, like going to the Parole Board, there's no reason to ever identify with where you came from. There is just that time, that instant.

". . . I wasn't surprised, nor was it a great pleasure to find my belief confirmed that 'people become the role they enact'; that guards become symbols of authority and cannot be challenged; and that there are no rules or no rights they are obliged to grant prisoners. This happens with prison guards, and this happens with college students playing at prison guards. The prisoner, on the other hand, who is left to consider his own situation in regard to how defiant he is, how effective he is in keeping the experience away from him, comes face-to-face daily with his own helplessness. He has to correlate both his own hatred and the effectiveness of his defiance with the reality that regardless of how heroic or how courageous he sees himself at a certain time—he will still be counted and still be subjected to the rules and regulations of the prison."[5]

I think it is appropriate to end these deliberations with a similarly insightful passage from the letters of the political prisoner George Jackson, written a bit before Carlo's statement. Recall that his lawyer wanted me to be an expert witness in his defense in the upcoming Soledad Brothers trial; however, Jackson was killed before I could do so, one day after our study ended.

It is strange indeed that a man can find anything to laugh at in here. Everyone is locked up twenty-four hours a day. They have no past, no future, no goal other than the next meal. They're afraid, confused and confounded by a world they know that they did not make, that they feel they cannot change, so they make those loud noises so they won't hear what their mind is trying to tell them. They laugh to assure themselves and those around them that they are not afraid, sort of like the superstitious individual who will whistle or sing a happy number as he passes the graveyard.[6]

CHAPTER EIGHT

Thursday's Reality Confrontations

Thursday's prison is full of woe, yet we have miles to go before our exploration is complete.

In the middle of the night, I awake from a terrible nightmare in which I am hospitalized in a strange town after an auto accident. I am struggling to communicate to the nurse that I had to go back to my work, but she cannot understand me. It is as though I were speaking in a foreign tongue. I scream out to let me go; "I have to be released." Instead, she puts me in restraints and tapes my mouth shut. In a kind of "lucid dream," where one is aware of being an actor in a dream while still dreaming, I envision that word of this incident gets back to the guards.[1] They are delighted that with the "bleeding-heart-liberal" superintendent out of the way, they are now totally free to deal with their "dangerous prisoners" in any way they feel necessary to maintain law and order.

That is indeed a scary thought. Imagine what might happen in that basement dungeon if the guards could now do whatever they wanted to the prisoners. Imagine what they could do knowing there was no oversight, no one observing their secret games of domination and submission, no one to interfere with their own little "mind experiments," which they could play out as wit and whimsy dictated. I jump off the convertible couch-bed in my upstairs office, wash, dress, and head back to the basement, glad to have survived that nightmare and to have my own freedom restored.

The 2:30 A.M. count is in full swing once again. The seven weary prisoners, awakened once more by loud, shrilling whistles and billy clubs rattling the bars on their stinking, barren cells, are lined up against the wall. Guard Vandy is reciting selected rules and then testing the prisoners' memories of them by delivering assorted punishments for memory lapses.

Guard Ceros would like the whole experience to be more like a tightly run military prison, so he has the prisoners march in place repeatedly, as though they were in the Army. After a brief discussion, the two comrades decide that these young men need to be more fully disciplined and to understand the importance of making their beds in the best military fashion. The prisoners are ordered to strip their beds completely and then remake them with precision and stand by them for inspection. Naturally, as in good boot camp style, they all fail the inspection, must restrip their beds, remake their beds, refail inspection, and then repeat the inane process until the guards grow bored with that game. Guard Varish adds his cute two cents: "Okay, men, now that you have made your beds, you can sleep in them—until the next count." Remember, this is only day five of our experiment.

VIOLENCE ERUPTS ON THE YARD

Amid the 7 A.M. count and seemingly more carefree singing required of the prisoners, violence suddenly erupts. Prisoner Paul-5704, exhausted from lack of sleep and irritated at having been singled out for abuse on almost all shifts, strikes back. He refuses to do sit-ups as commanded. Ceros insists that the others all continue to do sit-ups without stopping until 5704 agrees to join in; only by his submission can he stop their painful exercise. Prisoner 5704 does not take the bait.

In an extended interview with Curt Banks, Paul-5704 described his side of this incident and the hostility festering within him:

"I've got lousy thigh muscles, and I'm not supposed to stretch them. I told them that, but they said, 'shut up and do them anyway.' 'Fuck you, you little punk,' I said, while still laying on the ground. As I was getting up to be put in the

Hole once again, He [Ceros] pushed me against the wall. We scuffled, pushing each other hard and yelling. I wanted to swing at him and hit him in the face, but to me that would represent fighting. . . . I'm a pacifist, you know, I just don't think it was in me. But I hurt my foot when we hassled, and insisted on seeing a doctor, but was put in the Hole instead. I did threaten to 'flatten' him when I got out of the Hole, so they kept me in there until all others had breakfast. When they finally let me out of solitary, I was furious and did try to strike that guard [Ceros].

"It took two guards to restrain me. As they took me to a separate room for my solo breakfast, I complained about the pain in my foot and asked for a doctor. I did not let the guards examine my foot since what did they know about it?

"I ate alone but did apologize to [Varnish], who was least hostile toward me. But the guy I really want to crack is 'John Wayne,' that guy from Atlanta. I'm a Buddhist, and he keeps calling me a Communist just to provoke me, and it does. I now think that the good treatment on the part of some guards, like big Landry [Geoff], is only because they were ordered to act that way."[2]

Guard John Landry notes in the daily log that 5704 has been the one most in trouble or "at least he was the most punished prisoner":

> After each episode he [5704] has shown considerable depression, but his spirit, which he calls 'the freak mentality,' continues to rise. He is one of the strongest willed prisoners. He also refused to wash lunch dishes, so I recommend giving him lousy dinners and curtailed smoking privileges— he has a heavy habit.

Consider the following alternate and insightful perspective Guard Ceros had of this critical incident and of the psychology of imprisonment in general:

> One of the prisoners, 5704, was not cooperating at all, so I decided to put him in the Hole. By that time, it was regular routine. He reacted violently and I found that I had to defend myself, not as me, but as the guard. He hated *me* as the guard. He was reacting to the uniform; I felt that was the image he placed on me. I had no choice but to defend myself as a guard. I wondered why the other guards weren't rushing to help me. Everybody was stunned.
>
> I realized then that I was as much a prisoner as they were. I was just a reaction to their feelings. They had more of a choice in their actions. I don't think we did. We were both crushed by the situation of oppressiveness, but we guards had the illusion of freedom. I did not see that at the time, or else I would have quit. We all went in as slaves to the money. The prisoners soon became slaves to us; we were still slaves to the money. I realized later that we were all slaves to something in this environment. Thinking of it as "just an experiment" meant no harm could be done with reality. That was the illusion of freedom. I knew I could quit, but I didn't, because I couldn't as a slave to something there.[3]

Prisoner Jim-4325 agreed about the slavish nature of his condition: "The worst thing about this experience is the super structured life and the absolute obedience one must pay to the guards. The humiliation of being almost slaves to the guards is the worst."[4]

However, Guard Ceros did not let his sense of being trapped in his role interfere with exerting the power of his position. He noted, "I enjoyed bothering them. It bothered me that 'Sarge,' 2093, was so very sheepish. I did make him polish and wax my boots seven times, and he never complained."[5]

In his reflections, Guard Vandy revealed the dehumanizing perception of the prisoners that had crept into his thinking about them: "Prisoners were very sheepish by Thursday, except for a brief scuffle between Ceros and 5704, which was a small incident of violence that I did not like whatsoever. I thought of them as sheep and I did not give a damn as to their condition."[6]

In Guard Ceros's final evaluation report, he offered a different take on the emerging sense of dehumanization by the guards of the prisoners:

> There were a few times when I had forgotten the prisoners were people, but I always caught myself, realized that they were people. I simply thought of them as 'prisoners' losing touch with their humanity. This happened for short periods of time, usually when I was giving orders to them. I am tired and disgusted at times, this is usually the state of my mind. Also I make an actual try of my will to dehumanize them in order to make it easy for me.[7]

Our staff agree that of all the guards, the one who "goes by the book" most consistently is Varnish. He is one of the oldest guards, at twenty-four, like Arnett. Both of them are graduate students, so they should have a bit more maturity than the other guards, whose ages range from just eighteen for Ceros, Vandy, and J. Landry.

Varnish's daily shift reports are the most detailed and lengthy, including accounts of individual incidents of prisoner subordination. Yet he rarely comments on what the guards were doing and there is no sense of the psychological forces at work in any of these reports. He punishes prisoners only for rule violations and never arbitrarily. Varnish's role-playing has become so fully internalized that he is the prison guard whenever he is in this prison setting. He is not dramatic and abusive as some others are, like Arnett and Hellmann. On the other hand, he is not trying to get the prisoners to like him, as others, such as Geoff Landry, do. He merely does his job as routinely and efficiently as possible. I see from his background information that Varnish considers himself egotistical at times, with a streak of dogmatism on the side.

"There was at times a distinct tendency to minimize effort by not harassing prisoners as much as *we could have*," Varnish reported.

The way in which roles can come to rule not only one's emotions but also one's reason is interestingly revealed in Varnish's self-reflective analysis after the study:

I started out in the experiment thinking that I would probably be able to act in a manner appropriate to the experiment, but as the experiment progressed, I was rather surprised to find out that the feelings I had sought to impose on myself were beginning to take over. I was actually beginning to feel like a guard and had really thought I was incapable of this kind of behavior. I was surprised—no, I was dismayed—to find out that I could really be a—uh—that I could act in a manner so absolutely unaccustomed to anything I would really dream of doing. And while I was doing it I didn't feel any regret, I didn't feel any guilt. It was only afterwards, when I began to reflect on what I had done, that this behavior began to dawn on me and I realized that this was a part of me I had not noticed before."[8]

Prisoner 5704 Earns More Tormenting

Prisoner Paul-5704's assault on Ceros was the primary subject of talk in the guard station during the 10 A.M. transfer from the morning to the day shift, when they were taking off or putting on their uniforms to end a shift or start one. They agreed that he would need special attention and discipline since no such attack against guards could be tolerated.

Prisoner 5704 was not included in the 11:30 A.M. count because he was *chained* to his bed in Cell 1. Guard Arnett ordered everyone else down for seventy push-ups as group punishment for 5704's insubordination. Although the prisoners were getting weaker from their minimal diet and exhausted from lack of sleep, they were nevertheless able to perform this sizable number of push-ups—which I could not do when well fed and rested. They were getting into athletic condition reluctantly and miserably.

Continuing the ironic theme music from the previous day, the prisoners were made to sing, loud and clear, "Oh, What a Beautiful Morning" and "Amazing Grace," mixed in with a choral round of "Row, Row, Row Your Boat." Shortly after he joined his fellows for this chorus, Prisoner Paul-5704 continued his verbal insubordination, and once again he was thrown into the Hole. Screaming and cursing at the top of his lungs, he again kicked down the wooden partition that separated the two compartments of the Hole. The guards dragged him out, handcuffed him, chained both ankles together, and put him back into Cell 2 while they repaired the damage to the Hole. Solitary now had to have two separate cell units for whenever two prisoners had to be disciplined simultaneously.

As inventively determined as real prisoners can be, 5704 somehow was able to take the hinge bolts off the door to his cell, thereby locking himself in and taunting the guards. Once again, the guards broke into his cell, and carted him back to the now-repaired Hole until he was taken to the Parole Board later that day for a disciplinary hearing.

5704's riotous actions finally break through the appearance of equanimity that Guard Arnett has carefully cultivated. As one of the older guards, a graduate student in sociology, who has tutored in three juvenile jails and who has been charged (and acquitted) for "illegal assembly" in a civil rights protest, Arnett has the most relevant experience for being a conscientious guard. He is, but without compassion for the prisoners, as he behaves with a completely professional demeanor every moment he is on the Yard. He is as precise in delivering his verbal commands as he is in his controlled physical gestures. He has become a high-status authority figure, like a TV anchorman, with his unified movements of head, neck, and shoulders and his synchronized arm-wrist-hand gestures. Deliberate in word and deed, Arnett conveys a sense of economy of involvement with the scene around him. It is as hard to imagine him being ruffled by anything, as it is to imagine anyone challenging him.

> I am a little surprised myself at the equanimity that I felt throughout. I felt angry only once for a slash when 5704 took the lock off his door and poked me in the stomach with my own stick (which I had just poked him with). At all other times, I felt quite relaxed. I never experienced any sense of power or elation when pushing people or ordering them about.[9]

In this prison setting, Arnett used his understanding of some social science research to his advantage:

> I was aware from my reading that boredom and other aspects of prison life can be exploited to make people feel disoriented by being impersonal, giving boring work, punishing all prisoners for bad behavior by individuals, demeaning perfect execution of trivial demands in exercise sessions. I was sensitive to the power of those in control of social settings and I tried to heighten alienation [of the prisoners] by using some of these techniques. I could use it only in a very limited way because I didn't want to be brutal.[10]

In challenging the early parole release for 5704, Arnett wrote to the Board, "I can hardly list all 5704's infractions at this time. He is constantly and grossly insubordinate, with flare ups of violence and extreme mood swings, and constantly tries to incite the other prisoners to insubordination and general uncooperativeness. He acts badly even when he knows punishment for the other prisoners will result. He should be dealt with harshly by the discipline committee."

Prisoner 416 Confronts the System with a Hunger Strike

Prisoner 5704 wasn't the only disciplinary concern. The madness of this place, to which we have become accustomed over the few days since we began last Sunday, had also struck Prisoner 416 when he arrived yesterday as a replacement prisoner for first-to-be-released prisoner Doug-8612. He could not believe what he was witnessing and wanted to quit the experiment immediately. However, he was told by his cellmates that he could not quit. His cellmates passed along the false statement that Prisoner 8612 had asserted, that it was not possible to leave, that *"They"* would not allow anyone to leave before the time was up. I am reminded of the famous line from the song "Hotel California": "You can check out anytime you like, but you can never leave."

Instead of challenging that false assertion, Prisoner 416 would use a passive means of escape. "I developed a plan," he later said. "I would insist on the loophole in my hastily prepared contract. But what force beyond pleading could I exert on this system? I could rebel as Paul-5704 has. But by using legal tactics to get out, my feelings were of secondary importance, though I followed them in terms of achieving my goal. Instead, I chose to exhaust the resources of this simulation by being impossible, by refusing all rewards and accepting their punishments." (It is unlikely that 416 realized that he was adopting a strategy that organized labor has used in struggles against management, to "play by the rules," formally known as "work to rule," on every matter in order to expose inherent weaknesses in the system.[11])

416 decided to go on a fast because, by refusing the food the guards offered, he would take away one source of their power over the prisoners. Looking at his skinny body, his muscle-free body, 135 pounds on a five-foot-eight frame, made me think that he already looked like a starvation victim.

In some ways, Clay-416 was more powerfully impacted by his first day as a prisoner in the Stanford County Jail than anyone else was, as he told us in this personal, yet depersonalized analysis:

"I began to feel that I was losing my identity. The person I call 'Clay,' the person who put me in this place, the person who volunteered to go into this prison— 'cause it was a prison to me, it still is a prison to me—I don't look on it as an experiment or a simulation—it is a prison run by psychologists instead of run by the State. I began to feel that identity, the person I was, that decided to go to prison—was distant from me—was remote, until finally, I wasn't that. I was '416.' I was really my number, and 416 was going to have to decide what to do, and that was when I decided to fast. I decided to fast because that was the one reward the guards gave you. They always threatened they wouldn't let you eat, but they had to give you eats. And so I stopped eating. Then I had a sort of power over something because I found the one thing they couldn't crack me on. They were going to catch shit eventually if they didn't get me to eat. And so I was sort of humiliating them by being able to fast."[12]

He began by refusing to touch his lunch. Arnett reported that he overheard 416 telling his cellmates that he intended not to eat until he got the legal consultation that he had been demanding. He said that "After about twelve hours I'll probably collapse, and then what can they do? They'll have to give in." Arnett found him nothing more than a "sassy and back talkin' " prisoner. He sees nothing noble in this hunger strike.

Here was a new prisoner embarking on a daring plan of disobedience, directly challenging the guards' power. His act could potentially make him a nonviolent hero around whom the prisoners could rally, someone to rouse them from their mindlessly obedient stupor—like Mahatma Gandhi. By contrast, it is clear that the violence used by 5407 did not work in a place where the resources of power are so imbalanced in favor of the system. I was hoping that 416 would come up with another plan that would involve his cellmates and the others in communal disobedience, using a mass hunger strike as a tactic for remediation of their harsh treatment. Nevertheless, I worried that he was so internally focused that he had little awareness of the need to engage his fellows in fuller group opposition.

Two More Prisoners Break Down

It appeared that the problem caused by 5407 and 416 were the beginnings of a domino effect of confrontations. Prisoner 1037's mother had been right. Her son, Rich, had not looked good to her; now he did not look good to me. He had become increasingly depressed after his folks had left following visiting hours; he probably wished that they had insisted on taking him home with them. Instead of accepting his mother's accurate appraisal of his condition, Rich probably came to believe that his masculinity was at stake. He wanted to prove that he could take it, "like a man." He couldn't. Just like his cellmates 8612 and 819 from the original rebellious Cell 2, 1037 displayed symptoms of extreme stress to such an extent that I had him taken to the quiet room outside the prison yard and told him that it would be best if he were paroled at this time. He was pleased and surprised at this good news. As I helped him change into his civilian clothes, he was still shaky. I told him he would get full pay for the entire experiment and that we would be in contact with him and all the other students soon to go over the results of the study, complete the final surveys, and give them their payment.

Prisoner 1037 later said that the worst part of the experiment was the "time when the guards gave me the feeling that they were expressing their true inner feelings and not just the guard role they were playing. For example, there were some times during the exercise periods when we prisoners would be pushed to the point of real suffering. Some guards seemed to really enjoy our agony."[13]

When his parents came to get him during visiting hours, the news of 1037's imminent parole did not go down well with Prisoner 4325, who was more stressed than any of us had realized. "Big Jim," as our research team referred to 4325, seemed like a self-assured young man whose preselection assessment had indicated he was in the normal range on all measures. Nevertheless, on that afternoon he abruptly broke down.

"When the appearance before the Parole Board came up, I immediately became hopeful of getting released. But I fell a long way down when Rich [1037] was paroled and I was not. That one act worked its way into me and brought about an even heavier feeling of desperation. I 'broke' as a result. I learned that my emotions are much more present than I thought and realized what a great life I actually have. If prison is anything like what I went through here, I don't know how it could help anyone."[14]

I said the same things to him as I had said to 1037, namely, that we were going to parole him soon anyway for his good behavior, and that it was fine if he left sooner. I thanked him for his participation, told him I was sorry that it had been so tough on him, and invited him back soon to discuss what we found. I wanted to have all the students come back together to share their reactions after having had a bit of distance from this unusual experience. He gathered his belongings and left quietly after indicating that he did not need to see a psychological counselor in Student Health Services.

The Warden's Log noted, "4325 reacts badly and has to be released by 5:30 P.M. because of severe reactions like those displayed by 819 [Stew] and 8612 [Doug] before him." The log also adds the curious fact that there is no mention of 4325's release by any of the prisoners or by any of the guards. Gone and forgotten. Rest in Peace. Apparently, by this time in the grueling test of endurance all that matters is who is present and accounted for—not who used to be. Out of sight is definitely out of mind.

Letters Home from the Stanford Jail

"Today when the prisoners were writing letters home explaining what a fine time they were having, as they have done before, prisoner 5486 [Jerry] could not get his letter right until the third attempt," reported Guard Markus. "This prisoner's behavior and respect for authority have been steadily deteriorating from the early days when he was in the model cell #3. Since cell realignment, 5486 has been adversely affected by his new cellmates, and his behavior is now characterized by his new wise cracks, especially during counts. All of his behaviors have the sole purpose to undermine prison authority."

Arnett's report also singled out this formerly model prisoner as a new problem: "5486 has been in gradual downhill slide since being separated from 4325 and 2093 in cell #3. He has become something of a jokester and minor cutup. This unacceptable behavior should be rectified before leading to committing something serious."

The third guard on the day shift, John Landry, was similarly upset when "5486 made a joke out of letter writing as a sign of his general non-cooperation. I recommend, as punishment, that he be made to write 15 letters of this type."

Christina Joins the Mad Hatter's Party

After Thursday's Parole Board and Disciplinary Board finished their deliberations, Carlo had to return to the city for urgent business. I was glad that I did not have to take him to dinner because I wanted to be present for the early visiting hours scheduled for right after the prisoners had their dinner. I had to apologize to

Mrs. Y., Prisoner 1037's mother, for my insensitive behavior the other night. However, I also wanted to have a more relaxed dinner that night with the newcomer to those deliberations, Christina Maslach.

Christina had recently gotten her Ph.D. in social psychology at Stanford and was about to begin her career as an assistant professor at Berkeley, one of the first women to be hired by its Psychology faculty in decades. She was a diamond in the smooth—smart, serene, and self-contained. Hardworking and committed to a career as a research psychologist and educator, Christina had worked with me earlier as a teaching assistant and a valuable research collaborator as well as an informal editor of several of my books.

I imagine that I would have been in love with her even if she had not been stunningly beautiful. For a poor kid from the Bronx, this elegant "California Girl" was a dream come true. However, I had to maintain a respectful distance so that my recommendations for her employment would not be tainted by my personal involvement. Now that she had gotten one of the best jobs in the country on her own merits, we could pursue our relationship openly.

I had not told her much about this prison study because she and some other colleagues and graduate students were scheduled to do a thorough evaluation of the staff, prisoners, and guards the next day, Friday, about halfway through our scheduled two weeks. I had the sense that she had not been pleased by what she had seen and heard on the afternoon of the disciplinary deliberations. It was not anything she had said that disturbed me, but her saying nothing at all. We would discuss her reactions to Carlo and that scenario at our late dinner, as well as the kind of information I hoped she could obtain from her interviews on Friday.

The Priest Follows Through on His Promise of Pastoral Aid

The priest, who knows that this is just a simulated prison, has already done his part to add verisimilitude to this mock prison by his seriously intense role-playing the other day. Now he is forced to follow through on his priestly promise to give aid should anyone request his assistance. Sure enough, Father McDermott calls the mother of Hubbie-7258 and tells Mrs. Whittlow that her son needs legal representation if he wants to get out of the Stanford County Jail. Instead of just saying that if her son really wants out so badly, she will just take him back home with her when she sees him at the next Visitors' Night, Mrs. W. does what she is told. She calls her nephew Tim, a lawyer in the public defender's office. He in turn calls me, and we follow through on this script by agreeing to schedule his official lawyer's visit for Friday morning as one more realistic element in this experience that is growing ever more unreal. Our little drama, it would appear, is now being rewritten by Franz Kafka as a surreal supplement to *The Trial*, or perhaps by Luigi Pirandello as an update of his *Il fu Mattia Pascal*, or his better-known play *Six Characters in Search of an Author*.

A Hero in the Rearview Mirror

Sometimes it takes time and distance to realize the value of life's important lessons. Clay-416 might provide a counterpart of Marlon Brando's classic statement in *On the Waterfront,* "I coulda been a contender." Clay-416 might have said, "I coulda been a hero." However, in the heat of the moment he was thought to be just a "troublemaker" who caused hardships to his fellows—a rebel without an obvious cause.

Heroism often requires social support. We typically celebrate heroic deeds of courageous individuals, but we do not do so if their actions have tangible immediate cost to the rest of us and we can't understand their motives. Such heroic seeds of resistance are best sown if all members of a community share a willingness to suffer for common values and goals. We have seen such an instance, for example, in Nelson Mandela's resistance to apartheid when he was imprisoned in South Africa. Networks of people in many European nations organized escapes and hideouts for Jews to survive the Nazi Holocaust. Hunger strikes were employed for political purposes in the fasting to death of IRA leaders during their imprisonment in Belfast's Long Kesh prison. They and others from the Irish National Liberation Army used the hunger strike to gain attention to their status as political prisoners instead of being designated as ordinary criminals.[15] More recently, hundreds of detainees being held in the U.S. military prison in Guantánamo, Cuba, have gone on extended hunger strikes to protest the illegal and inhumane nature of their captivity and gain media attention to their cause.

As for Clay-416, although he had a personal plan for effective resistance, he did not take time to share it with his cellmates or the other prisoners so that they could decide to join forces with him. Had he done so, his plan might have represented a unifying principle rather than being dismissed as a personal pathology. It would have become a collective challenge to the evil system rather than a dispositional quirk. Perhaps because he came on the scene late, the other prisoners did not know him well enough or felt that he had not paid his dues as they had during those first hard days and nights. In any case, he was an "outsider," as Dave, our informer (replacement for 8612), had been. Though Dave had been quickly won over to the prisoners' side and aligned with their cause against the system that had hired him as its spy, not so with 416. However, I think it was also 416's introverted style that was alienating his fellows. He was used to going it alone, living his life in his own complex mind and not in the realm of interpersonal connections. Nevertheless, his defiance had a powerful impact on the thinking of at least one other prisoner, albeit after the prison experience was over.

Jerry-5486, the prisoner recently designated a "smart aleck" by the Parole Board, was clearly influenced by 416's heroism in the face of harsh abuse: "I was impressed with Clay's stoic determination and wish he would have been there from the beginning. He would have had a definite effect on the events that followed."

In his later reflections, 5486 added:

It was interesting that when Clay-416, who was the first real example of an obstinate person who had made up his mind when he absolutely refused to eat his sausages, people went against him. Earlier in the study, he would have been their ideal. Because a lot of people said they were going to be hard and fast and strike and all this, but when it finally came around to somebody having the guts to do that, they went against him. They wanted their own petty little comforts rather than see him hold on to his integrity.

Jerry-5486 went on to note how unpleasant it was to witness the clash between 416 and 7258, "between Hubbie and Clay over the sausages and the girlfriend." Later on, he had a better perspective on the true meaning of that confrontation, but he could not see the true nature of the event while it was unfolding and he could have taken action to intervene and defuse it:

I realized that everybody was so far into the whole thing that they were suffering and making others suffer as well. It was too sad to see them go through it, especially since [Hubbie] didn't realize that, if he had not gotten to see his girl, it would be 'John Wayne's' fault, not Clay's. [Hubbie] took the bait and let it tear him apart.[16]

Meanwhile, back in solitary confinement, Clay-416 was coping in a kind of Buddhist style that would have made Paul-5704 proud of him, had he known that Clay was using such a Zen-like tactic for mental survival.

"I meditated constantly. For example, when I was refusing dinner, the guard [Burdan] has all the prisoners out of their cells trying to convince me that visitors' day was going to be canceled and all this shit, which I calculated wouldn't happen. But I wasn't sure; I just had calculated that probability. I then continually stared at the droplet of water from the frankfurter that was glistening on my tin plate. I just stared at that droplet and focused myself first horizontally, then vertically. Nobody was then able to bother me. I had a religious experience in the Hole."[17]

This scrawny kid had found inner peace through his passive resistance, taking control over his body and directing himself away from the guards. Clay-416 offered this moving account of how he believed that he had won the contest of personal will against institutional power:

"Once I refused food before the dominant evening guard, I became content for the first time here. It pleased me to infuriate [Guard Hellmann]. Upon being thrown in the Hole for the night, I was jubilant. Jubilant because I felt all but sure that I had exhausted his resources (to be used against him). I was astonished to realize too that I had privacy in solitary confinement—it was luxurious. His punishment of the others did not concern me. I was gambling on the limits of the situation. I knew, I calculated, that visitors' privileges could not be removed. I prepared myself to stay in the Hole until probably ten the next morning. In the Hole

I was furthest from experiencing myself as 'Clay.' I was '416,' willing and proud even to be '416.' The number had an identity to me because 416 had found his own response to the situation. I felt no need to cling to the former manhood I had under my old name. In the Hole, there is a four-inch bar of light extending top to bottom, thrown by the crack between the closet doors. About the third hour there, I was filled with calm in regarding this bar of light. It is the most beautiful thing in the prison. I don't mean that only subjectively. It is, go look at it. When I was released around 11 P.M. and returned to a bed, I felt that I had won, that my will, so far, was stronger than the will of the situation as a whole. I slept well that night."

The Sidekick Shows a Little Soul

Curt Banks tells me that of all the guards the one he likes or respects least is Burdan because he is such a little toady, sucking up after Hellmann, living in the big guy's wake. I am feeling the same, although from a prisoner's point of view there were others who were much worse threats to their sanity and survival. One of the staff had overheard Burdan bragging that he had seduced his friend's wife last night. The three of them had been regular weekly bridge players, and although he had always been attracted to this twenty-eight-year-old mother of two children, he had never had the guts to move on her—until now. Perhaps it was his new-found sense of authority that gave him the courage to deceive and cuckold his old friend. If it were true, it was another reason not to like him. Then we found in his background information that his mother escaped from Nazi Germany, so we add some positive weight back into our evaluation of this complex young man.

Burdan's shift report is an amazingly accurate depiction of official corrections staff behavior:

> We have a crisis in authority, this rebellious conduct [416's fasting] potentially undermines the complete control we have over the others. I have gotten to know the idiosyncrasies of various numbers [interesting that he calls them "numbers"; a blatant deindividualization of the prisoners]; I attempt to utilize this information only for harassment while inside the cellblock.

He also points the finger at the lack of support he and the other guards were getting from our staff: "Real trouble started at dinner—we look to prison authority to find out how to handle this late revolt for the reason that we are worried about him not eating. . . . They are strangely absent." (We plead guilty to not providing oversight and training.)

My negative view of Guard Burdan is tempered by what he did next. "I can't stand the idea of him [416] being in the Hole any longer," he says. "It seems dangerous [since the rules limit solitary to one hour]. I argue with Dave, and then quietly put the new prisoner, 416, back in his cell." He adds, "but with a touch of malice, I order him to take the sausages to bed with him."[18]

A validation of this positive take on Burdan comes from a comment by Jerry-5486, who was the only prisoner to volunteer to give up his blanket for Clay-416: "I was upset at John Wayne's ranting and raving. [Burdan] came over to my cell knowing I sympathized with Clay and said that he won't be kept in there all night. 'We'll bring him out as soon as everyone is asleep,' he whispered to me, and then went back to pretending he was a hard guy. It was as if he needed to make some honest, sincere communication in the eye of the storm."[19]

Not only was Jerry-5486 in 416's corner, but he also came to feel that the best thing about this whole experience was meeting Clay: "Seeing one guy who knew what he wanted and was willing to endure whatever necessary to get it. He was the only guy with anything at stake who didn't sell out, or plead, or crack up."[20]

In that night's Shift Report, Burdan notes, "There is no solidarity between the remaining prisoners, with the exception of 5486 who has always demanded equal privileges for all." (I concur; that is one reason for respecting Jerry-5486 more than any of the other prisoners.)

This intense, extended experience is enriching my appreciation of the complexity of human nature because just when you think you understand someone, you realize you know only the smallest slice of their inner nature derived from a limited set of personal or mediated contacts. As I too come to respect Clay-416 for his willpower in the face of such strong opposition, I discover that he is not all Buddha. He tells us in his final interview what he thinks about the suffering his hunger strike caused the other prisoners: "If I am trying to get out and the guards create a situation where it is difficult on other people because I'm trying to get out, *I don't give a shit.*"

His friend Jerry-5486 provides a fascinating perspective on the complex mind games that he was playing—and losing—in this prison.

More and more as the experiment went on, I could justify my actions by saying "It's only a game, and I know it and I can endure it easy enough, and they can't bother my mind, so I'll go through the actions." Which was fine for me. I was enjoying things, counting my money, and planning my escape. I felt my head was pretty together and they couldn't upset me, because I was detached from it all, watching it happen. But I realize now that no matter how together I thought I was inside my head, my prison behavior was often less under my control than I realized. No matter how open, friendly and helpful I was with other prisoners I was still operating as an isolated, self-centered person, being rational rather than compassionate. I got along fine in my own detached way, but now I'm aware that frequently my actions hurt others. Instead of responding to their needs, I would assume that they were as detached as I and thereby rationalize my own selfish behavior.

The best example of this was when Clay [416] was in the closet with his sausages. . . . Clay and I were friends, he knew I was on his side during the fasting incident, and I felt I had helped him some at the supper table when the other prisoners were trying to make him eat. But when he went in the closet and we were told to yell things and pound on the door, I did it just like everyone else. I easily justified it by saying "It's just a game. Clay knows I'm on his side. My actions don't make any difference so I'll just keep humoring the guard." Later, I realized that the yelling and pounding was really hard on Clay. There I was tormenting the guy I liked most. And justifying it by saying "I'll go through the motions but they haven't got control of my mind." When what was really important was the other guy's mind. What was *he* thinking? How were my actions affecting him? I was blind to the consequences of my actions, and unconsciously assigning the responsibility for them to the guards. I had separated my mind from my actions. I probably would have done anything short of causing physical harm to a prisoner as long as I could shift the responsibility to the guards.

And so now I think, maybe you can't separate mind and actions as clearly as I did during the experiment. I prided myself on how unassailable my mind was—I didn't get upset, I didn't let them control my mind. But as I look back on the things I did it seems they had quite a strong, but subtle, control over my mind.[21]

"WHAT YOU ARE DOING TO THOSE BOYS IS A TERRIBLE THING!"

The last toilet run of Thursday night started at 10 P.M. Christina had been working at the library following her quiet stint earlier on the Parole and Disciplinary Board. She had come down to the prison for the first time to pick me up to drive over to the Town and Country Mall near campus for a late dinner at Stickney's Restaurant. I was in my Superintendent's Office going over some logistics for the next day's mass interviews. I saw her chatting with one of the guards, and when she finished, I motioned her in to have a seat near my desk. She later described her unusual encounter with that particular guard:

In August of 1971, I had just completed my doctorate at Stanford University, where I was the office mate of Craig Haney, and was preparing to start my new job as an assistant professor of psychology at the University of California, Berkeley. Relevant background also should include mention that I had recently gotten involved romantically with Phil Zimbardo, and we were even considering the possibility of marriage. Although I had heard from Phil and other colleagues about the plans for their prison simulation study, I had not participated in either the preparatory work or the initial days of the actual simulation. Ordinarily I would have been more interested and maybe become involved in some way, but I was in the process of moving, and my focus was on preparing for my first teaching job. However, I agreed when Phil asked me, as a favor, to help conduct some interviews with the study participants. . . .

When I went downstairs to the basement location of the prison . . . I then went to the other end of the hall, where the guards entered the yard; there was a room outside the yard entrance, which the guards used to rest and relax when not on duty or to change into or out of their uniforms at the start or end of their shifts. I talked to one of the guards there who was waiting to begin his shift. He was very pleasant, polite and friendly, surely a person anyone would consider a really nice guy.

Later on, one of the research staff mentioned to me that I should take a look at the yard again, because the new late-night guard shift had come on, and this was the notorious "John Wayne" shift. John Wayne was the nickname for the guard who was the meanest and toughest of them all; his reputation had preceded him in various accounts I had heard. Of course, I was eager to see who he was and what he was doing that attracted so much attention. When I looked through the observation point, I was absolutely stunned to see that their John Wayne was the "really nice guy" with whom I had chatted earlier. Only now, he was transformed into someone else. He not only moved differently, but he talked differently—with a Southern accent. . . . He was yelling and cursing at the prisoners as he made them go through "the count," going out of his way to be rude and belligerent. It was an amazing transformation from the person I had just spoken to—a transformation that had taken place in minutes just by stepping over the line from the outside world into that prison yard. With his military-style uniform, billy club in hand, and dark, silver-reflecting sunglasses to hide his eyes . . . this guy was an all-business, no-nonsense, really mean prison guard.[22]

Just then, I watched the last toilet run chain gang parading past the open door of my Superintendent's Office. As usual, their ankle chains were linked from inmate to inmate; big paper bags covered their heads, each prisoner's arm holding on to the shoulder of the one before him. A guard, big Geoff Landry, led the procession.

"Chris, look at this!" I exclaimed. She looked up, then right down.

"Did you see that? What do you think?"

"I already saw it." And she looked away again.

I was shocked by her seeming indifference.

"What do you mean? Don't you understand that this is a crucible of human behavior, we are seeing things no one has witnessed before in such a situation. What is the matter with you?" Curt and Jaffe also joined me against her.

She couldn't reply because she was so emotionally distressed. Tears ran down her cheeks. "I'm leaving. Forget dinner. I'm going home."

I ran out after her, and we argued on the front steps of Jordan Hall, home of the Psychology Department. I challenged whether she could ever be a good researcher if she was going to get so emotional from a research procedure. I told her that dozens of people had come down to this prison and no one had reacted as she had. She was furious. She didn't care if everyone in the world thought that what I was doing was okay. It was simply wrong. Boys were suffering. As principal investigator, I was personally responsible for their suffering. They were not prisoners, not experimental subjects, but boys, young men, who were being dehumanized and humiliated by other boys who had lost their moral compass in this situation.

Her recollection of this intense confrontation is filled with gems of wisdom and compassion, but at that time, it was a slap in my face, the wake-up call from the nightmare that I had been living day and night for the past week.

Christina recollects:

At around 11 P.M., the prisoners were being taken to the toilet prior to going to bed. The toilet was outside the confines of the prison yard, and this had posed a problem for the researchers, who wanted the prisoners to be 'in prison' 24 hours a day (just as in a real prison). They did not want the prisoners to see people and places in the outside world, which would have broken the total environment they were trying to create. So the routine for the bathroom runs was to put paper bags over the prisoners' heads so they couldn't see anything, chain them together in a line, and lead them down the hall into, around, and out of a boiler room and then to the bathroom and back. It also gave the prisoners an illusion of a great distance between the yard and the toilet, which was in fact only in a hallway around the corner.

Christina continues her recollection of that fateful night's reality confrontation:

When the bathroom run took place that Thursday evening, Phil excitedly told me to look up from some report I had been reading: "Quick, quick—look at what's happening now!" I looked at the line of hooded, shuffling, chained prisoners, with guards shouting orders at them—and then quickly averted my gaze. I was overwhelmed by a chilling, sickening feeling. 'Do you see that? Come on, look—it's amazing stuff!' I couldn't bear to look again, so I snapped back with, "I already saw it!" That led to a bit of a tirade by Phil (and other staff there) about what was the matter with me. Here was fascinating human behavior unfolding, and I, a psychologist, couldn't even look at it? They couldn't believe my reaction, which they may have taken to be a lack of interest. Their comments and teasing made me feel weak and stupid—the out-of-place woman in this male world—in addition to already feeling sick to my stomach by the sight of these sad boys so totally dehumanized.

She recalls our clash and its resolution:

A short while later, after we had left the prison setting, Phil asked me what I thought about the entire study. I'm sure he expected some sort of great intellectual discussion about the research and the events we had just witnessed. Instead, what he got was an incredibly emotional outburst from me (I am usually a rather contained person). I was angry and frightened and in tears. I said something like,

"What you are doing to those boys is a terrible thing!"

What followed was a heated argument between us. That was especially scary for me, because Phil seemed to be so different from the man I thought I knew, someone who loves students and cares for them in ways that were already legendary at the university. He was not the same man that I had come to love, someone who is gentle and sensitive to the needs of others and surely to mine. We had never had an argument before of this intensity. Instead of being close and in tune with each other, we seemed to be on opposite sides of some great chasm. Somehow, the transformation in Phil (and in me as well) and the threat to our relationship was unexpected and shocking. I don't remember how long the fight went on, but I felt it was too long and too traumatic.

What I do know is that eventually Phil acknowledged what I was saying, apologized for his treatment of me, and realized what had been gradually happening to him and everyone else in the study: that they had all internalized a set of destructive prison values that distanced them from their own humanitarian values. And at that point, he owned up to his responsibility as creator of this prison and made the decision to call the experiment to a halt. By then it was well past midnight, so he decided to end it the next morning, after contacting all the previously released prisoners, and calling in all the guard shifts for a full round of debriefings of guards, prisoners, and then everyone together. A great weight was lifted from him, from me, and from our personal relationship.[23]

YOU'RE MALE CAMELS, NOW HUMP THEM

I returned to the dungeon relieved and even exhilarated by the decision to abort the mission. I couldn't wait to share the news with Curt Banks, who had done yeoman's duty servicing the video patrol at various times of the day and night, despite having a family to tend to as well. He too was delighted and told me that he was going to recommend ending the study as soon as possible after what he had witnessed while I was gone. We were sorry Craig was not here tonight to share our end-game joy.

The calm demeanor displayed by Clay-416, after what should have been a stressful ordeal, has angered Hellmann. He cascades into a 1 A.M. count to end all counts. The sad, dwindling cadre of only five remaining prisoners (416, 2093, 5486, 5704, and 7258) wearily lines up against the wall to recite their numbers, rules, and songs. No matter how well they do their chores, someone is punished in various ways. They are yelled at, cursed, and made to say abusive things to each other. "Tell him he's a prick!" yells Hellman, and one prisoner turns to say that to the next. Then the sexual harassment that started to bubble up last night resumes as testosterone flows freely in every direction.

Hellman shouts out to all of them, "See that hole in the ground? Now do twenty-five push-ups, *fucking* that hole! You hear me!" One after another, the prisoners obey as Burdan shoves them down to do their duty.

After a brief consultation between John Wayne and his little sidekick, Burdan, a new sexual game is devised. "Okay, now pay attention. You three are going to be female camels. Get over here and bend over touching your hands to the floor." (When they do, their naked butts are exposed since they are wearing no underwear beneath their smock-dresses.) Hellmann continues with obvious glee, "Now you two, you're male camels. Stand behind the female camels and *hump* them."

Burdan giggles at this double entendre. Although their bodies never touch, the helpless prisoners are simulating sodomy by making thrusting motions of humping. They are dismissed back to their cells as the guards retreat to their quarters, clearly feeling that they have earned their night's salary. My nightmare from last night is coming true. I am glad that now I can control it by ending it all tomorrow.

It is hard to imagine that such sexual humiliation could happen in only five days, when the young men all know that this is a simulated prison experiment. Moreover, initially they all recognized that the "others" were also college students like themselves. Given that they were all randomly assigned to play these contrasting roles, there were no inherent differences between the two categories. They all began the experience as seemingly good people. Those who were guards knew that but for the random flip of a coin they could have been wearing the prisoner smocks and been controlled by those they were now abusing. They also knew that the prisoners had done nothing criminally wrong to deserve their lowly status. Yet, some guards have transformed into perpetrators of evil, and other guards have become passive contributors to the evil through their inaction. Still other normal, healthy young men as prisoners have broken down under the situational pressures, while the remaining surviving prisoners have become zombie-like followers.[24]

The power of this situation ran swiftly and deeply through most of those on this exploratory ship of human nature. Only a few were able to resist the situational temptations to yield to power and dominance while maintaining some semblance of morality and decency. Obviously, I was not among that noble class.

CHAPTER NINE

Friday's Fade to Black

We have so much to do to take down our prison in a matter of hours. Curt, Jaffe, and I are already exhausted from the hectic day and night we have just endured. In addition, in the middle of the night we have to decide on all the arrangements for debriefing sessions, final evaluations, and disbursement of payments and personal belongings, as well as cancellation of afternoon visits from colleagues who had planned to help us interview everyone connected with this study. We also have to cancel various arrangements with the cafeteria food service, return the rented cots and handcuffs to the campus police, and more.

We know that we each have to do double duty, monitoring the Yard action, taking short catnaps, and laying out the final day's logistics. We will announce the end of the study immediately after the public defender's visit. It was already scheduled for the morning, and it would be an appropriate event around which to wrap up the whole experience. We decide not to tell the guards before informing the prisoners of the good news from me directly. I anticipate that the guards will be angry to learn that the study is being terminated prematurely, especially now, when they believe that they are in total control and are anticipating an easy week ahead, with some new replacements. They have learned how to be "guards." Obviously, their learning curve has peaked.

Jaffe will contact the five prisoners who had been released earlier and invite them back around noontime to share in the debriefing and get their full week's pay. I have to ask all the guard shifts either to come by at noon or to hang around until then for a "special event." Having anticipated that there were supposed to be full staff interviews by outsiders on Friday, the guards expect some new element to be added, but not this abrupt end to their jobs.

If all goes as planned, there will be an hour of prisoner debriefing around one o'clock, then the same for the guards for an hour, and finally all the guards and prisoners will come together for a full encounter. While each group is engaged, the other group will complete our final evaluation forms, be paid, and have the opportunity either to keep their uniforms as souvenirs or to turn them in. If they wish, they can also take the various signs we posted in the Yard and on the Hole. We also have to arrange a big farewell lunch for everyone and make arrangements for them all to return soon to view selected videos and discuss their reactions from a more detached perspective.

Before taking my nap on the convertible couch in my upstairs professor's office, where I have been sleeping fitfully for most of the week, I tell the morning shift guards to let the prisoners sleep through the night and to minimize any further hostility against the prisoners. They shrug their shoulders and nod, as though Dad were telling them not to have fun on the playground.

FRIDAY'S FINAL COUNT

For the first time in a week, the prisoners have been allowed to sleep for nearly six unbroken hours. The accrued interest on their sleep debt must have been enormous. It is hard to determine the effects on their moods and their thinking that was caused by having their sleeping and dreaming disrupted so often every night. It was probably considerable. The emotional breakdown of some of the early-released prisoners may have been amplified by their sleep disturbances.

The 7:05 A.M. count lasts only ten minutes. Numbers are called out and other innocuous rituals observed. A good hot breakfast is served to the final five survivors. As might have been expected, Clay-416 refuses to eat any breakfast food, even when the other prisoners gently encourage him to do so.

Despite my instructions to go easy on the prisoners, the guards go ballistic at Clay's continued insubordination. "Everyone down for fifty push-ups if 416 don't eat his breakfast." Clay-416 does not budge but just stares down at his food plate. Vandy and Ceros try to force-feed him, stuffing food into his mouth as he spits it out. They enlist 5704 and 2093 to help them, but to no avail. Clay-416 is put back into his cell and forced to "make love" to his dinner sausages. Ceros orders him to caress them, to hug them, and then to kiss them. Clay-416 does all that. Yet he is true to his word and never eats a single bite of them.

Guard Vandy is upset at 416's defiance and also at his buddy's meanspiritedness. In his retrospective diary, Vandy said, "When 416 refused to eat I was once again angered specifically, since there was no way to force the food down his throat, even though we let some other prisoners try. Andre [Ceros] made the prisoner hug and kiss and caress a day-old sausage after being made to sleep with it. I thought this was uncalled for. I would never ever make the prisoner do this."[1]

What does Guard Ceros have to say about his own behavior? His retrospective diary noted, "I decided to force feed him, but he wouldn't eat. I let the food slide down his face. I didn't believe it was me doing it. I hated myself for making him eat. I hated him for not eating. I hated the reality of human behavior."[2]

The day shift came on at ten as usual. I told the lead guard, Arnett, to keep it cool and mellow in light of the coming legal representation. His day shift critical incident report indicated that Clay-416 was undergoing some strange changes in spite of his Zen meditation and earlier surface calm. Arnett's incident report noted:

> 416 is very jumpy. He jerked as I took the bag off his head for the toilet run. Had to pull him along when leading him to and from the bathroom, even though I told him I was not going to run him into anything [which the guards often did to prisoners for spite]. He was very nervous about being punished. I held his sausages when he went to the toilet. He tried to get me to give him back his sausages since another guard had ordered him to always have them."[3]

THE PUBLIC DEFENDER OF PRISONER RIGHTS AND WRONGS

I meet briefly with Tim B., a local lawyer working in the public defender's office. He is curious and skeptical about this whole affair. He has reluctantly given up his valuable time only because his aunt had asked him as a personal favor to check on his cousin. I describe the main features of the study and how serious it had become. I invite him to treat the matter exactly as he would if he had been called in to represent a group of real inmates. He agrees, and meets first with cousin Hubbie-7258 alone and then with all the prisoners. He allows us secretly to videotape the session in the same laboratory room on the first floor where the Parole Board had met.

The level of formality between these two kin surprises me. There is no hint of any previous relationship, if any existed. Maybe it was an Anglo thing, but I had expected at least a hug, not a formal handshake and "It's good to see you again." Attorney Tim goes through a standard list of items in a businesslike manner. He reads from a prepared list the categories of concern, stopping after each one to elicit the prisoner's responses, notes them, usually without comment, and moves on to the next in order:

Informed of rights upon arrest?
Harassment by guards?
Nature of any guard abuse?
Under pressure, mentally distraught?
Size and condition of cell?
Requests that have been denied?
Warden's behavior that was unacceptable?
Issues about bail?

Hubbie-7258 answers the questions in a good-humored way. I think he is assuming that his cousin was going through this standard routine prior to escorting him out of the jail. The prisoner tells his public defender that they have been told that there is no way for them to leave the prison, no way to break the contract. The PD reminds him that if the original contract were based on monetary return for services, by his being willing to forfeit that fee the contract would be null and void. "Yes, I told them that at the Parole Board hearing, but it did no good, I'm still here."[4] In listing his complaints, Hubbie-7258 makes it a point to note that Prisoner 416's troublemaking behavior had made them all mad.

The guards escort the remaining prisoners into the interview room, with bags over their heads as usual. The guards are joking as they remove the hoods. They leave, but I remain seated in the rear. The PD runs through the same set of questions as with Hubbie, inviting any of the prisoners to reply with their complaints as appropriate.

Clay-416 leads off, complaining first about the Parole Board pressuring him to plead guilty to the charges of his arrest, which he had refused to do because he was never officially charged. His fasting was, in part, a way to call attention to his illegal imprisonment given that he was being held without charges.

(Again this young man continued to confound me; clearly, he was functioning at multiple, incompatible levels. He was dealing with the whole experience in purely legalistic terms, mixing an experimental services contract with prisoner's rights and corrections formalities, not to mention a certain "new age" mystical meditation.)

Clay seems desperate to talk to someone who would actually listen to him. "Certain guards, who will go unnamed," he says, "misbehaved toward me up to the level of injurious behavior." He is willing to file an official complaint against them, if necessary. "Those guards also arranged for the other prisoners to be set against me by allegedly making my fasting a condition for their not getting visitors," he nods toward Hubbie-7258, who sheepishly looks the other way. "And I was frightened when they put me in the Hole and had the other prisoners bang against the door. Their own rule against violence was set, but I was afraid it would soon be overstepped."

Sarge-2093 speaks up next, describing some of the attempts various guards made to harass him, but he is proud to report that they had been unsuccessful. He then gives a precise clinical description and demonstration of when a particular guard had ordered him to do many push-ups—with two other prisoners sitting on his back.

The public defender is startled by that account, duly noting it down with a frown. Next, tall Paul-5704 complains about the guards manipulating him by using his smoking habit against him. Good guy Jerry-5486 complains at a less personal, more general level of the inadequate diet and missed meals, the exhaustion from endless middle-of-the-night counts, the out-of-control behavior of some guards, and the lack of supervision by the senior staff. I wince as he turns to look directly at me, but he was right on target: I was guilty.

When the public defender completes his note taking, he thanks them for this information, and says he would file a formal report on Monday and try to arrange for their bail. As he rises to leave, Hubbie-7258 loses it: "You can't go away and leave us here! We want to leave now with you. We can't stand another week or even weekend. I thought you were going to arrange for me, for us, to be bailed out now. Please!" Tim B. is taken aback by this sudden emotional outburst. He explains in a most formal way what his job entails, what its limits are, and how he could help them but is powerless to take action there and then. The five survivors appear to hit bottom at that point; their high hopes dashed by legal nonsense.

Tim B.'s reactions to this unique experience, conveyed to me in a letter shortly afterward, are informative:

On the Failure of the Prisoners to Demand Legal Rights

. . . [A]nother possible explanation of why the prisoners failed to request legal advice is that, as white middle-class Americans, they may not have ever envisioned the possibility that they would ever be thrust into the criminal arena, where their rights would be of paramount importance. Finding themselves in that position, they were disarmed of the ability to objectively appraise the situation and act as they otherwise knew they should.

On the Power of This Situation to Distort Reality

. . . The classical devaluation of money compared to such things as freedom and locomotion was clearly evident (in the activities which I witnessed). You will remember the great anticipation of release caused by my explanation of the bail offer. The reality of their imprisonment appeared to be quite penetrating even though they were intellectually aware that they were only involved in an experiment. Clearly confinement in itself seems to be painful regardless whether for legal reasons or otherwise.[5]

LISTEN CAREFULLY: THE EXPERIMENT IS OVER. YOU ARE FREE

The public defender's words darken the prisoners' hopes. A palpable cloak of gloom prevails over the sullen inmates. The public defender shakes their limp hands in turn as he leaves the room. I ask him to wait outside for me. Then I move to the head of the table and ask the prisoners to pay attention to what I am going to say next. They hardly have sufficient motivation left to pay attention to anything, now that their hopes for a quick dismissal have been dashed by the lawyer's officious reaction to their plight.

"I have something important to tell you, so please listen carefully: *The experiment is over. You are free to leave today.*"

There is no immediate reaction, no change in their facial expressions or body language. I have the sense that they are confused, skeptical, maybe even suspicious, and feel that this is another test of their reactions. I continue slowly and as clearly as possible, "I and the rest of the research staff have decided to terminate the experiment as of this moment. The study is officially over and the Stanford County Jail is closed. We all thank you for your important role in this study, and—"

Cheers replace the gloom. Hugs, slaps on backs, and wide smiles break through on those all-too-long-grim faces. Euphoria reverberates in Jordan Hall. It is a joyful moment for me as well to be able to liberate these survivors from their imprisonment and to give up my role as prison superintendent once and for all.

OLD POWER FAILURE, NEW POWER FOUND

There are few moments in my life that have given me more personal pleasure than being able to say those few words of liberation and to share in that total elation. I was overcome by the aphrodisiac of positive power, of being able to do something, to say something, that had such an unconditionally joyful impact on other people. Then and there I vowed to use whatever power that I had for good and against evil, to promote what is best in people, to work to free people from their self-imposed prisons, and to work against systems that pervert the promise of human happiness and justice.

The negative power on which I had been running for the past week, as superintendent of this mock prison, had blinded me to the reality of the destructive impact of the System that I was sustaining. Moreover, the myopic focus of a principal research investigator similarly distorted my judgment about the need to terminate the experiment much earlier, perhaps as soon as the second normal, healthy participant suffered an emotional breakdown. While I was focused on the abstract conceptual issue, the power of the behavioral situation versus the power of individual dispositions, I had missed seeing the all-encompassing power of the *System* that I had helped create and sustain.

Yes, indeed, Christina Maslach, it was terrible what I was allowing to be done to those innocent boys, not through any direct abuse but through my failure to stop abuse and my support of a system of arbitrary rules, regulations, and procedures that facilitated abuse. I was the "Iceman" in that hot house of inhumanity.

The System includes the Situation, but it is more enduring, more widespread, involving extensive networks of people, their expectations, norms, policies, and, perhaps, laws. Over time, Systems come to have a historical foundation and sometimes also a political and economic power structure that governs and directs the behavior of many people within its sphere of influence. Systems are the engines that run situations that create behavioral contexts that influence the human action of those under their control. At some point, the System may become an autonomous entity, independent of those who initially started it or even of those in apparent authority within its power structure. Each System comes to develop a culture of its own, as many Systems collectively come to contribute to the culture of a society.

While the Situation surely brought out the worst in many of these student volunteers, transforming some into perpetrators of evil and others into pathological victims, I was even more fully transformed by the System of domination. The others were kids, young men, without much real experience. I was a seasoned researcher, a mature adult, and a "street-smart" grown-up, still filled with my Bronx-boy acumen in sizing up situations and figuring out action-scenario to survive in the ghetto.

However, in the past week I had gradually morphed into a Prison Authority Figure. I walked and talked like one. Everyone around me responded to me as though I were one. Therefore, I became one of *them.* The very nexus of that authority figure is one that I have opposed, even detested, all my life—the high-status, authoritarian, overbearing boss man. Yet I had become that abstraction in the flesh. I could ease my conscience by noting that one of my principal activities as the good, kindly superintendent was restraining the overeager guards from committing physical violence. That restraint merely allowed them to divert their energies into more ingenious psychological abuses of the suffering prisoners.

It was surely my mistake to embrace the dual roles of researcher and superintendent because their different, sometimes conflicting, agendas created identity confusion in me. At the same time, those dual roles also compounded my power, which in turn influenced the many "outsiders" who came into our setting but did not challenge the System—parents, friends, colleagues, police, the priest, the media, and the lawyer. It is evident that one does not appreciate the power of Situations to transform one's thinking, feeling, and action when caught in its grip. A person in the claws of the System just goes along, doing what emerges as the natural way to respond at that time in that place.

If you were placed in a strange and novel cruel Situation within a powerful System, you would probably not emerge as the same person who entered that crucible of human nature. You would not recognize your familiar image if it were held next to the mirror image of what you had become. We all want to believe in our inner power, our sense of personal agency, to resist external situational forces of the kinds operating in this Stanford Prison Experiment. For some, that belief is valid. They are usually the minority, the rare birds, those who I will designate as heroic later in our journey. For many, that belief of personal power to resist powerful situational and systemic forces is little more than a reassuring illusion of invulnerability. Paradoxically, maintaining that illusion only serves to make one *more* vulnerable to manipulation by failing to be sufficiently vigilant against attempts of undesired influence subtly practiced on them.

ALL HANDS ON DECK FOR DEBRIEFING

It was evident that we had to use the short but vital debriefing time for several purposes. First, we needed to allow all the participants to express openly their emotions and reactions to this unique experience within a nonthreatening situation.[6] Next, it was important for me to make clear to both the prisoners and the guards that any extreme behavior they had displayed was diagnostic of the power of the situation and not diagnostic of any personal pathology in them. They had to be reminded that they had all been chosen precisely because they were normal and healthy to begin with. They had not brought any kind of personal defects into this prison setting; the setting had brought out the extremes in them that we all had witnessed. They were not the proverbial "bad apples"—rather, it was the "bad barrel" of the Stanford prison that was implicated in the transformations that had been demonstrated so vividly. Finally, it was crucial to use this opportunity as a time for moral reeducation. The debriefing was a means of exploring the moral choices that had been available to each of the participants and how they had dealt with them. We discussed what the guards could have done differently to be less abusive to the prisoners and what the prisoners could have done to deflect their abuse. I made it clear that I felt personally responsible for not having intervened a number of times during the study when the abuse was extreme. I had tried to contain physical aggression, but I had not acted to modify or stop the other forms of humiliation when I should have. I was guilty of the sin of omission—the evil of inaction—of not providing adequate oversight and surveillance when it was required.

The Ex-Cons Vent

The former prisoners displayed a curious mixture of relief and resentment. They were all pleased that the nightmare was finally over. Those who had survived the week did not show any overt pride in their accomplishment in the face of their peers who had been released early. They knew that at times they had been zombie-like in their mindless compliance, obeying absurd orders and totally conforming in chants against Prisoner Stewart-819, as well as engaging in hostile actions against Clay-416 and ridiculing Tom-2093, our most moral prisoner, "Sarge."

The five prisoners released early showed no negative signs of the emotional overload they had suffered. This was in part because they had a base level of stability and normality to which to return and in part because the source of their distress was centered on such an atypical setting, the basement jail, and its strange happenings. Being divested of their strange uniform and other prison attire had also helped detach them from that sordid situation. For the prisoners, the main issue was coping with the shame inherent in the submissive role they had played. They needed to establish a sense of personal dignity, to rise above the constraints of their submissive position that had been externally imposed on them.

However, Doug-8612, the first to be arrested and first to be released because of his deteriorating mental condition, was still angry with me in particular for having created a situation in which he lost control over his behavior and mind. Indeed, he had thought about leading a break-in with his friends to free the prisoners and had, in fact, come back to Jordan Hall the day after he was released to prepare for it. Fortunately, he had decided against that action for several reasons. He was amused to learn how seriously we had taken the rumor of his liberation plans and doubly pleased to learn of the lengths to which we, and especially I, had gone to safeguard our institution from his assault.

As expected, the newly freed former inmates railed against the guards, who they felt had gone far beyond the demands of their role to be creatively abusive to them or to single them out for particular abuse. Tops on their negative hit parade were Hellmann, Arnett, and Burdan, followed by Varnish and Ceros as less consistently "evil."

However, they were as quick to point out those guards whom they saw as "good guards," who had done little favors for them or who had never been so fully immersed in their role that they forgot that the prisoners were human beings. In this category, the two standouts were Geoff Landry and Markus. Geoff had done small favors for them, constantly distanced himself from the abusive actions of his night shift crewmates, and even stopped wearing his guard's sunglasses and military shirt. He even told us later that he had thought about asking to become a prisoner because he hated to be part of a system that was grinding other people down so badly.

Markus was not as obviously "wired" into the prisoners' suffering, but we learned that on a few early occasions he had brought in a gift of fresh fruit to supplement the prisoners' meager meals. After the warden had admonished him for not being sufficiently engaged during his shift, Markus, who had stayed on the sidelines during the prisoner revolt, began to yell at the prisoners and to issue scathing parole reports against them. As an aside, Markus's handwriting is quite beautiful, almost like calligraphy, so he showed it off a bit, using it to denounce the prisoners' parole requests. He is someone who loves the outdoors, hiking, camping, and yoga; therefore, he especially hated to be cooped up in our dungeon.

Between the "bad" and the "good" guards were those who had gone "by the book," done their job, played the role, and punished infractions but were rarely personally abusive toward individual prisoners. Here we find Varnish, the standby guards Morison and Peters, and, at times, the younger Landry brother. The initial aloofness and distancing himself from the Yard action that Varnish showed may in part have been due to his shyness, as revealed in his background information statement of "having few close friends."

John Landry played a vacillating role, at times as tough sidekick to Arnett and always as the one attacking rebellious prisoners with the skin-chilling, fire extinguisher carbon dioxide spray. At other times, he went by the book, and most prisoners reported that they liked him. John, a mature eighteen-year-old, was rather ruggedly handsome, and aspired to write fiction, live on a California beach, and continue dating a lot.

One mode of inaction that characterized the "good guards" was their reluctance to challenge the abusive actions of the "bad guards" on their shift. Not only did they never face up to them while on the Yard, but neither Geoff Landry nor Markus ever did so in private when they were in the guard quarters, as far as we were able to determine. Later on we will consider whether their failure to intervene as bystanders to abuse constituted an "evil of inaction."

One of the consistently rebellious prisoners, Paul-5704, reported this reaction upon discovering that the experiment was over:

> When we were notified the experiment was over, I felt a wave of relief and a wave of melancholy break inside of me at once. I was really glad the study was over, but also would have been much more happy that it lasted 2 weeks. The money is the only reason I was in the experiment. All the same, the feeling that I was glad to get out won, and I couldn't stop smiling till I got to Berkeley. Once I was there for a few hours, I forgot the whole thing and wouldn't talk to anybody about it.[7]

You will recall that this Paul was the prisoner who was proud to be the head of the Stanford County Jail Prisoners' Grievance Committee and the one who had also planned to write an exposé of the study for several alternative newspapers in Berkeley revealing how government-supported research was focused on ways in which to deal with student dissidents. His plan was totally forgotten; it never happened.

The Ex-Guards Resent

In the second hour of debriefing, the former guards presented a quite different group portrait. While a few of them, the "good guards" in the prisoner evaluations, were also glad that the ordeal was over, most were distressed to see the study terminated prematurely. Some focused on the easy money they had been anticipating for another week's work now that they had the situation clearly under their control. (They ignored the continuing problems posed by Clay-416's fast and Sarge's gaining the moral upper hand in his confrontations with Hellmann.) Some guards were ready to apologize openly for having gone too far, for fully enjoying their power. Others felt justified in what they had done, seeing their actions as necessary to fulfill the role they had been given. My main problem in dealing with the guards was to help them recognize that they should be experiencing some guilt since they had made others suffer, despite their understanding of the demands of the role they were playing. I made clear my strong guilt for failing to intervene more often, which had thereby given them implicit permission to go to the extremes they did. They might have avoided their abuses had they had better top-down surveillance.

It was easy for most guards to point to the prisoner rebellion on Day 2 as the turning point in their perception of the prisoners, who suddenly appeared to them as "dangerous" and needing to be suppressed. They also resented the negative personal references and cursing that some prisoners made to them during the rebellion, which they considered demeaning and which elicited their retaliation in kind.

A difficult element of the debriefing was allowing the guards to explain why they had done what they did, without sanctioning their justifications, for those were simply excuses for abusive, hostile, and even sadistic behavior. The end of the experiment also meant the end of enjoying having all that newfound guard power at their command. As Guard Burdan noted in his diary, "When Phil confides in me that the experiment was going to be over, I feel elated, but shocked to find some other guards disappointed somewhat because of the loss of money, but somewhat because they were enjoying themselves."[8]

A Final Mixing of the Categories

In the third hour of debriefing a lot of nervous laughter filled the laboratory room when we brought in the former prisoners to meet their captors, indistinguishable in their civilian clothes. Without their uniforms, numbers, and distinctive accessories, they were interchangeable, hard even for me to identify, having gotten so used to seeing them in their prison garb. (Remember, in 1971 there was hair everywhere, shoulder-length hair and long sideburns on most of the students in both categories, some of whom had full mustaches as well.)

The joint session was, in the words of one former prisoner, "stiffly polite," compared to the more relaxed and friendly prisoners' session. As each was scoping out the others, one prisoner asked whether some recruits had been selected to be guards because they were taller. Jerry-5486 said, "I had the feeling somewhere along the study that the guards were bigger than the prisoners, and I wonder if the average height of the guards is higher than the average height of the prisoners. I don't know if that's true or not or if that was my perception because of the uniforms." Before I answered "No," I asked all the students to line up in order of their height, from tallest to shortest. There was an almost perfect height match between the guards on one side and the prisoners on the other. What became evident is that the prisoners had come to perceive the guards as taller than they actually were, as though their guard power provided them with a two-inch shoe lift.

There were not any direct confrontations between abused prisoners and abusing guards, as I had anticipated there might be. In part, this was because such personal challenges would have been awkward in a group of more than twenty people. It is likely, however, that what remained of the strong emotions felt by some of the former prisoners had to be consciously suppressed now that the power grid had been deactivated. It also helped that a few of the guards openly apologized for submerging themselves too deeply into their role and taking it too seriously. Their apologies eased the tension and stood as proxy for the tougher guards who did not apologize openly, like Hellmann.

At this debriefing session, former Tough Guard Arnett, our sociology graduate student, recounted two events that had impressed him:

One was Zimbardo's observation of "prisoners'" immersion in their inmate roles . . . expressed by people staying inmates even when they said they'd give up their payment if they could be released [paroled]. The other impression is the seeming inability of former "prisoners" at the meeting to believe that "John Wayne" and I, and perhaps other guards (I felt that we were the two most disliked guards) had been completely acting in our roles. Some or many "prisoners" seemed to feel that we were actually sadistic or extremely authoritarian people and that our professions of acting were cover-ups, to hide the real nature of our behavior from them, or ourselves, or both. I am absolutely sure that for myself at least, this was *not* the case.[9]

One psychological observation that I offered was about the lack of humor in our prison and the failure to use humor to defuse tension or even to bring some reality to an unreal situation. For example, guards who were not pleased with the extreme behavior of their shift mates could have made a joke at their expense in guard quarters, saying that they should be getting double pay for overacting their role. Or the prisoners might have used humor to pull themselves out of the unreal basement jail by asking the guards what this place had been used for before it became a jail: a pigsty? Or a frat house, maybe? Humor breaks through the pretensions of person and place. However, in the past week there had been none to be found in this sad place.

Before we adjourned, I asked them all to be sure they had completed their final evaluations of the experience they had undergone and to complete some other forms that Curt Banks had available. I also invited them to write a short retrospective diary of the events that stood out in their memory during the following month. They would get a fee for doing so. Finally, they would all be invited back in a few weeks for a "Class of 1971" reunion to review some of the data we had gathered. A slide show and video clips would be available.

It should be added that I maintained contact with many of the participants over a number of years, all of them through correspondence whenever there was a publication or media show of the study. In addition, some of them participated in various television programs that featured our study for decades after this experience, a few even to this day. We will discuss the aftereffects of this experience on them later on.

What Does It Mean to Be a Prisoner or a Guard?

Before we turn in the next chapter to examining some of the objective data we collected over the six days of study and to reflect on the serious ethical issues raised by the experiment, I think it would be useful to review some of the insights we gathered from a selection of our participants.

On Being in the Role of Prisoner

Clay-416: "A good prisoner is one who knows how to strategically unify himself with other prisoners without getting put out of action himself. My cellmate, Jerry [5486], is a good prisoner. There are always bound to be some prisoners struggling to get out and others who are not at that point. Those who are not struggling at the time should learn to protect their interests without being a real obstacle to those who are struggling. A bad prisoner is one who cannot do this, who is only out for himself."[10]

Jerry-5486: "The most apparent thing that I noticed was how most of the people in this study derive their sense of identity and well-being from their immediate surroundings rather than from within themselves, and that's why they broke down—just couldn't stand the pressure—they had nothing within them to hold up against all of this."[11]

Paul-5704: "The way we had to degrade ourselves really brought me down and that's why we all got docile towards the end of the experiment. I gave up being a reactionary because I could see nothing was being changed by my attitude and behavior. After Stew and Rich [819 and 1037] left, I found myself thinking that I couldn't change everything that needed changing myself . . . that's another reason I settled down after they left, to accomplish what I wanted I would have needed others to work with me. I tried to talk to the other prisoners about a strike or something, but they wanted no part of it because of the punishment they had received for the first one."[12]

Guard Arnett: "I was profoundly surprised and impressed by the reactions of most of the prisoners to the experimental situation . . . particularly the individual breakdowns which did occur, and the impending ones which I feel surely would have happened had the experiment not been terminated when it was."[13]

Doug-8612: "The material conditions, like the guards, the cells, and such stuff, that didn't matter to me—like when I was nude and in chains, that never bothered me. It was the head part, the psychological part that was the worst. Knowing that I couldn't get out if I wanted . . . I didn't like not being able to go to the bathroom when I wanted to. . . . It's not having the choice that's the tearing apart thing."[14]

Substitute Prisoner Dave-"8612"—our spy, who knew that he was sent into our jail for only one day to find out about the nature of the escape plans—reveals how quickly and totally one can move into the role of prisoner: "The roles were infesting everyone from the lowliest prisoner to the warden himself." He very quickly identified himself with the prisoners, and in only a single day the simulated imprisonment had an enormous impact on Dave:

> I at times felt some guilt at being sent in to fink on these great guys—
> I was somewhat relieved that there was really nothing to tell about the
> escape. . . . And when the opportunity to fink did come up—I knew where

the handcuff key was after a while—I didn't tell. . . . I fell asleep that night feeling dirty, guilty, scared. When we were taken to the boiler room (in anticipation of the break in) I had taken off my foot cuff and seriously considered trying to escape (alone I might add) but I did not for fear of getting caught. . . . The experience of one full day as a prisoner had aroused sufficient anxiety to keep me away from the prison for the rest of the week. Even when I returned for the "debriefing" session, I was still feeling extremely anxious—I was not eating very much, felt mildly nauseous all the time, and was more nervous than I can ever remember being. The entire experience was so upsetting to me that I was unable to bring myself to discuss my experiences in depth with anyone—even my wife.[15]

I should add that we later discovered that the handcuff keys had been stolen from one of the guards by a prisoner. After the incident with the Wednesday-night transfer of all the prisoners up to the fifth-floor storage room, when they were returned to the Yard at 12:30 A.M., two of the prisoners had been cuffed together to prevent their trying to escape. Without the keys to unlock them, I had to call the Stanford Police to remove the cuffs, an embarrassment, to say the least. One of the prisoners had thrown the key into a heating vent. David knew this and never shared that information with any of the staff.

On the Power of the Guard Role

Guard Geoff Landry: "It's almost like a prison that you create yourself—you get into it, and it's just that it becomes the definitions you make of yourself, almost become walls, and you want to break out, and you want to be able to tell everyone that, 'this isn't really Me at all, and I'm a person who wants to get out and show that I'm free and I do have my own will, and I'm not the sadistic type of person that enjoys this type of thing."[16]

Guard Varnish: "This experience was worthwhile for me, absolutely. The idea that two roughly identical groups of college students each in only a week's time evolved into two totally disparate social groups with one group having and utilizing total power over the other to their detriment is chilling.

"I was surprised at myself. . . . I made them call each other names and clean out toilets with their bare hands. I practically considered the prisoners 'cattle,' and I kept thinking I have to watch out for them in case they try something."[17]

Guard Vandy: "My enjoyment in harassing and punishing prisoners was quite unnatural for me because I tend to think of myself as being sympathetic to the injured, especially animals. I think that it was an outgrowth from my total freedom to rule the prisoners, I began to abuse my authority."[18]

(An interesting carryover, or carryout, of this newfound guard power is revealed in Warden Jaffe's log. Vandy had reported to the others on his shift "that he had caught himself bossing his mother around at home.")

Guard Arnett: "Being superficially tough came easily to me. For one thing, I

am an authoritarian person in some ways (even though I strongly dislike the trait
in myself and others). Further, I felt that the experiment was important and my
being 'guard-like' was part of finding out how people react to real oppression. . . .
The main influence on my behavior was the feeling, even though vague, that real
prison is brutal in that it is dehumanizing. I tried to be that within the constraints
of my detachment and controlled commitment. . . . First, I tried to avoid ever
being personal or friendly. . . . I tried to be neutral and business like. Also, I was
aware from my readings that the boredom and other aspects of prison life can be
exploited to make people feel disoriented by being impersonal; giving boring
work; punishing all prisoners for 'bad' behavior by individuals; demanding perfect execution of trivial commands in exercise and at other times; speaking
harshly and mechanically during exercise sessions . . . within a social setting and
so very sensitive to those in control of that setting, and I tried to heighten prisoner
alienation by using some of those techniques. I could do this in only a limited way,
because I didn't want to be brutal."[19]

On Good and Bad Guards

Paul-5704: "I was pleased with John and Geoff [Landry]. They didn't really get
into the guard thing as much as the others. They always remained human beings
even when giving punishment to someone. I was surprised that the guards in general accepted their roles as much as they did after being able to go home each day
or night."[20]

   Guard John Landry: "After I talked to the other prisoners, they told me I was a
good guard and thanks for being that way. I knew inside I was a shit. Curt [Banks]
looked at me and I knew he knew. I knew also that while I was good and just to the
prisoners, I failed myself. I let cruelty happen and did nothing except feel guilty
and be a nice guy. I honestly didn't think I could do anything. I didn't even try. I
did what most people do. I sat in the guard's station and tried to forget about the
prisoners."[21]

   An even more remarkable testimony to the power of this simulated prison experience and its impact on one of the guards whom prisoners saw as the most fair
and just, Geoff Landry, the big brother of John Landry, occurred in an audio interview at the end of the study. He surprised us by indicating that he had been thinking of switching roles.

   Guard Geoff Landry: "The experience became more than just participating in
the experiment. What I mean to say is that if this was an experiment, the results
and products were almost too real. When a prisoner gives you a glassy stare, and
mumbles inaudibly, you just almost have to perceive the worst. It's almost because you fear that the worst will happen. It's almost as if I accepted it would happen, and the slightest indication of anxiety and breakdown is the beginning of
the worst possible effects. Specifically, the experience became more than just an
experiment when 1037 started acting as though he was breaking down. At this
time I was afraid and apprehensive and thought of quitting. And I also was think-

ing of asking to become a prisoner. I felt as though I didn't want to become part of the machine that beats down on other men and forces them to conform and continually harasses them. I almost wished that I was being harassed than having to be the harasser."[22]

In this context, it is interesting to note that on Wednesday night, this guard had reported to the Warden that his shirt was too tight and was irritating his skin, so he took it off. Obviously, since he had selected it, had tried it on for fit the day before we began, and had worn it for four days with no complaints, his problem was more mental than material. We arranged for him to get a larger size, which he put on reluctantly. He also kept taking off his sunglasses and not remembering where he had put them when the staff asked why he was not following standard guard protocol.

Guard Ceros: "I hated the whole fucking experiment. I walked out the door when the experiment was over. It was too real for me."[23]

On the Quiet Rage of Guard Sadism

Doug-8612, in an interview he did later for a student-directed film on our study, eloquently compared the Stanford Prison Experiment with real prisons he had come to know as a staff member working in a California prison:

"The Stanford Prison was a very benign prison situation, and it still caused the guards to become sadistic, prisoners to become hysterical, other prisoners to break out in hives. Here you have a benign situation, and it didn't work. It promoted everything a regular prison promotes. The guard role promotes sadism. The prisoner role promotes confusion and shame. Anybody can be a guard. It's harder to be on guard against the impulse to be sadistic. It's a *quiet rage*, malevolence, you can keep down but there's nowhere for it to go; it comes out sideways, sadistically. I think you do have more control as a prisoner. Everybody needs to [experience being] a prisoner. There are real prisoners I have met in jail who are people of exceptional dignity, who did not put down the guards, who were always respectful of the guards, who did not create in the guards a sadistic impulse, who could rise above the shame of the role. They knew how to preserve their dignity in that situation."[24]

On the Nature of Prisons

Clay-416: "The guards are as locked in as you are as prisoners. They just have the run of the cellblock, but they have a locked door behind them which they can't open, and so really you're all together and what you create, you create together. Prisoners have no society of their own and the guards don't have any society of their own. It's one thing and it's hideous."[25]

Guard Ceros: "[When] a prisoner reacted violently toward me, I found that I had to defend myself, not as me but as me the guard. . . . He hated me as the guard. He was reacting to the uniform. I had no choice but to defend myself as a guard. It shocked me. . . . I realized that I was just as much a prisoner as they were. I was just a reaction to their feelings. . . . We were both crushed by the oppressiveness, but we, the guards, had an illusion of freedom. That's just what it was, an illusion. . . . We all went in slaves to the money. The prisoners soon became slaves to us . . ."[26] As Bob Dylan sings in his song "George Jackson," sometimes the world seems like one big prison yard:

> Some of us are prisoners,
> The rest of us are guards.

ON CHARACTER TRANSFORMATION IN SIX DAYS

Reviewing some of the statements made before the start of the experiment and then again in our various daily records, we can see some fundamental transitions taking place in the mentality of the guards. A case in point is that of Guard Chuck Burdan, in his own words before, during, and after this experience.

Prior to the Experiment: "As I am a pacifist and non-aggressive individual, I cannot see a time when I might guard and/or maltreat other living things. I hope that I will be chosen as a prisoner rather than a guard. As an anti-establishment person continually involved in non-conforming political and social behavior, I can foresee a time when I may have to fill the role of a prisoner—and I am curious to see my capabilities in that direction."

After Guard Orientation Meeting: "Buying uniforms at the end of the meeting confirms the game-like atmosphere of this thing. I doubt whether many of us share the expectations of 'seriousness' that the experimenters seem to have. I am feeling a certain amount of relief at being only an alternate."

First Day: "My main fear at the outset of the experiment was that prisoners would see me as a real bastard, as a guard type, as all the things I am not and not the way I envision myself. . . . One of the reasons I have long hair is I don't want people to envision me in a manner that I am not. . . . Feel sure that the prisoners will make fun of my appearance and evolve my first basic strategy—mainly not to smile at anything they say or do which would be admitting it's all only a game. I stay outside the cage (while Hellmann and the tall blonde guard finish serving dinner, they seem much more self-assured in their roles than I feel). As I'm bracing myself to enter, I check my sunglasses, pick up my club—which provides a certain power and security—and walk in. I set my mouth rigidly into a semi scowl, determined to hold it there no matter what is said. At cell 3 I stop and setting my voice hard and low say to #5486, 'What are you smiling at?' 'Nothing, Mr. Correctional Officer.' 'Well see that you don't.' As I walk off I feel stupid."

Second Day: "Walking from my car I suddenly wanted people to notice my uniform, 'hey look what I'm doing'. . . . 5704 asked for a cigarette and I ignored him—because I am a non-smoker and could not empathize. . . . Meanwhile since I was feeling empathetic towards 1037, I determined NOT to talk with him. Later on, I am getting into the habit of hitting walls, chairs and bars [with Billy club] to show my power. . . . After we had Count and Lights Out [Guard Hellmann] and I held a loud conversation about going home to our girlfriends and what we were going to do to them (to irritate the prisoners)."

Third Day (Preparing for the first Visiting Night): "After warning the prisoners not to make any complaints unless they wanted the visit terminated fast, we finally brought in the first parents. I made sure I was one of the guards on the yard, because this was my first chance for the type of manipulative power that I really like—being a very noticed figure with almost complete control over what is said or not. While the parents and prisoners sat in chairs, I sat on the end of the table dangling my feet and contradicting anything I felt like. This was the first part of the experiment I was really enjoying. Prisoner 819 is being obnoxious and bears watching. . . . [Hellmann] and I both admire and dislike. As a guard (actor) he is fantastic, really getting into the sadism of the thing and this bugs me."

Fourth Day: "The psychologist [Craig Haney] rebukes me for handcuffing and blindfolding a prisoner before leaving the [counseling] office, and I resentfully reply that it is both necessary security and my business anyway. . . . At home I was having more and more trouble describing the reality of the situation."

Fifth Day: "I harass 'Sarge' who continues to stubbornly over-respond to all commands. I have singled him out for special abuse both because he begs for it and because I simply don't like him. The real trouble starts at dinner. The new prisoner [416] refuses to eat his sausages. We throw him into the Hole ordering him to hold sausages in each hand. We have a crisis of authority; this rebellious conduct potentially undermines the complete control we have over the others. We decide to play upon prisoner solidarity and tell the new one that all the others will be deprived of visitors if he does not eat his dinner. I walk by and slam my stick into the Hole door. . . . I am very angry at this prisoner for causing discomfort and trouble for the others. I decided to force feed him, but he wouldn't eat. I let the food slide down his face. I didn't believe it was me doing it. I hated myself for making him eat but I hated him more for not eating."

Sixth Day: "The experiment is over. I feel elated but am shocked to find some other guards disappointed somewhat because of the loss of money and some because they are enjoying themselves. . . . Talking during the detoxification session was very difficult; everything seems strained and uncomfortable. . . . I get on my bike and ride home through the sunshine. It feels damn good to be out of there."

Weeks later: "The absolute cruelty of this event (Hellmann's decision to leave 416 in the Hole all night) does not hit me until weeks later, but it must have hit Phil [Zimbardo] hard along with many other things at this point [that he decided to end the study].[27]

Another curious character transformation of someone only tangentially associated with our study is found among "additional anecdotes" in the Warden's Log. Recall my serious psychologist colleague who challenged me in the midst of my frantic efforts to deceive the anticipated intruders by alleging the study had been terminated. He demanded to know, "What is the independent variable?"

Jaffe's notes indicate that "Dr. B. visited on Tuesday night when the prisoners had been moved to the fifth floor closet. He and his wife went upstairs to see the prisoners. Mrs. B. passed out cupcakes, while Dr. B. made at least two comments ridiculing the prisoners, one concerning their manner of dress, and the other concerning the stench of the place. This pattern of 'getting into the act' occurred with almost every outside visitor."

While his wife gave the participants some "tea and sympathy," my usually reserved colleague unexpectedly treated these students in a dehumanized way that likely made them feel shamed.

On Hellmann's "Little Experiments"[28]

Let's look back at the Volunteer Background Form that Hellmann completed a week before the start of the experiment in order to get a sense of what he was like in his preguard status. I was amazed to learn that he was only an eighteen-year-old sophomore student, among our youngest participants. His counterpart, Arnett, was one of the oldest. Hellmann came from a middle-class academic family, the youngest sibling of four older sisters and a brother. At six feet two and 175 pounds, with green eyes and blond hair, he was an imposing figure. This young man identified himself as a musician and "a scientist at heart." His self-description indicated, "I live a natural life and love music and food and other people." He added, "I have a great love for my fellow human beings."

In response to the question "What do people like most about you?" Hellmann radiated confidence: "People at first admire me because of my talent and outgoing personality. Few know my real capabilities at human relationships."

In response to the negative version, "What do people like least about you?" Hellmann gave us an insight into this young man's complex character and a hint of what is to come when he is given absolute power. He wrote, "My impatience with stupidity, a total disregard for people whose life style I do not agree with. My exploitation of some people, my bluntness, my confidence." Finally, let's add to the mix that this volunteer said that he preferred to be assigned to the prisoner role rather than to be a guard "because people resent guards."

With that character reference in mind, it is now instructive to review his post-experiment reflections on what he perceived his role was in this study.

Guard Hellmann: "Yes it has been more than an experiment. I had a chance at testing people's capabilities, pushing them to the breaking point under the guise of a correctional officer. It was not pleasant but I felt compelled out of my own fascination to test their reactions. I was conducting experiments on my own on many occasions."[29]

"The best thing about the experiment was that I seemed to be the catalyst that brought out some startling results that gained interest from TV and the press. . . . I'm sorry if I caused more trouble than you wanted—It was an experiment of my own."[30]

"The worst thing about the experiment was that so many people took me so seriously and that I made them enemies. My words affected them, [the prisoners] seemed to lose touch with the reality of the experiment."[31]

A month after our study was terminated, this former guard was interviewed along with former prisoner Clay-416, his nemesis. They interacted as part of a TV documentary about our study on NBC's *Chronolog*, a forerunner of *60 Minutes*. It was titled, "819 Did a Bad Thing."

After Hellmann described his transformation into the guard role, Clay went on the offensive, finally being able to add to the adage of that era, "What comes around, goes around."

Hellmann: "Once you put a uniform on and are given a role, I mean, a job, saying 'Your job is to keep these people in line,' then you're certainly not the same person if you're in street clothes and in a different role. You really become that person once you put on the khaki uniform, you put on the glasses, you take the nightstick, and you act the part. That's your costume, and you have to act accordingly when you put it on."

Clay: "It harms me, I mean *harms*, I mean in the present tense, it harms me."

Hellmann: "How did it harm you? How does it harm you? Just to think that people can be like that?"

Clay: "Yeah. It let me in on some knowledge that I've never experienced firsthand. I've read about it, I've read a lot about it. But I've never experienced it first hand. I've never seen anyone turn that way. And I know that you're a *nice guy*. You know? You understand?"

Hellmann: [Smiling and shaking his head] "You don't know that."

Clay: "I do, I do know that you're a nice guy. I don't get bad—"

Hellmann: "Then why do you *hate* me?"

Clay: "Because I know what you can turn into. I know what you're willing to do if you say, 'Oh well, I'm not going to hurt anybody.' 'Oh well, it's a limited situation, or it's over in two weeks.' "

Hellmann: "Well, you in that position, what would you have done?"

Clay (slowly and carefully enunciating each word): I don't know. I can't tell you that I know what I'd do."

Hellmann: "Would you—"

Clay (now talking over Hellmann): "I don't think, I don't believe, I would have been as *inventive* as you. I don't think I would have applied as much *imagination* to what I was doing. Do you understand?"

Hellmann: "Yes, I—"

Clay [interrupting and seeming to enjoy his new sense of power]: "I think I would have been a guard, I don't think it would have been such a *masterpiece*!"

Hellmann: "I didn't see where it was really harmful. It was degrading, and that was part of my particular little experiment to see how I could, uh—"

Clay (in disbelief): "Your particular *little experiment*? Why don't you tell me about that?"

Hellmann: "I was running little experiments of my own."

Clay: "Tell me about your little experiments. I'm curious."

Hellmann: "Okay, I wanted to see just what kind of verbal abuse that people can take before they start objecting, before they start lashing back, under the circumstances. And it surprised me that no one said anything to stop me. No one said, 'Jeez, you can't say those things to me, those things are sick.' Nobody said that, they just accepted what I said. I said, 'Go tell that man to his face that he's the scum of the earth,' and they'd do it without question. They'd do push-ups without question, they'd sit in the Hole, they'd abuse each other, and here they're supposed to be together as a unit in jail, but here they're abusing each other because I requested them to and no one questioned my authority at all. And it really shocked me. [His eyes get teary.] Why didn't people say something when I started to abuse people? I started to get so profane, and still, people didn't say anything. Why?"

Why indeed?

CHAPTER TEN

The SPE's Meaning and Messages: The Alchemy of Character Transformations

We're all guinea pigs in the laboratory of God ...
Humanity is just a work in progress.

—Tennessee Williams, *Camino Real* (1953)

The Stanford Prison Experiment began as a simple demonstration of the effects that a composite of situational variables has on the behavior of individuals role-playing prisoners and guards in a simulated prison environment. For this exploratory investigation, we were not testing specific hypotheses but rather assessing the extent to which the external features of an institutional setting could override the internal dispositions of the actors in that environment. Good dispositions were pitted against a bad situation.

However, over time, this experiment has emerged as a powerful illustration of the potentially toxic impact of bad systems and bad situations in making good people behave in pathological ways that are alien to their nature. The narrative chronology of this study, which I have tried to re-create faithfully here, vividly reveals the extent to which ordinary, normal, healthy young men succumbed to, or were seduced by, the social forces inherent in that behavioral context—as were I and many of the other adults and professionals who came within its encompassing boundaries. The line between Good and Evil, once thought to be impermeable, proved instead to be quite permeable.

It is time now for us to review other evidence that we collected during the course of our research. Many quantitative sources of information shed additional light on what happened in that dark basement prison. Therefore, we must use all the available evidence to extract the meanings that have emerged from this unique experiment and to establish the ways in which humanity can be transformed by power and by powerlessness. Underlying those meanings are significant messages about the nature of human nature and the conditions that can diminish or enrich it.

SUMMING UP BEFORE DIGGING INTO THE DATA

As you have seen, our psychologically compelling prison environment elicited intense, realistic, and often pathological reactions from many of the participants. We were surprised both by the intensity of the guards' domination and the speed with which it appeared in the wake of the prisoner rebellion. As in the case of Doug-8612, we were surprised that situational pressures could overcome most of these normal, healthy young men so quickly and so extremely.

Experiencing a loss of personal identity and subjected to arbitrary continual control of their behavior, as well as being deprived of privacy and sleep, generated in them a syndrome of passivity, dependency, and depression that resembled what has been termed "learned helplessness."[1] (Learned helplessness is the experience of passive resignation and depression following recurring failure or punishment, especially when it seems arbitrary and not contingent upon one's actions.)

Half of our student prisoners had to be released early because of severe emotional and cognitive disorders, transient but intense at the time. Most of those who remained for the duration generally became mindlessly obedient to the guards' demands and seemed "zombie-like" in their listless movements while yielding to the whims of the ever-escalating guard power.

As with the rare "good guards," so too, a few prisoners were able to stand up to the guards' domination. As we have seen, Clay-416, who should have been supported for his heroic passive resistance, instead was harassed by his fellow prisoners for being a "troublemaker." They adopted the narrow dispositional perspective provided by the guards rather than generate their own metaperspective on Clay's hunger strike as emblematic of a path for their communal resistance against blind obedience to authority.

Sarge also behaved heroically at times by refusing to curse or verbally abuse a fellow prisoner when ordered to do so, but at all other times he was the model obedient prisoner. Jerry-486 emerged as our most evenly balanced prisoner; however, as he indicates in his personal reflections, he survived only by turning inward and not doing as much as he might to help the other prisoners, who could have benefited from his support.

When we began our experiment, we had a sample of individuals who did not deviate from the normal range of the general educated population on any of the dimensions we had premeasured. Those randomly assigned to the role of "prisoner" were interchangeable with those in the "guard" role. Neither group had any history of crime, emotional or physical disability, or even intellectual or social disadvantage that might typically differentiate prisoners from guards and prisoners from the rest of society.

It is by virtue of this random assignment and the comparative premeasures that I am able to assert that these young men did not import into our jail any of the pathology that subsequently emerged among them as they played either prisoners or guards. At the start of this experiment, there were no differences between the two groups; less than a week later, there were no similarities between them. It is reasonable, therefore, to conclude that the pathologies were elicited by the set of situational forces constantly impinging upon them in this prisonlike setting. Further, this Situation was sanctioned and maintained by a background System that I helped to create. I did so first when I gave the new guards their psychological orientation and then with the development of various policies and procedures that I and my staff helped to put into operation.

Neither the guards nor the prisoners could be considered "bad apples" prior to the time when they were so powerfully impacted by being embedded in a "bad barrel." The complex of features within that barrel constitute the situational forces in operation in this behavioral context—the roles, rules, norms, anonymity of person and place, dehumanizing processes, conformity pressures, group identity, and more.

WHAT DID WE LEARN FROM OUR DATA?

The around-the-clock direct observations that we made of behavioral interactions between prisoners and guards, and of special events, were supplemented by videotaped recordings (about twelve hours), concealed audiotape recordings (about thirty hours), questionnaires, self-reported individual difference personality measures, and various interviews. Some of these measures were coded for quantitative analyses, and some were correlated with outcome measures.

The data analyses present a number of problems in their interpretation: the sample size was relatively small; the recordings were selective and not comprehensive because of our limited budget and staff, and because of the strategic decision to focus on daily events of high interest (such as counts, meals, visitors, and parole hearings). In addition, the causal directions are uncertain because of the dynamic interplay among guards and prisoners within and across guard shifts. The quantitative data analysis of individual behavior is confounded by the obvious fact of the complex interactions of persons, groups, and time-based effects. In addition, unlike traditional experiments, we did not have a control group of comparable volunteers who did not undergo the experimental treatment of being a mock prisoner or mock guard but were given various pre–post assessments. We did not do so because we thought about our design as more a demonstration of a phenomenon, like Milgram's original obedience study, than as an experiment to establish causal associations. We imagined doing such control-versus-experimental group comparisons in future research if we obtained any interesting findings from this first exploratory investigation. Thus, our simple independent variable was only the main effect of the treatment of guard-versus-prisoner status.

Nevertheless, some clear patterns emerged that amplify the qualitative narrative I have presented thus far. These findings offer some interesting insights into the nature of this psychologically compelling environment and of the young men who were tested by its demands. Full details of the operational scoring of these measures and their statistical significance is available in the scientific article published in the *International Journal of Criminology and Penology*[2] and on the website www.prisonexp.org.

Personality Measures

Three kinds of measures of individual differences among the participants were administered when they came in for their pre-experiment assessment a few days prior to the start of the study. These measures were the F-Scale of authoritarianism, the Machiavellian Scale of interpersonal manipulation strategies, and the Comrey Personality Scales.

The F-Scale.[3] On this measure of rigid adherence to conventional values and a submissive, uncritical attitude toward authority, there was no statistically significant difference between the mean score of the guards (4.8) and that of the prisoners (4.4)—before they were divided into the two roles. However, a fascinating finding emerges when we compare the F-Scale scores of the five prisoners who remained for the duration of the study and the five who were released early. Those who endured the authoritarian environment of the SPE scored more than twice (mean = 7.8) as high on conventionality and authoritarianism than their early-released peers (mean = 3.2). Amazingly, when these scores are arranged in rank order from lowest to highest prisoner F-Scale values, a highly significant correlation is found with the number of days of staying in the experiment (correlation coefficient = .90). A prisoner was likely to remain longer and adjust more effectively to the authoritarian prison environment to the extent that he was high in rigidity, adherence to conventional values, and acceptance of authority—the features which characterized our prison setting. To the contrary, the prisoners who handled the pressures least well were the young men who were lowest on these F-Scale traits—which some would say are to their credit.

The Machiavellian Scale.[4] This measure, as its name implies, assesses one's endorsement of strategies for gaining effective advantage in interpersonal encounters. However, no significant differences were found between the guards' mean score (7.7) and the slightly higher mean of the prisoners (8.8), nor did this measure predict duration of the stay in prison. We expected that the skill of those high on this trait of manipulating others might be relevant in their daily interactions in this setting, but while two of the prisoners with the highest Machiavellian score were those we judged to have adjusted best to the prison, two others we evaluated as also adjusting well had the lowest Machiavellian scores.

The Comrey Personality Scales.[5] This self-report inventory consists of eight sub-scales that we used to predict dispositional variations between the guards and prisoners. These personality measures are: Trustworthiness, Orderliness, Conformity, Activity, Stability, Extroversion, Masculinity, and Empathy. On this measure, the average scores of the guards and those of the prisoners were virtually interchangeable; none even approached statistical significance. Furthermore, on every subscale, the group mean fell within the fortieth to sixtieth percentile range of the normative male population reported by Comrey. This finding bolsters the assertion that the personalities of the students in the two different groups could be defined as "normal" or "average." Craig Haney and Curt Banks did indeed do their preselection task of choosing a sample of student volunteers who were "ordinary men" well. In addition, there were no prior dispositional tendencies that could distinguish those individuals who role-played the guards from those who enacted the prisoner role.

A few interesting, though nonsignificant, differences were found between the prisoners who were released early and those who endured the full catastrophe. The "endurers" scored higher on Conformity ("acceptance of society as it is"), Extroversion, and Empathy (helpfulness, sympathy, generosity) than those who had to be released due to their extreme stress reactions.

If we examine the scores for those individual guards and prisoners that most deviated from the average of their group (by 1.5 standard deviations or more), some curious patterns appear.

First, let's look at some personality characteristics of particular prisoners. My impression of prisoner Jerry-5486 as "most together" was clearly supported by his being higher than any other prisoner on Stability, with nearly all his other scores very close to the population norm. When he does deviate from the others, it is always in a positive direction. He was also highest in Masculinity ("does not cry easily, not interested in love stories"). Stewart-819, who trashed his cell and caused grief to his cellmates who had to clean up his mess, scored lowest in Orderliness (the extent to which a person is meticulous and concerned with neatness and orderliness). Despite rules to the contrary, he did not care. Guess who scored highest on the measure of Activity (liking physical activity, hard work, and exercise)? Yes, indeed, it was Sarge-2093. Trustworthiness is the belief in the basic honesty and good intentions of others, and Clay-416 took the prize on that dimension. Finally, from the prisoner profiles, who do you suspect got the highest score on "Conformity" (a belief in law enforcement, acceptance of society as it is, and resentment of nonconformity in others)? Who reacted most strongly against Clay-416's resistance to the guards' demands? It was none other than our handsome youngster, Hubbie-7258!

Among the guards, there were only a few individual profile scores that were interesting as being "atypical" compared to their peers'. First, we see that the "good guard" John Landry, not his brother Geoff, was highest on Empathy. Guard

Varnish was lowest on Empathy and Trustworthiness but highest on concern for neatness and orderliness. He also had the highest Machiavellian score of any guard. Packaged together, that syndrome characterizes the coolly efficient, mechanical, and detached behavior he showed throughout the study.

While these findings suggest that personality measures do predict behavioral differences in some individual cases, we need to be cautious in overgeneralizing their utility in understanding individual behavior patterns in novel settings, such as this one. For example, based on all the measures we examined, Jerry-5486 was the most "supranormal" of the prisoners. However, second in line with personality inventory scores that would qualify him as "most normal" is Doug-8612. His disturbed account of acting and then becoming "crazy" was hardly predictable from his "most normal" pre-experimental status. Moreover, we could find no personality precursors for the difference between the four meanest guards and the others who were less abusive. Not a single personality predisposition could account for this extreme behavioral variation.

Now if we look at the personality scores of the two guards who were clearly the meanest and most sadistic toward prisoners, Hellmann and Arnett, both turned out to be ordinary, average on all but one of the personality dimensions. Where they diverged was on Masculinity. An intuitive personality theorist would seem justified in assuming that Hellmann, our badass "John Wayne," would top off the scale on Masculinity. Just the opposite was true: he scored lower on Masculinity than any other guard and, for that matter, lower than any prisoner did. In contrast, Arnett scored as the most masculine of all the guards. Psychodynamic analysts would most certainly assume that Hellmann's cruel, dominating behavior and his invention of homophobic exercises were motivated by a reaction formation against his nonmasculine, possibly latent-homosexual nature. However, before we wax analytically lyrical, I must hasten to add that there has been nothing in his subsequent lifestyle over the past thirty-five years that has characterized this young man as anything but appropriate and normal as a husband, father, businessman, and civic-minded citizen.

Mood Adjective Self-Reports. Twice during the study and immediately after the debriefing session, each of the students completed a checklist of adjectives that they felt best described their current mood state. We combined the mood adjectives into those that reflected negative versus positive moods and separately those that portrayed activity versus passivity. As might well be expected from all we have seen of the state of the prisoners, the prisoners expressed three times as much negative affect as positive and much more negativity overall than did the guards. The guards expressed slightly more negative than positive affect. Another interesting difference between the two groups is the greater fluctuation in the prisoners' mood states. Over the course of the study, they showed two to three times as much variation in their moods as did the relatively stable guards. On the dimension of activity-passivity, the prisoners tended to score twice as high, indicating twice as much internal "agitation" as the guards. While the prison experience had a negative emotional impact upon both guards and prisoners, the adverse effects upon the prisoners were more profound and unstable.

Comparing the prisoners who stayed to those who were released early, the mood of those who had to be terminated was marked by a decidedly more negative tone: depression and unhappiness. When the mood scales were administered for a third time, just *after* the subjects were told that the study had been terminated (the early-released subjects returned for the debriefing encounter session), elevated changes in positive moods were evident. All of the now "ex-convicts" selected self-descriptive adjectives that characterized their mood as less negative and much more positive—a decrease in negativity from the initially strong 15.0 to a low of 5.0, while their positivity soared from the initial low of 6.0 up to 17.0. In addition, they now felt less passive than before.

In general, there were no longer any differences on these mood subscales between prisoners released early and those who endured the six days. I am happy to be able to report the vital conclusion that by the end of the study both groups of students had returned to their pre-experiment baselines of normal emotional responding. This return to normality seems to reflect the "situational specificity" of the depression and stress reactions these students experienced while playing their unusual roles.

This last finding can be interpreted in several ways. The emotional impact of the prison experience was transient since the suffering prisoners quickly bounced back to a normal mood base level as soon as the study was terminated. It also speaks to the "normality" of the participants we had so carefully selected, and this bounce-back attests to their resilience. However, the same overall reaction among the prisoners could have come from very different sources. Those who remained were elated by their newfound freedom and the knowledge that they had survived the ordeal. Those who were released early were no longer emotionally distressed, having readjusted while away from the negative situation. Perhaps we can also attribute some of their newly positive reactions to gratification at seeing their fellow prisoners released, thus relieving them of the burden of guilt they may have felt for leaving early while their fellows had to stay on, enduring the ordeal.

Although some guards indicated that they wished the study had continued as planned for another week, as a group they too were glad to see it end. Their mean positivity score more than doubled (from 4.0 to 10.2), and their low negativity score (6.0) got even lower (2.0). Therefore, as a group, they also were able to regain their emotional composure and balance despite their role in creating the horrible conditions in this prison setting. This mood readjustment does not mean that some of these young men were not troubled by what they had done and by their failure to stop abuse, as we noted earlier in their postexperiment reactions and retrospective diaries.

Video Analysis. There were twenty-five relatively discrete incidents identifiable on the tapes of prisoner–guard interactions. Each incident or scene was scored for the presence of ten behavioral (and verbal) categories. Two raters, who had not been involved with the study, independently scored these tapes, and their level of agreement was satisfactory. These categories were: Asking Questions, Giving Commands, Offering Information, Using Individuating Reference (positive) or Deindividuating (negative), Making Threats, Giving Resistance, Helping Others, Using Instruments (for some goal), and Exhibiting Aggression.

As shown in the figure summarizing these results, overall there was an excess of negative, hostile interactions between the guards and prisoners. Assertive activity was largely the prerogative of the guards, while the prisoners generally assumed a relatively passive stance. Most characteristic of the guards across the

GUARD AND PRISONER BEHAVIOR[6]

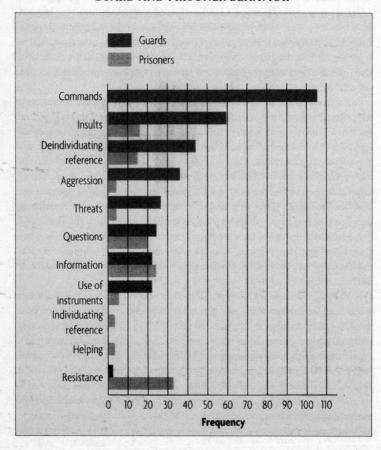

situations we recorded were the following responses: giving commands, insulting prisoners, deindividualizing prisoners, showing aggression toward prisoners, threatening, and using instruments against them.

At first, the prisoners resisted the guards, notably in the early days of the study and later, when Clay-416 went on his hunger strike. The prisoners tended to positively individuate others, asked questions of them, gave information to them, and rarely showed the negative behavior toward others that became typical of the dominating guards. Again, this occurred only in the first days of the study. On the other hand, the two most *infrequent* behaviors we observed over the six days of our study were individuating others and helping others. Only one such incident of helping was recorded—a solitary sign of human concern for a fellow human being occurred between two prisoners.

The recordings also underscore quantitatively what was observed over the course of the study: the guards continually escalated their harassment of the prisoners. If we compare two of the *first* prisoner–guard interactions during the counts with two of the *last*, we note that in an equivalent unit of time, no deindividuating references occurred initially, but a robust average of 5.4 occurred in the last counts. Similarly, the guards spoke few deprecating insults initially, only an average of 0.3, but by the last day they degraded the prisoners an average of 5.7 times in the same length of time.

According to the temporal analysis from this video data, what the prisoners did was simply to behave less and less over time. There was a general decrease across all behavioral categories over time. They did little initiating, simply becoming increasingly passive as the days and nights moved numbingly on.

The video analysis also clearly showed that the "John Wayne" night shift was hardest on the prisoners compared to the other two shifts. The behavior of the guards on this tough and cruel shift differed significantly from those that preceded and followed it in the following ways: issuing more commands (an average of 9.3 versus 4.0, respectively, for standardized units of time); giving more than twice as many deprecating insults toward the prisoners (5.2 versus 2.3, respectively). They also resorted more often to aggressively punishing the prisoners than did the guards on the other shifts. The more subtle verbal aggression in Arnett's shift is not detected in these analyses.

Audio Analysis. From time to time, audio recordings with concealed microphones were made of interviews between one of the staff with prisoners and guards, and of conversations among prisoners taking place in the cells. Nine categories were created to capture the general nature of this verbal behavior. Again, the recordings were classified into these categories by two independent judges, who did so reliably.

In addition to asking questions, giving information, making requests and demands and ordering commands, other categories focused on criticism; positive/negative outlook; positive/negative self-evaluation; individuating/deindividuating references; desire to continue in the study or abort; and intention to act in the future in positive or negative ways.

We were surprised to discover that the guards tended to have nearly as much negative outlook and negative self-regard as did most of the prisoners. In fact, the "good guard" Geoff Landry expressed more negative self-regard than did any prisoner and more general negative affect than all but one participant, namely Doug-8612. Our interviews with prisoners were marked by their general negativity in expressing affect and in their self-regard and intentions (primarily intention to be aggressive and having a negative outlook on their situation).

These interviews showed clear differences in the emotional impact of the experience between the prisoners who remained and those who were released early. We compared the mean number of expressions of negative outlook, negative affect, negative self-regard, and intention to aggress that were made by remaining versus released prisoners (per interview). Prisoners released early expressed expectations that were more negative and had more negative affect, more negative self-regard, and four times as many intentions to aggress as did their fellow prisoners who stuck it out. These interesting trends are close to being statistically significant.

Bugging the cells gave us information about what the prisoners were discussing in private during temporary respites from the counts, the menial work tasks, and other public events. Remember that the three inmates in each cell were initially total strangers. It was only when they were alone in the solitude of their cells that they could get to know one another since no "small talk" was allowed at public times. We assumed that they would seek common ground for relating to one another, given their close quarters and their expectation of interacting for two weeks. We expected to hear them talk about their college lives, majors, vocations, girlfriends, favorite teams, music preferences, hobbies, what they would do for the remainder of the summer once the experiment was over, or maybe what they would do with the money they would earn.

Not at all! Almost none of these expectations were borne out. Fully 90 percent of all conversations among prisoners related to prison issues. Only a mere 10 percent focused on personal or autobiographical exchanges that were not related to the prison experience. The prisoners were most concerned about food, guard harassment, establishing a grievance committee, forging plans of escape, visitors, and the behavior of prisoners in the other cells and those in solitary.

When they had the opportunity to distance themselves temporarily from the harassment by guards and the tedium of their schedules, to transcend the prisoner role and establish their personal identity in a social interaction, they did not do so. The prisoner role dominated all expressions of individual character. The prison setting dominated their outlook and concerns—forcing them into an expanded present temporal orientation. It did not matter whether the presentation of self was under surveillance or free from its glare.

By not sharing their pasts and future expectations, the only thing each prisoner knew about the other prisoners was based on observations of how they were behaving in the present. We know that what they had to see during counts and other menial activities was usually a negative image of one another. That image was all they had upon which to build a personality impression of their peers. Because they focused on the immediate situation, the prisoners also contributed to fostering a mentality that intensified the negativity of their experiences. Generally, we manage to cope with bad situations by compartmentalizing them into a temporal perspective that imagines a better, different future combined with recall of a reassuring past.

This self-imposed intensification of prisoner mentality had an even more damaging consequence: the prisoners began to adopt and accept the negative images that the guards had developed toward them. Half of all reported private interactions between the prisoners could be classified as nonsupportive and noncooperative. Even worse, whenever the prisoners made evaluative statements of, or expressed regard for, their fellow prisoners, 85 percent of the time they were uncomplimentary and deprecating! These frequencies are statistically significant: the greater focus on prison than nonprison topics would occur only one time in a hundred by chance, while the focus on negative attributions of fellow prisoners as opposed to positive or neutral terms would occur by chance only five times in a hundred. This means that such emerging behavioral effects are "real" and not likely to be attributed to random fluctuations in what the prisoners discussed in the privacy of their cells.

By internalizing the oppressiveness of the prison setting in these ways, the prisoners formed impressions of their mates primarily by watching them be humiliated, act like compliant sheep, or carry out mindlessly degrading orders. Without developing any respect for the others, how could they come to have any self-respect in this prison? This last unexpected finding reminds me of the phenomenon of "identification with the aggressor." The psychologist Bruno Bettelheim[7] used this term to characterize ways in which Nazi concentration camp prisoners internalized the power that was inherent in their oppressors (it was first used by Anna Freud). Bettelheim observed that some inmates acted like their Nazi guards, not only abusing other prisoners but even wearing bits of cast-off SS uniforms. Desperately hoping to survive a hostile, unpredictable existence, the victim senses what the aggressor wants and rather than opposing him, embraces his image and becomes what the aggressor is. The frightening power differential between powerful guards and powerless prisoners is psychologically minimized by such mental gymnastics. One becomes one with one's enemy—in one's own mind. This self-delusion prevents realistic appraisals of one's situation, inhibits effective action, coping strategies, or rebellion, and does not permit empathy for one's fellow sufferers.[8]

> Life is the art of being well-deceived; and in order that the
> deception may succeed it must be habitual and uninterrupted.

—William Hazlitt, "On Pedantry," *The Round Table*, 1817

THE SPE'S LESSONS AND MESSAGES

It is time to move from the specific behavioral reactions and personal attributes of these young men who enacted the roles of prisoners and guards to consider some broader conceptual issues raised by this research and its lessons, meaning, and messages.

The Virtue of Science

From one perspective, the SPE does not tell us anything about prisons that sociologists, criminologists, and the narratives of prisoners have not already revealed about the evils of prison life. Prisons can be brutalizing places that invoke what is worst in human nature. They breed more violence and crime than they foster constructive rehabilitation. Recidivism rates of 60 percent and higher indicate that prisons have become revolving doors for those sentenced for criminal felonies. What does the SPE add to our understanding of *society's failed experiment* of prisons as its instruments of crime control? I think the answer lies in the experiment's basic protocol.

In real prisons, defects of the prison situation and those of the people who inhabit it are confounded, inextricably intertwined. Recall my first discussion with the sergeant in the Palo Alto police station wherein I explained the reason we were conducting this research rather than going to a local prison to observe what was going on. This experiment was designed to assess the impact of a simulated prison situation on those who lived in it, both guards and prisoners. By means of various experimental controls, we were able to do a number of things, and draw conclusions, that would not have been possible in real-world settings.

Systematic selection procedures ensured that everyone going into our prison was as normal, average, and healthy as possible and had no prior history of antisocial behavior, crime, or violence. Moreover, because they were college students, they were generally above average in intelligence, lower in prejudice, and more confident about their futures than their less educated peers. Then, by virtue of random assignment, the key to experimental research, these good people were randomly assigned to the role of guard or prisoner, regardless of whatever inclination they might have had to be the other. Chance ruled. Further experimental control involved systematic observation, collection of multiple forms of evidence, and statistical data analyses that together could be used to determine the impact of the experience within the parameters of the research design. The SPE protocol disentangled person from place, disposition from situation, "good apples" from "bad barrels."

We must acknowledge, however, that all research is "artificial," being only an imitation of its real-world analogue. Nevertheless, despite the artificiality of controlled experimental research like the SPE, or that of the social psychological studies we will encounter in later chapters, when such research is conducted in sensitive ways that capture essential features of "mundane realism," the results can have considerable generalizability.[9]

Our prison was obviously not a "real prison" in many of its tangible features, but it did capture the central psychological features of imprisonment that I believe are central to the "prison experience." To be sure, any finding derived from an experiment must raise two questions. First, "Compared to what?" Next, "What is its external validity—the real-world parallels that it may help to explain?" The value of such research typically lies in its ability to illuminate underlying processes, identify causal sequences, and establish the variables that mediate an observed effect. Moreover, experiments can establish causal relationships that if statistically significant cannot be dismissed as chance connections.

The pioneering theorist-researcher in social psychology Kurt Lewin argued decades ago for a science of experimental social psychology. Lewin asserted that it is possible to abstract significant issues from the real world conceptually and practically and test them in the experimental laboratory. With well-designed studies and carefully executed manipulations of independent variables (the antecedent factors used as behavioral predictors), he thought, it was possible to establish certain causal relationships in ways that were not possible in field or observational studies. However, Lewin went further to advocate using that knowledge to effect social change, using research-based evidence to understand as well as attempt to change and improve society and human functioning.[10] I have tried to follow his inspiring lead.

Guard Power Transformations

> Our sense of power is more vivid when we break a man's spirit than when we win his heart.
>
> —Eric Hoffer, *The Passionate State of Mind* (1954)

Some of our volunteers who were randomly assigned to be guards soon came to abuse their newfound power by behaving sadistically—demeaning, degrading, and hurting the "prisoners" day in and night out. Their actions fit the psychological definition of evil proposed in chapter 1. Other guards played their role in tough, demanding ways that were not particularly abusive, but they showed little sympathy for the plight of the suffering inmates. A few guards, who could be classified as "good guards," resisted the temptation of power and were at times considerate of the prisoners' condition, doing little things like giving one an apple, another a cigarette, and so on.

Although vastly different from the SPE in the extent of its horror and complexity of the system that spawned and sustained it, there is one interesting parallel between the Nazi SS doctors involved in the death camp at Auschwitz and our SPE guards. Like our guards, those doctors could be categorized as falling into three groups. According to Robert Jay Lifton in *Nazi Doctors*, there were "zealots who participated eagerly in the extermination process and even did 'extra work' on behalf of killing; those who went about the process more or less methodically and did no more or no less than they felt that they had to do; and those who participated in the extermination process only reluctantly."[11]

In our study, being a good guard who did his job reluctantly meant "goodness by default." Doing minor nice deeds for the prisoners simply contrasted with the demonic actions of their shift mates. As noted previously, none of them ever intervened to prevent the "bad guards" from abusing the prisoners; none complained to the staff, left their shift early or came to work late, or refused to work overtime in emergencies. Moreover, none of them even demanded overtime pay for doing tasks they may have found distasteful. They were part of the "Evil of Inaction Syndrome," which will be discussed more fully later.

Recall that the best good guard, Geoff Landry, shared the night shift with the worst guard, Hellmann, and he never once made any attempt to get him to "chill out," never reminded him that this was "just an experiment," that there was no need to inflict so much suffering on the kids who were just role-playing prisoners. Instead, as we have seen from his personal accounts, Geoff simply suffered in silence—along with the prisoners. Had he energized his conscience into constructive action, this good guard might have had a significant impact in mitigating the escalating abuse of the prisoners on his shift.

In my many years of experience teaching at a variety of universities, I have found that most students are not concerned with power issues because they have enough to get by in their world, where intelligence and hard work get them to their goals. Power is a concern when people either have a lot of it and need to maintain it or when they have not much power and want to get more. However, power itself becomes a goal for many because of all the resources at the disposal of the powerful. The former statesman Henry Kissinger described this lure as "the aphrodisiac of power." That lure attracts beautiful young women to ugly, old, but powerful men.

Prisoner Pathologies

> Wherever anyone is against his will, that is to him a prison.
>
> —Epictetus, *Discourses*, second century A.D.

Our initial interest was not so much in the guards as in how those assigned the prisoner role would adapt to their new lowly, powerless status. Having spent the summer enmeshed in the psychology of imprisonment course I had just co-taught at Stanford, I was primed to be on their side. Carlo Prescott had filled us with vivid tales of abuse and degradation at the hands of guards. From other former prisoners, we heard firsthand the horror stories of prisoners sexually abusing other prisoners and gang wars. Thus, Craig, Curt, and I were privately pulling for the prisoners, hoping that they would resist any pressures the guards could muster against them and maintain their personal dignity despite the external signs of inferiority they were forced to wear. I could imagine myself a Paul Newman kind of wisely resistant prisoner, as portrayed in the movie *Cool Hand Luke*. I could never imagine myself as his jailor.[12]

We were pleased when the prisoners rebelled so soon, challenging the hassling of the menial tasks the guards assigned them, the arbitrary enforcement of rules, and the exhausting count lineups. Their expectations about what they would be doing in the "study of prison life" to which our newspaper ad had recruited them had been violated. They had anticipated a little menial labor for a few hours mixed with time to read, relax, play some games, and meet new people. That, in fact, was what our preliminary agenda called for—before the prisoners' rebellion and before the guards took control of matters. We had even planned to have movie nights for them.

The prisoners were particularly upset by the constant abuse rained on them day and night, the lack of privacy and relief from staff surveillance, the arbitrary enforcement of rules and random punishments, and being forced to share their barren, cramped quarters. When the guards turned to us for help after the rebellion started, we backed off and made it clear that their decisions would prevail. We were observers who did not want to intrude. I was not yet fully submerged in the superintendent's mentality at that early stage; rather, I was acting as the principal investigator, interested in data on how these mock guards would react to this emergency.

The breakdown of Doug-8612, coming so soon after he had helped to engineer a rebellion, caught us all off guard, if you will excuse the pun. We were all shaken by his shrill voice screaming opposition to everything that was wrong in the way the prisoners were being treated. Even when he shouted, "It's a fucking simulation, not a prison, and fuck Dr. *Zimbargo*!" I could not help but admire his spunk. We could not bring ourselves to believe that he was really suffering as much as he seemed to be. Recall my conversation with him when he first wanted to be released and I invited him to consider the option of becoming a "snitch" in return for a hassle-free time as a prisoner.

Recall further that Craig Haney had made the difficult decision to deal with Doug-8612's sudden breakdown by releasing him after only thirty-six hours into the experiment.

> As experimenters, none of us had predicted an event like this, and, of course, we had devised no contingency plan to cover it. On the other hand, it was obvious that this young man was more disturbed by his brief experience in the Stanford Prison than any of us had expected. . . . So, I decided to release Prisoner 8612, going with the ethical, humanitarian decision over the experimental one.

How did we explain this violation of our expectations that no one could have such a severe stress reaction so quickly? Craig remembers our wrong-headed causal attribution:

> We quickly seized on an explanation that felt as natural as it was reassuring—he must have broken down because he was weak or had some kind of defect in his personality that accounted for his oversensitivity and overreaction to the simulated prison conditions! In fact, we worried that there had been a flaw in our screening process that had allowed a "damaged" person somehow to slip through undetected. It was only later that we appreciated this obvious irony: we had "dispositionally explained" the first truly unexpected and extraordinary demonstration of situational power in our study by resorting to precisely the kind of thinking we had designed the study to challenge and critique.[13]

Let's go back and review the final reactions to this experience by Doug-8612 to appreciate his level of confusion at that time:

"I decided I want out, and then I went to talk to you guys and everything, and you said 'No' and you bullshitted me and everything, and I came back and I realized you were bullshitting me, and that made me mad, so I decided I'm getting out and I was going to do anything, and I made up several schemes whereby I could get out. The easiest one and that wouldn't hurt anybody or hurt any equipment was to just act mad or upset, so I chose that one. When I was in the Hole, I purposely kind of built it up and I knew that when I went to talk with Jaffe, I didn't want to release the energy in the Hole, I wanted to release in front of Jaffe, so I knew I'd get out, and then, even while I was being upset, I was manipulating and I was being upset, you know—how could you act upset unless you *were* upset . . . it's like a crazy person can't act crazy unless he really is kinda crazy, you know? I don't know whether I was upset or whether I was induced. . . . I was mad at the black guy, and what was his name, Carter? Something like that and you, Dr. Zimbardo, for making the contract like I was a serf or something . . . and the way you played with me afterwards, but what can you do, you had to do that, your people had to do it in an experiment."[14]

WHY SITUATIONS MATTER

Within certain powerful social settings, human nature can be transformed in ways as dramatic as the chemical transformation in Robert Louis Stevenson's captivating fable of Dr. Jekyll and Mr. Hyde. The enduring interest in the SPE over many decades comes, I think, from the experiment's startling revelation of "transformation of character"—of good people suddenly becoming perpetrators of evil as guards or pathologically passive victims as prisoners in response to situational forces acting on them.

Good people can be induced, seduced, and initiated into behaving in evil ways. They can also be led to act in irrational, stupid, self-destructive, antisocial, and mindless ways when they are immersed in "total situations" that impact human nature in ways that challenge our sense of the stability and consistency of individual personality, of character, and of morality.[15]

We want to believe in the essential, unchanging goodness of people, in their power to resist external pressures, in their rational appraisal and then rejection of situational temptations. We invest human nature with God-like qualities, with moral and rational faculties that make us both just and wise. We simplify the complexity of human experience by erecting a seemingly impermeable boundary between Good and Evil. On one side are Us, Our Kin, and Our Kind; on the other side of that line we cast Them, Their Different Kin, and Other Kind. Paradoxically, by creating this myth of our invulnerability to situational forces, we set ourselves up for a fall by not being sufficiently vigilant to situational forces.

The SPE, along with much other social science research (presented in chapters 12 and 13), reveals a message we do not want to accept: that most of us can undergo significant character transformations when we are caught up in the crucible of social forces. What we imagine we would do when we are outside that crucible may bear little resemblance to who we become and what we are capable of doing once we are inside its network. The SPE is a clarion call to abandon simplistic notions of the Good Self dominating Bad Situations. We are best able to avoid, prevent, challenge, and change such negative situational forces only by recognizing their potential power to "infect us," as it has others who were similarly situated. It is well for us to internalize the significance of the recognition by the ancient Roman comedy writer Terence that "Nothing by humans is alien to me."

This lesson should have been taught repeatedly by the behavioral transformation of Nazi concentration camp guards, and of those in destructive cults, such as Jim Jones's Peoples Temple, and more recently by the Japanese Aum Shinrikyo cult. The genocide and atrocities committed in Bosnia, Kosovo, Rwanda, Burundi, and recently in Sudan's Darfur region also provide strong evidence of people surrendering their humanity and compassion to social power and abstract ideologies of conquest and national security.

Any deed that any human being has ever committed, however horrible, is possible for any of us—under the right or wrong situational circumstances. That knowledge does not excuse evil; rather, it democratizes it, sharing its blame among ordinary actors rather than declaring it the province only of deviants and despots—of Them but not Us.

The primary simple lesson the Stanford Prison Experiment teaches is that *situations matter.* Social situations can have more profound effects on the behavior and mental functioning of individuals, groups, and national leaders than we might believe possible. Some situations can exert such powerful influence over us that we can be led to behave in ways we would not, could not, predict was possible in advance.[16]

Situational power is most salient in novel settings, those in which people cannot call on previous guidelines for their new behavioral options. In such situations the usual reward structures are different and expectations are violated. Under such circumstances, personality variables have little predictive utility because they depend on estimations of imagined future actions based on characteristic past reactions in familiar situations—but rarely in the kind of new situation currently being encountered, say by a new guard or prisoner.

Therefore, whenever we are trying to understand the cause of any puzzling, unusual behavior, our own or that of others, we should start out with a situational analysis. We should yield to dispositional analyses (genes, personality traits, personal pathologies, and so on) only when the situationally based detective work fails to make sense of the puzzle. My colleague Lee Ross adds that such an approach invites us to practice "attributional charity." That means we start not by blaming the actor for the deed but rather, being charitable, we first investigate the scene for situational determinants of the act.

However, attributional charity is easier said than practiced because most of us have a powerful mental bias—the "fundamental attribution error"—that prevents such reasonable thinking.[17] Societies that promote individualism, such as the United States and many other Western nations, have come to believe that dispositions matter more than situations. We overemphasize personality in explaining any behavior while concurrently underemphasizing situational influences. After reading this book, I hope you will begin to notice how often you see this dual principle in action in your own thinking and in decisions of others. Let's consider next some of the features that make situations matter, as illustrated in our prison study.

The Power of Rules to Shape Reality

Situational forces in the SPE combined a number of factors, none of which was very dramatic alone but that together were powerful in their aggregation. One of the key features was the power of rules. Rules are formal, simplified ways of controlling informal complex behavior. They work by externalizing regulations, by establishing what is necessary, acceptable, and rewarded and what is unacceptable and therefore punished. Over time, rules come to have an arbitrary life of their own and the force of legal authority even when they are no longer relevant, are vague, or change with the whims of the enforcers.

Our guards could justify most of the harm they did to the prisoners by referencing "the Rules." Recall, for example, the agony the prisoners had to endure to memorize the set of seventeen arbitrary rules that the guards and the warden had invented. Consider also the misuse of Rule 2 about eating at mealtimes to punish Clay-416 for refusing to eat his filthy sausages.

Some rules are essential for the effective coordination of social behavior, such as audiences listening while performers speak, drivers stopping at red traffic lights, and people not cutting into queues. However, many rules are merely screens for dominance by those who make them or those charged with enforcing them. Naturally, the last rule, as with the SPE rules, always includes punishment for violation of the other rules. Therefore, there must be someone or some agency willing and able to administer such punishment, ideally doing so in a public arena that can serve to deter other potential rule breakers. The comedian Lenny Bruce had a funny routine describing the development of rules to govern who could and could not throw shit over fences onto a neighbor's property. He described the creation of police as guardians of the "no-shit-in-my-backyard" rule. The rules and their enforcers are inherent in situational power. However, it is the System that hires the police and creates the prisons for convicted rule breakers.

When Roles Become Real

> Once you put a uniform on, and are given a role, I mean, a job, saying "your job is to keep these people in line," then you're certainly not the same person if you're in street clothes and in a different role. You really become that person once you put on the khaki uniform, you put on the glasses, you take the nightstick, and you act the part. That's your costume and you have to act accordingly when you put it on.

—Guard Hellmann

When actors enact a fictional character, they often have to take on roles that are dissimilar to their sense of personal identity. They learn to talk, walk, eat, and even to think and to feel as demanded by the role they are performing. Their professional training enables them to maintain the separation of character and identity, to keep self in the background while playing a role that might be dramatically different from who they really are. However, there are times when even for some trained professionals those boundaries blur and the role takes over even after the curtain comes down or the camera's red light goes off. They become absorbed in the intensity of the role and their intensity spills over to direct their offstage life. The play's audience ceases to matter because the role is now within the actor's mind.

A fascinating example of this effect of a dramatic role becoming a "tad too real" comes from the British television series *The Edwardian Country House*. Nineteen people, chosen from some eight thousand applicants, lived the lives of British servants working on a posh country estate in this "reality television" drama. Although the person chosen to play the head butler in charge of the staff expected to follow the period's rigidly hierarchical standards of behavior, he was "frightened" by the ease with which he became an autocratic master. This sixty-five-year-old architect was not prepared to slip so readily into a role that allowed him to exercise absolute power over a household of underservants whom he bossed: "Suddenly you realize that you don't have to speak. All I had to do was lift my finger up and they would keep quiet. And that is a frightening thought—it's appalling." A young woman who played the role of a housemaid but who in real life is a tourist information officer, began to feel like an invisible person. She described how she and the others so quickly adapted to their subservient role: "I was surprised, then scared at the way we all became squashed. We learned so quickly that you don't answer back, and you feel subservient."[18]

Typically, roles are tied to specific situations, jobs, and functions, such as being a professor, doorman, cab driver, minister, social worker, or porn actor. They are enacted when one is in that situation—at home, school, church, or factory, or onstage. Roles can usually be set aside when one returns to his or her "normal" other life. Yet some roles are insidious, are not just scripts that we enact only from time to time; they can become who we are most of the time. They are internalized even as we initially acknowledge them as artificial, temporary, and situationally bound. We become father, mother, son, daughter, neighbor, boss, worker, helper, healer, whore, soldier, beggar man, thief, and many more.

To complicate matters further, we all must play multiple roles, some conflicting, some that may challenge our basic values and beliefs. As in the SPE, what starts out as the "just playing a role" caveat to distinguish it from the real individual can have a profound impact when the role behavior gets rewarded. The "class clown" gets attention he can't get from displaying special academic talents but then is never again taken seriously. Even shyness can be a role initially enacted to avoid awkward social encounters, a situational awkwardness, and when practiced enough the role morphs into a shy person.

Just as discomfiting, people can do terrible things when they allow the role they play to have rigid boundaries that circumscribe what is appropriate, expected, and reinforced in a given setting. Such rigidity in the role shuts off the traditional morality and values that govern their lives when they are in "normal mode." The ego-defense mechanism of *compartmentalization* allows us to mentally bind conflicting aspects of our beliefs and experiences into separate chambers that prevent interpretation or cross talk. A good husband can then be a guiltless adulterer; a saintly priest can then be a lifelong pederast; a kindly farmer can then be a heartless slave master. We need to appreciate the power that role-playing can have in shaping our perspectives, for better as well as for worse, as when adopting the teacher or nurse role translates into a life of sacrifice for the good of one's students and patients.

Role Transitions from Healer to Killer

The worst-case scenario was the Nazi SS doctors who were assigned the role of selecting concentration camp inmates for extermination or for "experiments." They were socialized away from their usual healing role into the new role, assisting with killing, by means of a group consensus that their behavior was necessary for the common good, which led them to adopt several extreme psychological defenses against facing the reality of their complicity in the mass murder of Jews. Again we turn to the detailed account of these processes by social psychiatrist Robert Jay Lifton.

When a new doctor would come on the scene and be initially horrified by what he witnessed, he would ask:

> "How can these things be done here?" Then there was something like a general answer . . . which clarified everything. What is better for him [the prisoner]—whether he croaks [*verreckt*] in shit or goes to heaven in [a cloud of] gas? And that settled the whole matter for the initiates [*Eingeweihten*].
>
> Mass killing was the unyielding *fact of life* to which everyone was expected to adapt.

Framing the genocide of the Jews as the "Final Solution" (*Endlösung*) served a dual psychological purpose: "it stood for mass murder without sounding or feeling like it; and it kept the focus primarily on problem solving." It transformed the whole matter into a difficult problem that had to be solved by whatever means were necessary to achieve a pragmatic goal. The intellectual exercise deleted emotions and compassion from the doctor's daily rounds.

However, their job in selecting inmates for annihilation was both so "onerous, so associated with extraordinary evil" that these highly educated doctors had to utilize every possible psychological defense against avoiding the reality of their complicity in these murders. For some, "psychic numbing," detaching affect from cognition, became the norm; for others there was a schizophrenic solution of "doubling." The polarities of cruelty and decency in the same doctor at different times would "call forth two radically different psychological constellations within the self: one based on 'values generally accepted' and the education and background of a 'normal person'; the other based on 'this [Nazi-Auschwitz] ideology with values quite different from those generally accepted.' " These twin tendencies shifted back and forth from day to day.[19]

Reciprocal Roles and Their Scripts

It is also the case that some roles require reciprocal partnerships; for the guard role to have meaning, somebody has to play prisoner. One can't be a prisoner unless someone is willing to be the guard. In the SPE, no explicit training was required for the performance of roles, no manual of best practices. Recall on Day 1 the awkwardness of the guards and the prisoners' frivolity as each were feeling out their new strange roles. However, very soon, our participants were able to slip easily into their roles as the nature of the power differential at the base of the guard–prisoner symbiosis became clearer.

The initial script for guard or prisoner role-playing came from the participants' own experiences with power and powerlessness, of their observation of interactions between parents (traditionally, Dad is guard, Mom the prisoner), of their responses to the authority of doctors, teachers, and bosses, and finally from the cultural inscriptions written upon them by movie accounts of prison life. Society had done the training for us. We had only to record the extent of their improvisation with the roles they played—as our data.

There is abundant evidence that virtually all of our participants at one time or another experienced reactions that went well beyond the surface demands of role-playing and penetrated the deep structure of the psychology of imprisonment. Initially, some of the guards' reactions were probably influenced by their orientation, which outlined the kind of atmosphere we wished to create in order to simulate the reality of imprisonment. But whatever general demands those stage settings may have outlined for them to be "good actors," they should not have been operative when the guards were in private or believed that we were not observing them.

Postexperimental reports told us that some guards had been especially brutal when they were alone with a prisoner on a toilet run outside the Yard, pushing him into a urinal or against a wall. The most sadistic behaviors we observed took place during the late-night and early-morning shifts, when, as we learned, the guards didn't believe that we were observing or recording them, in a sense, when the experiment was "off." In addition, we have seen that guard abuse of prisoners escalated to new, higher levels each day despite the prisoners' nonresistance and the obvious signs of their deterioration as the full catastrophe of imprisonment was achieved. In one taped interview, a guard laughingly recalled apologizing for having pushed a prisoner on the first day, but by Day 4, he thought nothing of shoving them around and humiliating them.

Craig Haney's discerning analysis reveals the transformation in the power infusing the guards. Consider this encounter with one of them that took place after only a few days into the study:

> Just as with the prisoners, I also had interviewed all of [the guards] before the experiment began and felt I had gotten to know them as individuals, albeit only briefly. Perhaps because of this, I really felt no hostility toward them as the study proceeded and their behavior became increasingly extreme and abusive. But it was obvious to me that because I insisted on talking privately with the prisoners—ostensibly "counseling" them, and occasionally instructed the guards to refrain from their especially harsh and gratuitous mistreatment, they now saw me as something of a traitor. Thus, describing an interaction with me, one of the guards wrote in his diary: "The psychologist rebukes me for handcuffing and blindfolding a prisoner before leaving the (counseling) office, and I resentfully reply that

it is both necessary (for) security and my business anyway." Indeed, he had told me off. In a bizarre turn of events, I was put in my place for failing to uphold the emerging norms of a simulated environment I had helped to create by someone whom I had randomly assigned to his role.[20]

In considering the possible biasing of the guard orientation, we are reminded that the prisoners had no orientation at all. What did they do when they were in private and could escape the oppression they repeatedly experienced on the Yard? Rather than getting to know one another and discussing nonprison realities, we learned that they obsessed about the vicissitudes of their current situation. They embellished their prisoner role rather than distancing from it. So, too, with our guards: information we gathered about them when they were in their quarters preparing to enter or leave a shift reveals that they rarely exchanged personal, nonprison information. Instead, they talked about "problem prisoners," upcoming prison issues, reactions to our staff—never the usual guy stuff that college students might have been expected to share during a break. They did not tell jokes, laugh, or reveal any personal emotion to their peers, which they easily could have done to lighten the situation or distance themselves from the role. Recall Christina Maslach's earlier description of the transformation of the sweet, sensitive young man she had just met into the brutish John Wayne once he was in uniform and in his power spot on the Yard.

Adult Role-Playing in the SPE

I want to add two final points about the power of roles and the use of roles to justify transgression before moving to our final lessons. Let's go beyond the roles our volunteers played to recall the roles played to the hilt by the visiting Catholic priest, the head of our Parole Board, the public defender, and the parents on Visiting Nights. The parents not only accepted our show of the prison situation as benign and interesting rather than hostile and destructive, but they allowed us to impose a set of arbitrary rules on them, as we had done to their children, to constrain their behavior. We counted on their playing the embedded roles of conforming, law-abiding, middle-class citizens who respect authority and rarely challenge the system directly. Similarly, we knew that our middle-class prisoners were unlikely to jump the guards directly even when they were desperate and outnumbered them by as much as nine to two, when a guard was off the Yard. Such violence was not part of their learned role behavior, as it might have been with lower-class participants, who would be more likely to take matters into their own hands. There was not even evidence that the prisoners even fantasized such physical attacks.

The reality of any role depends on the support system that demands it and keeps it in bounds, not allowing alternate reality to intrude. Recall that when the mother of Prisoner Rich-1037 complained about his sad state, I spontaneously activated my Institutional Authority role and challenged her observation, imply-ing that there must have been a personal problem with 1037, not an operational problem with our prison.

In retrospect, my role transformation from usually compassionate teacher to data-focused researcher to callous prison superintendent was most distressing. I did improper or bizarre things in that new, strange role, such as undercutting this mother's justified complaints and becoming agitated when the Palo Alto police of-ficer refused my request to move our prisoners to the city jail. I think that because I so fully adopted the role it helped to make the prison "work" as well as it did. However, by adopting that role, with its focus on the security and maintenance of "my prison," I failed to appreciate the need to terminate the experiment as soon as the second prisoner went over the edge.

Roles and Responsibility for Transgressions

To the extent that we can both live in the skin of a role and yet be able to separate ourselves from it when necessary, we are in a position to "explain away" our per-sonal responsibility for the damage we cause by our role-based actions. We abdi-cate responsibility for our actions, blaming them on that role, which we convince ourselves is alien to our usual nature. This is an interesting variant of the Nurem-berg Trial defense of the Nazi SS leaders: "I was only following orders." Instead the defense becomes "Don't blame me, I was only playing my role at that time in that place—that isn't the real me."

Remember Hellmann's justification for his abusive behavior toward Clay-416 that he described in their television interview. He argued that he had been conducting "little experiments of my own" to see how far he could push the pris-oners so that they might rebel and stand up for their rights. In effect, he was proposing that he had been mean to stimulate them to be good; their rebellion would be his primary reward for being so cruel. Where is the fallacy in this post hoc justification? It can be readily exposed in how he handled the sausage rebel-lion by Clay-416 and Sarge's "bastard" rebellion; not with admiration for their standing up for rights or principles but rather with rage and more extreme abuse. Here Guard Hellmann was using the full power of being the ultimate guard, able to go beyond the demands of the situation to create his own "little experiment" to satisfy his personal curiosity and amusement.

In a recent interview with a reporter from the *Los Angeles Times* on a retro-spective investigation of the aftermath of the SPE, Hellmann and Doug-8612 both offered the same reasoning for why they acted as they did, the one being "cruel," the other "crazy"—they were merely *acting* those roles to please Zim-bardo.[21] Could be? Maybe they were acting new parts in the Japanese movie *Roshomon*, where everyone has a different view of what really happened.

Anonymity and Deindividuation

In addition to the power of rules and roles, situational forces mount in power with the introduction of uniforms, costumes, and masks, all disguises of one's usual appearance that promote anonymity and reduce personal accountability. When people feel anonymous in a situation, as if no one is aware of their true identity (and thus that no one probably cares), they can more easily be induced to behave in antisocial ways. This is especially so if the setting grants permission to enact one's impulses or to follow orders or implied guidelines that one would usually disdain. Our silver reflecting sunglasses were one such tool for making the guards, the warden, and me seem more remote and impersonal in our dealings with the prisoners. Their uniforms gave the guards a common identity, as did the necessity of referring to them in the abstract as, "Mr. Correctional Officer."

A body of research (to be explored in a later chapter) documents the excesses to which deindividuation facilitates violence, vandalism, and stealing in adults as in children—when the situation supports such antisocial actions. You may recognize this process in literature as William Golding's *Lord of the Flies.* When all members of a group of individuals are in a deindividuated state, their mental functioning changes: they live in an expanded-present moment that makes past and future distant and irrelevant. Feelings dominate reason, and action dominates reflection. In such a state, the usual cognitive and motivational processes that steer their behavior in socially desirable paths no longer guide people. Instead, their Apollonian rationality and sense of order yield to Dionysian excess and even chaos. Then it becomes as easy to make war as to make love, without considering the consequences

I am reminded of a Vietnamese saying, attributed to the Buddhist monk Thich Nhat Hanh: "in order to fight each other, baby chicks of the same mother hen paint their faces different colors." It is a quaint way to describe the role of deindividuation in facilitating violence. It is worth noticing, as we shall see, that one of the guards in the infamous Tier 1A at Abu Ghraib's torture center painted his face silver and black in the pattern of the rock group Insane Clown Posse, while he was on duty and posed for one of the many photos that documented prisoner abuse. We will have much more to say later about deindividuation processes as they contributed to the Abu Ghraib abuses.

Cognitive Dissonance That Rationalizes Evil

An interesting consequence of playing a role publicly that is contrary to one's private beliefs is the creation of *cognitive dissonance.* When there is a discrepancy between our behavior and beliefs, and when actions do not follow from relevant attitudes, a condition of cognitive dissonance is created. Dissonance is a state of tension that can powerfully motivate change either in one's public behavior or in one's private views in efforts to reduce the dissonance. People will go to remarkable lengths to bring discrepant beliefs and behavior into some kind of functional coherence. The greater the discrepancy, the stronger the motivation to achieve consonance and the more extreme changes we can expect to see. There is little dissonance if you harm someone when you have a lot of good reasons—your life was being threatened, it was part of your job as a soldier, you were ordered to act by a powerful authority, or you were given ample rewards for an action that was contrary to your pacifist beliefs.

Oddly enough, the dissonance effect becomes *greater* as the justification for such behavior *decreases*, for instance, when a repugnant action is carried out for little money, without threat, and with only minimally sufficient justification or inadequate rationale provided for the action. Dissonance mounts, and the attempts to reduce it are greatest, when the person has a sense of free will or when she or he does not notice or fully appreciate the situational pressures urging enactment of the discrepant action. When the discrepant action has been public, it cannot be denied or modified. Thus, the pressure to change is exerted on the softer elements of the dissonance equation, the internal, private elements—values, attitudes, beliefs, and even perceptions. An enormous body of research supports such predictions.[22]

How could dissonance motivate the changes we observed in our SPE guards? They had freely volunteered to work long, hard shifts for a small wage of less than $2 an hour. They were given minimal direction on how to play their difficult role. They had to sustain the role consistently over eight-hour work shifts for days and nights whenever they were in uniform, on the Yard, or in the presence of others, whether prisoners or parents or other visitors. They had to return to that role after sixteen-hour breaks from the SPE routine when they were off duty. Such a powerful source of dissonance was probably a major cause for internalizing the public role behaviors and for providing private supporting cognitive and affective response styles that made for the increasingly assertive and abusive behavior over time.

There is more. Having made the commitment to some action dissonant with their personal beliefs, guards felt great pressure to make sense of it, to develop reasons why they were doing something contrary to what they really believed and what they stood for morally. Sensible human beings can be deceived into engaging in irrational actions under many disguised dissonance commitment settings. Social psychology offers ample evidence that when that happens, smart people do stupid things, sane people do crazy things, and moral people do immoral things. After they have done them, they offer "good" rationalizations of why they did what they cannot deny having done. People are less rational than they are adept at *rationalizing*—explaining away discrepancies between their private morality and actions contrary to it. Doing so allows them to convince themselves and others that rational considerations guided their decision. They are insensitive to their own strong motivation to maintain consistency in the face of such dissonance.

The Power of Social Approval

Typically, people are also unaware of an even stronger force playing on the strings of their behavioral repertoire: the *need for social approval*. The need to be accepted, liked, and respected—to seem normal and appropriate, to fit in—is so powerful that we are primed to conform to even the most foolish and outlandish behaviors that strangers tell us is the right way to act. We laugh at the many *Candid Camera* episodes that reveal this truth, but rarely do we notice the times we ourselves are the *Candid Camera* "stars" in our own lives.

In addition to the dissonance effects, pressures to conform were also operative on our guards. Group pressure from other guards placed significant importance on being a "team player," conforming to an emergent norm that demanded dehumanizing the prisoners in various ways. The good guard was a group deviant, and he suffered in silence by being outside the socially rewarding circle of the other guards on his shift. The tough guard on each shift was emulated by at least one other guard on each shift.

THE SOCIAL CONSTRUCTION OF REALITY

The power that the guards assumed each time they donned their military-style uniforms was matched by the powerlessness the prisoners felt when wearing their wrinkled smocks with ID numbers sewn on their fronts. The guards had billy clubs, whistles, and sunglasses that disguised their eyes; the prisoners had a chained ankle and a stocking cap to contain their long hair. These situational differences were not inherent in the cloth or the hardware; rather, the source of their power is to be found in the psychological material that went into each group's subjective constructions of the meaning of these uniforms.

To understand how much situations matter, we need to discover the ways in which any given behavioral setting is perceived and interpreted by the people acting within it. It is the *meaning* that people assign to various components of the situation that creates its social reality. Social reality is more than a situation's physical features. It is the way actors view their situation, their current behavioral stage, which engages a variety of psychological processes. Such mental representations are beliefs that can modify how any situation is perceived, usually to make it fit or be assimilated into the actor's expectations and personal values.

Such beliefs create expectations, which in turn can gain strength when they become self-fulfilling prophecies. For example, in a famous experiment (by the psychologist Robert Rosenthal and the school principal Lenore Jacobson), when teachers were led to believe that certain children in their elementary school classes were "late bloomers," those children actually came to excel academically—even though researchers had chosen their names at random.[23] The teachers' positive conceptions of the latent talent of these children fed back to modify their behavior toward these children in ways that fostered the children's enhanced academic performance. Thus, this group of ordinary pupils proved the "Pygmalion Effect" by becoming what they were expected to be—academically outstanding. Sadly, the opposite is likely to occur even more frequently when teachers expect poor performance from certain kinds of pupils—from minority backgrounds or in some classes even from male students. Teachers then unconsciously treat them in ways that validate those negative stereotypes, and those students performing less well than they are capable.

In the SPE, the student volunteers could have elected to quit at any time. No guns or legal statutes bound them to their imprisonment, only a subject selection form on which they promised to do their best to last the full two weeks. The contract was merely a research contract between university researchers, a university human subjects research committee, and university students—all assumed initially that they could exercise free will and leave whenever they chose not to continue. However, as was obvious in the events that unfolded on the second day, the prisoners came to believe that it was a prison being run by psychologists and not by the State. They persuaded themselves, based on the quip by Doug-8612, that no one could leave of his own volition. Thus, none of them ever said, "I quit this experiment." Instead, the exit strategy for many became the passive one of forcing us to release them because of their extreme psychological distress. Their social construction of this new reality cemented them in the oppressive situation being created by the guards' capricious and hostile actions. The prisoners themselves became their own guards.

Another aspect of the way social reality was constructed in this research lies in the "release deal" that prisoners were offered at the end of their parole hearing. We framed the situation in terms of the power of the parole board to grant a parole if a prisoner were willing to forfeit all the money he had earned as a "prisoner." Even though most acquiesced to this deal, being willing to leave without any remuneration for the days they had in fact worked as "research subjects," none made the slightest attempt to leave at that point—to quit "the experiment." Instead, they accepted the social reality of parole over that of personal liberty to act in one's best self-interest. Each one allowed himself to be handcuffed, his head hooded, and led away from this near freedom back down to the prison dungeon.

Dehumanization: The Other as Nothing Worthwhile

> Kill a Gook for God
>
> —Penned on helmet of a U.S. soldier in Vietnam

One of the worst things that we can do to our fellow human beings is deprive them of their humanity, render them worthless by exercising the psychological process of dehumanization. This occurs when the "others" are thought not to possess the same feelings, thoughts, values, and purposes in life that we do. Any human qualities that these "others" share with us are diminished or are erased from our awareness. This is accomplished by the psychological mechanisms of intellectualization, denial, and the isolation of affect. In contrast to human relationships, which are subjective, personal, and emotional, dehumanized relationships are objectifying, analytical, and empty of emotional or empathic content.

To use Martin Buber's terms, humanized relationships are "I–Thou," while dehumanized relationships are "I–It." Over time, the dehumanizing agent is often sucked into the negativity of the experience, and then the "I" itself changes, to produce an "It–It" relationship between objects, or between agency and victim. The misperception of certain others as subhuman, bad humans, inhuman, infra-human, dispensable, or "animals" is facilitated by means of labels, stereotypes, slogans, and propaganda images.[24]

Sometimes dehumanization serves an adaptive function for an agent who must suspend his or her usual emotional response in an emergency, a crisis, or a work situation that demands invading the privacy of others. Surgeons may have to do so when performing operations that violate another person's body, as may first responders to a disaster. The same is often true when a job requires processing large numbers of people in one's caseload or daily schedule. Within some caring professions, such as clinical psychology, social work, and medicine, this process is called "detached concern." The actor is put into the paradoxical position of having to dehumanize clients in order to better assist or cure them.[25]

Dehumanization typically facilitates abusive and destructive actions toward those so objectified. It is hard to imagine that the following characterizations made by our guards were directed toward their prisoners—other college students who, but for a fateful coin flip, would have been wearing their uniforms: "I made them call each other names and clean toilets out with their bare hands. I practically considered the prisoners *cattle*, and I kept thinking I have to watch out for them in case they try something."

Or, from another of the SPE guards: "I was tired of seeing the prisoners in their rags and smelling the strong odors of their bodies that filled the cells. I watched them tear at each other on orders given by us."

The Stanford Prison Experiment created an ecology of dehumanization, just as real prisons do, in a host of direct, constantly repeated messages. It started with the loss of freedom and extended to the loss of privacy and finally to the loss of personal identity. It separated inmates from their past, their community, and their families and substituted for their normal reality a current reality that forced them to live with other prisoners in an anonymous cell with virtually no personal space. External, coercive rules and arbitrary decisions by guards dictated their behavior. More subtly, in our prison, as in all prisons I know about, emotions were suppressed, inhibited, and distorted. Tender, caring emotions were absent among both guards and prisoners after only a few days.

In institutional settings, the expression of human emotions is contained to the extent that they represent impulsive, often unpredictable individual reactions when uniformity of mass reactions is the expected norm. Our prisoners were dehumanized in many ways by the treatment of the guards and by degrading institutional procedures. However, they soon added to their own dehumanization by suppressing their emotional responses except when they "broke down." Emotions are essential to humanness. Holding emotions in check is essential in prisons because emotions are a sign of weakness that reveal one's vulnerability both to the guards and to other prisoners. We will explore more fully the destructive effects of dehumanization as it relates to moral disengagement in chapter 13.

SERENDIPITY SHINES ITS SPOTLIGHT ON THE SPE

What transformed our experiment into a major example of the psychology of evil was a series of dramatic, unexpected events that occurred shortly after our study ended—a massacre at California's San Quentin State Prison and a massacre at New York State's Attica Correctional Facility. These two events helped to catapult into national prominence a little academic experiment designed to test a theoretical notion of situational power. Here I will only outline key aspects of these events and their consequences for the SPE and me. Please see www.lucifereffect.com for a fuller treatment of the details along with the concurrent rise of the Black Panther Party and the Weather Underground radical student group.

The day after the SPE was terminated, a number of guards and prisoners were killed at San Quentin Prison in an alleged escape attempt headed by the black political prison activist George Jackson. Three weeks later, across the country in upstate New York, prisoners rioted at Attica Prison. They took over the prison and held nearly forty guards and civilian staff as hostages for five days. Instead of negotiating the prisoners' demands to change their conditions of oppression and the dehumanization they were experiencing, New York Governor Nelson Rockefeller ordered state troopers to retake the prison by all means necessary. They shot and killed more than forty of the inmates and hostages in the yard and wounded many others. The temporal proximity of these two events put prison conditions on center stage. I was invited to give testimonies to several congressional committees based on extensions of what I had learned from the SPE to prisons in general. I also became an expert witness for one of the six prisoners involved in the San Quentin State Prison massacre. Around that time, a media correspondent who saw me in a televised debate with San Quentin's associate warden decided to do a documentary on the SPE on national television (NBC's *Chronolog*, November 1971). A *Life* magazine feature soon followed, and the SPE was off and running.

PUTTING THE SPE INTO ITS ZEITGEIST FRAME

To appreciate more fully the extent of the character transformations in our student prisoners and guards that were induced by their experience in our mock
prison, it is well to consider the Zeitgeist of the late 1960s and early 1970s. It was
a time to reject authority, to "trust no one over thirty," to oppose the "military/
industrial establishment," to participate in antiwar rallies, to join in civil rights
and women's rights causes. It was a time for young people to rebel against the
rigid societal and parental conformity that had so restricted their parents in the
1950s. It was a time to experiment with sex, drugs, and rock and roll and to let
your hair grow long, "to let it all hang out." It was a time to be a "hippie," to go to
"be-ins" and "love-ins," to be a San Francisco "flower child" with flowers in your
hair, to be a pacifist, and especially to be an individualist. The Harvard psychologist Timothy Leary, that generation's intellectual acid guru, offered a triple pre-
scription for young people everywhere: "tune out" of traditional society; "turn
on" to mind-altering drugs; and "tune in" to one's inner nature.

The rise of the Youth Culture, with its dramatic rebellion against injustice
and oppression, was centered on the immorality of the Vietnam War, its obscene
daily body counts, and an administration unwilling to admit its error, cut bait and
exit for seven bloody years. These values were in the wind blowing across
European and Asian youth movements. Europeans were even more militant than
their American counterparts in vigorously challenging the establishment. They
openly rebelled against both political and academic orthodoxy. In direct opposition to what they considered reactionary, repressive regimes, students in Paris,
Berlin, and Milan "manned the barricades." Many were socialists who challenged
fascist and Communist totalitarianism, and they deplored the financial restrictions on access to higher education.

The student volunteers in our study, as a group, emerged from this youth culture of rebellion, personal experimentation, and the rejection of authority and
conformity. We might have expected the subjects in our experiment to be more resistant to institutional forces than they were, to resist complying with the dominance of the "System" that I imposed on them. We did not anticipate that they
would adopt such a power-prone mentality when they became guards because
none of our volunteers preferred to be a guard when he was given that option.
Even Tough Guard Hellmann wanted to be a prisoner rather than a guard, because, as he told us, "most people resent guards."

Virtually all of our student volunteers felt that becoming a prisoner was a
more likely possibility for them in the future; they were not going to college in
order to get jobs as prison guards, and they might get arrested for various minor
infractions someday. I take this to mean that there was not a predilection among
those assigned to be guards to be abusive or domineering in the ways they later

were. They did not bring into the Stanford Prison Experiment any tendencies to harm, abuse, or dominate others. If anything, we might say they brought in tendencies to be caring of other people in accordance with the contemporary social conditioning of their era. Similarly, there was no reason to expect the students role-playing prisoners to break down so quickly, if at all, given their initially positive mental and physical health. It is important to keep this temporal and cultural context in mind when considering later attempted replications of our study by researchers in totally different eras.

WHY SYSTEMS MATTER THE MOST

The most important lesson to be derived from the SPE is that Situations are created by *Systems*. Systems provide the institutional support, authority, and resources that allow Situations to operate as they do. After we have outlined all the situational features of the SPE, we discover that a key question is rarely posed: "Who or what made it happen that way?" Who had the power to design the behavioral setting and to maintain its operation in particular ways? Therefore, who should be held responsible for its consequences and outcomes? Who gets the credit for successes, and who is blamed for failures? The simple answer in the case of the SPE is—me! However, finding that answer is not such a simple matter when we deal with complex organizations, such as failing educational or correctional systems, corrupt megacorporations, or the system that was created at Abu Ghraib Prison.

System Power involves authorization or institutionalized permission to behave in prescribed ways or to forbid and punish actions that are contrary to them. It provides the "higher authority" that gives validation to playing new roles, following new rules, and taking actions that would ordinarily be constrained by preexisting laws, norms, morals, and ethics. Such validation usually comes cloaked in the mantle of *ideology*. Ideology is a slogan or proposition that usually legitimizes whatever means are necessary to attain an ultimate goal. Ideology is the "Big Kahuna," which is not challenged or even questioned because it is so apparently "right" for the majority in a particular time and place. Those in authority present the program as good and virtuous, as a highly valuable moral imperative.

The programs, policies, and standard operating procedures that are developed to support an ideology become an essential component of the System. The System's procedures are considered reasonable and appropriate as the ideology comes to be accepted as sacred.

During the era when fascist military juntas governed around the world from the Mediterranean to Latin America, from the 1960s to 1970s, dictators always sounded their call to arms as the necessary defense against a "threat to national security" allegedly posed by socialists or Communists. Eliminating that threat necessitated state-sanctioned torture by the military and civil police. It also legitimized assassination by death squads of all suspected "enemies of the state."

In the United States at the present time, the same alleged threats to national security have frightened citizens into willingly sacrificing their basic civil rights to gain an illusion of security. That ideology in turn has been the centerpiece justifying a preemptive war of aggression against Iraq. That ideology was created by the System in power, which in turn created new subordinate Systems of war management, homeland security management, and military prison management—or absence thereof, in default of serious postwar planning.

My scholarly fascination with the mind control strategy and tactics outlined in George Orwell's classic novel 1984[26] should have made me aware of System power sooner in my professional life. "Big Brother" is the System that ultimately crushes individual initiative and the will to resist its intrusions. For many years, discussion of the SPE did not even include a Systems-level analysis because the original dialogue was framed as the contest between the dispositional and situational ways of understanding human behavior. I ignored the bigger problem of considering that framing provided by the System. It was really only after I became engaged in understanding the dynamics of the widespread abuses in the many military prisons in Iraq, Afghanistan, and Cuba that the Systems level of analysis became glaringly obvious.

The Nobel Laureate physicist Richard Feynman showed that the tragic disaster of the space shuttle *Challenger* was due not to human error but to a systemic problem with "official management." NASA's top guns insisted on the launch despite the doubts of both of their engineers and the expressed concerns of the manufacturer of a critical component (which became the flawed O-ring that caused the disaster). Feynman argues that NASA's motivation may well have been "to assure the government of NASA perfection and success in order to ensure the supply of funds."[27] In later chapters, we will adopt the point of view that Systems as well as Situations matter to aid in our understanding of what went wrong at the Stanford and Abu Ghraib Prisons.

In contrast to NASA's system that failed when it tried to live up to its politically motivated slogan of "faster, better, cheaper" was the horrific success of the Nazi system of mass extermination. Here was a tightly integrated top-down system of Hitler's cabinet, the National Socialist politicians, bankers, Gestapo officers, SS troops, engineers, doctors, architects, chemists, educators, train conductors, and more, each doing its part in this concentrated attempt at the genocide of all European Jews and other enemies of the State.

Concentration camps had to be built, along with extermination camps and their specifically designed crematoria, and new forms of lethally effective poison gas had to be perfected. Propaganda specialists had to design campaigns in film, newspapers, magazines, and posters that denigrated and dehumanized the Jews as a menace. Teachers and preachers had to prepare the youth to become blindly obedient Nazis who could justify engaging in the "final solution of the Jewish question."[28]

A new language had to be developed with innocuous-sounding words concealing the truth of human cruelty and destruction, such as: *Sonderbehandlung* (special treatment); *Sonderaktion* (special action), *Umsiedlung* (resettlement), and *Evakuierrung* (evacuation). "Special treatment" was the code name for the physical extermination of people, sometimes shortened to SB for efficiency. SS head Reinhard Heydrich outlined basic principles of security during the war in a 1939 statement: "A distinction must be made between those who may be dealt with in the usual way and those who must be given special treatment [*Sonderbehandlung*]. The latter case covers subjects who, due to their most objectionable nature, their dangerousness, or their ability to serve as tools of propaganda for the enemy, are suitable for elimination, without respect for persons, by merciless treatment (usually by execution)."[29]

For the Nazi doctors who were enlisted to make the selections of inmates for extermination or experimentation, there was often a question of split loyalty—"of conflicting oaths, contradictions between murderous cruelty and momentary kindness which SS doctors seemed to manifest continuously during their time in Auschwitz. For the schism tended not to be resolved. Its persistence was part of the overall psychological equilibrium that enabled the SS doctor to do his deadly work. He became integrated into a large, brutal, highly functional system. . . . Auschwitz was a collective effort."[30]

CHAPTER ELEVEN

The SPE: Ethics and Extensions

We've traveled too far, and our momentum has taken over: We move idly towards eternity, without possibility of reprieve or hope of explanation.

—Tom Stoppard, *Rosencrantz and Guildenstern Are Dead*, Act 3 (1967)

We have seen the way in which the momentum of the simulated Stanford Prison took over the lives of those within its walls—mostly for the worse. In the previous chapter, I sketched a rough answer to the question of how people could be so swiftly and radically transformed. In particular, I pointed out the ways in which situational and systemic forces operated in tandem to spoil the fruits of human nature.

Our young research participants were not the proverbial "Bad Apples" in an otherwise good barrel. Rather, our experimental design ensured that they were initially good apples and were corrupted by the insidious power of the bad barrel, this prison. Of course, compared to the toxic and lethal nature of real civilian and military prisons, our Stanford Prison was relatively benign. The changes in the ways our volunteer participants thought, felt, and behaved in this environment were the consequences of known psychological processes that operate on all of us in various ways in many situations—albeit not so intensely, pervasively, and relentlessly. They were enmeshed in a "total situation" whose impact was greater than most ordinary situations that we move into and out of repeatedly at will.[1]

Consider the possibility that each of us has the potential, or mental templates, to be saint or sinner, altruistic or selfish, gentle or cruel, submissive or dominant, sane or mad, good or evil. Perhaps we are born with a full range of capacities, each of which is activated and developed depending on the social and cultural circumstances that govern our lives. I will argue that the potential for perversion is inherent in the very processes that make human beings do all the wonderful things we do. Each of us is the end product of the complex development and specialization that have grown out of millions of years of evolution, growth, adaptation, and coping. Our species has reached its special place on Earth because of our remarkable capacity for learning, for language, for reasoning, for inventing, and for imagining new and better futures. Every human being has the potential to perfect the skills, talents, and attributes we need to go beyond surviving to thrive in and enhance our human condition.

THE PERVERSION OF HUMAN PERFECTIBILITY

Could some of the world's evil result from ordinary people operating in circumstances that selectively elicit bad behavior from their natures? Let's answer such a question with a few general examples and then refocus on the normal human processes that became degraded in the SPE. Memory enables us to profit from mistakes and build upon the known to create better futures. However, with memory come grudges, revenge, learned helplessness, and the rumination over trauma that feeds depression. Likewise, our extraordinary ability to use language and symbols enables us to communicate with others personally, abstractly, over time and place. Language provides the foundation for history, planning, and social control. However, with language come rumors, lies, propaganda, stereotypes, and coercive rules. Our remarkable creative genius leads to great literature, drama, music, science, and inventions like the computer and the Internet. Yet that same creativity can be perverted into inventing torture chambers and torture tactics, into paranoid ideologies and the Nazis' efficient system of mass murder. Any one of our special attributes contains the possibility of its opposite negative, as in the dichotomies of love–hate; pride–arrogance; self-esteem–self-loathing.[2]

The fundamental human need to belong comes from the desire to associate with others, to cooperate, to accept group norms. However, the SPE shows that the need to belong can also be perverted into excessive conformity, compliance, and in-group versus out-group hostility. The need for autonomy and control, the central forces toward self-direction and planning, can be perverted into an excessive exercise of power to dominate others or into learned helplessness.

Consider three more such needs that can cut both ways. First, *needs for consistency and rationality* give meaningful and wise direction to our lives. Yet dissonant commitments force us to honor and rationalize wrong-headed decisions, such as prisoners remaining when they should have quit and guards justifying their abuse. Second, *needs to know and to understand our environment and our relationship to it* lead to curiosity, scientific discovery, philosophy, the humanities, and art. But a capricious, arbitrary environment that does not make sense can pervert those basic needs and lead to frustration and self-isolation (as it did in our prisoners). And finally, our *need for stimulation* triggers explorations and adventurous risk taking, but it can also make us vulnerable to boredom when we are placed in a static setting. Boredom, in turn, can become a powerful motivator of actions as we saw with the SPE night shift guards to have fun with their "playthings."

However, let me make clear one critical point: understanding the "why" of what was done does not excuse "what" was done. Psychological analysis is not "excusiology." Individuals and groups who behave immorally or illegally must still be held responsible and legally accountable for their complicity and crimes. However, in determining the severity of their sentence, the situational and systemic factors that caused their behavior must be taken into account.[3]

In the next two chapters, we will move beyond the SPE to review a large body of psychological research that complements and extends the arguments made so far about the power of situational forces in shaping human thinking and acting. Before moving on, we have go back to deal with some final, critical issues that were raised by this experiment. First, and most important, was the suffering worth it? There is no question that people suffered during this experiment. Those who made them suffer also had to deal with the recognition that they had gone beyond the demands of their role to inflict pain and humiliation on others for hours on end. Therefore, the ethics in this and similar research demand careful consideration.

Virtue, as Dante showed in the *Inferno*, is not simply refraining from sin; it requires action. Here I will discuss how paralysis of action worked in the SPE. In the next chapter, I will consider the broader implications of failure to act for society, as when passive bystanders fail to intervene when their help is needed.

In addition to dealing with the ethical errors of omission and with absolute ethics, we must focus in depth on the relative ethics that guide most scientific research. A central balance in the equation of relative ethics requires weighing pain against gain. Was the pain endured by the participants in this experiment offset by the gain to science and society generated by the research? In other words, did the scientific ends justify the experimental means? While there were many positive consequences that flowed from the study, the reader will have to decide for him or herself whether the study should ever have been done.

Research that provokes thought breeds other research and invites extensions, as the SPE did. After reflecting on the SPE's ethics, we will briefly review some of the replications and applications of this study that offer a broader context for appreciating its significance.

ETHICAL REFLECTIONS ON THE SPE

Was the SPE study unethical? In several ways, the answer must surely be "Yes." However, there are other ways of viewing this research that provide a reasonable "No." Before we look at evidence in this retrospective analysis in support of each of these alternatives, I need to make clear why I am even discussing these matters decades after the study is over and done. Having focused much personal attention on these ethical issues, I believe that I can bring a broader perspective to this discussion than is typical. Other researchers may benefit by avoiding similar pitfalls if they become aware of some subtle warning signs, and also by engaging greater sensitivity to ethical safeguards that the SPE highlighted. Without being defensive or rationalizing my role in this study, I will use this research as a vehicle for outlining the complexity of ethical judgments involved in research that entails interventions in human functioning. First, let us consider the category of the ethics of intervention. That will provide a foundation for comparing absolute ethics to the relative ethics that guide experimental research.

The Ethics of Intervention

Every act of intervention in the life of an individual, a group, or an environment is a matter of ethics (the radical therapist R. D. Laing would say it is a "political decision"). The following diverse groups share common objectives: therapists, surgeons, counselors, experimentalists, educators, urban planners, architects, social reformers, public health agents, cult leaders, used-car salespeople, and our parents. They all subscribe to one of these objectives: cure, behavior modification, recommendations for action, training, teaching, mind alteration, control, change, monetary allocation, construction, or discipline—in sum, various forms of intervention that directly affect our lives or do so indirectly by changing human environments.

Most agents of intervention initially intend benefits to the target of change and/or society. However, it is their subjective values that determine the cost-benefit ratio and raise critical ethical questions for us to consider. We take for granted the value of the powerful socializing influences parents exert on their children in shaping them to their image and toward a socially, politically, and religiously imposed ideal. Should we care that parents do so without obtaining their children's informed consent? Seems like an idle question until one considers parents who help indoctrinate their children into hate groups like the Ku Klux Klan, destructive cults, or terrorist cells, or into prostitution.

To put a finer point on the issue, "parental rights of domain" are usually not questioned—even when they teach children intolerance and prejudice—except when parents are excessively abusive in getting their way. But what can we say about the case of a father who wanted his son to be more patriotic, ostensibly a reasonable goal in almost all societies? The father in question wrote to a medical doctor whose advice column ran in a nationally circulated magazine: "I love my country and want my boy to love it too. Is it O.K. for me to give him a little pep talk while he's asleep; no big deal, just some patriotic stuff?"

At one level, Dad is asking if this tactic will work; is there evidence that sleep learning can be effective in delivering such below-consciousness persuasive messages? (The answer is that there is no supporting evidence.) At another level, Dad is raising an ethical question: Is it ethical for him to indoctrinate his defenseless child in this way? Would it be ethical if he did so when the child was awake or if he used monetary reinforcement or social approval instead of this dubious technique? Is it his goal or his means that some might find ethically offensive? Would it be preferable instead for this anxious father to rely upon the more subtle indoctrination devices that are disguised as "education" in the classroom: national flags; pictures of national leaders; national anthems; prayers; and being forced to read historical narratives and geography and civics textbooks that often give a biased view of history and are designed by every society as propaganda to maintain the status quo? The point here is that we must increase our collective sensitivity to the broad range of daily situations where interventions occur as a "natural" process of social life and where a violation of ethics goes unnoticed because of its prevalent and insidious presence.

ABSOLUTE ETHICS

For the sake of brevity, we may say that ethics can be categorized as "absolute" or "relative." When behavior is guided by absolute ethical standards, a higher-order moral principle that is invariant with regard to the conditions of its applicability can be postulated—across time, situations, persons, and expediency. Such absolute ethics are embodied in communal codes of conduct. These codes are often based upon adherence to a set of explicit principles, as in the Ten Commandments or the Bill of Rights. Such absolute ethics allow no degree of freedom that might justify means to an end or circumstances that might qualify instances where the principle is suspended or applied in an altered, watered-down form. In the extreme, no extenuating circumstances can justify an abrogation of the ethical standard.

An absolute ethical standard postulates that because human life is sacred it must not in any way be demeaned, however unintentionally. In the case of research, there is no justification for any experiment that induces human suffering. From such a position, it is even reasonable to maintain that no research should be conducted in psychology or medicine that violates the biological or psychological integrity of any human being regardless of the benefit that might, or even definitely accrue to the society at large.

Those who adopt this perspective argue that even if the actions that cause suffering are conducted in the name of science, for the sake of knowledge, "national security," or any other high-flying abstraction—they are unethical. Within psychology, those closely identified with the humanist tradition have been most vocal in urging that the basic concern for human dignity must take precedence over the stated goals of the discipline, namely, to predict and control behavior.

The SPE Was Absolutely Unethical

On the basis of such an absolute ethic, the Stanford Prison Experiment must certainly be judged unethical because human beings did suffer considerable anguish. People suffered much more than they could have reasonably anticipated when they volunteered for an academic study of "prison life" that was being conducted at a prestigious university. Moreover, that suffering escalated over time and resulted in such extreme stress and emotional turmoil that five of the sample of initially healthy young prisoners had to be released early.

The guards also suffered from the realization of what they had done under the cloak of their role and behind their anonymity-engendering sunglasses. They could see and hear the pain and humiliation they were causing to fellow students who had done nothing to deserve such brutality. Their realization of their unde- niably excessive abuse of the prisoners was much greater than the distress experi- enced by participants in Stanley Milgram's classic research on "blind obedience to authority," which we will review in depth in the next chapter.[4] That research has been challenged as unethical because participants could *imagine* the pain they were supposedly inflicting by shocking a remote victim, the "learner."[5] But as soon as the study ended they discovered that the "victim" was really an experi- mental confederate who had never been hurt but only pretended to be. Their dis- tress came from their awareness of what they *might have done* had the shocks been real. In contrast, the distress of our guards came from their awareness that their "shocks" to the prisoners were all real, direct, and continual.

An additional feature of the study that would qualify it as unethical was not disclosing in advance the nature of the arrests and formal booking at police head- quarters to the students who had been assigned to the prisoner role or to their parents, who were caught off guard by this unexpected Sunday intrusion into their lives. We were also guilty of manipulating parents into thinking the situa- tion of their sons was not as bad as it was by the various deceptive and control procedures we inaugurated on Visiting Nights. If you recall, we worried that par- ents would take their sons home if they fully realized the abusive nature of this mock prison. To forestall such action, which would have ended the study, we put on a "show" for them. We did so not only to keep our prison intact but also as a basic ingredient of our prison simulation, because such deceptions are usual in many systems under investigation by oversight committees. By putting out a good-looking red carpet, system managers counter complaints and concerns about the negative aspects of their situation.

Another reason for considering the SPE as unethical is the failure to termi- nate the study sooner than we did. I should have called it quits after the second prisoner suffered a severe stress disorder on Day 3. That should have been suffi- cient evidence that Doug-8612 was not faking his emotional reaction and break- down on the previous day. We should have stopped after the next and the next and the next prisoners suffered extreme disorders. But we did not. It is likely, however, that I would have terminated the study on Sunday, at the end of a full week, as a "natural ending," had not Christina Maslach's intervention forced premature clo- sure. I might have ended it after one week because I and the small staff of Curt Banks and David Jaffe were exhausted from dealing with the around-the-clock lo- gistics and the need to contain the guards' escalating abuses.

In retrospect, I believe that the main reason I did not end the study sooner, when it began to get out of hand, resulted from the conflict created in me by my dual roles as principal investigator, and thus guardian of the research ethics of the experiment, and as prison superintendent, eager to maintain the integrity and stability of my prison at all costs. I would like to believe that had someone else been playing the superintendent's role, I would have seen the light and blown the whistle sooner. I now realize that there should have been someone with authority above mine, someone in charge of oversight of the experiment.

However, neither the members of the Human Subjects Research Committee nor I imagined in advance that any such external authority was necessary in an experiment where college students had the freedom to stay or go anytime the going became rougher than they could handle. Before the experiment, it was just "kids going to play cops and robbers," and it was hard to imagine what could happen within a few days. It would have been good to have had advance hindsight operating.

I am sure that had this experiment been conducted in more recent times, the students and their parents would have filed lawsuits against the university and me. But the 1970s were a less litigious time in the United States than has existed since then. No legal charges were ever filed, and there were only a few attacks on the ethics of this research by professional colleagues.[6] Indeed, it was I who requested a postexperiment ethics evaluation by the American Psychological Association in July 1973, which determined that the existing ethical guidelines had been followed.

Nevertheless, I do feel responsible for creating an institution that gave permission for such abuses to occur within the context of the "psychology of imprisonment." The experiment succeeded all too well in creating some of what is worst in real prisons, but the findings came at the expense of human suffering. I am sorry for that and to this day apologize for contributing to this inhumanity.

RELATIVE ETHICS

Most research follows a utilitarian ethics model. When an ethical principle admits of contingent applications, its standard is relative and it is to be judged on pragmatic criteria weighted according to utilitarian principles. Obviously such a model guided this research, as it does most psychological experimentation. But what elements are considered in the cost-gain equation? How are the loss and gain to be proportionately weighted? Who is to judge whether the gain offsets the loss? These are some of the questions that must be faced if a position of relative ethics is deemed to be ethical at all.

Some solutions are resolved on the basis of conventional wisdom, meaning the present state of relevant knowledge, precedents in similar cases, social consensus, the values and sensitivity of the individual researcher, and the level of consciousness prevailing in the given society at a particular time. Research institutions, funding agencies, and governments also establish strict guidelines for and restrictions on all medical and nonmedical human research.

At the core of the ethical dilemma for social scientists is: Can a given researcher create a balance between what he or she believes is necessary for the conduct of socially or theoretically useful research and what is thought necessary to the well-being and dignity of the research participants? Since researchers' self-serving biases may push them more nearly toward the former than the latter, external reviewers, particularly grant reviewers and institutional review boards (IRBs), must serve as ombudspersons for the relatively powerless participants. However, these external reviewers must also act in the interest of "science" and "society" in determining whether, and to what degree, some deception, emotional arousal, or other aversive states can be permitted in a given experiment. They operate on the assumption that any negative impact of such procedures is transient and not likely to endure beyond the limits of the experiment. Let us consider next how those competing interests were served in the SPE.

On the relativist side of the ethical argument, one could contend that the SPE was not unethical because of the following: The legal counsel of Stanford University was consulted, drew up a formal "informed consent" statement, and told us of the work, safety, and insurance requirements we had to satisfy for them to approve the experiment. The "informed consent" statement signed by every participant specified that during the experiment there would be an invasion of his privacy; prisoners would have only a minimally adequate diet, would lose some of their civil rights, and would experience harassment. All were expected to complete their two-week contract to the best of their ability. The Student Health Department was alerted to our study and prior arrangements were made for any medical care subjects might need. Approval was officially sought and received in writing from the agency sponsoring the research, the Group Effectiveness Branch of the Office of Naval Research (ONR), the Stanford Psychology Department, and Stanford's Institutional Review Board (IRB).[7]

Aside from having the subjects arrested by police, there was no deception of the participants. Moreover, my staff and I repeatedly reminded the guards not to be physically abusive to the prisoners, individually or collectively. However, we did not extend the mandate to restrict psychological abuse.

Another factor that complicates assessing the ethics of this study is that our prison was open to inspection by outsiders, who should have protected the rights of the participants. Imagine you were a prisoner suffering in this setting. If you were a prisoner in our jail, who would you have wanted as your supporter? Who might have pressed the "Exit" button for you if you were unable to press it yourself? Would it have been the Catholic priest/prison chaplain when he saw you crying? Not a chance. How about your mom and pop, friends, family? Wouldn't they intervene after they noticed that your condition was deteriorating? None ever did. Maybe help would have come from one of the many professional psychologists, graduate students, secretaries, or staff of the Psychology Department, some of whom watched live-action videos of parts of the study, took part in Parole Board hearings, or spoke to participants during interviews or when they were in the storage closet during the "break-in" fiasco. No help for you from that source.

As noted, each of these onlookers fell into playing a passive role. They all accepted my framing of the situation, which blinded them to the real picture. They also intellectualized because the simulation seemed real; or because of the realism of the role-playing; or because they focused solely on the minutiae of the experimental design. Moreover, the bystanders did not see the more severe abuses as they were unfolding, nor were the participants willing to disclose them fully to outsiders, even to close friends and families. They were driven, perhaps, by embarrassment, pride, or a sense of "manliness." So many came and looked but did not see and just walked away.

Finally, what we did right was to engage in extensive debriefing, not just for three hours following the experiment but also on several subsequent occasions when most of the participants returned to review the videos and see a slide show of the study. I maintained contact with most of the participants for several years after the conclusion of the experiment, sending copies of articles, my congressional testimony, news clippings, and notices of upcoming TV shows on the SPE. Over the years, about a half dozen of the participants have joined me in some of these national broadcasts. I am still in contact with a few of them more than three decades later.

What was important about the extensive debriefing sessions was that they gave the participants a chance to openly express their strong feelings and to gain a new understanding of themselves and their unusual behavior in a novel, alien setting. Our method was a form of "process debriefing"[8] in which we made explicit that some effects and beliefs that are developed in an experiment can last beyond the limits of the experiment. We explained the reasons they should not in this special case. I emphasized that what they had done was diagnostic of the negative nature of the prison situation that we had created for them and was not diagnostic of their personalities. I reminded them that they had been carefully selected, precisely because they were normal and healthy, and that they had been assigned randomly to one or the other of the two roles. They did not bring any pathology into the place; rather, the place elicited pathology of various kinds from them. In addition, I informed them that their peers likewise had done almost anything that any one prisoner did that was demeaning or disordered. The same was true of most of the guards, who at some time were abusive of the prisoners. They behaved as they did in the role exactly as their shift mates had.

I also tried to make the debriefing a lesson on "moral education" by explicitly discussing the moral conflicts we all faced throughout the study. A pioneering theorist in moral development, Larry Kohlberg, has argued that such discussions within the context of moral conflict are the primary, perhaps the only way to increase an individual's level of moral development.[9]

Recall that the data from the mood adjective checklist showed that both prisoners and guards had returned to a more balanced emotional state following the debriefing session, to reach levels comparable to their emotional conditions at the start of the study. The relatively short duration of the negative impact of this intense experience on the participants can be ascribed to three factors: First, these youngsters all had a sound psychological and personal foundation to bounce back to after the study ended. Second, the experience was unique to and contained in that time, setting, costumes, and script, all of which could be left behind as a package of their "SPE adventure" and not reactivated in the future. Third, our detailed debriefing took the guards and prisoners off the hook for behaving badly and identified the features of the situation that had influenced them.

Positive Consequences to the Participants

In the traditional accounts of the relative ethics of research, in order for any research to be sanctioned it is necessary for the gain to science, medicine, and/or society to outweigh the cost to the participants. Although such a gain-cost ratio seems appropriate, I now want to challenge this method of accounting. The costs to the participants ("subjects" in the days of the SPE) were real, immediate, and often tangible. In contrast, whatever gains were anticipated when the study was designed or approval given were merely probable and distant and perhaps might never be realized. Much promising research does not yield significant results and thus is not even published and circulated in the scientific community. Even significant published findings may not translate into practice, and practice may not prove feasible or practical when scaled up to the level of social benefits. On the other hand, some basic research that had no obvious application when originally conceived has turned out to yield important applications. For example, basic research on the conditioning of the autonomic nervous system has led directly to the use of biofeedback as a therapeutic aid in health care.[10] Moreover, most researchers have shown little interest or talent in the "social engineering" applications of their findings to personal and social problems. Taken together, these criticisms say that the lofty "gain" side of the research ethical equation may not be met either in principle or practice, while the pain part remains a net loss as well as a gross loss to participants and society.

Also singularly missing from this ethical equation is concern for the net *gain* to the participants. Do they benefit in some way from having been part of a given research project? For instance, does their financial remuneration offset the distress they experience from taking part in medical research assessing aspects of pain? Do people value the knowledge they accrue as research participants? Do they learn something special about themselves from the research experience? Adequate, detailed debriefing is essential to realize this secondary objective of human subjects research. (For an example of how this can be achieved in one of my experiments on induced psychopathology, see notes.[11]) But such gains cannot be assumed or hoped for; they must be demonstrated empirically as outcome measures of any study conducted with a prior sense of its "questionable ethics." Also absent from most considerations of research ethics is the obligation incumbent on researchers to engage in a special kind of social activism that makes their research useful to their field of knowledge and to the improvement of their society.

I would like to balance the SPE's ethics slate a bit by first noting some remarkable profits it had to both its participants and staff. Then I will outline some of the social activism that I have engaged in over the past three or more decades to ensure that the value of this experiment has been realized as fully as possible.

Unexpected Personal Gains to SPE Participants and Staff

A number of unexpectedly positive effects emerged from this study that have had lasting impact on some of the participants and staff. In general, most of the participants indicated on their final follow-up evaluations (submitted from home at varying times after the study) that it was a valuable personal learning experience. These positives help balance, to some extent, the obvious negatives of the prison experience, as we note that none of the participants would volunteer for a similar study again. Let's examine some of the positive aftershocks of the SPE, taken from their evaluations.

Doug, Prisoner 8612, a ringleader of the prisoner rebellion, was the first prisoner to suffer an extreme emotional stress reaction. His response forced us to release him after only thirty-six hours. The experience was truly disturbing for him, as he said in an interview during the filming of our documentary, *Quiet Rage: The Stanford Prison Experiment:* "As an experience it was unique, I've never screamed so loud in my life; I've never been so upset in my life. It was an experience of being out of control, both of the situation and of my feelings. Maybe I've always had difficulties with losing control. I wanted to understand myself, so I went into psychology [after the SPE]. I'll go into psychology and I'll learn what makes a person tick so I won't be so afraid of the unknown."[12]

In a follow-up evaluation that he completed five years after the study, Doug revealed that he started to simulate extreme distress in order to be released, but then that role got to him. "I figured the only way I could get out of the experiment was to play sick, first physical. Then when that didn't work I played at mental fatigue. However, the energy it took to get into that space, and the mere fact that I *could* be so upset, upset me." How upset? He reported that his girlfriend told him that he was so upset and nervous that he talked about the experiment constantly for two months afterward.

Doug went on to get a Ph.D. in clinical psychology, in part to learn how to gain greater control over his emotions and behavior. He did his dissertation on shame (of the prisoner status) and guilt (of the guard status), completing his internship at San Quentin State Prison, rather than in the usual medical/clinical setting, and has been a forensic psychologist in the San Francisco and California corrections systems for more than twenty years. It was his moving testimony that gave us the title of our video, *Quiet Rage*, as he talked about the sadistic impulse in guards that must be guarded against because it is always there in situations of differential power—ready to slip out, to explode, as a kind of "quiet rage." Part of Doug's career has focused on helping inmates maintain a sense of dignity despite their surroundings, and to enable guards and prisoners to coexist more amicably. This is a case of the initial strongly negative effect of the SPE being transformed into insight that has had enduring consequences for the individual and society. There was much pain and much gain to the same research subject.

Guard Hellmann, the tough "John Wayne" macho guard, has been featured in all of the televised portrayals of the study for his dominating role and the "creatively evil" tasks and games he invented for the prisoners. We met recently at a lecture I was giving, and he confided that, unlike Andy Warhol's fifteen minutes of fame, which everyone gets once in a lifetime, the Stanford Prison Experiment has provided him with "fifteen minutes of infamy, permanently." In response to my request that he think about whether his participation may have had any positive consequences on his life, he sent me this note:

> Decades of carrying the baggage of life have softened the arrogant and insensitive teenager that I was in 1971. If someone had told me that my actions had harmed any of the prisoners, my likely response would have been "they're weaklings and sissies." But the memory of how I fell so deeply into my role that I was blind to the suffering of others serves today as a cautionary tale, and I think carefully about how I treat people. In fact, some might find me overly sensitive for my role as a business owner, as I sometimes hesitate to make decisions to, for example, fire non-performing employees for fear that it would be a hardship to them."[13]

Guard Vandy explained some of the personal insight he gained from his experience as the tough leader of his shift. During a follow-up evaluation a few months later, he told us, "My enjoyment in harassing and punishing prisoners was quite unnatural because I do tend to think of myself as being sympathetic to the injured, especially animals. I think it was an outgrowth from my total freedom to rule the prisoners; I began to abuse my authority. In view of this I have tried to realize when I am being pushy or authoritarian and then correct it. I find it much easier to examine it and realize just when I am behaving that way. I feel that now because of my ability to better understand it, that I have become less demanding and bossy than I was before the experiment."

Carlo Prescott, our prison consultant, was released from San Quentin State Prison only six months before his involvement in the SPE. He had been incarcerated in several California prisons as well as in a California Youth Authority facility for more than seventeen years of his life. The changes in his professional status and the enhanced self-esteem that accompanied his teaching at Stanford with me on the subject of the psychology of imprisonment, and his contributions to the SPE, have had salutary consequences for him. He landed a good job as the radio talk-show host of *Carlo's Corner* on San Francisco's KGO station, where he provoked his listeners to social consciousness and offered penetrating insights into racist and fascist trends in the United States. He also taught other college courses, lectured in the community, did community service, gave congressional testimony along with me, and has been a model citizen all these years.

Craig Haney went on to graduate from Stanford University's Law School with J.D., as well as a Ph.D. from our Psychology Department. He is a professor on the faculty of the University of California, Santa Cruz, where he teaches popular courses in psychology and law and in the psychology of institutions. Craig has become one of the nation's leading consultants on prison conditions and one of only a handful of psychological experts working with attorneys who represent prisoner class action suits in the United States. He has written extensively and brilliantly about many different aspects of crime, punishment, execution, and correction. We have collaborated on a number of professional journal articles, books, and trade magazines.[14] His statement of the impact that the SPE had on him clearly shows the worth of this experiment:

> For me, the Stanford Prison Experiment was a formative, career-altering experience. I had just finished my second year as a psychology graduate student at Stanford when Phil Zimbardo, Curtis Banks, and I began to plan this research. My interests in applying social psychology to questions of crime and punishment had just begun to crystallize, with Phil Zimbardo's blessing and support. . . . Not long after I finished my work on the SPE I began to study actual prisons and eventually focused also on the social histories that helped to shape the lives of the people who were confined inside them. But I never lost sight of the perspective on institutions that I gleaned from observing and evaluating the results of 6 short days inside our simulated prison.[15]

Christina Maslach, the heroine of the SPE, is now a psychology professor at the University of California, Berkeley, vice provost of undergraduate education, dean of letters and sciences, and a Carnegie Foundation Distinguished Professor of the Year. Her brief but powerful experience in the SPE also had a positive impact on her career decisions, as she said in this retrospective account:[16]

> For me, the important legacy of the prison experiment is what I learned from my personal experience and how that helped to shape my own subsequent professional contributions to psychology. What I learned about most directly was the psychology of dehumanization—how basically good

people can come to perceive and treat others in such bad ways; how easy it is for people to treat others who rely on their help or good will as less than human, as animals, inferior, unworthy of respect or equality. That experience in the SPE led me to do the pioneering research on burnout— the psychological hazards of emotionally demanding human service work that can lead initially dedicated and caring individuals to dehumanize and mistreat the very people they are supposed to serve. My research has tried to elucidate the causes and consequences of burnout in a variety of occupational settings; it has also tried to apply these findings to practical solutions. I also encourage analysis and change of the situational determinants of burnout rather than focusing on individual personalities of the human caregivers. So my own story in the Stanford Prison Experiment is not simply whatever role I played in ending the study earlier than planned, but my role in beginning a new research program that was inspired by my personal experience with that unique study.[17]

I might add that as the flip side to the deindividuation processes that were so potent in the SPE, Christina has also done pioneering research on its opposite, *individuation*, the ways in which people strive for uniqueness.[18]

Phil Zimbardo. And then there was me. (See notes for status of Curtis Banks and David Jaffee.[19]) The week in the SPE changed my life in many ways, both professionally and personally. The outcomes that can be traced to the unexpectedly positive consequences that this experience created for me were vast. My research was affected, as was my teaching and personal life, and I became a social change agent for improving prison conditions and highlighting other forms of institutional abuses of power.

My research focus for the following three decades has been stimulated by a variety of ideas I extracted from this prison simulation. They led me to study shyness, time perspective, and madness. It also changed my approach to teaching. Please allow me, at this point, to amplify on these three intersecting lines of research and the changes in my teaching style that were all stimulated by the SPE. Following that, I will reveal in a bit more detail how the experiment also helped to change my personal life.

Shyness as Self-Imposed Prison

> What other dungeon is so dark as one's own heart! What jailer
> so inexorable as one's self?
>
> —Nathaniel Hawthorne

In our basement jail, prisoners surrendered their basic freedoms in response to the coercive control of the guards. Yet in real life beyond the laboratory, many people voluntarily give up their freedoms of speech, action, and association without external guards forcing them to do so. They have internalized the demanding guard as part of their self-image; the guard who limits their options for spontaneity, liberty, and joy in life. Paradoxically, these same people have also internalized the image of the passive prisoner who reluctantly acquiesces to these self-imposed restrictions on all their actions. Any action that calls attention to one's person threatens her or him with potential humiliation, shame, and social rejection and thus must be avoided. In response to that inner guardian, the prisoner-self shrinks back from life, retreats into a shell, and chooses the safety of the silent prison of shyness.

Elaborating that metaphor from the SPE led me to think about shyness as a social phobia that breaks the bonds of the human connection by making other people threatening rather than inviting. The year after our prison study ended, I started a major research initiative, the Stanford Shyness Project, to investigate the causes, correlates, and consequences of shyness in adults and adolescents. Ours was the first systematic study of adult shyness; once we knew enough, we went on to develop a program for treating shyness in a unique Shyness Clinic (1977). The clinic, which has been in continuous operation over all this time in the Palo Alto community, has been directed by Dr. Lynne Henderson and is now part of the Pacific Graduate School of Psychology. My primary goal in the treatment and prevention of shyness has been to develop means to help shy people liberate themselves from their self-imposed, silent prisons. I have done so in part through writing popular books for the general public on how to deal with shyness in adults and children.[20] These activities are a counterpoint to the imprisonment to which I had subjected the participants in the SPE.

Time Perspective Biases

> People on the outside tend to live looking toward the future. The future for a convict is vague and sketchy. His past is gone; people stop writing after a while. The present becomes magnified.
>
> —Ken Whalen, ex-convict and playwright[21]

In the SPE, time sense became distorted in many ways. For the prisoners, their sleep cycle was disrupted by forced awakening for the counts; they were always tired, and that exhaustion was amplified by the tedious exercises and menial work regimes assigned to them. Their sense of time was also affected by the absence of external signs of day and night and lack of clocks. (The absence of clocks is part of the design strategy of gambling casinos to embed gamblers in an expanded present by removing any references to time.) As noted in the last chapter, the prisoners magnified their focus on the awful present by talking about the immediate situation and rarely about their past or future lives. Interestingly, after each of the prisoners who was released early was gone, the remaining prisoners made virtually no references to them. They were gone and forgotten, pushed out of immediate memory focus.

As for the staff, our time perspective also became distorted by the long shifts we had to endure, the short sleep episodes, and the many different logistical and tactical issues we had to deal with every day and night. I think that some of our misjudgments and indecisions can be traced in part to our distorted time sense. These experiences led to my need to understand how human behavior is influenced by our sense of time perspective, the way we partition the flow of our experiences into the temporal categories of past, present, and future. Using surveys, interviews, experiments, and cross-cultural studies, I learned many new things about time perspective that enabled me to develop a valid, reliable metric for assessing individual differences in time perspective.[22] The Zimbardo Time Perspective Inventory (ZTPI) is being used by researchers around the world to study a host of important phenomena, such as decision-making biases, health issues, stress, addiction, problem solving, environmental sustainability, and many more "time-tagged" phenomena.

Most people's lives are controlled by their overuse of one time frame—past, present, or future—and underreliance on the other frames, which they should be using in a more flexible, balanced fashion depending on the demands of any given situation. When there is work to be done, the discipline associated with future orientation is needed. When we need to connect to family and friends, the rooted positive past should be called upon. When we want to enjoy life's sensual pleasures and seek new adventures, a present orientation best enables us to do so. Many factors contribute to biasing people toward being excessively present-oriented—either hedonistic or fatalistic—excessively future-oriented, or excessively past-oriented—in either positive or negative focus. Among those factors are cultural influences, education, religion, social class, family modeling, and personal experiences. The SPE made it obvious that time perspective was not merely a personal trait or an outcome measure but could be altered by experiences in situations that expanded or contracted it.

When studying institutions, it also becomes apparent that time perspective plays a powerful, hidden role in shaping the minds of the those who become "institutionalized," whether in prisons, homes for the aged, or chronic care hospitals. Endless routines and undifferentiated daily activities create a seeming circularity of time—it just flows on, undivided into meaningful linear units but creeping onward as if it were an ant's journey on a Möbius strip of life. Among his insights into the meaning of imprisonment in *Soledad Brother*, George Jackson reflects on time and its distortion:

> The Time slips away from me. . . . There is no rest from it even at night. . . .
> The days, even the weeks lapse one into the other, endlessly into one another. Each day that comes and goes is exactly like the one that went before.[23]

Madness in Normal People

> Do you know what you have done? [Sherlock Holmes asked
> Sigmund Freud] You have succeeded in taking my methods—
> observation and inference—and applying them to the inside of
> a subject's head.
>
> —Nicholas Meyer, *The Seven Percent Solution*

One of the most dramatic outcomes of the SPE was the way in which many healthy, normal young men began to behave pathologically in a short time. Because our selection procedures ruled out preexistent, so-called premorbid, dispositions as causal factors, I wanted to understand the processes by which psychopathological symptoms first develop in ordinary people. Thus, in addition to stimulating me to study shyness and time perspective, my experiences in the SPE stimulated a new line of theorizing and experimental research on how normal people first begin to "go mad."

Most of what is known about abnormal functioning comes from retrospective analyses that attempt to figure out what factors might have caused the current mental disturbance in a given person—much like Sherlock Holmes's strategies of inferential reasoning from effects back to causes. Instead, I tried to develop a model that focuses on the processes involved in the development of symptoms of mental disorders, such as phobia and paranoia. People are motivated to generate explanations when they perceive that some expectation about their functioning is violated. They try to make sense of what went wrong when they fail in academic, social, business, athletic, or sexual situations—depending on how important such a discrepancy is to their self-integrity. The rational search process for meaning is distorted by cognitive biases that focus attention on classes of explanation that are not appropriate in the current analysis. Thus, overusing explanations that focus on "people" as the causes of one's reactions may bias the search for meaning toward developing symptoms characteristic of paranoid thinking. Similarly, explanations focused on "environments" as the causes of one's reactions may bias that search toward the symptom development typical of phobic thinking.

This new model of the cognitive and social bases of "madness" in normal, healthy people has been validated in our controlled laboratory experiments. We have found, for example, that pathological symptoms may develop in up to one third of normal participants in the rational process of their trying to make sense of unexplained sources of arousal.[24] We also demonstrated that college students with normal hearing who were made to experience partial temporary deafness by means of hypnotic suggestion soon began to think and act in paranoid ways, believing that others were hostile to them. Thus, undetected hearing impairment in the elderly may be a contributor to their development of paranoid disorders—and thus can be prevented or treated with hearing aids rather than psychotherapy or institutionalization.

Therefore, I have argued that the seeds of madness can be planted in anyone's backyard and will grow in response to transient psychological perturbations in the course of the lifetime of ordinary experience. Switching from a restrictive medical model of mental disturbances to a public health model encourages the search for situational vectors at play in individual and societal disturbances rather than restricting the search to within the head of the distressed individual. We are in a better position to prevent, as well as to treat, madness and psychopathology when we bring fundamental knowledge of cognitive, social, and cultural processes to bear on a fuller appreciation of the mechanisms involved in transforming normal into dysfunctional behavior.

Teaching by Powering Down

My awareness of the ease with which I became a dominating power figure in the SPE led me to restructure my teaching methods to give students more power and limit the teacher's role to his command of expertise in his field rather than social control. I instituted "open-mike" periods at the start of class when students in large lectures could criticize anything about the course or make personal statements about it. This evolved into online bulletin boards in which students were encouraged to speak openly about positive and negative aspects of the course every day throughout the term. I also reduced competition for top grades among students by not grading on a curve and instead developing absolute standards that derived from each student's mastery of material criteria, taking tests with a learning partner, and even eliminating grading altogether in some courses.[25]

The SPE's Personal Impact

The year after the end of the SPE (August 10, 1972), I married Christina Maslach at the Stanford Memorial Church, where we also renewed our marital vows on our twenty-fifth anniversary in the presence of our children. That heroine profoundly affects all that I do in the best ways imaginable. In this relationship, I was able to salvage one more bit of heaven from the hell of that prison experience.

Another personal impact that this little weeklong study had on me was in becoming an advocate for social change based on research-based evidence, in promoting prison reform, and in my dedicated efforts to maximize the reach of the SPE's significant messages. Let's review them in some detail.

Maximizing the Gain: Spreading the Social Gospel

While the SPE changed my life in many ways, one of the most abrupt changes occurred as the result of my invited appearance before a subcommittee of the U.S. House of Representatives: suddenly, I was transformed from an academic researcher to an advocate for social change. In its hearings on prison reform in

October 1971, the subcommittee wanted not only analysis but also recommendations for reform. In my statement in the *Congressional Record*, I clearly advocated congressional intervention into the prison structure to bring about improvements in the condition of inmates, as well as for correctional personnel.[26]

My advocacy has largely taken the form of consciousness raising about the necessity for ending the "social experiment" of prisons because, as demonstrated by the high rates of recidivism, the experiment has failed. We must find the reason for that through more thorough systems analyses and propose alternative solutions to incarceration. We must also break down resistance to meaningful prison reform. My second testimony before a congressional subcommittee, which focused on juvenile detention (September 1973), moved me further toward becoming a social advocate. I outlined nineteen separate recommendations for improved treatment of detained juveniles.[27] I was pleased to learn that a new federal law was passed that was in part stimulated by my testimony. Senator Birch Bayh, who headed this investigation, helped to put into law the rule that, to prevent their being abused, juveniles in pretrial detention should not be housed with adults in federal prisons. The SPE was about abuse of juveniles in pretrial detention. (Of course, we confused matters by having parole hearings, which in real life would not occur until one had been convicted and sentenced.)

One powerful legal impact of the SPE for me derived from my participation in the federal court trial of *Spain et al. v. Procunier et al.* (1973). The "San Quentin Six" prisoners had been isolated in solitary confinement for more than three years for their alleged involvement in the murder of guards and informer prisoners during the escape attempt of George Jackson on August 21, 1971. As an expert witness, I toured the facilities of San Quentin's maximum-adjustment center and interviewed each of the six prisoners a number of times. My prepared statement and two days of trial testimony concluded with the opinion that all of these prison conditions of involuntary, prolonged, indefinite confinement under dehumanizing conditions constituted "cruel and unusual punishment" and must therefore be changed. The court arrived at a similar conclusion. In addition, I served throughout the trial as a psychological consultant to the team of lawyers for the plaintiffs.

These and other activities that I have engaged in following the SPE were undertaken with the sense of an ethical mission. To balance the relative ethics equation, I felt it was necessary to compensate for the pain experienced by our SPE participants by maximizing the gain of this research to science and society. My early efforts are summarized in a book chapter written in 1983, "Transforming Experimental Research into Advocacy for Social Change."[28]

The Power of Media and Visual Images

Because the SPE was such a visual experience, we used its images to spread the message of situational power. First, I created a slide show of eighty images that were synchronized to my audiotaped narration, with the help of Gregory White in 1972; it was distributed mostly to college teachers as a lecture supplement. The advent of video enabled us to transfer these images and include in the presentation both archival footage from the study along with new footage, interviews, and my videotaped narration. This project was developed with a team of Stanford students headed by Ken Musen, the director of *Quiet Rage: The Stanford Prison Experiment* (1985). Recently, it was upgraded to DVD format with the assistance of Scott Plous in 2004. This fifty-minute presentation ensures the best quality and worldwide accessibility. Its many dramatic still and action images made it possible to further broaden the reach of the SPE by including a segment on it in Program 19 of the public television series that I helped to develop, *Discovering Psychology*, "The Power of the Situation." I was also able to feature images from the SPE in my introductory psychology textbooks, *Psychology and Life* and *Psychology: Core Concepts*. Those images have also been incorporated into my lectures on the psychology of evil before student, professional, and civic audiences.

The first publication of the SPE was in an article in the mainstream media, "The Mind Is a Formidable Jailer: A Pirandellian Prison," in *The New York Times Magazine* (April 8, 1973). This presentation was designed to reach beyond the usual limited academic audience for such experimental research. In this publication, the power of the story was amplified by the inclusion of many illustrative images. A story in *Life* magazine (October 15, 1971), entitled "I Almost Considered the Prisoners as Cattle," attracted further media attention.

The visual nature of the SPE made it ripe for television and other media coverage. I mentioned earlier that it was featured only a few months after its completion on NBC-TV's *Chronolog* series.[29] The illustrated story of the SPE was also aired on *60 Minutes* and the *National Geographic* TV series.[30] Most recently, it was featured in a well-made television program, "The Human Behavior Experiments."[31]

Other ways in which I have actively tried to extend the impact of our study include the following:

- Presenting the study to civic, judicial, military, law enforcement, and psychology groups to enlighten them and to arouse concern about prison life.
- Organizing conferences on corrections in the U.S. military (1972, 1973, and 1974) that examined the relationship of research programs to policy decisions and measured their impact on military correctional systems. One focus was on systemic problems, such as racial discrimination and the frustrations of ambition that are fostered by recruiters.[32]
- Helping a local community test out its new jail and its newly hired staff by creating a mock prison in which 132 citizens volunteered to role-play prisoners for three days: The power of role-playing we witnessed in the SPE was even more dramatic in this real jail setting—given that these guards realized that they were under public scrutiny, they behaved rather kindly.

A reporter noted some of the extreme reactions: "A housewife exhibited the symptoms of a nervous breakdown and had to be released." "A woman inmate took another hostage, held a knife to her throat, pierced the skin and refused to end the role she was supposed to be playing. Guards had to overpower her." "Many would later remark that within a day their minds grew foggy and they couldn't concentrate. They became irritated by the lack of privacy, especially the open toilets. Some felt abandoned and dehumanized. Others said they began to withdraw or wanted to rebel. Some lost track of time." This demonstration alerted the staff to several technical and operational problems that they fixed before opening the jail for local felons. One of the mock prisoners was an attorney who concluded that despite the good appearance of the jail and the courteous staff, prison "really is a miserable place to be."[33] As a result of this mock prison trial, the officials put into place remedial practices designed to counter such extreme reactions from future inmates.

- Exchanging letters (all *handwritten*, in those precomputer days!) with more than two hundred prisoners, a dozen of whom became regular correspondents. Even today, I answer many e-mail queries every day from students, notably British high school students, for whom the SPE is required learning in the social and cognitive psychology portion of their A Level courses (see www.revision-notes.co.uk).

Two of the most powerful letters that were stimulated by the SPE came from a psychologist colleague recently and from a prisoner right after the study. I'd like to share them before we move on to examine further extensions of our experiment in different realms. The psychologist described the parallels between the SPE and the military indoctrination he had experienced:

My interest in social psychology began when I was a cadet at the USAF Academy and read about (or saw the video of) the SPE study in my intro psych class. It spoke to what I saw going on all around me in the indoctrination of promising young minds into killing, dehumanizing, abuse machines. Your analysis is dead on: It is not a question of getting more moral soldiers. Instead it is a question of recognizing how the situation of war (and the cultural institutions/practices of the military that we have designed to "prepare" people for that situation) creates monsters out of us all.[34]

A prisoner in an Ohio state prison described the abuses he experienced and the rage they instilled in him:

I was recently released from "solitary confinement" after being held therein for 37 months [months!]. A silent system was imposed upon me and to even "whisper" to the man in the next cell resulted in being beaten by guards, sprayed with chemical mace, black-jacked, stomped, and thrown into a "strip-cell" naked to sleep on a concrete floor without bedding, covering, wash basin, or even a toilet. The floor served as toilet and bed, and even there the "silent system" was enforced. To let a "moan" escape your lips because of the pain and discomfort resulted in another beating. I spent not days, but months there during my 37 months in solitary.

I have filed every writ possible against the administrative acts of brutality. The State Courts have all denied the petitions. Because of my refusal to let the "things die down" and "forget" all that happened during my 37 months in solitary, I am the most hated prisoner in this Ohio Penitentiary and called a "hard-core incorrigible."

Professor Zimbardo, maybe I am an incorrigible, but if true, it's because I would rather die than to accept being treated as less than a human being. I have never complained of my prison sentence as being unjustified except through legal means of appeals. I have never put a knife on a guard's throat and demanded my release. I know that thieves must be punished and I don't justify stealing, even though I am a thief myself. But now I don't think I will be a thief when I am released.

No, I'm not rehabilitated. It's just that I no longer think of becoming wealthy by stealing. I now only think of "killing." Killing those who have beaten me and treated me as if I were a dog. I hope and pray for the sake of my own soul and future life of freedom, that I am able to overcome the bitterness and hatred which eats daily at my soul, but I know to overcome it will not be easy.

REPLICATIONS AND EXTENSIONS

We bring to an end our investigation into the Stanford Prison Experiment as a social phenomenon with a brief overview of the ways in which its results have been replicated or reproduced and have been extended in various domains. Beyond its utility within social science, the SPE has migrated far out into other realms, into the public arena of television shows, commercial film, and even artistic productions. Its basic findings about the ease with which good people can be transformed into perpetrators of evil if their institutional power is not restrained has led to some social and military applications designed to prevent such outcomes.

Because it is important for us to move on to consider the full range of psychological research that validates and broadens the conclusions of the SPE, at this point it is sufficient simply to outline these replications and extensions. A fuller presentation of this material, with detailed commentary and references, is available at www.lucifereffect.com.

A Solid Replication in Another Culture

A team of researchers at the University of New South Wales, Australia, extended the SPE by having one condition similar to ours and several other experimental variants to explore how social organizations influence the relationship between prisoners and guards.[35] Their "Standard Custodial" regime was modeled on medium-security prisons in Australia and was closest in its procedure to the SPE. The researchers' central conclusion of their rigorous experimental protocol notes: "Our results thus support the major conclusion of Zimbardo et al that hostile, confrontive relations in prisons result primarily from the nature of the prison regime, rather than the personal characteristics of inmates and officers" (p. 283). These results, within this research design, also help offset skepticism about the validity of such simulation experiments by providing baselines to assess behavioral changes from objectively defined structural characteristics of real-life prisons.[36]

The Mock Psychiatric Ward Experience

For three days, twenty-nine staff members at Elgin State Hospital in Illinois were confined to a ward of their own, a mental ward in which they performed the role of "patient." Twenty-two regular staff played their usual roles while trained observers and video cameras recorded what transpired. "It was really fantastic the things that happened in there," reported research director Norma Jean Orlando. In a short time the mock patients began acting in ways that were indistinguishable from those of real patients: six tried to escape, two withdrew into themselves, two wept uncontrollably, one came close to having a nervous breakdown. Most experienced a general increase in tension, anxiety, frustration, and despair. The vast majority of staff-patients (more than 75 percent) reported feeling each of the following: "incarcerated," without an identity, as if their feelings were not important, as if nobody were listening to them, not being treated as a person, nobody caring about them, forgetting it was an experiment, and really feeling like a patient. One staff-member-turned-patient who suffered during his weekend ordeal gained enough insight to declare: "I used to look at the patients as if they were a bunch of animals; I never knew what they were going through before."[37]

The positive outcome of this study, which was conceived as a follow-up to the Stanford Prison Experiment, was the formation of an organization of staff members who worked cooperatively with current and former patients. They became dedicated to raising the consciousness of the hospital personnel about the way patients were being mistreated, as well as working at personally improving their own relationship to patients and of patients' relationship with staff. They came to realize the power of their "total situation" to transform the behavior of patients and staff in unwelcome ways, and then in more constructive ways.

A Seeming Replication Failure in a TV Pseudoexperiment

An experiment was conducted for a BBC-TV show based on the SPE model. Its results challenged those of the SPE because the guards showed little violence or cruelty. Let's fast-forward to the end of the study and its remarkable conclusion: the prisoners dominated the guards! The *guards* became "increasingly paranoid, depressed and stressed and complained most of being bullied."[38] Repeat, not the prisoners but the guards were distressed by their experiences in this reality TV show. Several of the guards couldn't take it anymore and quit; none of the prisoners did so. The prisoners soon established the upper hand, working as a team to undermine the guards; then everyone got together and decided to form a peaceful "commune"—with the help of a labor union organizer! Our Lucifer Effect website contains a critical analysis of this pseudoexperiment.

The SPE as a Warning Against Abuse of Power

Two of the unexpected uses of our research have been in women's shelters and in the Navy's Survival, Evasion, Resistance, and Escape (SERE) program. Directors of a number of shelters for abused women have informed me that they use our *Quiet Rage* video to illustrate the ease with which masculine power can become abusive and destructive. Seeing the film and discussing its implications helps abused women not to blame themselves for their abuse but to better understand the situational factors that transformed their once loving mates into such abusing criminals. The experiment has also become absorbed into some versions of feminist theory of gender relations based on power.

Every branch of the military has a version of the SERE program. It was developed after the Korean War to teach those captured by the enemy how to withstand and resist extreme forms of coercive interrogation and abuse. Central to the training is the psychological and physical hardship trainees experience for days within a mock prisoner-of-war camp. This intense, grueling simulation prepares them to better cope with the terrors they might face if they are captured and tortured.

I have been informed by several sources in the Navy that the SPE's message of the ease with which command power can become excessive has been made explicit in its training through using both our video and our website. This serves to warn the SERE trainer-captors against the impulse to "go over the top" in abusing their "captives." So one use of the SPE is to guide training in "guard" restraint in a setting that gives permission for guards to abuse others "for their own eventual good."

On the other hand, the SERE program, as practiced by the Army at Fort Bragg, North Carolina, has been indicted by a number of critics as now being misused by the Pentagon. They argue that top officials have "flipped the switch" from focusing on ways to increase resistance by captured American soldiers to developing effective interrogation techniques to use against captured "enemy combatants" and other assumed enemies of America. According to several accounts, these techniques have migrated from the military SERE programs to Guantánamo Bay Prison, known as "Gitmo."

An American law professor, M. Gregg Bloche, and Jonathan H. Marks, a British barrister and bioethics fellow, have condemned the use of these interrogation procedures, which have been developed in part by behavioral scientists and physicians. They argue that "by bringing SERE tactics and the Guantanamo model onto the battlefield, the Pentagon opened a Pandora's box of potential abuse . . . the SERE model's embrace by the Pentagon's civilian leaders is further evidence that abuse tantamount to torture was national policy, not merely the product of rogue freelancers."[39] The investigative reporter Jane Mayer in a *New Yorker* essay, "The Experiment," has expressed similar concerns.[40] I will visit the issue of the misuse of the SPE by the Pentagon in chapter 15.

The tactics developed by SERE programs were part of the protocol for defensive training of military personnel in case of enemy capture; however, after the terrorist attacks of September 11, 2001, they were retrofit to be part of the arsenal of offensive tactics to elicit information from military personnel or civilians considered as enemies. Their objective was to make those being interrogated feel vulnerable, be pliable, and become cooperative in revealing desired information. Their techniques were developed with the help of behavioral scientist consultants and refined based on trial-and-error field practice in SERE drills at Fort Bragg, North Carolina, and other military training installations. In general, these tactics minimized the use of physical torture, substituting mental, "soft torture" instead. Five of the main tactics in the SERE program to render detainees or others being interrogated as amenable to yielding information and confessions are:

- Sexual humiliation and degradation
- Humiliation based on religious and cultural practices
- Sleep deprivation
- Sensory deprivation and sensory overload
- Physical torment to achieve the psychological advantages of fear and anxiety, such as "water-boarding," or hypothermia (exposure to freezing temperatures)

We see these tactics specifically proposed in memos of both Secretary Rumsfeld for use at Guantánamo and of General Sanchez at Abu Ghraib, and put into operation at those prisons and elsewhere. There is also documented evidence that a team of interrogators and other military personnel from Guantánamo visited the SERE training program at Fort Bragg in August 2002. Given the classified nature of this information, these statements are of course only reasonable inferences based on reports from various knowledgeable sources.

Is it possible that the SPE's main message of situational power was co-opted by the Pentagon and utilized in its torture training programs? I would not like to believe that; however, one recent critique makes that claim rather powerfully.

"This appears to be the experiment that informs torture in Iraq . . . A situation is created—made worse by understaffing, danger, and no outside independent controls—and with a little encouragement (never specific instructions to torture) guards do torture. This situation and this torture are now widely recognized in U.S. prisons in Iraq. . . . The U.S. administration's advantage in the Stanford experiment 'situation' is that it provides deniability—there are no orders to torture, but the situation can be predicted to cause it."[41]

The authors of this opinion go on to specify that this is more than mere speculation because the Stanford Prison Experiment is singled out in the Schlesinger Committee Report investigating the Abu Ghraib abuses. They argue that "[t]he publication of information about this experiment in an official document, linking it to conditions in U.S. military prisons, further reveals chain of command responsibility for policy." The key link to the SPE in the Schlesinger Report is how it highlighted the power of the pathological situation created in our experimental prison.

"The negative, anti-social reactions observed were not the product of an environment created by combining a collection of deviant personalities, but rather, the result of an intrinsically pathological situation which could distort and rechannel the behavior of essentially normal individuals. The abnormality here resided in the psychological nature of the situation and not in those who passed through it."[42]

Crossovers into Popular Culture

Three examples of how our experiment has crossed the boundary from the ivory tower into the realms of music, theater, and art come from a rock group, a German movie, and the art of a Polish artist whose "art form" was exhibited at the 2005 Venice Biennale. "Stanford Prison Experiment" (minus the "The") is the name of a rock band from Los Angeles whose intense music is "a fusion of punk and noise," according to its leader, who learned about the SPE as a student at UCLA.[43] *Das Experiment* is a German film based on the SPE that has been widely shown around the world. This attribution of *Das Experiment*, as inspired by the SPE, gives legitimacy and a real-world quality to this "fantasy," as the scriptwriter called it. It purposely confuses viewers about what did happen in our study with the liberties that were taken for the sake of sensationalism. It ends up being a vulgar display of sexism and gratuitous sexuality and violence with no redeeming value.

Although some viewers found the film exciting, the movie was panned in critical reviews, such as these by two well-known British film critics. *The Observer*'s reviewer concluded, " 'The Experiment' is an improbable thriller of no great originality that offers itself as a fable of national (possibly universal) inclination toward authoritarian fascism."[44] Harsher was the reviewer of *The Guardian:* "Any episode of Big Brother would have had more insight than this silly and obtuse nonsense."[45] An American film critic, Roger Ebert, extracted one valuable lesson from the movie, which applies to the SPE as well: "Perhaps uniforms turn us into packs, led by the top dog. There are few strays."[46]

A Polish artist, Artur Zmijewski, has made a forty-six-minute film, *Repetition*, that highlights the seven days paid volunteers spent in his mock prison. The film was screened every hour on the hour to large audiences in the Polish Pavilion at the June 2005 Venice Biennale, the world's oldest celebration of contemporary art, and also shown in Warsaw and San Francisco art venues.

According to one reviewer, this film "suggests that Zimbardo's experiment, which has as much intuition as strictly scientific method in its design, may have had the makings of a work of art. . . . In the simulated prison, however, artistic decorum soon gets left behind. The 'game' achieves a momentum of its own, so completely wrapping up its players in its dynamic that it starts to touch them at the core. Guards get more brutal and controlling. The disobedient are put in solitary; all heads are shaved. At this point a few prisoners, rather than simply seeing all this as annoying play that they can bear with for as long as it takes (at $40 a day), see it as a genuinely evil situation and quit the 'experiment' for good."[47]

THE STANFORD PRISON EXPERIMENT WEBSITE: INTERNET POWER

Using archival footage and a forty-two-page slide show, www.prisonexp.org tells the story of what happened during our experiment's six fateful days; it includes background documents, discussion questions, articles, interviews, and a wealth of other material for teachers, students, and anyone else interested in learning more about the experiment and corrections, in five languages. It was launched in December 1999, with the expert assistance of Scott Plous and Mike Lestik.

If you visit Google.com and do a keyword search for "Experiment," what you are likely to discover is that the SPE is the top-ranked website worldwide, out of 291 million results, as of August 2006. Similarly, an August 2006 Google keyword search for "Prison" places the Stanford Prison Experiment website second only to the Federal Bureau of Prisons of the United States, out of more than 192 million results.

On a typical day, www.prisonexp.org's pages are viewed more than 25,000 times, more than 38 million times since the site was launched. At the height of news coverage on the Abu Ghraib Prison abuses in May and June 2004, Web traffic to the Stanford Prison Experiment website (and its parent site, www.social psychology.org) exceeded 250,000 page views per day. This level of traffic attests not only to public interest in psychological research but to the need many people feel to understand the dynamics of imprisonment or, more generally, the dynamics of power and oppression. The data may also reflect the now-legendary status that this experiment has attained in many countries of the world.

One vivid, very personal consequence of visiting the SPE website can be seen in the following letter to me from a nineteen-year-old psychology student who describes the personal value he got from his exposure to it. It enabled him to better understand a terrible experience he had had during military boot camp:

> Not too far into it [watching the Stanford Prison Experiment], I was almost in tears. November 2001, I joined the United States Marine Corps, pursuing a childhood dream. To make a long story short, I had become the victim of repeated illegal physical and mental abuse. An investigation showed I suffered more than 40 unprovoked beatings. Eventually, as much as I fought it, I became suicidal, thus received a discharge from U.S.M.C. boot camp. I was in this base for just about 3 months.
>
> The point I am trying to make is that the manner in which your guards carried about their duties and the way that Military Drill Instructors do is unbelievable. I was amazed at all the parallels of your guards and one particular D.I. that comes to mind. I was treated much the same way and even worse in some cases.
>
> One incident that stands out was an effort to break platoon solidarity. I was forced to sit in the middle of my squad bay [living quarters] and shout to the other recruits "if you guys would have moved faster, we wouldn't be doing this for hours" referencing every single other recruit holding over their heads very heavy foot lockers. The event was very similar to the prisoners saying, "#819 was a bad prisoner." After my incident and after I was home safe some months later, all I could think about was how much I wanted to go back to show the other recruits that as much as the D.I.'s told the platoon that I was a bad recruit, I wasn't. [Just as our prisoner Stew-819 wanted to do.] Other behaviors come to mind like the push-ups for punishment, shaved heads, not having any identity other than being addressed as and referring to other people as "Recruit So-and-so" which replicates your study.
>
> The point of it all is even though your experiment was conducted 31 yrs. ago, my reading the study has helped me gain an understanding I was previously unable to gain before, even after therapy and counseling. What you have demonstrated really gave me insight into something I've been dealing with for almost a year now. Although, it is certainly not an excuse for their behavior, I now can understand the rationale behind the D.I.'s actions as far as being sadistic and power hungry.
>
> In short, Dr. Zimbardo, thank you.

A full, graphic depiction of the making of a Marine can be found in William Mares, *The Marine Machine.*[48]

It is reasonable to conclude that there is something about this little experiment that has enduring value not only among social scientists but also even more strongly among the general public. I now believe that special something is the dramatic transformation of human nature, not by Dr. Jekyll's mysterious chemicals, which turned him into the evil Mr. Hyde, but rather by the power of social situations and the Systems that create and sustain them. My colleagues and I are pleased that we have been able "to give psychology a way into the public consciousness" in an informative, interesting, and entertaining way that enables all of us to understand something so basic and disturbing about human nature.

Now it is time to broaden our empirical foundation beyond this one experiment as we turn in the next several chapters to review a variety of research from many sources that more fully informs us about how much situations can matter in turning good people into evildoers.

CHAPTER TWELVE

Investigating Social Dynamics: Power, Conformity, and Obedience

I believe that in all men's lives at certain periods, and in many men's lives at all periods between infancy and extreme old age, one of the most dominant elements is the desire to be inside the local Ring and the terror of being left outside. . . . Of all the passions the passion for the Inner Ring is most skilful in making a man who is not yet a very bad man do very bad things.

—C. S. Lewis, "The Inner Ring" (1944)[1]

Motives and needs that ordinarily serve us well can lead us astray when they are aroused, amplified, or manipulated by situational forces that we fail to recognize as potent. This is why evil is so pervasive. Its temptation is just a small turn away, a slight detour on the path of life, a blur in our sideview mirror, leading to disaster.

In trying to understand the character transformations of the good young men in the Stanford Prison Experiment, I previously outlined a number of psychological processes that were pivotal in perverting their thoughts, feelings, perceptions, and actions. We saw how the basic need to belong, to associate with and be accepted by others, so central to community building and family bonding, was diverted in the SPE into conformity with newly emergent norms that enabled the guards to abuse the prisoners.[2] We saw further that the basic motive for consistency between our private attitudes and public behavior allowed for dissonant commitments to be resolved and rationalized in violence against one's fellows.[3]

I will argue that the most dramatic instances of directed behavior change and "mind control" are not the consequence of exotic forms of influence, such as hypnosis, psychotropic drugs, or "brainwashing," but rather the systematic manipulation of the most mundane aspects of human nature over time in confining settings.[4]

It is in this sense, I believe what the English scholar C. S. Lewis proposed—that a powerful force in transforming human behavior, pushing people across the boundary between good and evil, comes from the basic desire to be "in" and not "out." If we think of social power as arrayed in a set of concentric circles from the most powerful central or inner ring moving outward to the least socially significant outer ring, we can appreciate his focus on the centripetal pull of that central circle. Lewis's "Inner Ring" is the elusive Camelot of acceptance into some special group, some privileged association, that confers instant status and enhanced identity. Its lure for most of us is obvious—who does not want to be a member of the "in-group"? Who does not want to know that she or he has been tried and found worthy of inclusion in, of ascendance into, a new, rarified realm of social acceptability?

Peer pressure has been identified as one social force that makes people, especially adolescents, do strange things—anything—to be accepted. However, the quest for the Inner Ring is nurtured from within. There is no peer-pressure power without that push from self-pressure for Them to want You. It makes people willing to suffer through painful, humiliating initiation rites in fraternities, cults, social clubs, or the military. It justifies for many suffering a lifelong existence climbing the corporate ladder.

This motivational force is doubly energized by what Lewis called the "terror of being left outside." This fear of rejection when one wants acceptance can cripple initiative and negate personal autonomy. It can turn social animals into shy introverts. The imagined threat of being cast into the out-group can lead some people to do virtually anything to avoid their terrifying rejection. Authorities can command total obedience not through punishments or rewards but by means of the double-edged weapon: the lure of acceptance coupled with the threat of rejection. So strong is this human motive that even strangers are empowered when they promise us a special place at their table of shared secrets—"just between you and me."[5]

A sordid example of these social dynamics came to light recently when a forty-year-old woman pleaded guilty to having sex with five high school boys and providing them and others with drugs and alcohol at weekly sex parties in her home for a full year. She told police that she had done it because she wanted to be a "cool mom." In her affidavit, this newly cool mom told investigators that she had never been popular with her classmates in high school, but orchestrating these parties enabled her to begin "feeling like one of the group."[6] Sadly, she caught the wrong Inner Ring.

Lewis goes on to describe the subtle process of initiation, the indoctrination of good people into a private Inner Ring that can have malevolent consequences, turning them into "scoundrels." I cite this passage at length because it is such an eloquent expression of how this basic human motive can be imperceptibly perverted by those with the power to admit or deny access to their Inner Ring. It will set the stage for our excursion into the experimental laboratories and field settings of social scientists who have investigated such phenomena in considerable depth.

> To nine out of ten of you the choice which could lead to scoundrelism will come, when it does come, in no very dramatic colors. Obviously bad men, obviously threatening or bribing, will almost certainly not appear. Over a drink or a cup of coffee, disguised as a triviality and sandwiched between

two jokes, from the lips of a man, or woman, whom you have recently been getting to know rather better and whom you hope to know better still—just at the moment when you are most anxious not to appear crude, or naive or a prig—the hint will come. It will be the hint of something, which is not quite in accordance with the technical rules of fair play, something that the public, the ignorant, romantic public, would never understand. Something which even the outsiders in your own profession are apt to make a fuss about, but something, says your new friend, which "we"—and at the word "we" you try not to blush for mere pleasure— something "we always do." And you will be drawn in, if you are drawn in, not by desire for gain or ease, but simply because at that moment, when the cup was so near your lips, you cannot bear to be thrust back again into the cold outer world. It would be so terrible to see the other man's face— that genial, confidential, delightfully sophisticated face—turn suddenly cold and contemptuous, to know that you had been tried for the Inner Ring and rejected. And then, if you are drawn in, next week it will be something a little further from the rules, and next year something further still, but all in the jolliest, friendliest spirit. It may end in a crash, a scandal, and penal servitude; it may end in millions, a peerage and giving the prizes at your old school. But you will be a scoundrel.

RESEARCH REVELATIONS OF SITUATIONAL POWER

The Stanford Prison Experiment is a facet of the broad mosaic of research that reveals the power of social situations and the social construction of reality. We have seen how it focused on power relationships among individuals within an institutional setting. A variety of studies that preceded and followed it have illuminated many other aspects of human behavior that are shaped in unexpected ways by situational forces.

Groups can get us to do things we ordinarily might not do on our own, but their influence is often indirect, simply modeling the normative behavior that the group wants us to imitate and practice. In contrast, authority influence is more often direct and without subtlety: "You do what I tell you to do." But because the demand is so open and bold-faced, one can decide to disobey and not follow the leader. To see what I mean, consider this question: To what extent would a good, ordinary person resist against or comply with the demand of an authority figure that he harm, or even kill, an innocent stranger? This provocative question was put to experimental test in a controversial study on blind obedience to authority. It is a classic experiment about which you have probably heard because of its "shocking" effects, but there is much more of value embedded in its procedures that we will extract to aid in our quest to understand why good people can be induced to behave badly. We will review replications and extensions of this classic study and again ask the question posed of all such research: What is its external validity, what are real-world parallels to the laboratory demonstration of authority power?

Beware: Self-Serving Biases May Be at Work

Before we get into the details of this research, I must warn you of a bias you likely possess that might shield you from drawing the right conclusions from all you are about to read. Most of us construct self-enhancing, self-serving, egocentric biases that make us feel special—never ordinary, and certainly "above average."[7] Such cognitive biases serve a valuable function in boosting our self-esteem and protecting against life's hard knocks. They enable us to explain away failures, take credit for our successes, and disown responsibility for bad decisions, perceiving our subjective world through rainbow prisms. For example, research shows that 86 percent of Australians rate their job performance as "above average," and 90 percent of American business managers rate their performance as superior to that of their average peer. (Pity that poor average dude.)

Yet these biases can be maladaptive as well by blinding us to our similarity to others and distancing us from the reality that people just like us behave badly in certain toxic situations. Such biases also mean that we don't take basic precautions to avoid the undesired consequences of our behavior, assuming it won't happen to us. So we take sexual risks, driving risks, gambling risks, health risks, and more. In the extreme version of these biases, most people believe that they are less vulnerable to these self-serving biases than other people, even after being taught about them.[8]

That means when you read about the SPE or the many studies in this next section, you might well conclude that *you* would not do what the majority has done, that you would, of course, be the exception to the rule. That statistically unreasonable belief (since most of us share it) makes you even more vulnerable to situational forces precisely because you underestimate their power as you overestimate yours. You are convinced that you would be the good guard, the defiant prisoner, the resistor, the dissident, the nonconformist, and, most of all, the Hero. Would that it were so, but heroes are a rare breed—some of whom we will meet in our final chapter.

So I invite you to suspend that bias for now and imagine that what the majority has done in these experiments is a fair base rate for you as well. At the very least, please consider that you can't be certain of whether or not you could be as readily seduced into doing what the average research participant has done in these studies—if you were in their shoes, under the same circumstances. I ask you to recall what Prisoner Clay-416, the sausage resister, said in his postexperimental interview with his tormenter, the "John Wayne" guard. When taunted with "What kind of guard would you have been if you were in my place?" he replied modestly, "I really don't know."

It is only through recognizing that we are all subject to the same dynamic forces in the human condition, that humility takes precedence over unfounded pride, that we can begin to acknowledge our vulnerability to situational forces. In this vein, recall John Donne's eloquent framing of our common interrelatedness and interdependence:

> All mankind is of one author, and is one volume; when one man dies, one chapter is not torn out of the book, but translated into a better language; and every chapter must be so translated. . . . As therefore the bell that rings to a sermon, calls not upon the preacher only, but upon the congregation to come: so this bell calls us all. . . . No man is an island, entire of itself . . . any man's death diminishes me, because I am involved in mankind; and therefore never send to know for whom the bell tolls; it tolls for thee.
>
> (*Meditations* 27)

Classic Research on Conforming to Group Norms

One of the earliest studies on conformity, in 1935, was designed by a social psychologist from Turkey, Muzafer Sherif.[9] Sherif, a recent immigrant to the United States, believed that Americans in general tended to conform because their democracy emphasized mutually shared agreements. He devised an unusual means of demonstrating conformity of individuals to group standards in a novel setting.

Male college students were individually ushered into a totally dark room in which there was a stationary spot of light. Sherif knew that without any frame of reference, such a light appears to move about erratically, an illusion called the "autokinetic effect." At first, each of these subjects was asked individually to judge the movement of the light. Their judgments varied widely; some saw movement of a few inches, while others reported that the spot moved many feet. Each person soon established a range within which most of his reports would fall. Next, he was put into a group with several others. They gave estimates that varied widely, but in each group a norm "crystallized" wherein a range of judgments and an average-norm judgment emerged. After many trials, the other participants left, and the individual, now alone, was asked again to make estimates of the movement of the light—the test of his conformity to the new norm established in that group. His judgments now fell in this new group-sanctioned range, "departing significantly from his earlier personal range."

Sherif also used a confederate who was trained to give estimates that varied in their latitude from a small to a very large range. Sure enough, the naive subject's autokinetic experience mirrored that of the judgments of this devious confederate rather than sticking to his previously established personal perceptual standard.

Asch's Conformity Research: Getting into Line

Sherif's conformity effect was challenged in 1955 by another social psychologist, Solomon Asch,[10] who believed that Americans were actually more independent than Sherif's work had suggested. Asch believed that Americans could act autonomously, even when faced with a majority who saw the world differently from them. The problem with Sherif's test situation, he argued, was that it was so ambiguous, without any meaningful frame of reference or personal standard. When challenged by the alternative perception of the group, the individual had no real commitment to his original estimates so just went along. Real conformity required the group to challenge the basic perception and beliefs of the individual— to say that X was Y, when clearly that was not true. Under those circumstances, Asch predicted, relatively few would conform; most would be staunchly resistant to this extreme group pressure that was so transparently wrong.

What actually happened to people confronted with a social reality that conflicted with their basic perceptions of the world? To find out, let me put you into the seat of a typical research participant.

You are recruited for a study of visual perception that begins with judging the relative size of lines. You are shown cards with three lines of differing lengths and asked to state out loud which of the three is the same length as a comparison line on another card. One is shorter, one is longer, and one is exactly the same length as the comparison line. The task is a piece of cake for you. You make few mistakes, just like most others (less than 1 percent of the time). But you are not alone in this study; you are flanked by a bunch of peers, seven of them, and you are number eight. At first, your answers are like theirs—all right on. But then unusual things start to happen. On some trials, each of them in turn reports seeing the long line as the same length as the medium line or the short line the same as the medium one. (Unknown to you, the other seven are members of Asch's research team who have been instructed to give incorrect answers unanimously on specific "critical" trials.) When it is your turn, they all look at you as you look at the card with the three lines. You are clearly seeing something different than they are, but do you say so? Do you stick to your guns and say what you know is right, or do you go along with what everyone else says is right? You face that same group pressure on twelve of the total eighteen trials where the group gives answers that are wrong, but they are accurate on the other six trials interspersed into the mix.

If you are like most of the 123 actual research participants in Asch's study, you would yield to the group about 70 percent of the time on some of those critical, wrong-judgment trials. Thirty percent of the original subjects conformed on the majority of trials, and only a quarter of them were able to maintain their independence throughout the testing. Some reported being aware of the differences between what they saw and the group consensus, but they felt it was easier to go along with the others. For others the discrepancy created a conflict that was resolved by coming to believe that the group was right and their perception was wrong! All those who yielded underestimated how much they had conformed, recalling yielding much less to the group pressure than had actually been the case. They remained independent—in their minds but not in their actions.

Follow-up studies showed that, when pitted against just one person giving an incorrect judgment, a participant exhibits some uneasiness but maintains independence. However, with a majority of three people opposed to him, errors rose to 32 percent. On a more optimistic note, however, Asch found one powerful way to promote independence. By giving the subject a partner whose views were in line with his, the power of the majority was greatly diminished. Peer support decreased errors to one fourth of what they had been when there was no partner—and this resistance effect endured even after the partner left.

One of the valuable additions to our understanding of why people conform comes from research that highlights two of the basic mechanisms that contribute to group conformity.[11] We conform first out of *informational needs:* other people often have ideas, views, perspectives, and knowledge that helps us to better navigate our world, especially through foreign shores and new ports. The second mechanism involves *normative needs:* other people are more likely to accept us when we agree with them than when we disagree, so we yield to their view of the world, driven by a powerful need to belong, to replace differences with similarities.

Conformity and Independence Light Up the Brain Differently

New technology, not available in Asch's day, offers intriguing insights into the role of the brain in social conformity. When people conform, are they rationally deciding to go along with the group out of normative needs, or are they actually changing their perceptions and accepting the validity of the new though erroneous information provided by the group? A recent study utilized advanced brain-scanning technology to answer this question.[12] Researchers can now peer into the active brain as a person engages in various tasks by using a scanning device that detects which specific brain regions are energized as they carry out various mental tasks. The process is known as functional magnetic resonance imaging (FMRI). Understanding what mental functions various brain regions control tells us what it means when they are activated by any given experimental task.

Here's how the study worked. Imagine that you are one of thirty-two volunteers recruited for a study of perception. You have to mentally rotate images of three-dimensional objects to determine if the objects are the same as or different from a standard object. In the waiting room, you meet four other volunteers, with whom you begin to bond by practicing games on laptop computers, taking photos of one another, and chatting. (They are really actors—"confederates," as they are called in psychology—who will soon be faking their answers on the test trials so that they are in agreement with one another but not with the correct responses that you generate.) You are selected as the one to go into the scanner while the others outside look at the objects first as a group and then decide if they are the same or different. As in Asch's original experiment, the actors unanimously give wrong answers on some trials, correct answers on others, with occasional mixed group answers thrown in to make the test more believable. On each round, when it is your turn at bat, you are shown the answers given by the others. You have to decide if the objects are the same or different—as the group assessed them or as you saw them?

As in Asch's experiments, you (as the typical subject) would cave in to group pressure, on average giving the group's wrong answers 41 percent of the time. When you yield to the group's erroneous judgment, your conformity would be seen in the brain scan as changes in selected regions of the brain's cortex dedicated to vision and spatial awareness (specifically, activity increases in the right intraparietal sulcus). Surprisingly, there would be no changes in areas of the forebrain that deal with monitoring conflicts, planning, and other higher-order mental activities. On the other hand, if you make independent judgments that go against the group, your brain would light up in the areas that are associated with emotional salience (the right amygdala and right caudate nucleus regions). This means that resistance creates an emotional burden for those who maintain their independence—autonomy comes at a psychic cost.

The lead author of this research, the neuroscientist Gregory Berns, concluded that "We like to think that seeing is believing, but the study's findings show that seeing is believing what the group tells you to believe." This means that other people's views, when crystallized into a group consensus, can actually affect how we perceive important aspects of the external world, thus calling into question the nature of truth itself. It is only by becoming aware of our vulnerability to social pressure that we can begin to build resistance to conformity when it is not in our best interest to yield to the mentality of the herd.

Minority Power to Impact the Majority

Juries can become "hung" when a dissenter gets support from at least one other person and together they challenge the dominant majority view. But can a small minority turn the majority around to create new norms using the same basic psychological principles that usually help to establish the majority view?

A research team of French psychologists put that question to an experimental test. In a color-naming task, if two confederates among groups of six female students consistently called a blue light "green," almost a third of the naive majority subjects eventually followed their lead. However, the members of the majority did not give in to the consistent minority when they were gathered together. It was only later, when they were tested individually, that they responded as the minority had done, shifting their judgments by moving the boundary between blue and green toward the green of the color spectrum.[13]

Researchers have also studied minority influence in the context of simulated jury deliberations, where a disagreeing minority prevents unanimous acceptance of the majority point of view. The minority group was never well liked, and its persuasiveness, when it occurred, worked only gradually, over time. The vocal minority was most influential when it had four qualities: it persisted in affirming a consistent position, appeared confident, avoided seeming rigid and dogmatic, and was skilled in social influence. Eventually, the power of the many may be undercut by the persuasion of the dedicated few.

How do these qualities of a dissident minority—especially its persistence—help to sway the majority? Majority decisions tend to be made without engaging the systematic thought and critical thinking skills of the individuals in the group. Given the force of the group's normative power to shape the opinions of the followers who conform without thinking things through, they are often taken at face value. The persistent minority forces the others to process the relevant information more mindfully.[14] Research shows that the decisions of a group as a whole are more thoughtful and creative when there is minority dissent than when it is absent.[15]

If a minority can win adherents to their side even when they are wrong, there is hope for a minority with a valid cause. In society, the majority tends to be the defender of the status quo, while the force for innovation and change comes from the minority members or individuals either dissatisfied with the current system or able to visualize new and creative alternative ways of dealing with current problems. According to the French social theorist Serge Moscovici,[16] the conflict between the entrenched majority view and the dissident minority perspective is an essential precondition of innovation and revolution that can lead to positive social change. An individual is constantly engaged in a two-way exchange with society—adapting to its norms, roles, and status prescriptions but also acting upon society to reshape those norms.

BLIND OBEDIENCE TO AUTHORITY: MILGRAM'S SHOCKING RESEARCH

"I was trying to think of a way to make Asch's conformity experiment more humanly significant. I was dissatisfied that the test of conformity was judgments about lines. I wondered whether groups could pressure a person into performing an act whose human import was more readily apparent; perhaps behaving aggressively toward another person, say by administering increasingly severe shocks to him. But to study the group effect . . . you'd have to know how the subject performed without any group pressure. At that instant, my thought shifted, zeroing in on this experimental control. Just how far would a person go under the experimenter's orders?"

These musings, from a former teaching and research assistant of Solomon Asch, started a remarkable series of studies by a social psychologist, Stanley Milgram, that have come to be known as investigations of "blind obedience to authority." His interest in the problem of obedience to authority came from deep personal concerns about how readily the Nazis had obediently killed Jews during the Holocaust.

"[My] laboratory paradigm . . . gave scientific expression to a more general concern about authority, a concern forced upon members of my generation, in particular upon Jews such as myself, by the atrocities of World War II. . . . The impact of the Holocaust on my own psyche energized my interest in obedience and shaped the particular form in which it was examined."[17]

I would like to re-create for you the situation faced by a typical volunteer in this research project, then go on to summarize the results, outline ten important lessons to be drawn from this research that can be generalized to other situations of behavioral transformations in everyday life, and then review extensions of this paradigm by providing a number of real-world parallels. (See the Notes for a description of my personal relationship with Stanley Milgram.[18])

Milgram's Obedience Paradigm

Imagine that you see the following advertisement in the Sunday newspaper and decide to apply. The original study involved only men, but women were used in a later study, so I invite all readers to participate in this imagined scenario.

Public Announcement

WE WILL PAY YOU $4.00 FOR ONE HOUR OF YOUR TIME

Persons Needed for a Study of Memory

*We will pay five hundred New Haven men to help us complete a scientific study of memory and learning. The study is being done at Yale University.

*Each person who participates will be paid $4.00 (plus 50c carfare) for approximately 1 hour's time. We need you for only one hour: there are no further obligations. You may choose the time you would like to come (evenings, weekdays, or weekends).

*No special training, education, or experience is needed. We want:

Factory workers	Businessmen	Construction workers
City employees	Clerks	Salespeople
Laborers	Professional people	White-collar workers
Barbers	Telephone workers	Others

All persons must be between the ages of 20 and 50. High school and college students cannot be used.

*If you meet these qualifications, fill out the coupon below and mail it now to Professor Stanley Milgram, Department of Psychology, Yale University, New Haven. You will be notified later of the specific time and place of the study. We reserve the right to decline any application.

*You will be paid $4.00 (plus 50c carfare) as soon as you arrive at the laboratory.

- -

TO:
PROF. STANLEY MILGRAM, DEPARTMENT OF PSYCHOLOGY, YALE UNIVERSITY, NEW HAVEN, CONN. I want to take part in this study of memory and learning. I am between the ages of 20 and 50. I will be paid $4.00 (plus 50c carfare) if I participate.

A researcher whose serious demeanor and gray laboratory coat convey scientific importance greets you and another applicant at your arrival at a Yale University laboratory in Linsly-Chittenden Hall. You are here to help scientific psychology find ways to improve people's learning and memory through the use of punishment. He tells you why this new research may have important practical consequences. The task is straightforward: one of you will be the "teacher" who gives the "learner" a set of word pairings to memorize. During the test, the teacher gives each key word, and the learner must respond with the correct association. When right, the teacher gives a verbal reward, such as

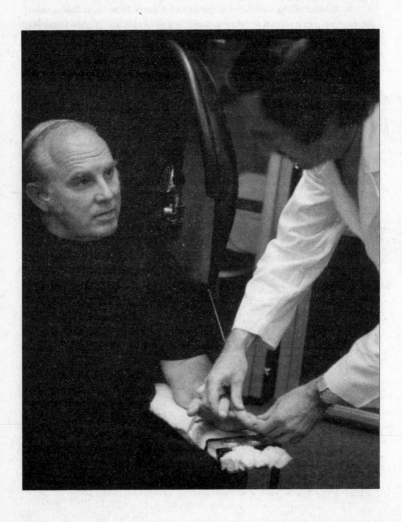

"Good" or "That's right." When wrong, the teacher is to press a lever on an impressive-looking shock apparatus that delivers an immediate shock to punish the error.

The shock generator has thirty switches, starting from a low level of 15 volts and increasing by 15 volts at each higher level. The experimenter tells you that every time the learner makes a mistake, you have to press the next higher voltage switch. The control panel indicates both the voltage level of each of the switches and a corresponding description of the level. The tenth level (150 volts) is "Strong Shock"; the 13th level (195 volts) is "Very Strong Shock"; the 17th level (255 volts) is "Intense Shock"; the 21st level (315 volts) is "Extremely Intense Shock"; the 25th level (375 volts) is "Danger, Severe Shock"; and at the 29th and 30th levels (435 and 450 volts) the control panel is simply marked with an ominous XXX (the pornography of ultimate pain and power).

You and another volunteer draw straws to see who will play each role; you are to be the teacher, and the other volunteer will be the learner. (The drawing is rigged, and the other volunteer is a confederate of the experimenter who always plays the learner.) He is a mild-mannered, middle-aged man whom you help escort to the next chamber. "Okay, now we are going to set up the learner so he can get some punishment," the researcher tells you both. The learner's arms are

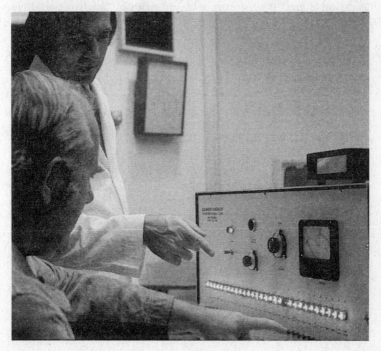

strapped down and an electrode is attached to his right wrist. The shock generator in the next room will deliver the shocks to the learner—if and when he makes any errors. The two of you communicate over the intercom, with the experimenter standing next to you. You get a sample shock of 45 volts, the third level, a slight tingly pain, so you now have a sense of what the shock levels mean. The experimenter then signals the start of your trial of the "memory improvement" study.

Initially, your pupil does well, but soon he begins making errors, and you start pressing the shock switches. He complains that the shocks are starting to hurt. You look at the experimenter, who nods to continue. As the shock levels increase in intensity, so do the learner's screams, saying he does not think he wants to continue. You hesitate and question whether you should go on, but the experimenter insists that you have no choice but to do so.

Now the learner begins complaining about his heart condition and you dissent, but the experimenter still insists that you continue. Errors galore; you plead with your pupil to concentrate to get the right associations, you don't want to hurt him with these very-high-level, intense shocks. But your concerns and motivational messages are to no avail. He gets the answers wrong again and again. As the shocks intensify, he shouts out, "I can't stand the pain, let me out of here!" Then he says to the experimenter, "You have no right to keep me here! Let me out!" Another level up, he screams, "I absolutely refuse to answer any more! Get me out of here! You can't hold me here! My heart's bothering me!"

Obviously you want nothing more to do with this experiment. You tell the experimenter that you refuse to continue. You are not the kind of person who harms other people in this way. You want out. But the experimenter continues to insist that you go on. He reminds you of the contract, of your agreement to participate fully. Moreover, he claims responsibility for the consequences of your shocking actions. After you press the 300-volt switch, you read the next keyword, but the learner doesn't answer. "He's not responding," you tell the experimenter. You want him to go into the other room and check on the learner to see if he is all right. The experimenter is impassive; he is not going to check on the learner. Instead he tells you, "If the learner doesn't answer in a reasonable time, about five seconds, consider it wrong," since errors of omission must be punished in the same way as errors of commission—that is a rule.

As you continue up to even more dangerous shock levels, there is no sound coming from your pupil's shock chamber. He may be unconscious or worse! You are really distressed and want to quit, but nothing you say works to get your exit from this unexpectedly distressing situation. You are told to follow the rules and keep posing the test items and shocking the errors.

Now try to imagine fully what your participation as the teacher would be. I am sure you are saying, "No way would I ever go all the way!" Obviously, you would have dissented, then disobeyed and just walked out. You would never sell out your morality for four bucks! But had you actually gone all the way to the last of the thirtieth shock levels, the experimenter would have insisted that you repeat that XXX switch two more times, for good measure! Now, that is really rubbing it in your face. Forget it, no sir, no way; you are out of there, right? So how far up the scale do you predict that *you* would you go before exiting? How far would the average person from this small city go in this situation?

The Outcome Predicted by Expert Judges

Milgram described his experiment to a group of forty psychiatrists and then asked them to estimate the percentage of American citizens who would go to each of the thirty levels in the experiment. On average, they predicted that less than 1 percent would go all the way to the end, that only sadists would engage in such sadistic behavior, and that most people would drop out at the tenth level of 150 volts. They could not have been more wrong! These experts on human behavior were totally wrong because, first, they ignored the situational determinants of behavior in the procedural description of the experiment. Second, their training in traditional psychiatry led them to rely too heavily on the dispositional perspective to understand unusual behavior and to disregard situational factors. They were guilty of making the fundamental attribution error (FAE)!

The Shocking Truth

In fact, in Milgram's experiment, two of every three (65 percent) of the volunteers went all the way up the maximum shock level of 450 volts. The vast majority of people, the "teachers," shocked their "learner-victim" over and over again despite his increasingly desperate pleas to stop.

And now I invite you to venture another guess: What was the dropout rate after the shock level reached 330 volts—with only silence coming from the shock chamber, where the learner could reasonably be presumed to be unconscious? Who would go on at that point? Wouldn't every sensible person quit, drop out, refuse the experimenter's demands to go on shocking him?

Here is what one "teacher" reported about his reaction: "I didn't know what the hell was going on. I think, you know, maybe I'm killing this guy. I told the experimenter that I was not taking responsibility for going further. That's it." But when the experimenter reassured him that he would take the responsibility, the worried teacher obeyed and continued to the very end.[19]

And almost everyone who got that far did the same as this man. How is that possible? If they got that far, why did they continue on to the bitter end? One reason for this startling level of obedience may be related to the teacher's not knowing how to exit from the situation, rather than just blind obedience. Most participants dissented from time to time, saying they did not want to go on, but the experimenter did not let them out, continually coming up with reasons why they had to stay and prodding them to continue testing their suffering learner. Usually protests work and you can get out of unpleasant situations, but nothing you say affects this impervious experimenter, who insists that you must stay and continue to shock errors. You look at the shock panel and realize that the easiest exit lies at the end of the last shock lever. A few more lever presses is the fast way out, with no hassles from the experimenter and no further moans from the now-silent learner. Voilà! 450 volts is the easy way out—achieving your freedom without directly confronting the authority figure or having to reconcile the suffering you have already caused with this additional pain to the victim. It is a simple matter of up and then out.

Variations on an Obedience Theme

Over the course of a year, Milgram carried out nineteen different experiments, each one a different variation of the basic paradigm of: experimenter/teacher/ learner/memory testing/errors shocked. In each of these studies he varied one social psychological variable and observed its impact on the extent of obedience to the unjust authority's pressure to continue to shock the "learner-victim." In one study, he added women; in others he varied the physical proximity or remoteness of either the experimenter-teacher link or the teacher-learner link; had peers rebel or obey before the teacher had the chance to begin; and more.

In one set of experiments, Milgram wanted to show that his results were not due to the authority power of Yale University—which is what New Haven is all about. So he transplanted his laboratory to a run-down office building in downtown Bridgeport, Connecticut, and repeated the experiment as a project, ostensibly of a private research firm with no apparent connection to Yale. It made no difference; the participants fell under the same spell of this situational power.

The data clearly revealed the extreme pliability of human nature: almost everyone could be totally obedient or almost everyone could resist authority pressures. It all depended on the situational variables they experienced. Milgram was able to demonstrate that compliance rates could soar to over 90 percent of people continuing the 450-volt maximum or be reduced to less than 10 percent—by introducing just one crucial variable into the compliance recipe.

Want maximum obedience? Make the subject a member of a "teaching team," in which the job of pulling the shock lever to punish the victim is given to another person (a confederate), while the subject assists with other parts of the procedure. Want people to resist authority pressures? Provide social models of peers who rebelled. Participants also refused to deliver the shocks if the learner said he wanted to be shocked; that's masochistic, and they are not sadists. They were also reluctant to give high levels of shock when the experimenter filled in as the learner. They were more likely to shock when the learner was remote than in proximity. In each of the other variations on this diverse range of ordinary American citizens, of widely varying ages and occupations and of both genders, it was possible to elicit low, medium, or high levels of compliant obedience with a flick of the situational switch—as if one were simply turning a "human nature dial" within their psyches. This large sample of a thousand ordinary citizens from such varied backgrounds makes the results of the Milgram obedience studies among the most generalizable in all the social sciences.

> When you think of the long and gloomy history of man, you will find far more hideous crimes have been committed in the name of obedience than have been committed in the name of rebellion.

—C. P. Snow, "Either-Or" (1961)

Ten Lessons from the Milgram Studies: Creating Evil Traps for Good People

Let's outline some of the procedures in this research paradigm that seduced many ordinary citizens to engage in this apparently harmful behavior. In doing so, I want to draw parallels to compliance strategies used by "influence professionals" in real-world settings, such as salespeople, cult and military recruiters, media advertisers, and others.[20] There are ten methods we can extract from Milgram's paradigm for this purpose:

1. Prearranging some form of contractual obligation, verbal or written, to control the individual's behavior in pseudolegal fashion. (In Milgram's experiment, this was done by publicly agreeing to accept the tasks and the procedures.)
2. Giving participants meaningful roles to play ("teacher," "learner") that carry with them previously learned positive values and automatically activate response scripts.
3. Presenting basic rules to be followed that seem to make sense before their actual use but can then be used arbitrarily and impersonally to justify mindless compliance. Also, systems control people by making their rules vague and changing them as necessary but insisting that "rules are rules" and thus must be followed (as the researcher in the lab coat did in Milgram's experiment or the SPE guards did to force prisoner Clay-416 to eat the sausages).
4. Altering the semantics of the act, the actor, and the action (from "hurting victims" to "helping the experimenter," punishing the former for the lofty goal of scientific discovery)—replacing unpleasant reality with desirable rhetoric, gilding the frame so that the real picture is disguised. (We can see the same semantic framing at work in advertising, where, for example, bad-tasting mouthwash is framed as good for you because it kills germs and tastes like medicine is expected to taste.)

5. Creating opportunities for the diffusion of responsibility or abdication of responsibility for negative outcomes; others will be responsible, or the actor won't be held liable. (In Milgram's experiment, the authority figure said, when questioned by any "teacher," that he would take responsibility for anything that happened to the "learner.")

6. Starting the path toward the ultimate evil act with a small, seemingly insignificant first step, the easy "foot in the door" that swings open subsequent greater compliance pressures, and leads down a slippery slope.[21] (In the obedience study, the initial shock was only a mild 15 volts.) This is also the operative principle in turning good kids into drug addicts, with that first little hit or sniff.

7. Having successively increasing steps on the pathway that are gradual, so that they are hardly noticeably different from one's most recent prior action. "Just a little bit more." (By increasing each level of aggression in gradual steps of only 15-volt increments, over the thirty switches, no new level of harm seemed like a noticeable difference from the prior level to Milgram's participants.)

8. Gradually changing the nature of the authority figure (the researcher, in Milgram's study) from initially "just" and reasonable to "unjust" and demanding, even irrational. This tactic elicits initial compliance and later confusion, since we expect consistency from authorities and friends. Not acknowledging that this transformation has occurred leads to mindless obedience (and it is part of many "date rape" scenarios and a reason why abused women stay with their abusing spouses).

9. Making the "exit costs" high and making the process of exiting difficult by allowing verbal dissent (which makes people feel better about themselves) while insisting on behavioral compliance.

10. Offering an ideology, or a big lie, to justify the use of any means to achieve the seemingly desirable, essential goal. (In Milgram's research this came in the form of providing an acceptable justification, or rationale, for engaging in the undesirable action, such as that science wants to help people improve their memory by judicious use of reward and punishment.) In social psychology experiments, this tactic is known as the "cover story" because it is a cover-up for the procedures that follow, which might be challenged because they do not make sense on their own. The real-world equivalent is known as an "ideology." Most nations rely on an ideology, typically, "threats to national security," before going to war or to suppress dissident political opposition. When citizens fear that their national security is being threatened, they become willing to surrender their basic freedoms to a government that offers them that exchange. Erich Fromm's classic analysis in *Escape from Freedom* made us aware of this trade-off, which Hitler and other dictators have long used to gain and maintain power: namely, the claim that they will be able to provide security in

exchange for citizens giving up their freedoms, which will give them the ability to control things better.[22]

Such procedures are utilized in varied influence situations where those in authority want others to do their bidding but know that few would engage in the "end game" without first being properly prepared psychologically to do the "unthinkable." In the future, when you are in a compromising position where your compliance is at stake, thinking back to these stepping-stones to mindless obedience may enable you to step back and not go all the way down the path—*their* path. A good way to avoid crimes of obedience is to assert one's personal authority and always take full responsibility for one's actions.[23]

Replications and Extensions of the Milgram Obedience Model

Because of its structural design and its detailed protocol, the basic Milgram obedience experiment encouraged replication by independent investigators in many countries. A recent comparative analysis was made of the rates of obedience in eight studies conducted in the United States and nine replications in European, African, and Asian countries. There were comparably high levels of compliance by research volunteers in these different studies and nations. The majority obedience effect of a mean 61 percent found in the U.S. replications was matched by the 66 percent obedience rate found across all the other national samples. The range of obedience went from a low of 31 percent to a high of 91 percent in the U.S. studies, and from a low of 28 percent (Australia) to a high of 88 percent (South Africa) in the cross-national replications. There was also stability of obedience over decades of time as well as over place. There was no association between when a study was done (between 1963 and 1985) and degree of obedience.[24]

Obedience to a Powerful Legitimate Authority

In the original obedience studies, the subjects conferred authority status on the person conducting the experiment because he was in an institutional setting and was dressed and acted like a serious scientist, even though he was only a high school biology teacher paid to play that role. His power came from being perceived as a representative of an authority system. (In Milgram's Bridgeport replication described earlier, the absence of the prestigious institutional setting of Yale reduced the obedience rate to 47.5 percent compared to 65 percent at Yale, although this drop was not a statistically significant one.) Several later studies showed how powerful the obedience effect can be when legitimate authorities exercise their power within their power domains.

When a college professor was the authority figure telling college student volunteers that their task was to train a puppy by conditioning its behavior using electric shocks, he elicited 75 percent obedience from them. In this experiment, both the "experimenter-teacher" and the "learner" were "authentic." That is, college students acted as the teacher, attempting to condition a cuddly little puppy, the learner, in an electrified apparatus. The puppy was supposed to learn a task, and shocks were given when it failed to respond correctly in a given time interval. As in Milgram's experiments, they had to deliver a series of thirty graded shocks, up to 450 volts in the training process. Each of the thirteen male and thirteen female subjects individually saw and heard the puppy squealing and jumping around the electrified grid as they pressed lever after lever. There was no doubt that they were hurting the puppy with each shock they administered. (Although the shock intensities were much lower than indicated by the voltage labels appearing on the shock box, they were still powerful enough to evoke clearly distressed reactions from the puppy with each successive press of the shock switches.)

As you might imagine, the students were clearly upset during the experiment. Some of the females cried, and the male students also expressed a lot of distress. Did they refuse to continue once they could see the suffering they were causing right before their eyes? For all too many, their personal distress did not lead to behavioral disobedience. About half of the males (54 percent) went all the way to 450 volts. The big surprise came from the women's high level of obedience. Despite their dissent and weeping, 100 percent of the female college students obeyed to the full extent possible in shocking the puppy as it tried to solve an insoluble task! A similar result was found in an unpublished study with adolescent high school girls. (The typical finding with human "victims," including Milgram's own findings, is that there are no male-female gender differences in obedience.[25])

Some critics of the obedience experiments tried to invalidate Milgram's findings by arguing that subjects quickly discover that the shocks are fake, and that is why they continue to give them to the very end.[26] This study, conducted back in 1972 (by psychologists Charles Sheridan and Richard King), removes any doubt that Milgram's high obedience rates could have resulted from subjects' disbelief that they were actually hurting the learner-victim. Sheridan and King showed that there was an obvious visual connection between a subject's obedience reactions and a puppy's pain. Of further interest is the finding that half of the males who disobeyed lied to their teacher in reporting that the puppy had learned the insoluble task, a deceptive form of disobedience. When students in a comparable college class were asked to predict how far an average woman would go on this task, they estimated 0 percent—a far cry from 100 percent. (However, this faulty low estimate is reminiscent of the 1 percent figure given by the psychiatrists who assessed the Milgram paradigm.) Again this underscores one of my central arguments, that it is difficult for people to appreciate fully the power of situational forces acting on individual behavior when they are viewed outside the behavioral context.

Physicians' Power over Nurses to Mistreat Patients

If the relationship between teachers and students is one of power-based authority, how much more so is that between physicians and nurses? How difficult is it, then, for a nurse to disobey an order from the powerful authority of the doctor—when she knows it is wrong? To find out, a team of doctors and nurses tested obedience in their authority system by determining whether nurses would follow or disobey an illegitimate request by an unknown physician in a real hospital setting.[27]

Each of twenty-two nurses individually received a call from a staff doctor whom she had never met. He told her to administer a medication to a patient immediately, so that it would take effect by the time he arrived at the hospital. He would sign the drug order then. He ordered her to give his patient 20 milligrams of the drug "Astrogen." The label on the container of Astrogen indicated that 5 milliliters was usual and warned that 10 milliliters was the maximum dose. His order doubled that high dose.

The conflict created in the minds of each of these caregivers was whether to follow this order from an unfamiliar phone caller to administer an excessive dose of medicine or follow standard medical practice, which rejects such unauthorized orders. When this dilemma was presented as a hypothetical scenario to a dozen nurses in that hospital, ten said they would refuse to obey. However, when other nurses were put on the hot seat where they were faced with the physician's imminent arrival (and possible anger at being disobeyed), the nurses almost unanimously caved in and complied. All but one of twenty-two nurses put to the real test started to pour the medication (actually a placebo) to administer to the patient—before the researcher stopped them from doing so. That solitary disobedient nurse should have been given a raise and a hero's medal.

This dramatic effect is far from isolated. Equally high levels of blind obedience to doctors' almighty authority showed up in a recent survey of a large sample of registered nurses. Nearly half (46 percent) of the nurses reported that they could recall a time when they had in fact "carried out a physician's order that you felt could have had harmful consequences to the patient." These compliant nurses attributed less responsibility to themselves than they did to the physician when they followed an inappropriate command. In addition, they indicated that the primary basis of social power of physicians is their "legitimate power," the right to provide overall care to the patient.[28] They were just following what they construed as legitimate orders—but then the patient died. Thousands of hospitalized patients die needlessly each year due to a variety of staff mistakes, some of which, I assume, include such unquestioning obedience of nurses and tech aides to physicians' wrong orders.

Deadly Obedience to Authority

This potential for authority figures to exercise power over subordinates can have disastrous consequences in many domains of life. One such example is found in the dynamics of obedience in commercial airline cockpits, which have been shown to lead to many airline accidents. In a typical commercial airline cockpit, the captain is the central authority over a first officer and sometimes a flight engineer, and the might of that authority is enforced by organizational norms, the military background of most pilots, and flight rules that make the pilot directly responsible for operating the aircraft. Such authority can lead to flight errors when the crew feels forced to accept the "authority's definition of the situation," even when the authority is wrong.

An investigation of thirty-seven serious plane accidents where there were sufficient data from voice recorders revealed that in 81 percent of these cases, the first officer did not properly monitor or challenge the captain when he had made errors. Using a larger sample of seventy-five plane accidents as the context for evaluating destructive obedience, the author of this study concludes, "If we assume that both monitoring and challenging errors are due to excessive obedience, we may conclude that excessive obedience may cause as many as 25% of all airplane accidents."[29]

Administrative Obedience to Authority

In modern society people in positions of authority rarely punish others with physical violence as in the Milgram paradigm. What is more typical is, *mediated violence,* where authorities pass along orders to underlings who carry them out or the violence involves verbal abuse that undercuts the self-esteem and dignity of the powerless. Authorities often take actions that are punitive and whose consequences are not directly observable. For example, giving hostile feedback to someone that knowingly will disrupt their performance and adversely affect their chances of getting a job qualifies as a form of such socially mediated violence.

A team of Dutch researchers assessed the extension of authority-based obedience to such a situation in a series of ingenious experiments involving twenty-five separate studies of nearly 500 participants from 1982 to 1985 at Utrecht University in the Netherlands.[30] In their "administrative obedience paradigm" the experimenter told the research participant, acting as administrator, to make a series of fifteen "stress remarks" to a job applicant (a trained accomplice) in the next room. Specifically, the subjects were instructed to administer a job selection test to the applicant—if he passed the test, he would get the job; if he failed, he would remain unemployed.

They were also instructed to disturb and stress the applicant while giving him the test. These fifteen graded remarks were critical of his test performance and also denigrated his personality, such as "That was really stupid of you." As the participant-administrators delivered these ever-more-hostile remarks, they "placed the applicant under such intense psychological strain that he did not perform satisfactorily and consequently failed to get the job." In addition, they were told by the researchers to continue despite any protests from the applicant. Any dissent by the participant-administrators was countered with up to four prods by the experimenter to continue the hostile remarks before they were finally permitted to stop if they were adamant. Finally, and most significantly, the subjects were informed that the ability to work under stress was *not* an essential job requirement, but the procedure had to be followed because it assisted the experimenter's research project, which was studying how stress affects test performance. Causing distress and hurting another person's job chances had no further use than the researcher's collection of some data. In the control condition, subjects could stop making the stress remarks at any point they chose.

When asked to predict whether they would make all the stress remarks under these circumstances, more than 90 percent of a separate set of comparable Dutch respondents said they would not comply. Again, the "outsider's view" was way off base: fully 91 percent of the subjects obeyed the authoritative experiment to the very end of the line. This same degree of extreme obedience held up even when personnel officers were used as the subjects despite their professional code of ethics for dealing with clients. Similarly high obedience was found when subjects were sent advance information several weeks before their appearance at the laboratory so that they had time to reflect on the nature of their potentially hostile role.

How might we generate *disobedience* in this setting? You can choose among several options: Have several peers rebel before the subject's turn, as in Milgram's study. Or notify the subject of his or her legal liability if the applicant-victim were harmed and sued the university. Or eliminate the authority pressure to go all the way, as in the control condition of this research—where no one fully obeyed.

Sexual Obedience to Authority: The Strip-Search Scam

"Strip-search scams" have been perpetrated in a number of fast-food restaurant chains throughout the United States. This phenomenon demonstrates the pervasiveness of obedience to an anonymous but seemingly important authority. The modus operandi is for an assistant store manager to be called to the phone by a male caller who identifies himself as a police officer named, say, "Scott." He needs their urgent help with a case of employee theft at that restaurant. He insists on being called "Sir" in their conversation. Earlier he has gotten relevant inside information about store procedures and local details. He also knows how to solicit the information he wants through skillfully guided questions, as stage magicians and "mind readers" do. He is a good con man.

Ultimately Officer "Scott" solicits from the assistant manager the name of the attractive young new employee who, he says, has been stealing from the shop and is believed to have contraband on her now. He wants her to be isolated in the rear room and held until he or his men can pick her up. The employee is detained there and is given the option by the "Sir, Officer," who talks to her on the phone, of either being strip-searched then and there by a fellow employee or brought down to headquarters to be strip-searched there by the police. Invariably, she elects to be searched now since she knows she is innocent and has nothing to hide. The caller then instructs the assistant manager to strip search her; her anus and vagina are searched for stolen money or drugs. All the while the caller insists on being told in graphic detail what is happening, and all the while the video surveillance cameras are recording these remarkable events as they unfold. But this is only the beginning of a nightmare for the innocent young employee and a sexual and power turn-on for the caller-voyeur.

In a case in which I was an expert witness, this basic scenario then included having the frightened eighteen-year-old high school senior engage in a series of increasingly embarrassing and sexually degrading activities. The naked woman is told to jump up and down and to dance around. The assistant manager is told by the caller to get some older male employee to help confine the victim so she can go back to her duties in the restaurant. The scene degenerates into the caller insisting that the woman masturbate herself and have oral sex with the older male, who is supposedly containing her in the back room while the police are slowly wending their way to the restaurant. These sexual activities continue for several hours while they wait for the police to arrive, which of course never happens.

This bizarre authority influence in absentia seduces many people in that situation to violate store policy, and presumably their own ethical and moral principles, to sexually molest and humiliate an honest, churchgoing young employee. In the end, the store personnel are fired, some are charged with crimes, the store is sued, the victims are seriously distressed, and the perpetrator in this and similar hoaxes—a former corrections officer—is finally caught and convicted.

One reasonable reaction to learning about this hoax is to focus on the dispositions of the victim and her assailants, as naive, ignorant, gullible, weird individuals. However, when we learn that this scam has been carried out successfully in sixty-eight similar fast-food settings in thirty-two different states, in a halfdozen different restaurant chains, and with assistant managers of many restaurants around the country being conned, with both male and female victims, our analysis must shift away from simply blaming the victims to recognizing the power of situational forces involved in this scenario. So let us not underestimate the power of "authority" to generate obedience to an extent and of a kind that is hard to fathom.

Donna Summers, assistant manager at McDonald's in Mount Washington, Kentucky, fired for being deceived into participating in this authority phone hoax, expresses one of the main themes in our *Lucifer Effect* narrative about situational power. "You look back on it, and you say, I wouldn't a done it. But unless you're put in that situation, at that time, how do you know what you would do. You don't."[31]

In her book *Making Fast Food: From the Frying Pan into the Fryer,* the Canadian sociologist Ester Reiter concludes that obedience to authority is the most valued trait in fast-food workers. "The assembly-line process very deliberately tries to take away any thought or discretion from workers. They are appendages to the machine," she said in a recent interview. Retired FBI special agent Dan Jablonski, a private detective who investigated some of these hoaxes, said, "You and I can sit here and judge these people and say they were blooming idiots. But they aren't trained to use common sense. They are trained to say and think, 'Can I help you?' "[32]

THE NAZI CONNECTION: COULD IT HAPPEN IN YOUR TOWN?

Recall that one of Milgram's motivations for initiating his research project was to understand how so many "good" German citizens could become involved in the brutal murder of millions of Jews. Rather than search for dispositional tendencies in the German national character to account for the evil of this genocide, he believed that features of the situation played a critical role; that obedience to authority was a "toxic trigger" for wanton murder. After completing his research, Milgram extended his scientific conclusions to a very dramatic prediction about the insidious and pervasive power of obedience to transform ordinary American citizens into Nazi death camp personnel: "If a system of death camps were set up in the United States of the sort we had seen in Nazi Germany, one would be able to find sufficient personnel for those camps in any medium-sized American town."[33]

Let us briefly consider this frightening prediction in light of five very different but fascinating inquiries into this Nazi connection with ordinary people willingly recruited to act against a declared "enemy of the state." The first two are class-room demonstrations by creative teachers with high school and grade school children. The third is by a former graduate student of mine who determined that American college students would indeed endorse the "final solution" if an au-thority figure provided sufficient justification for doing so. The last two directly studied Nazi SS and German policemen.

Creating Nazis in an American Classroom

Students in a Palo Alto, California, high school world history class were, like many of us, not able to comprehend the inhumanity of the Holocaust. How could such a racist and deadly social-political movement have thrived, and how could the average citizen have been ignorant of or indifferent to the suffering it imposed on fellow Jewish citizens? Their inventive teacher, Ron Jones, decided to modify his medium in order to make the message meaningful to these disbelievers. To do so, he switched from the usual didactic teaching method to an experiential learning mode.

He began by telling the class that they would simulate some aspects of the German experience in the coming week. Despite this forewarning, the role-playing "experiment" that took place over the next five days was a serious matter for the students and a shock for the teacher, not to mention the principal and the students' parents. Simulation and reality merged as these students created a totalitarian system of beliefs and coercive control that was all too much like that fashioned by Hitler's Nazi regime.[34]

First, Jones established new rigid classroom rules that had to be obeyed without question. All answers must be limited to three words or less and preceded by "Sir," as the student stood erect beside his or her desk. When no one challenged this and other arbitrary rules, the classroom atmosphere began to change. The more verbally fluent, intelligent students lost their positions of prominence as the less verbal, more physically assertive ones took over. The classroom movement was named "The Third Wave." A cupped-hand salute was introduced along with slogans that had to be shouted in unison on command. Each day there was a new powerful slogan: "Strength through discipline"; "Strength through community"; "Strength through action"; and "Strength through pride." There would be one more reserved for later on. Secret handshakes identified insiders, and critics had to be reported for "treason." Actions followed the slogans—making banners that were hung about the school, enlisting new members, teaching other students mandatory sitting postures, and so forth.

The original core of twenty history students soon swelled to more than a hundred eager new Third Wavers. The students then took over the assignment, making it their own. They issued special membership cards. Some of the brightest students were ordered out of class. The new authoritarian in-group was delighted and abused their former classmates as they were taken away.

Jones then confided to his followers that they were part of a nationwide movement to discover students who were willing to fight for political change. They were "a select group of young people chosen to help in this cause," he told them. A rally was scheduled for the next day at which a national presidential candidate was supposed to announce on TV the formation of a new Third Wave Youth program. More than two hundred students filled the auditorium at Cubberly High School in eager anticipation of this announcement. Exhilarated Wave members wearing white-shirted uniforms with homemade armbands posted banners around the hall. While muscular students stood guard at the door, friends of the teacher posing as reporters and photographers circulated among the mass of "true believers." The TV was turned on, and everyone waited—and waited—for the big announcement of their next collective goose steps forward. They shouted, "Strength through discipline!"

Instead, the teacher projected a film of the Nuremberg rally; the history of the Third Reich appeared in ghostly images. "Everyone must accept the blame—no one can claim that they didn't in some way take part." That was the final frame of the film and the end of the simulation. Jones explained the reason to all the assembled students for this simulation, which had gone way beyond his initial intention. He told them that the new slogan for them should be "Strength through understanding." Jones went on to conclude, "You have been manipulated. Shoved by your own desires into the place you now find yourselves."

Ron Jones got into trouble with the administration because the parents of the rejected classmates complained about their children being harassed and threatened by the new regime. Nevertheless, he concluded that many of these youngsters had learned a vital lesson by personally experiencing the ease with which their behavior could be so radically transformed by obeying a powerful authority within the context of a fascistlike setting. In his later essay about the "experiment," Jones noted that "In the four years I taught at Cubberly High School, no one ever admitted to attending the Third Wave rally. It was something we all wanted to forget." (After leaving the school a few years later, Jones began working with special education students in San Francisco. A powerful docudrama of this simulated Nazi experience, titled "The Wave," captured some of this transformation of good kids into pseudo Hitler Youth.[35])

Creating Little Elementary School Beasties: Brown Eyes Versus Blue Eyes

The power of authorities is demonstrated not only in the extent to which they can command obedience from followers, but also in the extent to which they can define reality and alter habitual ways of thinking and acting. Case in point: Jane Elliott, a popular third-grade schoolteacher in the small rural town of Riceville, Iowa. Her challenge: how to teach white children from a small farm town with few minorities about the meaning of "brotherhood" and "tolerance." She decided to have them experience personally what it feels like to be an underdog and also the top dog, either the victim or the perpetrator of prejudice.[36]

This teacher arbitrarily designated one part of her class as superior to the other part, which was inferior—based only on their eye color. She began by informing her students that people with blue eyes were superior to those with brown eyes and gave a variety of supporting "evidence" to illustrate this truth, such as George Washington's having blue eyes and, closer to home, a student's father (who, the student had complained, had hit him) having brown eyes.

Starting immediately, said Ms. Elliott, the children with blue eyes would be the special "superior" ones and the brown-eyed ones would be the "inferior" group. The allegedly more intelligent blue-eyes were given special privileges, while the inferior brown-eyes had to obey rules that enforced their second-class status, including wearing a collar that enabled others to recognize their lowly status from a distance.

The previously friendly blue-eyed kids refused to play with the bad "brown-eyes," and they suggested that school officials should be notified that the brown-eyes might steal things. Soon fistfights erupted during recess, and one boy admitted hitting another "in the gut" because, "He called me brown-eyes, like being a black person, like a Negro." Within one day, the brown-eyed children began to do more poorly in their schoolwork and became depressed, sullen, and angry. They described themselves as "sad," "bad," "stupid," and "mean."

The next day was turnabout time. Mrs. Elliott told the class that she had been wrong—it was really the brown-eyed children who were superior and the blue-eyed ones who were inferior, and she provided specious new evidence to support this chromatic theory of good and evil. The blue-eyes now switched from their previously "happy," "good," "sweet," and "nice" self-labels to derogatory labels similar to those adopted the day before by the brown-eyes. Old friendship patterns between children temporarily dissolved and were replaced by hostility until this experiential project was ended and the children were carefully and fully debriefed and returned to their joy-filled classroom.

The teacher was amazed at the swift and total transformation of so many of her students whom she thought she knew so well. Mrs. Elliott concluded, "What had been marvelously cooperative, thoughtful children became nasty, vicious, discriminating little third-graders. . . . It was ghastly!"

Endorsing the Final Solution in Hawaii: Ridding the World of Misfits

Imagine that you are a college student at the University of Hawaii (Manoa campus) among 570 other students in any of several large evening school psychology classes. Tonight your teacher, with his Danish accent, alters his usual lecture to reveal a threat to national security being created by the population explosion (a hot topic in the early 1970s).[37] This authority describes the emerging threat to society posed by the rapidly increasing number of people who are physically and mentally unfit. The problem is convincingly presented as a high-minded scientific project, endorsed by scientists and planned for the benefit of humanity. You are then invited to help in "the application of scientific procedures to eliminate the mentally and emotionally unfit." The teacher further justifies the need to take action with an analogy to capital punishment as a deterrent against violent crime. He tells you that your opinions are being solicited because you and the others assembled here are intelligent and well educated and have high ethical values. It is flattering to think that you are in this select company. (Recall the lure of C. S. Lewis's "Inner Ring.") In case there might be any lingering misgivings, he provides assurances that much careful research would be carried out before action of any kind would be taken with these misfit human creatures.

At this point, he wants only your opinions, recommendations, and personal views on a simple survey to be completed now by you and the rest of the students in the auditorium. You begin answering the questions because you have been persuaded that this is a new vital issue about which your voice matters. You diligently answer each of the seven questions and discover that there is a lot of uniformity between your answers and those of the rest of the group.

Ninety percent of you agree that there will always be some people more fit for survival than others.

Regarding killing of the unfit: 79 percent wanted one person to be responsible for the killing and another to carry out the act; 64 percent preferred anonymity for those who pressed the button with only one button causing death though many were pressed; 89 percent judged that painless drugs would be the most efficient and humane method of inducing death.

If required by law to assist, 89 percent wanted to be the one who assisted in the decisions, while 9 percent preferred to assist with the killings or both. Only 6 percent of the students *refused* to answer.

Most incredibly, fully 91 percent of all student respondents agreed with the conclusion that "under extreme circumstances it is entirely just to eliminate those judged most dangerous to the general welfare"!

Finally, a surprising 29 percent supported this "final solution" even if it had to be applied to their own families![38]

So these American college students (night school students and thus older than usual) were willing to endorse a deadly plan to kill off all others who were judged by some authorities to be less fit to live than they were—after only a brief presentation by their teacher-authority. Now we can see how ordinary, even intelligent Germans could readily endorse Hitler's "Final Solution" against the Jews, which was reinforced in many ways by their educational system and strengthened by systematic government propaganda.

Ordinary Men Indoctrinated into Extraordinary Killing

One of the clearest illustrations of my exploration of how ordinary people can be made to engage in evil deeds that are alien to their past history and moral values comes from a remarkable discovery by the historian Christopher Browning. He recounts that in March 1942 about 80 percent of all victims of the Holocaust were still alive, but a mere eleven months later about 80 percent were dead. In this short period of time, the *Endlösung* (Hitler's "Final Solution") was energized by means of an intense wave of mobile mass murder squads in Poland. This genocide required mobilization of a large-scale killing machine at the same time that able-bodied German soldiers were needed on the collapsing Russian front. Because most Polish Jews lived in small towns and not large cities, the question that Browning raised about the German high command was "where had they found the manpower during this pivotal year of the war for such an astounding logistical achievement in mass murder?"[39]

His answer came from archives of Nazi war crimes, which recorded the activities of Reserve Battalion 101, a unit of about five hundred men from Hamburg, Germany. They were elderly family men, too old to be drafted into the Army; they came from working-class and lower-middle-class backgrounds, and they had no military police experience. They were raw recruits sent to Poland without warning of, or any training in, their secret mission—the total extermination of all Jews living in the remote villages of Poland. In just four months they shot to death at point-blank range at least 38,000 Jews and had another 45,000 deported to the concentration camp at Treblinka.

Initially, their commander told them that this was a difficult mission that must be obeyed by the battalion. However, he added that any individual could refuse to execute these men, women, and children. The records indicate that at first about half the men refused and let the other police reservists engage in the mass murder. But over time, social modeling processes took over, as did guilt-induced persuasion by those reservists who had been doing the shooting, along with the usual group conformity pressures of "how would they be seen in the eyes of their comrades." By the end of their deadly journey, up to 90 percent of the men in Battalion 101 were blindly obedient to their battalion leader and were personally involved in the shootings. Many of them posed proudly for photographs of their up-close and personal killing of Jews. Like those who took photos of the prisoner abuse at Abu Ghraib Prison, these policemen posed in their "trophy photos" as proud destroyers of the Jewish menace.

Browning makes it clear that there was no special selection of these men, nor self-selection, nor self-interest or careerism that could account for these mass murders. Instead, they were as "ordinary" as can be imagined—until they were put into a novel situation in which they had "official" permission and encouragement to act sadistically against people who were arbitrarily labeled as the "enemy." What is most evident in Browning's penetrating analysis of these daily acts of human evil is that these ordinary men were part of a powerful authority system, a political police state with ideological justifications for destroying Jews and intense indoctrination of the moral imperatives of discipline and loyalty and duty to the state.

Interestingly, for the argument that I have been making that experimental research can have real-world relevance, Browning compared the underlying mechanisms operating in that far-off land at that distant time to the psychological processes at work in both the Milgram obedience studies and our Stanford Prison Experiment. The author goes on to note, "Zimbardo's spectrum of guard behavior bears an uncanny resemblance to the groupings that emerged within Reserve Police Battalion 101" (p. 168). He shows how some became sadistically "cruel and tough," enjoying the killing, whereas others were "tough, but fair" in "playing the rules," and a minority qualified as "good guards" who refused to kill and did small favors for the Jews.

The psychologist Ervin Staub (who as a child survived the Nazi occupation of Hungary in a "protected house") concurs that most people under particular circumstances have a capacity for extreme violence and destruction of human life. From his attempt to understand the roots of evil in genocide and mass violence around the world, Staub has come to believe that "Evil that arises out of ordinary thinking and is committed by ordinary people is the norm, not the exception. . . . Great evil arises out of ordinary psychological processes that evolve, usually with a progression along the continuum of destruction." He highlights the significance of ordinary people being caught up in situations where they can learn to practice evil acts that are demanded by higher-level authority systems: "Being part of a system shapes views, rewards adherence to dominant views, and makes deviation psychologically demanding and difficult."[40]

Having lived through the horrors of Auschwitz, John Steiner (my dear friend and sociologist colleague) returned for decades to Germany to interview hundreds of former Nazi SS men, from privates to generals. He needed to know what had made these men embrace such unspeakable evil day in and day out. Steiner found that many of these men were high on the F-Scale measure of authoritarianism, which attracted them to the subculture of violence in the SS. He refers to them as "sleepers," people with certain traits that are latent and may never be expressed except when particular situations activate these violent tendencies. He concludes that "the situation tended to be the most immediate determinant of SS behavior," rousing "sleepers" into active killers. However, from his massive interview data Steiner also found that these men had led normal—violence-free—lives both before and after their violent years in the concentration camp setting.[41]

Steiner's extensive experience with many of the SS men at a personal and scholarly level led him to advance two important conclusions about institutional power and the role enactment of brutality: "Institutional support for roles of violence has apparently far more extensive effects than generally realized. When implicit, and especially explicit, social sanctions support such roles, people tend to be attracted to them who may not only derive satisfaction from the nature of their work but are quasiexecutioners in feeling as well as action."

Steiner goes on to describe how roles can trump character traits: "[It] has become evident that not everyone playing a brutal role has to have sadistic traits of character. Those who continued in roles originally not conducive to their personality often changed their values (i.e., had a tendency to adjust to what was expected of them in these roles). There were SS members who clearly identified with and enjoyed their positions. Finally there were those who were repulsed and sickened by what they were ordered to do. They tried to compensate by helping inmates whenever possible. (This writer's life was saved by SS personnel on several occasions.)"

It is important to acknowledge that the many hundreds of thousands of Germans who became perpetrators of evil during the Holocaust were not doing so simply because they were following the orders given by authorities. Obedience to an authority system that gave permission and reward for murdering Jews was built on a scaffold of intense anti-Semitism that existed in Germany and other European nations at that time. This prejudice was given direction and resolve by the German chain of command to ordinary Germans, who became "Hitler's willing executioners," in the analysis by the historian Daniel Goldhagen.[42]

Although it is important to note the motivating role of Germans' hatred of Jews, Goldhagen's analysis suffers from two flaws. First, historical evidence shows that from the early nineteenth century on there was less anti-Semitism in Germany than in neighboring countries such as France and Poland. He also errs in minimizing the influence of Hitler's authority system—a network that glorified racial fanaticism and the particular situations created by the authorities, like the concentration camps, which mechanized genocide. It was the interaction of personal variables of German citizens with situational opportunities provided by a System of fanatical prejudice that combined to empower so many to become willing or unwilling executioners for their state.

THE BANALITY OF EVIL

In 1963, the social philosopher Hannah Arendt published what was to become a classic of our times, *Eichmann in Jerusalem: A Report on the Banality of Evil.* She provides a detailed analysis of the war crimes trial of Adolf Eichmann, the Nazi figure who personally arranged for the murder of millions of Jews. Eichmann's defense of his actions was similar to the testimony of other Nazi leaders: "I was only following orders." As Arendt put it, "[Eichmann] remembered perfectly well that he would have had a bad conscience only if he had not done what he had been ordered to do—to ship millions of men, women, and children to their death with great zeal and the most meticulous care" (p. 25).[43]

However, what is most striking in Arendt's account of Eichmann is all the ways in which he seemed absolutely ordinary:

> Half a dozen psychiatrists had certified him as "normal"—"More normal, at any rate, than I am after having examined him," one of them was said to have exclaimed, while another had found that his whole psychological outlook, his attitude toward his wife and children. mother and father, brothers, sisters, and friends, was "not only normal but most desirable" (pp. 25–26).

Through her analysis of Eichmann, Arendt reached her famous conclusion:

> The trouble with Eichmann was precisely that so many were like him, and that the many were neither perverted nor sadistic, that they were, and still are, terribly and terrifyingly normal. From the viewpoint of our legal institutions and our moral standards of judgment, this normality was much more terrifying than all the atrocities put together, for it implied . . . that this new type of criminal . . . commits his crimes under circumstances that make it well-nigh impossible for him to know or feel that he is doing wrong (p. 276).
>
> It was as though in those last minutes [of Eichmann's life] he was summing up the lesson that this long course in human wickedness had taught us—the lesson of the fearsome, word-and-thought-defying banality of evil (p. 252).

Arendt's phrase "the banality of evil" continues to resonate because genocide has been unleashed around the world and torture and terrorism continue to be common features of our global landscape. We prefer to distance ourselves from such a fundamental truth, seeing the madness of evildoers and senseless violence of tyrants as dispositional characters within their personal makeup. Arendt's analysis was the first to deny this orientation by observing the fluidity with which social forces can prompt normal people to perform horrific acts.

Torturers and Executioners: Pathological Types or Situational Imperatives?

There is little doubt that the systematic torture by men of their fellow men and women represents one of the darkest sides of human nature. Surely, my colleagues and I reasoned, here was a place where dispositional evil would be manifest among torturers who did their daily dirty deeds for years in Brazil as policemen sanctioned by the government to get confessions by torturing "subversive" enemies of the state.

We began by focusing on the torturers, trying to understand both their psyches and the ways they were shaped by their circumstances, but we had to expand our analytical net to capture their comrades in arms who chose or were assigned to another branch of violence work: death squad executioners. They shared a "common enemy": men, women, and children who, though citizens of their state, even neighbors, were declared by "the System" to be threats to the country's national security—as socialists and Communists. Some had to be eliminated efficiently, while others, who might hold secret information, had to be made to yield it up by torture, confess to their treason, and then be killed.

In carrying out this mission, these torturers could rely in part on the "creative evil" embodied in torture devices and techniques that had been refined over centuries since the Inquisition by officials of the Catholic Church and later of many nation-states. However, they had to add a measure of improvisation when dealing with particular enemies to overcome their resistance and resiliency. Some of them claimed innocence, refused to acknowledge their culpability, or were tough enough not to be intimidated by most coercive interrogation tactics. It took time and emerging insights into human weaknesses for these torturers to become adept at their craft. By contrast, the task of the death squads was easy. With hoods for anonymity, guns, and group support, they could dispatch their duty to country swiftly and impersonally: "just business." For a torturer, the work could never be just business. Torture always involves a personal relationship; it is essential for the torturer to understand what kind of torture to employ, what intensity of torture to use on a certain person at a certain time. Wrong kind or too little—no confession. Too much—the victim dies before confessing. In either case, the torturer fails to deliver the goods and incurs the wrath of the senior officers. Learning to determine the right kind and degree of torture that yields up the desired information elicits abounding rewards and flowing praise from one's superiors.

What kind of men could do such deeds? Did they need to rely on sadistic impulses and a history of sociopathic life experiences to rip and tear the flesh of fellow beings day in and day out for years on end? Were these violence workers a breed apart from the rest of humanity, bad seeds, bad tree trunks, and bad flowers? Or is it conceivable that they could be ordinary people, programmed to carry out their deplorable acts by means of some identifiable and replicable training programs? Could we identify a set of external conditions, situational variables, that had contributed to the making of these torturers and killers? If their evil actions were not traceable to inner defects but rather attributable to outer forces acting on them—the political, economic, social, historical, and experiential components of their police training—we might be able to generalize across cultures and settings and discover some of the operative principles responsible for this remarkable human transformation.

The sociologist and Brazil expert Martha Huggins, the Greek psychologist and torture expert Mika Haritos-Fatouros, and I interviewed several dozen of these violence workers in depth at various venues in Brazil. (For a summary of our methods and detailed findings about these violence workers, see Huggins, Haritos-Fatouros, and Zimbardo[44]). Mika had done a similar, earlier study of torturers trained by the Greek military junta, and our results were largely congruent with hers.[45] We found that sadists are selected out of the training process by trainers because they are not controllable, get off on the pleasure of inflicting pain, and thus do not sustain the focus on the goal of extraction of confessions. Thus, from all the evidence we could muster, torturers and death squad executioners were not unusual or deviant in any way prior to practicing their new roles, nor were there any persisting deviant tendencies or pathologies among any of them in the years following their work as torturers and executioners. Their transformation was entirely explainable as being the consequence of a number of situational and systemic factors, such as the training they were given to play this new role; their group camaraderie; acceptance of the national security ideology; and their learned belief in socialists and Communists as enemies of their state. Other situational influences contributing to the new behavioral style included being made to feel special, above and better than their peers in public service by being awarded this special assignment; the secrecy of their duties being shared only with comrades in arms; and the constant pressure to produce results regardless of fatigue or personal problems.

We reported many detailed case studies that document the ordinariness of the men engaged in these most heinous of acts, sanctioned by their government, and secretly supported by the CIA at that point in the Cold War (1964–1985) against Soviet communism. The account *Torture in Brazil*, by members of the Catholic Archdiocese of São Paulo, provides detailed information of the extensive involvement of CIA agents in the torture training of Brazilian police.[46] Such information is consistent with all that is known of the systematic instruction in interrogation and torture offered at the "School of the Americas" to operatives from countries sharing a common enemy in communism.[47]

However, my colleagues and I believe that such deeds are reproducible at any time in any nation when there is an obsession with threats to national security. Before the fears and excesses engendered by the recent "war against terrorism," there was the nearly perpetual "war against crime" in many urban centers. In

New York City's police department, that "war" spawned "the commandos of the NYPD." This insular police team was given free rein to hunt down alleged rapists, robbers, and muggers as local conditions dictated. They wore T-shirts with their motto, "There is no hunting like the hunting of men." Their battle cry was "We own the night." Such a professionalized police culture was comparable to that of the Brazilian police-torturers we had studied. One of their notable atrocities was the murder of an African immigrant (Amadou Diallo, from Guinea), gunning him down with more than forty bullets while he tried to pull out his wallet to give them his ID.[48] Sometimes "bad shit happens," but usually there are identifiable situational and systemic forces operating to make it happen.

Suicide Bombers: Mindless Fanatics or Mindful Martyrs?

Amazingly, what holds true for these violence workers is comparable to the transformation of young Palestinians from students into suicide bombers intent on killing innocent Israeli civilians. Recent media accounts converge on the findings from more systematic analyses of the process of becoming a suicidal killer.[49]

Who adopts this fatalistic role? Is it poor, desperate, socially isolated, illiterate young people with no career and no future? Not at all. According to the results of a recent study of four hundred al-Qaeda members, three quarters of that sample came from the upper or middle class. This study by the forensic psychiatrist Marc Sageman also found other evidence of the normality and even superiority of these youths turned suicide bombers. The majority, 90 percent, came from caring, intact families. Two thirds had gone to college; two thirds were married; and most had children and jobs in science and engineering. "These are the best and brightest of their society in many ways," Sageman concludes.[50]

Anger, revenge, and outrage at perceived injustice are the motivational triggers for deciding to die for the cause. "People desire death when two fundamental needs are frustrated to the point of extinction," according to the psychologist Thomas Joiner in his treatise *Why People Die by Suicide*. The first need is one we have pointed to as central to conformity and social power, the need to belong with or connect to others. The second need is the need to feel effective with or to influence others.[51]

Ariel Merari, an Israeli psychologist who has studied this phenomenon extensively for many years, outlines the common steps on the path to these explosive deaths.[52] First, senior members of an extremist group identify young people who appear to have an intense patriotic fervor based on their declarations at a public rally against Israel or their support of some Islamic cause or Palestinian action. Next, they are invited to discuss how seriously they love their country and hate Israel. They are asked to commit to being trained. Those who do commit become part of a small secret cell of three to five youths. They learn the tricks of the trade from their elders: bomb making, disguise, and selecting and timing targets.

Finally, they make public their private commitment by making a videotape, declaring themselves to be "the living martyr" for Islam (*"al-shahid-al-hai"*). In one hand they hold the Koran, in the other a rifle; the insignia on their headband declares their new status. This video binds them to the final deed, because it is sent to their families. The recruits are also told the Big Lie that not only will they earn a place beside Allah, but their relatives will also be entitled to a high place in Heaven because of their martyrdom. The suicidal pie is sweetened with a sizable financial incentive, or a monthly pension, that goes to their family.

Their photo is emblazoned on posters that will be put on walls everywhere in the community the moment they succeed in their mission—to become inspirational models for the next round of suicide bombers. To stifle their concerns about the pain from wounds inflicted by exploding nails and other bomb parts, the recruits are assured that before the first drop of their blood touches the ground they will already be seated at the side of Allah, feeling no pain, only pleasure. The die is cast; their minds have been carefully prepared to do what is ordinarily unthinkable. Of course, the rhetoric of dehumanization serves to deny the humanity and innocence of their victims.

In these systematic ways a host of normal, angry young men and women become transformed into heroes and heroines. Their lethal actions model self-sacrifice and total commitment as true believers to the cause of the oppressed. That message is sent loud and clear to the next cadre of young suicide bombers in waiting.

We can see that this program utilizes a variety of social psychological and motivational principles to assist in turning collective hatred and general frenzy into a dedicated, seriously calculated program of indoctrination and training for individuals to become youthful living martyrs. It is neither mindless nor senseless, only a very different mind-set and with different sensibilities than we have been used to witnessing among young adults in most countries.

For his new film, *Suicide Killers*, the French filmmaker Pierre Rehov interviewed many Palestinians in Israeli jails who were caught before detonating their bombs or had abetted would-be attacks. His conclusion about them resonates with the analyses presented here: "Every single one of them tried to convince me it was the right thing to do for moralistic reasons. These aren't kids who want to do evil. These are kids who want to do good. . . . The result of this brainwashing was kids who were very good peope inside (were) believing so much that they were doing something great."[53]

The suicide, the murder, of any young person is a gash in the fabric of the human family that we elders from every nation must unite to prevent. To encourage the sacrifice of youth for the sake of advancing the ideologies of the old must be considered a form of evil that transcends local politics and expedient strategies.

"Perfect 9/11 Soldiers" and "Ordinary British Lads" Are Bombing Us

Two final examples of the "ordinariness" of mass murderers are worth mentioning. The first comes from an in-depth study of the 9/11 hijackers, whose suicidal terrorist attacks in New York and Washington, D.C., resulted in the deaths of nearly three thousand innocent civilians. The second comes from the London police reports of suspected suicide bombers of London's Underground and a double-decker bus in June 2005 that resulted in scores of deaths and serious injuries.

The carefully researched portraits of several of the 9/11 terrorists by the reporter Terry McDermott in *Perfect Soldiers* underscores just how ordinary these men were in their everyday lives.[54] His research led McDermott to an ominous conclusion: "It is likely that there are a great many more men just like them" out there throughout the world. One review of this book takes us back to Arendt's banality-of-evil thesis, updated for our new era of global terrorism. *The New York Times*' reviewer Michiko Kakutani offers us a scary postscript: "Perfect Soldiers replaces the caricatures of outsize 'evil geniuses' and 'wild-eyed fanatics' with portraits of the 9/11 plotters as surprisingly mundane people, people who might easily be our neighbors or airplane seatmates."[55]

That frightening scenario was played out in the subsequent coordinated attacks on London's transit system by a team of suicide bombers, "mundane murderers," who anonymously rode a subway train or a bus. To their friends, relatives, and neighbors in the northern England city of Leeds, these young Muslim men were "ordinary British lads."[56] Nothing in their past history would mark them as dangerous; indeed, everything about them enabled these "ordinary lads" to fit in seamlessly in their town, at their jobs. One was a skilled cricket player who gave up drinking and women to lead a more devout life. Another was the son of a local businessman who ran a fish-and-chips shop. Another was a counselor who worked effectively with disabled children and had recently become a father and moved his family into a new home. Unlike the 9/11 hijackers, who had raised some suspicions as foreigners seeking flight training in the United States, these young men were homegrown, flying well below any police radar. "It's completely out of character for him. Someone must have brainwashed him and made him do it," reflected a friend of one of them.

"The most terrifying thing about suicide bombers is their sheer normality," concludes Andrew Silke, an expert on the subject.[57] He notes that in all the forensic examinations of the bodies of dead suicide bombers there have never been traces of alcohol or drugs. Their mission is undertaken with a clear mind and dedication.

And as we have seen, whenever there has been a student shooting in a school, as in Columbine High School in the United States, those who thought they knew the perpetrators typically report, "He was such a good kid, from a respectable family . . . you just can't believe he would do it." This harkens back to the point I raised in our first chapter—how well do we really know other people?—and its corollary—how well do we know ourselves to be certain of how we would behave in novel situations under intense situational pressures?

THE ULTIMATE TEST OF BLIND OBEDIENCE TO AUTHORITY: KILLING YOUR CHILDREN ON COMMAND

Our final extension of the social psychology of evil from artificial laboratory experiments to real-world contexts comes to us from the jungles of Guyana, where an American religious leader persuaded more than nine hundred of his followers to commit mass suicide or be killed by their relatives and friends on November 28, 1978. Jim Jones, the pastor of Peoples Temple congregations in San Francisco and Los Angeles, set out to create a socialist utopia in this South American nation, where brotherhood and tolerance would be dominant over the materialism and racism he loathed in the United States. But over time and place Jones was transformed from the caring, spiritual "father" of this large Protestant congregation into an Angel of Death—a truly cosmic transformation of Luciferian proportions. For now I want only to establish the obedience to authority link between Milgram's basement laboratory in New Haven and this jungle–killing field.[58]

The dreams of the many poor members of the Peoples Temple for a new and better life in this alleged utopia were demolished when Jones instituted extended forced labor, armed guards, total restriction of all civil liberties, semistarvation diets, and daily punishments amounting to torture for the slightest breach of any of his many rules. When concerned relatives convinced a congressman to inspect the compound, along with a media crew, Jones arranged for them to be murdered as they were leaving. He then gathered almost all of the members who were at the compound and gave a long speech in which he exhorted them all to take their lives by drinking poison, cyanide-laced Kool-Aid. Those who refused were forced to drink by the guards or shot trying to escape, but it appears as though most obeyed their leader.

Jones was surely an egomaniac; he had all of his speeches and proclamations, and even his torture sessions tape-recorded—including this last-hour suicide drill. In it Jones distorts reality, lies, pleads, makes false analogies, appeals to ideology and to transcendent future lives, and outright insists that they follow his orders, as his staff is efficiently distributing the deadly poison to the more than nine hundred members gathered around him. Some excerpts from that last hour convey a sense of the death-dealing tactics he used to induce total obedience to an authority gone mad:

> Please get us some medication. It's simple. It's simple. There's no convulsions with it [of course there are, especially for the children]. . . . Don't be afraid to die. You'll see, there'll be a few people land out here. They'll torture some of our children here. They'll torture our people. They'll torture our seniors. We cannot have this. . . . Please, can we hasten? Can we hasten with that medication? You don't know what you've done. I tried. . . . Please. For God's sake, let's get on with it. We've lived—we've lived as no

other people lived and loved. We've had as much of this world as you're gonna get. Let's just be done with it. Let's be done with the agony of it. [Applause.]. . . . Who wants to go with their child has a right to go with their child. I think it's humane. I want to go—I want to see you go, though. . . . It's not to be afeared. It is not to be feared. It is a friend. It's a friend . . . sitting there, show your love for one another. Let's get gone. Let's get gone. Let's get gone. [Children crying.]. . . . Lay down your life with dignity. Don't lay down with tears and agony. There's nothing to death. . . . it's just stepping over to another plane. Don't be this way. Stop this hysterics. . . . No way for us to die. We must die with some dignity. We must die with some dignity. We will have no choice. Now we have some choice. . . . Look children, it's just something to put you to rest. Oh, God. [Children crying.]. . . . Mother, Mother, Mother, Mother, Mother, please. Mother, please, please, please. Don't—don't do this. Don't do this. Lay down your life with your child. [The full transcript is available online; see the Notes.[59]]

And they did, and they died for "Dad." The power of charismatic tyrannical leaders, like Jim Jones and Adolf Hitler, endures even after they do terrible things to their followers, and even after their demise. Whatever little good they may have done earlier somehow comes to dominate the legacy of their evil deeds in the minds of the faithful. Consider the example of a young man, Gary Scott, who followed his father into the Peoples Temple but was expelled for being disobedient. In his statement as he called the National Call-In following the broadcast of the NPR show "Father Cares: The Last of Jonestown," by James Reston, Jr., Gary describes how he was punished for an infraction of the rules. He was beaten, whipped, sexually abused, and forced to endure his worst fear of having a boa constrictor crawling all over him. But, more important, listen to the articulation of his enduring reaction to this torment. Does he hate Jim Jones? Not one bit. He has become a "true believer," a "faithful follower." Even though his father died in Jonestown at that poison fount, and he himself was brutally tortured and humiliated, Gary publically states that he still admires and even loves his "dad"—Jim Jones. Not even George Orwell's omnipotent *1984* Party could honestly claim such a victory.

Now we need to go beyond conformity and authority obedience. Powerful as these are, they are only starters. In the confrontation of potential perpetrators and victims, like guard and prisoner, torturer and sufferer, suicide bomber and civilian victims, there are processes that operate to change the psychological makeup of one or the other. Deindividuation makes the perpetrator anonymous, thereby reducing personal accountability, responsibility, and self-monitoring. This allows perpetrators to act without conscience-inhibiting limits. Dehumanization takes away the humanity of potential victims, rendering them as animallike, or as nothing. We will also inquire about conditions that make bystanders to evil become passive observers and not active intruders, helpers, or whistle-blowing he-

roes. That slice of the evil of inaction is really a cornerstone of evil because it allows perpetrators to believe that others who knew what was going on accepted
and approved it even if only by their silence.

A fitting conclusion to our investigation of the social dynamics of conformity
and obedience comes from the Harvard psychologist Mahrzarin Banaji:

> What social psychology has given to an understanding of human nature
> is the discovery that forces larger than ourselves determine our mental life
> and our actions—chief among these forces [is] the power of the social
> situation.[60]

Investigating Social Dynamics: Deindividuation, Dehumanization, and the Evil of Inaction

The historical account of humans is a heap of conspiracies, rebellions, murders, massacres, revolutions, banishments, the very worst effects that avarice, faction, hypocrisy, perfidiousness, cruelty, rage, madness, hatred, envy, lust, malice, and ambition could produce.... I cannot but conclude the bulk of your natives to be the most pernicious race of little odious vermin that nature ever suffered to crawl upon the surface of the earth.

—Jonathan Swift, *Gulliver's Travels* (1727)[1]

Perhaps Jonathan Swift's total condemnation of our human race—of us Yahoos—is a bit extreme, but consider that he wrote this critique several hundred years before the advent of genocides throughout the modern world, before the Holocaust. His views reflect a basic theme in Western literature that "Mankind" has suffered a great fall from its original state of perfection, starting with Adam's act of disobedience against God when he succumbed to Satan's temptation.

The social philosopher Jean-Jacques Rousseau elaborated this theme of the corrupting influence of social forces by envisioning human beings as "noble, primitive savages" whose virtues were diminished by contact with corrupting society. In stark opposition to this conception of human beings as the innocent victims of an all-powerful, malignant society is the view that people are born evil—genetic bad seeds. Our species is driven by wanton desires, unlimited appetites, and hostile impulses unless people are transformed into rational, reasonable, compassionate human beings by education, religion, and family, or controlled by the discipline imposed upon them by the authority of the State.

Where do you stand in this ages-old debate? Are we born good and then corrupted by an evil society or born evil and redeemed by a good society? Before casting your ballot, consider an alternative perspective. Maybe each of us has the capacity to be a saint or a sinner, altruistic or selfish, gentle or cruel, dominant or submissive, perpetrator or victim, prisoner or guard. Maybe it is our social circumstances that determine which of our many mental templates, our potentials, we develop. Scientists are discovering that embryonic stem cells are capable of becoming virtually any kind of cell or tissue and ordinary skin cells can be turned into embryonic stem cells. It is tempting to expand these biological concepts and what is now known about the developmental plasticity of the human brain to the "plasticity" of human nature.[2]

What we are is shaped both by the broad systems that govern our lives—wealth and poverty, geography and climate, historical epoch, cultural, political and religious dominance—and by the specific situations we deal with daily. Those forces in turn interact with our basic biology and personality. I have argued earlier that the potential for perversion is inherent in the complexity of the human mind. The impulse toward evil and the impulse toward good together comprise the most fundamental duality in human nature. This conception offers a complex, richer portrait of the pride and puzzles in human actions.

We have examined the power of group conformity and obedience to authority that can dominate and subvert individual initiative. Next, we add insights from research into the domains of deindividuation, dehumanization, and bystander apathy, or the "evil of inaction." This information will complete the foundation for us to fully appreciate how ordinary, good individuals—perhaps even you, gentle reader—can be led at times to do bad things to others, even bad deeds that violate any sense of common decency or morality.

DEINDIVIDUATION: ANONYMITY AND DESTRUCTIVENESS

William Golding's novel *Lord of the Flies* asks how a simple change in one's external appearance can trigger dramatic changes in overt behavior. Good British choirboys are transformed into murderous little beasts by simply painting their faces. When food runs out on their desert island, a group of boys, led by Jack Merridew, try to kill a pig—but they can't complete the act because killing has been inhibited by their Christian morality. Then Jack decides to paint his face into a mask, and as he does, a frightening metamorphosis occurs as he sees his reflection in the water:

> He looked in astonishment, no longer at himself but at an awesome stranger. He spilt the water and leapt to his feet, laughing excitedly. Beside the pool his sinewy body held up a mask that drew their eyes and appalled them [the other boys]. He began to dance and his laughter became a bloodthirsty snarling. He capered toward Bill, and the mask was a thing on its own, behind which Jack hid, liberated from shame and self-consciousness.

After the other boys in Jack's gang also disguise themselves with painted masks, they are readily able to "Kill the pig. Cut her throat. Spill her blood."[3] Once that alien deed of killing another creature is accomplished, they then relish the fun of killing both animals and their human enemies, notably the intellectual boy nicknamed "Piggy." Might makes right, and all hell breaks loose as Ralph, the good-boy leader, is hunted down by the herd.

Is there any psychological validity to the notion that disguising one's external appearance can drastically infect behavioral processes? I attempted to answer that question with a set of studies that helped stimulate a new field of inquiry on the psychology of deindividuation and antisocial behavior.[4]

The Shocking Behavior of Anonymous Women

The basic procedure in this first experiment involved having female college students believe they were delivering a series of painful electric shocks to other women, under the guise of a believable "cover story." They would have multiple opportunities to shock each of two other young women whom they saw and heard from behind a one-way mirror. Half of the student volunteers were randomly assigned to a condition of anonymity, or *deindividuation*, half to a condition where their identity was made salient, or *individuation*. The four college student subjects, in each of the ten separately tested deindividuation groups, had their appearance concealed by hoods and loose, oversized lab coats, their names replaced by numbers, one to four. The experimenter treated them as an anonymous group, not as individuals. These procedures were performed allegedly to mask their nonverbal behavior so that others could not detect their reactions. The comparison group, by contrast, was given name tags that helped to make them feel unique, but everything else was the same for them as for those in the deindividuated groups. Both the deindividuated and the comparison subjects were in four-woman groups, and both were asked to repeatedly shock each of two women "victims" over the course of twenty trials.

The cover story was that the target women were subjects in a study of creativity under stress. The job of our participants was to stress them by administering painful electric shocks while I, as the experimenter in the next room, also behind the mirror, administered the creativity test.

Unlike in the Milgram paradigm, there was no authority directly pressuring them to act aggressively by delivering these painful shocks because I did not interact with them at all during the shock episodes. The students could see me through the observation window along with each of the two women in the alleged creativity study. In addition, there was no group conformity pressure exerted on them because they did not interact with one another, being in separate cubicles adjacent to one another. Finally, there was not even pressure on them to perform the task in order not to violate the rationale for the study. If any one of the four group members delivered a shock, the target woman would act hurt, so there would be sufficient stress induced to impact her creativity. Thus, not shocking would be neither disobedient nor confrontational—one could be merely a passive observer of teammates' shocking instead of an active perpetrator.

The behavior of interest was the *duration* of shock administered—how long each student continued to hold down the shock button after the shock-ready signal appeared. Their decision was not whether to press the shock switch but how quickly to pull their finger off the switch or to keep pressing it down and deliver longer shocks to the victims. Of course, they could choose not to follow the instructions and refuse to even press the shock switch at all (no one ever did that).

One of the complicit women had been portrayed as very nice, the other as "bitchy," in their tape-recorded interviews. This was done to create divergent attitudes toward them in the minds of their "stress inducers." Actually, they were both research confederates, trained to act as though they were in pain when a shock light lit up and to give a convincing performance that the students in the other room could witness.

Before the experiment began, each of the students in the study was given a sample of the painful shock (of 75 volts) so they knew that it would hurt—but of course, no shock was actually given in the experiment. For each of twenty trials, the women had to decide whether and for how long they would administer this standard level of painful shock to a woman who was seemingly suffering in pain from their actions. Then, after the first target woman left, she was replaced by the second target woman for yet another round of twenty shock trials. Because each member of the four-person experimental and comparison groups was tested in adjacent individual cubicles, their "teammates" could not directly influence their behavior. Nevertheless, they had a sense of being in a group from having been together initially while they listened together to the tape recordings. It is important to note that except for the manipulation of anonymity versus identifiability, everything in the study was identical for both groups.

The results were clear: The women in the deindividuation condition delivered twice as much shock to both victims as did the comparison women who had been randomly assigned to the individuated condition. Moreover, the women who were anonymous shocked both victims equally, the one they had previously rated as pleasant and the other they had rated as unpleasant. It did not matter what they had previously felt about them once they had their finger on the trigger. They also increased shock time for both over the course of the twenty trials, holding their finger down ever longer on the shock switch as their victims twisted and moaned right before them. In contrast, the individuated women discriminated between the likeable and unpleasant targets, shocking the pleasant woman less over time than they did the unpleasant one.

That the anonymous women ignored their previous liking or disliking of the two target women when they had the chance to harm them speaks to a dramatic change in their mentality when in this psychological state of deindividuation. The escalation of shock, with repeated opportunities to administer its painful consequences, appears to be an upward-spiraling effect of the emotional arousal that is being experienced. The agitated behavior becomes self-reinforcing, each action stimulating a stronger, less controlled next reaction. Experientially, it comes not from sadistic motives of wanting to harm others but rather from the energizing sense of one's domination and control over others at that moment in time.

This basic paradigm has been repeated with comparable results in a host of laboratory and field studies, using deindividuating masks, administering white noise, or throwing Styrofoam balls at the target victims, and with military personnel from the Belgian Army as well as with schoolchildren and a variety of college students. Similar escalations of shock over time were also found in a study where teacher-shockers were supposed to be educating their pupil-victims—they too delivered increasing levels of shock across training sessions.[5]

The Stanford Prison Experiment, as you recall, relied on the deindividuating silver reflecting sunglasses for the guards and staff along with standard military-style uniforms. One important conclusion flows from this body of research: anything, or any situation, that makes people feel anonymous, as though no one knows who they are or cares to know, reduces their sense of personal accountability, thereby creating the potential for evil action. This becomes especially true when a second factor is added: if the situation or some agency gives them *permission* to engage in antisocial or violent action against others, as in these research settings, people are ready to go to war. If, instead, the situation conveys merely a reduction of self-centeredness with anonymity and encourages prosocial behavior, people are ready to make love. (Anonymity in party settings often makes for more socially engaging parties.) So William Golding's insight about anonymity and aggression was psychologically valid—but in more complex and interesting ways than he depicted.

> Sure, this robe of mine doth change my disposition.
>
> —William Shakespeare, *The Winter's Tale*

Anonymity can be conferred on others not only with masks but also by the way that people are treated in given situations. When others treat you as if you are not a unique individual but just an undifferentiated "other" being processed by the System, or your existence is ignored, you feel anonymous. The sense of a lack of personal identifiability can also induce antisocial behavior. When a researcher treated college student research volunteers either humanely or as "guinea pigs" in an experiment, guess who ripped him off when he wasn't looking? Later on, these students found themselves alone in the professor-researcher's office with the opportunity to steal coins and pens from a bowl full of them. Those who were in the anonymity condition stole much more often than did the humanely treated students.[6] Kindness can be more than its own reward.

Halloween Aggression by Schoolchildren

What happens when children go to an unusual Halloween party where they put on costumes and are given permission by their teacher to play aggressive games for prizes? Will anonymity plus opportunity to aggress lead children to engage in more aggression over time?

Elementary school children attended a special, experimental Halloween party given by their teacher and supervised by a social psychologist, Scott Fraser.[7] There were many games to play, and the children could win tokens for each game they won. These tokens could be exchanged for gifts at the end of the party. The more tokens you won, the better the toys you could get, so the motivation to win as many tokens as possible was high.

Half the games were nonaggressive in nature, and half involved confrontations between two children to reach the goal. For example, a nonaggressive game might have individual students trying to speedily retrieve a beanbag in a tube, while a potentially aggressive game would entail two students competing to be the first one to get that one beanbag out of the tube. The aggression observed typically involved the competitors' pushing and shoving each other. It was not very extreme but was characteristic of first-stage physical encounters between children.

The experimental design used only one group, in which each child served as his or her own control. This procedure is known as the A-B-A format—pre-baseline/change introduced/post-baseline. The children first played the games without costumes (A), then with costumes (B), then again without costumes (A). Initially, while the games were played, the teacher said the costumes were on the way so they would start the fun while they waited for them to arrive. Then, when the costumes arrived, they were put on in different rooms so the children's identities were not known to each other, and they played the same games but now in costume. In the third phase, the costumes were removed (allegedly to be given to other children in other parties) and the games continued as in the first phase. Each phase of the games lasted about an hour.

The data are striking testimony to the power of anonymity. Aggression among these young schoolchildren increased significantly as soon as they put the costumes on. The percentage of the total time that these children played the aggressive games more than doubled from their initial base level average, up from 42 percent (in A) to 86 percent (in B). Equally interesting was the second major result: aggression had a high negative payoff. The more time a child spent engaged in the aggressive games, the fewer tokens she or he won during that phase of the party. Being aggressive thus cost the children a loss of tokens. Acting in the aggressive games took more time than the nonaggressive games and only one of two contestants could win, so overall, being aggressive lost valued prizes. However, that did not matter when the children were costumed and anonymous. The smallest number of tokens won was during the second, anonymity B, phase, where aggression was highest; only an average of 31 tokens were won, compared to 58 tokens in the A phase.

A third important finding was that there was no carryover of aggressive behavior from the high level in the B phase to the last A-phase level, which was comparable to the initial A phase. The percentage of aggressive acts dropped to 36 percent, and the number of tokens won soared to 79. Thus, we can conclude that the behavior change brought on by anonymity did not create a dispositional, internal change, but only an outward response change. Change the situation, and behavior changes in lockstep fashion. The use of this A-B-A design also makes apparent that perceived anonymity was sufficient to dramatically alter behavior in each time frame. Anonymity facilitated aggression even though the consequences of that physical aggression were not in the child's best immediate interest of winning tokens exchangeable for fine prizes. Aggression became its own reward. Goals that were distant took a backseat to "the fun and games" of the present moment. (We will see a similar phenomenon operating in some of the Abu Ghraib abuses.)

In a related field study, Halloween trick-or-treaters visiting local homes in their own costumes were more likely to steal goodies when they were anonymous than when identifiable. Friends of the researchers put out bowls filled with candies and others with coins, each of which was labeled "Take one." Going beyond that limit constituted a transgression, stealing. Some children arrived alone, others in groups of friends. In the anonymous condition, the homeowner made it evident that he or she could not tell who they were. With their identities concealed by their costumes, the majority of those in groups stole the candy and money (just as did those college students in the study where they were treated as "guinea pigs"). This was in contrast to the nonanonymous condition, wherein the adult host had first asked them to reveal their identity behind their masks.[8]

Among the more than seven hundred children studied in this natural situation, more transgressions were found when they were in anonymous groups (57 percent) than when anonymous and alone (21 percent). Fewer transgressions occurred when nonanonymous children were alone (8 percent) than when they were in groups of other nonanonymous trick-or-treaters (21 percent). Even when alone and identifiable, the temptation of easy money and delicious treats was too great for some children to pass up. However, adding the full-anonymity dimension turned that singular temptation into an overwhelming passion for most children to take all the goodies they could.

Cultural Wisdom: How to Make Warriors Kill in War but Not at Home

Let's leave the laboratory and the games at children's parties to go back to the real world, where these issues of anonymity and violence may take on life-and-death significance. Specifically, let's look at the differences between societies that go to war without having young male warriors change their appearance and those that always include ritual transformations of appearance by painting faces and bodies or masking the warriors (as in *Lord of the Flies*). Does a change in external appearance make a significant difference in how warring enemies are then treated?

A cultural anthropologist, R. J. Watson,[9] posed that question after reading my earlier work on deindividuation. His data source was the Human Relations Area Files, where information on cultures around the world is archived in the form of reports of anthropologists, missionaries, psychologists, and others. Watson found two pieces of data on societies in which warriors did or did not change their appearance prior to going to war and the extent to which they killed, tortured, or mutilated their victims, a decidedly deadly dependent variable—the ultimate in outcome measures.

The results are striking confirmation of the prediction that anonymity promotes destructive behavior—when permission is also given to behave in aggressive ways that are ordinarily prohibited. War provides the institutionally approved permission to kill or wound one's adversaries. This investigator found that, of the twenty-three societies for which these two data sets were present, in fifteen warriors changed their appearance. They were the societies that were the most destructive; fully 80 percent of them (twelve of fifteen) brutalized their enemies. By contrast, in seven of eight of the societies in which the warriors did *not* change their appearance before going into battle, they did not engage in such destructive behavior. Another way to look at this data is that 90 percent of the time when victims of battle were killed, tortured, or mutilated, it was by warriors who had first changed their appearance and deindividuated themselves.

Cultural wisdom dictates that a key ingredient in transforming ordinarily nonaggressive young men into warriors who can kill on command is first to change their external appearance. Most wars are about old men persuading young men to harm and kill other young men like themselves. For the young men, it becomes easier to do so if they first change their appearance, altering their usual external façade by putting on military uniforms or masks or painting their faces. With the anonymity thus provided in place, out go their usual internal compassion and concern for others. When the war is won, the culture then dictates that the warriors return to their peacetime status. This reverse transformation is readily accomplished by making the warriors remove their uniforms, take off their masks, wash away the paint, and return to their former personae and peaceful demeanor. In a sense, it is as though they were in a macabre social ritual, unknowingly using the A-B-A paradigm of Fraser's Halloween experiment. Peaceful when identifiable, murderous when anonymous, peaceful again when returned to the identifiable condition.

Certain environments convey a sense of transient anonymity in those who live or behave in their midst, without changing their physical appearance. To demonstrate the impact of the anonymity of place in facilitating urban vandalism, my research team did a simple field study. Recall from chapter 1 that we abandoned cars on the streets near the uptown campus of New York University in the Bronx, New York, and near Stanford University's campus in Palo Alto, California. We photographed and videotaped acts of vandalism against these cars, which were clearly abandoned (license plates removed, hoods raised). In the anonymity of the Bronx setting, several dozen passersby, on the street or in cars, stopped to vandalize the car within forty-eight hours. Most were reasonably well-dressed adults, who stripped the car of any valuable items or simply destroyed it—all in the daytime. By contrast, over a week's time, not a single passerby engaged in any act of vandalism against the car abandoned in Palo Alto. This demonstration was the only empirical evidence cited in support of the "Broken Windows Theory" of urban crime. Environmental conditions contribute to making some members of society feel that they are anonymous, that no one in the dominant community knows who they are, that no one recognizes their individuality and thus their humanity. When that happens, we contribute to their transformation into potential vandals and assassins. (For full details of this research and Broken Windows Theory, see our Lucifer Effect website.)

Deindividuation Transforms Our Apollonian Nature into a Dionysian Nature

Let's assume that the "good" side of people is the rationality, order, coherence, and wisdom of Apollo, while the "bad" side is the chaos, disorganization, irrationality, and libidinous core of Dionysus. The Apollonian central trait is constraint and the inhibition of desire; it is pitted against the Dionysian trait of uninhibited release and lust. People can become evil when they are enmeshed in situations where the cognitive controls that usually guide their behavior in socially desirable and personally acceptable ways are blocked, suspended, or distorted. The suspension of cognitive control has multiple consequences, among them the suspension of: conscience, self-awareness, sense of personal responsibility, obligation, commitment, liability, morality, guilt, shame, fear, and analysis of one's actions in cost-benefit calculations.

The two general strategies for accomplishing this transformation are: (a) reducing the cues of social accountability of the actor (no one knows who I am or cares to) and (b) reducing concern for self-evaluation by the actor. The first cuts out concern for social evaluation, for social approval, doing so by making the actor feel anonymous—the process of deindividuation. It is effective when one is functioning in an environment that conveys anonymity and diffuses personal responsibility. The second strategy stops self-monitoring and consistency monitoring by relying on tactics that alter one's state of consciousness. This is accomplished by means of taking alcohol or drugs, arousing strong emotions, engaging in hyperintense actions, getting into an expanded present-time orientation where there is no concern for past or future, and projecting responsibility outward onto others rather than inward toward oneself.

Deindividuation creates a unique psychological state in which behavior comes under the control of immediate situational demands and biological, hormonal urges. Action replaces thought, seeking immediate pleasure dominates delaying gratification, and mindfully restrained decisions give way to mindless emotional responses. A state of arousal is often both a precursor to and a consequence of deindividuation. Its effects are amplified in novel or unstructured situations where typical response habits and character traits are nullified. One's vulnerability to social models and situational cues is heightened; therefore, it becomes as easy to make love as to make war—it all depends on what the situation demands or elicits. In the extreme, there is no sense of right and wrong, no thoughts of culpability for illegal acts or Hell for immoral ones.[10] With inner restraints suspended, behavior is totally under external situational control; outer dominates inner. What is possible and available dominates what is right and just. The moral compass of individuals and groups has then lost its polarity.

The transition from Apollonian to Dionysian mentalities can be swift and unexpected, making good people do bad things, as they live temporarily in the expanded present moment without concerns for the future consequences of their actions. Usual constraints on cruelty and libidinal impulses melt away in the excesses of deindividuation. It is as if there were a short circuit in the brain, cutting off the frontal cortex's planning and decision-making functions, while the more primitive portions of the brain's limbic system, especially its emotion and aggression center in the amygdala, take over.

The Mardi Gras Effect: Communal Deindividuation as Ecstasy

In ancient Greece, Dionysus was unique among the gods. He was seen as creating a new level of reality that challenged traditional assumptions and ways of living. He represented both a force for the liberation of the human spirit from its staid confinement in rational discourse and orderly planning, and a force of destruction: lust without limits and personal pleasure without societal controls. Dionysus was the god of drunkenness, the god of insanity, the god of sexual frenzy and battle lust. Dionysus' dominion includes all states of being that entail the loss of self-awareness and rationality, the suspension of linear time, and the abandonment of the self to those urges in human nature that overthrow codes of behavior and public responsibility.

Mardi Gras has its origins as a pagan, pre-Christian ceremony now recognized by the Roman Catholic Church as occurring on the Tuesday (Fat Tuesday, or Shrove Tuesday) just before Ash Wednesday. That holy day marks the start of the Christian liturgical Season of Lent with its personal sacrifices and abstinence leading to Easter Sunday, forty-six days later. Mardi Gras celebrations begin on the Twelfth Night Feast of the Epiphany, when the three kings visited the newborn Jesus Christ.

In practice, Mardi Gras celebrates the excess of libidinous pleasure seeking, of living for the moment, of "wine, women, and song." Cares and obligations are forgotten while celebrants indulge their sensual nature in communal revelries. It is a Bacchanalian festivity that loosens behavior from its usual constraints and reason-based actions. However, there is always the preconscious awareness that this celebration is transitory, soon to be replaced by even greater than usual limits on personal pleasures and vices with the advent of Lent. "The Mardi Gras effect" involves temporarily giving up the traditional cognitive and moral constraints on personal behavior when part of a group of like-minded revelers bent on having fun now without concern for subsequent consequences and liabilities. It is deindividualization in group action.

DEHUMANIZATION AND MORAL DISENGAGEMENT

Dehumanization is the central construct in our understanding of "man's inhumanity to man." Dehumanization occurs whenever some human beings consider other human beings to be excluded from the moral order of being a human person. The objects of this psychological process lose their human status in the eyes of their dehumanizers. By identifying certain individuals or groups as being outside the sphere of humanity, dehumanizing agents suspend the morality that might typically govern reasoned actions toward their fellows.

Dehumanization is a central process in prejudice, racism, and discrimination. Dehumanization stigmatizes others, attributing to them a "spoiled identity." For example, the sociologist Erving Goffman[11] described the process by which those who are disabled are socially discredited. They become not fully human and thus tainted.

Under such conditions, it becomes possible for normal, morally upright, and even usually idealistic people to perform acts of destructive cruelty. Not responding to the human qualities of other persons automatically facilitates inhumane actions. The golden rule then becomes truncated: "Do unto others as you would." It is easier to be callous or rude toward dehumanized "objects," to ignore their demands and pleas, to use them for your own purposes, even to destroy them if they are irritating.[12]

A Japanese general reported that it had been easy for his soldiers to brutally massacre Chinese civilians during Japan's pre–World War II invasion of China, "because we thought of them as *things*, not people like us." This was obviously so during the "Rape of Nanking" in 1937. Recall the description (in chapter 1) of the Tutsis by the woman who orchestrated many of the rapes of them—they were nothing more than "insects," "cockroaches." Similarly, the Nazi genocide of the Jews began by first creating through propaganda films and posters a national perception of these fellow human beings as inferior forms of animal life, as vermin, as voracious rats. The many lynchings of black people by mobs of whites in cities throughout the United States were likewise not considered crimes against humanity because of the stigmatization of them as only "niggers."[13]

Behind the My Lai massacre of hundreds of innocent Vietnamese civilians by American soldiers was the dehumanizing "gooks" label that GIs had for all of those different-looking Asian people.[14] Yesterday's "gooks" have become today's "hajjis" and "towel heads" in the Iraq War as a new corps of soldiers derogates these different-looking citizens and soldiers. "You just sort of try to block out the fact that they're human beings and see them as enemies," said Sergeant Mejia, who refused to return to action in what he considered an abominable war. "You call them 'hajis', you know? You do all the things that make it easier to deal with killing them and mistreating them."[15]

That such labels and their associated images can have powerful motivating effects was demonstrated in a fascinating controlled laboratory experiment (mentioned in chapter 1, elaborated here).

Experimental Dehumanization: Animalizing College Students

My Stanford University colleague Albert Bandura and his students designed a powerful experiment that elegantly demonstrates the power of dehumanizing labels to foster harm against others.[16]

Seventy-two male volunteers from nearby junior colleges were divided into three-member "supervisory teams" whose task was to punish the inadequate decision making of other college students who were allegedly serving as a group of decision makers. The real subjects of the study were, of course, the students playing the role of supervisors.

On each of twenty-five bargaining trials, the supervisors heard the decision-making team (reported to be in an adjacent room) supposedly formulating collective decisions. The supervisors were given information they used to evaluate the adequacy of the decision on each trial. Whenever a bad decision was made, it was the job of this supervisory team to punish the error by administering a shock. They could choose the shock intensity from a mild level of 1 to a maximum level of 10 on any trial, which all the members of the decision-making team would receive.

The supervisors were told that participants from different social backgrounds were included in this project to increase its generality, but each group of decision makers was composed of people with similar attributes. This was done so that the positive or negative labels soon to be applied to them would hold for the entire group.

The researchers varied two features of this basic situation: how the "victims" were labeled and how personally responsible the supervisors were for the shocks they administered. The volunteers were randomly assigned to three conditions of labeling—dehumanized, humanized, or neutral—and two conditions of responsibility—individualized or diffused.

Let's first consider how the labeling was imposed and its effects. Then we will see how the responsibility variations operated. After settling into the study, each group of participants believed they were overhearing an interchange over the intercom between the research assistant and the experimenter about the questionnaires the decision makers had allegedly completed. The assistant remarked in a brief aside that the personal qualities exhibited by this group confirmed the opinion of the person by whom they had been recruited. In the *dehumanized* condition, the decision makers were characterized as "an animalistic, rotten bunch." By contrast, in the *humanized* condition, they were characterized as a "perceptive, understanding, and otherwise humanized group." No evaluative references were made about those in the third, *neutral* condition.

It should be made clear that the participants never interacted with their shock victims and therefore could not make such evaluations personally or evaluate their adequacy. The labels were secondhand attributions made about other young college men, supposedly also volunteers functioning in an assigned role in this situation. So did the labels have any effect on how these college students punished those they were allegedly supervising? (There were, in fact, no actual "others," only standardized tape feedback.)

Indeed, the labels stuck and had a big impact on the extent to which the students punished their supervisees. Those labeled in the dehumanizing way, as "animals," were shocked most intensively, and their shock level increased linearly over ten trials. It also climbed higher and higher over trials, up to an average of 7 out of the maximum of 10 for each group of participants. Those labeled "nice" were given the smallest amount of shock, while the unlabeled, neutral group fell in the middle of these two extremes.

Further, during the first trial, there was no difference at all between the three experimental treatments in the level of shock administered—they all administered the same low level of shock. Had the study ended then, the conclusion would have been that the labels made no difference. However, with each successive trial, as the errors of the decision makers allegedly multiplied, the shock levels of the three groups diverged. Those shocking the so-called animals shocked them more intensely over time, a result comparable to the escalating shock level of the deindividuated female college students in my earlier study. That rise in aggressive responding over time, with practice, or with experience illustrates a self-reinforcing effect. Perhaps the pleasure is not so much in inflicting pain as in the sense of power and control one feels in such a situation of dominance—giving others what they deserve to get. The researchers point to the disinhibiting power of labeling to divest other people of their human qualities.

On the plus side in this study, that same arbitrary labeling also resulted in others being treated with greater respect if someone in authority had labeled them positively. Those perceived as "nice" were harmed the least. Thus, the power of humanization to counteract punitiveness is of equal theoretical and social significance as the phenomenon of dehumanization. There is an important message here about the power of words, labels, rhetoric, and stereotyped labeling, to be used for good or evil. We need to refashion the childhood rhyme "Sticks and stones may break my bones, but names will never harm me," to alter the last phrase to "but bad names can kill me, and good ones can comfort me."

Finally, what about the variations in *responsibility* for the level of shock that was being administered? Significantly higher levels of shock were given when participants believed that the shock level was an average response of their team rather than when it was the direct level of each individual's personal decision. As we have seen before, diffusion of responsibility, in any form it takes, lowers the inhibition against harming others. As one might predict, the very highest levels of shock—and anticipated harm—were administered both when participants felt less personally responsible and when their victims were dehumanized.

When Bandura's research team evaluated how the participants had justified their performance, they found that dehumanization promoted the use of self-absolving justifications, which in turn were associated with increasing punishment. These findings about how people disengage their usual self-sanctions against behaving in ways that are detrimental to others led Bandura to develop a conceptual model of "moral disengagement."

Mechanisms of Moral Disengagement

This model begins by assuming that most people adopt moral standards because of undergoing normal socialization processes during their upbringing. Those standards act as guides for prosocial behavior and deterrents of antisocial behavior as defined by their family and social community. Over time, these external moral standards imposed by parents, teachers, and other authorities become internalized as codes of personal conduct. People develop personal controls over their thoughts and actions that become satisfying and provide a sense of self-worth. They learn to sanction themselves to prevent acting inhumanely and to foster humane actions. The self-regulatory mechanisms are not fixed and static in their relation to a person's moral standards. Rather, they are governed by a dynamic process in which moral self-censure can be selectively activated to engage in acceptable conduct; or, at other times, moral self-censure can be disengaged from reprehensible conduct. Individuals and groups can maintain their sense of moral standards by simply disengaging their usual moral functioning at certain times, in certain situations, for certain purposes. It is as if they shift their morality into neutral gear and coast along without concern for hitting pedestrians until they later shift back to a higher gear, returning to higher moral ground.

Bandura's model goes further in elucidating the specific psychological mechanisms individuals generate to convert their harmful actions into morally acceptable ones as they selectively disengage the self-sanctions that regulate their behavior. Because this is such a fundamental human process, Bandura argues that it helps to explain not only political, military, and terrorist violence but also "everyday situations in which decent people routinely perform activities that further their interests but have injurious human effects."[17]

It becomes possible for any of us to disengage morally from any sort of destructive or evil conduct when we activate one or more of the following four types of cognitive mechanisms.

First, we can redefine our harmful behavior as honorable. Creating moral justification for the action, by adopting moral imperatives that sanctify violence, does this. Creating advantageous comparisons that contrast our righteous behavior to the evil behavior of our enemies also does this. (We only torture them; they behead us.) Using euphemistic language that sanitizes the reality of our cruel actions does this as well. ("Collateral damage" means that civilians have been bombed into dust; "friendly fire" means that a soldier has been murdered by the stupidity or intentional efforts of his buddies.)

Second, we can minimize our sense of a direct link between our actions and its harmful outcomes by diffusing or displacing personal responsibility. We spare ourselves self-condemnation if we do not perceive ourselves as the agents of crimes against humanity.

Third, we can change the way we think about the actual harm done by our actions. We can ignore, distort, minimize, or disbelieve any negative consequences of our conduct.

Finally, we can reconstruct our perception of victims as deserving their punishment, by blaming them for the consequences, and of course, by dehumanizing them, perceiving them to be beneath the righteous concerns we reserve for fellow human beings.

Understanding Dehumanization Is Not Excusing It

It is important once again to add here that such psychological analyses are never intended to excuse or make light of the immoral and illegal behaviors of perpetrators. By making explicit the mental mechanisms people use to disengage their moral standards from their conduct, we are in a better position to reverse the process, reaffirming the need for moral engagement as crucial for promoting empathic humaneness among people.

However, before moving on it is important to make concrete the notion that people in positions of power and authority often reject attempts at causal situational analyses in matters of great national concern. Instead, at least in one recent instance, they have endorsed simplistic dispositional views that would have made Inquisition judges smile.

Secretary of State Condoleezza Rice is a Stanford University professor of political science with a specialization in the Soviet military. Her training should have made her sensitive to systems-level analyses of complex political problems. However, not only was that perspective missing during an interview with Jim Lehrer on his *NewsHour* (July 28, 2005), but instead she championed a dogmatic, simplistic dispositional view. In response to her interviewer's question about whether U.S. foreign policy is promoting rather than eliminating terrorism, Rice attacked any such thinking as "excuse mongering," as she makes it clear that terrorism is simply about "evil people": "When are we going to stop making excuses for the terrorists and saying that somebody is making them do it? No, these are simply evil people who want to kill. And they want to kill in the name of a perverted ideology that really is not Islam, but they somehow want to claim that mantle to say that this is about some kind of grievance. This isn't about some kind of grievance. This is an effort to destroy, rather than to build. And until everybody in the world calls it by name—the evil that it is—stops making excuses for them, then I think we're going to have a problem."

I Am More Human than You: The Infrahumanization Bias

Beyond perceiving and derogating others in the "out-group" with animallike qualities, people also deny them any "human essence." *Out-group infrahumanization* is a newly investigated phenomenon in which people tend to attribute uniquely human emotions and traits to their in-group and deny their existence in out-groups. It is a form of emotional prejudice.[18]

However, we go further in declaring that the essence of humanness resides primarily in ourselves, more so than in any others, even our in-group members. While we attribute infrahumaness to out-groups, as less than human, we are motivated to see ourselves as more human than others. We deny uniquely human traits and even human nature to others, relative to our own egocentric standard. This *self-humanization bias* is the complement of the other-infrahumanization bias. These tendencies appear to be rather general and multifaceted. A team of Australian researchers concluded their investigation into the perception of humanness with a variant of the famous quote by the ancient Roman writer Terence. He proudly proclaimed, "Nothing human is alien to me." Its ironic twist notes, "Nothing human may be alien to me, but something human is alien to you."[19] (It is unlikely that such an imperial "I" exists among members of collectivist cultures, but we await new research to inform us of the limits of such egocentrism.)

Creating Dehumanized Enemies of the State

Among the operational principles we must add to our arsenal of weapons that trigger evil acts by ordinarily good men and women are those developed by nation-states to incite their own citizens. We learn about some of these principles by considering how nations prepare their young men to engage in deadly wars while also preparing citizens to endorse engaging in wars of aggression. A special form of cognitive conditioning through propaganda helps accomplish this difficult transformation. "Images of the enemy" are created by national media propaganda (in complicity with governments) to prepare the minds of soldiers and citizens to hate those who fit the new category "your enemy." Such mental conditioning is a soldier's most potent weapon. Without it, he might never put another young man in the crosshairs of his gun sight and fire to kill him. It induces a fear of vulnerability among citizens who can imagine what it would be like to be dominated by that enemy.[20] That fear becomes morphed into hatred and a willingness to take hostile action to reduce its threat. It extends its reaches into a willingness to send our children to die or be maimed in battle against that threatening enemy.

In *Faces of the Enemy*, Sam Keen[21] shows how archetypes of the enemy are created by visual propaganda that most nations use against those judged to be the dangerous "them," "outsiders," "enemies." These visual images create a consensual societal paranoia that is focused on the enemy who would do harm to the women, children, homes, and God of that nation's way of life, destroying its fundamental beliefs and values. Such propaganda has been widely practiced on a worldwide scale. Despite national differences in many dimensions, it is still possible to categorize all such propaganda into a select set utilized by *"homo hostilis."* In creating a new evil enemy in the minds of good members of righteous tribes, "the enemy" is: aggressor, faceless, rapist, godless, barbarian, greedy, criminal, torturer, murderer, an abstraction, or a dehumanized animal. Scary images reveal one's nation being consumed by the animals that are most universally feared: snakes, rats, spiders, insects, lizards, gigantic gorillas, octopi, or even "English pigs."

A final point on the consequences of adopting a dehumanized conception of selected others is the unthinkable things that we are willing to do to them once they are officially declared different and undesirable. More than 65,000 American citizens were sterilized against their will during an era (1920s–1940s) when eugenics advocates used scientific justifications to purify the human race by ridding it of all those with undesirable traits. We expect that view from Adolf Hitler but not from one of America's most revered jurists, Oliver Wendell Holmes. He ruled in a majority opinion (1927) that compulsory sterilization laws, far from being unconstitutional, were a social good:

> It is better for all the world, if instead of waiting to execute degenerate offspring for crime, or let them starve for their imbecility, society can prevent those who are manifestly unfit from continuing their kind. Three generations of imbeciles are enough.[22]

Please recall the research cited in chapter 12 on students at the University of Hawaii who were willing to endorse the "final solution" to eliminate the unfit, even their own family members if necessary.

Both the United States and England have had a long history of involvement in the "war against the weak." They have had their fair share of vocal, influential proponents of eugenics advocating and scientifically justifying plans to rid their nation of the misfits while enhancing the privileged status of the most fit.[23]

THE EVIL OF INACTION: PASSIVE BYSTANDERS

> The only thing necessary for evil to triumph is for good men to do nothing.
>
> —British statesman Edmund Burke

> [W]e must learn that passively to accept an unjust system is to cooperate with that system, and thereby to become a participant in its evil.
>
> —Martin Luther King, Jr.[24]

Our usual take on evil focuses on the violent, destructive actions of perpetrators, but the failure to act can also be a form of evil, when helping, dissent, disobedience, or whistle-blowing are required. One of the most critical, least acknowledged contributors to evil goes beyond the protagonists of harm to the silent chorus who look but do not see, who hear but do not listen. Their silent presence at the scene of evil doings makes the hazy line between good and evil even fuzzier. We ask next: Why don't people help? Why don't people act when their aid is needed? Is their passivity a personal defect of callousness, of indifference? Alternatively, are there identifiable social dynamics once again at play?

The Kitty Genovese Case: Social Psychologists to the Rescue, Belatedly

In a major urban center, such as New York City, London, Tokyo, or Mexico City, one is surrounded by literally tens of thousands of people. We walk beside them on the streets, sit near them in restaurants, movies, buses, and trains, wait in line with them—but remain unconnected, as if they do not really exist. For a young woman in Queens, they did not exist when she most needed them.

> For more than half an hour, 38 respectable, law-abiding citizens in Queens [New York] watched a killer stalk and stab a woman in three separate attacks in Kew Gardens. Twice the sound of their voices and the sudden glow of their bedroom lights interrupted him and frightened him off. Each time he returned, sought her out and stabbed her again. Not one person telephoned the police during the assault; one witness called the police after the woman was dead. [*The New York Times*, March 13, 1964]

A recent reanalysis of the details of this case casts doubt upon how many people actually saw the events unfolding and whether they really comprehended what was happening, given that many were elderly and had awoken suddenly in the middle of the night. Nevertheless, there seems to be no question that many residents of this well-kept, usually quiet, almost suburban neighborhood heard the chilling screams and did not help in any way. Kitty died alone on a staircase, where she could no longer elude her crazed murderer.

Yet only a few months later, there was an even more vivid and chilling depiction of how alienated and passive bystanders can be. An eighteen-year-old secretary had been beaten, choked, stripped, and raped in her office. When she finally broke away from her assailant, naked and bleeding, she ran down the stairs of the building to the doorway screaming "Help me! Help me! He raped me!" A crowd of about forty persons gathered on the busy street and watched as the rapist dragged her back upstairs to continue his abuse. No one came to her aid! Only the chance arrival of passing police prevented her further abuse and possible murder (*The New York Times*, May 6, 1964).

Researching Bystander Intervention

Social psychologists heeded the alarm by initiating a series of pioneering studies on bystander intervention. They countered the usual slew of dispositional analyses about what is wrong with the callous New York bystanders by trying to understand what in the *situation* freezes the prosocial actions of ordinary people. At the time, both Bibb Latané and John Darley[25] were professors at New York City universities—Columbia and NYU, respectively—so they were close to the heart of the action. Their field studies were done in a variety of New York City venues, such as on subways and street corners, and in laboratories.

Their research generated a counterintuitive conclusion: the more people who witness an emergency, the *less* likely any of them will intervene to help. Being part of a passively observing group means that each individual assumes that others are available who could or will help, so there is less pressure to initiate action than there is when people are alone or with only one other observer. The mere presence of others diffuses the sense of personal responsibility of any individual to get involved. Personality tests of participants showed no significant relationship between any particular personality characteristics and the speed or likelihood of intervening in staged emergencies.[26]

New Yorkers, like Londoners or others from big cities around the world, are likely to help and will intervene if they are directly asked or when they are alone or with a few others. The more people present who might help in an emergency situation, the more we assume that someone else will step forward, so we do not have to become energized to take any personal risk. Rather than callousness, failure to intervene is not only because one fears for one's life in a violent scenario, but also because one denies the seriousness of the situation, fears doing the wrong thing and looking stupid or worries about the costs of getting involved in "someone else's business." There is also an emergent group norm of passive nonaction.

Want Help? Just Ask for It

A former student of mine, Tom Moriarity, conducted a convincing demonstration that a simple situational feature can facilitate active bystander intervention among New Yorkers.[27] In two scenarios, Tom arranged for a confederate to leave her purse on a table in a public, busy restaurant or her radio on a blanket at a crowded beach. Then another member of his research team would pretend to steal the purse or the radio as Tom recorded the actions of those near the scene of the simulated crime. Half the time virtually no one intervened and let the criminal escape with the goods. However, the other half of the time virtually everyone stopped the criminal in his tracks and prevented the crime. What made the difference?

In the first case, the woman merely asked the person nearby for the time, making minimal social contact, before leaving the scene temporarily. However, in the second case, she made a simple request to a nearby person to keep an eye on her purse or her radio until she returned. That direct request created a social obligation to protect this stranger's property—an obligation that was honored fully. Want help? Ask for it. Chances are good that you will get it, even from allegedly callous New Yorkers or other large-city folks.

The implications of this research also highlight another theme we have been developing, that social situations are created by and can be modified by people. We are not robots acting on situational demand programs but can change any programming by our creative and constructive actions. The problem is that too often we accept others' definition of the situation and their norms, rather than being willing to take the risk of challenging the norm and opening new channels of behavioral options. One interesting consequence of the line of research on passive and responsive bystanders has been the emergence of a relatively new area of social psychological research on helping and altruism (well summarized in a monograph by David Schroeder and his colleagues).[28]

How Good Are Good Samaritans in a Hurry?

A team of social psychologists staged a truly powerful demonstration that the failure to help strangers in distress is more likely due to situational variables than to dispositional inadequacies.[29] It is one of my favorite studies, so let's role-play with you once again as a participant.

Imagine you are a student studying for the ministry at Princeton University's Theological Seminary. You are on your way to deliver a sermon on the Good Samaritan so that it can be videotaped for a psychology experiment on effective communication. You know the passage from the Gospel of Luke, chapter 10, quite well. It is about the only person who stopped to help a victim in distress on the side of the road from Jerusalem to Jericho. The Gospel tells us that he will reap his just rewards in Heaven for having been the Good Samaritan on Earth—a biblical lesson for all of us to heed about the virtues of altruism.

Imagine further that as you are heading from the Psychology Department to the videotaping center, you pass a stranger huddled up in an alley in dire distress, on the ground moaning, clearly in need of some aid. Now, can you imagine any conditions that would make you *not* stop to be that Good Samaritan, especially when you are mentally rehearsing the Good Samaritan parable at that very moment?

Rewind to the psychology laboratory. You have been told that you are late for the appointed taping session and so should hurry along. Other theology students were randomly assigned to conditions in which they were told that they had a little time or a lot more time to get to the taping center. But why should time pressure on you (or the others) make a difference if you are a good person, a holy person, a person thinking about the virtue of intervening to help strangers in distress, as did that old-time Good Samaritan? I am willing to wager that you would like to believe it would *not* make a difference, that in that situation you would stop and help, no matter what the circumstances. And so would the other seminary students come to the aid of the victim in distress.

Guess again: if you took the bet, you lost. The conclusion from the point of view of the victim is this: Don't be a victim in distress when people are late and in a hurry. Almost every one of those seminary students—fully 90 percent of them—passed up the immediately compelling chance to be a Good Samaritan because they were in a hurry to give a sermon about it. They experienced the clash in task demands: to help science or to help a victim. Science won, and the victim was left to suffer. (As you would now expect, the victim was an acting confederate.)

The more time the seminarians believed they had, the more likely they were to stop and help. Thus, the situational variable of *time pressure* accounted for the major variations in who helped and who were passive bystanders. There was no need to resort to dispositional explanations about theology students being callous, cynical, or indifferent, as the nonhelping New Yorkers were assumed to be in the case of poor Kitty Genovese. When the research was replicated, the same result occurred, but when the seminarians were on their way to fulfill a less important task, the vast majority did stop to help. The lesson from this research is to not ask *who* does or does not help but rather *what* the social and psychological features of that situation were when trying to understand situations in which people fail to help those in distress.[30]

The Institutionalized Evil of Inaction

In situations where evil is being practiced, there are perpetrators, victims, and survivors. However, there are often observers of the ongoing activities or people who know what is going on and do not intervene to help or to challenge the evil and thereby enable evil to persist by their inaction.

It is the good cops who never oppose the brutality of their buddies beating up minorities on the streets or in the back room of the station house. It was the good bishops and cardinals who covered over the sins of their predatory parish priests because of their overriding concern for the image of the Catholic Church. They knew what was wrong and did nothing to really confront that evil, thereby enabling these pederasts to continue sinning for years on end (at the ultimate cost to the Church of billions in reparations and many disillusioned followers).[31]

Similarly, it was the good workers at Enron, WorldCom, Arthur Andersen, and hosts of similarly corrupt corporations who looked the other way when the books were being cooked. Moreover, as I noted earlier, in the Stanford Prison Experiment it was the good guards who never intervened on behalf of the suffering prisoners to get the bad guards to lighten up, thereby implicitly condoning their continually escalating abuse. It was I, who saw these evils and limited only physi-

cal violence by the guards as my intervention while allowing psychological violence to fill our dungeon prison. By trapping myself in the conflicting roles of researcher and prison superintendent, I was overwhelmed with their dual
demands, which dimmed my focus on the suffering taking place before my eyes. I
too was thus guilty of the evil of inaction.

At the level of nation-states, this inaction, when action is required, allows
mass murder and genocide to flourish, as it did in Bosnia and Rwanda and has
been doing more recently in Darfur. Nations, like individuals, often don't want to
get involved and also deny the seriousness of the threat and the need for immediate action. They also are ready to believe the propaganda of the rulers over the
pleas of the victims. In addition, there often are internal pressures on decision
makers from those who "do business there" to wait it out.

One of the saddest cases I know of the institutional evil of inaction occurred
in 1939, when the U.S. government and its humanitarian president, Franklin D.
Roosevelt, refused to allow a ship loaded with Jewish refugees to embark in any
port. The SS *St. Louis* had come from Hamburg, Germany, to Cuba with 937 Jewish refugees escaping the Holocaust. The Cuban government reversed its earlier
agreement to accept them. For twelve days these refugees and the ship's captain
tried desperately to get permission from the U.S. government to enter a port in
Miami, which was in clear view. Denied permission to enter this or any other port,
the ship turned back across the Atlantic. Some refugees were accepted in Britain
and other countries, but many finally died in Nazi concentration camps. Imagine
being so close to freedom and then dying as a slave laborer.

When incompetence is wedded to indifference and indecision, the outcome is
the failure to act when action is essential for survival. The Katrina hurricane disaster in New Orleans (August 2005) is a classic case study in the total failure of
multiple, interlocking systems to mobilize the enormous resources at their disposal to prevent the suffering and deaths of many citizens. Despite advance warnings of the impending disaster of the worst kind imaginable, city, state, and
national authorities did not engage in the basic preparations needed for evacuation and for the safety of those who could not leave on their own. In addition to
the municipal and state authority systems failing to communicate adequately
(because of political differences at the top), the response from the Bush administration was nil, too late, and too little when it did come. Incompetent, inexperienced heads of the Federal Emergency Management Association (FEMA) and of
the Department of Homeland Security failed to engage the National Guard, Army
reserve units, Red Cross, state police, or Air Force personnel to provide food,
water, blankets, medicine, and more for the hundreds of thousands of survivors
living in squalor for days and nights on end. A year later, much of the city is still
in shambles, with entire neighborhoods decimated and deserted, thousands of
homes marked for destruction, but little help has been forthcoming. Touring
these desolate areas was heartbreaking for me. Critics contend that the systems'

failed response can be traced to class and racial issues, because most of the survivors who could not evacuate were lower-class African Americans. This evil of
inaction has been responsible for the deaths, despair, and disillusion of many citizens of New Orleans. Perhaps as many as half of those who did finally leave may
never come home again.[32]

Et tu, Brute?

Each of us has to wonder if, and hope that when the time comes, we will have the
courage of our convictions to be a responsive bystander who sounds the alarm
when our countrymen and -women are violating their oath of allegiance to
country and to humanity. However, we have seen in these chapters that pressures
to conform are enormous, to be a team player, not to rock the boat, and not to risk
the sanctions against confronting any system. Those forces are often coupled
with the top-down power of authority systems to convey expectations indirectly
to employees and underlings that unethical and illegal behavior is appropriate
under special circumstances—which they define. Many of the recently uncovered
scandals at the highest levels of government, in the military, and in business involve the toxic mix of unverbalized authority expectations conveyed to subordinates who want to be accepted in the "Inner Ring," with the tacit approval of a
horde of knowingly silent partners.

"Toxic leaders cast their spell broadly. Most of us claim we abhor them. Yet we
frequently follow—or at least tolerate—them, be they our employers, our CEOs,
our senators, our clergy, or our teachers. When toxic leaders don't appear on
their own, we often seek them out. On occasion, we even create them by pushing
good leaders over the toxic line." In Jean Lipman-Blumen's penetrating analysis of
the dynamic relationship between leaders and followers in *The Allure of Toxic
Leaders*, we are reminded that recognizing the early signs of toxicity in our leaders
can enable us to take preventive medicine, not passively imbibe their seductive
poison.[33]

> Throughout history, it has been the inaction of those who could
> have acted; the indifference of those who should have known
> better; the silence of the voice of justice when it mattered most;
> that has made it possible for evil to triumph.
>
> —Haile Selassie, former emperor of Ethiopia

WHY SITUATIONS AND SYSTEMS MATTER

It is a truism in psychology that personality and situations interact to generate behavior; people are always acting within various behavioral contexts. People are
both products of their different environments and producers of the environments
they encounter.[34] Human beings are not passive objects simply buffeted about by

environmental contingencies. People usually select the settings they will enter or avoid and can change the setting by their presence and their actions, influence others in that social sphere, and transform environments in myriad ways. More often than not, we are active agents capable of influencing the course of events that our lives take and also of shaping our destinies.[35] Moreover, human behavior and human societies are greatly affected by fundamental biological mechanisms as well as by cultural values and practices.[36]

The individual is the coin of the operating realm in virtually all of the major Western institutions of medicine, education, law, religion, and psychiatry. These institutions collectively help create the myth that individuals are always in control of their behavior, act from free will and rational choice, and are thus personally responsible for any and all of their actions. Unless insane or of diminished capacity, individuals who do wrong should know that they are doing wrong and be punished accordingly. Situational factors are assumed to be little more than a set of minimally relevant extrinsic circumstances. In evaluating various contributors to any behavior of interest, the dispositionalists put the big chips on the Person and the chintzy chips on the Situation. That view seemingly honors the dignity of individuals, who should have the inner strength and will power to resist all temptations and situational inducements. Those of us from the other side of the conceptual tracks believe that such a perspective denies the reality of our human vulnerability. Recognizing such common frailties in the face of the kinds of situational forces we have reviewed in our journey thus far is the first step in shoring up resistance to such detrimental influences and in developing effective strategies that reinforce the resilience of both people and communities.

The situationist approach should encourage us all to share a profound sense of humility when we are trying to understand "unthinkable," "unimaginable," "senseless" acts of evil—violence, vandalism, suicidal terrorism, torture, or rape. Instead of immediately embracing the high moral ground that distances us good folks from those bad ones and gives short shrift to analyses of causal factors in that situation, the situational approach gives those "others" the benefit of "attributional charity." It preaches the lesson that any deed, for good or evil, that any human being has ever done, you and I could also do—given the same situational forces.

Our system of criminal legal justice over-relies on commonsense views held by the general public about what things cause people to commit crimes—usually only motivational and personality determinants. It is time for the legal justice system to take into account the substantial body of evidence from the behavioral sciences about the power of the social context in influencing behavior, criminal actions as well as moral ones. My colleagues Lee Ross and Donna Shestowsky have offered a penetrating analysis of the challenges that contemporary psychology poses to legal theory and practice. Their conclusion is that the legal system might adopt the model of medical science and practice by taking advantage of current research on what goes wrong, as well as right, in how the mind and body work:

The workings of the criminal justice system should not continue to be guided by illusions about cross-situational consistency in behavior, by erroneous notions about the impact of dispositions versus situations in guiding behavior, or by failures to think through the logic of "person by situation" interactions, or even comforting but largely fanciful notions of free will, any more than it should be guided by once common notions about witchcraft or demonic possession.[37]

Situated Identities

Our personal identities are socially situated. We are *where* we live, eat, work, and make love. It is possible to predict a wide range of your attitudes and behavior from knowing any combination of "status" factors—your ethnicity, social class, education, and religion and where you live—more accurately than by knowing your personality traits.

Our sense of identity is in large measure conferred on us by others in the ways they treat or mistreat us, recognize or ignore us, praise us or punish us. Some people make us timid and shy; others elicit our sex appeal and dominance. In some groups we are made leaders, while in others we are reduced to being followers. We come to live up to or down to the expectations others have of us. The expectations of others often become self-fulfilling prophecies. Without realizing it, we often behave in ways that confirm the beliefs others have about us. Those subjective beliefs can create new realities for us. We often become who other people think we are, in their eyes and in our behavior.[38]

Can You Be Judged Sane in an Insane Place?

Situations confer their social identities on us even when it should be obvious that it is not our true personal identity. Recall in the "mock ward" study at Elgin State Mental Hospital (chapter 12) that hospital staff mistreated the "mental patients" on their ward in a variety of ways; however, they were not actually patients but fellow staff members dressed as and playing the role of patients. Similarly, in the Stanford Prison Experiment, everyone knew that the guards were college kids pretending to be guards and that the prisoners were college kids pretending to be prisoners in that mock prison. Did it matter what their real identity was? Not really, as you saw; not after a day or so. They became their situated identities. In addition, I too became The Prison Superintendent in walk, talk, and distorted thought—when I was in that place.

Some situations "essentialize" the roles people are assigned; each person must be what the role demands when he is on that stage set. Image, if you will, that you are a totally normal person who finds yourself hospitalized in a psychiatric ward in a mental hospital. You are there because a hospital admissions officer mistakenly labeled you as "schizophrenic." That diagnosis was based on the fact that you complained to him about "hearing voices," nothing more. You believe that you do not deserve to be there and realize that the way to be released is to act as normal and as pleasant as you can. Obviously the staff will soon realize there has been some mistake, you are not a mentally ill patient, and send you back home. Right?

Don't count on this happening if you were in that setting. You might never be released, according to a fascinating study conducted by another of my Stanford colleagues, David Rosenhan, with the wonderful title "On Being Sane in Insane Places."[39]

David and seven associates each went through the same scenario of making an appointment with a different mental hospital admissions officer and complaining of hearing voices or noises, "thuds," but giving no other unusual symptoms. Each of them was admitted to their local mental hospital, and as soon as they were dressed in the patient's pajamas and scuffies, they behaved in a pleasant, apparently normal fashion at all times. The big question was how soon the staff would catch on, realize they were really sane, and bid them adieu.

The simple answer in every one of the eight cases, in each of the eight mental wards, was *Never!* If you are in an Insane Place, you must be an Insane Person because Sane People are not Patients in Insane Asylums—so the situated-identity reasoning went. To be released took a lot of doing, after several weeks, and only with help from colleagues and lawyers. Finally, after the suitably sane Eight were checked out, written across each of their hospital charts was the same final evaluation: "Patient exhibits schizophrenia in remission." Meaning that, no matter what, the staff still believed that their madness could erupt again some day—so don't throw away those hospital scuffies!

Assessing Situational Power

At a subjective level, we can say that you have to be embedded within a situation to appreciate its transformative impact on you and others who are similarly situated. Looking in from the outside won't do. Abstract knowledge of the situation, even when detailed, does not capture the affective tone of the place, its nonverbal features, its emergent norms, or the ego involvement and arousal of being a participant. It is the difference between being an audience member at a game show and being the contestant onstage. It is one reason that experiential learning can have such potent effects, as in the classroom demonstrations by Ms. Elliott and Ron Jones we visited earlier. Do you recall that when forty psychiatrists were asked to predict the outcome of Milgram's experimental procedure, they vastly underestimated its powerful authority impact? They said that only 1 percent would go all the way up to the maximum shock level of 450 volts. You have seen just how far off they were. They failed to appreciate fully the impact of the social psychological setting in making ordinary people do what they would not do ordinarily.

How important is situational power? A recent review of 100 years of social psychological research compiled the results of more than 25,000 studies including 8 million people.[40] This ambitious compilation used the statistical technique of *meta-analysis,* which is a quantitative summary of findings across a variety of studies that reveals the size and consistency of such empirical results. Across 322 separate meta-analyses, the overall result was that this large body of social psychological research generated substantial effect sizes—that the power of social situations is a reliable and robust effect.

This data set was reanalyzed to focus only on research relevant for understanding the social context variables and principles that are involved when ordinary people engage in torture. The Princeton University researcher Susan Fiske found 1,500 separate effect sizes that revealed the consistent and reliable impact of situational variables on behavior. She concluded, "Social psychological evidence emphasizes the power of the social context, in other words, the power of the interpersonal situation. Social psychology has accumulated a century of knowledge across a variety of studies about how people influence each other for good or ill."[41]

LOOKING AHEAD TO APPLES, BARRELS, WHEELERS, AND DEALERS

Now the time has come to collect our analytical gear and move our journey to the far-off foreign land of Iraq to try to understand an extraordinary phenomenon of our times: the digitally documented abuses of Iraqis detained in the prison at Abu Ghraib. Revelations of these violations against humanity moved out from that secret dungeon in Tier 1A, that little shop of horrors, to reverberate around a shocked world. How could this happen? Who was responsible? Why had photographs been taken that implicated the torturers in the act of committing their crimes? These and more questions filled the media for months on end. The president of the United States vowed "to get to the bottom of this." A host of politicians and pundits knowingly proclaimed that it was all the work of a few "bad apples." The abusers were nothing more than a band of sadistic "rogue soldiers."

Our plan is to reexamine what happened and how it happened. We are now adequately prepared to contrast this standard dispositional analysis of identifying the evil perpetrators, the "bad apples," in the otherwise presumably good barrel, with our search for situational determinants—the nature of that bad barrel. We will also review some of the conclusions from various independent investigations into these abuses that will take us beyond situational factors to implicate the System—military and political—in our explanatory mix.

CHAPTER FOURTEEN

Abu Ghraib's Abuses and Tortures: Understanding and Personalizing Its Horrors

The landmark Stanford study provides a cautionary tale for all military detention operations. . . . Psychologists have attempted to understand how and why individuals and groups who usually act humanely can sometimes act otherwise in certain circumstances.

—Schlesinger Independent Panel report[1]

Washington, D.C., April 28, 2004. I was in the nation's capital representing the American Psychological Association at a meeting of the Council of Scientific Society Presidents. Except when I am traveling, I rarely have time to watch TV news midweek. When I began flipping through channels in my hotel room, I came across something that froze me. Unbelievable images were flashing across the screen from CBS's program *60 Minutes II*.[2] Naked men were stacked high in a pyramid, and American soldiers stood grinning over their prisoner pile. A female soldier was leading a naked prisoner around by a dog leash tied around his neck. Other prisoners looked horrified as they seemed on the verge of being attacked by vicious-looking German shepherd dogs. On and on they went, like a pornographic slide show: naked prisoners were made to masturbate in front of a cigarette-smoking female soldier who stood giving a high-five approval salute; prisoners were made to simulate fellatio.

It seemed inconceivable that American soldiers were tormenting, humiliating, and torturing their captives by forcing homoerotic poses upon them. Yet here they were. Still other unbelievable images buzzed by: prisoners standing or bent over in stress positions with green hoods or women's pink panties covering their heads. Were these the fine young men and women sent overseas by the Pentagon on the glorious mission of bringing democracy and freedom to an Iraq recently liberated from the tyrant/torturer Saddam Hussein?

It was amazing to see that in many of the images in this horror show the perpetrators themselves appeared along with their victims. It is one thing to do evil deeds, quite another to document one's culpability in graphic, enduring photos.

What had they been thinking as they made their "trophy photos"? Finally, the soon-to-be-iconic image of psychological torture appeared. A hooded prisoner was precariously perched on a cardboard box with his arms outstretched and electric wires attached to his fingers. He had been led to believe (by Sgt. Davis) that if his legs gave way and he fell off the perch, he would be electrocuted. His hood was lifted briefly to see the wires leading from the wall to his body. They were false electrodes that aimed at inducing anxiety, not physical pain. How long he shuddered in absolute fear for his life we don't know, but we can readily imagine the trauma of his experience and empathize with this hooded man.

At least a dozen images swept across the screen; I wanted to turn off the TV but could not look away because I was captured by the vivid power of the pictures and their violation of expectation. Before even beginning to entertain hypotheses about what could possibly have induced such behavior in these soldiers, I was assured, along with the rest of the nation, that the torture was the work of only a few "bad apples." General Richard B. Myers, chairman of the Joint Chiefs of Staff, in a television interview declared his surprise at these allegations and astonishment at the images of criminal abuse. However, he said, he was certain that there was no evidence that the abuses were "systemic." To the contrary, he asserted that they were the isolated work of a handful of "rogue soldiers." According to this authoritative military spokesperson, fully 99.9 percent of American soldiers were performing in exemplary fashion overseas—meaning that there was no

need to be alarmed at the less than 1 percent of them who were defective soldiers carrying out these abominable abuses.

"Frankly, I think all of us are disappointed by the actions of the few," said Brigadier General Mark Kimmitt, interviewed on the *60 Minutes II* show. "Every day we love our soldiers, but frankly, some days we're not always proud of our soldiers." It was comforting to know that only a few rotten soldiers, serving as prison guards in America's many military prisons, were engaged in such unthinkable acts of wanton torture.[3]

Wait a minute. How could General Myers know that this was an isolated incident before having conducted a thorough investigation of his system of military prisons in Iraq, Afghanistan, and Cuba? The exposé had just been revealed; there had not been sufficient time for anyone to have done a thorough investigation in order to make such an assertion. There was something troubling about this authoritative declaration to absolve the System and blame the few at the bottom of the barrel. His claim was reminiscent of what police chiefs tell the media whenever police abuse of criminal suspects is revealed—blame the few rotten-apple-bad-cops—to deflect the focus away from the norms and usual practices in the back rooms of police stations or the police department itself. This rush to attribute a "bad-boy" dispositional judgment to the few offenders is all too common among the guardians of the System. In the same way, school principals and teachers use that device to blame particularly "disruptive" students instead of taking the time to evaluate the alienating effects of boring curricula or poor classroom practices of specific teachers that might provoke such disruptions.

Secretary of Defense Donald Rumsfeld denounced the acts as "terrible" and "inconsistent with the values of our nation." "The photographic depictions of U.S. military personnel that the public has seen have unquestionably offended and outraged everyone in the Department of Defense," he said. "Any wrongdoers need to be punished, procedures evaluated, and problems corrected." Then he added a statement that obliquely took the heat off the military for their lack of appropriate training and preparation of Army Reserve Military Police for such a difficult mission: "[I]f someone doesn't know that doing what is shown in those photos is wrong, cruel, brutal, indecent, and against American values, I am at a loss as to what kind of training could be provided to teach them."[4] However, Rumsfeld was also quick to redefine the nature of these acts as "abuse" and not "torture." He said, "What has been charged so far is abuse, which I believe technically is different from torture. I'm not going to address the 'torture' word."[5] Time out for another pause in this narrative: To what technicality is Rumsfeld referring?[6]

As media carried these images worldwide on prime-time TV, on the front pages of newspapers, in magazines, and on websites for days on end, President Bush launched an immediate and unprecedented damage control program to protect the reputation of his military and his administration, especially his secretary of defense. He dutifully declared that he would form independent investigations that would get to the "bottom of this." I wondered if the president would also order investigations that might get to the "top" of this scandal so that we could see the full picture and not just its frame? It would seem so, given that his deputy director for coalition operations in Iraq, Brigadier General Mark Kimmitt, publicly declared, "I'd like to sit here and say that these were the only prisoner abuse cases that we're aware of, but we know that there have been some other ones since we've been here in Iraq." (Doesn't this contradict General Myers's assertion that it was an isolated incident and not systemic?)

In fact, there have been so many cases of abuse, torture, and homicide uncovered since the Abu Ghraib scandal blew the lid off that by April 2006 more than four hundred separate military investigations had been launched into such allegations, according to Lieutenant Colonel John Skinner, U.S. Department of Defense.

Two other public reactions to the abuse photos are worthy of our notice, one by a famous media personality, another expressing the "outrage" of a United States congressman. To the archconservative talk-show host Rush Limbaugh, the photos, such as the one of a pyramid of naked prisoners, seemed little more than a college prank: "This is no different than what happens at the Skull and Bones [a Yale University secret society] initiation, and we're going to ruin people's lives over it, and we're going to hamper our military effort, and then we are going to really hammer them [the accused soldiers] because they had a good time. You know these people are being fired at every day. I'm talking about people having a good time, these people. You ever heard of emotional release? You heard of need to blow some steam off?"[7]

Torture as emotional release? Catharsis for the stressed soldiers? Having a good time by just blowing off a little steam? Those were the justifications by this influential celebrity for terrible acts of torture. One slight difference between the fraternity "hell night" scene and the Abu Ghraib torture scene is, of course, that fraternity pledges have the choice of whether to endure hazing as a testament of their commitment to joining a college society. They are not forcibly subjected, without their prior consent, to such humiliation and torment by a hostile, enemy occupation force.

Senator James Inhofe (Republican, Oklahoma), a member of the Senate Armed Services Committee, before which Secretary Rumsfeld had testified, was outraged. However, he avowed that he was "more outraged by the outrage" caused by the photographs than by what they depicted. He blamed the victims for deserving their abuse and the media for publicizing the images. "These prisoners, you know they're not there for traffic violations. If they're in Cellblock 1-A or 1-B, these prisoners, they're murderers, they're terrorists, they're insurgents. Many of them probably have American blood on their hands, and here we're so concerned about the treatment of those individuals." He continued his attack by arguing that the media were provoking further violence against Americans around the world by publicizing the outrage caused by showing the photos.[8]

The Pentagon used similar reasoning in its effort to block the release of these images. However, Major General Donald Ryder's internal Army report challenged the view that these prisoners were violent, noting that some Iraqis were held for long periods simply because they had expressed "displeasure or ill will" toward U.S. forces. Other accounts make it evident that many of the inmates were "innocent civilians" (according to the prison superintendent, Brigadier General Janis Karpinski). They had been picked up in military sweeps of towns where insurgent activity had occurred. In these sweeps, all the male family members, including young boys, were incarcerated in the nearest military prison and then often taken to Abu Ghraib for questioning.

Although I have seen many horrifying images of extreme abuse in conducting research on torture in Brazil and in preparing lectures on torture, something at once struck me as being different and yet familiar about the images that were emerging from the exotically named Abu Ghraib Prison. The difference had to do with the playfulness and shamelessness displayed by the perpetrators. It was just "fun and games," according to the seemingly shameless Private Lynndie England, whose smiling face belied the chaos going on around her. Nevertheless, a sense of the familiar was haunting me. With a shock of recognition, I realized that watching some of these images made me relive the worst scenes from the Stanford Prison Experiment. There were the bags over prisoners' heads; the nakedness; the sexually humiliating games that entailed camels humping or men leapfrogging over each other with their genitals exposed. These comparable abuses had been imposed by college student guards on their college student prisoners. In addition, just as in our study, the worst abuses had occurred during the night shift! Moreover, in both cases the prisoners were being held in pretrial detention.

It was as though the worst-case scenario of our prison experiment had been carried out over months under horrendous conditions, instead of in our brief, relatively benign simulated prison. I had seen what could happen to good boys when they were immersed in a situation that granted them virtually absolute power in dealing with their charges. In our study, the guards had had no prior training for their roles and been given only minimal staff supervision to curtail their psychological abuse of prisoners. Imagining what could happen when all the constraints that operated in our experimental setting were removed, I knew that in the Abu Ghraib Prison, powerful situational forces must have been in play, and even more dominating systemic forces had to have been at work. How could I ever know the truth about the behavioral context in that far-off situation or uncover any truth about the System that had created and maintained it? It was apparent to me that the System was now struggling mightily to conceal its own complicity in torture.

MAKING SENSE OF SENSELESS ABUSES

The design of the Stanford Prison Experiment made it evident that initially our guards were "good apples," some of whom became soured over time by powerful situational forces. In addition, I later realized that it was I, along with my research team, who was responsible for the System that made that situation work so effectively and so destructively. We failed to provide adequate top-down constraints to prevent prisoner abuse, and we set an agenda and procedures that encouraged a process of dehumanization and deindividuation that stimulated guards to act in creatively evil ways. Further, we could harness the System's power to terminate the experiment when it began to spin out of control and when a whistle-blower forced recognition of my personal responsibility for the abuses.

In contrast, in trying to understand the abuses that took place at Abu Ghraib, we are starting at the end of the process, with documented evil deeds. Therefore, we have to do a reverse analysis. We have to determine what these guards might have been like as people *before* they were assigned to guard the prisoners on those tiers of that Iraqi prison. Can we establish what pathologies, if any, the guards might have brought into the prison in order to separate their dispositional tendencies from what that particular situation might have brought out in them? Next, can we uncover what the behavioral context into which they were thrust was like? What was the social reality for the guards in that particular setting at that particular time?

Finally, we must discover something about the power structure that is responsible for creating and sustaining the working and living conditions of all the inhabitants of that dungeon—Iraqi prisoners and American guards alike. What justification can the System provide for using this particular prison to house "detainees" indefinitely without legal recourse and to interrogate them using "coercive tactics"? At what levels was the decision made to suspend the safeguards of the Geneva Conventions and the military's own rules of conduct regarding prisoners, namely, banning any actions that are cruel, inhuman, and degrading in the treatment of them? Those regulations provide the most basic standards of conduct in the treatment of prisoners in any democracy whether in times of war or peace. Nations put them into practice not so much out of charitable goodwill but to ensure the decent treatment of their own soldiers should they be captured as prisoners of war.

Not trained as an investigative reporter and not having the means to travel to Abu Ghraib or to interview the key participants in these abuses, I had little reason to expect that I would be able to get to the top or to the bottom of this intriguing psychological phenomenon. It would be a shame not to be able to bring to bear an understanding of this seemingly senseless violence based on my unique, "insider" knowledge from having been the superintendent of the Stanford prison. What I learned from the SPE paradigm about investigating institutional abuses is the need to evaluate various factors (dispositional, situational, and systemic) that lead to the behavioral outcome we want to understand. I was also curious as to who it was who had shined the spotlight on the abuses going on in that prison dungeon.

Joe Darby, Heroic Whistle-Blower, Ordinary Guy

The young soldier who blew the whistle on that "little shop of horrors" and exposed its dark deeds to public scrutiny was a twenty-four-year-old Army Reservist, Joe Darby. That young man is a hero because he forced the military officials to acknowledge the existence of such abusive practices and act to rein them in in all their prisons. Darby was in the same 372nd Military Police Company as the Military Police on night shift duty in the prison, but he was not working on that assignment.

One day, his buddy Corporal Charles Graner gave Darby a CD filled with hundreds of digital images and video clips that he and the other guards had taken. A few of the images had already made the rounds in their unit; some were even displayed on computer screen savers. Darby was at first amused looking at the pictures, thinking it was "pretty funny" to see a pile of naked Iraqis in a pyramid showing their asses. But the more he looked, the more distressed he felt at what he saw. "It didn't sit right with me," he said. He felt it was wrong for Americans to be doing such terrible things to other people even if they were foreigners imprisoned in a war zone. "I couldn't stop thinking about it. After about three days, I made a decision to turn the pictures in," Darby reported. He agonized over that decision, torn between loyalty to his friends and the urging of his moral conscience. Darby had known Lynndie England since basic training. Nevertheless, he said, what he saw "violated everything I personally believed, and all I'd been taught about the rules of law."

So on that day in January 2004, Joe Darby made a giant leap for moral mankind by first handing over a copy of the CD, with an anonymous note in a manila envelope, to an agent at the Criminal Investigation Division (CID). He later confided to Special Agent Tyler Pieron (U.S. Army Criminal Investigation Command at Abu Ghraib Prison) that he was the one who put the CD in the envelope and was willing to talk to CID more fully. Darby wanted to remain anonymous as long as he continued working at Abu Ghraib, for fear of retaliation for having ratted on his buddies in this way.[9]

It took enormous personal courage for Darby to blow the whistle so loudly, knowing that it would surely make trouble for his buddies in the 372nd who appeared on the CD. Nevertheless, when others were doing the wrong thing, Darby did the right thing.

We must also take into account that his military status was at the bottom rung, a specialist in the Army Reserve. He was openly challenging what was going on in a military-run prison—a prison, as I later discovered, a section of which was a special interrogation center created by the secretary of defense himself to elicit "actionable intelligence from terrorists and insurgents." It took fortitude for Darby to challenge the system.[10]

Apple Blossom Time in the Nation's Capital

Chance suddenly sent good fortune my way. A former Stanford student, working at National Public Radio in Washington, D.C., recognized the parallels between the photos of Abu Ghraib and those I had shown in my course lectures about the Stanford Prison Experiment. He tracked me down in my D.C. hotel to do an NPR interview shortly after the story surfaced. The main point of my interview was to challenge the administration's "bad apple" excuse with an alternative "bad barrel" metaphor that I derived from the similarity between the Abu Ghraib situation and the Stanford Prison Experiment. Many other TV, radio, and newspaper interviews soon fed off this first NPR interview to provide neat sound bites about assorted Apples and sordid Barrels. My commentary was sought by the media because it could be dramatized by vivid video and still footage from our experimental prison.

This national publicity, in turn, reminded Gary Myers, counsel for one of the MP guards, that my research was relevant in highlighting the external determinants of his client's alleged abusive behavior. Myers invited me to be an expert witness for Staff Sergeant Ivan "Chip" Frederick II, the military policeman who was in charge of the night shift on Tiers 1A and 1B. I agreed, in part so that I could have access to all the information I needed to fully understand the role of the triadic elements in the attributional analysis of this alien behavior: the Person, the Situation, and the System that had put this person in that place to commit such crimes.

With that background information, I hoped to more fully appreciate the dynamic transactions that had fueled these aberrations. In the process, I agreed to offer appropriate assistance to Myers's client. However, I made it clear that my sympathies were more with Joe Darby, who had been brave enough to expose the abuses, than with anyone involved in perpetrating them.[11] Under these conditions, I then joined Staff Sergeant Frederick's defense team and embarked on a journey into this new heart of darkness.

Let's begin our analysis by getting a better sense of what that place was like, that Abu Ghraib Prison—geographically, historically, politically, and in its recent operational structure and function. Then we can move on to examine the soldiers and prisoners in their behavioral context.

THE PLACE: THE ABU GHRAIB PRISON

Twenty miles (32 kilometers) west of Iraq's capital city, Baghdad, and a few miles from Fallujah lies the Iraqi city of Abu Ghraib (or Abu Ghurayb), where the prison is located. It lies within the Sunni triangle, the center of violent insurgency against the American occupation. In the past, the prison was designated by the Western media "Saddam's Torture Central" because it was the place where, during the reign of the Ba'athist government, Saddam Hussein arranged for the torture and murder of "dissidents" in twice-weekly public executions. There are allegations that some of these political and criminal prisoners were used in Nazi-like experiments as part of Iraq's chemical and biological weapons program.

At any one time, as many as fifty thousand people were held in the sprawling prison complex, whose name could translate into "House of Strange Fathers" or "Father of the Strange." It had always had an unsavory reputation because it had served as an insane asylum for severely disturbed inmates in the pre-Thorazine era. Built by British contractors in 1960, it covered 280 acres (1.15 square kilometers) and had a total of twenty-four guard towers encircling its perimeter. It was a sprawling small city, partitioned into five walled compounds each meant to hold particular kinds of prisoners. In the center of its open yard stood a huge 400-foot tower. Unlike most American prisons, which are built in remote rural areas, Abu Ghraib is located within sight of large apartment houses and offices (perhaps built after 1960). Inside, its cells were jammed with as many as forty people confined in a 12-foot-square (4-meter-square) space and living under vile conditions.

Colonel Bernard Flynn, Commander, Abu Ghraib Prison, described just how close the prison was to those attacking it: "It's a high-visibility target because we're in a bad neighborhood. All of Iraq is a bad neighborhood. . . . There's one tower where it's built so close to the neighborhood that we can look into the bedrooms, you know, right there on the porches. There were snipers on those roofs and on those porches firing at the soldiers who were up there on the towers. So we're constantly on guard and trying to defend this and trying to keep the insurgents away from coming inside."[12]

After the U.S. forces overthrew Saddam's government in March 2003, the name of the prison was changed from Abu Ghraib—to dissociate it from its unsavory past—to the Baghdad Central Confinement Facility (BCCF)—initials seen in many of the investigative reports. When Saddam's regime collapsed, all prisoners, including many criminals, were released, and the prison was looted; whatever could be removed was stolen—doors, windows, bricks: you name it and someone stole it. Incidentally—and not reported in the media—the Abu Ghraib city zoo was also opened and all the wild animals released. For a time, lions and tigers roamed the streets until they were captured or killed. A former CIA bureau chief, Bob Baer, described the scene he witnessed at this notorious prison: "I visited Abu Ghraib a couple of days after it was liberated. It was the most awful sight I've ever seen. I said, 'If there's ever a reason to get rid of Saddam Hussein, it's because of Abu Ghraib.'" His grim account adds, "There were bodies that were eaten by dogs, torture. You know, electrodes coming out of the walls. It was an awful place."[13]

Although senior U.K. officials recommended that the prison be demolished, U.S. authorities decided to rebuild the prison as quickly as possible so that it could be used to detain all those who were suspected of vaguely defined "crimes against the Coalition," suspected insurgency leaders, and assorted criminals. In charge of this motley group of detainees were Iraqi guards of dubious character. Many of those held in security were blameless assorted Iraqi civilians who had been picked up in random military sweeps or at highway checkpoints for "suspicious activity." They included whole families—men, women, and adolescents—to be interrogated for information they might have about the unanticipated growing insurgency against the Coalition. Once arrested and found innocent after interrogation, they were not released because the military feared that they would then join the insurgency, or because nobody wanted to take the reponsibility for making such decisions.

The Towering Target of Mortar Attacks

The imposing four-hundred-foot tower in the center of the prison soon became the sighting focus of almost nightly mortar attacks that were launched from the tops of nearby buildings. In August 2003, a mortar attack killed eleven soldiers who were sleeping in tents outside in the yard on the "soft site." In another attack, an explosive ripped through a tent filled with soldiers, among them Colonel Thomas Pappas, the head of one of the military intelligence brigades stationed at the prison. Although Pappas was unharmed, the young soldier who was his driver was shredded and died, along with other soldiers. Pappas was so affected by this sudden horror that he never again took off his flak jacket. It was reported to me that he always wore his jacket and hard helmet even while showering. He was later declared "not combat fit" and relieved of his duties. His deteriorating mental condition did not permit him to provide the vitally necessary supervision of his soldiers working in the prison. After the terrifying mortar attack, Pappas housed most of his soldiers inside the prison walls on the "hard site," which meant that they were usually sleeping in small prison cells, just like those of the prisoners.

Stories of their comrades' deaths and the constant continuing sniper, grenade, and mortar attacks created an ambient sense of fear among everyone assigned to the prison, which came under hostile attack as many as twenty times a week. Both American soldiers and Iraqi prisoners and detainees were killed by this hostile fire. Over time, the attacks destroyed some of the prison complex and left buildings burned out and debris everywhere in sight.

The mortar shelling was so frequent that it became part of the surreal surrounding of the Abu Ghraib madness. Joe Darby recalls discussions with buddies as they tried to figure out the size and location of the mortar after hearing the boom of its launch; whether it was 60 or 80 mm. or even big enough to be a 120 mm. explosion. However, that psychic numbness in the face of death did not last forever. Darby confesses that "a few days before my unit left Abu Ghraib, all of a sudden people started worrying about mortar attacks for the first time. It was weird. They'd be huddling against the wall together. I found myself crouched in a corner, praying. The numbness was wearing off. That's one of the things you have to keep in mind when you look at the pictures. We all got numb in different ways."

According to one high-ranking informant who worked there for several years, the prison remained a very dangerous place in which to work or be housed. In 2006, the military command finally decided to abandon it, but a bit too late to undo the damage caused by its earlier decision to resurrect it.*

Compounding the woes of the soldiers, the war-torn Abu Ghraib Prison had no sewage system—only holes in the ground and porta-potties. Even so, there were not enough outside porta-potties to accommodate all the prisoners and soldiers. Because they were not regularly emptied, they overflowed, and in the extreme summer temperatures, the stench was horrible for everyone all the time. There was also no adequate shower system; water was rationed; there was no soap; electricity went down regularly because there were no reliably operating generators. The prisoners stank, as did the whole facility that enclosed them. Under the heavy rains of summer, when temperatures soared well above 110 degrees F. (45 C.), the prison became a baking oven, or sauna. During a windstorm, fine dust participles got into everyone's lungs, causing congestion and viral infections.

After it was decided to demolish the tall tower in order to eliminate it as a sighting target for insurgents, mortar attacks were on target less frequently, but that huge demolition added to the permanent debris in and degradation of the prison site.

Nor did the quality of the food make up for the other deficiencies in the accommodations. Even though this large facility had recently been renovated by the U.S. Army, there were no mess halls. For more than two years after the occupation of Abu Ghraib, soldiers assigned to duty there were obliged to eat T-Rations and

---

*Abu Ghraib Prison was officially closed as of August 15, 2006, and all remaining prisoners shipped to Camp Cropper, near the Baghdad airport.

MREs (Meals Ready to Eat) out of containers. A mess hall was finally constructed in December 2003. In summary, I cannot express the scene better than did a warrant officer in charge of military investigations there who told me just how terrible it was to work in such a place "that for a long time resembled hell on earth."[14]

Eighty Acres of Hell

American history buffs will remind us at this point that an even more hellish prison was created and maintained by the U.S. military during and after the Civil War. Camp Douglas was the prison a few miles outside of Chicago where thousands of captured Confederate prisoners were sent for safekeeping. It was poorly conceived on reclaimed swampland, with inadequate resources, indecisive and lax leadership, no clear guidelines for dealing with POWs, and great hostility against these Confederate "traitors" on the part of local civilians and the small battalion of guards who supervised as many as five thousands prisoners. Camp Douglas became known as "eighty acres of Hell" because thousands of prisoners died there, as slave laborers, from starvation, brutal beatings, torture, willful mistreatment, and a host of contagious diseases and viral disorders. The equivalent Hell on Earth in the South for captured Union soldiers was the better-known Andersonville Prison.[15]

The New Commander Arrives On-site, But Sight Unseen

In June 2003 a new officer was put in charge of the Iraqi prison disaster. Army Reserve Brigadier General Janis Karpinski was made commander of the 800th Military Police Brigade, which operated Abu Ghraib Prison and was in charge of all other military prisons in Iraq. The appointment was strange for two reasons: Karpinsky was the only female commander in the war zone, and she had absolutely no experience in running any kind of prison system. Now she was supposed to command three large jails, seventeen prisons throughout Iraq, eight battalions of soldiers, hundreds of Iraqi guards, and thirty-four hundred inexperienced Army Reservists, as well as the special Interrogation Center in Tier 1A. It was an overwhelming demand to be put on the shoulders of such an inexperienced Army Reserve officer.

According to several sources, Karpinski soon abandoned her post at Abu Ghraib because of its dangers and awful living conditions and retreated to the safety and security of Camp Victory, near the Baghdad airport. Because Karpinski was off-site much of the time, traveling often to Kuwait, there was no top-down authoritative supervision of the facility on a day-to-day basis. Moreover, she claims that those higher up in the chain of command told her that Tier 1A was a "special site" and was not under her direct supervision—so she never visited it.

Having a woman who was only nominally in charge also encouraged sexist attitudes among the soldiers that led to a breakdown in ordinary military discipline and order. "General Karpinski's subordinates at Abu Ghraib at times disregarded her commands and didn't enforce codes on wearing uniforms and saluting superiors, which added to the lax standards that prevailed at the prison," said one member of the brigade. The soldier, who spoke on the condition of anonymity, also said that commanders in the field routinely ignored General Karpinski's orders, saying that they didn't have to listen to her because she was a woman."[16]

One task she did perform, after a fashion, consisted of weekly "scrubs," where she made decisions about which prisoners should be released either because they were not dangerous or because they probably had no useful information and were neither insurgents nor criminals. However, I was told that Karpinski played it safe by releasing relatively few detainees, while many new prisoners were being brought in daily; therefore, the prison population continued to swell. To make matters worse, though few were leaving, there was a constant influx of new prisoners from other prisons, as, for example, when Camp Bucca was overcrowded.

As the prison population swelled to more than ten thousand during the first six months of Karpinski's tenure, there were, among those imprisoned, thirty juveniles, ages ten to seventeen. For these children not only were there no educational programs, but there were also no separate facilities. "It was heartbreaking to see the conditions under which these young children were living for months on end," said one observer. In addition, nothing was done to provide separate arrangements for prisoners who were mentally ill or were suffering from a variety of contagious diseases, like TB.

It is curious, then, that given the terrible conditions at Abu Ghraib, General Karpinski would give a thumbs-up report in an interview with the *St. Petersburg Times* in December 2003. She said that for many of the Iraqis imprisoned at Abu Ghraib, "living conditions now are better in prison than living at home." She added, "At one point we were concerned that they wouldn't want to leave." However, at that very moment, as General Karpinski was giving such a cheery pre-Christmas interview, Major General Antonio Taguba was conducting an investigation of reports of numerous incidents of "sadistic, blatant, and wanton criminal abuses" perpetrated by her Army Reserve soldiers in the 372nd Military Police Company, from the night shift on Tier 1A.

General Karpinski was later admonished, suspended from duty, officially reprimanded, and removed from this command. She was also demoted to the rank of colonel and retired from the service. She was the first officer to be found blameworthy in the investigation of prisoner abuses, for her sins of omission and ignorance—not for anything she did, but for what she did not do.

In her autobiography, *One Woman's Army*, Karpinski tells her side of the story.[17] She recounts the visit of an Army team from Guantánamo, headed by Major General Geoffrey Miller, who told her, "We're going to change the nature of the interrogation at Abu Ghraib." That meant "taking off the kid gloves," to stop being so soft on these suspected insurgents, and to start using tactics that would get "actionable intelligence" needed in the war against terrorists and insurgents.

Miller also insisted that the official name of the prison cease to be the Baghdad Central Confinement Facility (BCCF) and return to its original designation, which was still feared among the Iraqi population: Abu Ghraib Prison.

She also notes that Lieutenant General Ricardo Sanchez, the commander of U.S. forces in Iraq, repeated the theme that General Miller had laid down about prisoners and detainees being nothing more than "like dogs," and the need to get tougher in dealing with them. In Karpinski's view, her superior officers, Generals Miller and Sanchez, set a new agenda for dehumanization and torture at Abu Ghraib.[18]

THE PERSON: I'D LIKE TO INTRODUCE "CHIP" FREDERICK

I first met Chip Frederick on September 30, 2004, when his legal counsel, Gary Myers, arranged for me to spend a day with him and his wife, Martha, in San Francisco. While we engaged in an in-depth, four-hour interview, Martha did a bit of sightseeing, after which we had lunch at my home in Russian Hill. Since that time I have had an active correspondence with Chip Frederick, and I have been in phone and e-mail contact with Martha and with Chip's older sister, Mimi Frederick.

After having examined all of his records and all available reports about him, I arranged to have a military clinical psychologist (Dr. Alvin Jones) conduct a full psychological assessment of Frederick in September 2004.[19] I reviewed those data as well as the independent blind evaluation of the MMPI testing that had been done by an assessment expert. In addition, I administered a measure of psychological burnout at the time of our interview, and an expert on job stress independently evaluated its results. Let's start with some general background, add some personal input from family and some of Frederick's recent self-evaluations, and then review the formal psychological assessments.

Chip was thirty-seven years old at that time, the son of a seventy-seven-year-old West Virginia coal miner father and a seventy-three-year-old homemaker mother. He grew up in the small town of Mt. Lake Park, Maryland. He describes his mother as very supportive and caring and his father as very good to him. One of his favorite memories is working on vehicles in the garage alongside his father. His older sister, Mimi, forty-eight, is a registered nurse. He married Martha in Virginia in June 1999; they met when she was a trainer at the correctional facility where he worked. He has become the stepfather of her two grown daughters.

All his life, Chip has attended Baptist Church services regularly, at least every other Sunday. He considers himself a moral and spiritual person, even after his involvement in the abuses at Abu Ghraib. Before going to Iraq, he attended the local community college and went on to take courses at Allegheny College in Maryland but did not finish his degree. He was an average-C student, never failed a course, and liked to learn new skills. Chip, however, is more a jock than an intellectual; he played basketball, baseball, football, and soccer in high school. As an adult, he continued to play softball as a left fielder, hitting for a good average rather than distance. His main hobbies are hunting and fishing. He is also a "people person" who has a great many close longtime friends with whom he has stayed in touch over the years. He is very close to these friends, who are, he said, the kind of people "that you would die for." Chip indicated that he also has close relations with his niece and nephew. In general, he is a family man; he counts on his family, and they have always been able to count on him. He loves his wife, Martha, whom he describes as "perfect" and a "very strong woman," and he loves her daughters "as if they were my own."

Chip is in good health and is physically fit. He has never had surgery, psychological counseling, or medication for mental problems. His only run-in with the law came when he was nineteen as a "disturbing the peace" arrest that carried a fine of $5.00, which he received for hollering too loud and long at a night game of "hide-and-seek." He rarely smokes, drinks only a few beers a week, and has never used illegal drugs.

Chip describes himself in the following way: "very quiet, sometimes shy, down to earth, softhearted, very agreeable, an overall good person."[20] However, it is important for us to note some additional self-descriptions: Chip usually fears being rejected by others, and so, in any disagreement, he often gives way in order to be accepted; he changes his mind to accommodate others so that they will not be "mad at me or hate me." Others can influence him even when he believes that he has made up his mind. He does not like to be alone; he likes to be around others, and he becomes depressed when he is alone for any length of time.

Some of my research on shyness provides empirical support for this shyness-conformity link. We have found that shy college students were likely to give in to and agree with others whose opinions were discrepant from their own when they believed they might have to defend their point of view openly, whereas they did not conform when they did not have to fear a public confrontation.[21]

The man is superpatriotic—every day he flies the American flag in his front yard and takes it down at sunset. He gives the flag as a gift to friends and family. "I bought several flags to give to family, my place of business, and I flew them in Kuwait, every one of them. I think I had nine or ten, I flew them when I was in Baghdad, and I'd send them to my wife," he said during our interview. Chip Frederick gets "goose bumps" and "teary-eyed" when he hears the National Anthem. He wrote to me recently from his prison cell, "I am proud to say that I served most of my adult life for my country. I was very prepared to die for my country, my family and friends. . . . I wanted to be the one to make a difference."[22] (I must admit that such feelings seem a bit over the top to someone with my more cautious brand of patriotism.)

His sister, Mimi, has this to say about her kid brother:

Growing up with Chip was a delight for me. I am 3 months shy of being 11 years older than he is. Chip was a quiet person. He was considerate of his peers. Chip always was thoughtful of others' feelings and was never a vengeful type person. Chip was ornery and liked practical jokes. He would always feed the dog peanut butter and would laugh so hard he would be on the ground rolling! Chip played sports and was a team player. His philosophy of life is fairness, and he still has a strong belief in that, responsibility and accountability, he was taught good morals and values by our parents. I remember watching him go off to the army at the young age of 17, just a kid, only to return a young man all grown up and demonstrating these same skills that he values so much. Chip likes to hunt and fish in his spare time. He enjoys sports, NASCAR, motorcycling and spending time with his family.[23]

Frederick's Corrections and Army Service Record

Before being activated for duty in Iraq, Chip Frederick worked as a correctional officer in a small, medium-security prison, the Buckingham Correctional Center, in Dillwyn, Virginia, for five years from December 1996. He was a floor officer in charge of supervising 60 to 120 inmates at any given time. While he was in institutional training, he met Martha, who was his trainer. The only blemish on his record is a reprimand he received for once wearing the wrong uniform. However, that is balanced by a citation he received for preventing an inmate's suicide. Before becoming a correctional officer, Frederick worked making eyeglasses at Bausch & Lomb.

I was able to review many of his performance evaluations, which had been conducted annually by the Virginia Department of Corrections. A summary of key observations by various evaluating officers provides a sense of how well Chip progressed through probationary training to become a corrections officer. He typically exceeded expectations on almost all specific performance dimensions.

"C/O Frederick has been proficient in performing this [sic] assigned duties for this probationary period. Has met all established performance standards." "Officer Frederick shows initiative and does a very good job." (April 1997)

One negative blemish on his performance record with the Virginia Department of Corrections reads: "Employee needs to be more consistent on post assignments and enforce standing counts." (November 1997)

On all other six dimensions, he is rated as "Meets expectations" but as only "Fair, but needs improvement" on the dimension of initiating and completing count procedures. (Recall the count procedure ordeal of the SPE?)

Otherwise, the comments are uniformly positive: "He is a very good officer and shows leadership abilities." "His appearance exceeds expectations." (November 1998) (This was also true of his handling keys and equipment. All the rest of the dimensions "meet expectations.")

"Officer Frederick meets all criteria and has the potential to be an excellent officer." "Officer Frederick does an excellent job in controlling the custody, control, and safety of inmates." "Officer Frederick is always neat and clean, shoes polished and appears that he takes pride in his uniform." (November 1999)

"Officer Frederick operates and maintains post in a safe, secure and clean manner. When assigned to special housing he keeps his area clean and prepared for inspections." "Officer Frederick is always dressed properly for his shift assignment. He maintains his professional appearance." "He works well with both his co-workers and inmates. He has a thorough knowledge of the work to be done and established policies and procedures. He has no problem assisting others in completing their job assignments." (October 2000)

Overall, these evaluations are increasingly positive up to the point that Chip Frederick's performance "exceeds expectations." However, it is instructive to note a key conclusion in one of these final reports: "There were no factors beyond the employee's control which affected his performance." It is important to keep this in mind precisely because I will argue that "situational factors beyond his control" did undermine his performance at Abu Ghraib.

In the final evaluations of Frederick, in May 2001, his ratings were high: "Officer Frederick does a very good job as the floor officer. He communicates well with the inmates in his area and on the strike force." "Officer Frederick displays a high standard of professional conduct and appearance." "Officer Frederick does a very good job enforcing all written policies." "Officer Frederick does a very good job taking counts."

It is obvious that Chip Frederick became a valuable corrections officer who was highly effective when he had explicit procedures and written policies to follow. He clearly learned on the job and benefited from the surveillance and feed-back of his supervisors. He is also someone for whom appearance and grooming is important, as is maintaining a professional demeanor. Those qualities, which are central in Chip's personal identity, would be under assault by the horrible con-ditions we have noted existed at Abu Ghraib Prison and were even worse on the night shift on Tier 1A.

Chip joined the armed forces in 1984 for the money and the experience, and to be with friends. It also seemed the patriotic thing to do at that time. He served for more than eleven years in the National Guard in a combat engineer unit and added to that service ten more years in the Military Police of the Army Reserve. The only negative mark on his record was one he got for being late for formation early in his career. After being activated, his first tour of duty was in Kuwait in May 2003, and then in a small town, Al-Hillah, south of Baghdad, where he served with half a dozen close buddies in the 372nd MP Company. He was an op-eration sergeant charged with sending out patrols.[24]

> The mission was great, the locals loved us. There were no major incidents or injuries. It was peaceful till we left [and Polish Coalition forces took over]. I made it a point to learn about the culture, I learned a little Arabic, and I made sure I interacted with the people. I sent packets full of candies to my kids [in that village]. My kids were always cheering for me.

Frederick also reported that he continues to be proud that he was able to make those children smile just by listening to them and taking the time to play with them.[25]

During that time, he was able to satisfy his overwhelming desire for neatness by "semipressing" his uniform. This meant that after washing and drying his uni-form, he put it under a plywood board underneath his mattress and slept on it for a week. He was the only soldier who had creases in his pants, and he was ragged for it, but he didn't care, "because that's just me; I don't like to be sloppy." He de-scribes himself as a perfectionist who always likes things to be "nice, neat and clean." His penchant for being neat was so extreme that it would sometimes "drive his wife crazy." Unfortunately, there was little time and no reason for such neatness in Abu Ghraib Prison, where he arrived early in October 2003.

One indication of Chip Frederick's exemplary service as a soldier for his na-tion comes from a review of the many awards he has earned over the years. They include: Army Achievement Medal (awarded three times); Army Reserve Compo-nents Medal (awarded four times); National Defense Medal (awarded twice); Armed Forces Reserve Medal with "M" Device; Noncommissioned Officer's Pro-fessional Development Ribbon; Army Service Ribbon; Army Reserve Components Overseas Training Ribbon (awarded twice); Global War on Terrorism Medal; and Global War on Terrorism Expeditionary Medal. He was also about to re-ceive a Bronze Star for the effective way he had dealt with a shooting incident with a Syrian detainee in Abu Ghraib, but which was not awarded after the abuse revelations surfaced. These are some rather impressive credentials as far as I am concerned, especially for someone later alleged to be a "rogue soldier."

Psychological Assessments[26]

Chip's IQ falls in the average range on the combined measures of verbal and performance intelligence on standard tests.

Three measures of personality and emotional functioning contain validity scales that assess how the person being tested portrays him or herself across all test items, picking up lying, defensiveness, and falsifying answers. Chip showed no tendency to present himself in either an overly positive or overly negative light in regard to psychological functioning. However, it is important to highlight the conclusion: "Validity scales indicate the patient presented himself as a morally virtuous individual," according to the military psychologist conducting the assessment. In addition, these standardized test results indicate that Chip Frederick has "no sadistic or pathological tendencies." That conclusion strongly suggests that the "bad apple" dispositional attribution of blame made against him by military and administration apologists has no basis in fact.

> Test results suggest a core motivation for the patient to obtain and maintain nurturance and supportive relationships. He is expected to be obliging, docile, and placating, while seeking relationships in which he can lean on others for emotional support, affection, nurture, and security. His temperament will likely be pacifying and he will try to avoid conflict. In this regard, he will have a general tendency to hesitate in expressing negative feelings for fear of alienating others. He will exhibit an excessive need for both security and attachment and to be taken care of, and he will likely feel uneasy when alone. This underlies, in part, his tendency to submit to the wishes of others in order to maintain security.[27]

The independent evaluation of Chip Frederick's personality assessment by an expert clinical psychologist, Dr. Larry Beutler, indicates substantial agreement with the conclusions by the Army clinical psychologist. First, he notes that "The results of the assessment can be considered reasonably reliable and valid indicators of his [Frederick's] current functioning."[28] Dr. Beutler goes on to say, in bold type, "It should also be noted that there is no evidence of gross pathology. . . . [He] is not manifesting serious personality or Axis 1 pathology."

This means that Chip shows no evidence at all of a psychopathic personality that would predispose him to be abusive without guilt in his work setting. He also falls into the "normal, healthy range" with regard to schizophrenia, depression, hysteria, and all other major forms of psychological pathology.

However, Dr. Beutler also says that in his considered opinion a syndrome of underlying psychological traits raises concerns about Chip's leadership in complex, demanding situations, such as those he encountered at Abu Ghraib:

These symptoms [of Frederick's] are likely to impede his ability to respond to new situations and may reduce his flexibility and ability to adapt to change. He is likely to be indecisive, insecure and to rely on others to help him make decisions. . . . He seeks assurance of his worth and acknowledgment of his efforts, and is quite dependent on others to help him set and keep an agenda or make decisions. . . . He is easily led by others and in spite of his best efforts to "do what is right," is likely to be over controlled by circumstances, authorities, and peer pressures.

These reports make evident that Staff Sergeant Chip Frederick would make a good "social-emotional leader" but not as good a "task leader," a distinction that researchers on leadership use to distinguish two contrasting leadership styles. A social-emotional leader is sensitive to the needs of those in his organization and engages in activities that will promote a positive quality of group membership. On the other hand, a task leader focuses on the more formal aspects of leadership, setting agendas and standards, providing assignments, and giving informational feedback to achieve the group's goals. Ideally, a group leader should possess both traits, but often the job is divided among several leaders, each of whom is best at one or the other set of attributes. Groups need effective task leaders more than they do good social-emotional ones in situations that are ambiguous, that involve shifting demands, and that lack explicit objectives—a classic example of the night shift job setting on Tier 1A. As good as Chip may have been in previous leadership or correctional circumstances, he was simply the wrong person for the complex job of leader on that shift at that time in that place.

Chip Frederick also completed the primary assessment of an individual's extent and type of psychological burnout within an organizational setting. He did so by imaging his work situation as it was when he was at Abu Ghraib. The Maslach Burnout Inventory (MBI) identifies three aspects of a person's relationship with a specific work setting: emotional exhaustion, cynicism, and personal efficacy. It was developed by Christina Maslach (recall the heroine of the Stanford Prison Experiment). The measure was later refined and extended in her research with Dr. Michael Leiter, who provided a "blind" analysis of Frederick's reactions (that is, he was unaware of who the "client" was and of his specific work setting).[29]

According to Dr. Leiter, Chip's scores reveal an unusual profile of burnout on these three dimensions. Ordinarily, a high degree of exhaustion, elevated cynicism, and a reduced sense of personal effectiveness at work go together in characterizing job burnout. However, Chip showed few signs of cynicism or a negative evaluation of his personal work effectiveness. Nonetheless, he does show extreme emotional exhaustion:

The profile indicated a person experiencing extreme exhaustion, which is the defining quality of burnout. Specifically, the assessment indicates a person who is emotionally drained and chronically tired. His recovery cycles are not providing sufficient rest or relief from work to permit him to replenish his energy, leading to a condition of chronic weariness. It is evident that his current state is contrary to the individual's identity: He thinks of himself as capable of managing serious demands, but is overwhelmed in his current circumstances. . . . Overall, this profile indicates a person experiencing job burnout that is specific to the work situation in question. The profile suggests that under different work circumstances, he could be a productive and enthusiastic contributor.

Research in cognitive psychology shows that performance on a variety of tasks is undermined by conditions, such as chronic stress and multitasking, that impose an excessive load on a person's cognitive resources. Memory and problem solving, as well as judgment and decision making, all suffer when the mind's usual capacity is overextended.[30] I will argue that Chip's ordinary level of cognitive capacities was indeed overwhelmed by the inordinate load imposed on him by the situational demands he faced nightly at his new, overwhelming job.

With these clues in mind, let us now turn our focus on the "work circumstance" alluded to in Dr. Leiter's report. From Chip's perspective, what was it like to work on Tier 1A during the night shift? I invite you, the reader, to assume the same mind-set that you used earlier in our journey, when you imagined that you were a participant, or a subject, in various social psychological experiments. Try walking in Chip Frederick's boots for a few months, from October to December 2003.

A Bad Apple or a Chip off the Best Block?

Before we leave our dispositional analysis to consider the situational forces at play, we must keep in mind that this young man brought *no* pathology into that situation. There is absolutely nothing in his record that I was able to uncover that would predict that Chip Frederick would engage in any form of abusive, sadistic behavior. On the contrary, there is much in his record to suggest that had he not been forced to work and live in such an abnormal situation, he might have been the military's All-American poster soldier on its recruitment ads. He could have been used honestly in place of the military's fabricated psuedoheroes, Privates Jessica Lynch and Pat Tillman.[31] The military could have used Staff Sergeant Ivan Frederick as a superpatriot who loved his country and was ready to serve it to the last drop of his blood. He could have been the best of apples in their good barrel.

In a sense, Chip Frederick also could have been one of the participants in our Stanford Prison Experiment, who we knew were good young men, normal and healthy—before they went down into that prison basement. Although he does not share their intelligence level or middle-class background, Chip can be compared with them in starting out as a *tabula rasa*, a clean slate, which would soon become boldly etched upon by a pathological prison setting. What was the Situation that brought out the worst in this otherwise good soldier? How could it have indelibly etched itself on him, distorting his usual mental and behavioral functioning? What was the nature of the "barrel" into which this once "good apple" was dropped?

THE SITUATION: NIGHTMARES AND NIGHT GAMES ON TIER 1A

Because he had prior experience in corrections, Staff Sergeant Frederick was assigned to be in charge of a small group of other Army Reserve Military Police on the night shift at Abu Ghraib. He had to oversee activities on four tiers in the "hard site," that is, inside the concrete structure rather than outside in the tent camps surrounded by barbed wire. One of those camps was Camp Vigilant (later changed to Camp Redemption), which had four separate compounds. Within Tier 1A (Alpha) was a special facility designed for inmate, or "detainee," interrogations. They were usually conducted by civilian contract interrogators, some aided by translators (hired by the Titan Corporation) and only loosely supervised by military intelligence, the CIA, and other service branches.

At first, Staff Sergeant Frederick was responsible for about four hundred prisoners. That was in early October 2003, when his 372nd Military Police Army Reserve Company (based in Cresaptown, Maryland) replaced the 72nd Military Police National Guard Company. Initially, he was able to handle the complex assignments handed to him, even though it was an escalation from the hundred or so medium-security prisoners he had had under his command back home. However, not long after President Bush had declared "mission accomplished," instead of the Iraqi citizenry being supportive, all hell broke loose. Insurgency and foreign terrorism against the U.S. and Coalition occupation surged out of control. No one had anticipated how extensive, coordinated, and deadly it would be and would continue to grow out of control.

Revenge for the deaths of so many soldiers mixed freely with fear and uncertainty about how to contain this eruption. Orders were sent out to round up all likely suspects in towns where any insurgent violence had erupted. That meant widespread arrests of whole families, especially adult males. The detention system was not able to process this new load adequately. Record keeping on detainees and their likely interrogation value fell by the wayside, and basic resources became completely inadequate under the pressure of an inmate population that doubled in November and nearly tripled to more than a thousand by December.

Chip was required to be in charge of all of them and, in addition to being in charge of a dozen or so MPs, to oversee the fifty to seventy Iraqi police who were guarding more than 1,000 Iraqis imprisoned on various criminal charges. The Iraqi police, who worked Tiers 2, 3, and 4, were notorious for smuggling in weapons and other contraband to inmates for a fee. Although the average age of the prisoners was in the range of twenty, there were also up to fifty adolescents, as well as children as young as ten years old and seniors in their sixties—all housed *together* in huge cells. Female prisoners, prostitutes, and the wives of generals and men who had been important leaders in Saddam's party were housed in Tier 1B (Bravo). Each of the Alpha and Bravo tiers held about fifty prisoners at any one time. In short, being in charge of this complex facility without adequate resources and a suddenly erupting foreign prisoner population placed a heavy burden upon someone whose prior experience had been limited to policing a small number of medium-security civilian prisoners in a small town in Virginia.

Training and Accountability

Zimbardo: "Please tell me about your training to be a guard, a guard leader, in this prison."[32]

Frederick: "None. No training for this job. When we mobilized at Fort Lee, we had a cultural awareness class, maybe it was about forty-five minutes long, and it was basically about not to discuss politics, not to discuss religion, and not to call 'em 'Aayrabs,' don't call 'em 'Camel Jockeys,' 'Towel Heads,' or not to call 'em 'Rag Heads, Aayrabs.' "

Z: "How would you describe the supervision you received and the accountability you felt you had toward your superior officers?"

Frederick: "None."

Z: "Who was your direct superior officer to whom you reported?"

Frederick: "Sergeant First Class Snyder. I was in charge of the four tiers, and he was in charge of me and it keeps going up the chain. Next in line is Captain Brinson. Above Captain Brinson is Captain Reese; above Reese is Lieutenant Colonel Phillabaum."

Frederick's shift began at 4 P.M. and lasted for twelve hours, until 4 A.M. He went on to report that few of these officers were ever present on Alpha Tier at night or made even brief appearances early in the shift. He had no supervision from Sergeant Snyder because his superior had no professional training in corrections. However, at various times Chip did offer suggestions and recommended changes to Snyder, Brinson, and Reese.

Z: "You would make recommendations?"

Frederick: "Yes, about operation of the facility. Not to handcuff prisoners to cell doors, should not have prisoners nude except for self-mutilators, can't handle prisoners with mental conditions. . . . One of the first things that I asked for as soon as I got there was regulations, operating procedures. . . . I was housing juveniles, men, women, and mentally ill prisoners all in the same thing, it's a violation of the military code."

Z: "So you would try to get up the chain of command?"

Frederick: "I would tell anybody that would come in who I thought had some ranking. . . . Usually they would tell me, 'Just see what you can come up with, keep up the good work,' this is the way Military Intelligence wants it done."

At other times, Chip said that he would be scoffed at or reprimanded by higher-ups for complaining. Given the combat zone conditions, they told him, he would have to make do as best possible. He was surely not in Kansas or the Dill-wyn, Virginia, Prison. There would never be any clear written procedures, no for-mal policies, and no structured guidelines. There was none of the procedural support that Chip Frederick needed to follow in order to be the kind of leader he hoped to be in this most important mission in his life. He was on his own, without any support system upon which he could rely. This was exactly the worst working condition for him, given Chip Frederick's basic needs and values, which we have just reviewed from his assessments. It was a sure recipe for failure. And that was only the beginning.

Nonstop Night Work

Not only did this soldier work half around the clock, he did so seven days a week with not a single day off for a full forty days! Then he had only one day off, fol-lowed by two more solid weeks on, before he could get a regular day off after four nights on. I can't imagine any job where such a work schedule would not be seen as inhumane. Given the shortage of trained corrections personnel and perhaps the failure of his superiors to appreciate the extent of this overwhelming daily workload, there was no recognition of or concern for Chip Frederick's job stress and burnout potential. He had to do what they wanted him to do and simply stop complaining to his superiors.

Where did he go at 4 A.M. when his long twelve-hour shift was over? He sim-ply went to sleep in another part of the prison—in a prison cell! He slept in a six-by-nine-foot prison cell that had no toilet but did have plenty of rodents running around it. It was dirty because there were not enough cleaning supplies and not enough water to clean it up. Chip Frederick told me during our interview, "I couldn't find supplies to keep the facilities clean. The plumbing was bad. Shit was backed up in the porta-potties. There was trash and mold everywhere. . . . It was nasty in there. There were human body parts in the facility. . . . There was a pack of wild dogs running around [still present from the days when prisoners executed by Saddam were buried in part of the prison and wild dogs would dig up their re-mains]. You know I was so mentally drained when I got off in the morning, all I wanted to do is sleep."

He missed breakfast, lunch, often had only one meal a day, which consisted of T-rations and not-so-tasty MREs—the Army-issue meals ready to be eaten out of containers. "Portions were small due to the large number of soldiers that had to be fed. I ate a lot of cheese and crackers," Chip reported. Other emerging health problems for this athletic, socially minded young man were that he stopped exer-cising because he was always tired and he was not able to socialize with buddies because of work schedule conflicts. More and more his life revolved entirely around his prison supervision and the MP Reservists working there under his command. They soon became what social psychologists refer to as his "reference group," a new in-group that would come to have a big influence on him. He was enmeshed in a "total situation," of the kind that the psychologist Robert Jay Lifton had earlier described as facilitating mind control in cults and in the North Korean prisoner-of-war camps.

Many Others on the All-Night Scene

The two MP reservists who served most often on the night shift in Alpha Tier were Corporal Charles Graner, Jr., and Specialist Megan Ambuhl. Graner was put in direct charge of Tier 1A during the night shift, given that Chip had to move around to supervise the other tiers. When they were off duty, Specialist Sabrina Harman replaced them. Sometimes Sergeant Javal Davis would fill in. Private First Class Lynndie England was a file clerk who was not assigned to this duty but visited often to be with her boyfriend, Charles Graner. She celebrated her twenty-first birthday on the tier. Specialist Armin Cruz, of the 325th Military Intelligence Battalion, was also frequently around that tier.

There were also "dog handlers," soldiers who came on the tier to use their dogs either to intimidate prisoners into talking or to force prisoners out of their cells if they were suspected of having weapons, or just for a show of force. Five such teams were sent to Abu Ghraib in November 2003, having had practice at the Guantánamo Bay Prison. (Two of these dog handlers, who were later found guilty of prisoner abuse, were Sergeant Michael Smith and Staff Sergeant Santos Cardona.) Nurses and medics also visited on occasion, when some special medical problem arose. Also present were a number of civilian contractors from the Titan Corporation, who did the interrogation of those detainees suspected of having information about insurgency activities or knowledge of terrorist activities. They often required translators to assist them in their interactions with the detainee-suspects. FBI, CIA, and military intelligence personnel were also around at times for special interrogations.

As might be expected, high-ranking military visitors were rarely around in the middle of the night. Commander Karpinski never visited Tiers 1 A/B during the months that Chip was on duty, except once when giving a TV tour. One reservist in that unit reported seeing Karpinski only twice in the five months he was at Abu Ghraib. A few other officers made brief appearances in the late afternoon. Chip used those rare occasions to report problems with the facility and to suggest changes he hoped could be made; none ever was. Various other people, who were not in uniform and had no identification, came and went to and from these two tiers. No one was supposed to ask to see their credentials, so they operated in total anonymity. Against the rules of military conduct, civilian contractors gave orders to the MP guards about things they wanted done to prepare particular prisoners for interrogation. Soldiers on duty are not supposed to take orders from civilians. This line has become increasingly blurred with the rise in use of civilian contract personnel to fulfill roles previously handled by military intelligence.

Chip's letters and e-mail messages home clearly told that a key function that he and the other MP reservists on Tier 1 Alpha served was to help the interrogators do their job more effectively. "Military intelligence has encouraged and told us, 'Great job.' " "They usually don't allow others to watch them interrogate. But since they like the way I run the prison, they have made an exception." He was proud to report that his men were good at doing what they were asked to do, softening up detainees so they would give up the information interrogators wanted. "We help getting them to talk with the way we handle them. . . . We've had a very high rate with our style of getting them to break. They usually end up breaking within hours."

Chip's messages home repeatedly noted that military intelligence teams, which included CIA officers and linguists and interrogators from private defense contractors, dominated all of the action that occurred in that dungeon facility of Abu Ghraib. He told me that he could not identify any of these interrogators because they had deliberately made themselves anonymous. They rarely gave their names and had no IDs on their uniform; in fact, most of them did not even wear a military outfit. Chip's account squares with media accounts about the climate created by General Sanchez's insistence that the best way to get actionable intelligence from detainees was by extreme methods of interrogation and secrecy.

Some rules for U.S. military personnel at the prison made it easy for people to duck responsibility for their actions, a factor that may also have opened the door to abuse. According to an undated prison memo titled "Operational Guidelines," which covered the high-security cell block (Tier 1A), the acronym "MI [Military Intelligence] will not be used in the area."

"Additionally, it is recommended that all military personnel in the segregation area reduce knowledge of their true identities to these specialized detainees. The use of sterilized uniforms [cleansed of all identification] is highly suggested and personnel should NOT address each other by true name and rank in the segregation area."[33]

The Army's own investigations revealed the truth of Frederick's descriptions about the extreme strategies that were employed in the prison. They found that interrogators had encouraged MP reservists working in the prison to prepare Iraqi detainees for questioning, physically and mentally.[34] The traditionally established line between MPs dealing only with detention procedures and military intelligence personnel working on intelligence gathering was blurred when these reservists were recruited to assist in prepping detainees for coercive interrogation. Military intelligence agents were also guilty of some of the worst abuses. For example, in order to obtain information from one Iraqi general, interrogators soaked down his sixteen-year-old son, smeared him with mud, and then drove him naked out into the cold. Sergeant Samuel Provenance (Alpha Company, 302nd Military Intelligence Battalion) reported to several news agencies that two of the interrogators had sexually abused a female teenager and that other personnel were aware of this abuse. We will see in the next chapter that much worse abuses were committed by any number of soldiers and civilians, in addition to those by Chip Frederick's MP night shift crew.

"I hope the investigation [of inmate abuses] is including not only the people who committed the crimes, but some of the people that might have encouraged these crimes as well," said Brigadier General Mark Kimmitt, deputy director for Coalition operations in Iraq, in an interview with Dan Rather on *60 Minutes II*. "Because they certainly share some level of responsibility as well." (We will note that the System has been slow in accusing and investigating its own officials.)

Chip Frederick also had general custody of fifteen to twenty "ghost detainees," prisoners who were listed only as OGA—Other Government Agency—property. Because they were assumed to be high-ranking officials who had valuable information to give, the interrogators were given latitude to use all means necessary to extract that actionable information. These detainees were "ghosts" because there was no official record of them ever having been at that site, never officially listed, without any ID. During our interview, Chip confided, "I saw one of them after he was killed by Delta Force soldiers. They killed this guy. I got the impression that nobody cared. Nobody cared what happened in there."[35]

That "guy" was a ghost detainee who had been severely beaten by a Navy SEALs unit, then hung on a rack during interrogation by a CIA agent, suffocated to death, then packed in ice and put into a body bag with an IV inserted in his arm (by a medic) so that his murderers could pretend he was sick and being taken to the hospital in the morning. Before he was dumped somewhere by a cab driver, some of the MPs (Graner and Harman) on the night shift had their pictures taken with him as souvenirs, just for the record. (We will revisit this case in more detail in the following chapter.) However, the effect of the MPs on night shift witnessing these and other instances of grim abuse by a variety of visitors to their Tier 1A was certainly to establish a new social norm of abuse acceptability. If it were possible to get away with murder, what harm was there in just smacking around some resistant detainees or embarrassing them by making them take humiliating positions? they reasoned.

The Fear Factor

There was much to fear within those prison walls—not only for the prisoners but also for Chip Frederick and all the other guards. As is the case in most prisons, prisoners with time on their hands and ingenuity will fashion weapons out of virtually anything available to them. Here their weapons were made from metal broken off from beds or windows, broken glass, and sharpened toothbrushes. With less ingenuity and some money, prisoners could bribe the Iraqi guards to supply them with guns, knives, bayonets, and ammunition. For a fee, these guards would also transfer notes and letters to and from family members. Frederick had been warned by guys in the 72nd MP Company, which his unit replaced, that many of the Iraqi guards were very corrupt—they even assisted escape attempts by providing security information, facility maps, clothes, and weapons. They also smuggled in drugs to the detainees. Although Frederick was nominally in charge of these guards, they would refuse to make rounds of the tiers, and usually they just sat around on tables outside the tier smoking and talking. This must be added to all the other sources of Chip Frederick's constant frustrations and stress in running a secure facility.

Prisoners regularly assaulted the guards verbally and physically; some threw feces at them, and others used their long fingernails to scratch the guards' faces. One of the most frightening and unexpected series of events on the tier happened on November 24, 2003, when Iraqi police smuggled a handgun, ammo, and bayonets into the cell of a suspected Syrian insurgent. Chip's small force had a shootout with him, and they were able to subdue him without killing him. However, that event raised the bar for everyone in that place to be eternally vigilant and even more fearful of lethal attacks against them.

Prisoner riots occurred over the poor quality of the food, which was often inedible and insufficient. Riots were also likely to erupt when mortar attacks exploded nearby in Abu Ghraib's "soft site." As noted earlier, the facility was under daily bombardment, and both guards and prisoners were wounded and some killed by these mortar attacks. "I was always fearful," Chip confessed to me. "The mortar and rocket attacks and the firefights were very scary for me. I had never been in a combat zone before Iraq." Nevertheless, he had to suck it up and act brave, given his position of authority over the detainees, his fellow MPs, and the Iraqi police. The situation demanded that Chip Frederick pretend not to be afraid but instead to appear calm, cool, and collected. This conflict between his outer, seemingly composed manner and his inner turmoil worsened as more inmates were constantly added to the ranks and demands from higher-ups escalated to get more "actionable intelligence" from the detainees.

In addition to his bottled-up fear, Chip Frederick endured the stress and exhaustion generated by the excessive demands of this complex new job, for which he was totally unprepared and untrained. Consider, too, the wide discrepancy between his core values—order, neatness, and cleanliness—and the chaos, filth, and disorder that surrounded him all the time. Although he was supposed to be in charge of the entire compound, he reported that he had felt "weak" because "no one would work with me. I couldn't make any changes about how to run this place." He also began to feel anonymous because "no one was listening to my position. It was clear that there was no accountability." Moreover, the physical setting in which he found himself conferred total anonymity by its barren ugliness. Anonymity of place combined with anonymity of person, given that it became the norm to stop wearing their full military uniforms while on duty. And all around them, most visitors and the civilian interrogators came and went unnamed. No one in charge was readily identifiable, and the seemingly endless mass of prisoners, wearing orange jumpsuits or totally naked, were also indistinguishable from one another. It was as extreme a setting for creating deindividuation as I can imagine.

Parallels with the Guards in the Stanford Prison Experiment

Now that we have surveyed the work setting, we can begin to see parallels between the psychological states experienced by Chip Frederick and his fellow guards with those of the guards in the Stanford Prison Experiment. Deindividuation processes created by anonymity of person and anonymity of place are evident. Dehumanization of prisoners is apparent by virtue of their sheer numbers, enforced nakedness, and uniform appearance, as well as by the guards' inability to understand their language. One of the night shift MPs, Ken Davis, reported in a later television documentary about how dehumanization had been bred into their thinking: "We were never trained to be guards. The higher-ups said, 'Use your imagination. Break them. We want them broke by the time we come back.' As soon as we'd have prisoners come in, sandbags instantly on their head. They would flexicuff 'em; throw 'em down to the ground; some would be stripped. It was told to all of us, they're nothing but dogs [familiar phrase?]. So you start breeding that picture to people, then all of a sudden, you start looking at these people as less than human, and you start doing things to 'em that you would never dream of. And that's where it got scary."[36]

Boredom operated in both prison settings, bred by long shift hours on those nights when everything was under control. Boredom was a potent motivator to take actions that might bring some excitement, some controlled sensation seeking. Both sets of guards decided on their own initiative "to make things happen" that they thought would be interesting or fun.

All this was aggravated, of course, by the lack of mission-specific training for a difficult and complex job and the lack of oversight by a supervisory staff, which rendered accountability unnecessary. In both prisons, the system's operatives gave permission for the guards to maintain total power over the prisoners. In addition, the guards feared that the prisoners would escape or riot, as did our Stanford guards, although of course with less deadly consequences. Obviously, Abu Ghraib Prison was a far more lethal environment than our relatively benign prison at Stanford. However, as the experiment showed, the abusiveness of guards and their aggression toward the prisoners escalated nightly, culminating in a series of sexual, homophobic acts imposed upon the prisoners. The same was true, in even more perverse and extreme ways, on Tier 1A. Moreover, in both cases, the worst abuses occurred during the night shift, when the guards felt that the authorities noticed them least; thus, free from their elemental constraints.

It should be made clear that such situational forces as those described here did not directly prod the guards into doing bad things, as in the Milgram research paradigm. Except for the encouragement given by some civilian interrogators to "soften up" detainees in order to render them vulnerable, it was the situational forces at Abu Ghraib—as in the Stanford prison—that created *freedom* from the usual social and moral constraints on abusive actions. It became apparent to both sets of night shift guards that they could get away with many taboo behaviors because responsibility was diffused; no one challenged them when newly emergent norms made acceptable once unthinkable behavior. It is the phenomenon of "when the cat's away, the mice will play." It is reminiscent of Golding's *Lord of the Flies*, where supervising grown-ups were absent as the masked marauders created havoc. It should also remind you of the research on anonymity and aggression reported in the previous chapter.

It is instructive to note some of the conclusions reached by the independent panel headed by James Schlesinger that compared the two prison situations. I was surprised to discover the parallels drawn in that report between our simulated prison conditions at Stanford and the all-too-real prison conditions at Abu Ghraib. In a three-page Appendix (G), the report describes psychological stressors, the bases for inhumane treatment of prisoners, and the social psychological factors that are involved when ordinarily humane people behave inhumanely toward others:

> The potential for abusive treatment of detainees during the Global War on Terrorism was entirely predictable based on a fundamental understanding of social psychology principles coupled with an awareness of numerous known environmental risk factors. [Most of the leaders were unacquainted with these risk factors.]

> Such conditions neither excuse nor absolve the individuals who engaged in deliberate immoral or illegal behaviors [even though] certain conditions heightened the possibility of abusive treatment.

> Findings from the field of social psychology suggest that the conditions of war and the dynamics of detainee operations carry inherent risks for human mistreatment, and therefore must be approached with great caution and careful planning and training.

> [The] landmark Stanford study . . . provides a cautionary tale for all military detention operations, which were relatively benign. In contrast, in military detention operations, soldiers work under stressful combat conditions that are far from benign.

> Psychologists have attempted to understand how and why individuals and groups who usually act humanely can sometimes act otherwise in certain circumstances.

Among the social psychological concepts identified by the Schlesinger investigation that help explain why abusive behaviors occur include deindividuation, dehumanization, enemy image, groupthink, moral disengagement, and social facilitation. We have discussed all of these processes earlier with regard to the Stanford Prison Experiment, and they were operating as well in Abu

Ghraib, with the exception of "groupthink." I do not believe that this biased way of thinking (that promotes a group's consensus with the leader's position) was at play among the night shift guards, because they were not systematically planning their abuses.

"Groupthink" is a concept developed by my former Yale teacher, the psychologist Irving Janis to account for bad decisions made in groups composed of intelligent people. Such groups suppress dissent in the interest of group harmony, when they are an amiable, cohesive group that does not include dissenting viewpoints and has a directive leader. The disastrous Bay of Pigs invasion of Cuba (1961) is a prime example of groupthink by President John Kennedy's cabinet. More recently, groupthink was at work in the shared belief within the American intelligence community (IC) and the Bush cabinet that Iraq possessed weapons of mass destruction (which, in turn, led to the war against Iraq): "IC personnel involved in the Iraq WMD issue demonstrated several aspects of groupthink: examining few alternatives, selective gathering of information, pressure to conform within the group or withhold criticism, and collective rationalization." The background for this conclusion by the Senate Intelligence Committee is available online; see the Notes.[37]

In an independent analysis published in the journal *Science*, the social psychologist Susan Fiske and her colleagues supported the position taken by the Schlesinger investigation. They concluded that "Abu Ghraib resulted in part from ordinary social processes, not just extraordinary individual evil." Among the social processes identified are conformity, socialized obedience to authority, dehumanization, emotional prejudices, situational stressors, and gradual escalation of abuses from minimal to extreme.[38]

A former soldier in Iraq offers further documentation of the relevance of the SPE to understanding the behavioral dynamics at work in Iraq military prisons, and also why strong leadership is crucial.

Professor Zimbardo,

I was a soldier [lead counterintelligence agent] in the unit that established Camp Cropper, the first detention facility set up in Baghdad after the Baath Regime fell. I can definitely relate the lessons from your prison study to my observations on the ground in Iraq. I dealt extensively with both the Military Police and detainees throughout my tour and saw many examples of the situations you described from the study.

However, unlike the soldiers at Abu Ghraib our unit had very competent leadership and things never got anywhere near the level as at Abu Ghraib. Our leaders knew the rules, set the standards, and supervised to ensure that the rules were followed. Infractions of the rules were investigated and when appropriate, violators were punished. Detention missions are dehumanizing for everyone involved. I think I went numb after the first two weeks. Active involvement by our leaders kept us from forgetting who we were and why we were there. Anyhow, I enjoyed reading the summary of your experiment; it brought more clarity to my thinking.

Sincerely,
Terrence Plakias[39]

Sexual Dynamics on Tier 1A

One of the unusual features of the night shift staff on Alpha Tier was the mixture of young female and male guards. It is noteworthy that, in this culture of unsupervised young adults, the women were quite attractive. Add to this emotionally charged mix young Lynndie England, who hung out with that shift to be with her new boyfriend, Charles Graner. England and Graner soon began engaging in torrid sexual escapades, which they documented in digital photos and videos. Eventually she became pregnant and subsequently gave birth to his child. However, there must have been something else going on between Graner and the twenty-nine-year-old MP guard Megan Ambuhl, because they later got married—after he was sentenced to prison.

The media, which focused on the England-Graner-Ambuhl triangle, gave little coverage to the fact that there were prostitutes among the Iraqi criminal prisoners, who are seen posing with bared breasts for the Army Reservists who took their pictures. In addition, there were scores of naked Iraqi male detainees, partly because of the humiliation strategy imposed upon them by orders from higher authorities and partly because there were not enough orange prison suits to go around. Ironically, some of the prisoners had to wear women's pink panties instead of male underwear because of a mistake in the supply order. It was a short step down to force some prisoners to wear them over the head as a funny form of humiliation.

Despite Chip Frederick's requests to separate young and adult detainees, a group of Iraqi prisoners allegedly raped a fifteen-year-old boy who had been housed with them. Specialist Sabrina Harman marked one of these men on his leg with a Sharpie pen, "I am a Rapeist" [sic]. On another of them, a lipstick face was drawn around his nipples with his prison ID number also marked with lipstick across his bare chest. The sexual atmosphere was explosive. There is evidence that one MP sodomized a male detainee with a chemical light and perhaps with a broomstick as well. Male detainees were frequently threatened with rape by certain guards. Other evidence implicates a male MP in raping a female detainee. It was becoming ever more like a porn palace than a military prison.

James Schlesinger, who headed one of the many independent investigations, described what he saw and heard about that night shift's nightly activities: "It was like *Animal House*" (the movie). It was a Situation spiraling out of the control of any person.

Chip Frederick remembers that the abuses occurred in the following clus-
tered chronological order:

1–10 October 2003: Nudity, handcuffing to cell doors, wearing women's underwear. This was carried over from the relief in place with the 72nd MP
Company.

1 October to 25 October. Sexual poses (in presence of MI—handcuffed together naked). Also an unknown soldier who was there claimed he was
from GITMO and showed Graner some stress positions that were used at
GITMO.

8 November. Riot at Ganci compound [one of the separate compounds
within Abu Ghraib Prison]. Seven detainees being moved to the hard site
(Tier 1A). Were in possession of multiple weapons and was planning to take
an MP Hostage and kill the MP. This was the night of the pyramid, assaults,
sexual poses and masturbation. Dogs came around this time.

Following a thorough investigation, General Antonio Taguba's report item-
izes a long set of abuses and torture practices attributed to various members of
this MP unit on Tiers 1A and 1B. The charges in his damning report include the
following:

a. Breaking chemical lights and pouring the phosphoric liquid on detainees;

b. Threatening detainees with a charged 9mm pistol;

c. Pouring cold water on naked detainees;

d. Beating detainees with a broom handle and a chair;

e. Threatening male detainees with rape;

f. Allowing a military police guard to stitch the wound of a detainee who was injured after being slammed against the wall in his cell;

g. Sodomizing a detainee with a chemical light and perhaps a broomstick;

h. Using military working dogs to frighten and intimidate detainees with threats of attack, who in one instance actually bit a detainee.

Intentional abuse of detainees by military police personnel included the following acts:

a. Punching, slapping, and kicking detainees; jumping on their naked feet;

b. Videotaping and photographing naked male and female detainees;

c. Forcibly arranging detainees in various sexually explicit positions for photographing;

d. Forcing detainees to remove their clothing and keeping them naked for several days at a time;

e. Forcing naked male detainees to wear women's underwear;

f. Forcing groups of male detainees to masturbate themselves while being photographed and videotaped;

g. Arranging naked male detainees in a pile and then jumping on them;

h. Positioning a naked detainee on a MRE Box, with a sandbag on his head, and attaching wires to his fingers, toes, and penis to simulate electric torture;

i. Placing a dog chain or strap around a naked detainee's neck and having a female soldier pose for a picture;

j. A male MP guard having sex with a female detainee;

k. Using military working dogs (without muzzles) to intimidate and frighten detainees, and in at least one case biting and severely injuring a detainee;

l. Taking photographs of dead Iraqi detainees.

"These findings are amply supported by written confessions provided by several of the suspects, written statements provided by detainees, and witness statements," concludes General Taguba.[40]

Cautionary Notes

It would seem that such a list of military infractions and crimes would close the case on the accused. However, in that same report, General Taguba concludes that these MPs were set up to engage in some of these abuses by higher-ups. He states that "Military Intelligence (MI) interrogators and other US Government agency's interrogators actively requested that MP guards set physical and mental conditions for favourable interrogation of witnesses."

Major General George Fay's investigative report goes even further in providing a more damning statement about the active role that MI personnel played in these abuses. His report notes that for a period of seven months, "Military intelligence personnel allegedly requested, encouraged, condoned or solicited Military Police personnel [the Army Reserve night shift guards] to abuse detainees, and/or participated in detainee abuse, and/or violated established interrogation procedures and applicable law."[41] We will review both generals' reports more fully in the next chapter to highlight our focus on system failures and command complicity in the abuses.

The Night of October 25, 2003

Around midnight on Tier 1A, three Iraqi detainees were dragged from their cells, made to crawl on the floor naked, chained together, and forced into simulated sexual acts. One of the abuse photos shows this cluster of prisoners surrounded by about seven soldiers looking down on them. The key protagonists were an interrogator, Ramon Kroll, and MI Specialist Armin Cruz. Among those identified as a passive observer was MP Ken Davis. He watched it all and just walked away from it (forever sorry now that he did not intervene immediately). Another observer was MI Reservist Israel Rivera, who described it as a *Lord of the Flies* incident. He also did not intervene, but the next day Rivera blew the whistle on Cruz and Kroll. They were subsequently court-martialed, with Cruz getting eight months in prison and Kroll ten months in detention. Cruz's father had been the first Cuban to graduate from the United States Military Academy at West Point. Graner was also reported to have taken part in this incident but was not singled out as one of the abusers.

The trigger of this particular abuse was the rumor circulating that these prisoners had raped a boy detainee, and this was payback for that offense. Frederick also noted that he too had been upset by this incident because he had complained to superiors that such rapes would happen if youths were housed with adult prisoners. Ironically, a subsequent military investigation indicated that the rumor was false, or at least that these three prisoners had not been involved in any rape.

A powerful documentary about this event as an example of the night shift abuses was aired by the Canadian Broadcast Company's *Fifth Estate* television news (November 16, 2005). The full story, with moving testimonies and detailed background, is available from its website (see Notes).[42]

The Graner Catalyst

Reserve Corporal Charles Graner is to the Abu Ghraib Prison night shift what our "John Wayne" guard was to the night shift in the Stanford prison. Both were catalysts for making things happen. "John Wayne" went far beyond the margins of the role assigned him as he concocted "little experiments" of his own. Corporal Graner far exceeded his role in abusing prisoners both physically and psychologically. Significantly, both Graner and "John Wayne" are charismatic characters who radiated confidence and a tough-nosed, no-nonsense attitude that influenced others on their shift. Although Staff Sergeant Frederick was his military superior, Graner really took charge of Tier 1A even when Chip was present. It seems as though the original idea of taking the photos came from him, and many of the photos were made with his digital camera.

Graner, a member of the Marine Corps Reserve, had served as a prison guard in the Persian Gulf War—without incident. During Operation Desert Storm he worked the largest prisoner-of-war camp for about six weeks, again without incident. "He was one of the guys who kept our spirits up," a member of that company recalled. Another buddy remembered Graner as "a funny guy, outgoing, and quick to crack a joke." He added, "From what I saw, he did not have a malevolent side." However, according to another member of Graner's unit, a potentially violent confrontation between him and some other soldiers with Iraqi prisoners was averted solely by field commanders who took charge and directed the unit's well-disciplined soldiers to take over.

A longtime neighbor who had known Graner for thirty years added to the positive evaluation: "He was a real good guy. I have nothing but good things to say about Chuck. Never once did he give anyone a problem." His mother recorded her pride in his high school yearbook: "You have always made your father and me proud of you. You are the best."[43]

However, on the other side of the ledger is a Graner who is reported to have physically abused his wife, who finally divorced him. Media accounts indicate that he was also disciplined several times when he worked as a maximum-security prison corrections officer.

On the Tier 1A night shift, all external constraints on Graner's antisocial behavior were gone with the wind. Chaos and casual intimacies replaced military discipline; any semblance of a strong authority structure was nowhere in sight; and with the constant encouragement by military intelligence and civilian contract interrogators for him to "soften up" detainees prior to interrogation, Graner was readily led into temptation.

Charles Graner was totally sexualized in that permissively volatile setting. He was having a sexual affair with Lynndie England, documenting it in many photos. He made an Iraqi women prisoner expose her breasts and genitals while he photographed her. It is reported that Graner forced group masturbation among the prisoners and ordered naked male prisoners to crawl around on the ground "so that their genitalia had to drag along the floor," while he shouted at them that they were "fucking fags."[44] In addition, Graner was the one who first thought of piling naked prisoners in a pyramid. And when a group of naked prisoners with bags over their heads was forced to masturbate in front of male and female soldiers, Graner jokingly told Lynndie England that "the line of masturbating detainees was a gift for her birthday."[45]

After his trial, Chip Frederick wrote to me about Graner, "I don't put all the blame on him. He just had a way about him to get you to think that everything was Okay. I am very sorry for my actions and if I could go back to Oct 2003, I would do things differently. . . . I wish that I could have been stronger . . ."[46]

Specialist Matthew Wisdom, who first reported the abuses to his superiors in November 2003 (though his complaint was ignored), gave testimony in Graner's trial. He said that Graner enjoyed beating inmates and moreover that he had laughed, whistled, and sung while abusing them. When Specialist Joe Darby asked Graner about a shooting that had taken place on the tier, Graner handed him two CDs filled with the incriminating photographs. Upset at the immorality of the scenes they depicted, Darby asked Graner what they signified to him. Graner replied, "The Christian in me says it's wrong, but the corrections officer in me says, I love to make a grown man piss himself."

Chip Frederick still regrets coming under Graner's influence. Here is one instance where there was predictive validity of Chip's personality tendencies to conform and comply. Recall the conclusions from his psychological assessment: Chip usually fears being rejected by others, and so in any disagreement, he often gives way in order to be accepted; he changes his mind to accommodate others so that they will not be "mad at me or hate me." Others can influence him even when he believes that he has made up his mind. Sadly, his mind was undermined by stress, fear, exhaustion, and Graner's influence.

An Alternative Take on Charles Graner

In Akira Kurosawa's classic Japanese movie *Rashomon*, the same event is described in very different ways by a group of people who all experienced it. I have mentioned that that was the case with the Stanford Prison Experiment. Guard "John Wayne" and Prisoner Doug-8612 later told the media that they had only been "acting" sadistic or pretending to go crazy, respectively. More recently, former Guard Hellmann, gave yet another version of his actions:

> At the time, if you had questioned me about the effect I was having, I would say, well, they must be a wimp. They're weak or they're faking. Because I wouldn't believe that what I was doing could actually cause somebody to have a nervous breakdown. It was just us sorta getting our jollies with it. You know. Let's be like puppeteers here. Let's make these people do things.[47]

Other SPE prisoners and guards reported that it was either a terrible experience or no big deal. Reality, to some extent, is in the mind of the beholder. However, at Abu Ghraib, people's lives were dramatically impacted by the reality consensus of the military, the military court, and the media.

Charles Graner was portrayed from the outset of the investigation as the true "bad apple," in the bunch—sadistic, evil, engaging in wanton abuses against detainees. His past record of trouble in a previous corrections facility in the United States was presented as evidence that he had brought a violent, antisocial nature into Tier 1A. It was irresponsible media hype.

To the contrary, an examination of Graner's performance file from the Corrections Institute in Greene County, Pennsylvania, reveals that he had *never* been accused, suspected of, or disciplined for any offense or maltreatment of any inmate.

An even more dramatic contrast between Graner as irresponsible monster and Graner as good soldier is found in his performance evaluation during the key month of the prisoner abuses. On November 16, 2003, in a Developmental Counseling Form (4856) given to Graner by the platoon leader Captain Brinson, he is singled out for the fine job he has been doing:

> Cpl. Graner, you are doing a fine job in Tier 1 of the BCF as the NCOIC of the "MI Hold" area. You have received many accolades from the MI units here and specifically from LTC [blackened; likely Lt. Col. Jordan]. Continue to perform at this level and it will help us succeed at our overall mission.

He is then cautioned to wear his military uniform and to maintain proper military appearance (which no one on that tier had been doing). A second caution recognizes the high stress level that he and others have been operating under on that tier. Graner is asked to be aware of effects that such stress might have on his behavior, specifically with regard to the use of force in dealing with a particular detainee. However, Graner's version of the appropriate use of forces is accepted by this officer. "I 100 percent support your decision when you believe you must defend yourself," adds the officer. (A PDF file of this counseling statement is available; see the Notes, p. 518.[48])

MP Reservist Ken Davis recently gave a surprisingly supportive account of an interaction he had with Graner:

> One evening, after he got off of his shift, he [Graner] was hoarse.
>
> And I said: "Graner, are you getting sick?"
>
> And he goes, "No."
>
> And I said, "Well, what's going on?"
>
> And, he said, "Well, I'm havin' to yell, and do other things to detainees that I feel are morally and ethically wrong. What do you think I should do?"
>
> I said, "Then don't do 'em."
>
> And he goes, "I don't have a choice."
>
> And I said, "What do you mean?"
>
> He says, "Every time a bomb goes off outside the wire, or outside the fence, they come in, and they tell me, that's another American losin' their life. And unless you help us, their blood's on your hands as well."[49]

Given this awareness of the high stress levels on Tier 1A, one might assume that some mental health personnel would be called in to help the soldiers in dealing constructively with the turmoil. A psychiatrist was assigned to Abu Ghraib for several months, but he did not treat or counsel any of the MPs who needed such expertise or work with any of the mentally ill detainees. Instead, it is reported that his main function was to assist military intelligence in making its interrogations more effective. Megan Ambuhl has asserted that "There were no credible claims of sodomy, or rape, nor were there pictures or videos of such, at least not by any of the 7 MP's involved in this investigation." She continued, "I have all the pictures and videos from the beginning of the investigation. I spent almost 13 hours a day on that block. No rapes or sodomy occurred."[50] Will we ever know what really happened there, and who and what was to blame for the horrors of Abu Ghraib?

THE "TROPHY PHOTOS": DIGITALLY DOCUMENTED DEPRAVITY

In wars between nations and in confrontations with criminals, soldiers, police, and prison guards have often been brutal in their abuse, torture, and murder of their "enemies," suspects, or captives. Such actions are to be expected (but not accepted) in war zones, when lives are risked in the line of duty and when "foreigners" conduct the abuse against our soldiers. We do not expect or accept such behavior by agents of democratic governments when there is no imminent threat to their lives and when captives are vulnerable and unarmed.

Accordingly, many Americans were distressed some years back, in March 1991, when a televised videotape showed a group of Los Angeles police officers (LAPD) repeatedly beating an unarmed African-American motorist, Rodney King. More than fifty blows of their nightsticks were inflicted upon him as he lay on the ground helpless, while two dozen law enforcement officers watched the beating, and some of them assisted in holding King down by placing their feet on his back.

In her analysis of the power of visual images in modern society, novelist Susan Sontag wrote:

> For a long time—at least six decades—photographs have laid down the tracks of how important conflicts are judged and remembered. The Western memory museum is now mostly a visual one. Photographs have an insuperable power to determine what we recall of events, and it now seems probable that the defining association of people everywhere with the war that the United States launched pre-emptively in Iraq last year will be photographs of the torture of Iraqi prisoners by Americans in the most infamous of Saddam Hussein's prisons, Abu Ghraib.[51]

Sontag went on to highlight the content of those images as indicative of the worst excesses of a culture grown *shameless* as its citizens are exposed daily to TV shows like Jerry Springer's and others where participants are vying to humiliate themselves publicly. She indicts American culture as one that admires unrestrained power and dominance. Sontag illustrates its shamelessness further with reference to the Pentagon's "Shock and Awe" label of its assault against Baghdad in March 2003 in advance of the battle. (Since then, some critics have proposed an alternative of "Shame and Awful" to characterize what has been done since then to Iraq by the military and irresponsible civilian corporations.)

The digital images coming out of Abu Ghraib had a unique impact on people throughout the world. Never before had we seen such visual evidence of sexual abuse and torture by prison guards or of men and women apparently enjoying their heinous deeds and then having the audacity to pose themselves and record their brutal actions. How could they have done it? Why did they give these abuses their personal visual signatures? Let's consider some possible explanations.

Digital Power

One simple answer is that new digital technology makes everyone an instant photographer. It provides immediate feedback and no development waiting time, and its images can easily be readily shared online without being censored by film-developing laboratories. Because these cameras are conveniently small in size, large in capacity, and relatively inexpensive, they are so ubiquitous that it is easy for anyone to take hundreds of photos on the spot. Just as Web logs (blogs) and personal webcasts allow ordinary people to experience unedited moments of fleeting fame, so too does "owning" unusual photo images that can be distributed worldwide via a host of websites gives others their moment of glory.

Consider the fact that one amateur porn site encouraged its male viewers to submit nude images of their wives and girlfriends to be posted in exchange for free access to the porn videos it made available.[52] Soldiers were invited also to exchange war zone photos for the same free access to porn, and many did. A "gore" warning was put on some of those images, such as the one of a group of American soldiers smiling and giving high fives in front of the burned remains of an Iraqi, with the caption "Burn Baby Burn."

Trophy Photos from Other Eras

Such images are reminiscent of the "trophy photos" of black men and women being lynched or burned alive in the United States between the 1880s and 1930s as onlookers and perpetrators posed for the camera. We saw in the last chapter that such images are emblematic of dehumanization at its worst, because, in addition to depicting the torture and murder of black Americans for often spurious "crimes" against whites, the photos that documented these unholy events were made into postcards to be bought and sent to friends and relatives. Some of the images included smiling young children brought along by their parents to witness the torment of black men and women being violently murdered. A documentary catalogue of many of these postcards is found in the recent book *Without Sanctuary.*[53]

Other such trophy photos were taken by German soldiers during the Second World War of their personal atrocities against Polish Jews and Russians. We noted in the previous chapter that even "ordinary men," old reserve German policeman who had initially resisted shooting to death families of Jews, over time came to document their murderous deeds as executioners.[54] Still other visual repositories exist of such executions with their executioners, as can be seen in Janina Struk's *Photographing the Holocaust.*[55] The Turks' massacre of Armenians is also documented in photographs contained in a website devoted to that genocide.[56]

Another genre of trophy photos common in pre-animal-rights eras is that of big-game hunters and sports fishermen exulting over their marlin, tigers, or grizzly bears. I recall seeing a photo of Ernest Hemingway in such a pose. However, the classic iconic image of the fearless safari hunter is that of the American president Teddy Roosevelt proudly standing behind a huge rhino that he had just bagged. Another shows the former president and son Kermit sitting atop a water buffalo in a nonchalant pose with legs crossed, big gun in hand.[57] Such trophy photos were public statements of man's power and mastery over nature's mighty beasts—overcome by his skill, courage, and technology. Curiously, in those photos, the victors appear rather grim, rarely are they smiling; they are victors in a battle against formidable adversaries. In a sense, they pose like the young David with his slingshot before the fallen giant Goliath.

Exhibitionists Performing for Voyeurs

The grinning faces of many of the night shift guards at Abu Ghraib suggest a different dimension of trophy photos: the exhibitionistic. Some photos seem as though the abuses were merely available props for the exhibitionists to document the extremes to which they could go in that unusual setting. These exhibitionists also seem to anticipate an audience of eager voyeurs who would enjoy the sight of these antics. However, they failed to realize that file sharing and easy distribution would make the digital images independent of the photographers; they would lose control over who would get to view them—and thus they were caught red-handed by the authorities.

With the exception of the iconic image of torture of the hooded man with electrodes on his hands and the photos of dogs menacing prisoners, most of the other trophy pictures are sexual in nature. The link between torture and sexuality gives them a pornographic quality that is disturbing, yet fascinating, for many viewers. We are all invited down into that sadomasochistic dungeon to get a close look at these excesses in action. Though it is horrible to view these abuses, people keep looking at them.

I was surprised to discover the extent of voyeurism that is now being satisfied via the World Wide Web. A website named simply www.voyeurweb.com claims to attract 2.2 million unique visitors daily to its free amateur porn site for Web surfers.

Complex Motives and Social Dynamics

Human behavior is complex, so there is often more than one reason for any given act, and in Abu Ghraib, I believe these digital images were the product of multiple

motives and interpersonal dynamics in addition to the sexuality and exhibitionism. Status and power, revenge and retaliation, deindividuation of the helpless— it is likely that all were involved in the abuses and the photo taking. In addition, we must consider that some of them were actually condoned and staged by the interrogators.

Staged Photos Used to Threaten Detainees

There is one simple reason for the trophy photos at Abu Ghraib: the MPs were told to pose for them by the interrogators, civilian, and military. One version of the story, according to retired officer Janis Karpinski and reported earlier by some of the accused soldiers, was that initially the idea for taking the posed photos was to use them as threats to aid interrogations. "They set those photos up to get confessions, 'to cut to the chase,' " said Karpinski on May 4, 2006, during a panel held at Stanford University. "They would take out the laptops, show the photos, and tell the prisoners, 'Start talking or tomorrow you are at the bottom of the pile.' It was done intentionally, methodically."[58]

Surely, some of the photos are clearly posed for someone's camera, with MPs smiling for the camera, giving high fives, and pointing at something to notice in the scene. The dehumanizing photo of Lynndie England dragging a detainee on the ground with a dog leash around his neck is most likely of that origin. It is unlikely she went to Iraq with a dog leash in her duty bag. However, all that was necessary for social facilitation to take over was for any official to give the MPs permission to take even one such photo of abuse. That permission opened the doors to this new nightly activity of ever more scenes of creative evil at work. Once started, there was no end in sight because it was relieving the MPs' boredom, getting revenge, demonstrating mastery, and having fun and sex games—until Joe Darby blew the whistle and shut down the show.

Abu Ghraib Photos

Comparative literature professor Judith Butler invites us to reconsider the significance of the Abu Ghraib photographs not as coming from the whims of the particular MPs taking them. Rather, she argues that the MPs were "embedded photographers" whose images reflected the basic values of their military— homophobia, misogyny, and dominance over all enemies.[59]

Gaining Status, Getting Revenge

Let's acknowledge the generally low status of Army Reservists within the military hierarchy, which was further degrading for a reservist MP assigned to the night shift in a horrible prison. They realized that they were at the bottom of the barrel, working under awful conditions, taking orders from civilians, and without recourse to authorities who cared enough to check out what was going on there. The only ones on the scene with lower status were the prisoners themselves.

Therefore, the nature of the abuses as well as their documentation served to establish the unequivocal social dominance of every guard over all of their prisoners through this downward comparison. The torture and abuse were an exercise of pure power for the sake of demonstrating their absolute control over their inferiors. The photos were needed by some of these guards to convince themselves of their superiority, as well as to broadcast their dominant status to their peers. The photos gave them "bragging rights." It is also likely that racism was involved to some extent, with generally negative attitudes toward Arabs as a very different "other." This was a carryover of hostility from the September 11, 2001, terrorist attacks against all brown-skinned men of any Arabic background.

A more immediate motive shared by many soldiers was revenge for fellow soldiers who had been killed or seriously wounded by Iraqi insurgents. It is apparent that revenge led to retaliation against inmates who had rioted or who had allegedly raped a boy. For example, the seven prisoners arrayed in the pyramid had been sent to Tier 1A after rioting in Camp Ganci and hurting a female MP in the process. Humiliating and beating them up was "teaching them a lesson" about the consequences of getting out of control. For instance, the only prisoner Chip Frederick ever hit was the one he punched hard in the chest because he allegedly threw a rock that hurt the female MP. Forcing detainees to simulate fellatio or to masturbate in public in front of women soldiers and then documenting this humiliation was more than just a tactic of embarrassment. It was the MPs' sexual scenarios as payback for detainees they felt had gone over the line.

Deindividuation and the Mardi Gras Effect

Nevertheless, how do we account for Lynndie England's conception that it was all just "fun and games"? In this case, I believe, *deindividuation* is involved. The anonymity of person and place that we noted earlier can create an altered state of mind, which, when combined with diffused responsibility for one's actions, induces deindividuation. Actors become immersed in their high-intensity physical actions without rational planning or regard for consequences. The past and future give way to an immediate-present, hedonistic time perspective. It is a mind space in which emotion rules reason, and constraints on passion are loosened.

It is the "Mardi Gras effect" of living for the moment behind a mask that conceals one's identity and gives vent to libidinous, violent, and selfish impulses that are ordinarily contained. Behavior then erupts in response to immediate situational demands, without planned conspiracy or malicious forethought. We saw what happened when this *Lord of the Flies* phenomenon was brought into my NYU laboratory as deindividuated women gave ever-increasing shocks to innocent victims. It was also re-created by some of the guards in our Stanford prison. In these situations, as in Abu Ghraib, standard social constraints against aggression and antisocial action were suspended as people experienced extended latitudes of behavioral freedom.

Just as I did not encourage my guards to act sadistically, neither did the military encourage its guards to engage in sexual abuse against prisoners. Nevertheless, in both situations a general norm of permissiveness prevailed that created a sense that the guards could do pretty much whatever they felt like doing because they were not personally accountable and could get away with anything because no one was watching. In that context, traditional moral reasoning is diminished, actions speak louder than old learned lessons, and Dionysian impulses suppress Apollonian rationality. Moral disengagement operated then to change the mental and emotional landscape of those caught up in its web.

Comparable Abuses by British and Elite U.S. Soldiers

If the social psychological principles that I argue were operating on that Tier 1A night shift are not *person*-specific but *situation*-specific, we should find similar abuses in other similar settings perpetrated by very different soldiers in that same combat zone. Indeed, there are at least two verified instances of such behavior— both of which were hardly noticed by the U.S. media.

British soldiers stationed at the Basra Prison in Iraq also sexually abused their captives, forcing them to simulate sodomy on each other after stripping them naked. Their photos shocked the British public, who could not believe that their young men would ever do such terrible deeds and then even document them. The fact that one of the abusers was a decorated hero from earlier combat was an even greater violation of the British public's expectations. Even worse and more to the point was what BBC News reported on June 29, 2004: "UK troops swapped abuse photos." The subtitle added, "British soldiers have swapped hundreds of photos showing brutality against Iraqi captives." Several soldiers who were serving as members of the elite Queen's Lancashire Regiment gave some of the images to the *Daily Mirror,* one of which showed a hooded prisoner being struck with a rifle butt, urinated on, and with a gun held to his head. The soldiers claimed that there were many more pictures of such abuse that they shared in a "culture of trading pictures." However, their Army commanders destroyed them when they were found in their luggage as they were leaving Iraq.

On the May 12, 2004, edition of *60 Minutes II,* CBS's Dan Rather ran a home video made by an American soldier that revealed what conditions were like at both Camp Bucca and Abu Ghraib. The video segment shows a young soldier's disdain for the Iraqi prisoners. She says: "We've already had two prisoners die . . . but who cares? That's two less for me to worry about." Several other soldiers who were at Camp Bucca and are accused of abusing prisoners there told Rather that "the problems began with the chain of command—the same chain of command that was in charge of Abu Ghraib when the pictures of torture and abuse were taken."[60]

Another documented instance of this loss of control involved U.S. soldiers from the 82nd Airborne Division who were stationed at the forward operating base (FOB) Mercury, near Fallujah. It was the place where insurgents and other captives were temporarily imprisoned before being shipped off to Abu Ghraib. "The murderous maniacs" is what they [Fallujah citizens] called us because they knew that if they got caught by us and detained by us before they went to Abu Ghraib then it would be hell to pay." This sergeant's account goes on to describe how they would "fuck a PUC" (Person under Control) by beating him or torturing him severely. He goes on to report that "Everyone in camp knew if you wanted to work out your frustration you show up at the PUC tent. In a way it was sport."

Another sergeant from the same unit elaborated on his motives for the abuse, which included breaking detainees' legs with a metal baseball bat. "Some days we would get bored, so we would have everyone sit in a corner and then make them get into a pyramid. This was before Abu Ghraib but just like it. We did it for amusement."

Army Captain Ian Fishback, an officer in this "elite unit," also testified to Human Rights Watch in September 2005 about the extensive prisoner abuse that was going on in that prison setting. He revealed that his soldiers had also documented their terrible deeds in digital images. "[At FOB Mercury] they said that they had pictures that were similar to what happened at Abu Ghraib, and because they were so similar to what happened at Abu Ghraib, the soldiers destroyed the pictures. They burned them. The exact quote was, 'They [the soldiers at Abu Ghraib] were getting in trouble for the same things we were told to do, so we destroyed the pictures.' "[61]

We will meet the captain again in the next chapter, where his detailed description of the abuses perpetrated by his unit matches those in Tier 1A, with the exception of the sexual abuse.

PUTTING SERGEANT IVAN FREDERICK ON TRIAL

The team of military investigators and prosecutors invested considerable zeal in preparing the cases against each of the seven accused MPs. (Had the military command responsible for Abu Ghraib invested a fraction of that attention, concern, and resources in oversight and maintenance of discipline, there would have been no need for these trials.) Their game plan was simple and compelling: After gathering sufficient evidence and testimonies, they worked out plea bargain deals with each of the defendants whereby the most extreme sentences possible would be reduced if they pled guilty and testified against their fellow MPs. The trials began with those most minimally involved, such as Specialist Jeremy Sivits, to "give it up" on each of the others, working up to the big three: Frederick, Graner, and England.

Five charges were leveled against Frederick. In a Stipulation of Fact, as part of his plea bargain, the accused accepted them as true, susceptible to proof, and also admissible in evidence:

Conspiracy to Maltreat Detainees. Conspiracy charges are usually difficult to prove in civilian courts without hard evidence, in writing or in audio- or videotape of

the planning. However, in this case the MPs' conspiracy consisted of entering into a "nonverbal agreement" with other MPs on Tier 1A of the hard site. That means a "wordless conspiracy" existed among the accused and with Davis, Graner, Ambuhl, Harman, Sivits, and England. They are alleged to have agreed as a group "to engage in specific acts which served to maltreat detainees (subordinates), which is a violation of Article 93 of the Uniform Code of Military Justice" (Stipulation of Fact, p. 3). Does that mean by a wink and a nod or hand gestures? Alternatively, does it mean that they engaged in these documented activities in concert and therefore, in retrospect, there must have been an a priori conspiracy?

Dereliction of Duty. As the noncommissioned officer in charge, Frederick "had a duty to treat all detainees with dignity and respect and to protect detainees and prisoners in his presence from illegal abuse, cruelty, and maltreatment" (Stipulation of Fact, p. 6). He was derelict in all these duties.

Maltreatment of Detainees. This refers to the hooded prisoner with electrodes attached to his fingers, who was led to believe that if he fell off the box he was forced to stand on, he would be electrocuted. Frederick attached one of those wires to the prisoner's left hand and took a photo of it as a "souvenir." (Also mentioned in this charge as background is the reason that this detainee, nicknamed "Gilligan," was made to stand on the box for long periods in a stress position. He was being kept "awake as part of a sleep management program. Sleep management normally includes rigorous physical exercise to keep a detainee awake before being interrogated" [Stipulation of Fact, p. 6]). There are other specifications of maltreatment of several detainees in the human pyramid and putting a detainee, nicknamed "shitboy" (because he covered himself with feces), between two medical litters (in an attempt to get him to stop defecating) and then Frederick had his photo taken sitting on top of the detainee. (It should be mentioned that the medics advised this treatment of putting the mentally unstable detainee strapped between two litters to keep him from harming himself; it was not Frederick's idea but rather following medical protocol.)

Assault Consummated by Battery. Frederick once punched a detainee in the chest "with enough force to cause the detainee to have difficulty breathing" (Stipulation of Fact, p. 8). (This detainee was one of the rioters brought to Tier 1A after their attempted escape and battery against a female MP at Camp Ganci.)

Indecent Acts with Another. This refers to the accused forcing several detainees to masturbate in front of male and female soldiers and other detainees, while they were being photographed. "Under the circumstances, the conduct of the accused was of a nature to bring discredit upon the armed forces and was prejudicial to good order and discipline," the stipulation goes on. "These photographs and other images captured by the accused and his co-conspirators were taken for personal reasons. The images were saved on personal computers and not for official purposes" (Stipulation of Fact, p. 9).

The Trial

Frederick's trial was held in Baghdad on October 20 and 21, 2004, despite the defense counsel's motion for a change of venue to the United States. Since I refused to go to such a dangerous place, I went instead to the naval base in Naples, Italy, where I gave my testimony in a videoconference in a highly secured room. It was a difficult setting because, first, my testimony was being disrupted by delayed audio feedback, and second, the images of the trial on the video screen sometimes froze. Compounding the difficulty was the fact that I was talking to a TV screen and not interacting directly with the judge. To make it even more difficult, I was told not to use notes during my testimony, which meant that I had to recall from memory the hundreds of pages of the five investigative reports that I had carefully read plus all the other background information I had amassed on Frederick and the Tier 1A conditions.

Given that Frederick had already entered a guilty plea, my testimony was focused entirely on specifying the situational and systemic influences on his behavior that had been induced by the impact of an abnormal setting on a very normal young man. I also outlined the psychological assessment results, the positive aspects of his background before he was assigned to Tier 1A, and highlights from my interview with him. This was done in an effort to support the conclusion that Frederick had brought no pathological tendencies into that behavioral context. Rather, I argued that the *situation* had brought out the aberrant behaviors in which he engaged and for which he is both sorry and guilty.

I also made clear that, in trying to understand how Frederick's actions were impacted by situational social dynamics, I was engaging not in "excusiology" but rather in a conceptual analysis that is not usually considered seriously enough in sentencing decisions. In addition, in giving my credentials and relevance to this case, I outlined the main features and findings and some parallels between the Stanford Prison Experiment and the environment of abuse at Abu Ghraib Prison. (My full testimony appears on pages 294 to 330 of "Ivan 'Chip' Frederick's Trial Transcripts," October 2004. Unfortunately, it is not available online.)

The prosecutor, Major Michael Holley, dismissed the thrust of my situational argument. He argued that Frederick knew right from wrong, had adequate military training for the job, and essentially had made a rational decision to engage in the immoral, detrimental behaviors with which he was charged. Thus he put all the blame on Frederick's disposition to knowingly do evil, while pushing any situational or systemic influences out of consideration by the court. He also implied that the Geneva Conventions was in effect and that these soldiers should have known its constraints. That is not true, as we will see in the next chapter: President George Bush and his legal advisers changed the definition of these detainees and of torture in a set of legal memos that rendered the Geneva Conventions obsolete during this "war on terror."

The Verdict

The military judge, Colonel James Pohl, took only one hour to return his verdict of guilty as charged on all counts. Frederick's prison sentence was set at eight years. My testimony apparently had a minimal effect on the severity of his sentence, as did the eloquent plea of his attorney, Gary Myers. All of the situational and systemic factors that I detailed were worth little on the international public relations stage that had been established by the military and the Bush administration chains of command. They had to show the world and the Iraqi people that they were "tough on crime" and would swiftly punish these few rogue soldiers, the "bad apples" in the otherwise good U.S. Army barrel. Once all of them had been tried, sentenced, and jailed, only then might this stain on the American military fade away.[62]

Charles Graner refused to plead guilty and got a ten-year sentence. Lynndie England, in a complicated series of trials, was sentenced to three years in prison. Jeremy Sivits got one year, while Javal Davis got six months. Sabrina Harman got off with a light sentence of six months based on evidence of her prior kindness to Iraqis before she was assigned to Abu Ghraib. Finally, Megan Ambuhl was discharged without any prison time.

Some Relevant Comparisons

There is no question that the abuses engaged in by Chip Frederick brought physical and emotional suffering to prisoners under his charge and enduring humiliation and anger to their families. He pled guilty, was found guilty as charged and given a stern sentence. From the Iraqis' perspective it was too lenient; from my perspective it was too severe, given the circumstances that had precipitated and sustained the abuses. However, it is instructive to compare his sentence to that of another soldier in another war who was found guilty of capital offenses against civilians.

One of the earlier stains on the pride of the U.S. military came during the Vietnam War, when soldiers in Charlie Company invaded the village of My Lai in search of Viet Cong fighters. None were found there, but the chronic stresses, frustrations, and fears of these soldiers erupted in unimaginable fury against the local civilians. More than five hundred Vietnamese women, children, and elderly people were murdered in close-up machine-gun barrages or burned alive in their huts, and many women were raped and disemboweled. Some of them were even scalped! Terrifying descriptions of these cruelties were voiced in a matter-of-fact way by some of the soldiers in the film, *Interviews with My Lai Vets.* Seymour Hersh provided a detailed account of the atrocities in his book, *My Lai 4,* which publicly exposed them for the first time a year later.

Only one soldier was found guilty for these crimes, Lieutenant William Calley, Jr. His senior officer, Captain Ernest Medina, who was on site during this "search-and-destroy mission," and reported to be personally firing at the civilians, was acquitted of all charges and he resigned from service. Captain Medina, nicknamed "Mad Dog," had been really proud of his men in Charlie Company, claiming, "We had become the best company in the battalion." Perhaps this was a premature rush to judgment.

Lieutenant Calley was found guilty of the premeditated murder of more than a hundred Vietnamese civilians at My Lai. His original life sentence was reduced to three and a half years, which he served in the barracks under house arrest, never spending a day in prison. Most people don't know that he subsequently received a pardon for these mass murders and returned to his community to become a paid after-dinner speaker and honored businessman. Might it have been different if Calley had been just an enlisted man and not an officer? Might it have also been different if "trophy photos" had been taken by the soldiers of Charlie Company that would have made vivid and real what words about such brutal atrocities failed to convey? I think so.

Another set of relevant comparisons comes from lining up some of these night shift MPs against other soldiers who have been recently charged and sentenced by military courts for various crimes. It becomes apparent that though convicted for similar or even worse crimes, the sentences handed down to these other soldiers were much more lenient.

Staff Sergeant Frederick's maximum sentence for his crimes was 10 years in prison, dishonourable discharge (DD), and reduction to the lowest rank, E1. With his plea bargain, he received 8 years in prison, DD, demotion to E1, and forfeiture of all pay and allowances, including 22 years of his saved retirement income.

Corporal Berg was found guilty of negligent homicide, self-injury, and false statements. Maximum sentence: 11 years in prison. Received: 18 months and E1.

Sergeant First Class Price was found guilty of assault, maltreatment, and obstruction of justice. Maximum sentence: 8 years in prison, DD, and E1. Received: reduction in rank to SSG, no prison time, no DD.

Corporal Graner was found guilty of assault, maltreatment, nonverbal conspiracy, indecent acts, and dereliction of duty. Maximum sentence: 15 years in prison, DD, and E1. Received: 10 years in prison, DD, E1, and a fine.

Private Brand was found guilty of assault, maltreatment, false swearing, and maiming. Maximum sentence: 16 years in prison, DD, and E1, Received: only reduction in rank to E1.

Sergeant (name withheld) was found guilty of assault, unlawful discharge of firearm, robbery, and dereliction of duty. Maximum sentence: 24.5 years in prison, DD, and E1. Received: only a letter of reprimand.

Private England was found guilty of conspiracy, maltreatment, and indecent act. Maximum sentence: 10 years in prison, DD, and E1. Received: 3 years in prison.

Sergeant First Class Perkins was found guilty of aggravated assault, assault and battery, and obstruction of justice. Maximum sentence: 11.5 years in prison, DD, and E1. Received: 6 months in prison and reduction in rank to staff sergeant.

Captain Martin was found guilty of aggravated assault, assault, obstruction of justice, and conduct unbecoming of an officer. Maximum sentence: 9 years in prison. Received: 45 days in prison.

Clearly, then, the scales of military justice were not even balanced for these comparable crimes. I believe it was the trophy photos that added considerable weight to bias the legal decisions against the night shift MPs. For a fuller set of such comparisons and a listing of sixty soldiers who have been court-martialed and their dispositions, as well as other clarifications to the record on the Abu Ghraib abuses, please see the interesting website www.supportmpscapegoats.com.

THE TRANSFORMATION OF PRISON GUARD IVAN FREDERICK INTO PRISONER NUMBER 789689

Our focus in attempting to describe the Lucifer Effect has been on understanding transformations of human character. Perhaps one of the most extreme and rare transformations imaginable takes place in someone going from a position of power as a prison guard to a position of total powerlessness as a prisoner. That is sadly so in the case of this once fine corrections officer, dedicated soldier, and loving husband. He has been battered and nearly broken by the verdict against him from the military court and his subsequent cruel treatment in confinement. Chip Frederick is now reduced to a number—789689—as an inmate on "Warehouse Road" in the U.S. Disciplinary Barracks at Fort Leavenworth. After being sentenced in Baghdad, Chip was shipped off to Kuwait, where he was put in solitary confinement, even though he posed no danger to himself or others. He describes conditions there as being reminiscent of his tiers at Abu Ghraib, but his situation got worse when he was imprisoned at Fort Leavenworth.

Chip had been given medications for the insomnia, depression, and anxiety attacks that he suffered in the year since the scandal broke. However, in the Kansas prison he was denied all meds, forced to "go cold turkey." That meant not sleeping and being under constant stress. "I don't think I can do it, I don't think that I can take it anymore," he wrote to me on Christmas 2004.[63] He was put in a small, cold cell, given only two thin blankets and no pillow, and forced to wear dirty, worn socks and underwear with fecal and urine stains. His subhuman treatment was extended when he went to Texas for the trial of a fellow MP. The military publically stripped his uniform of the nine honor medals and ribbons he had won over twenty years of military service while he watched in tears. Moreover, to rub salt into his wounds, he was brought in front of the courthouse so that the media could see him in his shackles. He is reminded daily that you do not do things that humiliate the U.S. Army without suffering payback.

Now that all the trials of the "Abu Ghraib Seven" are over, Chip Frederick's treatment has improved. He is going to barber school in the prison to learn a new trade because he can never serve as a corrections officer again. "I would love to be reinstated back into the Army to go back over there and prove myself. I was the one to never give up on anything and that it was me that could make a difference. . . . I was very prepared to die for my country, my family and my friends. I wanted to be the one to make a difference. . . . I am proud that I served much of my adult life for my country."[64]

Do you see the parallel with Stew-819, the SPE prisoner who insisted on going back into our prison to show his mates that he was not a bad prisoner? It is also reminiscent of a classic social psychological experiment that showed greater loyalty to one's group the more severe was the initiation into it.[65]

Martha Frederick's life has also been shattered by these trials and tribulations. You may recall that she is a corrections officer in the Pennsylvania prison where they met. "Abu-Iraq is the pit of inhumanity and Abu has become the graveyard where my life as I know it was laid to rest 'Uncle Phil.' . . . Normal life as I once knew it will NEVER be again. Life has become a constant struggle to rise above the rubble of that place financially and mentally."[66]

Another side effect of this sad story is Martha's recent decision to divorce Chip because of the financial and emotional burdens she has had to endure. The decision has been yet another devastating blow to him. However, she remains steadfast in her support of him. She wrote me, "I have stood beside him, in front of him and behind him through all that has occurred. And I will continue to do so even separate from the bonds of marriage. But I just can't go on living in this vacuum."[67]

Finally, there is another sad answer to the question of whether the abusive interrogations were worth it. Did they yield the actionable intelligence being sought by the military and civilian command? Perhaps, but no, not likely, maybe a bit, but hardly worth justifying the irrefutable damage to America's moral image, or the suffering of those interrogated and the lasting psychological impact on the interrogators. Of course, administration sources will say that they did get what they were looking for, but it is classified so they can never tell us how much the coercive interrogations helped in their war on terror and secondary war on insurgents. They are not immune to lying to cover their tracks. However, most experts on torture and on police interrogations agree that such physical abuse committed with humiliating and degrading tactics rarely yields trustworthy evidence. You get confessions and admissions by building rapport not by bullying, by earning trust not by fostering hatred.

We have seen earlier the negative reactions of some of the soldiers who participated in these military interrogations. Too many innocents were detained who had no useful information to offer; too few trained interrogators, fewer trained translators, and too great a demand from top down to get information immediately—no questions asked. Political scientist and torture expert Darius Rejali has gone on record doubting the reliability of such interrogation procedures used throughout military bases in Iraq, Gitmo, and Afghanistan. He contends there is a consensus that people will say anything under conditions of physical coercion. You will find statements to this effect from official U.S. government documents, including the U.S. Army Field Manual for Interrogation (FM 30-15), the CIA Kubark Manual (1963), and the Human Resources Exploitation Manual (1985). In one of his essays on Salon.com, Rejali asserts that torture may have a dark allure, giving the interrogator a druglike rush while immersed in the process, but leaving a legacy of destruction that takes generations to undo.[68]

FINAL NOTES

In the next chapter, we will move from our focus on individual soldiers caught up in an inhuman behavioral setting to consider the role that the System played in creating the conditions that fostered the abuses and tortures at Abu Ghraib and in many other military prisons. There we will examine the complexities of systemic influences that operated to create and sustain a "culture of abuse." First, we will review highlights of the many independent military investigations into these abuses. That will allow us to measure the extent to which those investigations implicate System variables, such as leadership failures, little or no mission specific training, inadequate resources, and interrogation-confession priorities, as major contributors to what occurred on that night shift in Abu Ghraib. Then we will examine reports from Human Rights Watch of other comparable—and some even worse—abuses reported by officers in the Army's elite 82nd Airborne Division in Iraq. We will broaden our search to investigate the ways in which military and government chains of command created similar situations in other military prisons to facilitate their "war on terrorism" and "war on insurgency." We will do so with the help of interviews and analyses reported in a PBS *Frontline* documentary, "A Question of Torture" (October 18, 2005), which details the role of the Bush administration and the military's chain of command in first sanctioning such torture in Guantánamo Bay Prison and then transporting it to Abu Ghraib and beyond.

I will shift roles from behavioral scientist turned pyschological investigative

reporter in the current chapter to that of prosecutor in the next. I will charge selected members of the military chain of command with misusing their authority
to make torture operational at Guantánamo Bay Prison and then exporting those
tactics to Abu Ghraib. They gave permission to the Military Police and military intelligence to employ these torture tactics—under sanitized terms—and failed to
provide the leadership, oversight, accountability, and mission-specific training
necessary for the MPs on the night shift on Tier 1A. I will argue that they are thus
guilty of sins of both commission and omission.

In putting the System on hypothetical trial, we end by putting President Bush
and his advisers in the dock for their role in redefining torture as an acceptable,
necessary tactic in their ubiquitous and nebulous war on terror. They are also
charged with exempting captured insurgents and all "foreigners" under military
arrest from the safeguards provided by the Geneva Conventions. Secretary of Defense Rumsfeld is charged with creating the interrogation centers where "detainees" were subjected to a host of extremely coercive "abuses" for the dubious
purpose of eliciting confessions and information. He is probably also responsible
for other violations of American moral standards, such as "outsourcing the torture" of high-value detainees to foreign countries in the government's "extraordinary rendition" program.

I intend to show that the System, from Bush to Cheney to Rumsfeld and down
the hierarchy of command, laid the foundation for these abuses. If so, then we, as
a democratic society, have much to do to ensure that future abuses are prevented
by insisting that the System modify the structural features and operational policies of its interrogation centers.

We will end the next chapter on an upbeat note because in fact, a plan was
put into place at Abu Ghraib to better train MPs, MI personnel, and interrogators
in the exercise of their power. My psychologist colleague Colonel Larry James was
sent to that prison recently (May 2004) to install a new set of operational procedures intended to deter the kind of violence we have examined in this chapter. Of
special interest is the provision that all MPs and other relevant personnel view the
DVD of the Stanford Prison Experiment as part of their training. How that came
about and what effects it is having will be part of the good news to come out of
this bad-news place.

That positive outlook will then carry us into the final chapter. There, I will try
to balance some of the negativity with which we have been dealing in our long
journey by offering two encouraging perspectives on learning ways to resist unwanted influences and on celebrating heroes and heroism.

Finally, I recognize that it may seem a stretch to some readers that I emphasize parallels between our little Stanford experiment in a simulated prison and the
dangerous realities of a combat zone prison. It is not the physical dissimilarities
that matter but the basic psychological dynamics that are comparable in both.[69] I
would point out further that several independent investigators have made such
comparisons, as in the Schlesinger report (quoted at the start of this chapter) and

in a report by former Naval Cryptologist Alan Hensley. In his analysis of the defendants charged with the abuses, he concluded:

> In the case of Abu Ghraib, a model described in detail in the Zimbardo Study, constructed of virtually identical factors, and resulting empirical evidence existed beforehand to predict with utmost certainty this chain of events would occur without conscious deliberation on the part of the participants."[70]

I want to end this phase of our journey with the analysis of *Newsweek* magazine's Baghdad bureau chief, Ron Nordland, about what he thinks went wrong in a war that began with good intentions:

> What went wrong? A lot, but the biggest turning point was the Abu Ghraib scandal. Since April 2004, the liberation of Iraq has become a desperate exercise in damage control. The abuse of prisoners at Abu Ghraib alienated a broad swatch of the Iraqi public. On top of that it didn't work. There is no evidence that all the mistreatment and humiliation saved a single American life or led to the capture of any major terrorist, despite claims by the military that the prison produced "actionable intelligence."[71]

CHAPTER FIFTEEN

Putting the System on Trial: Command Complicity

Army prosecutor Major Michael Holley's patriotic closing statement in the trial of Sergeant Ivan Frederick helps set the stage for our analysis of the use of torture on "unlawful combatants" and detainees imprisoned in military prisons in Iraq, Afghanistan, and Cuba:

> And I would remind you, sir, that the enemy fights on morale like we do, and this can form a rallying point for our enemies now and in the future. And I would also ask you to think about enemies who might surrender in the future. That's what we ideally want. We want them to be so intimidated by the combat power of the United States Army that they surrender. But if a prisoner—or an enemy, rather, believes that he will be humiliated and subjected to degrading treatment, why wouldn't he continue to fight until [his] last breath? And in fighting, might he not take the lives of soldiers, lives that might not otherwise be spent. This type of behavior [of the accused MPs] has long-term impact including, and lastly, it has the impact on soldiers, our soldiers and sailors and marines, airmen, who may be captured in the future and their treatment, and I'll leave it at that.

The prosecutor continues to make evident that what is at stake in this and the other trials of the "Abu Ghraib Seven" is nothing less than the Honor of the Military:

> Finally, sir, the honor of our United States Army is both precious and perishable. We have a sacred trust in the United States Army, of all armies, but in particular, our Army, is that we bear this great responsibility and power, the power to impose force on others. And the only thing that separates us imposing power unjustly and becoming a rival, a mob, a group of thugs, is that we have this sense of honor that we do what's right, we fol-

low those orders that are given to us and we do the honorable thing, and
this behavior [the Abu Ghraib Prison abuses and torture] degrades that.
And we also, just like any other Army, we need a moral high ground, as
well, to rally ourselves.[1]

My closing statement in the Frederick trial was spontaneous and unscripted.
It foreshadowed some key arguments that will be developed in this chapter, which
provides fuller scope for the theses that powerful situational and systemic forces
were operating to cause these abuses. Moreover, in the time since that trial (October 2004), further evidence has emerged that clearly shows the complicity of a
host of military commanders in the abuses and torture on Tier 1A, Abu Ghraib
Prison. Here is the text of my statement:

> The Fay Report, the Taguba Report indicate that this [abuse] could have
> been prevented had the military put in any of the resources or any of the
> concern that they're putting into these trials—Abu Ghraib never would
> have happened. But Abu Ghraib was treated with indifference. It had no
> priority, the same low priority in security as the archaeological museum in
> Baghdad [whose treasures were looted after Baghdad was "liberated"
> while soldiers passively watched]. These are both low-priority [military]
> items, and this one happened to erupt under these unfortunate circum-
> stances. So I think that the military is on trial, particularly all of the offi-
> cers who are above Sergeant Frederick who should have known what was
> going on, should have prevented it, should have stopped it, and should
> have challenged it. They are the ones who should be on trial. Or, if
> Sergeant Frederick is responsible to some extent, whatever his sentence is,
> has to be, I think, mitigated by the responsibility of the whole chain of
> command.[2]

In this chapter, our path will follow several different directions that should
lead us to draw out from behind the dark screen of concealment the central role
of many key players in the drama at Abu Ghraib—the directors, scriptwriters,
and stage managers who made this tragic play possible. In a sense, the MPs were
merely bit actors, "seven characters in search of an author," or a director.

Our task is to determine what were the systemic pressures that existed outside of the situation that existed inside Abu Ghraib's hard site of interrogation.
We need to identify the particular parties involved at all levels in the chain of command for creating the conditions responsible for the implosion of human character in those MPs. In presenting the chronology of these intertwined forces, I will
switch roles from that of defense expert to that of prosecutor. In that capacity, I
introduce a new kind of modern evil, "administrative evil," that constitutes the
foundation of complicity of the chain of political and military command in these
abuses and tortures.[3] Both public and private organizations, because they operate
within a legal framework, not an ethical framework, can inflict suffering, even

death, on people by following cold rationality for achieving the goals of their ideology, a master plan, a cost-benefit equation, or the bottom line of profit. Under those circumstances, their ends always justify efficient means.

INVESTIGATIONS OF ABU GHRAIB ABUSES EXPOSE SYSTEM FAULTS

In response to numerous reports of abuse, not only at Abu Ghraib but also at military prisons throughout Iraq, Afghanistan, and Cuba, the Pentagon has conducted at least a dozen official investigations. I closely reviewed half of them in preparation for my role in the defense of Sergeant Ivan Frederick. In this section, I will outline chronologically some of those key reports and highlight their conclusions with exact quotes from them. Doing so will give us a sense of how high-ranking officers and government officials evaluated the causes of torture and abuse. Because all but one of these investigations were ordered by the military with specific instructions to focus on perpetrators, most of them failed to indict military and political leaders for their roles in creating conditions conducive to these abuses. The only exception was the Schlesinger Report, ordered by Secretary Rumsfeld.

By looking down rather than up the chain of command, these reports are limited in scope and neither as independent nor as nonpartisan as one would wish. However, they provide us with a starting point in our case against the military and administration chains of command that we will then supplement with additional media and agency reports complemented by firsthand testimonies of soldiers involved in torture. (For a full chronology of the Abu Ghraib abuses and investigative reports, please see the website in the Notes.[4])

The Ryder Report Was the First to Send Up Warning Signals

The Army's chief law enforcement officer, Provost Marshal Donald Ryder, a major general, prepared the first report (November 6, 2003) by order of General Sanchez. Ryder was appointed in August to head an assessment team, as requested by the Army criminal investigation unit. That unit is identified as CJTF-7—Combined Joint Task Force 7, a multiservice and Department of Defense (DoD) task force that included Army, Navy, Marine Corps, Air Force, and DoD civilian staff.

This document reviewed the entire prison system in Iraq and recommended ways to improve it. At the end, Ryder concluded that there had been serious human rights violations, as well as training and manpower inadequacies that were "system-wide." His report also raised concerns about the fuzzy boundaries between the MPs, who were supposed only to guard prisoners, and the military intelligence (MI) teams assigned to interrogate prisoners. It noted that the MIs tried to enlist the MPs to engage in activities that would "prepare" detainees for interrogation.

This MI–MP tension dated back to the Afghanistan War, during which MPs worked with MIs to "set favorable conditions for subsequent interviews," a euphemism for breaking the will of prisoners. Ryder called for the establishment of procedures "to define the role of military police soldiers . . . clearly separating the actions of the guards from those of the military intelligence personnel." His report should have put on notice all those in charge of the military's prison systems.

Despite this valuable contribution, "Ryder undercut his warning," according to the journalist Seymour Hersh, "by concluding that the situation had not yet reached a crisis point. Though some procedures were flawed, he said, he found 'no military police units purposely applying inappropriate confinement practices.' " Remember that this report appeared at the height of the most flagrant abuses going on in Tier 1A during the fall of 2003 but before Specialist Joe Darby's exposé (January 13, 2004). Hersh's *New Yorker* magazine article (May 5, 2004), which broke open the scandal, concluded about the Ryder report that "His investigation was at best a failure and at worst a coverup."[5]

The Taguba Report Is Thorough and Tough[6]

Once the notorious photos surfaced among military higher-ups and the criminal investigating team in January 2004, General Sanchez was forced to move beyond Ryder's whitewash job. He assigned Major General Antonio M. Taguba to do a fuller investigation into allegations of detainee abuse, undocumented prisoner escapes, and widespread failures in discipline and accountability. Taguba did an admirable job in a detailed, extensive investigation that was published in March 2004. Although it was intended to remain classified because it made direct accusations of officer dereliction of duty, leveled other strong charges against fellow officers, and contained as evidence some of "The Photos," it was too juicy not to be leaked to the media (probably for big bucks).

The Taguba Report was leaked to *The New Yorker,* where its main findings and the photos were published in Hersh's story, but this occurred only after the photos were also leaked to the producers of *60 Minutes II* and shown in its April 28, 2004, broadcast. (You will recall that this was what started me on this adventure.)

Taguba wasted no time in refuting his fellow general's report. "Unfortunately, many of the *systemic problems* that surfaced during [Ryder's] assessment are the very same issues that are the subject of this investigation," he wrote. (Italics added for emphasis.) "In fact, many of the abuses suffered by detainees occurred during, or near to, the time of that assessment." The report continued, "Contrary to the findings of MG [Major General] Ryder's report, I find that personnel assigned to the 372nd MP Company, 800th MP Brigade were directed to change facility procedures to 'set the conditions' for MI interrogations." His report made it clear that Army intelligence officers, CIA agents, private contractors, and OGAs [other government agencies] "actively requested that MP guards set physical and mental conditions for favorable interrogation of witnesses."

In support of this assertion, Taguba cited sworn statements from several guards about the complicity of the military intelligence personnel and of the interrogators.

SPC [Specialist] Sabrina Harman, 372nd MP Company, stated in her sworn statement regarding the incident where a detainee was placed on a box with wires attached to his fingers, toes, and penis, "that her job was to keep detainees awake." She said that MI was talking to CPL [Corporal] Grainer [sic]. She stated, "MI wanted to get them to talk. It is Grainer [sic] and Frederick's job to do things for MI and OGA to get these people to talk."

Taguba presented testimony from Sergeant Javal Davis about what he observed regarding the influence of military intelligence and OGAs on the MP guards:

"I witnessed prisoners in the MI hold section, wing 1A, being made to do various things that I would question morally. In Wing 1A we were told that they had different rules and different SOP [standard operating procedures] for treatment. I never saw a set of rules or SOP for that section just word of mouth. The Soldier in charge of 1A was Corporal Granier [sic]. He stated that the Agents and MI Soldiers would ask him to do things, but nothing was ever in writing he would complain [sic]." When asked why the rules in 1A/1B were different than those in the rest of the wings, Sergeant Davis stated: "The rest of the wings are regular prisoners and 1A/B are Military Intelligence (MI) holds." When asked why he did not inform his chain of command about this abuse, Sergeant Davis stated: "Because I assumed that if they were doing things out of the ordinary or outside the guidelines, someone would have said something. [Observe the evil of inaction at work again.] Also the wing belongs to MI and it appeared MI personnel approved of the abuse." Sergeant Davis also stated that he had heard MI insinuate to the guards to abuse the inmates. When asked what MI said he stated: "Loosen this guy up for us." "Make sure he has a bad night." "Make sure he gets the treatment." He claimed these comments were made to CPL Granier [sic] and SGT Frederick. Finally, SGT Davis stated that [sic] "the MI staffs to my understanding have been giving Granier [sic] compliments on the way he has been handling the MI holds. Examples being statements like, 'Good job, they're breaking down real fast. They answer every question. They're giving out good information, Finally,' and Keep up the good work. Stuff like that."

Reminiscent of my SPE guards' taking away the prisoners' mattresses, sheets, clothes, and pillows for rule violations is the statement made to Taguba by Specialist Jason Kennel, 372nd MP Company:

"I saw them nude, but MI would tell us to take away their mattresses, sheets, and clothes." He could not recall who in MI had instructed him to do this, but commented that, "if they wanted me to do that they needed to give me paperwork." He was later informed that "We could not do anything to embarrass the prisoners."

This is just one example of the continuous inconsistencies between the reality of the abusive situation and the unofficial encouragement of the MPs to abuse detainees by MIs and other agents on that tier. As they gave orders for abuse spoken from one side of the mouth, the official public statement from the other side of the mouth insisted that "We do not condone prisoner abuse or anything but their humane treatment." Such an approach created the case for plausible deniability later on.

Also of passing interest in establishing parallels with the SPE is the Taguba Report's emphasis on the need for uniformity in the "counts." Recall the central role that the "counts" came to play as occasions for abuse of our SPE prisoners. "There is a lack of standardization in the way the 320th MP Battalion conducted physical counts of their detainees." The report goes on to complain of the lack of count standardization:

> Each compound within a given encampment did their headcounts differently. Some compounds had detainees line up in lines of 10, some had them sit in rows, and some moved all the detainees to one end of the compound and counted them as they passed to the other end of the compound.

The Taguba Report specifies that top military leaders who were made aware of extreme detainee abuse had recommended court martial, but they never followed through. Their inaction, given their awareness of the abuses, thereby strengthened the impression that there would be no payback for abusing prisoners:

> Another obvious example of the Brigade Leadership not communicating with its Soldiers or ensuring their tactical proficiency concerns the incident of detainee abuse that occurred at Camp Bucca, Iraq, on May 12, 2003. . . . An extensive CID [Criminal Investigative Division] investigation determined that four soldiers from the 320th MP Battalion had kicked and beaten these detainees following a transport mission from Talil Air Base. . . .
>
> Formal charges under the UCMJ were preferred against these Soldiers and an Article-32 Investigation conducted by LTC [Lieutenant Colonel] Gentry. He recommended a general court martial for the four accused, which BG [Brigadier General] Karpinski supported. Despite this documented abuse, there is no evidence that BG Karpinski ever attempted to re-

mind 800th MP Soldiers of the requirements of the Geneva Conventions regarding detainee treatment or took any steps to ensure that such abuse was not repeated. Nor is there any evidence that LTC(P) Phillabaum, the commander of the Soldiers involved in the Camp Bucca abuse incident, took any initiative to ensure his Soldiers were properly trained regarding detainee treatment.

What We Have Here is a Failure to Communicate, to Educate, and to Provide Leadership

Taguba offers many instances of ways in which the soldiers and Army Reserve MPs were not properly trained and were not given the resources and information they needed to perform their difficult functions as guards in Abu Ghraib Prison. The report states:

> There is a general lack of knowledge, implementation, and emphasis of basic legal, regulatory, doctrinal, and command requirements within the 800th MP Brigade and its subordinate units. . . .
>
> The handling of detainees and criminal prisoners after in-processing was inconsistent from detention facility to detention facility, compound to compound, encampment to encampment, and *even shift to shift throughout the 800th MP Brigade AOR* (Area of Responsibility). [Italics added to emphasize shift differences from day to night on Tier 1A.]

The report also states:

> The Abu Ghraib and Camp Bucca detention facilities are significantly over their intended maximum capacity while the guard force is undermanned and under resourced. This imbalance has contributed to the poor living conditions, escapes, and accountability lapses at the various facilities. The overcrowding of the facilities also limits the ability to identify and segregate leaders in the detainee population who may be organizing escapes and riots within the facility.

The report goes on to identify one of the problems raised by Chip Frederick in policing his tier, that of numerous unidentified civilians and unknown others coming and going, and giving orders to him and his staff.

> In general, US civilian contract personnel (Titan Corporation, CACI, etc.), third country nationals, and local contractors do not appear to be properly supervised within the detention facility at Abu Ghraib. During our on-site inspection, they wandered about with too much unsupervised free access in the detainee area. Having civilians in various outfits (civilian and DCUs [Desert Camouflage Units]) in and about the detainee area causes confusion and may have contributed to the difficulties in the accountability process and with detecting escapes.

Taguba documents many instances of prisoners escaping and rioting and describes lethal encounters between MPs and detainees. In every case, the report repeats its conclusion: "No information on findings, contributing factors, or corrective action has been provided to this investigation team." The report also takes note of one major prisoner riot that had lethal consequences, one of those that Chip Frederick mentioned as a prelude to a transfer to his Tier 1A of the riot ringleaders, who were then abused there:

> 24 November 03- Riot and shooting of 12 detainees ... Several detainees allegedly began to riot at about 1300 in all of the compounds at the Ganci encampment. This resulted in the shooting deaths of 3 detainees, 9 wounded detainees, and 9 injured US Soldiers. A 15-6 investigation by COL Bruce Falcone (220th MP Brigade, Deputy Commander) concluded that the detainees rioted in protest of their living conditions, that the riot turned violent, the use of non-lethal force was ineffective, and, after the 320th MP Battalion CDR [Commander] executed "Golden Spike," the emergency containment plan, the use of deadly force was authorized.

What or who was to blame for this riot and the use of deadly force to contain it? Taguba concludes that a host of problems were involved. He notes:

> Contributing factors were lack of comprehensive training of guards, poor or non-existent SOPs, no formal guard-count conducted prior to shift, no rehearsals or ongoing training, the mix of less than lethal rounds with lethal rounds in weapons, no AARs [after action reports] being conducted after incidents, ROE [rules of engagement] not posted and not understood, overcrowding, uniforms not standardized, and poor communication between the command and Soldiers.

Taguba was especially concerned that the obviously inadequate training of the MP brigade, well-known by military command, was never corrected:

> I find that the 800th MP Brigade was not adequately trained for a mission that included operating a prison or penal institution at Abu Ghraib Prison Complex. As the Ryder Assessment found, I also concur that units of the 800th MP Brigade did not receive corrections-specific training during their mobilization period. MP units did not receive pinpoint assignments prior to mobilization and during the post mobilization training, and thus could not train for specific missions. The training that was accomplished at the mobilization sites were [sic] developed and implemented at the company level with little or no direction or supervision at the Battalion and Brigade levels, and consisted primarily of common tasks and law enforcement training. However, I found no evidence that the Command, although aware of this deficiency, ever requested specific corrections training from the Commandant of the Military Police School, the US Army Con-

finement Facility at Mannheim, Germany, the Provost Marshal General of the Army, or the US Army Disciplinary Barracks at Fort Leavenworth, Kansas. . . .

This investigation indicates that BG Karpinski and her staff did a poor job allocating resources throughout the Iraq JOA [Joint Operations Area]. Abu Ghraib (BCCF [Baghdad Central Confinement Facility]) normally housed between 6000 and 7000 detainees, yet it was operated by only one battalion. In contrast, the HVD [High Visibility Detainees] Facility maintains only about 100 detainees, and is also run by an entire battalion. . . .

In addition to being severely undermanned, the quality of life for Soldiers assigned to Abu Ghraib (BCCF) was extremely poor. There was no DFAC [dining facility], PX [post exchange], barbershop, or MWR [morale, welfare, and recreation] facilities. There were numerous mortar attacks, random rifle and RPG [rocket-propelled grenade] attacks, and a serious threat to Soldiers and detainees in the facility. The prison complex was also severely overcrowded and the Brigade lacked adequate resources and personnel to resolve serious logistical problems. Finally, because of past associations and familiarity of Soldiers within the Brigade, it appears that friendship often took precedence over appropriate leader and subordinate relationships.

Taguba Targets Derelict, Deficient Commanders

One of the exceptional features of General Taguba's report, compared with all the other investigations into the Abu Ghraib abuses, is its willingness to identify the commanders who failed to exercise their military leadership—and who deserve some form of military punishment. It is worth our time to lay out some of the reasons that the general targeted many military leaders for their roles in creating a command that was a mockery rather than a model of military leadership. These were the leaders who were supposed to provide the disciplinary structure for the hapless MPs:

With respect to the 800th MP Brigade mission at Abu Ghraib (BCCF), I find that there was clear friction and lack of effective communication between the Commander, 205th MI Brigade, who controlled FOB [Forward Operations Base] Abu Ghraib (BCCF) after 19 November 2003, and the Commander, 800th MP Brigade, who controlled detainee operations inside the FOB. There was no clear delineation of responsibility between commands, little coordination at the command level, and no integration of the two functions. Coordination occurred at the lowest possible levels with little oversight by commanders. . . .

The 320th MP Battalion was stigmatized as a unit due to previous detainee abuse which occurred in May 2003 at the Bucca Theater Internment Facility (TIF), while under the command of LTC (P) Phillabaum.

Despite his proven deficiencies as both a commander and leader, BG Karpinski allowed LTC (P) Phillabaum to remain in command of her most troubled battalion guarding, by far, the largest number of detainees in the 800th MP Brigade. . . .

Numerous witnesses stated that the 800th MP Brigade S-1, MAJ Hinzman and S-4, MAJ Green, were essentially dysfunctional, but that despite numerous complaints, these officers were not replaced. This had a detrimental effect on the Brigade Staff's effectiveness and morale. Moreover, the Brigade Command Judge Advocate, LTC James O'Hare, appears to lack initiative and was unwilling to accept responsibility for any of his actions. LTC Gary Maddocks, the Brigade XO (Executive Officer) did not properly supervise the Brigade staff by failing to lay out staff priorities, take overt corrective action when needed, and supervise their daily functions. . . .

In addition, numerous officers and senior NCOs have been reprimanded/disciplined for misconduct during this period.

From my reading of Taguba's analysis, I must conclude that Abu Ghraib was an "animal house" at the *officer* level, as well as among the night shift Army Reserve MPs on Tier 1A. Twelve officers and NCOs were reprimanded or disciplined (mildly) for their misconduct, dereliction of duty, lack of leadership, and alcohol abuse. One glaring example involved Captain Leo Merck, commander of the 870th MP Company, who was alleged to have taken nude photographs of his own female soldiers without their knowledge. A second example involved NCOs who were found derelict in duty for fraternizing with junior commissioned officers and for gratuitously shooting off their M-16 rifles while exiting their cars, unintentionally and negligently blowing up a fuel tank!

Taguba recommended that a dozen of the individuals in command positions, who should have been positive role models for the ordinary soldiers and reservists functioning under them, deserved to be relieved from command or relieved from Duty and given a General Officer Memorandum of Reprimand.

His report cites many specific instances of failure of leadership for each of the following principals:

Brigadier General Janis L. Karpinski, Commander, 800th MP Brigade; Colonel Thomas M. Pappas, Commander, 205th MI Brigade; Lieutenant Colonel (P) Jerry L. Phillabaum, Commander, 320th MP Battalion; Lieutenant Colonel Steven L. Jordan, former director, Joint Interrogation and Debriefing Center, and liaison officer to 205th MI Brigade; Major David W. DiNenna, S-3, 320th MP Battalion; and Captain Donald J. Reese, commander, 372nd MP Company.

Other lower-level officers also cited by Taguba are important for their positions in Tier 1A. They include: First Lieutenant Lewis C. Raeder, Platoon Leader, 372nd MP Company; Sergeant Major Marc Emerson, operations Sergeant Major 320th MP Battalion; First Sergeant Brian G. Lipinski, 372nd MP Company; and Sergeant First Class Shannon K. Snider, platoon sergeant, 372nd MP Company.

The Taguba Report issued a common justification for reprimanding those who should have been in charge of operations at Tier 1A: Reese, Raeder, Emerson, Lipinski, and Snider. Each of them was charged with one or more of the following:

- Failing to ensure that Soldiers under his direct command knew and understood the protections afforded to detainees in the Geneva Convention Relative to the Treatment of Prisoners of War.
- Failing to properly supervise his Soldiers working and "visiting" Tier 1 of the Hard-Site at Abu Ghraib (BCCF).
- Failing to properly establish and enforce basic soldier standards, proficiency, and accountability.
- Failing to ensure that Soldiers under his direct command were properly trained in Internment and Resettlement Operations.

Here, then, is further support for the pleadings made by Chip Frederick and other MP guards on his shift that they were essentially clueless as to what was appropriate and what was not acceptable when preparing detainees for interrogation.

However, culpability lay not just with the military. This investigation also shows that several civilian interrogators and interpreters who wrongly involved the MPs in their interrogation of detainees on Tier 1A were personally implicated in the abuse. Among them, the Taguba Report identifies the following culprits: Steven Stephanowicz, contract U.S. civilian interrogator, CACI, 205th Military Intelligence Brigade, and John Israel, contract U.S. civilian interpreter, CACI, 205th Military Intelligence Brigade.

Stephanowicz is accused of having "Allowed and/or instructed MPs, who were not trained in interrogation techniques, to facilitate interrogations by 'setting conditions' which were neither authorized and [*sic*] in accordance with applicable regulations/policy. He clearly knew his instructions equated to *physical abuse*." (Italics added for emphasis.) That is exactly what Frederick and Graner reported that they had been encouraged to do by these civilians who seemed to be in charge of the main action of Tier 1A: to get actionable intelligence through detainee interrogation by any means necessary.

The effect of the negative modeling of the "evil of inaction" is also revealed by Taguba's admonition of Sergeant Snider for "Failing to report a Soldier, who under his direct control, abused detainees by stomping on their bare hands and feet in his presence."

Before we leave the Taguba Report to move on to some of the findings in several other independent investigations, we must note its powerful conclusion about the culpability of some military officers and civilian workers who have not yet been tried, or even charged, for the abuses at Abu Ghraib:

Several US Army Soldiers have committed egregious acts and grave breaches of international law at Abu Ghraib/BCCF and Camp Bucca, Iraq.

Furthermore, key senior leaders in both the 800th MP Brigade and the 205th MI Brigade failed to comply with established regulations, policies, and command directives in preventing detainee abuses at Abu Ghraib (BCCF) and at Camp Bucca during the period August 2003 to February 2004. . . .

Specifically, I suspect that COL Thomas M. Pappas, LTC Steve L. Jordan, Mr. Steven Stephanowicz, and Mr. John Israel were either *directly or indirectly responsible for the abuses at Abu Ghraib* (BCCF) and strongly recommend immediate disciplinary action as described in the preceding paragraphs as well as the initiation of a Procedure 15 Inquiry to determine the full extent of their culpability. [Italics added for emphasis.]

The Milolashek Report Blames Only the Few

Lieutenant General Paul T. Milolashek, Army inspector general, reviewed ninety-four confirmed cases of detainee abuse in Afghanistan and Iraq and the conditions contributing to these violations of U.S. military policy; (the report was issued on February 10, 2004). Even though the report identifies the many instances of flawed decisions by senior commanders and military officers that contributed to the abuses, General Milolashek concluded that the abuses did not result from any military *policy*, nor were they the fault of any senior officers. Instead, he turned his blame laser on only low-ranking soldiers for committing these abuses. Let Milolashek's record show that these ninety-four cases of detainee abuse in military prisons in Afghanistan and Iraq were due simply to the "unauthorized actions taken by a few individuals." Thus, the inspector general cleanly absolved the entire chain of command of any responsibility for the damages. The ninety-four cases of abuse also go far beyond the confines of the night shift on Tier 1A.

This top-level "whitewash" should be packaged with the Ryder Report as a Tweedledee-Tweedledum boxed set. However, before moving on, it is valuable to set this general's conclusion of no top dogs responsible against inconsistencies in his report's other findings. The report notes that troops received "ambiguous guidance from command on the treatment of detainees" and, further, that established interrogation policies were "not clear and contained ambiguity." It also notes that the decision by senior commanders in Iraqi prisons to rely on the Guantánamo Bay Prison ("Gitmo") guidelines was wrong. The detainees at Gitmo were considered high value "alien combatants" who may have had actionable intelligence necessary to extract in order to combat terrorism and insurgency. Secretary Rumsfeld outlined a set of stiff interrogation tactics to be used on those detainees; however, they were somehow transported overseas to Iraq prisons and to run-of-the-mill detainees. Milolashek's report states that this action by senior military officers "appears to contradict the terms of Rumsfeld's decision, which explicitly stated that the guidelines were applicable only to interrogations at Guantánamo; and this led to the use of 'high risk' interrogation techniques that left considerable room for misapplication, particularly under high-stress combat conditions."

The Fay/Jones Report Scales the Blame Upward and Outward[7]

Lieutenant General Anthony R. Jones assisted Major General George R. Fay in leading an investigation of allegations that the 205th Military Intelligence Brigade was involved in detainee abuse at Abu Ghraib. They also investigated whether any organizations or personnel higher than that brigade command were involved in those abuses in any way.[8] Although their report advances the standard dispositional attribution of putting the blame on the individual perpetrators of the abuses—once again that "small groups of morally corrupt soldiers and civilians"—it does extend the causation to situational and systemic factors in revealing ways.

"The events at Abu Ghraib cannot be understood in a vacuum," is the Fay/Jones lead-in to outlining how the "operational environment" contributed to those abuses. Compatible with the social psychological analysis that I have been proposing, their report goes on to detail both the powerful situational and systemic forces operating within and around the behavioral setting. Consider the significance of the following three paragraphs extracted from the final report:

> LTG Jones found that while senior level officers did not commit the abuse at Abu Ghraib they did bear responsibility for lack of oversight of the facility, failing to respond in a timely manner to the reports of the International Committee of the Red Cross and for issuing policy memos that failed to provide clear, consistent guidance for execution at the tactical level.
>
> MG Fay has found that from 25 July 2003 to 6 February 2004, twenty-seven 205 MI BDE [Brigade] Personnel allegedly requested, encouraged, condoned or solicited Military Police (MP) personnel to abuse detainees and/or *participated in detainee abuse* and/or violated established interrogation procedures and applicable laws and regulations during interrogation operations at Abu Ghraib. [Italics added for emphasis.]
>
> The leaders from units located at Abu Ghraib or with supervision over Soldiers and units at Abu Ghraib failed to supervise subordinates or provide direct oversight of this important mission. These leaders failed to properly discipline their Soldiers. These leaders failed to learn from their mistakes and failed to provide continued mission-specific training. . . . The absence of effective leadership was a factor in not sooner discovering and taking actions to prevent both the violent/sexual abuse incidents and the misinterpretation/confusion incidents. . . . *Abuses would not have occurred had doctrine been followed and mission training conducted.* [Italics added for emphasis.]

The joint report of these generals summarizes multiple factors that they found as having contributed to the abuses at Abu Ghraib. Seven factors are identified as primary contributors to the abuses:

- "Individual criminal propensities" (the alleged dispositions of the reserve MPs)
- "leadership failures" (systemic factors)
- "dysfunctional command relationships at brigade and higher echelons" (systemic factors)
- "multiple agencies/organizations involvement in interrogation operations at Abu Ghraib" (systemic factors)
- "failure to effectively screen, certify, and then integrate contractor interrogators/analysts/linguists" (systemic factor)
- "lack of a clear understanding of the MP and MI roles and responsibilities in interrogation operations" (situational and systemic factors)
- "lack of safety and security at Abu Ghraib" (situational and systemic factors)

The Fay/Jones Report thus specifies six of seven contributing factors to the abuses as traceable to systemic or situational factors, and but one to dispositional factors. It then proceeds to expand on this overview by highlighting numerous systemic failures that played key roles in facilitating the abuses:

> Looking beyond personal responsibility, leader responsibility and command responsibility, systemic problems and issues also contributed to the volatile environment in which abuse occurred. The report lists several dozen specific systemic failures ranging from doctrine and policy concerns to leadership and command and control issues to resource and training issues.

Cooperating with Illegal CIA Activities as "Teamwork"

I was surprised to discover in this report open, public criticism of the CIA's role in the abusive interrogations, which was supposed to be clandestine:

> The systematic lack of accountability for interrogator actions and detainees plagued detainee operations at Abu Ghraib. It is unclear how and under what authority the CIA could place prisoners like DETAINEE-28* in Abu Ghraib because no memorandums of understanding existed on the subject between the CIA and CJTF-7. Local CIA officers convinced COL Pappas and LTC Jordan that they should be allowed to *operate outside the established local rules and procedures.* [Italics added for emphasis.]

Let's pause for a moment to let that statement resonate before considering how this matter of the military's links with the CIA was resolved. Fay/Jones noted that "When COL Pappas raised the issue of CIA use of Abu Ghraib with COL Blotz,

---

*We will have more to say about this detainee, Manadel al-Jamadi, later on.

COL Blotz encouraged COL Pappas to cooperate with the CIA because everyone was all one team. COL Blotz directed LTC Jordan to cooperate [as well]."

Creating an Unhealthy Work Environment

The way in which such "above and beyond the law" undercover work by CIA operatives contributed to a cancerous environment is elaborated in Fay/Jones with a psychological analysis:

> The death of DETAINEE-28 and incidents such as the loaded weapon in the interrogation room, were widely known within the US community (MI and MP alike) at Abu Ghraib. Speculation and resentment grew out of a lack of personal responsibility, of some people being above the laws and regulations. The resentment contributed to the unhealthy environment that existed at Abu Ghraib. The death of DETAINEE-28 remains unresolved.

> The operational use of anonymity as a protective shield to get away with murder is noted in passing: "CIA officers operating at Abu Ghraib used alias [*sic*] and never revealed their true names."

When the Self-Serving Claims of the MPs Turn Out to Be True

The Fay/Jones investigation offers support for the claims by Chip Frederick and other night shift MPs that many of their abusive actions were encouraged and supported by a variety of individuals working for military intelligence in their unit:

> The MPs being prosecuted claim that their actions came at the direction of MI. Although self-serving, these claims do have some basis in fact. *The environment created at Abu Ghraib contributed to the occurrence of such abuse and the fact that it remained undiscovered by higher authority for a long period of time.* What started out as nakedness and humiliation, stress and physical training [exercise], carried over into sexual and physical assaults by a small group of morally corrupt and unsupervised Soldiers and civilians. [Italics added for emphasis.]

> These investigating generals repeatedly make evident the major roles played by systemic and situational factors in the abuses. However, they cannot give up the dispositional attribution of the perpetrators as the few "morally corrupt" individuals, the so-called bad apples in an otherwise flawless barrel filled to the brim with "the noble conduct of the vast majority of our Soldiers."

Decent Dogs Doing Dirty Deeds

The Fay/Jones Report was one of the first to detail and fault some of the "accepted" tactics used to facilitate effective interrogations. For example, it notes that the use of dogs was imported by Major General Geoffrey Miller from Gitmo prison in Cuba, but the report adds, "The use of dogs in interrogations to 'fear up' detainees was utilized without proper authorization."

Once muzzled dogs were officially made available to induce fear in prisoners, it did not take long to unofficially unmuzzle them in order to rev up the fear factor. The Fay/Jones Report identifies a civilian interrogator [number 21, a private CACI employee] who used an unmuzzled dog during an interrogation and who yelled to MPs where a dog was being used against a detainee to "take him home." To show that the dogs could chew things up, that dog had just torn apart the detainee's mattress. Another interrogator (Soldier 17, 2nd MI Battalion) is accused of failing to report the improper use of dogs that he saw when the handler allowed the dog to "go nuts" in scaring two juvenile detainees by sending an unmuzzled dog into their cell. This interrogator also failed to report the dog handlers discussing their competition to scare detainees to the point that they would defecate in their pants. They claimed to have already made several detainees urinate on themselves when threatened by their dogs.

Naked Prisoners Are Dehumanized Prisoners

The use of nudity as an incentive to maintain detainee cooperation was imported from prisons in Afghanistan and Guantánamo. When it came time to use that tactic at Abu Ghraib, the Fay/Jones Report noted "the lines of authority and the proper legal opinions blurred. They simply carried forward the use of nudity into the Iraqi theater of operations. The use of clothing as an incentive [nudity] is significant in that it likely contributed to an escalating 'de-humanization' of the detainees and set the stage for additional and more severe abuses to occur [by the MPs]."

When Segregation Becomes Isolation

Although Lieutenant General Sanchez had approved the tactic of "isolation" over extended periods of time for specific detainees, it appears that he really meant "segregation" of them from fellow prisoners. However, at the Abu Ghraib hard site, Sanchez was taken at his word, and many detainees were totally isolated and completely removed from all outside contact, as in solitary confinement, "other than the required care and feeding by MP guards and interrogation by MI." The Fay/Jones Report notes that "These cells had limited or poor ventilation, no light, and were often made excessively hot or cold. Use of isolation rooms in the Abu Ghraib Hard Site was not closely controlled or monitored. Lacking proper training, clear guidance, or experience in this technique, both MP and MI stretched the bounds into further abuse; sensory deprivation and unsafe or unhealthy living conditions."

Assigning Blame: Officers, MI, Interrogators, Analysts,
Interpreters, Translators, and Medics

The Fay/Jones Report concludes by declaring as culpable all those its investigation found responsible for detainee abuse at Abu Ghraib—fully twenty-seven individuals by name or identity code. What is significant to me is the number of people who knew of the abuses, witnessed them, even participated in them in various ways and did nothing to prevent, stop, or report them. They provided "social proof" to the MPs that it was acceptable to continue doing whatever they wanted to do. Their smiling, silent faces provided social support from the surrounding network of the general interrogation team that gave thumbs up to abuses that should have received reprimands. Once again, we see the evil of inaction facilitating the evil of action.

Medics and nurses often were guilty of not helping victims in distress, of observing brutality and looking the other way, and worse. They signed off on false death certificates and lied about the nature of wounds and broken limbs. They violated their Hippocratic oath and "sold their souls for dross," according to professor of medicine and bioethics Steven H. Miles, in his book *Oath Betrayed.*[9]

At the top of the Fay/Jones blame list is again the inept Colonel Pappas, with twelve separate charges against him, and again Lieutenant Colonel Steven Jordan (director of the Joint Interrogation Debriefing Center). The following officers, not on Taguba's hit list, are singled out by Fay and Jones as also culpable: Major David Price (operations officer at that center), Major Michael Thompson (deputy operations officer at that center), and Captain Carolyn Wood, officer in charge of Interrogation Control Element (ICE) at that center.

Before reviewing some of the reprehensible actions of the lower-level cast of characters who played both directors and audience for the "Abu Ghraib Seven" perpetrators, it is well to stop for a moment to consider the fate of Captain Carolyn Wood. As leader of the 519th Military Intelligence Brigade when she was only a lieutenant, Wood had an important role to play, but she misplayed it badly. At Bagram Prison in Afghanistan, Wood authorized new, tougher interrogation guidelines that somehow ended up in detainees being severely beaten; one was killed, and a female detainee was sexually assaulted by three of her MI interrogators. The Fay/Jones Report notes that "CPT Wood should have been aware of the potential for detainee abuse at Abu Ghraib," given her knowledge of prior abuses by her MI soldiers. However, Wood received a Bronze Star for Valor after her duty in Afghanistan and another Bronze Star, along with a promotion, following revelation of the abuses in Abu Ghraib.[10] If such leadership wins high distinctions, what, then, constitutes bad leadership in that military corps?

Failures of bystander intervention by numerous observers of the abuse on Tier 1A helped to perpetuate that abuse. Among those who were identified as witnessing abuses and doing nothing about them were the following:

- Soldier 15, MI interrogator, and Soldier 22 (who also heard MPs say they were using detainees as "practice dummies" by striking them unconscious)
- Soldier 24, intelligence analyst (present during abuse of detainees in many photographs)

- Soldier 25, interrogator (who "thought it was funny" when dog handlers scared detainees into running into their cells as dogs attacked; she was also present when a pyramid of naked prisoners was formed)
- Soldier 20, Medic (who witnessed prisoner abuse and saw photos of the naked pyramid)
- Soldier 01, Medic (she also saw the human pyramid when called to provide medical treatment).

Also included are those mentioned earlier who watched the dog attacks and never challenged the dog handlers or reported the abuses.

Not content to observe in silence, many others eagerly joined the fray. One Army analyst (Soldier 10) threw water on three naked detainees; one interrogator (Soldier 19) actively participated in the abuse of three detainees depicted in the photographs, threw foam balls at their genitals, poured water over them, and gave instructions to MPs to abuse a detainee who was later found "naked and hooded on the floor whimpering." The Fay/Jones Report identifies another personally involved interrogator: "Soldier-29 saw Graner slap a detainee; she saw a computer screen saver with the image of seven naked detainees in a human pyramid; she saw the photos being taken; she knew that MPs gave a detainee a cold shower, made him roll in dirt, and then forced him to stand in the cold until he was dry; she stripped a prisoner naked and walked him outside in the cold on a winter night."

Most tellingly in support of Chip Frederick's defense, this female interrogator is charged with giving MPs instructions to mistreat and abuse detainees. It was proven that she told that to SSG Frederick when detainees had not cooperated in an interrogation—which "appeared to result in [their] subsequent abuse" (according to Fay and Jones).

This thorough investigation by two Army generals should lay to rest any claims that the MPs on the night shift of Tier 1A abused and tortured the prisoners solely out of their personally deviant motivations or sadistic impulses. Instead, the picture that is emerging is one of complex multiple causality. Many other soldiers and civilians are identified and implicated in various ways in the torture and abuse process. Some were perpetrators, some facilitators, and some observers who failed to report abuses. In addition, we see that a legion of officers is also fingered as responsible for these abuses by their failures of leadership, and by creating the chaotic, impossible situation in which Chip Frederick and those serving under him found themselves enmeshed.

However, General Sanchez was not directly implicated in any wrongdoing by this investigation. Yet, he was not entirely off the hook, according to General Paul J. Kern, who told reporters, "We did not find General Sanchez culpable but we found him responsible for what did or did not happen."[11] Now, that is really elegant wordplay: General Sanchez is not "culpable" but merely "responsible for" everything! We will not be as charitable to this officer.

Next we turn to a special investigation ordered by Rumsfeld and headed not by another general, but by former defense secretary James Schlesinger. This committee did not conduct new, independent investigations; rather, they interviewed top military and Pentagon leaders, and their report offers us many important features for the case we are building.

The Schlesinger Report Identifies Culpability[12]

This is the final investigative report we will present. It offers valuable evidence to our case for the situational and systemic influences contributing to the abuses at Abu Ghraib. Of special interest are its specification of many shortfalls in the detention center operation, its pointing out leadership and command culpabilities, and its revelation of the cover-up of the photos of abuse by the military after Joe Darby took the photo CD to a military criminal investigator.

What struck me as most unexpected, and what was much appreciated in this report, is the section devoted to detailing the relevance of social psychological research to understanding the abuses at Abu Ghraib. Unfortunately, it is tucked away in an Appendix (G) and is therefore likely not to be widely read. This addendum to the Schlesinger Report also presents the apparent parallels between the Abu Ghraib situation and the abuses that occurred during the Stanford Prison Experiment.

Widespread Military Abuses

First, the report notes the widespread nature of "abuse" across all U.S. military facilities. (The term "torture" is never used.) At that time, November 2004, there were three hundred incidents of alleged detainee abuse in joint operation areas, with sixty-six established as "abuse" by forces at Guantánamo and in Afghanistan, and fifty-five more in Iraq. A third of these incidents were related to interrogation, and at least five deaths of detainees were reported as having happened during interrogation. Two dozen additional cases of detainee deaths were still under investigation at that time. This grim account seems to fill up the "vacuum" that Fay and Jones referred to in their report about the abuses on Tier 1A. Albeit they were the most visible instance of the abuses perpetrated by soldiers, they may have been less horrible than the murders and mayhem in other military detention facilities that we will visit later.

Major Problem Areas and Exacerbating Conditions

The Schlesinger Report identified five areas as major problems that fed into the context of the abuses. They are:

- Inadequate mission-specific training of MPs and MI soldiers
- Equipment and resources shortfalls
- Pressure on interrogators to produce "actionable intelligence" (with inexperienced, untrained personnel and detainees who were in custody for as long as ninety days before being interrogated)

- Leadership that was "weak," inexperienced, and operating within a confused, overly complex structure
- The CIA operating under its own rules, without accountability to anyone in the military command structure

The report also specifies a number of prevailing conditions that exacerbated the difficult task facing the soldiers in the Abu Ghraib Prison, notably those on the hard site in Tier 1A. It lists the following conditions that impacted the MPs and MIs on that tier:

- The fear besetting MPs given that the facility was under frequent hostile fire from mortar and rocket-propelled grenades
- Detainee escape attempts were numerous
- Several riots in the prison
- MI and MP seriously underresourced
- MI and MP lack of unit cohesion and midlevel leadership
- Reserve MI and MP units had lost senior NCOs and other personnel through rotation back to the United States and/or reassignment
- 372nd MP soldiers were not trained for prison guard duty
- Thinly stretched in dealing with the large number of detainees
- 800th MP was among the lowest units in priority and did not have the capability to overcome the shortfalls it confronted
- Lack of discipline and standards of behavior were not established or enforced
- No clear delineation of responsibility between commands and little coordination; lax and dysfunctional command structure
- Weak and ineffective leaders; top leaders failed to ensure that subordinates were properly trained and supervised
- Some medical personnel failed to report detainee abuses that they had witnessed and provided tacit approval as bystanders
- "Secretary Rumsfeld publicly declared he directed one detainee be held secretly at the request of the Director of Central Intelligence." That action provided a model of deception at the highest levels of command, which was emulated in various ways by others in command at Abu Ghraib.

What We Have Here Is Again a Failure of Leadership

Again and again, this report makes evident the total failure of leadership at every level and its contribution to the abuses by the MPs on the notorious night shift:

The aberrant behavior on the night shift in cell block 1 at Abu Ghraib would have been avoided with proper training, leadership, and oversight.

These abuses . . . represent deviant behavior and a failure of leadership and discipline.

There were other abuses not photographed during interrogation sessions and abuses during interrogation sessions elsewhere than Abu Ghraib.

Still, the abuses were not just the failure of some individuals to follow known standards. And they are more than the failure of a few leaders to enforce proper discipline. *There is both institutional and personal responsibility at higher levels.* [Italics added for emphasis.]

At the tactical level, we concur with the Jones/Fay investigations conclusion that military intelligence personnel share responsibility for the abuses at Abu Ghraib.

The unclear command structure at Abu Ghraib was further exacerbated by the confused relationships up the chain.

The unclear chain of command established by CJTF-7 combined with the poor leadership and lack of supervision contributed to the atmosphere at Abu Ghraib that allowed the abuses to take place.

At the leadership level there was friction and a lack of communication between the 800th MP Brigade and the 205th MI Brigade through the summer and fall of 2003. . . . There was a lack of discipline and standards of behavior were not established or enforced. A lax and dysfunctional command climate took hold.

There were serious lapses of leadership in both units from junior non-commissioned officers to battalion and brigade levels. The commanders at both brigades knew, or should have known, abuses were taking place and taken measures to prevent them.

By not communicating standards, policies, and plans to soldiers, their leaders conveyed a tacit approval of abusive behaviors toward prisoners.

Weak and ineffectual leadership of the Commanding General of the 800th MP Brigade, and the Commanding Officer of the 205 MI Brigade, allowed the abuses at Abu Ghraib.

We concur with the Jones finding that LTG Sanchez and MG Wojdakowski failed to insure proper staff oversight of detention and interrogation operations.

The Independent Panel finds BG Karpinski's leadership failures helped set the conditions at the prison which led to the abuses.

Cover-up of the Abuse Photos

The Schlesinger Panel also mentions in passing how the military responded to the revelation of abuse and torture in the "trophy photos." Interestingly, the committee uses language that takes all the officials off the hook for negligence and malfeasance. There was an attempt at a cover-up by downplaying the meaning and significance of this damning photographic evidence of torture and abuse:

"The officials who saw the photos on January 14, 2004, not realizing their likely significance, did not recommend the photos be shown to more senior officials." Based on the interim report to CJTF-7 and CENTCOM commanders in mid-March 2004, "their impact was not appreciated by these officers or their staff officers as indicated by the failure to transmit them in a timely fashion to more senior officials. Again, the reluctance to move bad news up the chain of command was a factor impeding notification of the Secretary of Defense.

General Richard Myers, chairman of the Joint Chiefs of Staff, tried to delay public showing of the photos by CBS Television in April 2004, so he must have realized that they had some "likely significance." Nevertheless, as I have mentioned previously, this top general felt free to say publicly that he knew these events were not "systematic" but rather were due to the criminal actions of a "few bad apples."

The Social Psychology of Inhumane Treatment of Others

Among the dozen investigations of abuses in military detention facilities, the Schlesinger Report is unique in offering a detailed consideration of the ethical issues involved and in summarizing the psychological stressors and the situational forces operating in Abu Ghraib Prison. Unfortunately, both of these special features are tucked away at the end of the report in Appendices H, "Ethics," and G, "Stressors and Social Psychology," when they should have been highlighted.

Of personal relevance is the committee's identification of parallels between the Stanford Prison Experiment and the Abu Ghraib abuses. Let's briefly review the main points raised in this section of the Schlesinger Report:

> The potential for abusive treatment of detainees during the Global War on Terrorism was entirely predictable based on a fundamental understanding of the principle of social psychology principles [sic] coupled with an awareness of numerous known environmental risk factors. . . . Findings from the field of social psychology suggest that the conditions of war and the dynamics of detainee operations carry inherent risks for human mistreatment, and therefore must be approached with great caution and careful planning and training.

However, the report noted that most military leaders are unacquainted with such important risk factors. In addition, the Schlesinger Report made clear that understanding the psychological foundations of the abusive behaviors does not excuse the perpetrators—as I have stated previously throughout this book: "Such conditions neither excuse nor absolve the individuals who engaged in deliberate immoral or illegal behaviors" even though "certain conditions heightened the possibility of abusive treatment."

The Lessons of the Stanford Prison Experiment

The Schlesinger Report boldly proclaimed that the "landmark Stanford study provides a cautionary tale for all military detention operations." In contrasting the Abu Ghraib environment to the relatively benign environment of the Stanford Prison Experiment, the report makes it evident that "in military detention operations, soldiers work under stressful combat conditions that are far from benign." The implication is that those combat conditions might be expected to generate even more extreme abuses of power by military police than were observed in our mock prison experiment. The Schlesinger Report continues to explore the central issue we have been dealing with throughout our Lucifer Effect journey.

"Psychologists have attempted to understand how and why individuals and groups who usually act humanely can sometimes act otherwise in certain circumstances." Among the concepts the report outlined to help explain why abusive behaviors occur among ordinarily humane individuals are the following: deindividuation, dehumanization, enemy image, groupthink, moral disengagement, social facilitation, and other environmental factors.

One such environmental factor singled out was the widespread practice of stripping detainees. "The removal of clothing as an interrogation technique evolved into something much broader, resulting in the practice of groups of detainees being kept naked for extended periods of time at Abu Ghraib." In its very sensitive analysis of why this practice of enforced nakedness played a causal role in the abuses of detainees by MPs and others in Tier 1A, the Schlesinger Report noted that the initial intention was to make detainees feel more vulnerable and to become more compliant with interrogators. However, it describes how this tactic eventually fostered dehumanizing conditions on that tier.

Over time, "this practice is likely to have had a psychological impact on guards and interrogators as well. The wearing of clothes is an inherently social practice, and therefore the stripping away of clothing may have had the unintended consequence of dehumanizing detainees in the eyes of those who interacted with them. . . . Dehumanization lowers moral and cultural barriers that usually preclude . . . the abusive treatment of others."

Common to these investigative reports, and the others not included here, are two key elements: they specify a variety of situational and environmental contributors to the abuses at Abu Ghraib; they also identify many systemic and structural contributors to those abuses. However, because top military brass or the secretary of defense, Donald Rumsfeld, commissioned them, the authors of these dozen reports stop short of attributing blame to higher levels in the chain of command.

For a clearer focus on that bigger picture, we leave this evidentiary foundation for our case and turn next to a recent report from Human Rights Watch, the largest such organization that works to defend human rights worldwide. (See www.hrw.org.)

HUMAN RIGHTS WATCH REPORT:
"GETTING AWAY WITH TORTURE?"[13]

"Getting Away with Torture?" is the provocative title of the Human Rights Watch (HRW) report (April 2005), which stresses the need for a truly independent investigation of the many abuses, tortures, and murders of prisoners by U.S. military and civilian personnel. It calls for an investigation of all those who were the architects of such policies that have led to wanton violations of human rights.

We can think of the torture dungeon at Abu Ghraib and similar facilities at Gitmo and other military prisons in Afghanistan and Iraq as having been designed by the senior "architects" Bush, Cheney, Rumsfeld, and Tenet. Next came the "justifiers," the lawyers who came up with new language and concepts that legalized "torture" in new ways and means—the president's legal counselors Alberto Gonzales, John You, Jay Bybee, William Taft, and John Ashcroft. The "foremen" on the torture construction job were the military leaders, such as Generals Miller, Sanchez, Karpinski, and their underlings. Finally, came the technicians, the grunts in charge of carrying out the daily labor of coercive interrogation, abuse, and torture—the soldiers in military intelligence, CIA operatives, civilian contract and military interrogators, translators, medics, and military police, including Chip Frederick and his night shift buddies.

Shortly after the photographic revelations of abuses at Abu Ghraib, President Bush vowed that the "wrongdoers will be brought to justice."[14] However, the HRW report points out that only the lowly MPs were brought to justice and that none of those who created the policies and provided the ideology and permission for those abuses to take place ever were. "In the intervening months," the HRW report concludes:

> It has become clear that torture and abuse have taken place not solely at Abu Ghraib but rather in dozens of detention facilities worldwide, that in many cases the abuse resulted in death or severe trauma, and that a good number of the victims were civilians with no connection to al-Qaeda or terrorism. There is also evidence of abuse at controlled "secret locations" abroad and of authorities sending suspects to third-country dungeons around the world where torture was likely to occur. To date, however, the only wrongdoers being brought to justice are those at the bottom of the chain-of-command. The evidence demands more. Yet a wall of impunity surrounds the architects of the policies responsible for the larger pattern of abuses.
>
> As this report shows, evidence is mounting that high-ranking civilian and military leaders—including Secretary of Defense Donald Rumsfeld, former CIA Director George Tenet, Lieutenant General Ricardo Sanchez, formerly the top commander in Iraq, and Major General Geoffrey Miller, the

former commander of the prison camp at Guantánamo Bay, Cuba—made decisions and issued policies that facilitated serious and widespread violations of the law. The circumstances strongly suggest that they either knew or should have known that such violations took place because of their actions. There is also mounting data that, when presented with evidence that abuse was in fact taking place, they failed to act to stem the abuse.

The coercive methods approved by senior officials and widely employed over the last three years include tactics that the United States has repeatedly condemned as barbarity and torture when practiced by others. Even the Army field manual condemns some of these methods as torture.

Although much relevant evidence remains secret, a series of revelations over the past twelve months, brought together here, already makes a compelling case for a thorough, genuinely independent investigation of what top officials did, what they knew, and how they responded when they became aware of the widespread nature of the abuses.

As upsetting as were the images of abuse and torture by the Tier 1A night shift MPs, they pale in comparison to the many murders of detainees by soldiers, CIA, and other civilian personnel. "If the United States is to wipe out the stain of Abu Ghraib, it needs to investigate those at the top who ordered or condoned abuse and come clean on what the president has authorized," said Reed Brody, special counsel for Human Rights Watch. He adds, that "Washington must repudiate, once and for all, the mistreatment of detainees in the name of the war on terror."[15]

Many Abusers, Few Punished, Officers Get Free Ride

Let's set the record straight on the extent of abuses of detainees in Iraq, Afghanistan, and Guantánamo Bay, Cuba. A recent Army statement indicates that more than 600 accusations of abuse of detainees have been reported since October 2001. Of those, 190 have never been investigated or there is no known investigation of them—the "ghost abusers." At least 410 other accusations have been investigated with the following consequences: 150 faced disciplinary action, 79 were court-martialed, 54 were found guilty, 10 were sentenced to more than one year in prison, 30 were sentenced to less than one year, 14 got no prison time, 10 were acquitted, 15 cases are still pending or charges were dropped, 71 were administratively disciplined or nonjudicially disciplined. If one does the addition, that leaves at least 260 investigations closed or whose ongoing status was unclear as of April 2006, the time the report was published.[16] One of the dog handlers, Sergeant Michael Smith, was sentenced to six months in prison for using his unmuzzled dog to torment prisoners. He maintained that he had been "following orders to soften up prisoners for interrogation." He is also reported to have said that "Soldiers are not supposed to be soft and cuddly," and he was not that.[17]

As of April 10, 2006, there was no evidence that the military has even attempted to prosecute a single officer under the doctrine of command responsibility for personally directed abuses or for those of their subordinates. In the detailed report of all investigated abuses only five officers have been criminally charged, none under the command responsibility doctrine. One Army captain was charged with dereliction of duty for the deaths of two detainees in Afghanistan; the charges were dropped. A Navy lieutenant was charged with assault and dereliction of duty in the death of a ghost detainee Manadel al-Jamadi; he was acquitted. Three other officers, a lieutenant, a captain, and a major, were convicted at court-martial of detainee abuse, either directly participating in abusing prisoners or ordering their troops to do so; one received a sentence of only 45 days in prison, another got two months, and the third was discharged with no prison sentence at all. The military command goes soft on its errant officers by using nonjudicial hearings and administrative reprimands that are usually meant for minor offenses and carry weak sentences. This is so even in more than 70 cases of serious criminal abuse, including 10 homicides and 20 assault cases. Such leniency extends also to CIA operatives in at least 10 abuse cases and 20 civilian contractors working for the CIA or the military. Thus, it becomes evident that detainee abuse was widespread far beyond Abu Ghraib and further that there is a general failure of command responsibility in any of the many cases of abuse and torture. (See the Notes for access to the full report of the abuses and failures of prosecution of guilty officers.[18])

HRW Goes up the Command Chain

After its detailed documentation of the widespread abuses perpetrated by soldiers in MP and MI brigades, the CIA, and civilian contractors serving as interrogators, the HRW goes nearly all the way up the chain of command in its accusation of criminal responsibility for war crimes and torture:

> While there are obviously steep political obstacles in the way of investigating a sitting defense secretary and other high-ranking officials, the nature of crimes is so serious, and mounting evidence of wrongdoing is now so voluminous, that it would be an abdication of responsibility for the United States not to push this to the next level. Unless those who designed or authorized the illegal policies are held to account, all the protestations of "disgust" at the Abu Ghraib photos by President George W. Bush and others will be meaningless. If there is no real accountability for these crimes, for years to come the perpetrators of atrocities around the world will point to their treatment of prisoners to deflect criticism of their own conduct. Indeed, when a government as dominant and influential as the United States openly defies laws against torture, it virtually invites others to do the same. Washington's much-needed credibility as a proponent of human

rights was damaged by the torture revelations and will be further damaged if torture continues to be followed by complete impunity for the policy-makers.[19]

Stripping Away Immunity for the Architects of Illegal Policy

Both U.S. and international law recognize the principle of "command responsibility" or "superior responsibility," by which individuals in civilian or military authority may be criminally liable for crimes committed by those under their command. Three elements are required for such liability to be established. First, there must be a clear superior-subordinate relationship. Second, the superior must have known or had reason to know that the subordinate was about to commit a crime or had already committed a crime. Third, the superior must have failed to take necessary and reasonable measures to prevent the crime or to punish the perpetrator.

War crimes and torture are punishable under the terms of the War Crimes Act of 1996, the Anti-Torture Act of 1996, and the Uniform Code of Military Justice (UCMJ). Human Rights Watch goes on record arguing that a *prima facie* case exists that warrants the opening of criminal investigations with respect to four officials: Secretary of Defense Donald Rumsfeld, former CIA director George Tenet, Lieutenant General Ricardo Sanchez, and Major General Geoffrey Miller.

Here I can only outline some of the justifications for holding each of these officials liable for the acts of torture and abuse committed under their watch—a full description and supporting evidence is provided in the HRW report.

On Trial: Secretary of Defense Donald Rumsfeld

Rumsfeld told the Senate Armed Services Committee: "These events occurred on my watch. As Secretary of Defense, I am accountable for them. I take full responsibility."[20]

HRW asserts that "Secretary Rumsfeld should be investigated for war crimes and torture by US troops in Afghanistan, Iraq, and Guantánamo under the doctrine of 'command responsibility.' Secretary Rumsfeld created the conditions for troops to commit war crimes and torture by sidelining and disparaging the Geneva Conventions.[21] He did so by approving interrogation techniques that violated the Geneva Conventions as well as the Convention against Torture and by approving the hiding of detainees from the International Committee of the Red Cross." HRW continues:

> From the earliest days of the war in Afghanistan, Secretary Rumsfeld was on notice through briefings, ICRC reports, human rights reports, and press accounts that troops were committing war crimes, including acts of torture. However, there is no evidence that he ever exerted his authority and warned that the mistreatment of prisoners must stop. Had he done so, many of the crimes committed by forces could have been avoided.

An investigation would also determine whether the illegal interrogation techniques that Secretary Rumsfeld approved for Guantánamo were actually used to inflict inhuman treatment on detainees there before he rescinded his approval to use them without requesting his permission. It would also examine whether Secretary Rumsfeld approved a secret program that encouraged physical coercion and sexual humiliation of Iraqi prisoners, as alleged by the journalist Seymour Hersh. If either were true, Secretary Rumsfeld might also, in addition to command responsibility, incur liability as the instigator of crimes against detainees.

Rumsfeld authorized a list of interrogation methods that violated the Geneva Convention and the Convention against Torture used on detainees at Guantánamo, which then migrated to other military prisons in Afghanistan and Iraq. Among his directives for preparing detainees for interrogation were the following:

The use of stress positions (like standing) for a maximum of four hours in isolation up to 30 days

The detainee may also have a hood placed over his head during transportation and questioning

Deprivation of light and auditory stimuli

Removal of all comfort items (including religious items)

Forced grooming (shaving of facial hair, etc)

Removal of clothing

Using detainees' individual phobias (such as fear of dogs) to induce stress

In addition, standard operating procedures advocated exposing detainees to extremes of heat, cold, light, and noise.

The Department of Defense was repeatedly warned about torture and abuse of detainees by the International Committee of the Red Cross (ICRC) in May and July 2003 (prior to the public exposé at Abu Ghraib) and again in February 2004.[22]

The ICRC reported on hundreds of allegations of prisoner abuse at a number of military venues, making repeated requests to take immediate steps to correct these abuses. These concerns were ignored, the abuses worsened, and inspections by the ICRC were curtailed. In its February 2004 report, presented confidentially to officials of the Coalition forces, the following violations against "protected persons deprived of their liberty" during their internment by Coalition forces, the ICRC highlighted the following:

- Brutality upon capture and initial custody, sometimes causing death or serious injury
- Physical or psychological coercion during interrogation to secure information

- Prolonged solitary confinement in cells devoid of light
- Excessive and disproportionate use of force resulting in death or injury during their period of internment

The ICRC report concludes with a stern warning that the secretary of defense should have heeded but apparently did not: "The practices described in this [twenty-four-page] report are prohibited under International Humanitarian Law. They warrant serious attention by CF [Correctional Facilities]. In particular, CF should review their policies and practices, take corrective action and improve the treatment of prisoners of war and other protected persons under their authority."

Amnesty International has also weighed in with its own in-depth report on detention and torture in Iraq. It calls upon the Iraqi, U.S., and U.K. authorities to "take urgent, concrete steps to ensure that the fundamental human rights of all detainees in Iraq are respected. In particular, these authorities must urgently put in place adequate safeguards to protect detainees from torture or ill-treatment."[23]

Mark Danner, a journalism professor at the University of California, Berkeley, reviewed all the relevant documents for his book *Torture and Truth: America, Abu Ghraib and the War on Terror.* Danner concludes from his detailed investigation that "When you read the documents, Secretary of Defense Donald Rumsfeld was involved very personally in approving procedures that went beyond the line of what is allowed in military law, and for that matter, in civilian law, when it comes to what can be done to prisoners."[24]

On Trial: Former CIA Director George Tenet

HRW accuses former CIA director George Tenet of a variety of violations. Under George Tenet's direction, and reportedly with his specific authorization, the CIA tortured detainees through "waterboarding" (the near drowning of a suspect) and by withholding their medicines. Other tactics reportedly used by the CIA include feigning suffocation, making prisoners hold "stress positions," light and noise bombardment, sleep deprivation, and making detainees believe they are in the hands of foreign governments known to torture routinely. Under Director Tenet, the CIA "rendered" detainees to other governments, which tortured the detainees. Under Director Tenet's direction, the CIA also put detainees beyond the protection of the law, in secret locations in which they were rendered completely defenseless, with no resource or remedy whatsoever, with no contact with the outside world, and completely at the mercy of their captors. These detainees, in long-term incommunicado detention, have effectively been "disappeared."

Recall that the Fay/Jones investigation concluded that "CIA detention and interrogation practices led to a loss of accountability, abuse, reduced interagency cooperation and an unhealthy mystique that further poisoned the atmosphere at Abu Ghraib." In effect, the CIA operated under its own rules and beyond the law.

Under Director Tenet, the CIA also developed the widespread practice of using "ghost detainees." How many? We will never know for sure, but General Paul Kern, the senior officer who oversaw the Fay/Jones inquiry, told the Senate Armed Services Committee, "The number [of ghost detainees] is in the dozens, perhaps up to 100." The CIA kept a number of detainees off the books at Abu Ghraib, hiding them from the ICRC.

Army Lieutenant Colonel Steven Jordan, who was second in command of the intelligence-gathering effort at Abu Ghraib while the abuse was occurring, told military investigators that "other government agencies" and a secretive elite task force "routinely brought in detainees for a short period of time" and that the detainees were held without internment numbers, with their names kept off the books. Such practices are violations of international law.[25]

The "Ice Man" Goeth

The Fay/Jones Report mentions one of these "ghosted" cases: In November 2003 an Iraqi detainee by the name of Manadel al-Jamadi, brought to the prison by Navy SEALs and interrogated by a CIA agent, was never formally registered. Jamadi was "tortured to death," but the cause of his death was concealed in a most unusual way.

The investigative reporter Jane Mayer has shed light on the sinister role the CIA played in this homicide and its grisly cover-up. Her fascinating account "A Deadly Interrogation" in *The New Yorker* magazine (November 14, 2005) raises the question "Can the CIA legally kill a prisoner?"

The al-Jamadi case is especially important for us in our effort to understand the behavioral context at Abu Ghraib in which Chip Frederick and his other "rogue soldiers" worked. They were enmeshed in an environment where they observed ghost detainees routinely being brutalized, tortured, and some even murdered. They witnessed perpetrators literally "getting away with murder."

By comparison with what happened to the ghost detainee Manadel al-Jamadi, the so-called Ice Man, what they did to the run-of-the-mill detainees must have seemed much more like just "fun and games." They knew him to have been battered, suffocated to death, and then iced away.

Al-Jamadi was a so-called high-value target for interrogation because he allegedly supplied explosives to insurgents. A team of Navy SEALs captured him at his home outside Baghdad on November 4, 2003, at 2 A.M. He ended up with a black eye, a cut on his face, and perhaps half a dozen fractured ribs following a violent struggle. The SEALs turned al-Jamadi over to CIA custody at Abu Ghraib for interrogation, led by Mark Swanner. This CIA operative, accompanied by a translator, took al-Jamadi into a holding cell in the prison, stripped him naked, and began yelling at him to tell him where the weapons were.

According to Mayer's *New Yorker* story, Swanner told the MPs to take the prisoner to Tier 1 Alpha, into the shower room for interrogation. Two of the MPs were ordered (by this anonymous civilian) to shackle the prisoner to the wall, even

though he was by now totally passive. They were told to hang him from his arms in a torture position known as "Palestine Hanging." (First practiced during the Spanish Inquisition, when it was known as *strappado*.) After they left the room, one MP recalled, "we heard a lot of screaming." Less than an hour later, Manadel al-Jamadi was dead.

Walter Diaz, the MP on guard duty, said that there was no need to hang him up like that, given that he was handcuffed and offered no resistance. When the MPs were told by Swanner to take the dead man down from the wall, "blood came gushing out of his nose and mouth, as if a faucet had been turned on," Diaz reported.

Now the problem for the CIA was what to do with the victim's body. Captain Donald Reese, the MP commander, and Colonel Thomas Pappas, the MI commander, were alerted to this "unfortunate incident" on their shift. They needn't have worried, because the CIA took matters into its own stealthy hands. Al-Jamadi was kept in the shower room until the next morning, packed in ice and bound with clear tape to retard decomposition of the corpse. The next day a medic inserted an IV into the "Ice Man's" arm and had him carried out of the prison on a stretcher as if he were alive but merely ill, so as not to upset the other detainees, who were told he had had a heart attack. A local taxi driver carted the corpse away to an unknown destination. All evidence was destroyed, and there was no paper trail because al-Jamadi had never officially been registered. The Navy SEALS were exonerated for their part in manhandling al-Jamadi, the medic was not identified, and, several years later, Mark Swanner continues to work for the CIA, with no criminal charge against him! Case almost closed.

Among all the other horror images in Corporal Graner's digital camera were several photos of that very same "Ice Man" that were recorded for posterity. First, there was a photo of an attractive, smiling Specialist Sabrina Harman bending over al-Jamadi's battered body with a thumbs-up sign. Then Graner got into the mix to add his approving smile to hers, before the "Ice Man" melted away. For sure, Chip and the other night shift MPs knew what had just gone down. If such things could happen and be so deftly handled, then the dungeon of Tier 1 Alpha was the "Romper Room," where anything went. Had they not taken those photos and had Darby not sounded the alarm, the world might never have learned what had happened in that once secret place.

Nonetheless, the CIA continues unshackled in any way by laws that should restrain its agents from torturing and murdering people, even in its global war on terrorism. *Ironically, Swanner has admitted that he obtained* no *useful information from this murdered ghost detainee.*

This involvement of the CIA in torture is nothing new and is evident in the analysis by the historian Alfred McCoy in his recent book documenting its role from the Cold War to the Terror War. According to McCoy, the shocking photographs of abuse from Abu Ghraib are nothing new. In his view:

> If we look closely at these grainy images, we can see the geneology of CIA torture techniques, from their origins in the 1950s to their present-day perfection. Indeed, the photographs from Iraq illustrate standard interrogation practice inside the global gulag of secret CIA prisons that have operated, on executive authority, since the start of the war on terror. These photos, and later investigations they prompted, offer telltale signs that the CIA was both the lead agency at Abu Ghraib and the source of systematic tortures practiced in Guantánamo, Afghanistan, and Iraq. In this light, the nine soldiers court-martialed for the abuse at Abu Ghraib were simply following orders. Responsibility for their actions lies much higher, much higher, up the chain of command.[26]

On Trial: Lieutenant General Ricardo Sanchez

Like Rumsfeld, Lieutenant General Ricardo Sanchez also loudly acknowledged his responsibility: "As senior commander in Iraq, I accept responsibility for what happened at Abu Ghraib."[27] However, such responsibility should bear appropriate consequences and not be employed as photo op public gesturing. Human Rights Watch includes this top commander among the big four who should stand trial for torture and war crimes. Its report states:

> Lt. Gen. Sanchez should be investigated for war crimes and torture either as a principal or under the doctrine of "command responsibility." Gen. Sanchez authorized interrogation methods that violate the Geneva Conventions and the Convention against Torture. According to Human Rights

Watch, he knew, or should have known, that torture and war crimes were committed by troops under his direct command, but failed to take effective measures to stop these acts.

I am putting General Sanchez on trial in this book because of the fact that, in the words of the HRW report, "he promulgated interrogation rules and techniques that violated the Geneva Conventions and the Convention against Torture, and further that he knew or should have known about torture and war crimes committed by troops under his command."

Given the lack of "actionable intelligence" being gathered at Guantánamo Bay Prison despite months of interrogations, there was pressure on everyone to get the goods on the terrorists, and to do so immediately, by all means necessary. Mark Danner reported an e-mail sent by the military intelligence officer Captain William Ponce to his colleagues, urging them to provide an "interrogation wish list" by mid-August 2003. The captain infused his message with an ominous foreshadowing of what was to come at Abu Ghraib: "The gloves are coming off gentlemen regarding these detainees." His message continued, "Col Boltz [the second-ranking MI commander in Iraq] has made it clear that we want these individuals broken. Casualties are mounting and we need to start gathering info to help protect our fellow soldiers from any further attacks."[28]

General Geoffrey Miller, then recently put in charge of the detention facilities at Gitmo, headed a visiting team of specialists to Iraq from August to September 2003. His mission was to spread the new get-tough interrogation policies to Generals Sanchez, Karpinski, and other officers. "General Miller put his finger in Sanchez' chest and told him he wanted the information," according to Karpinski.[29] Miller was able to push these other officers around only with obvious support from Rumsfeld and other high-ranking generals, based on his so-called successes at Gitmo.

Sanchez formalized his rules for interrogation in a memo on September 14, 2003, introducing more extreme measures than had been practiced by his MPs and MIs.[30] Some of his explicitly stated goals were to "create fear, disorient detainees and capture shock." These newly approved techniques that came by way of Rumsfeld via Miller, included:

Presence of Military Working Dog: Exploits Arab fear of dogs while maintaining security during interrogations. Dogs will be muzzled and under control of . . . handler at all times to prevent contact with detainee.

Sleep Management: Detainee provided minimum 4 hours of sleep per 24 hour period, not to exceed 72 continuous hours.

Yelling, Loud Music and Light Control: Used to create fear, disorient detainee and prolong capture shock. Volume controlled to prevent injury.

Stress Positions: Use of physical postures (sitting, standing, kneeling, prone, etc.) for no more than 1 hour per use. Use of technique(s) will not exceed 4 hours and adequate rest between use of each position will be provided.

False Flag: Convincing the detainee that individuals from a country other than the United States are interrogating him.

The Schlesinger Report indicated that a dozen of Sanchez's techniques went beyond those acceptable in Army Field Manual 34-52 and were even more extreme than those that had been approved for Guantánamo. Sanchez's memo was released publicly in March 2005 in response to a FDIA lawsuit. It came about a year after General Sanchez had lied to Congress in sworn testimony (in May 2004) that he had never ordered or approved the use of intimidation by dogs, sleep deprivation, excessive noise, or inducing fear. He should be tried for all the reasons outlined above.

One soldier's view about the extent to which there was direct involvement of the military command in directing abuses against detainees comes from Joe Darby, our heroic whistleblower: "Nobody in command knew about the abuse, because nobody in command cared enough to find out. That was the real problem. The entire command structure was oblivious, living in their own little worlds. So it wasn't a conspiracy—it was negligence, plain and simple. They were fucking clueless."[31] General Sanchez has been forced to retire early (November 1, 2006) by the top military brass because of his role in the Abu Ghraib scandal. He admitted, "That's the key reason, the sole reason, that I was forced to retire." (*Guardian Unlimited*, November 2, 2006, "U.S. General Says Abu Ghraib Forced Him Out.")

On Trial: Major General Geoffrey Miller

Human Rights Watch asserts that "Major General Geoffrey Miller, as commander at the tightly-controlled prison camp at Guantánamo Bay, Cuba, should be investigated for his potential responsibility in the war crimes and acts of torture committed against detainees there." Furthermore, he "knew or should have known that troops under his command were committing war crimes and acts of torture against detainees at Guantánamo." Additionally, "Gen. Miller may have proposed interrogation methods for Iraq that were the proximate cause of the torture and war crimes committed at Abu Ghraib."

General Miller was commander of Joint Task Force–Guantánamo (JTF–GTMO) from November 2002 until April 2004, when he became the deputy commanding general of Detention Operations in Iraq, the position he held until 2006. He was sent to Gitmo to replace General Rick Baccus, who higher-ups considered was "coddling" prisoners by insisting that the Geneva Conventions guidelines be strictly followed. In short order, "Camp X-Ray" was transformed into "Camp Delta" with 625 inmates, 1,400 MIs and MPs, and lots of tension.

Miller was an innovator and developed specialized interrogation teams that for the first time integrated military intelligence (MI) personnel with the military police (MP) guard force—blurring a line that had previously been impermeable in the Army. To get inside the heads of the prisoners, Miller relied on experts. "He brought in behavioral scientists, who were psychologists and psychiatrists [both civilian and military]. And they were looking for psychological vulnerabilities, soft spots, ways to manipulate the detainees to kind of get them to cooperate, and looking for sort of psychic vulnerabilities and cultural vulnerabilities."[32]

Using prisoners' medical records, Miller's interrogators tried to induce depression, to disorient detainees, and to break them. The prisoners resisted: there were hunger strikes, at least fourteen prisoners committed suicide early on, and over the next few years, several hundred prisoners attempted suicide.[33] Recently, three Gitmo detainees committed suicide by hanging themselves in their cells with bedsheets; none had been formally charged after having been held there for many years. Instead of recognizing such acts as signs of desperation, one government spokesperson derided them as a public relations move to gain attention.[34] A Navy rear admiral contended that they had not been acts of desperation but rather "an act of asymmetrical warfare against us."

Miller's new interrogation teams were encouraged to get more aggressive, given Secretary Rumsfeld's official authorization of the harshest techniques ever sanctioned for use by U.S. soldiers. Abu Ghraib was to become Miller's new experimental laboratory to test his hypotheses about the means necessary to get "actionable intelligence" from resistant prisoners. Rumsfeld went to Gitmo with his aide Stephen Cambone to meet with Miller and be sure they were all playing the same game.

Recall that General Karpinski said that Miller told her, "You have to treat the prisoners like dogs. If . . . they believe that they're any different than dogs, you have effectively lost control of your interrogation from the very start. . . . And it works. This is what we do down at Guantánamo Bay."[35]

Karpinski is also on record as saying that Miller "came up there and told me that he was going to "Gitmo-ize" the detention operation (at Abu Ghraib)."[36] Colonel Pappas reported that Miller told him the use of dogs at Gitmo had proven effective in setting the atmosphere for getting information from prisoners and that the use of dogs "with or without a muzzle" was okay.[37]

To be certain that his orders were followed, Miller wrote a report and saw to it that his team left behind a compact disc with detailed instructions to be followed. General Sanchez then authorized his tough new rules, which elaborated on many of the techniques being used in Guantánamo. The veteran Army general Paul Kern made evident the problems created by such application of Gitmo-approved tactics to Abu Ghraib: "I think it became confusing. I mean, we found in computers in Abu Ghraib SECDEF [Secretary of Defense Rumsfeld's] memos that were written for Guantánamo, not for Abu Ghraib. And that caused confusion."[38] For all the reasons outlined above, General Geoffrey Miller is added to our list of defendants on trial for their crimes against humanity.[39]

In its accusations, Human Rights Watch stopped short of going up to the pinnacle of system responsibility for the abuses and torture at Abu Ghraib: Vice President Dick Cheney and President George W. Bush. I will not be so hesitant. A bit later, I will add these two to our list of defendants put on trial here. They will be accused for their role in setting the agenda that redefined the nature of torture, suspended protections afforded prisoners under international law, and encouraged the CIA to engage in a series of illegal and lethal tactics because of their obsession with the so-called war on terror.

However, first we need to explore further the question of whether the Tier 1A abuses were an isolated incident by those few rotten apples or whether their offensive behavior was part of a broader pattern of tacitly approved, and widely practiced, abuses by many in the military and civilian cadre involved with capture, detention, and interrogation of suspected insurgents. My contention will be that this barrel of apples began rotting from the top down.

TORTURE, TORTURE EVERYWHERE, WITH MAYHEM ON THE SIDE

As he did on the day after the abuse photos were first revealed publicly, General Richard Myers, the Joint Chiefs chairman, continues to deny any systemwide involvement in the abuses; instead he continues to lay all the blame on the "Abu Ghraib Seven MPs." He said publicly (on August 25, 2005), "I think we've had at least fifteen investigations on Abu Ghraib, and we've dealt with that. I mean, just a little snapshot—if it was only the night shift at Abu Ghraib, which it was, it was only a small section of the guards that participated in this, it's a pretty good clue that it wasn't a more widespread problem."[40]

Did he ever read any of those reports? From only the sections of the independent investigative reports that I have summarized here, it could not be clearer that the abuses went well beyond those few MPs emerging in the images from Tier 1A. Those investigations implicate the military leadership, civilian interrogators, military intelligence, and the CIA in creating the conditions that spawned the abuses. Even worse, they participated in other, even more deadly abuses.

You will recall that the Schlesinger panel detailed fifty-five cases of detainee abuse throughout Iraq, as well as twenty instances of detainee deaths still under slow investigation. The Taguba Report found numerous instances of wanton criminal abuses constituting "*systematic* and illegal abuse of detainees" at Abu Ghraib (my italics). Another Pentagon report documented forty-four allegations of such war crimes at Abu Ghraib. The International Committee of the Red Cross told the government that its treatment of detainees in many of its military prisons has involved psychological and physical coercion that is "tantamount to torture."

Further, it reports that such methods being used by interrogators at Abu Ghraib "appeared to be part of the standard operating procedures by military intelligence personnel to obtain confessions and extract information." And we have just reviewed the more recent statistics of more than six hundred cases of abuse reported throughout the U.S. military prisons in Iraq, Afghanistan, and Cuba. Does this sound like only "a few bad apples" in one bad dungeon, in one bad prison?

Revelations of Widespread Prisoner Abuses *Before* Abu Ghraib

Although both military and civilian administrative commands sought to isolate the abuses and tortures in Iraq to an aberration of a few bad soldiers working the night shift in Tier 1A in the fall of 2003, new Army documents belie such assertions. On May 2, 2006, the ACLU released Army documents revealing that senior government officials were aware of extreme cases of detainee abuse in Iraq and Afghanistan two weeks *before* the Abu Ghraib scandal broke. An information paper entitled "Allegations of Detainee Abuse in Iraq and Afghanistan," dated April 2, 2004, detailed sixty-two ongoing investigations of abuse and *homicides* of detainees by U.S. forces.

Cases include assaults, punching, kicking and beating, mock executions, sexual assault of a female detainee, threatening to kill an Iraqi child to "send a message to other Iraqis," stripping detainees, beating them and shocking them with a blasting device, throwing rocks at handcuffed Iraqi children, choking detainees with knots of their scarves, and interrogations at gunpoint. At least twenty-six cases involved detainee deaths. Some of the cases had already gone through a court-martial proceeding. The abuses went beyond Abu Ghraib and touched Camp Cropper, Camp Bucca, and other detention centers in Mosul, Samarra, Baghdad, and Tikrit in Iraq, as well as Orgun-E in Afghanistan (see Notes for the full report by the ACLU).[41]

A Pentagon report of the twelfth investigation into military abuses, led by Army brigadeer general Richard Formica, noted that U.S. Special Operations troops continued to use a set of harsh, unauthorized interrogation tactics against detainees during a four-month period in early 2004. This was long *after* the 2003 Abu Ghraib abuses, and after approval for their use had been rescinded. Some were given only crackers and water for as long as seventeen days, kept naked, locked in cells so small they could neither stand or lie down for a week, frozen, deprived of sleep, and subjected to sensory overload. Despite these findings, none of the soldiers received even a reprimand. Formica believed the abuse was not "deliberate" or due to "personal failure," but to "inadequate policy failure." He also added to this whitewash that, based on his observations, "none of the detainees seemed to be the worse for wear because of the treatment."[42] *Amazing!*

Marines Murder Iraqi Civilians in Cold Blood

I have focused on understanding the nature of the bad barrel of prisons that can corrupt good guards, but there is a larger, more deadly barrel, that of war. In all wars, at all times, in every country, wars transform ordinary, even good men into killers. That is what soldiers are trained to do, to kill their designated enemies. However, under the extreme stresses of combat conditions, with fatigue, fear, anger, hatred, and revenge at full throttle, men can lose their moral compass and go beyond killing enemy combatants. Unless military discipline is strictly maintained and every soldier knows he bears personal responsibility for his actions, which are under surveillance by senior officers, then the furies are released in unimaginable orgies of rape and murder of civilians as well as enemy soldiers. We know such loss was true at My Lai and in other less well-known military massacres, such as those of the "Tiger Force" in Vietnam. This elite fighting unit left a seven-month-long trail of executions of unarmed civilians.[43] Sadly, the brutality of war that spills over from the battlefield to the hometown has become true again in Iraq.[44]

Military experts warn that as soldiers have to fight more against elusive enemies in asymmetrical warfare it will become increasingly difficult for them to maintain discipline under such stresses. Wartime atrocities occur in all wars and are committed by most occupying forces, even high tech ones. "Combat is about stress, and criminal behavior toward civilians is a classic combat stress symptom. If you get enough soldiers into enough combat, some of them are going to murder civilians," according to a senior official at a Washington military think tank.[45]

We must acknowledge that soldiers are well-trained killers who have successfully completed an intense learning experience in boot camp, with the battlefield as their testing ground. They must learn to suppress their prior moral training guided by the commandment "thou shalt not kill." New military training that works to rewire their brains to accept killing in wartime as a natural response is known as the science of "killology." This term, coined by retired lieutenant colonel Dave Grossman, now a West Point professor of military science, is elaborated in his book *On Killing* and in his website.[46]

However, sometimes the "science of creating killers" can get out of hand and make murder become ordinary. Consider the reactions of a twenty-one-year-old soldier who just killed a civilian in Iraq who refused to stop at a traffic check. "It was like nothing. Over here, killing people is like squashing an ant. I mean, you kill somebody, and it's like, 'All right, let's go get some pizza. I mean, I thought killing somebody would be this life-changing experience. And then I did it, and it was like, 'All right, whatever.' "[47]

On November 19, 2005, a roadside bomb went off in the town of Haditha, Iraq, killing a U.S. Marine and injuring two other soldiers. In the following hours, fifteen Iraqi civilians are reported to have been killed by an improvised explosive device, according to a Marine investigation. Case closed, as many Iraqis are killed in this way almost every day. However, a townsperson (Taher Thabet) made a videotape of the bullet-ridden bodies of the dead civilians and turned it over to the *Time* magazine bureau in Baghdad. That prompted a more serious investigation into the murders of twenty-four civilians by that Marine battalion. It appears that the Marines entered three homes and methodically killed most of the occupants, including seven children and four women, by gunshots and grenades. They also shot dead a taxi driver and four students who had stopped their taxi on the road nearby.

There was clearly an attempted cover-up by senior Marine officers when they realized that these were unprovoked murders of civilians by Marines who had abandoned the rules of engagement. In March 2006 the battalion commander and two of his company commanders were relieved of command; one said that he was a "political casualty." Several more investigations are under way at this writing and may even find more senior commanders culpable. It is important to add to this terrible tale that these Marines from the 3rd Platoon, Kilo Company, were experienced soldiers, on their second and third tour of duty. They had engaged in fierce fighting earlier in Fallujah where nearly half their buddies were killed or seriously wounded in combat. So, there was a lot of anger and feelings of revenge building up before the Haditha massacre.[48]

War is hell on soldiers, but it is always worse on civilians and especially children in battle zones, when the soldiers stray off the moral path, acting cruelly against them. In another recent incident under investigation, U.S. forces killed as many as thirteen civilians in the hamlet of Ishaqi, Iraq. Some were found tied up and shot in the head, including several children. U.S. military officials, acknowledging that "noncombatants" had been killed, called the casualties "collateral deaths" (again this is an instance of euphemistic labeling associated with moral disengagement).[49]

Imagine what happens when a senior officer gives soldiers permission to kill civilians. Four soldiers accused of killing three unarmed Iraqi men during a house raid in the city of Tikrit, Iraq, were told by their brigade commander, Colonel Michael Steele, to "kill all the male insurgents, terrorists." The soldier who reported this new rule of engagement was threatened by his colleagues if he told anyone about the shooting deaths.[50]

One of the worst horrors of war is the rape of innocent civilian women by soldiers, as was documented in the massacre of the Tutsi women by Hutu militia in Rwanda, described in chapter 1. A new allegation of similarly horrible brutality has surfaced in Iraq, where a group of U.S. soldiers (101st Airborne Division) are accused in federal court of raping a fourteen-year-old girl after killing her parents and four-year-old sister, then shooting her in the head and burning all the bodies. The evidence is clear that they intended this bloody assault by first changing out of uniform (so as not to be identified) after eyeing the young girl at their traffic checkpoint and proceeding to murder her family before abusing her. The military had initially blamed the murders on insurgents.[51]

This suspension of self-constraints against cruelty that is all too common among soldiers in combat zones is not limited to the U.S. military. British soldiers were videotaped as they beat up Iraqi youths. The cameraman, a corporal in that unit, can be heard laughing as he urges his comrades to enjoy their abuses. Obviously, the prime minister, Tony Blair, has promised a probe into what one of his military spokesmen describes as the actions limited to a "tiny number of soldiers."[52] At least he had the decency not to use the "bad apples" metaphor.

Let us next go beyond abstract generalizations, statistics, and military investigations to listen to the confessions of several U.S. Army interrogators about what they saw and what they themselves did in abusing detainees. As we will see, they go on record as reporting on the widespread abuse and patterns of torture they witnessed and which they personally practiced.

We will also briefly review the recently revealed program at Gitmo that enabled young female interrogators, nicknamed "torture chicks" by the media, to employ a variety of sexual lures in their arsenal of interrogation tactics. Their presence and tactics must have been done with commanders' approval; they did not just decide to "sex out" in Cuba on their own initiative. We will learn that not only did the lowly Army Reserve MPs on Tier 1A engage in despicable acts of abuse, but even elite soldiers and military officers performed many even more brutal acts of violence against prisoners.

Finally, we will see the scope of torture as virtually boundless, because the United States "outsources" torture to other countries in programs known as "renditions," "extraordinary renditions," and even "reverse renditions." We will discover that not only did Saddam torture his people, the United States did so, and the new Iraqi regime also has been torturing its countrymen and women in secret prisons throughout Iraq. One can only feel sorrow for Iraqis when their torturers come packaged in so many different guises.

Next Up: Witnesses for the Prosecution

Specialist Anthony Lagouranis (retired) was an Army interrogator for five years (2001 to 2005) with a tour of duty in Iraq during 2004. Although first stationed at Abu Ghraib, Lagouranis was assigned to a special intelligence-gathering unit that serviced detention facilities throughout Iraq. When he talks about the "culture of abuse" that permeated interrogations throughout Iraq, his database is countrywide and not Tier 1A–specific.[53]

Then there is Sergeant Roger Brokaw (retired), who worked at Abu Ghraib for six months as an interrogator, starting in spring 2003. Brokaw reports that few of those with whom he talked, maybe only 2 percent, were dangerous or were insurgents; most had been brought in or singled out by Iraqi police who had a grudge against somebody or simply didn't like him. Both men say that one of the reasons intelligence gathering was so ineffective was that detention facilities were overflowing with people who had no good information to give. Many had been picked up in roundups of all the males in entire families in an area of insurgent activity. Because there were relatively few trained interrogators or translators available, by the time these detainees were interviewed any information they might have had was cold and outdated.

A lot of frustration arose from expending so much effort for so few solid results. That frustration also led to a lot of aggression, as the old frustration-aggression hypothesis would predict. Time was running; the insurgency was growing; pressure was building from the military commanders, who were feeling the heat from their civilian bosses up the command chain. Extraction of information was vital.

Brokaw: "Because they were picking up people for anything, just the drop of a hat. There was [*sic*] quotas, quotas on interrogating so many people per week and sending reports up the chain of command."

Lagouranis: "We rarely got good intel from the prisoners, and I blame that on that we were getting prisoners who were innocent and didn't have intel to give us."

Brokaw: "And ninety-eight percent of the people I talked to had no reason being in there. They would just take them at face value and go in and raid this house and pull these people out and throw them in the detention camps. Colonel Pappas [said], there was pressure from him to get information. Get information. 'Let's get this information, save another GI's life. If we have, you know, if we find these weapons, if we find these insurgents, we'll save soldiers' lives.' And I think that led to this idea of condoning whatever the interrogators or the MPs wanted to do to these people to soften them up."

Brokaw also reported that the message about "taking the gloves off" spiraled down the chain of command to give meaning to that boxing metaphor.[54]

Brokaw: "I heard the phrase, 'We're going to take the gloves off.' Colonel Jordan said that one night in one of our meetings. 'We're taking the gloves off. We're going to show these people, you know, that we're in charge.' And he was talking about the detainees."

As the insurgency against the Coalition forces became ever more lethal and extensive, pressure on the MIs and MPs to get that elusive actionable intelligence was ever greater. An anonymous interviewee told PBS *Frontline* (October 18, 2005):

"Most of the abuses around Iraq are not photographed, and so they'll never get any outrage out of it. And this makes it even harsher because around Iraq, in the back of a Humvee or in a shipping container, there's no camera. There are no cameras. There are [*sic*] no still photography. There's no video cameras. And there's no one looking over your shoulder, so you can do anything you want."

Lagouranis added some details: "Now it's all over Iraq. It's—as I said, people are torturing people in their homes. The infantry units are torturing people in their homes. They were using things like, as I said, burns. They would smash people's feet with the back of an axe-head. They would break bones, ribs. You know, that was—that was serious stuff." He added, "When the units would go out into people's homes and do these raids, they would just stay in the house and torture them." Brokaw witnessed some of the same abuses: "I saw black eyes and fat lips, and some of them had to be treated for bad abrasions on legs and arms."

Just how far were MIs and MPs allowed to go in their quest for information?

Lagouranis: "Part of it is, they were trying to get information, but part of it is also just pure sadism. You just kept wanting to push and push and push and see how far you could go. It's natural for people to reach an intense level of frustration when you're sitting there with somebody that you feel you have total control over and total power over, and you can't get him to do what you want. And that you do that all day, every day. And at some point, you want to start raising the stakes."

What happens when you add high fear and revenge as psychological catalysts to the volatile mix?

Lagouranis: "If you're really angry because you're getting mortared all the time—I mean, rockets, they're shooting RPGs [rocket-propelled grenades] at us, there's nothing you can do. And people are dying around you because of this unseen enemy. And so you get in the interrogation booth with this guy who you think might be doing this stuff, and you know, you want to go as far as you can."

How far did they actually go?

Lagouranis: "I remember the chief warrant officer in charge of the interrogation facility. He'd heard about how the SEALs were using just ice water to lower the body temperature of the prisoner. And they would give him—you know, they would take his rectal temperature to make sure he didn't die. They would keep him hovering on hypothermia." The reward for giving up the information demanded was de-icing the prisoner before he died!

Social modeling, another potent psychological tactic, was put into practice when this interrogator used a similar strategy throughout the night inside a cold metal shipping container that served as the interrogation cell.

Lagouranis: "So we were keeping them hovering around hypothermia in this environment of what they call 'environmental manipulation,' with the [loud blaring] music and strobe lights. And then we would bring in military working dogs and use those on the prisoners. Even though it was controlled—like, the dogs were muzzled, they were being held by a handler. But the prisoner didn't know that because he was blindfolded. These are big German shepherds. So, when I would ask the prisoner a question and I didn't like the answer, I would cue the handler, so the dog would bark and jump on the prisoner, but he wasn't able to bite him. . . . sometimes they wet their jumpsuits because they were so scared, you know? Especially because they're blindfolded. They can't figure out—you know, that's a pretty terrifying position to be in. That was something I was ordered to do, and I made the chief warrant officer sign off on every single thing that I was asked to do."

Moral disengagement facilitates behaving in ways that would ordinarily be self-censured by moral people.

Lagouranis: "It is because you really do feel like you're outside of normal society, you know? Your family, your friends, they're not there to see what's going on. And everybody is sort of participating in this I don't know what—psychosis, or for want of a better word, this delusion about what you're doing there. And what becomes OK as you look around gets broken down, you know? And I mean, I felt it myself. I remember being in that shipping container in Mosul. You know, I'd been with a guy [an interrogated prisoner] all night long. And you just feel so isolated, and morally isolated, that you felt like you could do whatever you want to this guy, and maybe you even want to."

This young interrogator, who must live the rest of his life with the knowledge of the evil he did as part of his service to his country, describes how violence has a way of escalating, of feeding upon itself.

Lagouranis: "You just kept wanting to push and push and push, and see how far you could go. And it seems like that's just part of human nature. I mean, I'm sure you've read studies conducted in American prisons where you put a group of people in charge of another group of people, and give them control over them, and pretty soon it turns into cruelty and torture, you know? So it's pretty common." [Can we assume that he is referring to the prison at Stanford University? If so, the SPE has assumed an urban-myth status as a "real prison."]

The need for strong leadership to curtail abuse is essential:

Lagouranis: "And I saw it [cruelty and abuse] in every detention facility I went to. If there wasn't really strong, strong leadership that said, 'We're not going to tolerate abuse,' . . . in every facility there would have been abuse. And even among people like the MPs who aren't trying to get intel—they just do it because it's something people do there, if they're not controlled either inwardly or from above."

After seeing even worse cases of "abuse coming out of the Force Recon Marines in North Babel," Lagouranis couldn't take it anymore. He began writing reports about the abuses, documenting them with photos of the wounds and sworn prisoner statements, and then sent all this information through the Marine chain of command. How were his charges received? As with the complaints that Chip Frederick raised to his superiors about the dysfunctional conditions at Abu Ghraib, no one in the Marine command responded to the complaints of this interrogator.[55]

Lagouranis: "Nobody ever came to look at that stuff; no one ever came to talk to me about it. I just felt like I was sending these abuse reports to nowhere. And no one was investigating them, or they had no way to investigate them, or maybe no desire." [Such official silence adds its fecal touch to all dissent.]

Perhaps a reason for higher-ups failing to respond to this young interrogator's pleas for help and redress in dealing with his assignment was the uncertainty and conflict going on at top agency levels. There were disagreements about just how far "torture" should be allowed to go in coercive interrogations.

The FBI clashed with the CIA over what it considered wrongheaded ways of dealing with suspects, especially "high-value" ones. One such critical report of CIA tactics is found in an FBI memo:

To FBIHQ. I entered interview rooms to find a detainee chained hand and foot in the fetal position to the floor, with no chair, food, or water. Most

times, they had urinated or defecated on themselves, and had been left
there for 18 to 24 hours or more.

A special case that points out just how far an interrogation team at Guantánamo Prison would go is that documented for "Prisoner 063." His name was Mohammed al-Qahtani, believed to be "the twentieth hijacker" from the 9/11
terrorist attacks. He was abused in almost every imaginable way. He was made to
urinate on himself, was deprived of sleep and food for days on end, and was terror-
ized by a fierce attack dog. His continued resistance was met with further abuse.
Prisoner 063 was forced to wear a woman's bra and had a woman's thong placed
on his head. Interrogators made fun of him, calling him a homosexual. They even
put on a dog leash and made him do animal tricks. A female interrogator strad-
dled al-Qahtani in the hope of sexually exciting him and then castigated him for
violating his religious beliefs. Investigative reporters for *Time* magazine have revealed in vivid detail the hour-by-hour, even minute-by-minute log book of al-
Qahtani's month-long secret interrogation.[56] It is a mixture of crude and brutal
tactics with some sophisticated ones combined with many that are simply silly or
stupid. Any experienced police detective could have gotten more out of this prisoner in less time using less immoral tactics.

On learning of this interrogation, Navy General Counsel Alberto Mora was
appalled by what he considered unlawful practices not worthy of any military or
a government that condones it. In an eloquent statement that provides the essential frame for appreciating what it means to condone such abusive interrogations,
Mora said:

> If cruelty is no longer declared unlawful, but instead is applied as a matter
> of policy, it alters the fundamental relationship of man to government. It
> destroys the whole notion of individual rights. The Constitution recog-
> nizes that man has an inherent right, not bestowed by the state or laws, to
> personal dignity, including the right to be free of cruelty. It applies to all
> human beings, not just in America—even those designated as "unlawful
> enemy combatants." If you make this exception, the whole Constitution
> crumbles. It's a transformative issue."[57]

What I ask you to consider now, dear reader, in your role as juror, is the comparison of some of these planned tactics with those supposedly originating from
the allegedly "perverted minds" of the Tier 1A MPs as shown in their photos. In
addition to the many photos of detainees with women's panties over their heads
is the horrific image of Lynndie England dragging a prisoner along the ground
with a dog leash around his neck. It now seems reasonable to conclude that the
panties on the head, the leash, and that dehumanizing scenario were all borrowed from their earlier use by the CIA, by General Miller's special Gitmo interrogation teams, and had become generally accepted interrogation tactics being
practiced throughout the war zones. But no photography allowed!

Elite Soldiers Do It: 82nd Airborne Break Bones, Burn Photos

Perhaps the most impressive witness for my case against the entire command structure is Captain Ian Fishback, a decorated West Point graduate and captain of an elite airborne unit serving in Iraq. His recent letter to Senator John McCain complaining of rampant abuses being perpetrated against prisoners began:

> I am a graduate of West Point currently serving as a Captain in the Army Infantry. I have served two combat tours with the 82nd Airborne Division, one each in Afghanistan and Iraq. While I served in the Global War on Terror, the actions and statements of my leadership led me to believe that United States policy did not require application of the Geneva Conventions in Afghanistan or Iraq.

During a number of interviews with Human Rights Watch, Captain Fishback revealed in specific detail the disturbing consequences of that confusion over the legal limits imposed on interrogators. His account is supplemented by two sergeants in his unit at the Forward Operating Base (FOB) of Camp Mercury near Fallujah.[58] (Although mentioned in the previous chapter, here I will provide a fuller version of and context for Captain Fishback's revelations.)

In his letter to Senator McCain, Fishback testified to habitual beatings to the face and body of prisoners before interrogation, the pouring of burning chemicals on prisoners' faces, their routine shackling in positions that led to physical collapse, and forced exercises that led them to lose consciousness. They even stacked prisoners in pyramids, à la Abu Ghraib. Such abuses occurred before, during, and after the scandal erupted about the abuses at Abu Ghraib.

> When we were at FOB Mercury, we had prisoners that were stacked in pyramids, not naked but they were stacked in pyramids. We had prisoners that were forced to do extremely stressful exercises for at least two hours at a time. . . . There was a case where a prisoner had cold water dumped on him and then he was left outside in the night. [Again, as Lagouranis reported, here is the tactic of exposure to extreme elements.] There was a case where a soldier took a baseball bat and struck a detainee on the leg hard. This is all stuff that I'm getting from my NCOs [Non-Commissioned Officers].

Fishback testified that commanders directed and condoned the abuse: "I would be told, 'These guys were IED [improvised explosive device] trigger men last week.' So we would fuck them up. Fuck them up bad . . . But you gotta understand, this was the norm." (Recall our earlier discussion of *emergent norms* in particular situations where some new practice quickly becomes the standard that must be complied with and conformed to.)

One of Fishback's sergeants testified, "Everyone in camp knew if you wanted to work out your frustration you show up at the PUC tent [prisoners were called

PUCs, "persons under control"]. In a way, it was sport. One day [another sergeant] shows up and tells a PUC to grab a pole. He told him to bend over and broke the guy's leg with a mini–Louisville slugger, a metal bat. As long as no PUCs came up dead, it happened. We kept it to broken arms and legs."

Amazingly, Fishback reports that his soldiers also digitally documented their prisoner abuses.

> [At FOB Mercury] they said that they had pictures that were similar to what happened at Abu Ghraib, and because they were so similar to what happened at Abu Ghraib, the soldiers destroyed the pictures. They burned them. They [the soldiers at Abu Ghraib] were getting in trouble for the same things we were told to do, so we destroyed the pictures.

Finally, Captain Fishback started a seventeen-month-long campaign of reporting his concerns and complaints to his superiors—with the same absence of reaction that Interrogator Anthony Lagouranis and Sergeant Ivan Frederick had received. He went public with his letter to Senator McCain, which helped to fortify McCain's opposition to the suspension of the Geneva Conventions by the Bush administration.

Of course, Fishback's heroic whistle-blowing has not endeared him to his superiors. He was brought home to Fort Bragg, North Carolina, and sequestered there for interrogation by the military. However, he is unlikely to yield to their pressure, as can be inferred from the last sentence in his letter to Senator McCain:

> If we abandon our ideals in the face of adversity and aggression, then those ideals were never really in our possession. I would rather die fighting than give up even the smallest part of the idea that is "America."

"Torture Chicks" Lap Dance Prisoners in the Gitmo Confessional

Our next witness reveals a new wrinkle in depravity that the military (probably in alliance with the CIA) developed in its Gitmo prison. "Sex was used as a weapon to create a wedge between the detainee and his Islamic faith," reported Erik Saar, a military translator working at that prison camp. This young soldier went to Guantánamo Bay full of patriotic fervor, believing he could help in the war on terrorism. However, he soon realized that he was not helping at all; that what was happening there was all "a mistake." In a radio interview on Amy Goodman's *Democracy Now* show on April 4, 2005, Saar offered vivid details about the sexual tactics used against prisoners, tactics he witnessed firsthand. He elaborated on this interview in a book-length exposé, *Inside the Wire: A Military Intelligence Soldier's Eyewitness Account of Life at Guantanamo.*[59]

During the six months he served there, Saar, who is fluent in Arabic, had to translate for the prisoner what the official interrogator asked and said and then repeat the prisoner's replies to the interrogator in English. He was in a "Cyrano-type role" demanding that he use precisely the proper words to convey the exact meaning of both the interrogator's and prisoner's intentions to each other. The new trick involved the use of a seductive female interrogator. Saar reported: "The female interrogator would sexually entice prisoners being interrogated to make them feel unclean. . . . She would rub her breast on his back, talk about her body parts. . . . The prisoner was shocked and infuriated."

Saar quit his post because he became convinced that such an interrogation strategy "was totally ineffective and not in keeping with the values of our democracy."[60] *The New York Times* columnist Maureen Dowd coined the nickname "Torture Chicks" for the female interrogators at Gitmo who used sexual lures on prisoners to gain information and confessions.[61] Let us go "inside the wire" for fuller details of what such an interrogation was like.

Saar reports one particularly dramatic encounter that could be classified under the military rubric "Invasion of Space by Female." The victim was a twenty-one-year-old Saudi of "high value" who spent a great deal of time praying in his cell. Before the procedure began, the female interrogator, "Brooke," and Saar were both "sanitized" by taping over their names on their uniforms to preserve their anonymity. Then Brooke said, "The detainee we're going to talk to is a piece of shit and we might have to turn things up a bit" because, as she made evident, "I'm starting to take shit from above because he's not talking. We need to try something new tonight." This Saudi detainee was believed to have taken flight lessons with the 9/11 hijackers, so was very high value. Saar noted "that when military interrogators were questioning a detainee who was uncooperative, they very quickly wanted to 'turn up the heat': shout, be confrontational, play the bad cop, forget building rapport."

Interrogator Brooke continued: "I just need to make him feel that he absolutely must cooperate with me and has no other options. I think we should make him feel so fucking dirty that he can't go back to his cell and spend the night praying. We have to put up a barrier between him and his God."[62] When the prisoner did not respond to her questioning, the interrogator decided to turn up the heat.

"To my surprise," Saar exclaimed, "she started to unbutton her top slowly, teasingly, almost like a stripper, revealing a skin-tight brown Army T-shirt stretching over her chest. . . . She walked slowly behind him and began rubbing her breasts against his back." She taunted the prisoner: "Do you like these big American tits, Fareek? I see that you are starting to get hard. How do you think Allah feels about that?" She then moved around to sit right in front of him and placing her hands over her breasts, teased the prisoner with "Don't you like these big tits?" When the prisoner looked away toward Saar, she challenged his masculinity: "Are you gay? Why do you keep looking at him? . . . . He thinks I have great tits. Don't you?" (Saar nods affirmatively.)

The prisoner resists, spitting at her. Unfazed, the interrogator turns up the screw another notch. As she unbuttons her pants, she asks the prisoner:

"Fareek, did you know that I am having my period? . . . How do you feel about me touching you now?" [As she withdrew her hand from her panties, it appeared as if it were covered with her blood. She asked him one last time who told him to learn to fly, who sent him to flight school.] "You fuck," she hissed, wiping what he believed was menstrual blood on his face. . . . "What do you think your brothers will think of you in the morning when they see an American woman's menstrual blood on your face?" Brooke said, standing up, "By the way, we've shut off the water to your cell for tonight, so the blood will still be there tomorrow," she tossed out as we left the booth. . . . She had done what she thought was best to get the information her bosses were asking for. . . . What the fuck did I just do? What the fuck were we doing in this place?

Yes, indeed, a very good question. However, there was never a clear answer for Saar or for anyone else.

Other Revelations of Gitmo Crimes and Misdemeanors

Erik Saar reveals a number of other practices that were deceptive, unethical, and illegal. He and the others on the interrogation teams were under strict orders never to speak to the International Red Cross observers. He was ordered to stay away from them. Of "ghost detainees" he says, "There were a chunk of them, we had no idea how or why they came to Gitmo. There was no evidence of their culpability. Many were despondent." He also reported, "There were also young children at Gitmo, kept outside of the main Camp Delta. They had no interrogation value, but were kept there for a long time." No one has ever reported on children prisoners at Gitmo, who had to have been brought there from Iraq and Afghanistan.

"False setups" were arranged when visiting dignitaries were scheduled to visit to observe a "typical" interrogation. A fictional setting was arranged that would make the scene look normal and ordinary. It was reminiscent of the model Jewish camp created by the Nazis in their concentration camp at Teresienstadt, Czechoslovakia, where they fooled the International Red Cross observers and others into believing the inmates were all happy with their relocation. Erik Saar describes that everything was sanitized in the "A-OK" setup:

> One of the things I learned when I joined the intelligence team was that when a V.I.P. visit would take place, meaning it could be a general or could be an executive from the senior government service, one of the intelligence agencies, maybe, or even a Congressional delegation, there was a concerted effort to explain to the interrogators that they were to find a detainee who had previously been cooperative and put him in the interrogation booth at the time when the V.I.P. would be visiting and sitting in the observation room. Essentially, they were to find someone who had been

cooperative, who they were able to sit across a table with and have a regular dialogue, and someone who would also had in the past provided adequate intelligence, and then they were to replay that interrogation for the visiting VIP's.

And essentially, as an intelligence professional, this was insulting. And I don't think I was alone in feeling this way, to be honest with you, because in the intelligence community your whole existence is in order to provide policymakers with the right information to make the right decisions. So, that's really the existence of the intelligence community, to simply provide the right information. And this concept of creating this fictitious world so Gitmo [would look] like one thing to those visiting, when in reality it was something far different, completely undermined everything that we, as professionals, were trying to do in intelligence.

It was possible for supervisors to watch any interrogation through a one-way mirror in each room, but "they rarely did so," according to Saar. Important sessions with high-value detainees were supposed to be recorded on concealed video cameras. If they had been, senior officers might have been as distressed as this translator was by such sexually perverse tactics and put a stop to them. Not so, says Saar:

> There were also cameras in the booths, but the sessions were not recorded;
> General [Geoffrey] Miller thought taping could only cause legal problems.
> The video was simply fed to a screen in the observation room. For the overwhelming majority of sessions, the only ones who ever knew what took place in the booth [were] the interrogator, the linguist, and the detainee.

"Outsourcing" Torture

Additional evidence of the spread of stealth torture as a means of forcing intelligence from resistant suspects is revealed in secret CIA programs that whisked prisoners to foreign countries that had agreed to do the dirty job for the United States. In a policy known as "renditions," or "extraordinary renditions," dozens, perhaps hundreds, of "high-value terrorists" (HVTs) were taken to a number of foreign countries, often in business jets leased by the CIA.[63] President Bush apparently authorized the CIA to have detainees in custody "disappeared" or "rendered" to countries where the use of torture is well-known (and documented by Amnesty International).[64] Such prisoners were kept incommunicado in longterm secret detention facilities in "undisclosed locations." In "reverse renditions," foreign authorities arrested "suspects" in noncombat, nonbattlefield settings and transferred them into custody, usually to Guantánamo Bay Prison, without the basic legal protections afforded by international law.

The president of the Center for Constitutional Rights, Michael Ratner, said of this program:

I call it outsourcing torture. What it really means is that in the so-called war on terror, the C.I.A. picks up people anywhere in the world that it wants, and if it doesn't want to engage in the torture itself, or in the interrogation, whatever term you want to use, it will send them to another country that our intelligence agencies have a close relationship with. That can be Egypt, it can be Jordan.[65]

One CIA senior officer in charge of this rendition program was Michael Scheuer. He reports matter-of-factly:

We took people to the countries of their origin in the Middle East, if those countries had a legal process outstanding for them and were willing to take them. That person would be treated according to the laws of that country, not to the laws of the United States, but to the laws of, take your pick, Morocco, Egypt, Jordan.[66]

Obviously, the interrogation tactics used in those countries would include torture techniques that the CIA did not want to know about, as long as there was any useful "intel" coming out of them. However, it is difficult in our high-tech era to keep such a program concealed for long. Some of America's allies have led a probe into at least thirty flights suspected of being engaged by the CIA in the outsourcing-torture program. The investigation has revealed that key suspects were transported to Soviet-era compounds in Eastern Europe.[67]

In my judgment, these programs of outsourcing torture indicate not that the CIA and military intelligence operatives were reluctant to torture prisoners but that they believed that agents in those countries knew how to do it better. They have been perfecting the practice of the "third degree" longer than the Americans have. I have outlined here only a small sample of the far more extensive abuses heaped upon all sorts of detainees in American military prisons in order to refute the administration's assertion that such abuse and torture were not "systematic."

Autopsies and death reports on detainees held in facilities in Iraq and Afghanistan reveal that nearly half of the forty-four deaths reported occurred during or after interrogations by Navy SEALs, military intelligence, or the CIA. These homicides resulted from abusive interrogation tactics that included hooding, gagging, strangulation, beating with blunt objects, water boarding, sleep deprivation, and extreme temperature manipulations. The executive director of the ACLU, Anthony Romero, has made it clear that "There is no question that interrogations have resulted in deaths. High-ranking officials who knew about the torture sat on their hands and those who created and endorsed these policies must be held accountable."[68]

TAKING IT TO THE TOP: HOLDING DICK CHENEY AND GEORGE W. BUSH ACCOUNTABLE

> As became increasingly obvious in the months after the [Abu Ghraib] pho-
> tos came to public light, this pattern of abuse did not result from the acts
> of individual soldiers who broke the rules. It resulted from decisions made
> by the Bush administration to bend, ignore, or cast rules aside. Adminis-
> tration policies created the climate for Abu Ghraib and for abuse against
> detainees worldwide in a number of ways.

This summary statement by Human Rights Watch in its report "United States: Getting Away with Torture?" focuses our attention at the very top of the long chain of command—all the way up to Vice President Dick Cheney and President George W. Bush.

The War on Terror Framed the Torture Paradigm Shift

In line with previous presidential failures—in their "War on Nouns"—on Poverty and Drugs—the Bush administration declared a "War on Terror" following the attacks of September 11, 2001. The central premise of this new war was that terrorism is the primary threat to "national security," and to the "homeland," and that it must be opposed by all means necessary. This ideological foundation has been used by virtually all nations as a device for gaining popular and military support for aggression, as well as repression. It was used freely by right-wing dictatorships in Brazil, Greece, and many other nations in the 1960s and '70s to justify torture and death-squad executions of their citizens who were positioned as the "enemies of the state."[69] Italy's right-wing Christian Democrats used the "strategy of tension" during the late 1970s to exaggerate the fear of terrorism by the Red Brigades (radical Communists) as a means of political control. Of course, the classic example is that of Hitler's labeling Jews the originators of Germany's economic collapse of the 1930s. They were the internal threat that justified an external program of conquest and demanded their extermination both in Germany and in all the countries the Nazis occupied.

Fear is the State's psychological weapon of choice to frighten citizens into sacrificing their basic freedoms and rule-of-law protections in exchange for the security promised by their all-powerful government. Fear was the linchpin that gained the majority support of the U.S. public and Congress first for a preemptive war against Iraq and later for the mindless maintenance of a variety of Bush administration policies. First, fear was spread in Orwellian fashion by predicting a nuclear attack against the United States and its allies by Saddam Hussein's arsenal of "weapons of mass destruction." For example, on the eve of the congressional vote on the Iraq War resolution, President Bush told the nation and Congress that Iraq was an "evil nation" that threatened America's security. "Knowing these realities," Bush remarked, "Americans must not ignore the threat gathering against us. Facing clear evidence of peril, we cannot wait for the final proof—the smoking gun—that could come in the form of a mushroom cloud."[70] That mushroom cloud was spread over America not by Saddam but by Bush's team.

Over the next several years, all key members of the Bush administration echoed such dire warnings in speech after speech. A report was prepared by the Special Investigations Division of the Committee on Government Reform for Representative Henry A. Waxman on the Bush administration's public statements on Iraq. It used a public database of all such statements by Bush, Cheney, Rumsfeld, Secretary of State Colin Powell, and National Security Advisor Condoleezza Rice. According to the report, these five officials made 237 specific "false and misleading" statements on the Iraqi threat in 125 public appearances, an average of about 50 for each disciple. In the month of September 2002, the first anniversary of the 9/11 attacks, the Bush administration is on record as having made nearly 50 misleading and deceptive statements to the public.[71]

In his investigative analysis, Pulitzer Prize–winning author Ron Suskind traces much of the Bush administration's framing of the war on terror to Cheney's statement right after 9/11. Cheney defined it: "If there's a 1% chance that Pakistani scientists are helping al-Qaeda build or develop a nuclear weapon, we have to treat it as a certainty in terms of our response. It's not about our analysis . . . it's about our response." Suskind writes in his book *The One Percent Doctrine,* "So, now spoken, it stood: a standard of action that would frame events and responses from the Administration for years to come." He goes on to note that unfortunately, the vast federal government does not operate efficiently or effectively under new forms of stress, like this war on terror, and under cognitive dissonance from the unexpected insurgency and rebellion of captive peoples. "It has protective urges, competing agendas, rules for who does what and who represents actions to the citizenry, the sovereign, the bosses; it accomplishes a great deal, yes, but is defined often by its dysfunctions. And that means it lies and dissembles, hides what it can, and sometimes out of self-preservation, because without your trust [of citizens] it is nothing but office space."[72]

A different method of fearmongering can be seen in the politicization of the terror alarm (color code) warning system by the Bush administration's Department of Homeland Security. I believe that initially its intention was to serve, as all disaster warnings do, to mobilize citizens to prepare for a threat. However, over time, the eleven vague warnings never carried any realistic advice for citizen action. Warned of a hurricane, people are told to evacuate; warned of a tornado, we know that we must retreat to the storm cellar; but warned of a terrorism attack coming sometime, somewhere, we are told simply to be "more watchful," and, of course, to go about our business as usual. There was never any public explanation or debriefing when each of these many threats failed to materialize despite their alleged "credible sources." Mobilizing national forces for each rise in threat level costs at least a billion dollars a month and creates unnecessary anxiety and stress in the population. In the end, broadcasting the color-coded threat levels was less a valid warning system than the government's costly way of ensuring and sustaining the nation's fear of terrorists—in the absence of any terror attacks.

French existentialist author Albert Camus has pointed out that fear is a method; terror makes fear, and fear stops people from thinking rationally. It makes people think in abstractions about the enemy, the terrorists, the insurgents who threaten us, who thus must be destroyed. Once we begin thinking of people as a class of entities, as abstractions, then they meld into "faces of the enemy," and primitive impulses to kill and torture them surface even among ordinarily peaceful people.[73]

I am on record with my criticism of these "phantom alarms" as dysfunctional and dangerous, but there is evidence that increases in Bush's poll ratings were closely correlated with the sounding of these warnings.[74] The issue here is that by arousing and sustaining fear of an enemy at our gates, the Bush administration was able to position the president as the Almighty Commander in Chief of a nation at war.

By calling himself "commander in chief" and vastly expanding the powers granted him by Congress, President Bush and his advisers came to believe that they were above national and international law and that therefore any of their policies were legal simply by asserting them in a newly recast official legal interpretation. The seeds for the flowers of evil that blossomed in that dark dungeon of Abu Ghraib were planted by the Bush administration in its triangular framing of national security threats, citizen fear and vulnerability, and interrogation/torture to win the war on terror.

Vice President Dick Cheney as "The Vice President of Torture"

A *Washington Post* editorial called Dick Cheney "The Vice President of Torture" because of his efforts to defeat and finally to modify the McCain amendment to the Department of Defense's budget authorization bill.[75] That amendment demanded the humane treatment of prisoners in American military custody. Cheney had lobbied hard to get an exception to the law granted for the CIA in order to enable it to use whatever means it deemed necessary to extract information from its suspects. Cheney argued that such a bill would tie the hands of CIA operatives and expose them to potential prosecution for their efforts in the global war on terror. (And we have gotten a glimpse of how extremely brutal and lethal their efforts can be.)

The legislation proposed by Senator John McCain, a former prisoner of war in Vietnam who himself experienced the horrors of torture, bans the use of torture and cruel, inhuman, and degrading treatment by any government agency. It also requires all military interrogations to conform to the Army's Field Manual on Intelligence Interrogation (FM 34-52). Not only was the bill passed 90 to 9 in the Senate, it was endorsed strongly in a personal letter to McCain by more than a dozen top military commanders from the Marines, Army, and Navy. They asserted that the Army field manual is the tried and true "gold standard" that should be followed consistently.

As a postscript, these generals and admirals believe that "when agencies other than DoD [Department of Defense] detain and interrogate prisoners, there should be no legal loopholes permitting cruel and degrading treatment."[76]

McCain takes a broad perspective on torture and the need to right America's moral compass. In a *Newsweek* magazine essay on "The Truth About Torture," McCain held that:

> This is a war of ideas, a struggle to advance freedom in the face of terror in places where oppressive rule had bred the malevolence that creates terrorists. Prisoner abuses extract a terrible toll on us in this war of ideas. They inevitably become public, and when they do they threaten our moral standing. . . . The mistreatment of prisoners harms us more than our enemies.[77]

It is unlikely that passage of this legislation will dim Cheney's passionate support for the CIA's use of all the means at its disposal to get confessions and intelligence from secretly held terror suspects. This must be so when we consider Cheney's steadfast adherence to the beliefs he expressed shortly after the 9/11 attacks. In a televised interview on NBC's *Meet the Press*, Cheney made a remarkable statement:

> We also have to work, though, sort of the dark side, if you will. We've got to spend time in the shadows in the intelligence world. A lot of what needs to be done here will have to be done quietly, without any discussion, using sources and methods that are available to our intelligence agencies, if we're going to be successful. That's the world these folks operate in, and so it's going to be vital for us to use any means at our disposal, basically, to achieve our objective.[78]

In an NPR interview, the former chief of staff for Secretary of State Colin Powell, Colonel Lawrence Wilkerson, charged that the Cheney-Bush team of neoconservatives issued directives that led to the prisoner abuses by soldiers in Iraq and Afghanistan. Wilkerson outlined the path such directives took:

> It was clear to me that there was a visible audit trail from the vice president's [Cheney's] office through the secretary of defense [Rumsfeld] down to the commanders in the field that in carefully couched terms—that to a soldier in the field meant two things: We're not getting enough good intelligence and you need to get that evidence—and, oh, by the way, here's some ways you can probably get it.

Wilkerson also referred to David Addington, Cheney's counsel, as "a staunch advocate of allowing the president in his capacity as commander in chief to deviate from the Geneva Conventions."[79] This leads us right up to the pinnacle of power.

President George W. Bush as "The Commander in Chief of War"

As commander in charge of an open-ended war on global terrorism, President George W. Bush has relied on a team of legal advisers to establish a legitimate basis for a preemptive war of aggression against Iraq, to redefine torture, to create new rules of engagement, to restrict citizens' freedoms through the so-called PATRIOT Act, and to authorize illegal eavesdropping, wiretapping, and spying on the phone calls of American citizens. As usual, all this is done in the name of protecting the sacred homeland national security in the global war against you-know-what. Bush's legal advisory team consisted of: Alberto R. Gonzalez, counsel to the president (subsequently promoted to attorney general); John You, deputy assistant attorney general, and Jay S. Bybee, assistant attorney general (both of the Department of Justice); Attorney General John Ashcroft; and William H. Taft IV, legal adviser, State Department.

Alberto Gonzales offered the following legal judgment to the president (memo, January 25, 2002): "The nature of the new war places a high premium on other factors, such as the ability to quickly obtain information. . . . In my judgment, this new paradigm renders obsolete Geneva's strict limitations on questioning of enemy prisoners."

The Torture Memos

An August 1, 2002, Department of Justice memo, referred to in the press as the "Torture Memo," narrowly defined "torture" in terms not of what it constitutes but only in terms of its most extreme consequences. It held that physical pain must be "equivalent in intensity to the pain accompanying serious physical injury, such as organ failure, impairment of bodily function, or even death." In line with this memo, in order to prosecute anyone charged with torture crimes, it is necessary that it must have been the "specific intent" of the defendant to cause "severe physical or mental pain or suffering." "Mental torture" was narrowly defined to include only acts that would result in "significant psychological harm of significant duration, e.g., lasting for months or years."

The memo went on to assert that the earlier ratification of the 1994 anti-torture statute could be considered unconstitutional because it would interfere with the president's power as commander in chief. Other guidelines from the Justice Department's lawyers gave the president the power to reinterpret the Geneva Conventions to suit the administration's purposes in the war on terror. Belligerents captured in Afghanistan, Taliban soldiers, al-Qaeda suspects, insurgents, and all those rounded up and taken into custody would not be considered POWs, and therefore not granted any of the legal protections to which a prisoner of war is entitled. As "enemy noncombatants," they could be held indefinitely at any facility in the world, without counsel or specific charges leveled against them. In addition, the president apparently approved the CIA's program of "disappearing" high-value terrorists.

The evidence is circumstantial, but it is convincing. For example, in his book *State of War: The Secret History of the C.I.A. and the Bush Administration*, James Risen concludes that there is "a secret agreement among very senior administration officials to insulate Bush and to give him deniability" in regard to the CIA's involvement in the extreme new interrogation tactics.[80]

A less gracious description of the relationship between President Bush and his team of legal advisers came from the legal scholar Anthony Lewis, after he had thoroughly reviewed all the available memoranda:

> The memos read like the advice of a mob lawyer to a mafia don on how to skirt the law and stay out of prison. Avoiding prosecution is literally a theme of the memoranda. . . . Another theme in the memoranda, an even more deeply disturbing one, is that the President can order the torture of prisoners even though it is forbidden by a federal statute and by the international Convention Against Torture, to which the United States is a party.[81]

Readers are invited to read all the relevant materials I have outlined here (the investigative reports, ICRC report, and more) along with all twenty-eight "torture memos" by President Bush's legal advisers, Rumsfeld, Powell, Bush, and others that prepared the way for the legitimization of torture in Afghanistan, Guantánamo, and Iraq. In a remarkable 1,249-page volume, *The Torture Papers: The Road to Abu Ghraib*, edited by Karen Greenberg and Joshua Dratel, the full paper trail of memoranda is laid out, exposing the perversion of legal skills by government lawyers.[82] It provides us with an insight into how such "skills that have done so much to protect Americans in this most legalized of countries—can be misused in the cause of evil."[83] The editors conclude in no uncertain terms what the significance of these documents should be for citizens to understand the motives and intentions of their elected leaders and other government officials:

> While the proverbial road to hell is paved with good intentions, the internal government memos collected in this publication demonstrate that the path to the purgatory that is Guantánamo Bay, or Abu Ghraib, has been paved with decidedly bad intentions. The policies that resulted in rampant abuse of detainees first in Afghanistan, then at Guantánamo Bay, and later in Iraq, were the product of three pernicious purposes designed to facilitate the unilateral and unfettered detention, interrogation, abuse, judgment, and punishment of prisoners: (1) the desire to place the detainees beyond the reach of any court or law; (2) the desire to abrogate the Geneva Convention with respect to the treatment of persons seized in the context of armed hostilities; and (3) the desire to absolve those implementing the policies of any liability for war crimes under U.S. and international law.

Indeed, any claim of good faith—that those who formulated the policies were merely misguided in their pursuit of security in the face of what
is certainly a genuine terrorist threat—is belied by the policy makers'
more than tacit acknowledgment of their unlawful purpose. . . . The message that these memoranda convey in response is unmistakable: these
policy makers do not like our system of justice, with its checks and balances, and rights and limits, that they have been sworn to uphold. That
antipathy for and distrust of our civilian and military justice systems is
positively un-American.[84]

Law Professor Jordan Paust (former captain, U.S. Army Judge Advocate General's Corps) wrote of George W. Bush's legal advisers, who prepared these justifications for torture against detainees, "Not since the Nazi era have so many
lawyers been so clearly involved in international crimes concerning the treatment and interrogation of persons detained during war."

Heading that list of advisers is Attorney General Alberto Gonzales, who
helped develop a legal memo that reinterpreted "torture" as noted above. Not
until the Abu Ghraib photos were disclosed did Gonzales and President Bush repudiate this memo offering the most extreme conception of torture. Gonzales's
dedication to expanding presidential powers within the framework of the war on
terror has been compared to that of the influential Nazi lawyer Carl Schmitt.
Schmitt's ideas about freeing the nation's executive from legal constraints in
times of emergency helped suspend Germany's constitution and gave Hitler total
power. Gonzales's biographer noted that Gonzales is a likable man who comes
across as an "ordinary man" without sadistic or psychopathic tendencies.[85] However, in his institutional role, Gonzales's legal memos have been responsible for
suspension of civil liberties and brutal interrogation of terror suspects in violation of international law.[86]

Gitmo Interrogations Opposed by the Defense Department's Criminal Investigation Task Force

According to a recent MSNBC report, leaders of the Defense Department's Criminal Investigation Task Force said that they had repeatedly warned senior Pentagon officials (beginning in early 2002 and continuing for years after) that the
harsh interrogation techniques used by a separate intelligence team would not
produce reliable information, could constitute war crimes, and would embarrass
the nation when they became public knowledge. The concerns and advice of
these experienced criminal investigators were largely ignored by all those in the
chain of command directing the interrogations at Gitmo and Abu Ghraib in favor
of their preferred intense, coercive forms of interrogation. Alberto J. Mora, the
former general counsel of the Navy, has gone on record supporting the members
of this task force: "What makes me intensely proud of all these individuals was
that they said, 'We will not be party to this, even if we are ordered to do so.' They

are heroes, and there's no other way to describe them. They demonstrated enormous personal courage and personal integrity in standing up for American values and the system we all live for." In the end, these investigators were not able to stop the abuses, but only to slow them down by getting Secretary of Defense Rumsfeld to roll back some of his harshest interrogation tactics.[87]

Obsession with the War on Terror

We can see that Bush's obsession with the war on terror has propelled him further down the dangerous path laid out in the late Senator Barry Goldwater's dictum "Extremism in the defense of liberty is no vice . . . moderation in the pursuit of justice is no virtue." Accordingly, President Bush has authorized domestic surveillance of American citizens by the National Security Agency (NSA) without legally mandated warrants. In what amounts to a large data-mining operation, a huge volume of telephone and Internet traffic has been gathered by the NSA and sent to the FBI for analysis—actually overwhelming its capacities for effective processing of such information.[88]

Such surveillance requires "backdoor access" to the major telecommunications switches on American soil that route international calls and the secret cooperation of the nation's largest telecommunications companies, according to a detailed *New York Times* report of January 2006.[89] The *Times'* exposé has revealed the excesses inherent in vesting such power in the president without the restraints of legal or congressional checks and balances. A case has been made for comparing Bush's sense of being above the law with that of President Richard Nixon, who "unleashed the dogs of domestic surveillance in the 1970s" and defended doing so by his assertion "When the President does it, that means it is not illegal."[90] Bush now says the very same thing with the same sense of impunity.

This sense of being above the law is seen also in Bush's unprecedented use of "signing statements." In the process of approving a law passed by Congress, the president affirms his prerogative *not* to follow the law he has just signed. President Bush has used this tactic more than any other president has in U.S. history, more than 750 times, to disobey statutes passed by Congress when they conflict with his interpretation of the Constitution. This included placing this personal restraint on the McCain Amendment against torture.[91]

However, President Bush's assertion of executive power has been challenged in a recent decision of the Supreme Court that limits his authority. It repudiated the Bush administration's plans to put Guantánamo detainees on trial before military commissions (tribunals), because they were unauthorized by federal statute and they violated international law. According to *The New York Times*, "The ruling marked the most significant setback yet for the administration's broad expansion of presidential power."[92]

Paradoxically, in its desire to rid the world of the evil of terrorism, the Bush administration has itself become a glaring exemplar of "administrative evil." It is an organization that inflicts pain and suffering unto death while willingly using formal, rational, and efficient procedures to disguise the substance of what it does—ignoring the means to justify what its members consider to be higher-order ends.[93]

Other examples of this mechanism of administrative evil at work include the Nazis' extermination of Jews in the Holocaust, NASA's role in the *Challenger* disaster, the promotion of addictive cigarettes by American tobacco company executives and their hired "scientific experts," and the deceptive business practices of Enron and other crooked companies. Administrative evil is systemic, in the sense that it exists beyond any one person once its policies are in place and its procedures take control. Nevertheless, I would argue, organizations must have leaders, and those leaders must be held accountable for creating or maintaining such evil.

I believe that a system consists of those agents and agencies whose power and values create or modify the rules of and expectations for "approved behaviors" within its sphere of influence. In one sense, the system is more than the sum of its parts and of its leaders, who also fall under its powerful influences. In another sense, however, the individuals who play key roles in creating a system that engages in illegal, immoral, and unethical conduct should be held accountable despite the situational pressures on them.

President Bush and his advisers have been able to alter the War Crimes Act (of 1996) by pushing Congress to pass the United States Military Commissions Act of 2006 (Senate Bill 3930) that he signed on October 17, 2006. It was drafted in part to rebuff the Supreme Court's decision on *Hamdan v. Rumsfeld* that has challenged the administration's use of military tribunals in trials of detainees at Guantánamo Prison. This new Military Commissions Act provides for a host of controversial practices relating to the U.S. government's detention and treatment of *"unlawful enemy combatants."* All those so designated are afforded neither the military rights of soldiers nor those of civilians in civil law. The president is given broad war-time powers to designate anyone as fitting that category, including American citizens, thereby losing their right of habeas corpus and protections provided by the Geneva Conventions. They may be imprisoned indefinitely, tried only by a military tribunal whose judge may use hearsay evidence even when obtained without a search warrant, and whose finding of guilt requires only a two-thirds majority of tribunal members. In addition, it harbors at least two more objectionable features: permitting many interrogation tactics that qualify as only "humiliating," and retroactively protecting all government officials who may have been involved in "crimes against humanity," including the murder of interrogated detainees by CIA operatives and others. (Thus, virtually all the abuses by the MPs at Abu Ghraib are now allowable because they would qualify as merely "humiliating," not as torture.)

Upholding the War Crimes Act and the Geneva Conventions should be indispensable for all civilized nations that choose to live by the rule of law and not by the rule of power and tyranny. The Military Commissions Act is "a tyrannical law that will be ranked with the low points in American democracy, our generation's version of the Alien and Sedition Acts," according to a *New York Times* editorial (September 28, 2006). Where is the outrage by citizens and freedom loving people everywhere?[94]

MEMBERS OF THE JURY, YOUR VERDICT, PLEASE

You have read here the testimony of many eyewitnesses as well as key sections of the summary reports by the major independent investigative panels, along with parts of the extensive analyses by Human Rights Watch, the Red Cross, the ACLU, Amnesty International, and PBS's *Frontline* about the nature of the abuse and torture of prisoners in the custody of the U.S. Military.

Do you now believe that the mistreatment of detainees in Abu Ghraib's Tier 1A by Sergeant Ivan "Chip" Frederick and the other MPs on night shift duty was an aberration, an isolated incident caused solely by a few "bad apples," allegedly "rogue soldiers"?

Further, do you now believe that such abuse and torture was or was not part of a "systematic" program of coercive interrogation? Did the extent of the abuses and torture in these interrogations go far deeper and well beyond the limited time, place, and set of actors in the Abu Ghraib Tier 1A night shift?

Given the acknowledged guilt of those MPs charged with the photographed abuses, do you now believe that there were sufficient situational forces (a "bad barrel") and system pressures ("bad barrel makers") acting on them that should have mitigated the extent of their prison sentences?

Are you willing and ready to make a judgment of complicity in the abuses at Abu Ghraib and many other military facilities and secretly run CIA jails of each of the following high-ranking members of the military command: Major General Geoffrey Miller, Lieutenant General Ricardo Sanchez, Colonel Thomas Pappas, and Lieutenant Colonel Steven Jordan? [95]

Are you willing and ready to make a judgment of complicity in the abuses at Abu Ghraib and many other military facilities and secretly run CIA jails of each of the following top members of the political command: former CIA director George Tenet and Secretary of Defense Donald Rumsfeld?

Are you willing and ready to make a judgment of complicity in the abuses at Abu Ghraib and many other military facilities and secretly run CIA jails of each of the following top members of the political command: Vice President Dick Cheney and President George W. Bush?

The Prosecution Rests

(However, you might also want to look at a note about a recent tribunal that tried the Bush administration for its "crimes against humanity."[96])

While you are deliberating, consider this final section about a positive attempt by the military system to acknowledge the necessity of proper guard training and effective institutional constraints on abuses of power in interrogating prisoners. Had such procedures been in place from the start, it is likely that the abuses at Abu Ghraib would not have happened.

THE SPE GOES TO ABU GHRAIB AS A TRAINING GUIDE AGAINST POWER OVERLOAD AND HUMANITY OUTAGES

On the long flight from Hawaii to Baghdad, Army Colonel Larry James watched the DVD of the Stanford Prison Experiment, *Quiet Rage*, over and over, maybe "as many as twenty-four times." "What did Zimbardo do wrong?" "What should he have done differently to prevent the abuses in his prison?" He raised these questions because he was en route to a special mission: *Fix Abu Ghraib!* Dr. James is a distinguished clinical psychologist, who for years was chair of the Department of Psychology, Walter Reed Army Medical Center. He was given this unique task in May 2004, at the command of Major General Geoffrey Miller, with whom he had worked in the Guantánamo Bay Prison. (Yes, the very same general whose earlier strategies and tactics had done so much damage in the prisons in both Cuba and Iraq.)

As chief behavioral science director, James reported directly to Major General Miller. As one of the highest-ranking officers in the prison, James was able to get his policies and procedures enacted almost immediately. I had given James several sets of our newly made DVD when I learned he was headed to Abu Ghraib. He had suggested that I join him on the mission, but I was too fearful of the danger to go with him. I would have gladly joined him had it not been for the lethal environment that existed in that prison and throughout Iraq. I interviewed James upon his return, asking him what he had decided would be the best set of prevention strategies to safeguard against new abuses.[97]

In general, his goal was to set up procedures that would create and maintain good order and discipline in this prison setting and would meet the criteria of the American Correctional Association. He arranged for site visits at Abu Ghraib Prison and also at Camp Bucca by an Army lieutenant colonel who was the chief of the Behavioral Science Department, Disciplinary Barracks (Leavenworth, Kansas), and also by a site reviewer for the American Correctional Association. All of their findings and recommendations were implemented. Because of their survey of conditions, a mental health hospital was built for the prisoners and a large team of mental health professionals was detailed to Abu Ghraib to provide services to detainees—for the first time.

Next, he established some basic ground rules for himself:

1. Do no harm.
2. Keep everything safe; physically and psychologically; health care should mirror the standards adopted by the American Correctional Association.

3. Keep everything legal; meet all principles of the Uniformed Code of Military Justice.

4. Keep everything ethical; be sure no one is ever harmed, and continually ask, "Did I do anything to violate the ethical standards of the American Psychological Association?"

5. Make interrogations effective; create conditions that transform "interrogations" into detectivelike "interviews" of inmates that are designed to acquire the intelligence necessary to save American lives in nonabusive ways.

Colonel James walked the grounds at night and at random times, talking with guards and staff, always being cognizant of abuses, wrongdoing, or conduct inconsistent with good order and discipline. He worked personally to stop problems or misconduct, or, if he could not resolve any issue, reported his concerns directly to the general.

After examining every aspect of the prison, Colonel James established the following seven layers of Prison Oversight and Rules Governing the Treatment and Interrogation of Prisoners at Abu Ghraib Prison, presumably to be extended to other facilities:

1. There must be supervision by senior officers at all times, including night shifts.

2. "Interrogations" must be replaced by "interviews" following the model of a U.S. detective investigation at a police headquarters. One person alone must never conduct the interviews; there must be at least two present in the interview booth, the interviewer and translator, at a minimum. This way they can check on each other and have dual feedback available.

3. A written "no-go" policy must make explicit what actions are prohibited and what are permitted during these prisoner interviews, eliminating any ambiguity about what can and cannot be done or justified.

4. Mandatory "mission-specific training" must be required of all those involved in these interviews.

5. Interview booths must be open to surveillance through one-way observation mirrors enabling viewing from hall corridors by officers and others, and all interviews must be videotaped for subsequent analysis and administrative review.

6. Military police will regularly rove the entire facility at random intervals, reporting regularly to higher-ups and making guards and interviewers aware that they are always under surveillance. (James also arranged for two military psychologists to be his "roving ambassadors" in this way.)

7. Multiple layers of supervision and oversight are required, with medical inspection of each prisoner interviewed, pre- and again postinterview, to

report any signs of changed medical status as a consequence of the interview procedure. Similarly, a military attorney must review all procedures, along with other layers of regular supervision built into the system.

Although it was not part of these official procedures, Larry James encouraged the MPs to watch *Quiet Rage: The Stanford Prison Experiment* and discuss its message about abuse of power as it might relate to their new role of being a guard within that prison setting.

Would he have been able to install such strong oversight procedures *before* the revelation of the abuses? It's hard to say, but I think it is unlikely that anyone would have even thought to create this mission. Had this set of procedures been in place, is it less likely the abuses would have occurred? That seems certainly to be so because such conditions would have eliminated the confusion and the diffusion of responsibility, while also making it apparent that everyone's behavior was under surveillance. (Of course, that also extends to what should have been happening at the SPE.)

It's good that many seemingly effective practices are in place, but have they made a difference? James's answer was "My dependent variable is there have been no abuses since these rules have been put in place [as of November 2005]."

Since then, the Pentagon has decided to shut down the prison at Abu Ghraib, releasing some of its detainees and transferring others to Camp Cropper, near the Baghdad airport. Britain's top legal adviser has recently called for the United States to close the prison at Guantánamo Bay (which over the years has held a total of 759 prisoners, according to the Department of Defense).[98] He believes that this detention center has become an international symbol of injustice. Attorney General Peter Goldsmith said that the reliance of that camp on military tribunals does not meet the British commitment to the principle of "a fair trial in accordance with international standards."[99] Spain's most prominent investigative magistrate, Baltasar Garzón, also called on the United States to shut down this prison, as "an insult to countries that respect laws." He says Spain learned the lesson from the evils of the Inquisition that "torture and degradation do not work as investigative techniques."[100]

Colonel Larry James was awarded the Bronze Star for this special military service. It is a great pleasure for me to be able to end this chapter celebrating this singular accomplishment of my colleague and friend. I wish that he had been empowered to do so a few years earlier.

LET THE SUNSHINE IN

Well, we've made it to the end of our long journey together. I appreciate your staying power to continue on despite these confrontations with some of what is worse in human nature. It has been especially difficult for me to revisit the scenes of abuse in the Stanford Prison Experiment. It has also been tough to face up to my ineffectiveness in helping achieve a better resolution in the case of Chip Frederick. As a perennial optimist, facing all the evils of genocide, massacres, lynchings, torture, and other horrible things that people do to other people is starting to dim my positive outlook on the human condition.

In the final phase of our journey, we will let the sunshine in to illuminate these dark corners of the human psyche. It is time to accentuate the positive and eliminate the negative. I shall do so in two ways. First, you will get some well-reasoned advice on how to resist the social influences that you don't want and don't need but that bombard you, and most of us, daily. While acknowledging the power of situational forces to influence most of us to behave badly in many contexts, I also make evident that we are not slaves to their power. It is through understanding how such forces operate that we can resist, oppose, and prevent them from leading us into undesirable temptation. Such knowledge can liberate us from subjugation to the mighty grasp of conformity, compliance, persuasion, and other forms of social influence and coercion.

Having explored the weaknesses, frailties, and all-too-easy transformations of human character throughout our journey, we end on a most positive note by celebrating heroism and heroes. By now I hope you are willing to accept the premise that ordinary people, even good ones, can be seduced, recruited, initiated into behaving in evil ways under the sway of powerful systematic and situational forces. If so, are you also ready to endorse the reverse premise: that any of us is a potential hero waiting for a situation to arise that will enable us to show that we have "the right stuff"? Let's now learn how to resist temptation and celebrate heroes.

CHAPTER SIXTEEN

Resisting Situational Influences and Celebrating Heroism

Every exit is an entry somewhere else.

—Tom Stoppard, *Rosencrantz and Guildenstern Are Dead*

We have come to the end of our journey through the dark places that imprison the minds of our fellow travelers. We have witnessed the conditions that reveal the brutal side of human nature and have been surprised by the ease and the extent to which good people can become so cruel to others. Our conceptual focus has been on trying to understand better how such transformations take place. Although evil can exist in any setting, we have looked most closely into its breeding ground in prisons and wars. They typically become crucibles, in which authority, power, and dominance are blended and, when covered over by secrecy, suspend our humanity, and rob us of the qualities we humans value most: caring, kindness, cooperation, and love.

Much of our time was spent in the simulated prison that my colleagues and I created in the basement of Stanford University's Psychology Department. In just a few days and nights the virtual paradise that is Palo Alto, California, and Stanford University became a hellhole. Healthy young men developed pathological symptoms that reflected the extreme stress, frustration, and hopelessness they were experiencing as prisoners. Their counterparts, randomly assigned to the role of guards, repeatedly crossed the line from frivolously playing that role to seriously abusing "their prisoners." In less than a week, our little "experiment," our mock prison, receded into the background of our collective consciousness, to be replaced by a reality of prisoners, guards, and prison staff that seemed remarkably real to all. It was a prison run by psychologists rather than by the State.

The detailed scrutiny that I brought to the nature of these transformations, which have never before been fully elaborated, is aimed at bringing each reader as close as possible to that special place where we can pit person power against institutional power. I tried to convey a sense of the unfolding processes by which a host of seemingly minor situational variables, such as social roles, rules, norms, and uniforms, came to have so powerful an impact on all those caught up in its system.

At a conceptual level, I have proposed that we give greater consideration and more weight to situational and systemic processes than we typically do when we are trying to account for aberrant behaviors and seeming personality changes. Human behavior is always subject to situational forces. This context is embedded within a larger, macrocosmic one, often a particular power system that is designed to maintain and sustain itself. Traditional analyses by most people, including those in legal, religious, and medical institutions, focus on the actor as the sole causal agent. Consequently, they minimize or disregard the impact of situational variables and systemic determinants that shape behavioral outcomes and transform actors.

Hopefully, the examples and supporting information in this book will challenge the rigid Fundamental Attribution Error that locates the inner qualities of people as the main source of their actions. We have added the need to recognize both the power of situations and the behavioral scaffolding provided by the System that crafts and upholds the social context.

We have journeyed from a make-believe prison to the nightmare reality that was Iraq's Abu Ghraib Prison. Surprising parallels emerged between the social psychological processes at work in both of those prisons, the mock one and the all-too-real one. In Abu Ghraib, our analytical spotlight focused on one young man, Staff Sergeant Ivan Chip Frederick, who made a dual transformation: from good soldier to bad prison guard and then to suffering prisoner. Our analysis revealed, just as in the Stanford Prison Experiment, the dispositional, situational, and systemic factors that played a crucial role in fostering the abuse and torture that Frederick and other military and civilian personnel heaped on the prisoners in their custody.

I moved then from my position as an impartial social science researcher to assume the role of a prosecutor. In doing so, I exposed to you, readers-as-jurors, the crimes of the top brass in the military command and in the Bush administration that make them complicit in creating the conditions that in turn made possible such wide-ranging wanton abuse and torture throughout most U.S. military prisons. As noted repeatedly, the view I have provided does not negate the responsibility of these MPs, nor their guilt; explanation and understanding do not excuse such misdeeds. Rather, understanding how the events happened and appreciating what were the situational forces operating on the soldiers can lead to proactive ways to modify the circumstances that elicit such unacceptable behavior. Punishing is not enough. "Bad systems" create "bad situations" create "bad apples" create "bad behaviors," even in good people.

For the last time, let's define Person, Situation, and System. The Person is an actor on the stage of life whose behavioral freedom is informed by his or her makeup—genetic, biological, physical, and psychological. The Situation is the behavioral context that has the power, through its reward and normative functions, to give meaning and identity to the actor's roles and status. The System consists of the agents and agencies whose ideology, values, and power create situations and dictate the roles and expectations for approved behaviors of actors within its spheres of influence.

In this, the final phase of our journey, we will consider advice about how to prevent or combat negative situational forces that act upon all of us from time to time. We will explore how to resist influences that we neither want nor need but that rain upon us daily. We are not slaves to the power of situational forces. But we must learn methods of resisting and opposing them. In all the situations we have explored together, there were always a few, a minority, who stood firm. The time has come to try to expand their numbers by thinking about how they were able to resist.

If I have in some measure brought you to appreciate that under some circumstances *You* might behave in the ways that participants did in the research conditions outlined here and in the real prison of Abu Ghraib, I ask you to consider now, could you also accept a conception of *You* as a Hero? We will celebrate also the good in human nature, the heroes among us, and the heroic imagination in all of us.

LEARNING HOW TO RESIST UNWANTED INFLUENCES

People with paranoid disorders have great difficulty in conforming to, complying with, or responding to a persuasive message, even when it is offered by their well-meaning therapists or loved ones. Their cynicism and distrust create an isolating barrier that shields them from involvement in most social encounters. Because they are adamantly resistant to social pressures, they provide an extreme model for immunity to influence, though obviously at great psychic cost. At the other end of the scale are the overly gullible, unconditionally trusting people who are easy marks for any and every scam artist.

Among them are the many people who fall prey to frauds, scams, and confidence games at some time in their lives. A full 12 percent of Americans are defrauded by con-artist criminals each year, sometimes losing their life savings. It is likely that this figure is shared by people in most nations. Although the majority of those defrauded are over fifty years old, at a time of life when wisdom should prevail, many people of all ages are regularly duped by tricksters in telemarketing, health care, and lottery scams.[1]

Remember the phony authority hoax perpetrated on an innocent teenager at a McDonald's restaurant that was described in chapter 12? Surely you asked yourself, "How could she and those adults duped by this caller be so stupid?" Well, this same hoax was effective in getting many other fast-food restaurant personnel to follow that false authority blindly. How many? Recall in a dozen different restaurant chains in nearly seventy different establishments, in thirty-two states![2] We noted that one assistant manager in a McDonald's restaurant, who was totally duped by the phony caller–con man, asks us all, "Unless you are in that situation, at that time, how do you know what you would do? You don't know what you would do."[3]

The point is that instead of distancing ourselves from the individuals who were deceived by assuming negative dispositional attributes in them—stupidity, naiveté—we need to understand why and how people like us were so completely seduced. Then we will be in a position to resist and to spread awareness of methods of resisting such hoaxes.

The Duality of Detachment Versus Saturation

A basic duality exists in the human condition of detachment versus saturation, of cynical suspicion versus engagement. Detaching ourselves from others in the fear of being "taken in" is an extreme defensive posture, but it is true that the more open we are to other people's persuasion, the more likely we are to be swayed by them. Nevertheless, open, passionate involvement with others is essential to human happiness. We want to feel strongly, to trust completely, to act spontaneously, and to feel connected to others. We want to be fully "saturated" in living. At least some of the time, we want to suspend our evaluative faculties and abandon our primitive fearful reserve. We want to dance with passion along with Zorba the Greek.[4]

Yet, we must regularly assess the worth of our social involvements. The challenge for each of us is how best to oscillate between two poles, immersing fully and distancing appropriately. Knowing when to stay involved with others, when to support and be loyal to a cause or a relationship rather than dismissing it, is a delicate question that we all face regularly. We live in a world in which some people aim to use us. In that same world are others who genuinely want us to share what they believe are mutually positive goals. How to tell which is which? That is the question, dear Hamlet and dear Ophelia.

Before we begin to deal with specific means for combating mind-controlling influences, we must consider another possibility: the old illusion of *personal invulnerability*.[5] Them? Yes. Me? *No!* Our psychological journey should have convinced you to appreciate how the array of situational forces that we've highlighted can suck in the majority of people. But not You, right? It is hard to extend the lessons we have learned from an intellectual assessment to affect our own codes of conduct. What is easily applied in the abstract to "those others" is not easily applied in the concrete to oneself. We are different. Just as no two fingerprints have identical patterns, no two people have identical genetic, developmental, and personality patterns.

Individual differences should be celebrated, but in the face of strong, common situational forces, individual differences shrink and are compressed. In such instances, behavioral scientists can predict what the majority of people will do knowing nothing about the particular people who comprise a group, only the nature of their behavioral context. It should be clear that not even the best psychology can predict how each and every individual will behave in a given situation; some degree of individual variance always exists that cannot be accounted for. Therefore, you may reject the lessons that we are about to learn as inapplicable to yourself; you are the special case, the special end of the tail of the normal distribution. However, know that you do so at the cost of being caught with your defenses down and your tail twisted.

My advice about what to do in case you encounter a "dirty, rotten scoundrel," disguised as a nice guy or a sweet old lady, has been accumulated over many decades from many personal experiences. As a scrawny, sickly kid trying to survive on the mean streets of my South Bronx ghetto, I had to learn basic street smarts; these consisted of figuring out quickly how certain people would be likely to act in certain situations. I got good enough at the skill to become a leader of the gang, the team, or the class. Then I was trained by an unscrupulous boss, a Fagin-like character in drag, on how to deceive Broadway theatergoers into checking their hats and coats when they did not want to and to manipulate them into paying tips to get them back, when tipping was not required. As her apprentice, I became experienced in selling expensive show programs when free versions were available and in overdosing kids with loads of candy and drinks if their parents were not chaperoning them to our candy counter. I was also trained to sell magazines door to door, eliciting pity from, and thereby sales to, sympathetic tenement dwellers. Later on, I studied formally the tactics police use to get confessions from suspects, that state-sanctioned torturers use to get anything they want from their victims, and that cult recruiters use in seducing the innocent into their dens. My scholarship extended to studying the mind control tactics used by the Soviets and the methods used by the Chinese Communists in the Korean War and in their massive national thought reform programs. I also studied our own homegrown mind manipulators in the CIA, the state-sponsored MKULTRA program,[6] and Jim Jones's lethal charismatic power over his religious followers (described in earlier chapters).

I have both counseled and learned from those who survived various cult experiences. In addition, I have engaged in a lifetime of investigative research on persuasion, compliance, dissonance, and group processes. My writing on some of these topics includes a training manual for peace activists during the Vietnam War, as well as several basic texts on attitude change and social influence.[7] These credentials are offered only to bolster the communicator credibility of the information provided next.

Promoting Altruism via the Virtuous Authority Experiment

Let us first imagine a "Reverse-Milgram" authority experiment. Our goal is to create a setting in which people will comply with demands that intensify over time *to do good.* The participants would be guided gradually to behave in ever-more-altruistic ways, slowly but surely moving further than they could have imagined toward ever-more-positive, prosocial actions. Instead of the paradigm arranged to facilitate a slow descent into evil, we could substitute a paradigm for a slow ascent into goodness. How could we formulate an experimental setting in which that was possible? Let us design such a thought experiment. To begin, imagine that we arrange for each participant a hierarchy of experiences or actions that range from slightly more positive acts than he or she is used to doing to ever-more-extreme "good" actions. The extremes of virtue push him or her upward all the way to engaging in actions that at first seemed unimaginable.

There might be a time-based dimension in the design for those busy citizens who do not practice virtue because they have convinced themselves that they just don't have time to spare for good deeds. The first "button" on the "Goodness Generator" might be to spend ten minutes writing a thank-you note to a friend or a get-well card to a colleague. The next level might demand twenty minutes of giving advice to a troubled child. Increasing the pressure in this paradigm might then entail the participant's agreeing to give thirty minutes of his time to read a story to an illiterate housekeeper. Then the altruism scale moves upward to spending an hour tutoring a needy student, then to babysitting for a few hours to allow a single parent to visit her sick mother, working for an evening in a soup kitchen, helping unemployed veterans, devoting part of a day to taking a group of orphaned children to the zoo, being available to talk with returning wounded veterans, and on and on upward, a step-by-step commitment to giving precious time every week to ever-more-worthy causes. Providing social models along the way who are already engaged in the requested task, or who take the initiative to ante up to the next level, should work to encourage obedience to virtuous authority, should it not? It's worth a try, especially since, as far as I know, nothing like this experiment has ever been done.

Ideally, our experiment in social goodness would end when the person was doing something that he or she could never have imagined doing before. Our goodness track could also include contributions to creating a healthy and sustainable environment that might go from minimal acts of conservation or recycling to ever more substantial activities, such as giving money, time, and personal involvement to "green" causes. I invite you to expand on this notion in a host of domains in which society would benefit as more citizens "went all the way"—doing good without any supporting ideology, for, as we know from dissonance theory, beliefs follow behavior. Get people to perform good actions, and they will generate the necessary underlying principles to justify them. Talmudic scholars are supposed to have preached not to require that people believe before they pray, only to do what is needed to get them to begin to pray; then they will come to believe in what and to whom they are praying.

Research Supports a Reverse-Milgram Altruism Effect

As noted, this reverse-Milgram experiment has never been done. Suppose we actually attempted to perform such an experiment in the laboratory or, better yet, in our homes and communities. Would it work? Could we use the power of authority and of the situation to produce virtue? Based on what I know about human beings and the principles of social influence, I am confident that we could do a better job of bringing about righteousness in our world, employing basic principles of social influence (see Notes for some references).[8]

The reverse-Milgram experiment described here combines three simple influence tactics that have been extensively studied and documented by social psychologists: the foot-in-the-door tactic, social modeling, and self-labeling of helpfulness. I've merely brought them together in one situation for promoting altruism. Moreover, researchers have found that these tactics can be used to promote all sorts of prosocial behavior—from donating one's hard-earned money to charity to increasing recycling and even to giving blood at the next Red Cross blood drive.

Our "slow ascent into goodness step by step" makes use of what social psychologists call the *"foot-in-the-door"* (FITD) tactic. This tactic begins by first asking someone to do a small request (which most people readily perform) and then later on to ask them to comply with a related but much bigger request (which was the actual goal all along).[9] The classic demonstration of this tactic was done more than forty years ago by Jonathan Freedman and Scott Fraser.[10] They asked suburbanites to put a big, ugly sign urging "Drive Carefully" in their nice suburban yard. Fewer than twenty percent of the homeowners did so. However, three fourths of the homeowners agreed to place that sign in their yards if two weeks earlier they had taken a small step and posted in their windows an unobtrusive three-inch sign urging safe driving. The same approach works with other prosocial behavior. For example, researchers have found that merely signing a petition leads to increased monetary support of the handicapped, filling out a brief questionnaire increases the willingness of people to donate their organs to others after death, conserving a small amount of energy induces homeowners to subsequently conserve more energy, and making a small public commitment increases the recycling of paper products.[11] What is more, this FITD effect can be enhanced by chaining together a series of increasingly larger requests, putting two feet in the door—just as in our reverse-Milgram experiment on promoting altruism.[12]

Our reverse-Milgram experiment would also employ *social models* to encourage prosocial behavior. In the SPE and Abu Ghraib Prison, there was an abundance of negative models that supported abusive behavior. Turning the power of social models around to enhance positive acts can be as effective in achieving the opposite, desirable outcomes. Researchers have found that altruistic role models increase the likelihood that those around them will engage in positive, prosocial behavior. Here is just a sampling of findings: social role models have been shown to increase donations to the Salvation Army; to promote helping a stranger with a flat tire; to lower rates of aggression and promote nonviolent responses; to reduce littering; and to increase donating money to poor children and a willingness to share one's resources with others.[13] But one word of advice: Remember to practice what you preach. Models persuade far more effectively than words. For example, in one set of experiments, children were exposed to an adult model that preached either greed or charity to them in a persuasive sermon. However, that adult then went on to practice either greedy or charitable actions. The results showed that the children were more likely to do what the model did than what the model had said.[14]

The wisdom of the Talmudic scholars previously mentioned is consistent with another social influence principle underlying our reverse-Milgram experiment: Give someone an *identity label* of the kind that you would like them to have as someone who will then do the action you want to elicit from them. When you tell a person that he or she is helpful, altruistic, and kind, that person is more likely to do helpful, altruistic, and kind behaviors for others. In the Stanford Prison Experiment, we randomly assigned young men to the roles of prisoner and guard, and they soon took on the manners and the behaviors of those roles. So, too, if we tell someone that he or she is a helpful person, he or she will take on the manners and actions consistent with that identity label. For example, researchers have found that telling someone that he or she is "a generous person" increases compliance with a request to make a large contribution to prevent multiple sclerosis; giving people feedback that they are kind makes them more likely to help someone who has dropped a large number of cards; and those given a salient identity as "blood donors" are more likely to continue to donate their own blood to a stranger whom they don't expect ever to know or meet.[15]

One of the great advantages of our species is the ability to explore and understand our social world and then to use what we know to make our lives better. Throughout this book, we have seen the power of the situation to produce evil. I now argue that we can take those same basic principles and use the power of the situation to produce virtue. I fear for the future of humanity if my argument on this point is a failure or if I fail in making my argument acceptable to you. Might I suggest that you take a small step today in carrying out the reverse-Milgram experiment in your own life? I think you are just the person to do it and to serve as a role model for others in transforming our world to one with a more positive future. If not you, then who?

A Ten-step Program to Resist Unwanted Influences

If we consider some of the social psychological principles that fostered the evils we saw during the course of our journey, then once again—as we have just done in constructing the Goodness Generator example—let us use variants of those principles to get people to accentuate the positive and eliminate the negative in their lives. Given the range of different types of influence, it would be necessary to tailor resistance to each type. Combating wrong dissonant commitments requires different tactics from opposing compliance-gaining strategies used on us. Confronting persuasive speeches and powerful communicators forces us to use different principles than we need for dealing with those who would dehumanize us or deindividuate us. Ways of undercutting groupthink are also different from ways of modifying the impact of intense recruiters.

I have developed such a compendium for you; however, it offers more depth and specifics than is possible to deal with in this chapter. The solution is to make it all available to you free, online in the special website developed as a companion to this book: www.LuciferEffect.com. That way, you can read it at your leisure, take notes, check out the reference sources on which it is based, and contemplate scenarios in which you will put these resistance strategies into practice in your life. Also, after you have encountered a particular social influence tactic used on you or on others you know, you can turn to this handy guide for solutions about what to do next time around to be in a better position to master that challenge.

Here is my ten-step program for resisting the impact of undesirable social influences and at the same time promoting personal resilience and civic virtue. It uses ideas that cut across various influence strategies and provides simple, effective modes of dealing with them. The key to resistance lies in development of the three Ss: self-awareness, situational sensitivity, and street smarts. You will see how they are central to many of these general strategies of resistance.

"I made a mistake!" Let's start out by encouraging admission of our mistakes, first to ourselves, then to others. Accept the dictum that to err is human. You have made an error in judgment; your decision was wrong. You had every reason to believe it was right when you made it, but now you know you were wrong. Say the six magic words: "I'm sorry"; "I apologize"; "Forgive me." Say to yourself that you will learn from your mistakes, grow better from them. Don't continue to put your money, time, and resources into bad investments. Move on. Doing so openly reduces the need to justify or rationalize our mistakes and thereby to continue to give support to bad or immoral actions. Confession of error undercuts the motivation to reduce cognitive dissonance; dissonance evaporates when a reality check occurs. "Cutting bait" instead of resolutely "staying the course" when it is wrong has an immediate cost, but it always results in long-term gain. Consider how many years the Vietnam War continued long after top military and administration officials, such as Secretary of Defense Robert McNamara, knew that the war was wrong and could not be won.[16] How many thousands of lives were lost to such wrongheaded resistance, when acknowledging failure and error could have saved them? How much good could come to all of us were our political leaders able to admit their similar errors in Iraq? It is more than a political decision to "save face" by denying errors instead of saving soldiers' and civilian lives—it is a moral imperative.

"I am mindful." In many settings smart people do dumb things because they fail to attend to key features in the words or actions of influence agents and fail to notice obvious situational clues. Too often we function on automatic pilot, using outworn scripts that have worked for us in the past, never stopping to evaluate

whether they are appropriate in the here and now.[17] Following the advice of the Harvard researcher Ellen Langer, we must transform our usual state of mindless inattention into "mindfulness," especially in new situations.[18] Don't hesitate to fire a wake-up shot to your cortex; when we are in familiar situations old habits continue to rule even though they have become obsolete or wrong. We need to be reminded not to live our lives on automatic pilot but always to take a Zen moment to reflect on the meaning of the immediate situation, to think before acting. Never go mindlessly into situations where angels and sensible people fear to tread. For the best results, add "critical thinking" to mindfulness in your resistance.[19] Ask for evidence to support assertions; demand that ideologies be sufficiently elaborated to allow you to separate rhetoric from substance. Try to determine whether the recommended means ever justify potentially harmful ends. Imagine end-game scenarios of the future consequences of any current practice. Reject simple solutions as quick fixes for complex personal or social problems. Support critical thinking from the earliest times in children's lives, alerting them to the deceptive TV ads, biased claims, and distorted perspectives being presented to them. Help them become wiser and warier knowledge consumers.[20]

"I am responsible." Taking responsibility for one's decisions and actions puts the actor in the driver's seat, for better or for worse. Allowing others to compromise their own responsibility, to diffuse it, makes them powerful backseat drivers and makes the car move recklessly ahead without a responsible driver. We become more resistant to undesirable social influence by always maintaining a sense of personal responsibility and by being willing to be held accountable for our actions. Obedience to authority is less blind to the extent that we are aware that diffusion of responsibility merely disguises our individual complicity in the conduct of questionable actions. Your conformity to antisocial group norms is undercut to the extent that you do not allow displacement of responsibility, when you refuse to spread responsibility around the gang, the frat, the shop, the battalion, or the corporation. Always imagine a future time when today's deed will be on trial and no one will accept your pleas of "only following orders," or "everyone else was doing it."

"I am Me, the best I can be." Do not allow others to deindividuate you, to put you into a category, a box, a slot, to turn you into an object. Assert your individuality; politely state your name and your credentials, loud and clear. Insist on the same behavior in others. Make eye contact (remove all eye-concealing sunglasses), and offer information about yourself that reinforces your unique identity. Find common ground with dominant others in influence situations and use it to enhance similarities. Anonymity and secrecy conceal wrongdoing and undermine the human connection. They can become the breeding grounds that generate dehumanization, and, as we now know, dehumanization provides the killing ground for bullies, rapists, torturers, terrorists, and tyrants. Go a step beyond self-individuation.

Work to change whatever social conditions make people feel anonymous. Instead, support practices that make others feel special, so that they too have a sense of personal value and self-worth. Never allow or practice negative stereotyping; words, labels, and jokes can be destructive, if they mock others.

"I respect just authority but rebel against unjust authority." In every situation, work to distinguish between those in authority who, because of their expertise, wisdom, seniority, or special status, deserve respect, and the unjust authority figures who demand our obedience without having any substance. Many who assume the mantel of authority are pseudo-leaders, false prophets, confidence men and women, self-promoters who should not be respected but rather disobeyed and openly exposed to critical evaluation. Parents, teachers, and religious leaders should play more active roles in teaching children this critical differentiation. They should be polite and courteous when such a stance is justified, yet be good, wise children by resisting those authorities who do not deserve their respect. Doing so will reduce our mindless obedience to self-proclaimed authorities whose priorities are not in our best interests.

"I want group acceptance, but value my independence." The lure of acceptance into a desired social group is more powerful than that of the mythical golden ring in *Lord of the Rings*. The power of that desire for acceptance will make some people do almost anything to be accepted and go to even further extremes to avoid rejection by the Group. We are indeed social animals, and usually our social connections benefit us and help us to achieve important goals that we could not achieve alone. However, there are times when conformity to a group norm is counterproductive to the social good. It is imperative to determine when to follow the norm and when to reject it. Ultimately, we live within our own minds, in solitary splendor, and therefore we must be willing and ready to declare our independence regardless of the social rejection it may elicit. It is not easy, especially for young people with a shaky self-image or adults whose self-image is isomorphic with that of their job. Pressures on them to be a "team player," to sacrifice personal morality for the good of the team, are nearly irresistible. What is required is that we step back, get outside opinions, and find new groups that will support our independence and promote our values. There will always be another, different, better group for us.

"I will be more frame-vigilant." Who makes the frame becomes the artist, or the con artist. The way issues are framed is often more influential than the persuasive arguments within their boundaries. Moreover, effective frames can seem not to be frames at all, just sound bites, visual images, slogans, and logos. They influence us without our being conscious of them, and they shape our orientation toward the ideas or issues they promote. For example, voters who favored reducing estate tax benefits for the rich were urged to vote against a "death tax"; the tax was exactly

the same, but its defining term was different. We desire things that are framed as being "scarce," even when they are plentiful. We are averse to things that are framed as potential losses and prefer what is presented to us as a gain, even when the ratio of positive to negative prognoses is the same.[21] We don't want a 40 percent chance of losing X over Y, but we do want the 60 percent chance of gaining Y over X. The linguist George Lakoff clearly shows in his writings that it is crucial to be aware of frame power and to be vigilant in order to offset its insidious influence on our emotions, thoughts, and votes.[22]

"I will balance my time perspective." We can be led to do things that are not really what we believe in when we allow ourselves to become trapped in an expanded present moment. When we stop relying on our sense of past commitments and our sense of future liabilities, we open ourselves to situational temptations to engage in *Lord of the Flies* excesses. By not "going with the flow" when others around you are being abusive or out of control, you are relying on a temporal perspective that stretches beyond present-oriented hedonism or present-oriented fatalism. You are likely to engage in a cost-benefit analysis of your actions in terms of their future consequences. Or you may resist by being sufficiently conscious of a past time frame that contains your personal values and standards. By developing a balanced time perspective in which past, present, and future can be called into action depending on the situation and task at hand, you will be in a better position to act responsibly and wisely than when your time perspective is biased toward reliance on only one or two time frames. Situational power is weakened when past and future combine to contain the excesses of the present.[23] For example, research indicates that righteous Gentiles who helped to hide Dutch Jews from the Nazis did not engage in the kind of rationalizing their neighbors did in generating reasons for *not* helping. These heroes depended upon moral structures derived from their past and never lost sight of a future time when they would look back on this terrible situation and be forced to ask themselves whether they had done the right thing when they chose not to succumb to fear and social pressure.[24]

"I will not sacrifice personal or civic freedoms for the illusion of security." The need for security is a powerful determinant of human behavior. We can be manipulated into engaging in actions that are alien to us when faced with alleged threats to our security or the promise of security from danger. More often than not, influence peddlers gain power over us by offering a Faustian contract: You will be safe from harm if you will just surrender some of your freedom, either personal or civic, to that authority. The Mephistophelian tempter will argue that his power to save you depends upon all the people making small sacrifices of this little right or that small freedom. Reject that deal. Never sacrifice basic personal freedoms for the promise of security because the sacrifices are real and immediate and the security is a distant illusion. This is as true in traditional marital arrange-

ments as it is in the commitment of good citizens to the interests of their nation when its leader promises personal safety and national security at the cost of a collective sacrifice of suspending laws, privacy, and freedoms. Erich Fromm's classic *Escape from Freedom* reminds us that this is the first step a fascist leader takes even in a nominally democratic society.

"I can oppose unjust systems." Individuals falter in the face of the intensity of the systems we have described: the military and prison systems as well as those of gangs, cults, fraternities, corporations, and even dysfunctional families. But individual resistance in concert with that of others of the same mind and resolve can combine to make a difference. The next section in this chapter will portray individuals who changed systems by being willing to take the risk of blowing the whistle on corruption within them or by constructively working to change them. Resistance may involve physically removing one's self from a total situation in which all information, rewards, and punishments are controlled. It may involve challenging the groupthink mentality and being able to document all allegations of wrongdoing. It may involve getting help from other authorities, counselors, investigative reporters, or revolutionary compatriots. Systems have enormous power to resist change and withstand even righteous assault. Here is one place where individual acts of heroism to challenge unjust systems and their bad barrel makers are best performed by soliciting others to join one's cause. The system can redefine individual opposition as delusional, a pair of opponents as sharing a *folie à deux*, but with three on your side, you become a force of ideas to be reckoned with.

This ten-step program is really only a starter kit toward building individual resistance and communal resilience against undesirable influences and illegitimate attempts at persuasion. As mentioned, a fuller set of recommendations and relevant research-based references can be found on the Lucifer Effect website under *"Resisting Influence Guide."*

Before moving to the final stop in our journey, celebrating heroes and heroism, I would like to add two final general recommendations. First, be discouraged from venal sins and small transgressions, such as cheating, lying, gossiping, spreading rumors, laughing at racist or sexist jokes, teasing, and bullying. They can become stepping-stones to more serious falls from grace. They serve as minifacilitators for thinking and acting destructively against your fellow creatures. Second, moderate your in-group biases. That means accepting that your group is special but at the same time respecting the diversity that other groups offer. Fully appreciate the wonder of human variety and its variability. Assuming such a perspective will help you to reduce group biases that lead to derogating others, to prejudice and stereotyping, and to the evils of dehumanization.

THE PARADOXES OF HEROISM

A young woman challenges an authority older than she, forcing him to recognize his complicity in reprehensible deeds that are being perpetrated on his watch. Her confrontation goes further and helps to terminate the abuse of innocent prisoners by their guards. Does her action qualify as "heroic," given that scores of others who had witnessed the prisoners' distress all failed to act against the system when they realized its excesses?

We would like to celebrate heroism and heroes as special acts by special people. However, most people who are held up to this higher plane insist that what they did was not special, was really what everyone should have done in the situation. They refuse to consider themselves "heroes." Maybe such a reaction comes from the ingrained notion we all have—that heroes are supermen and -women, a cut or more above the common breed. Perhaps more than their modesty is at work. Perhaps, rather, it is our general misconception of what it takes to be heroic.

Let's now look at the best in human nature and the transformation of the ordinary into the heroic. We will examine alternative conceptions and definitions of heroism and propose a way to classify different kinds of heroic action; then elaborate on some examples that fall into these categories; and finally design a table of contrasts between the banalities of evil and of heroism. But first, let's go back to the person and the act that started this section and ended the Stanford Prison Experiment.

Recall (from chapter 8) that Christina Maslach was a recently graduated Ph.D. from the Stanford Psychology Department with whom I had become romantically involved. When she saw a chain gang of prisoners being carted to the toilet with bags over their heads as guards shouted orders at them and she witnessed my apparent indifference to their suffering, she exploded.

Her later account of what she felt at the time, and how she interpreted her actions, tells us a good deal about the complex phenomenon of heroism.[25]

> What he [Zimbardo] got was an incredibly emotional out-burst from me (I am usually a rather contained person). I was angry and frightened and in tears. I said something like, *"What you are doing to those boys is a terrible thing!"*
>
> So what is the important story to emerge from my role as "the Terminator" of the Stanford Prison Experiment? I think there are several themes I would like to highlight. First, however, let me say what the story is not. Contrary to the standard (and trite) American myth, the Stanford Prison Experiment is not a story about the lone individual who defies the majority. Rather, it is a story about the majority—about how everyone who had some contact with the prison study (participants, researchers, observers, consultants, family, and friends) got so completely sucked into it. The

power of the situation to overwhelm personality and the best of intentions is the key story line here.

So why was my reaction so different? The answer, I think, lies in two facts: I was a late entrant into the situation, and I was an "outsider." Unlike everyone else, I had not been a consenting participant in the study. Unlike everyone else, I had no socially defined role within that prison context. Unlike everyone else, I was not there every day, being carried along as the situation changed and escalated bit by bit. Thus the situation I entered at the end of the week was not truly the "same" as it was for everyone else—I lacked their prior consensual history, place, and perspective. For them, the situation was construed as being still within the range of normalcy; for me, it was not—it was a madhouse.

As an outsider, I did not have the option of specific social rules that I could disobey, so my dissent took a different form—of challenging the situation itself. This challenge has been seen by some as a heroic action, but at the time it did not feel especially heroic. To the contrary, it was a very scary and lonely experience being the deviant, doubting my judgment of both situations and people, and maybe even my worth as a research social psychologist.

Christina then raises a profound qualification. For an act of personal defiance to be worthy of being considered "heroic," it must attempt to change the system, to correct an injustice, to right a wrong:

> I had to consider also in the back of my mind what I might do if Phil continued with the SPE despite my determined challenge to him. Would I have gone to the higher authorities, the department chair, dean, or Human Subjects Committee, to blow the whistle on it? I can't say for sure, and I am glad it never came to that. But in retrospect, that action would have been essential in translating my values into meaningful action. When one complains about some injustice and the complaint only results in cosmetic modifications while the situation flows on unchanged, then that dissent and disobedience are not worth much.

She expands on a point that was raised in our discussion of the Milgram research, where it was argued that verbal dissent was only ego balm for the "teacher," to make him feel better about the terrible things he was doing to his "learner." *Behavioral disobedience* was necessary to challenge authority. However, in the Milgram experiment case there was never disobedience more significant than a silent retreat as each teacher-perpetrator exited from the distressing situation without changing it in any meaningful way. Christina's take on what the heroic minority should have done after they opposed the authority figure has never been framed so eloquently:

What did it matter to the classic original Milgram study that one third of the participants disobeyed and refused to go all the way? Suppose it was not an experiment; suppose Milgram's "cover story" were true, that researchers were studying the role of punishment in learning and memory and would be testing about one thousand participants in a host of experiments to answer their practical questions about the educational value of judiciously administered punishment. If you disobeyed, refused to continue, got paid, and left silently, your heroic action would not prevent the next 999 participants from experiencing the same distress. It would be an isolated event without social impact unless it included going to the next step of challenging the entire structure and assumptions of the research. Disobedience by the individual must get translated into systemic disobedience that forces change in the situation or agency itself and not just in some operating conditions. It is too easy for evil situations to co-opt the intentions of good dissidents or even heroic rebels by giving them medals for their deeds and a gift certificate for keeping their opinions to themselves.

What Is the Stuff of Heroism and Heroes?

When does a person who engages in an action that qualifies as a heroic act, on the basis of criteria we will lay out next, not become a "hero"? Further, under what circumstances might her or his act be considered not heroic but cowardly?

Christina's action had the positive consequence of terminating a situation that had spiraled out of control and began to do more harm than had been intended at its inception. She does not consider herself a hero because she was simply expressing her personal feelings and beliefs that were translated (by me as principal investigator) into the outcome she desired. She did not have to "blow the whistle" to higher authorities to intervene in order to stop the runaway experiment.

Compare her condition to that of two potential heroes in that study, Prisoner Clay-416 and Prisoner "Sarge." Both of them openly defied the authority of the guards and suffered considerably for doing so. Clay's hunger strike and refusal to eat the sausages challenged the guards' complete control and should have rallied his peers to stand up for their rights. It did not. Sarge's refusal to utter public obscenities despite the harassment by Guard "John Wayne" also should have been viewed as heroic defiance by his peers and rallied them not to yield to such abuse. It did not. Why not? In both cases, they acted alone, without sharing their values or intentions with the other prisoners, without asking for their support and recognition. Therefore, it was easy for the guards to label them "troublemakers" and to brand them as the culprits responsible for the guards' deprivations of the rest of the prisoners. Their acts could be considered heroic, but they cannot be considered heroes because they never acted to change the whole abusive system by bringing other dissidents on board.

Another aspect of heroism is raised by their example. Heroism and heroic status are always social attributions. Someone other than the actor confers that honor on the person and the deed. There must be social consensus about the significance and meaningful consequence of an act for it to be deemed heroic, and for its agent to be called a hero. Wait! Not so fast! A Palestinian suicide bomber who is killed in the act of murdering innocent Jewish civilians is given heroic status in Palestine and demonic status in Israel. Similarly, aggressors may be construed as heroic freedom fighters or as cowardly agents of terrorism, depending on who is conferring the attribution.[26]

This means that definitions of heroism are always culture-bound and time-bound. To this day, puppeteers enact the legend of Alexander the Great before children in remote villages of Turkey. In the towns where his command posts were set up and his soldiers intermarried with villagers, Alexander is a great hero, but in towns that were simply conquered on his relentless quest to rule the known world, Alexander is portrayed as a great villain, more than a thousand years after his death.[27]

What is more, to become part of any culture's history a hero's acts must be recorded and preserved by those who are literate and who have the power to write history or to pass it on in an oral tradition. Poor, indigenous, colonized, illiterate people have few widely acknowledged heroes because there is no record of their acts.

Defining Heroes and Heroism

Heroism has never been systematically investigated in the behavioral sciences.[28] Heroes and heroism seem to be best explored by literature, art, myth, and cinema. Multiple data sources document the ills of human existence: homicides and suicides, crime rates, prison populations, poverty levels, and the base rate of schizophrenia in a given population. Similar quantitative data for positive human activities are not easy to come by. We don't keep records of how many acts of charity, kindness, or compassion occur in a community in the course of a year. Only occasionally do we learn of a heroic act. Such apparently low base rates lead us to believe that heroism is rare and that heroes are the truly exceptional. Nevertheless, renewed interest in the importance of addressing the good in human nature has arisen from the new research and empirical rigor of the Positive Psychology movement. Spearheaded by Martin Seligman and his colleagues, this movement has created a paradigm shift toward accentuating the positive in human nature and minimizing psychology's long-held focus on the negative.[29]

Currently accepted conceptions of heroism emphasize primarily its physical risk without adequately addressing other components of heroic acts, such as nobility of purpose and nonviolent acts of personal sacrifice. Emanating from the analyses of human virtues by positive psychologists is a set of six major categories of virtuous behavior that enjoy almost universal recognition across cultures. The classification includes: wisdom and knowledge, courage, humanity, justice, temperance, and transcendence. Of these, courage, justice, and transcendence are the central characteristics of heroism. Transcendence includes beliefs and actions that go beyond the limits of self.

Heroism focuses us on what is right with human nature. We care about heroic stories because they serve as powerful reminders that people are capable of resisting evil, of not giving in to temptations, of rising above mediocrity, and of heeding the call to action and to service when others fail to act.

Many modern dictionaries describe heroism as "gallantry" or "bravery," and these in turn are described as courage, and courage returns us, once again, to heroics. However, older dictionaries were at pains to break down the concept, offering subtle distinctions among words used to describe heroic acts. For example, the *1913 Webster's Revised Unabridged Dictionary* associates heroism with courage, bravery, fortitude, intrepidity, gallantry, and valor.[30] As part of the entry for each of these words, the dictionary's editor tried to ensure that the reader understood how they differed.

Courage is that firmness of spirit and swell of soul, that meets danger without fear. Bravery is daring and impetuous courage, like that of one who has the reward continually in view and displays his courage in daring acts. Fortitude has often been styled "passive courage" and consists in the habit of encountering danger and enduring pain with a steadfast and unbroken spirit. Valor is courage exhibited in war (against living opponents) and cannot be applied to single combat; it is never used figuratively. Intrepidity is firm, unshaken courage. Gallantry is adventurous courage, which courts danger with a high and cheerful spirit.

The dictionary goes on to elaborate, in footnote examples, that a man may show courage, fortitude, or intrepidity in the common pursuits of life, as well as in war. Valor, bravery, and gallantry are displayed in the contest of arms. Valor belongs only to battle; bravery may be shown in single combat; gallantry may be manifested either in attack or defense; but in the latter case, the defense is usually turned into an attack. Heroism may call into exercise all these modifications of courage. It is a contempt of danger, not from ignorance or inconsiderate levity but from a noble devotion to some great cause and a just confidence of being able to meet danger in the spirit of such a cause.[31]

Military Heroes

Historically, most examples of heroism have emphasized acts of courage that involved bravery, gallantry, and risk of serious physical injury or death. According to the psychologists Alice Eagly and Selwyn Becker, the combination of courage and nobility of purpose is more likely to result in someone being considered a hero than just courage alone.[32] The idea of nobility in heroism is often tacit and elusive. Generally the risk of life and limb or of personal sacrifice is much more conspicuous. The heroic ideal of the war hero has served as a theme from ancient epics to modern journalism.

Achilles, commander of Greek forces in the Trojan War, is often held up as an archetypal war hero.[33] Achilles' engagement in combat was based on his commitment to a military code that defined his actions as gallant. Yet, while his acts were heroic, his overriding motivation was the pursuit of glory and renown that would make him immortal in the minds of men after his death.

The historian Lucy Hughes-Hallett argued that "A hero may sacrifice himself so that others might live, or so that he himself may live forever in other's memories. . . . Achilles will give anything, including life itself, to assert his own uniqueness, to endow his particular life with significance, and to escape oblivion."[34] The desire to risk one's physical being in exchange for lasting recognition across generations may seem a relic from another era, yet it still warrants serious consideration in our evaluation of modern heroic behavior.

This historical view of the hero also suggests that there is something innately special about heroes. Hughes-Hallett wrote, "There are men, wrote Aristotle, so godlike, so exceptional, that they naturally, by right of their extraordinary gifts, transcend all moral judgment or constitutional control: 'There is no law which embraces men of that caliber: they are themselves law.' " One definition of heroism arises from this Aristotelian conception: "It is the expression of a superb spirit. It is associated with courage and integrity and a disdain for the cramping compromises by means of which the unheroic majority manage their lives—attributes that are widely considered noble. . . . [Heroes are] capable of something momentous—the defeat of an enemy, the salvation of a race, the preservation of a political system, the completion of a voyage—which *no one else* [italics added] could have accomplished."[35]

This concept of conspicuous service that distinguishes a warrior from his peers persists to this day in our military services. The U.S. Department of Defense recognizes heroism by awarding a number of medals for acts considered to be above and beyond the call of duty. The highest of these is the Medal of Honor, which has been awarded to about 3,400 soldiers.[36] Rules governing the Medal of Honor emphasize the role of gallantry and intrepidity, the willingness to enter into the heart of a battle without flinching that clearly distinguishes the individual's performance from that of his fellow soldiers.[37] Similarly, the British military awards the Victoria Cross as its highest medal for heroism, defined as valorous conduct in the face of an enemy.[38]

The ideal of the military hero is clearly echoed in other contexts, and it includes those who routinely risk their health and lives in the line of duty, such as police officers, firefighters, and paramedics. The insignia worn by firefighters is a version of the Maltese Cross, a symbolic acknowledgment of the creed of heroic service that Knights of Malta were sworn to live by in the Middle Ages. The Maltese Cross in its original form remains a symbol of gallantry for the military in the British Victoria Cross, and from 1919 to 1942 in the U.S. Navy's version of the Medal of Honor, the Tiffany Cross.

Civilian Heroes

If Achilles is the archetypal war hero, Socrates holds the same rank as a civic hero. His teaching was so threatening to the authorities of Athens that he became the target of government censure and was eventually tried and sentenced to death for refusing to renounce his views. When we equate the military heroism of Achilles with the civil heroism of Socrates, it becomes clear that while heroic acts are usually made in service to others or the fundamental moral principles of a society, the hero often works at the nexus of constructive and destructive forces. Hughes-Hallett suggests that "the wings of opportunity are fledged with the feathers of death." She proposes that heroes expose themselves to mortal danger in pursuit of immortality. Both Achilles and Socrates, powerful exemplars of heroism, go to their deaths in service of the divergent codes of conduct by which they chose to live.

Socrates' choice to die for his ideals serves as an eternal normative reminder of the power of civil heroism. We are told that at the hour of Socrates' sentencing, he invoked the image of Achilles in defending his decision to die rather than to submit to an arbitrary law that would silence his opposition to the system he opposed. His example brings to mind the similar heroism of the U.S. Revolutionary War patriot Nathan Hale, whose defiant dying stand will later be used to illustrate one type of heroic action.

Consider the daring deed of the "unknown rebel" who confronted a line of seventeen oncoming tanks that were aimed at smashing the freedom rally of the Chinese Democracy Movement at Tiananmen Square, Peking, on June 5, 1989.

This young man stopped the deadly advance of a column of tanks for thirty minutes and then climbed atop the lead tank, reportedly demanding of its driver, "Why are you here? My city is in chaos because of you. Go back, turn around and stop killing my people." The anonymous "Tank Man" became an instant international symbol of resistance; he faced the ultimate test of personal courage with honor and delineated forever the proud image of an individual standing in defiance against a military juggernaut. The image of that confrontation was broadcast around the world and made him a universal hero. There are conflicting stories about what happened to him as a consequence of his act, some reporting his imprisonment, others his execution, others his anonymous escape. Regardless of what became of him, his status as a civil hero was acknowledged when the Tank Man was included in the list of *Time* magazine's 100 most influential people of the twentieth century (April 1998).

The physical risk demanded of civilians who act heroically differs from a soldier's or first responder's heroic acts, because professionals are bound by duty and a code of conduct and because they are trained. Thus, the standard for duty-bound and non-duty-bound physical-risk heroism may differ, but the style of engagement and potential sacrifice the action demands is very similar.

Civilian heroes who perform acts that involve immediate physical risk are recognized in awards, such as the Carnegie Hero Award in the United States and the George Cross in Britain.[39] British and Australian authorities also recognize heroic actions that involve groups.[40] For example, Australia recognized "a group of students who tackled and restrained an armed offender after a crossbow attack on a fellow student at Tomaree High School, Salamander, New South Wales" in 2005 by awarding a group bravery citation. The citation is, "For a collective act of bravery, by a group of persons in extraordinary circumstances, that is considered worthy of recognition." Once again, a seemingly simple concept is broadened from the behavior of a solitary hero to that of a collective hero, which we will consider shortly.

Physical-Risk Heroes Versus Social-Risk Heroes

One definition offered by psychologists cites physical risk as the defining feature of heroes. For Becker and Eagly, heroes are "individuals who choose to take risks on behalf of one or more other people, despite the possibility of dying or suffering serious physical consequences from these actions."[41] Other motives for heroism, such as principle-driven heroism, are acknowledged but not elaborated on. It seems curious that psychologists would promote so narrow a prototype of heroism and exclude other forms of personal risk that might qualify as heroic acts, such as risks to one's career, the possibility of imprisonment, or the loss of status. A challenge to their definition came from the psychologist Peter Martens, who noted that it singled out only heroes who stood for an idea or principle—the nobility component of heroism that betokens the Aristotelian hero among the proletariat.[42]

Senator John McCain, himself a hero who resisted giving any military information in spite of being subjected to extreme torture, believes that the concept of heroism might be broadened beyond physical risk and suffering. McCain contends that "the standard of courage remains, as I think it should, acts that risk life or limb or other very serious personal injuries for the sake of others or to uphold a virtue—a standard often upheld by battlefield heroics but one that is certainly not limited to martial valor."[43] Each of these descriptions of heroic behavior equates the characteristics found in physical and civil heroism while pointing out critical differences between them.

The various conceptions of heroism also roughly map onto ideas of courage, justice, and transcendence that Seligman and his colleagues developed as part of their classification system for virtues and strengths. For example, the virtue of courage is erected on four character strengths that include authenticity, bravery (roughly similar to intrepidity), persistence (similar to fortitude), and zest. Justice is noted as another virtue. Fairness, leadership, and teamwork are subsumed within this virtue. In practice, the concept of service to a noble cause or ideal is often ultimately a matter of justice, for example, the abolition of slavery. Finally, transcendence is another of the virtues that touches on heroism insofar as it is the strength that forces connection to the larger universe and gives meaning to our actions and existence. While not articulated in the literature on heroism, transcendence may be related to Webster's 1913 conception of fortitude in heroic behavior. Transcendence may allow an individual involved in a heroic act to remain detached from the negative consequences, anticipated or revealed, that are associated with his or her behavior. In order to be heroic, one must rise above the immediate risks and perils that heroism necessarily entails, either by reframing the nature of the risks or by altering their significance relevant to "higher-order" values.

A New Taxonomy of Heroism

Stimulated by thinking about the heroic behaviors associated with the Stanford Prison Experiment, I began a fuller exploration of this intriguing topic in dialogues with my psychology colleague Zeno Franco. We first broadened the conception of heroic risk, then proposed an enhanced definition of heroism, and finally generated a new taxonomy of heroism. It seemed apparent that risk or sacrifice should not be limited to an immediate threat to physical integrity or death. The risk component in heroism can be any serious threat to the quality of life. For example, heroism might include persistent behavior in the face of known long-term threats to health or serious financial consequences; to the loss of social or economic status; or to ostracism. Because this broadens the definition of heroism considerably, it also seemed necessary to rule out some forms of apparent heroism that might, in fact, not be heroic but "pseudoheroic."

In his book *The Image: A Guide to Pseudo-Events in America*, Daniel Boorstin deflates the modern confluence of heroism with celebrity. "Two centuries ago when a great man appeared, people looked for God's purpose in him; today we look for his press agent. . . . Among the ironic frustrations of our age, none is more tantalizing than these efforts of ours to satisfy our extravagant expectations of human greatness. Vainly do we make scores of artificial celebrities grow where nature planted only a single hero."[44]

Another example of what heroism is *not* can be seen in a children's book on American heroes that offers fifty examples.[45] Its stories of heroism actually point to a group of activities or roles that are necessary but insufficient to warrant true heroic status. All of the examples are role models upheld as worthy of emulation, but only a fraction meet the definitional requirements of hero status. Not all mavericks, warriors, or saints are heroes. The hero must embody a combination of deliberate nobility and potential sacrifice. Sometimes individuals are accorded hero status when not deserved by their actions, but they become so for some purpose of an agency or government. These "pseudoheroes" are media creations promoted by powerful systemic forces.[46]

Heroes are rewarded in various ways for their heroic deeds, but if they anticipate secondary gain at the time of their act they must necessarily be disqualified from heroic status. However, if secondary gains are accrued subsequent to their act without prior anticipation of or motivation to attain them, the act still qualifies as heroic. The point is that a heroic act is *sociocentric* and not egocentric.

Heroism can be defined as having four key features: (a) it must be engaged in voluntarily; (b) it must involve a risk or potential sacrifice, such as the threat of death, an immediate threat to physical integrity, a long-term threat to health, or the potential for serious degradation of one's quality of life; (c) it must be conducted in service to one or more other people or the community as a whole; and (d) it must be without secondary, extrinsic gain anticipated at the time of the act.

Heroism in service of a noble idea is usually not as dramatic as physical-risk heroism. However, physical-risk heroism is often the result of a snap decision, a moment of action. Further, physical-risk heroism usually involves a probability, not the certainty, of serious injury or death. The individual performing the act is generally removed from the situation after a short period of time. On the other hand, it might be argued that some forms of civil heroism are more heroic than physical risk forms of heroism. People such as Nelson Mandela, Martin Luther King, Jr., and Dr. Albert Schweitzer willingly and knowingly submitted to the trials of heroic civil activity day after day for much of their adult lives. In this sense, the risk associated with physical-risk heroism is better termed *peril*, while the risk involved in civil heroism is considered *sacrifice.*

Sacrifice entails costs that are not time-limited. Typically, civil heroes have the opportunity to carefully review their actions and to weigh the consequences of their decisions. Each might have chosen to retreat from the cause he championed because the cost of his or her actions had become too burdensome, yet they did not. Each of these individuals risked their quality of life on many levels. Their activities had serious consequences: arrest, imprisonment, torture, and risk to family members, and even assassination.

Returning to Webster's 1913 definition of heroism, we may say that upholding the highest civil ideas in the face of danger is the core concept of heroism. Taking physical risk is only one means of meeting the dangers that can be encountered in performing heroic acts. We are reminded that heroism "is a contempt of danger, not from ignorance or inconsiderate levity, but from a *noble devotion to some great cause* [italics added], and a just confidence of being able to meet danger in the spirit of such a cause." The danger may be immediately life threatening, or it may be insidious. Consider one of Nelson Mandela's statements at the beginning of his twenty-seven-year-long imprisonment for opposing the tyranny of apartheid:

> During my lifetime I have dedicated myself to the struggle of the African people. I have fought against white domination, and I have fought against black domination. I have cherished the ideal of a democratic and free society in which all persons live together in harmony and with equal opportunities. It is an ideal which I hope to live for and to achieve. But, if needs be, it is an ideal for which I am prepared to die.[47]

Based on this more flexible definition of heroism, Zeno Franco and I created a working taxonomy that includes twelve subcategories of heroism, distinguishing two subcategories within the military, physical-risk heroic type and ten subcategories with the civilian, social-risk type. In addition, the taxonomy identifies discriminating characteristics of each of the dozen hero types, as well as the form of risk they encounter, and gives a few examples drawn from historical and contemporary sources.

The taxonomy was developed a priori, based on reasoning and literature reviews. It is neither empirically grounded nor fixed but is rather a working model that is open to modification by new research findings and readers' qualifications and additions. It will be obvious that the subcategories, definitions, risks, and exemplars offered are all deeply culturally and temporally bound. They reflect a largely European-American, middle-class, adult, postmodern perspective. Incorporating other perspectives will surely expand and enrich it.

		Subtype	Definition	Risk/ Sacrifice	Exemplars
	Military Heroism— Gallantry, Bravery, Valor	1. Military and Other Duty-bound Physical-Risk Heroes	Individuals involved in military or emergency response careers that involve repeated exposure to high-risk situations; heroic acts must exceed the call of duty	Serious Injury Death	Achilles Medal of Honor recipients Hugh Thompson Adm. James Stockdale
	Civil Heroism	2. Civil Heroes— Non-duty-bound Physical-Risk Heroes	Civilians who attempt to save others from physical harm or death while knowingly putting their own life at risk	Serious Injury Death	Carnegie heroes
	Social Heroism—Fortitude, Courage, Intrepidity	3. Religious figures	Dedicated, life-long religious service embodying highest principles or breaks new religious/ spiritual ground. Often serves as a teacher or public exemplar of service	Sacrifice of self in ascetic path Upsetting religious orthodoxy	Buddha Mohammed St. Francis of Assisi Mother Teresa

		Subtype	Definition	Risk/ Sacrifice	Exemplars
Social Heroism—Fortitude, Courage, Intrepidity		4. Politico-Religious figures	Religious leaders who have turned to politics to affect wider change, or politicians who have a deep spiritual belief system that informs political practice	Assassination Imprisonment	Mohandas Gandhi Martin Luther King, Jr. Nelson Mandela Rev. Desmond Tutu
		5. Martyrs	Religious or political figures who knowingly (sometimes deliberately) put their lives in jeopardy in the service of a cause	Certain or near certain death in the service of a cause or ideal	Jesus Socrates Joan of Arc José Martí Steve Biko
		6. Political or Military leaders	Typically lead a nation or group during a time of difficulty; serve to unify nation, provide shared vision, and may embody qualities that are seen as necessary for the group's survival	Assassination Opposition Being voted out of office Smear campaigns Imprisonment	Abraham Lincoln Robert E. Lee Franklin Roosevelt Winston Churchill Václav Havel

	Subtype	Definition	Risk/ Sacrifice	Exemplars
Social Heroism—Fortitude, Courage, Intrepidity	7. Adventurer/ Explorer/ Discoverer	Individual who explores unknown geographical area or uses novel and unproven transportation methods	Physical health Serious injury Death Opportunity costs (length of journey)	Odysseus Alexander the Great Amelia Earhart Yuri Gagarin
	8. Scientific (Discovery) heroes	Individual who explores unknown area of science, uses novel and unproven research methods, or discovers new scientific information seen as valuable to humanity	Inability to convince others of the importance of findings Professional ostracism Financial losses	Galileo Edison Madam Curie Einstein
	9. Good Samaritan	Individuals who step in to help others in need; situation involves considerable disincentives for altruism; may not involve immediate physical risk	Punitive sanctions from authorities Arrest Torture Death Opportunity costs Ostracism	Holocaust rescuers Harriet Tubman Albert Schweitzer Richard Clark Richard Rescorla

		Subtype	Definition	Risk/ Sacrifice	Exemplars
Social Heroism—Fortitude, Courage, Intrepidity		10. Odds beater/ Underdog	Individuals who overcome handicap or adverse conditions and succeed in spite of circumstances and provide model for others	Failure Rejection Scorn Envy	Horatio Alger Helen Keller Eleanor Roosevelt Rosa Parks
		11. Bureau-cracy heroes	Employees in large organizations in controversial arguments within or between agencies; typically involves standing firm on principle despite intense pressures	Jeopardize carefully groomed career Professional ostracism Loss of social status Financial losses Loss of credibility Risk to health	Louis Pasteur Edward Tolman Barry Marshall
		12. Whistle-blowers	Individuals who are aware of illegal or unethical activities in an organization who report the activity without expectation of reward	Jeopardize carefully groomed career Professional ostracism Loss of social status Financial losses Loss of credibility Physical reprisal	Ron Ridenhour Cynthia Cooper Coleen Rowley Deborah Layton Christina Maslach Joe Darby Sherron Watkins

A Sampling of Hero Profiles

Putting some flesh on the bare bones of heroism both humanizes the conception and illustrates its many forms. I will profile a dozen individuals that are particularly interesting or that I know personally. Having argued that situations make heroes, we can use some major situational markers to cluster some of them, such as apartheid, McCarthyism, Vietnam and Iraq wars, and the Jonestown mass suicides/murders.

Apartheid Heroes

At the vanguard of efforts to promote freedom and human dignity are special kinds of heroes who are willing to engage in lifelong battles against systemic oppression. In recent times, Mohandas Gandhi and Nelson Mandela took heroic paths that led to their engaging and dismantling two systems of apartheid. In 1919, Gandhi began passive resistance to Britain's authority over India. He was imprisoned for two years. Over the next twenty years, he struggled for the liberation of India, for equal treatment of members of the Hindu class system, and for religious tolerance. World War II delayed the advent of India's self-determination, but in 1948 the country finally celebrated its independence from Great Britain. Gandhi was assassinated shortly thereafter, but he became the exemplar of enduring nonviolent resistance to oppression.[48]

South Africa developed a formalized, legalized apartheid structure in 1948 that prevailed until 1994 and that virtually enslaved the native black population. Nelson Mandela was tried for inciting strikes and protest meetings and on other charges in 1962. He spent the next twenty-seven years incarcerated in the notorious Robben Island prison. During the time he was imprisoned, Mandela and his fellow political prisoners used the prison system itself to create both a real and symbolic resistance situation that served to galvanize the people of South Africa and the world to end the system of apartheid. He was able to transform the self-generated identities of several generations of prisoners by leading them to understand that they were political prisoners acting with dignity to support a just cause. But in the process of doing so, he helped to transform the attitudes and beliefs of many of the guards, and to challenge the entire prison system as well.[49]

Anti-McCarthyism Heroes

The menace of global communism was from the 1950s until the 1989 fall of the Berlin Wall what the fear of global terrorism is now: it dictated national policy, it fomented wars, and it entailed an enormous waste of resources and lives. It is important to remember McCarthyism because it was a form of repressive, authoritarian quasi-government control that occurred in a mature democracy. Those who defused the anti-Communist hysteria propelled by Senator Joe McCarthy and the House Un-American Activities Committee in the United States never received the enduring, universal recognition that Gandhi or Mandela enjoyed. Nevertheless, their opposition to injustice meets our definitional criteria.

At the height of the McCarthy era, the University of California initiated a "loyalty oath" that all faculty members were required to sign. A psychology professor, Edward Tolman, refused to sign the oath and led a small group of professors who opposed the policy. On July 18, 1950, Tolman submitted a letter of protest to the president of the University of California, Robert Sproul. In August of that year, the Regents of the University of California fired thirty-one professors, including Tolman, for their refusal to sign the loyalty oath. Later that month, the professors filed suit for reinstatement under *Tolman vs. Underhill*. In 1952, the State Supreme Court found in favor of these nonsigners. During the loyalty oath dispute, Tolman encouraged other young faculty members to sign the oath and leave the fight against it to him and others who could (financially) afford to continue the struggle. Tolman, a soft-spoken academician with no prior history of political involvement, became deeply respected for his courageous stance by many professors and staff in the University of California system.[50]

Other heroes of the McCarthy era included investigative journalists such as George Seldes and I. F. Stone and the cartoonists Herb Block and Daniel Fitzpatrick. During this period, I. F. Stone's name was listed on a Senate Internal Security Subcommittee list of eighty-two "most active and typical sponsors of Communist-front organizations." As a consequence of being blacklisted, Stone was forced to sue in order to get his press card.[51]

Moving from the imaginary Communist menace that faced the United States to the palpable daily menace and cruelty of national domination by a Communist regime, we meet Václav Havel. Havel is extraordinary in the sense that the Dalai Lama is, and is ordinary in the sense that a former stagehand and writer is. However, he was the architect of the "Velvet Revolution" that toppled the Czech Communist regime in 1989. Before finally convincing the government that its totalitarian brand of communism was destructive of all that Czechoslovakia stood for, Havel was imprisoned repeatedly for nearly five years. He was a leading figure in drafting the Charter 77 manifesto and organizing the Czechoslovak human rights movement of intellectuals, students, and workers. As a passionate supporter of nonviolent resistance, Havel is famous for having articulated the concept of "post-totalitarianism," which challenged his countrymen to believe they had the power to change a repressive regime that they inadvertently upheld by passively submitting to its authority. In letters he wrote from prison to his wife and in speeches, Havel made it evident that the first step in overthrowing an unacceptable social and political order is for citizens to realize that they are comfortably living within a lie. This unpretentious, shy man was made president by the Federal Assembly, and when the Communist government finally yielded to the power of the people, Václav Havel was democratically elected the first president of the new Czech Republic. He continues now, as a famous private citizen, to oppose political injustice and to support efforts for global peace.[52]

Vietnam War Heroes

Two very different kinds of military heroism under conditions of extreme duress appear in the actions of James Stockdale and Hugh Thompson. Stockdale, a former Stanford colleague at the Hoover Institute (and guest lecturer in my course on mind control), rose to the rank of vice admiral before his death at eighty-one in July 2005. He is considered by many to be one of the clearest examples of military heroism in the twentieth century for having endured extreme torture sessions repeatedly over seven years of imprisonment and never giving in to his Viet Cong captors. His key to survival was relying on his earlier training in philosophy, which enabled him to call to mind the teaching of the Stoic philosophers, notably Epictetus and Seneca. Stockdale's focus enabled him to distance himself psychologically from the torture and pain that he could not control and galvanize his thinking around those things he could control in his prison surroundings. He created a self-willed code of conduct for himself and others imprisoned with him. Survival under conditions of extreme trauma requires that one's will never be broken by the enemy, as when Epictetus was tortured by Roman rulers thousands of years earlier.[53]

Hugh Thompson is distinguished for his extreme courage in a nearly lethal battle—against his own soldiers! One of the most terrible events in the history of the U.S. military was the My Lai massacre, which took place on March 16, 1968, during the Vietnam War. An estimated 504 Vietnamese civilians were rounded up and killed in Son My village (My Lai 4 and My Khe 4) by American soldiers and their Charlie Company officers, Captain Ernest Medina and Lieutenant William Calley, Jr.[54] In response to military losses from ambushes and booby traps, the military command issued an order for the destruction of "Pinkville," a code name for a Communist Viet Cong village. Finding no enemy warriors there, the soldiers gathered up all the inhabitants of the village—elderly men, woman, children, and babies—and machine-gunned them to death (some they burned alive, raped, and scalped).

While this massacre was unfolding, a helicopter, piloted by Warrant Officer Hugh Thompson, Jr., which was flying overhead to provide air cover, set down to help a group of Vietnamese civilians who appeared to still be alive. As Thompson and his two-man crew returned to their helicopter after having set smoke signal markers, they saw Captain Medina and other soldiers running over to shoot the wounded. Thompson flew his helicopter back over My Lai village, where soldiers were about to blow up a hut full of wounded Vietnamese. He ordered the massacre to stop and threatened to open fire with the helicopter's heavy machine guns on any American soldier or officer who refused his order.

Although the commissioned lieutenants outranked Thompson, he did not let rank get in the way of morality. When he ordered that civilians be taken out of the bunker, a lieutenant countered that they would be taken out with grenades. Refusing to back down, Thompson replied, "I can do better than that. Keep your people in place. My guns are on you." He then ordered two other helicopters to fly in for medical evacuation of the eleven wounded Vietnamese. His plane returned to rescue a baby he had spotted still clinging to her dead mother. Only after Thompson reported the massacre to his superiors were cease-fire orders given.[55]

For his dramatic intervention and the media coverage it received, Thompson became persona non grata in the military and for punishment was required to fly the most dangerous helicopter missions again and again. He was shot down five times, breaking his backbone and suffering lasting psychological scars from his nightmare experience. It took thirty years before the military recognized his heroic deeds and those of his companions, Glenn Andreotta and Lawrence Colburn, with the Soldier's Medal for Heroism, the Army's highest award for bravery not involving direct contact with the enemy. Hugh Thompson died in January 2006. (Paradoxically, Lieutenant Calley was treated as a hero in some quarters, even with a song in his honor that cracked *Billboard*'s Top 40 in 1971.[56])

Whistle-Blowers in the Vietnam and Iraq Wars and Women on the Home Front

Less dramatic forms of heroism occur when an individual verbally confronts a system with news it does not want to hear, in this case of the complicity of officers and enlisted men in the abuse and murder of civilians. Two such soldiers are Ron Ridenhour, who exposed the My Lai massacre, and Joe Darby, the Army Reservist whose heroic action exposed the Abu Ghraib abuses and tortures.

Although the officers involved in the My Lai episode sought to cover up the atrocity, Ron Ridenhour, a twenty-two-year-old private newly sent to Vietnam, did all he could to uncover it. He had heard about the event from five eyewitness accounts of soldiers who had been at the bloody scene, had independently investigated it in Vietnam, and had continued to do so after returning home. Ridenhour sent a letter to President Nixon, members of Congress, and officials within the Department of Defense and the Department of the Army arguing that a public investigation of the My Lai massacre was needed. In his letter, Ridenhour made it clear that "as a conscientious citizen I have no desire to besmirch the image of American servicemen in the eyes of the world." However, he insisted that an investigation was essential (a year after the incident). He was largely ignored, but persisted until his righteous cause was recognized. Ridenhour demonstrates the principled heroic stance in his letters to these officials: "I remain irrevocably persuaded that if you and I do truly believe in the principles of justice and equality for every man, however humble, before the law, that form the very backbone that this country is founded on, then we must press forward a widespread and public investigation of this matter with all our combined efforts."[57]

Following the exposé by a young investigative reporter, Seymour Hersh, who got valuable material from Ridenhour, a major investigation was ordered and its findings fill four volumes of the Peers Report, released on March 14, 1970. Although up to twenty officers and enlisted men were identified as in various ways being involved in this massacre, only Lieutenant William Calley, Jr., was convicted and sentenced for the crimes. Although given a life sentence, his punishment was limited to a light term of three and a half years under house arrest, and he was later pardoned by the Secretary of the Army.[58] Incidentally, Ridenhour went on to a career as a journalist, but he told me in conversation that he always felt distrusted by many people in Washington, D.C. for having exposed the My Lai massacre.

By now we know too well the events surrounding the abuses heaped upon prisoners at Abu Ghraib's hard site, Tier 1A, by MPs and others involved in intelligence gathering. This scandalous behavior was brought to a sudden halt when dramatic images of the torture, humiliation, and violence were forced upon the attention of military commanders. It was a most ordinary young man who did an extraordinary thing that caused the halt to the horror. What he did took great personal fortitude, in the opinion of my military contacts, because he was a lowly Army Reserve specialist who put a superior officer on notice that something horrendous was happening on his watch.

When Darby first looked at the pictures on a CD that buddy Charles Graner had given him, he thought they were pretty funny. "To me, that pyramid of naked Iraqis, when you first see it, is hilarious. . . . When it came up out of nowhere like that, I just laughed," Darby recalled in a recent interivew.[59] However, as he viewed more of them—the sexually explicit ones, the ones showing the beatings, and the others—his affect shifted. "It just didn't sit right with me. I couldn't stop thinking about it. After about three days, I made a decision to turn the pictures in." It was a tough decision for Darby, because he realized fully the moral conflict facing him. "You have to understand: I'm not the kind of guy to rat somebody out. . . . But this crossed the line to me. I had the choice between what I knew was morally right and my loyalty to other soldiers. I couldn't have it both ways."[60]

Darby was afraid of retaliation against him by soldiers in his company unless he remained anonymous in this action.[61] He burned another CD copy of the pictures, typed an anonymous letter about them, put them in a plain manila envelope, and handed it to an agent at the Criminal Investigation Division (CID), remarking simply that they were left in his office. Shortly after, Special Agent Tyler Pieron grilled him and got Darby to admit: "I'm the one who put them in there," and then he gave a sworn statement. He was able to maintain his anonymity until Secretary of Defense Donald Rumsfeld unexpectedly "outted" Darby during the 2004 congressional hearings on these abuses—while Darby was having dinner with hundreds of soldiers in the mess hall. He was whisked away, and eventually concealed in military protective custody for the next several years. "But I don't regret any of it," Darby said recently. "I made my peace with the decision before I turned the pictures in. I knew that if people found out that it was me, I wouldn't be liked."

The revelations led to a host of formal investigations into abuses in that prison and at all other military facilities where detainees were being held. Darby's actions stopped much of the torture and abuse and led to significant changes in the way the Abu Ghraib Prison was run.[62]

But not everyone thinks that what Darby did was the right thing to do. For many, even in his hometown in the Allegheny Mountains, Darby's calling attention to the abuses was unpatriotic, un-American, and even faintly treasonous. "Hero a Two-Timing Rat," ran a headline in the *New York Post*. Even those who are not angry at his whistle-blowing are surprised that he could be a hero because he was such an ordinary kid from a poor family, an average student and even bullied in school. Darby's high school history teacher and football coach, Robert Ewing, a Vietnam veteran, eloquently summed up the mixed reactions:

> Some people are upset with what he did—ratting them out—and also because of what happened to those contractors, the beheading. They might say what the guards did pales in comparison. But . . . if we as a country, as a culture, believe certain values then you can't excuse that behavior. If I ever do see him again, I'll tell him I'm very proud. And as time goes on, most Americans are going to realize that, too.[63]

I helped arrange for Darby to receive a Presidential Citation from the American Psychological Association in 2004. He was unable to accept this honor personally because he, his wife, and his mother had to remain in military protective custody for several years in the wake of the many retaliation threats they received. Darby was finally recognized as a hero nationally when he received the 2005 John F. Kennedy Profile in Courage Award. In bestowing the award, Caroline Kennedy, president of the John F. Kennedy Library Foundation, said, "Individuals who are willing to take personal risk to further the national interest and uphold the values of American democracy should be recognized and encouraged in all parts of government. Our nation is indebted to U.S. Army Specialist Joseph Darby for standing up for the rule of law that we embrace as a nation."

Challenges to authority systems are not gender-bound; women are as likely to blow the whistle against crimes and injustice as men are. *Time* magazine honored three such women in choosing its "Persons of the Year" (2002) for their bold confrontation of major corporate fraud and FBI incompetence. Cynthia Cooper, an internal auditor at WorldCom, was responsible for revealing fraudulent accounting practices that kept $3.8 billion of losses off the company's books. After months of intensive investigation, often conducted during the night to avoid detection, Cooper and her team of auditors exposed the deceptive practices, which resulted in the firing and indictment of senior company officers.[64]

Sherron Watkins, a vice president at the high-flying Enron Corporation, also blew the whistle on the extensive corporate corruption taking place there, which involved "cooking the books" to give the appearance of great success to cover up failure. The formerly reputable Arthur Andersen accounting firm was also implicated in the huge scandal.[65] An FBI staff attorney, Colleen Rowley, blew the whistle on the FBI for its failure to follow up on pleas from her office that they check out a person whom it identified as a potential terrorist and who turned out to be one of the co-conspirators in the September 11, 2001, terror attacks. These "three woman of ordinary demeanor but extraordinary guts and sense" risked a great deal in challenging their established power base.[66]

Jonestown Heroes

Debbie Layton and Richard Clark were two survivors among the 913 American citizens who died in the mass suicides and murders that took place in Jonestown, Guyana, on November 18, 1978. Debbie came from a relatively affluent, educated white family in Oakland, California, while Richard came to San Francisco from humble African-American origins in Mississippi. They both became my personal friends when they arrived in the Bay area after having escaped the horrors of the Jonestown nightmare. Both qualify as heroes in different ways, Debbie as a whistle-blower and Richard as a Good Samaritan.

Debbie joined Reverend Jim Jones's Peoples Temple congregation as an eighteen-year-old. She was a loyal follower for many years and eventually became the Temple's finance secretary. As such, she was entrusted with moving millions of dollars out of Jonestown to deposits in secret Swiss bank accounts. Her mother and brother, Larry, were also Temple members. But over time she realized that Jonestown was more like a concentration camp than the promised utopia where racial harmony and a sustainable lifestyle would prevail. Nearly a thousand faithful members were subjected to hard labor, semistarvation, and physical and sexual abuse. Armed guards surrounded them, and spies infiltrated their lives. Jones even forced them to practice regular suicide drills, called "White Nights," that frightened Debbie into understanding that he was actually preparing them for a mass suicide.

At great personal peril, she decided to flee Jonestown and take the message of its potential destructive power to concerned relatives and to the government. She could not even alert her sick mother to her escape plan for fear that her emotional reaction that might tip off Jones. After executing a complex set of maneuvers, Debbie did escape and immediately did all she could to alert authorities to the abusive conditions at Jonestown and to warn them of what she believed was an imminent tragedy.

In June 1978, she issued an affidavit to the U.S. government warning of a potential mass suicide. Its thirty-seven detailed points began: "RE. The Threat And Possibility Of Mass Suicide By Members Of The People's Temple. I, Deborah Layton Blakey, declare the following under penalty of perjury: The purpose of this affidavit is to call to the attention of the United States government the existence of a situation which threatens the lives of United States citizens living in Jonestown, Guyana."

Six months later, her Cassandra-like prediction was eerily validated. Sadly, her pleas for aid were met by the skepticism of government officials who refused to accept that such a bizarre tale could be true. However, some concerned relatives did believe her and encouraged California Congressman Leo Ryan to investigate. Reporters, a cameraman, and some relatives accompanied Ryan on his visit. As he was about to return home with a positive evaluation of what he had been duped into believing were ideal living conditions, several families who decided to defect under his protection joined Ryan. But it was too late. Jones, by now very paranoid, believed the defectors would reveal the truth about Jonestown to the outside world. He had the congressman and some of his entourage murdered and then arranged for cyanide-laced Kool-Aid to be given to his weary followers. His infamous last-hour speech was outlined in Chapter 12; a full version is available online at the Jonestown website.[67]

Debbie Layton has written an eloquent account of how she and so many others were trapped by the persuasive lures of this diabolical preacher man. Jim Jones's Lucifer-like transformation from benevolent religious minister to angel of death unfolds chillingly in her book, *Seductive Poison*.[68] I have argued elsewhere that there are remarkable parallels between the mind control tactics used by Jones and those depicted in George Orwell's classic novel *1984* that might make the Jonestown phenomenon a field experiment of the most extreme mind control imaginable—and perhaps even sponsored by the CIA.[69]

I helped counsel Richard Clark and his girlfriend, Diane Louie, after they returned to San Francisco, having escaped the mass suicide. Richard was a simple, pragmatic man, a slow-speaking but sensitive observer of people and places. He said that the moment he got to Jonestown he could detect that something was seriously wrong. No one in the Promised Land was smiling. Everyone in the supposed land of plenty was hungry. People whispered and never laughed. Work not only came before play but also never left time for play. Jones's voice boomed out over the compound day and night, in person or on tape. The sexes were segregated into different barracks, and sex, even among married couples, was forbidden without Jones's approval. No one could leave because no one could figure out where they were in the midst of a jungle in a foreign land thousands of miles from home.

Richard Clark hatched a plan. He volunteered for a job that no one wanted in the "piggery," which was in an isolated smelly part of the sprawling compound. The place was ideal for Richard to escape Jones's mind-numbing rhetoric and to seek out a path through the jungle to freedom. Once he had slowly and carefully laid out his escape, he told Diane about it and said that when the time was ripe, they would flee together. In defiance of Jones's extensive spy system, Richard made the decidedly risky decision to tell the members of a few families about the planned escape. On the morning of Sunday, November 18, Jones ordered everyone to have a holiday in celebration of Congressman Ryan's return to America with the message about the good works being accomplished in this agricultural socialist utopia. That was Richard's exit cue. He assembled his party of eight and, pretending they were off on a picnic, led them through the jungle to safety. By the time they reached the capital at Georgetown, every one of their friends and other family members was dead.

Richard Clark died recently of natural causes, knowing that he made the right decision to trust his intuition, his street smarts, and his "discrepancy detectors." But most of all, he was pleased that he had saved the lives of those who followed him, an ordinary hero, out of the heart of darkness.[70]

A Four-Dimensional Model of Heroism

Based on the concepts of courage and examples of heroic behavior presented here, an elementary model of heroism can be generated. Within the overall motivational framework of a particular person, heroism can be described on three continua: Risk Type/Sacrifice; Engagement Style or Approach; and Quest. The axis of Risk Type/Sacrifice is anchored at one end by physical risk and at the other by social risk. Similarly, Engagement Style or Approach is anchored at one end by active (gallant) and, at the other end, passive (with fortitude) approaches. On the third dimension, the Quest is described as being in service of the preservation of life or in the preservation of an ideal. Although they are synonymous in some ways—the preservation of life is also a noble idea—the distinction is important within this context. The first three dimensions of this model are depicted in this illustration. We will add a fourth later.

Let's position three different types of heroes in this model space, Nathan Hale, Mother Teresa, and Richard Rescorla. The American Revolutionary War hero Nathan Hale had been operating as a spy in the British ranks for some time,

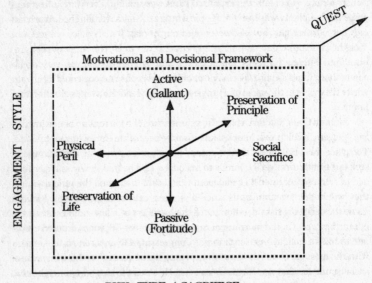

before he was caught. While his activities were patriotic, they were not in them-selves heroic. Had his clandestine activities gone unnoticed, he would never have become an American hero. It was in the moment of his execution at the hands of the British, a death he accepted with dignity, that he became a heroic figure. "I regret that I have but one life to give for my country" was his classic farewell. In that moment, Hale showed great fortitude, sacrificing his life in the service of a principle.

A very different kind of heroism is found in the life and work of Mother Teresa. Her activities cannot be not summed up in a single act, as was Nathan Hale's defiance at his execution. Rather, her heroic acts span the course of decades. Her dedication to enable the dying poor to die in a state of grace, Catholic grace, was based on service to a principle (compassion), in which she was actively and perpetually involved, and the sacrifices she made took the ascetic path to glory: her poverty, her chastity, and her denial of herself for the sake of others.

Our third hero to be placed in our multidimensional hero grid is Richard Rescorla. He was the director of security in Morgan Stanley's World Trade Center (WTC) offices in New York City at the time of the terrorist attacks of 9/11. A decorated Vietnam veteran (Silver Star, Purple Heart, and Bronze Stars for Valor and Meritorious Service), Rescorla is credited with saving the lives of thousands of Morgan Stanley employees by his decisive actions. Rescorla defied WTC authorities in ordering the employees in his offices to evacuate rather than to follow the order to remain at their desks. During the evacuation of the forty-fourth to seventy-fourth floors of WTC Tower 2, reports indicate, Rescorla verbally calmed the employees over a bullhorn and told them to stop talking on cell phones and to keep moving down the stairs. Rescorla, two security guards whom he had trained, and three other Morgan Stanley employees died when the building imploded. Rescorla and his team are credited with saving the lives of an estimated 2,800 employees who exited WTC-2 before it collapsed.[71] In contrast to the heroism of a figure like Nathan Hale, Rescorla's act was active and was performed directly in the service of preserving life, yet his glory too demanded the ultimate physical sacrifice.

Nathan Hale, Richard Rescorla, and Mother Teresa represent different aspects of the heroic ideal. The distinctions among their actions illuminate the diversity of acts that meet the enigmatic standard of heroic. Their actions are mapped on to our model of heroism.

A fourth dimension to be added to this model is that of Chronicity. Heroes can be made in instantaneous actions, or their heroism can accrue over time. Acute heroism, the heroism shown in a single act, is described in the martial context as bravery—an act of courage in a single combat. In contrast, chronic military heroism, courage that is displayed time and again in battle, is called valor. There are not yet comparable terms to denote duration in civil heroism, perhaps because the dramatic quality of heroism that is demonstrated in perilous situations is not as easily evident in the civic sphere. Among civic heroes we might con-

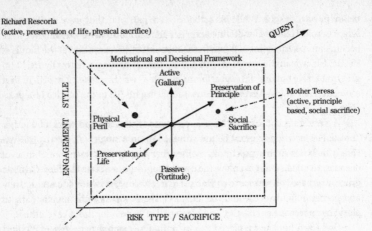

Richard Rescorla
(active, preservation of life, physical sacrifice)

QUEST

Motivational and Decisional Framework

ENGAGEMENT STYLE

Active
(Gallant)

Preservation of
Principle

Mother Teresa
(active, principle
based, social sacrifice)

Physical
Peril

Social
Sacrifice

Preservation of
Life

Passive
(Fortitude)

RISK TYPE / SACRIFICE

Nathan Hale (at the moment of execution)
(passive, principle based, physical sacrifice)

trast a time-limited, situationally specific heroism of the moment, like that of whistle-blowers, with the chronic heroism demonstrated by an enduring engagement in service to society, like that of Martin Luther King, Jr.

Collective Heroism as a Matter of Degree

The solitary heroic figure, like the brave marshal in a western movie who faces down a band of renegades, is supported, more often than not, by groups of people working in unison in emergencies, disasters, and situations that demand concerted action. The Underground Railroad, which took southern slaves to freedom in northern towns, could function only with the coordinated efforts of many people who worked in peril of their lives. Similarly, first responders to disasters are typically citizen volunteers working in loosely organized teams. As the "Tank Man" was, many individuals working in collective harmony are anonymous. They brave danger without expectation of personal notoriety but for the sake of answering a call to community service.

A special instance of this kind of collective heroism occurred on United Airlines flight 93, which was hijacked by terrorists on September 11, 2001. At first, passengers, believing the plane was returning to the airport, followed the norm by staying in their seats. But when some passengers were alerted by cell phone calls about the crash of other planes into the World Trade Center and the Pentagon, a new norm emerged. A small group of them gathered in the back of the plane and planned to get control of the cockpit. One of them was on the phone with a GTE operator, who heard him say, "Let's roll!" before he was disconnected. Their concerted action prevented the plane from reaching its intended target, either the White House or the Capitol. That field now stands as a memorial to collective heroism of the highest order.[72]

HEROIC CONTRASTS: THE EXTRAORDINARY
VERSUS THE BANAL

Fame is no plant that grows on mortal soil.

—John Milton

To the traditionally accepted notion that heroes are exceptional people, we can now add an opposing perspective—that some heroes are ordinary people who have done something extraordinary. The first image is the more romantic and is favored in ancient myth and modern media. It suggests that the hero has done something that ordinary people in the same position would not or could not have done. These superstars must have been born with a hero gene. They are the exception to the rule.

A second perspective, which we might call "the rule is the exception," directs us to examine the interaction between situation and person, the dynamic that impelled an individual to act heroically at a particular time and place. A situation may act either as a catalyst, encouraging action, or it may reduce barriers to action, such as the formation of a collective social support network. It is remarkable that in most instances people who have engaged in heroic action repeatedly reject the name of hero, as we saw was the case with Christina Maslach.

Such doers of heroic deeds typically argue that they were simply taking an action that seemed necessary at the time. They are convinced that anybody would have acted similarly, or else they find it difficult to understand why others did not. Nelson Mandela has said, "I was not a messiah, but an ordinary man who had become a leader because of extraordinary circumstances."[73] Phrases like this are used by people at all levels of society who have acted heroically: "It was nothing special"; "I did what had to be done." These are the refrains of the "ordinary" or everyday warrior, our "banal hero." Let's contrast such positive banality with what Hannah Arendt has taught us to call "the banality of evil."

On the Banality of Evil

This concept emerged from Arendt's observations at the trial of Adolf Eichmann, indicted for crimes against humanity because he helped to orchestrate the genocide of European Jews. In *Eichmann in Jerusalem: A Report on the Banality of Evil*, Arendt formulates the idea that such individuals should not be viewed as exceptions, as monsters, or as perverted sadists. She argues that such dispositional attributes, typically applied to perpetrators of evil deeds, serves to set them apart from the rest of the human community. Instead, Eichmann and others like him, Arendt says, should be exposed in their very ordinariness. When we realize this, we become more aware that such people are a pervasive, hidden danger in all societies. Eichmann's defense was that he was simply following orders. Of this mass murderer's motives and conscience, Arendt notes:

As for his base motives, he was perfectly sure that he was not what he called an *innerer Schweinehund*, a dirty bastard in the depths of his heart; and as for his conscience, he remembered perfectly well that he would have had a bad conscience only if he had not done what he had been ordered to do—to ship millions of men, women, and children to their death with great zeal and the most meticulous care.

What is most striking in Arendt's account of Eichmann is all the ways in which he seemed absolutely normal and totally ordinary:

Half a dozen psychiatrists had certified him as "normal"—"More normal, at any rate, than I am after having examined him," one of them was said to have exclaimed, while another had found that his whole psychological outlook, his attitude toward his wife and children, mother and father, brothers, sisters, and friends was "not only normal but most desirable."[74]

Arendt's now-classic conclusion:

The trouble with Eichmann was precisely that so many were like him, and that the many were neither perverted nor sadistic, that they were, and still are, terribly and terrifyingly normal. From the viewpoint of our legal institutions and our moral standards of judgment, this normality was much more terrifying than all the atrocities put together, for it implied . . . that this new type of criminal, who is in actual fact *hostis generis humani*, commits his crimes under circumstances that make it well-nigh impossible for him to know or feel that he is doing wrong.[75]

Then came her punch line, describing Eichmann's dignified march to the gallows:

It was as though in those last minutes he was summing up the lesson that this long course in human wickedness had taught us—the lesson of the fearsome, word-and-thought-defying banality of evil.[76]

The notion that "ordinary men" can commit atrocities has been more fully developed by the historian Christopher Browning, as we noted earlier. He uncovered the systematic and personal annihilation of Jews in remote Polish villages that were committed by hundreds of men in Reserve Police Battalion 101, sent to Poland from Hamburg, Germany. These middle-aged, family men of working-class and lower-middle-class backgrounds shot thousands of unarmed Jews—men, women, the elderly, and children—and arranged for the deportation to death camps of thousands more. Yet Browning contends in his book that they were all "ordinary men." He believes that the mass-murder policies of the Nazi regime "were not aberrational or exceptional events that scarcely ruffle the surface of everyday life. As the story of Reserve Battalion 10 demonstrates, mass murder and routine had become one. Normality itself had become exceedingly abnormal."[77]

The psychologist Ervin Staub holds a similar view. His extensive research led him to the conclusion that "Evil that arises out of ordinary thinking and is committed by ordinary people is the norm, not the exception."[78] Cruelty should be attributed to its social origins more than to its "characterological" determinants or "faulty personalities," according to Zygmunt Bauman's analysis of the horrors of the Holocaust. Bauman believes further that the exception to this norm is the rare individual who has the capacity to assert moral autonomy in resisting the demands of destructive authorities. Such a person is rarely aware that he or she possesses this hidden strength until put to the test.[79]

Another quality of the banality of evil ushers us into the torturers' den to consider whether such people, whose mission is to use all means necessary to break the will, resistance, and dignity of their victims, are anything other than pathological villains. The consensus among those who have studied torturers is that in general they were not distinguishable from the general population in their backgrounds or dispositions prior to taking on their sordid job. John Conroy, who studied men involved in torture in three different venues in Ireland, Israel, and Chicago, concluded that in all cases "unspeakable acts" were committed by "ordinary people." He maintains that torturers act out the will of the community they represent in suppressing its foes.[80]

From her in-depth analysis of soldiers trained by the Greek military junta to be state-sanctioned torturers (1967–1974), my colleague the Greek psychologist Mika Haritos-Fatouros concluded that torturers are not born but made by their training. "Anybody's son will do" is her answer to the question "Who will make an effective torturer?" In a matter of a few months, ordinary young men from rural villages became "weaponized" by their training in cruelty to act like brute beasts capable of inflicting the most horrendous acts of humiliation, pain, and suffering on anyone labeled "the enemy," who, of course, were all citizens of their own country.[81] Such conclusions are not limited to one nation, but are common in many totalitarian regimes. We studied "violence workers" in Brazil, policemen who tortured and murdered other Brazilian citizens for the ruling military junta. They too were "ordinary men," based on all the evidence we could amass.[82]

On the Banality of Heroism[83]

We may now entertain the notion that most people who become perpetrators of evil deeds are directly comparable to those who become perpetrators of heroic deeds, alike in being just ordinary, average people. The banality of evil shares much with the banality of heroism. Neither attribute is the direct consequence of unique dispositional tendencies; there are no special inner attributes of either pathology or goodness residing within the human psyche or the human genome. Both conditions emerge in particular situations at particular times when situational forces play a compelling role in moving particular individuals across a decisional line from inaction to action. There is a decisive decisional moment when a person is caught up in a vector of forces that emanate from a behavioral context. Those forces combine to increase the probability of one's acting to harm others or acting to help others. Their decision may or may not be consciously planned or mindfully taken. Rather, strong situational forces most often impulsively drive the person to action. Among the situational action vectors are: group pressures and group identity, the diffusion of responsibility for the action, a temporal focus on the immediate moment without concern for consequences stemming from the act in the future, presence of social models, and commitment to an ideology.

A common theme in the accounts of European Christians who helped the Jews during the Holocaust could be summed up as the "banality of goodness." What is striking over and over again is the number of these rescuers who did the right thing without considering themselves heroic, who acted merely out of a sense of common decency. The ordinariness of their goodness is especially striking in the context of the incredible evil of the systematic genocide by Nazis on a scale the world had never before experienced.[84]

I have tried to show throughout our journey that the military police guards who abused prisoners at Abu Ghraib and the prison guards in my Stanford Prison Experiment who abused their prisoners illustrate a *Lord of the Flies*–type temporary transition of ordinary individuals into perpetrators of evil. We must set them alongside those whose evil behavior is enduring and extensive, tyrants such as Idi Amin, Stalin, Hitler, and Saddam Hussein. Heroes of the moment also stand in contrast to lifetime heroes.

The heroic action of Rosa Parks's refusal to sit in the "colored" section in the back of an Alabama bus, of Joe Darby's exposing the Abu Ghraib tortures, or of the first responders' rush to the World Trade Center disaster are acts of bravery that occur at particular times and places. In contrast, the heroism of Mohandas Gandhi or Mother Teresa consists of valorous acts repeated over a lifetime. Chronic heroism is to acute heroism as valor is to bravery.

This perception implies that any of us could as easily become heroes as perpetrators of evil depending on how we are influenced by situational forces. The imperative becomes discovering how to limit, constrain, and prevent the situational and systemic forces that propel some of us toward social pathology. But equally important is the injunction for every society to foster a "heroic imagination" in its citizenry. It is achieved by conveying the message that every person is a hero in waiting who will be counted upon to do the right thing when the moment of decision comes. The decisive question for each of us is whether to act in help of others, to prevent harm to others, or not to act at all. We should be preparing many laurel wreaths for all those who will discover their reservoir of hidden strengths and virtues enabling them to come forth to act against injustice and cruelty and to stand up for their principled values.

The large body of research on situational determinants of antisocial behavior that we reviewed here, bookended by Milgram's investigations of authority power and the SPE's institutional power, reveals the extent to which normal, ordinary people can be led to engage in cruel acts against innocent others.[85] However, in those studies and many others, while the majority obeyed, conformed, complied, were persuaded, and were seduced, there was always a minority who resisted, dissented, and disobeyed. In one sense, heroism lies in the ability to resist powerful situational forces that so readily entrap most people.

Are the personalities of the resisters different from those of the blindly obedient?[86] Are they like Clark Kent, whose normal appearance conceals Superman's extraordinary powers? Not at all. Rather, our banality of heroism conception maintains that doers of heroic deeds of the moment are not essentially different from those who comprise the base rate of the easily seduced. There is not much empirical research on which to base such assertions. Because heroism is not a simple phenomenon that can be studied systematically, it defies clean definitions and on-the-spot data collection. Heroic acts are ephemeral and unpredictable, and appreciation of them is decidedly retrospective. Because heroes are usually interviewed months or years after their heroic behavior has occurred, there are no prospective studies of what the photographer Henri Cartier-Bresson might call the "decisive moment" of heroic action.[87] Generally we do not know what the decision matrix for heroes is at the time they elect to engage in risk-laden activities.

What seems evident is that heroic behavior is rare enough not to be readily predictable by any psychological assessments of personality. They measure individual differences between people in their usual, standard behavioral settings, not in the atypical settings that often elicit heroic deeds.

Lieutenant Alexander (Sandy) Nininger is a case example of a heroic soldier who engaged in extraordinarily fearless and ferocious fighting during World War II's infamous Battle of Bataan. This twenty-three-year-old West Point graduate volunteered to go hunting for Japanese snipers where the fighting was most intense. With grenades, a rifle, submachine gun, and bayonet, Nininger killed many Japanese soldiers single-handedly in intense close combat, and kept fighting although repeatedly wounded. Only after he had destroyed an enemy bunker did he collapse and die. His heroism earned him the Medal of Honor, posthumously, the first given in that war.

What makes this hero an object of our concern is that nothing from his past would have predicted that he would engage in such killing. This quiet, sensitive, intellectual young man had gone on record as saying that he could never kill anyone out of hatred. Yet, he had done so repeatedly without regard for his own safety. Had he been given all available personality tests, would they have helped predict this unexpectedly violent behavior? In his review of personality testing, the author Malcolm Gladwell surmises that Nininger's file might be as thick as a phone book, but "his file will tell us little about the one thing we're most interested in. For that, we have to join him in the jungles of Bataan." In short, we have to understand the Person in the Situation.[88]

HEROISM VALIDATES THE HUMAN CONNECTION

For reasons we do not yet fully understand, thousands of ordinary people in every country around the world, when they are placed in special circumstances, make the decision to act heroically. On the face of it, the perspective we take here seems to deflate the myth of the hero and to make something special into something banal. This is not so, however, because our position still recognizes that the act of heroism is indeed special and rare. Heroism supports the ideals of a community and serves as an extraordinary guide, and it provides an exemplary role model for prosocial behavior. The banality of heroism means that we are all heroes in waiting. It is a choice that we may all be called upon to make at some point in time. I believe that by making heroism an egalitarian attribute of human nature rather than a rare feature of the elect few, we can better foster heroic acts in every community. According to journalist Carol Depino "Everyone has the capability of becoming a hero in one degree or another. Sometimes you might not realize it. To someone it could be as small as holding a door open and saying 'hello' to them. We are all heroes to someone."[89]

This new theme of the universality of ordinary heroes encourages us to rethink about the common heroes among us, those whose daily sacrifices enrich our lives. Daniel Boorstin's earlier noted cynical view of media-crafted celebrities as heroes gives way before his deep appreciation of the everyday unsung heroes living and working among us:

> In this life of illusion and quasi-illusion, the person with solid virtues who can be admired for something more substantial than his well-knownness often proves to be the unsung hero: the teacher, the nurse, the mother, the honest cop, the hard worker at lonely, under-paid, unglamorous, unpublicized jobs. Topsy-turvily, these can remain heroes precisely because they remain unsung.[90]

And so, the parting message that we might derive from our long journey into the heart of darkness and back again is that heroic acts and the people who engage in them should be celebrated. They form essential links among us; they forge our Human Connection. The evil that persists in our midst must be countered, and eventually overcome, by the greater good in the collective hearts and personal heroic resolve of Everyman and Everywoman. It is not an abstract concept, but, as we are reminded by the Russian poet and former prisoner in Stalin's Gulag Aleksandr Solzhenitsyn: "The line between good and evil is in the center of every human heart."[91]

Thanks for sharing this journey with me.

Ciao, Phil Zimbardo

M. C. Escher's "Circle Limit IV" © 2006 The M. C. Escher Company-Holland.
All rights reserved. www.mcescher.com.

Notes

CHAPTER ONE: The Psychology of Evil: Situated Character Transformations

1. John Milton, *Paradise Lost*, in *John Milton: Complete Poems and Major Prose*, ed. M. Y. Hughes (New York: Odyssey Press, 1667/1957) quote in Book 1, p. 254; description of Satan's Demonic Conference in Book 2, ll. 44–389.

2. Elaine Pagels, *The Origin of Satan* (New York: Random House, 1995), p. xvii.

3. D. Frankfurter, *Evil Incarnate: Rumors of Demonic Conspiracy and Satanic Abuse in History* (Princeton, NJ: Princeton University Press, 2006), pp. 208–9.

4. Some worthwhile books to examine for other psychological perspectives on evil include: R. F. Baumeister, *Evil: Inside Human Cruelty and Violence* (New York: Freeman, 1997); A. G. Miller, ed., *The Social Psychology of Good and Evil* (New York: Guilford Press, 2004); M. Shermer, *The Science of Good & Evil: Why People Cheat, Gossip, Care, Share and Follow the Golden Rule* (New York: Henry Holt, 2004); E. Staub, *The Roots of Evil: The Origins of Genocide and Other Group Violence* (New York: Cambridge University Press, 1989); J. Waller, *Becoming Evil: How Ordinary People Commit Genocide and Mass Killing* (New York: Oxford University Press, 2002).

5. There is a growing body of literature in cultural psychology comparing behavioral and value differences between societies that can be described as fostering a more independent, individualistic orientation and those that are more interdependent and collectivist. A good starting point on how these different perspectives influence conceptions of the self is found in Hazel Markus and Shinobu Kitayama, "Models of Agency: Sociocultural Diversity in the Construction of Action," in *Nebraska Symposium on Motivation*, ed. V. Murphy-Berman and J. Berman, *Cross-Cultural Differences in Perspectives on Self.* (Lincoln: University of Nebraska Press, 2003).

6. One of the best references on the concept of essentialism as used by psychologists is found in Susan Gelman, *The Essential Child: Origins of Essentialism in Everyday Life* (New York: Oxford University Press, 2003).

   Another valuable source on the ways in which our mind-set about intelligence as essential (fixed) versus incremental (variable) qualities affects success in many domains is found in Carol Dweck's summary of her decades of original research, *Mindset: The New Psychology of Success* (New York: Random House, 2006).

7. A constructive approach for dealing with such school violence is found in the work of my psychological colleague Elliot Aronson. He uses the power of social psychological knowledge to offer a road map for changing a school's social environment so that compassion and cooperation replace competition and rejection: E. Aronson, *Nobody Left to Hate: Teaching Compassion After Columbine* (New York: Worth, 2000).

8. Heinrich Kramer and Jakob Sprenger, *The Malleus Maleficarum of Kramer and Sprenger* (*"The Witches' Hammer"*), edited and translated by Rev. Montague Summers (New York:

Dover, 1486/1948). Written by German Dominican monks. An interesting summary is available online in the commentary of Stephanie du Barry (1994), http://users.bigpond.net.au/greywing/Malleus.htm.

9. We must credit this ill-fated flight of theological fancy for the legacy of violence against women. The historian Anne Barstow traces the systemic use and widespread acceptance of male violence against women to its endorsement by male powers behind church and state that started this "witch craze" in Anne L. Barstow, *Witchcraze: A New History of European Witch Hunts* (San Francisco: HarperCollins, 1995).

10. C. Wright Mills, *The Power Elite.* (New York: Oxford University Press, 1956), pp. 3–4.

11. Sam Keen, *Faces of the Enemy: Reflections on the Hostile Imagination* (enlarged ed.) (New York: Harper & Row, 1986/2004). Also see the powerful companion DVD produced by Bill Jersey and Sam Keen. Further information is available at www.samkeen.com.

12. L. W. Simons, "Genocide and the Science of Proof," *National Geographic,* January 2006, 28–35. See also the insightful analyses of mass homicides in the chapter by D. G. Dutton, E. O. Doyankowski, and M. H. Bond, "Extreme Mass Homicide: From Military Massacre to Genocide," *Aggression and Violent Behavior,* vol. 10 (May–June, 2005): 437–473.

    These psychological scholars argue that political and historical factors shape the selection of a target group in military massacres, genocide, and political slaughter. That selection is based on a belief of prior unfair advantage taken or received in the past by that target group. Violence is then justified as revenge against this "cancerous group." In turn, that perception justifies killing nonviolent people on the basis of their assumed future risk and danger to the offender group, now the offensive attackers.

13. Some of the sad story of using rape as a weapon of terror revolves around one woman, who has been called "The Minister of Rape" by the investigator Peter Landesman in his thorough 2003 report in *The New York Times Magazine,* September 15, 2003, pp. 82–ff. 131. (All the following quotes are from this report.)

14. Jean Hatzfeld, *Machete Season: The Killers in Rwanda Speak.* (New York: Farrar, Straus and Giroux, 2005).

15. R. Dallaire with B. Beardsley, *Shake Hands with the Devil: The Failure of Humanity in Rwanda* (New York: Carroll and Graf, 2004).

16. The psychologist Robert Jay Lifton, author of *The Nazi Doctors,* argues that rape is often a deliberate tool of war to set into motion continuous suffering and extreme humiliation that will affect not just the individual victim but also everyone around her. "A woman is seen as a symbol of purity. The family revolves around that symbol. Then here is the brutal attack on that, stigmatizing them all. All this perpetuates the humiliation, reverberating among survivors and their whole families. In this way, rape is worse than death." Landesman, p. 125. See also A. Stiglmayer, ed, *Mass Rape: The War Against Women in Bosnia-Herzegovina* (Lincoln: University of Nebraska Press, 1994).

17. Iris Chang, *The Rape of Nanking: The Forgotten Holocaust of World War II.* (New York: Basic Books, 1997), p. 6.

18. A. Badkhen, "Atrocities Are a Fact of All Wars, Even Ours," *San Francisco Chronicle,* August 13, 2006, pp. E1–E6, and D. Nelson and N. Turse, "A Tortured Past," *Los Angeles Times,* August 20, 2006, pp. A1, ff.

19. A. Bandura, B. Underwood, and M. E. Fromson, "Disinhibition of Aggression Through Diffusion of Responsibility and Dehumanization of Victims," *Journal of Research in Personality* 9 (1975): 253–69. Participants believed the other students allegedly in the next room were being shocked by their lever presses; no shocks were given to the fictitious "animals," or others.

20. Quoted in a *New York Times* article on our study of moral disengagement among all those prison personnel associated with death penalty executions. Benedict Casey, "In the Execution Chamber the Moral Compass Wavers," *The New York Times,* February 7, 2006.

See M. J. Osofsky, A. Bandura, & P. G. Zimbardo, "The Role of Moral Disengagement in the Execution Process," *Law and Human Behavior,* 29 (2005): 371–93.

21. I recently explored these themes in my acceptance speech for the Havel Foundation Vision 97 Award that I received on October 5, 2005, on the birthday of Václav Havel, former president of the Czech Republic and its heroic revolutionary leader. See Philip G. Zimbardo, "Liberation Psychology in a Time of Terror," Prague: Havel Foundation, 2005. Online: www.zimbardo.com.havelawardlecture.pdf.

22. Rabindranath Tagore, *Stray Birds* (London: Macmillan, 1916), p. 24.

CHAPTER TWO: Sunday's Surprise Arrests

1. This early research and theory on deindividuation was summarized in my 1970 chapter "The Human Choice: Individuation, Reason, and Order Versus Deindividuation, Impulse, and Chaos," *1969 Nebraska Symposium on Motivation,* ed. W. J. Arnold and D. Levine (Lincoln: University of Nebraska Press, 1990), pp. 237–307. A more recent article on vandalism can be seen in P. G. Zimbardo, "Urban Decay, Vandalism, Crime and Civic Engagement," in *Schrumpfende Städte/Shrinking Cities,* ed. F. Bolenius (Berlin: Philipp Oswalt, 2005).

2. Graduate researcher Scott Fraser led the Bronx research team, and his counterpart, Ebbe Ebbesen, led the Palo Alto research team.

3. "Diary of an Abandoned Automobile," *Time,* October 1, 1968.

4. We had to get local police approval to do this field study, so they notified me of the neighbors' concern about the abandoned car now being stolen—by me.

5. The "Broken Windows Theory" of reducing crime by restoring neighborhood order was first presented in James Q. Wilson and George L. Kelling, "The Police and Neighborhood Safety," *The Atlantic Monthly,* March 1982, pp. 22–38.

6. I had helped develop a program to train antiwar activists to create citizen support for peace candidates in upcoming elections, using basic social psychological strategies and tactics of persuasion and compliance. Bob Abelson, my former Yale teacher, and I put these ideas together in an operational manual: R. P. Abelson and P. G. Zimbardo, *Canvassing for Peace: A Manual For Volunteers* (Ann Arbor, Mich.: Society for the Psychological Study of Social Issues, 1970).

7. The first of these violent police-campus confrontations took place at the University of Wisconsin in October 1967, when students protested the on-campus recruiting by Dow Chemical, the maker of the infamous napalm firebombs that were scorching the earth and civilians in Vietnam. There too, the university president acted in haste, relying on city police to contain the student demonstrators, who instead inflamed them with tear gas, baton bashing, and all-out mayhem. I recall a particularly vivid media image of a dozen cops beating up a single crawling student, most with their identities concealed by tear gas masks or having removed their identifying jackets. Anonymity plus authority is a recipe for disaster. The spin-off of that event was the mobilization of students across the United States. Most of them were students who had been nonpolitical and uninvolved in such activities—unlike their European counterparts, who had literally gone to the ramparts in defiance of their governments' restrictions on free access to public education and other complaints of injustice.

It was May Day 1970 at Kent State University, Ohio, when students began protesting the escalation of the Vietnam War by Richard Nixon and Henry Kissinger into Cambodia. Some students set the ROTC building on fire. A thousand National Guardsmen, ordered to occupy the campus, fired tear gas at protesters. Ohio Governor James Rhodes said on television, "We are going to eradicate the problem, not treat the symptom." That unfortunate remark set in place the conceptual groundwork for extreme reactions by the Guardsmen toward the students who were creating the problem—to be "eradicated," without negotiation or reconciliation.

When a group of unarmed students gathered on May 4 and was moving toward a group of seventy Guardsmen with bayonets readied on their rifles, one of the soldiers panicked and fired directly at them. In a blind flash, there was a sudden volley by most other Guardsmen shooting at the students. In three seconds, sixty-seven shots were fired! Four students were killed; eight were wounded, some seriously. Included in the dead and injured were some not even near the scene of confrontation, on their way to class, but in the distant line of fire. Some, like Sandra Schewer, who was shot 400 feet away, and, ironically, Bill Schroeder, an ROTC student, were also shot, not protesting, but just victims of "collateral damage."

One soldier later said, "My mind was telling me this is not right, but I fired on the individual, he dropped." No one was ever held responsible for these murders. An iconic photo of this event showed a young woman screaming in horror over the body of a fallen student. It also mobilized further antiwar sentiment in the United States.

Less well-known than the Kent State massacre was a similar event occurring only ten days later at Jackson State College in Mississippi, where three students were killed and twelve wounded by hundreds of shots fired on black students by National Guardsmen occupying their campus.

In contrast to these lethal encounters, most of the activities during the nationwide student strikes in May 1970 were relatively peaceful, although there were some cases of disruption and violence. In many cases, state authorities took measures to avert violence. In California, Governor Ronald Reagan shut down all twenty-eight campuses of the university and state college systems for four days. Guardsmen were sent onto the campuses of the universities of Kentucky, South Carolina, Illinois at Urbana, and Wisconsin at Madison. There were confrontations at Berkeley, the University of Maryland at College Park, and other places. At Fresno State College in California, a firebomb destroyed a million-dollar computer center.

8. This program was started by a Stanford faculty and student group and supported by the Palo Alto City Council, before which I had appeared in a town hall meeting to urge proactive reconciliation efforts.

9. This description of the preparations for the Sunday arrests by the Palo Alto police is based not on documented recordings of our transactions at that time but rather on my subsequent recall blended with the intention of creating a reasonable story line. My depiction of the experimental procedures and theoretical rationale for our research combines what I had previously explained to Captain Zurcher, to the TV executive at station KRON to engage its cooperation in filming the arrests, and to the cameraman before we got to the police station, in addition to what I recall saying to the arresting officers that morning. It is my attempt to convey this vital information to the reader without engaging in a pedantic time-out to do so formally. The full reason for conducting this study was based on more theoretical grounds, that of testing the relative impact of dispositional, or personality, factors versus situational factors in understanding behavioral transformations in novel behavioral contexts. That will become evident in subsequent chapters.

10. The following three scenarios were created based on available information on three of our mock prisoners from their initial background information and later interviews, along with observations made at the time of their Sunday arrests. Clearly, I have taken creative license in extending that information to form these imaginative scenarios. However, we will see that there are some parallels with their subsequent behavior as mock prisoners.

CHAPTER THREE: Let Sunday's Degradation Rituals Begin

1. Unless otherwise noted, all prisoner and guard dialogue is taken from verbatim transcripts of video footage made during the experiment. The names of prisoners and guards have been modified to conceal their true identities. Stanford Prison Experiment materials referred to in this book, and all original data and analyses, are preseved at the Archives of the

History of American Psychology in Akron, Ohio. Future materials will also be donated and permanently housed at the Archives as the Philip Zimbardo Papers. The first installment will be devoted to the Stanford Prison Experiment. Contact information for the Archives is www.uakron.edu or ahap@uakron.edu. The SPE has been the subject of extensive media discussion, and some of the participants have chosen to disclose their identities. However, this is the first time I have written about the experiment in such detail for a general audience. Therefore, I have determined to change the names of all prisoners and guards to conceal their true identities.

2. These rules were an expansion of those that Jaffe and his fellow students had developed for their project in my Social Psychology in Action course the past spring. In it, they created a mock prison in their dormitory. For that course, students chose from among a set of ten experiential projects that I suggested, each of which would investigate aspects of individuals in institutions, such as elderly entering homes for the aged, people joining cults, and the socialization into the roles of prisoners and guards. Jaffe and a dozen or so other students chose prisons as their topic, and as part of their research, they designed and ran a mock prison in their dormitory over a weekend—with dramatic results that stimulated the present formal experiment.

    In the mock prison arranged by these students, I provided some advice but did not know what they had experienced until they presented their course project in class the day after their prison weekend. I was amazed at the intensity of the feelings, expressed openly before a large lecture class, of anger, frustration, shame, and confusion about their behavior and that of their friends in their new roles. I followed up with a debriefing of all of them, where it became evident that the situation had packed a wallop. But given the self-selection of these students into this topic, it was not clear if there was something unusual about them or about the prisonlike setting. Only a controlled experiment with random assignment to the roles of guards and prisoners could separate dispositions from situational factors. That became one of the instigations for designing this experiment that we did the following summer.

    Jaffe's final report of the group study on May 15–16, 1971, is entitled simply "A Simulated Prison." Unpublished report, Stanford University, Spring 1971.

3. Guard's Shift Report.
4. Prisoner's taped final evaluation.
5. First week's planned meals with food services at Stanford's Tressider Student Union:

    | 1. Sunday | Beef stew |
    | 2. Monday | Chili Beans |
    | 3. Tuesday | Chicken Pot Pie |
    | 4. Wednesday | Turkey a la King |
    | 5. Thursday | Corn Fritters with bacon strips |
    | 6. Friday | Spaghetti with meatballs |

    Breakfasts: 5 oz. juice, cereal or hard-boiled eggs, and an apple.
    Lunches: 2 slices of bread with one of the following cold cuts—bologna, ham, or liverwurst. An apple, a cookie, milk or water.

6. Prisoner's retrospective dairy.
7. Prisoner's retrospective dairy.
8. Prisoner's retrospective dairy
9. Prisoner's letter in archives.
10. Guard's quote from NBC *Chronolog* interview, aired November 1971.
11. Guard's retrospective diary.
12. Verbatim transcript from video footage of the guards' meeting. See DVD *Quiet Rage: The Stanford Prison Experiment.*

CHAPTER FOUR: Monday's Prisoner Rebellion

1. The quotes in this and the other chapters on the Stanford Prison Experiment come from a variety of data sources that I try to identify specifically when pertinent. Among these archival data are verbatim transcripts of video footage filmed during various times of the experiment; Guard Shift Reports, which some guards wrote at the end of their shift; final interviews at the end of the study; final evaluation reports made after the participants went home and returned, usually within a few weeks; retrospective diaries, which some of them sent to us at various times subsequent to the termination of the study; audiotaped interviews; interviews done for an NBC TV program, *Chronolog*, September 1971 (aired November, 1971); and personal observations, as well as subsequent recollections that Craig Haney, Christina Maslach, and I made in a published chapter. This quote comes from a final evaluation report.
2. Unless otherwise noted, these and other prisoner and guard dialogues are taken from verbatim transcripts of video footage made during the experiment.
3. Guard's Shift Report.
4. Guard's retrospective diary.
5. Guard's retrospective diary.
6. This utterance by Prisoner 8612 is one of the most dramatic events in the entire study. In order for this simulation to work, everyone must agree to act as if it were a prison and not an experimental simulation of a prison. In a sense, that involves a communal self-censorship of tacitly agreeing to frame all events in prison metaphors and not experimental ones. It involves everyone knowing it is all just an experiment but all acting as if it were a real prison. 8612 shatters that frame by shouting out that it is not a prison, only a simulated experiment. Amid the chaos surrounding that moment, there was a sudden silence when he added a concrete, but strange, example of why this was not a prison—because in real prisons they don't take your clothes and bed away. Then another prisoner openly challenges him by simply adding, "They do." After that exchange, the self-censorship rule is reinforced, and the rest of the prisoners, guards, and staff all go on with the self-imposed limit on expressing the obvious truth. For a full presentation of the operation of self-censorship, see Dale Miller's recent text, *An Invitation to Social Psychology: Expressing and Censoring the Self* (Belmont, CA: Thomson Wadsworth, 2006).
7. Prisoner's retrospective diary.
8. Prisoner's taped interview.
9. Not clear what the "contract" means in this case. See the prison study website information at www.prisonexp.org for the following experimental materials: The description of the research given to the participants; the consent form they signed; and the application to the Human Subjects Research Committee at Stanford.
10. Prisoner's retrospective diary.
11. Prisoner's retrospective diary.
12. Prisoner's retrospective diary.
13. Quoted from our chapter on our subsequent recollections of the SPE: P. G. Zimbardo, C. Maslach, and C. Haney, "Reflections on the Stanford Prison Experiment: Genesis, Transformations, Consequences," in ed. T. Blass, *Obedience to Authority: Current Perspectives on the Milgram Paradigm,* (Mahwah, NJ: Erlbaum, 1999), pp. 193–237.
14. Ibid., p. 229.
15. Prisoner's final interview.

CHAPTER FIVE: Tuesday's Double Trouble: Visitors and Rioters

1. Unless otherwise noted, all prisoner and guard dialogue is taken from verbatim transcripts of video footage made during the experiment.
2. Guard's Shift Report.

3. NBC *Chronolog* interview (November 1971).
4. Guard's retrospective diary.
5. Prisoner's retrospective diary.
6. Spy's taped final interview with Dr. Zimbardo.
7. Prisoner's retrospective diary.
8. Prisoner's retrospective diary.
9. This O.N.R. grant funded my deindividuation research (see chapter 13) and was extended to cover the prison experiment. It was O.N.R. grant: N001447-A-0112-0041.
10. See Leon Festinger, *A Theory of Cognitive Dissonance* (Stanford, CA: Stanford University Press, 1957). See also my edited volume of research by my NYU students, colleagues, and me, Philip G. Zimbardo, ed., *The Cognitive Control of Motivation* (Glenview, IL: Scott, Foresman, 1969).
11. See Irving Janis and Leon Mann, *Decision Making: A Psychological Analysis of Conflict, Choice, and Commitment* (New York: Free Press, 1977).

CHAPTER SIX: Wednesday Is Spiraling Out of Control

1. All of the dialogue in these exchanges between guards, prisoners, staff, and the priest is from our verbatim transcripts composed from videos taken at the time, supplemented with log notes and my personal recollections. The priest's name has been changed to mask his identity, but everything else about him and his interactions with the prisoners and me is as accurate as possible.
2. We will see the same exact reaction in Chapter 14, when a real guard, Staff Sergeant Frederick at Abu Ghraib, complains about the lack of clear guidelines as to what was permissible to do to the prisoners.
3. Guard's Shift Report.
4. Prisoner's retrospective diary.
5. Spy's final taped interview with Dr. Zimbardo.
6. NBC *Chronolog* interview (November 1971).
7. As an aside, I note that one person who did see me discussing the issues of prisoner dehumanization and guard power was the lawyer for the famous black radical political prisoner George Jackson. I got a letter from him on Saturday afternoon (August 21, 1971) inviting me to be an expert witness on behalf of his client, who was going to trial soon for the alleged murder of a guard in the Soledad Brothers case. He wanted me to interview his client, who was in lockdown in nearby San Quentin Prison's solitary confinement, ironically called "The Maximum Adjustment Center" (perhaps borrowing from George Orwell's *1984*). On Saturday, events conspired to prevent me from accepting his invitation, since Jackson was killed in an alleged escape, but I did get heavily involved in several later trials. One federal trial challenged the Adjustment Center as a place of "cruel and unusual punishment." In addition, I was also an expert witness in a second trial that came to be known as the "San Quentin Six" murder-conspiracy case, held at the Marin County Courthouse—with its elegant lines designed by Frank Lloyd Wright presenting an almost comic contrast to those of the Maximum Adjustment Center.
8. Prisoner's final evaluation.
9. We had a Parole Board hearing earlier on Wednesday that will be presented in full detail in the next chapter. However, as no prisoners were actually paroled, I am not sure what Sarge is referring to, other than that two prisoners were released because of extreme stress reactions. Maybe the guards told the rest of the prisoners that they had been paroled to keep their hopes up. "Maximum security" must mean they are in the Hole.
10. Prisoner's final evaluation.
11. When I replay the tape of this scene again, I suddenly realize that this guard, who is acting out his version of the role made famous by Strother Martin as the cruel warden in *Cool Hand Luke*, actually looks and moves more like actor Powers Boothe playing the infamous

Rev. Jim Jones in the movie *Guyana Tragedy*. That monstrous tragedy would occur only six years later. *Cool Hand Luke* (1967), screenplay by Donn Pearce, directed by Stuart Rosenberg, featuring Paul Newman as Luke Jackson. *Guyana Tragedy* (1980), directed by William Graham.

CHAPTER SEVEN: The Power to Parole

1. Carlo Prescott opened the day with the following monologue to the other board members: "Parole boards have been known to turn down ideal candidates for parole, that is guys who have come in to the board having taken school, therapy, counseling. They turn this guy down because he's poor, because he's a repeated offender, because the neighborhood he comes from doesn't give him any support, because his parents are dead, because he doesn't have any means of income, just because they don't like his face, or because he shot a cop in the finger. And then they take some guy who's an ideal prisoner who has never been any trouble . . . an ideal prisoner—and they turn him down three, four, five, and six times. Young kids, who seem most likely to come back to prison, who are most likely to be completely shaped and confused by the prison setting that they will never reenter society, are released a great deal more swiftly than individuals who act naturally, who never get into any trouble, and can manage to thieve or hustle enough to stay out of prison. Now, that sounds crazy, but what it amounts to is this—prison's a big business. Prisons need prisoners. The people who come into prison and get their heads together are not coming back into prison, there's too many things they can do. But people who come in on indefinite sentences . . . when you say to them [as a Parole Board], "I have this much leeway to play games," you're saying, in effect, that the parole board must not look at the most obvious circumstances, which are . . ."

2. Unless otherwise noted, all prisoner and guard dialogue is taken from verbatim transcripts of video footage made during the experiment; this includes all the quotes from the Parole Board hearings.

3. I attended a number of California Parole Board hearings in Vacaville Prison as part of a public defender project headed by the San Francisco law offices of Sidney Wollinsky. The project was designed to assess the function of parole boards in the indeterminate sentencing system that was then in contested operation in the California Department of Corrections. In that system, judges could establish a range of sentence lengths for a conviction, such as five to ten years, instead of a fixed sentence. However, prisoners typically ended up serving the maximum time, not the average of the range times.

   It was chilling and sad for me to observe each prisoner desperately trying to convince the two-man Board that he deserved to be released, and doing so in the few minutes' time allotted to his appeal. One of the board members was not even paying attention because he was reading the file of the next prisoner in the long line that had to be processed each day, and the other was glancing at his file for perhaps the first time. If parole was denied, as it most often was, the prisoner had to wait another year to come back to the Board. My notes indicated that a major determinant of the probability of parole was in the time dimension framed by the opening question. If it were about the prisoner's past—details about the crime, the victim, the trial, or troubles in the prison system—there would be no parole. However, if he was questioned about what he was doing now that was constructive to gain early release or his future plans after release, the likelihood of parole was increased. It may be that the parole officer had already made up his mind and unconsciously framed his question to get more evidence of why a prisoner did not deserve parole by his making the past crime more salient. If, on the other hand, he saw some promise in the prisoner's file, a focus on the future would enable the prisoner a few minutes' time to elaborate on this optimistic potential.

4. Jane Elliott's blue-eyes/brown-eyes demonstration is told in: W. Peters, *A Class Divided, Then and Now* (Expanded Edition) (New Haven, CT: Yale University Press, 1971/1985).

Peters was involved in the filming of both prizewinning documentaries, the ABC News documentary "The Eye of the Storm" (available from Guidance Associates, New York) and the follow-up PBS *Frontline* documentary, "A Class Divided" (available online at www.pbs.org/wgbh/pages/frontline/shows/divided/etc/view.html).

5. This extended quote from Carlo is from an NBC *Chronolog* interview by producer Larry Goldstein, recorded at Stanford in September 1971, typed by my secretary Rosanne Saussotte, but sadly not used in the final program that was aired.

6. George Jackson, *Soledad Brother: The Prison Letters of George Jackson* (New York: Bantam Books, 1970), pp. 119–20.

CHAPTER EIGHT: Thursday's Reality Confrontations

1. Lucid dreaming is a state of semiawareness that the dreamer has of monitoring, and even coming to control, his or her dream as it is unfolding. A good recent reference to this interesting phenomenon is found in my colleague's book, S. LaBerge, *Lucid Dreaming: A Concise Guide to Awakening in Your Dreams and in Your Life* (Boulder, CO: Sounds True Press, 2004).

2. Prisoner's taped interview with Curt Banks.

3. Guard's final evaluation.

4. Prisoner's final evaluation.

5. Guard's final evaluation.

6. Guard's final evaluation.

7. Guard's final evaluation.

8. NBC *Chronolog* interview, November 1971. "Varnish" was a third-year graduate student in economics.

9. Guard's final evaluation.

10. Guard's retrospective diary.

11. "Work to rule" (for a basic definition, see http://en.wikipedia.org/wiki/Work_to_rule): As a policy, the work to rule was organized labor's alternative to striking for public servants. Because emergency workers such as police officers and firefighters would be fired immediately or replaced if they were to strike, they had to find other alternatives. Apparently, the first U.S precedent was the famous 1919 Boston Police Strike. The then-governor of Massachusetts, Calvin Coolidge, dismissed 1,200 men because of the strike and stated, "There is no right to strike against the public safety by anybody, anywhere, anytime," which is now widely quoted. He gained popularity, which helped catapult him into the vice presidency and eventually presidency of the United States. There was a case in 1969 involving the Atlanta Police Department when the Fraternal Order of Police (FOP) used a similar "slowdown" tactic, which seems identical to the work to rule. At the time, "hippie" activists were usually not arrested and were given lenient treatment by the police, which was a widely accepted, yet unofficial policy. Protesting for better wages and hours (among other issues), the FOP started a "slowdown" by issuing massive numbers of tickets to "hippies" and other mild transgressors, which jammed the administrative system and made it virtually impossible for the police force to continue working effectively. At the time, there was a scare about an outbreak of crime, and the police eventually bargained for better wages and conditions. See M. Levi, *Bureaucratic Insurgency: The Case of Police Unions* (Lexington, MA: Lexington Books, 1977), and International Association of Chiefs of Police, *Police Unions and Other Police Organizations* (New York: Arno Press and *The New York Times*, 1971) (Bulletin no. 4, September 1944).

12. Prisoner's final interview.

13. Prisoner's postexperiment questionnaire.

14. Prisoner's final evaluation.

15. The tactic of using hunger strikes as a political tool is traced by the political historian Sheila Howard to the first-ever hunger striker, Terence MacSwiney, MP (Member of Parliament). He was a newly elected lord mayor of Cork, who died during a hunger strike in 1920 in

search of political status as a prisoner. Gerry Adams (the leader of Sinn Fein) notes that MacSwiney directly inspired Mahatma Gandhi (see Foreword in Bobby Sands's book). Between 1976 and 1981 there were various periods of such hunger strikes among Irish political prisoners, the last of which became the most famous when ten men died as a result. They included seven members of the IRA, notably one of its leaders, Bobby Sands, and three members of the INLA (Irish National Liberation Army). Republican (i.e., IRA/INLA) prisoners went on a hunger strike in Long Kesh Prison (the "Maze" prison), just south of Belfast. Among other protests they conducted during their hunger strike was a "blanket protest": they refused to wear prison uniforms because they were a symbol of one's criminal status; instead, they wore blankets to keep them warm during their hunger strike.

Bobby Sands wrote a series of inspiring poems and other pieces from prison; they have inspired international support for the political cause of occupied peoples, notably in Iran and in Palestine in the Middle East. Likewise, Palestinian flags are flown alongside Irish tricolors in Derry town (predominantly Catholic/nationalist/republican) and in areas of Belfast.

Some relevant references are Shelia Howard, *Britain and Ireland 1914–1923* (Dublin: Gill and Macmillan, 1983); Gerry Adams, Foreword to *Bobby Sands Writings from Prison* (Cork: Mercier Press, 1997); and Michael Von Tangen Page, *Prisons, Peace, and Terrorism: Penal Policy in the Reduction of Political Violence in Northern Ireland, Italy, and the Spanish Basque Country, 1968–1997* (New York: St. Martin's Press, 1998).

16. Prisoner's final evaluation.
17. Prisoner's final interview, also source of next extended quote.
18. Guard's retrospective diary.
19. Prisoner's retrospective diary.
20. Prisoner's postexperiment questionnaire.
21. Prisoner's retrospective diary.
22. This extended quote and the following one are from Christina Maslach's essay in a collection of three, along with those of Craig Haney and myself: P. G. Zimbardo, C. Maslach, and C. Haney, "Reflections on the Stanford Prison Experiment: Genesis, Transformations, Consequences," in *Obedience to Authority: Current Perspectives on the Milgram Paradigm*, ed. T. Blass (Mahwah, NJ: Erlbaum, 1999), pp. 193–237. Quote is on pp. 214–16.
23. Ibid., pp. 216–17.
24. Bruno Bettelheim reports on a similar phenomenon among prisoners in the Nazi concentration camp in which he was interned during the early stages of the Holocaust, before the concentration camps became extermination camps. He relates how some inmates gave up trying to survive, becoming like zombies. His moving description of survival and surrender under horrendous conditions is worth including in full. It is from part of his essay "Owners of Their Face," in his book *Surviving and Other Essays* (New York: Alfred A. Knopf, 1979):

My reading of Paul Celan's poem was informed by what I had learned about survival in the camps from observing others and myself: even the worst mistreatment by the SS failed to extinguish the will to live—that is, as long as one could muster the wish to go on and maintain one's self-respect. Then tortures could even strengthen one's resolution not to permit the mortal enemy to break one's desire to survive, and to remain true to oneself as much as conditions permitted. Then the actions of the SS tended to make one livid with rage, and this gave one the feeling of being very much alive. It made one all the more determined to go on living, so as to be able someday to defeat the enemy.

. . . All this worked only up to a point. If there was no or only little indication that someone, or the world at large, was deeply concerned about the fate of the prisoner, his ability to give positive meaning to signs from the outside world eventually vanished and he felt forsaken, usually with disastrous consequences for his will and with it his ability to survive. Only a very clear demonstration that one was not abandoned—and the SS saw to it that one received this only very rarely, and not at all in the extermination camps—restored, at least momentarily, hope even to those who otherwise by and large had lost it. But those who had reached the utmost state of depression and disintegration, those who had turned into walking corpses because their life drives had become inoperative—the so-called "Muslims" (Muselmänner) could not believe in what others would have viewed as tokens that they had not been forgotten" (pp. 105–6).

CHAPTER NINE: Friday's Fade to Black

1. Guard's retrospective diary.
2. Ceros was an eighteen-year-old freshman who was thinking about becoming a social worker.
3. Guard's incident report.
4. Unless otherwise noted, all prisoner and guard dialogue is taken from verbatim transcripts of video footage made during the experiment.
5. Public defender's letter to me, August 29, 1971.
6. Critical Incident Stress Debriefing (CISD) has been the primary treatment in dealing with victims of traumatic stress, such as terrorist attacks, natural disasters, rape, and other abuses. However, recent empirical evidence challenges its therapeutic value, even pointing to instances where it is counterproductive by increasing and prolonging the negative emotional component of the stress. Having people vent their emotions, in some cases, serves to revivify the negative thoughts rather than relieve them.
   Some relevant references include
   B. Litz, M. Gray, R. Bryant, and A. Adler, "Early Intervention for Trauma: Current Status and Future Directions," *Clinical Psychology: Science and Practice* 9 (2002): 112–34. R. McNally, R. Bryant, and A. Ehlers, "Does Early Psychological Intervention Promote Recovery from Posttraumatic Stress?" *Psychological Science in the Public Interest* 4 (2003): 45–79.
7. Prisoner's retrospective diary.
8. Guard's retrospective diary. The participants were paid for only a full week, not for the second week, which was terminated, at the rate of $15.00 for each day served as prisoners and guards.
9. Guard's retrospective diary.
10. Prisoner's final evaluation.
11. Prisoner's final evaluation.
12. Prisoner's retrospective diary.
13. Guard's retrospective diary.
14. Prisoner's final evaluation.
15. Prisoner's retrospective diary.
16. Guard's final interview.
17. Guard's postexperiment questionnaire.
18. Guard's retrospective diary.
19. Guard's retrospective diary.
20. Prisoner's postexperiment questionnaire.
21. Guard's retrospective diary.
22. Guard's audio interview.
23. Guard's retrospective diary.
24. Transcript of interview for *Quiet Rage: The Stanford Prison Experiment.*
25. NBC *Chronolog* interview, November 1971.

26. Guard's retrospective diary.
27. Guard's retrospective diary.
28. Guard Hellmann's nickname, "John Wayne," has an interesting parallel that I learned from my colleague John Steiner. John Steiner, an emeritus professor of sociology at Sonoma State University and a Holocaust survivor, was as a teenager a prisoner in Buchenwald concentration camp for several years. When he learned that our prisoners had nicknamed one of the worst guards "John Wayne," he recounted a parallel with his own experience: "Well, the guards in the camps were all anonymous to us. We called them 'Herr Lieutenant' or 'Mr. S.S. Officer,' but they had no name, no identity. However, one of the guards, who was the most vicious of all, we gave him a nickname too. He was shooting the people for no reason, killing them, and pushing them into the electric fence. His violence was like a Wild West cowboy. So we called him 'Tom Mix,' but only behind his back." Tom Mix was the tough movie cowboy of the 1930s and '40s that John Wayne subsequently became for future generations.
29. Guard's final evaluation.
30. Guard's postexperiment questionnaire.
31. Guard's postexperiment questionnaire.

CHAPTER TEN: The SPE's Meaning and Messages: The Alchemy of Character Transformations

1. The concept of learned helplessness originally came from animal research by Martin Seligman and his associates. Dogs in conditioning experiments that were given inescapable shocks that they could do nothing to avoid soon stopped trying to escape, seemed to give up, and took the shocks—even when they then were given the opportunity to escape easily. Later research revealed parallels with humans who, having experienced inescapable noise, did nothing to stop a stressful new noise when they could have done so. Parallels are also evident in clinical depression, abused children and spouses, prisoners of war, and some residents of nursing homes for the aged. Some references include M.E.P. Seligman, *Helplessness: On Depression, Development and Death* (San Francisco: Freeman, 1975); D. S. Hiroto, "Loss of Control and Learned Helplessness," *Journal of Experimental Psychology* 102 (1974): 187–93; J. Buie, " 'Control' Studies Bode Better Health in Aging," *APA Monitor*, July 1988, p. 20.
2. The best reference for the data we collected and its statistically analyzed results is the first scientific article we published: Craig Haney, Curtis Banks, and Philip Zimbardo, "Interpersonal Dynamics in a Simulated Prison," *International Journal of Criminology and Penology* 1 (1973): 69–97. This journal is now defunct and, not being a publication of the American Psychological Association, there is not an available archive. However, a PDF file of that article is available at www.prisonexp.org and www.zimbardo.com. See also P. G. Zimbardo, C. Haney, W. C. Banks, and D. Jaffe, "The Mind is a Formidable Jailer: A Pirandellian Prison." *The New York Times Magazine*, April 8, 1973, pp. 36ff; and P. G. Zimbardo, "Pathology of Imprisonment," *Society* 6 (1972): 4, 6, 8.
3. T. W. Adorno, E. Frenkel-Brunswick, D. J. Levinson, and R. N. Sanford, *The Authoritarian Personality* (New York: Harper, 1950).
4. R. Christie, and F. L. Geis, eds. *Studies in Machiavellianism* (New York: Academic Press, 1970).
5. A. I. Comrey, *Comrey Personality Scales* (San Diego: Educational and Industrial Testing Service, 1970).
6. Figure 16.1, "Guard and Prisoner Behavior," in P. G. Zimbardo and R. J. Gerrig, *Psychology and Life*, 14th ed., (New York: HarperCollins, 1996), p. 587.
7. B. Bettelheim, *The Informed Heart: Autonomy in a Mass Age* (Glencoe, IL: Free Press, 1960).
8. J. Frankel. "Exploring Ferenczi's Concept of Identification with the Aggressor: Its Role in

Trauma, Everyday Life, and the Therapeutic Relationship," *Psychoanalytic Dialogues* 12 (2002): 101–39.

9. E. Aronson, M. Brewer, and J. M. Carlsmith, "Experimentation in Social Psychology," in *Handbook of Social Psychology*, vol. 1, ed. G. Lindzey and E. Aronson (Hillsdale NJ: Erlbaum, 1985).

10. K. Lewin, *Field Theory in Social Science* (New York: Harper, 1951). K. Lewin, R. Lippitt, and R. K. White, "Patterns of Aggressive Behavior in Experimentally Created 'Social Climates.' " *Journal of Social Psychology* 10 (1939): 271–99.

11. Robert Jay Lifton, *The Nazi Doctors: Medical Killing and the Psychology of Genocide* (New York: Basic Books, 1986), p. 194.

12. The movie *Cool Hand Luke* was released in the United States in November 1967.

13. P. G. Zimbardo, C. Maslach, and C. Haney, "Reflections on the Stanford Prison Experiment: Genesis, Transformations, Consequences," in *Obedience to Authority: Current Perspectives on the Milgram Paradigm*, ed. T. Blass (Mahwah, NJ: Erlbaum, 1999), pp. 193–237; quote on p. 229.

14. Prisoner's final interview, August 19, 1971.

15. R. J. Lifton, *Thought Reform and the Psychology of Totalism* (New York: Harper, 1969).

16. L. Ross, and R. Nisbett, *The Person and the Situation* (New York: McGraw-Hill, 1991).

17. L. Ross, "The Intuitive Psychologist and His Shortcomings: Distortions in the Attribution Process," *Advances in Experimental Social Psychology*, vol. 10, ed. L. Berkowitz (New York: Academic Press, 1977), pp. 173–220.

18. See the fuller account of these role transformations in Sarah Lyall's description in "To the Manor Acclimated," *The New York Times*, May 26, 2002, p. 12.

19. R. J. Lifton, *The Nazi Doctors* (1986) pp. 196, 206, 210–11.

20. Zimbardo, Maslach, and Haney, "Reflections on the Stanford Prison Experiment," p. 226.

21. A. Zarembo, "A Theater of Inquiry and Evil," *Los Angeles Times*, July 15, 2004, pp. A1, A24–A25.

22. L. Festinger, *A Theory of Cognitive Dissonance* (Stanford, CA: Stanford University Press, 1957); P. G. Zimbardo and M. R. Leippe, *The Psychology of Attitude Change and Social Influence* (New York: McGraw-Hill, 1991); P. G. Zimbardo, *The Cognitive Control of Motivation* (Glenview, IL: Scott, Foresman, 1969).

23. R. Rosenthal and L. F. Jacobson, *Pygmalion in the Classroom: Teacher Expectation and Pupils' Intellectual Development* (New York: Holt, 1968).

24. V. W. Bernard, P. Ottenberg, and F. Redl, "Dehumanization: A Composite Psychological Defense in Relation to Modern War," in *The Triple Revolution Emerging: Social Problems in Depth*, eds. R. Perruci and M. Pilisuck (Boston: Little, Brown, 1968), pp. 16–30.

25. H. I. Lief and R. C. Fox, "Training for 'Detached Concern' in Medical Students," in *The Psychological Basis of Practice*, ed. H. I. Lief, V. F. Lief, and N. R. Lief (New York: Harper & Row, 1963); C. Maslach, " 'Detached Concern' in Health and Social Service Professions," paper presented at the American Psychological Association annual meeting, Montreal, Canada, August 30, 1973.

26. P. G. Zimbardo, "Mind Control in Orwell's *1984*: Fictional Concepts Become Operational Realities in Jim Jones' Jungle Experiment," in *1984: Orwell and Our Future*, eds. M. Nussbaum, J. Goldsmith, and A. Gleason (Princeton, NJ: Princeton University Press, 2005), pp. 127–54.

27. Quote from Feynman's Appendix to the Rogers Commission Report on the Space Shuttle *Challenger* Accident. See his discussion of this experience in the second volume of his autobiographical *What Do You Care What Other People Think? Further Adventures of a Curious Character* (as told to Ralph Leighton) (New York: Norton, 1988).

28. G. Ziemer, *Education for Death: The Making of the Nazi* (New York: Farrar, Staus and Giroux, 1972).

29.   E. Kogon, J. Langbein, and A. Ruckerl, eds., *Nazi Mass Murder: A Documentary History of the Use of Poison Gas* (New Haven, CT: Yale University Press, 1993), pp. 5, 6.

30.   Lifton, *The Nazi Doctors* (1986), pp. 212, 213.

CHAPTER ELEVEN: The SPE: Ethics and Extensions

1.   The concept of "total situation" as one that exerts a powerful impact on human functioning was used by Erving Goffman in depicting the impact of institutions on mental patients and prisoners, and by Robert Jay Lifton in describing the power of Chinese Communist interrogation settings. Total situations are those in which one is physically and then psychologically confined to the extent that all information and reward structures are contained within its narrow boundaries. Craig Haney and I have extended that conception to cover high schools, which sometimes act as prisons. See E. Goffman, *Asylums: Essays on the Social Situation of Mental Patients and Other Inmates* (New York: Doubleday, 1961); R. J. Lifton, *Thought Reform and the Psychology of Totalism* (New York: Norton, 1969); C. Haney and P. G. Zimbardo, "Social Roles, Role-playing and Education: The High School as Prison," *Behavioral and Social Science Teacher,* vol. 1 (1973): 24–45.

2.   P. G. Zimbardo, *Psychology and Life,* 12th ed. (Glenview, IL: Scott, Foresman, 1989), Table "Ways We Can Go Wrong," p. 689.

3.   L. Ross and D. Shestowsky, "Contemporary Psychology's Challenges to Legal Theory and Practice," *Northwestern Law Review* 97 (2003): 108–14,

4.   S. Milgram, *Obedience to Authority* (New York: Harper & Row, 1974).

5.   D. Baumrind, "Some Thoughts on Ethics of Research: After Reading Milgram's 'Behavioral Study of Obedience,' " *American Psychologist* 19 (1964): 421–23.

6.   H. B. Savin, "Professors and Psycho-logical Researchers: Conflicting Values in Conflicting Roles," *Cognition* 2 (1973): 147–49. My reply to Savin is "On the Ethics of Intervention in Human Psychological Research: With Special Reference to the Stanford Prison Experiment," *Cognition* 2 (1973): 213–56.

7.   See copy of the Human Subjects Research Review approval at www.prisonexp.org, under Links.

8.   See L. Ross, M. R. Lepper, and M. Hubbard, "Perseverance in Self-Perception and Social Perception: Biased Attributional Processes in the Debriefing Paradigm," *Journal of Personality and Social Psychology* 32 (1975): 880–92.

9.   L. Kohlberg, *The Philosophy of Moral Development* (New York: Harper & Row, 1981).

10.   See Neal Miller's research on biofeedback and autonomic conditioning and his examples of how basic research can pay applied dividends: N. E. Miller, "The Value of Behavioral Research on Animals," *American Psychologist* 40 (1985): 423–40; and N. E. Miller, "Introducing and Teaching Much-Needed Understanding of the Scientific Process," *American Psychologist* 47 (1992): 848–50.

11.   P. G. Zimbardo, "Discontinuity Theory: Cognitive and Social Searches for Rationality and Normality—May Lead to Madness," in *Advances in Experimental Social Psychology,* vol. 31, ed. M. Zanna (San Diego: Academic Press, 1999), pp. 345–486.

12.   Details about *The Quiet Rage* video: P. G. Zimbardo, (writer and producer) and K. Musen, (co-writer and co-producer), *Quiet Rage: The Stanford Prison Experiment* (video) (Stanford, CA: Stanford Instructional Television Network, 1989).

13.   Personal communication, e-mail, June 5, 2005.

14.   C. Haney, "Psychology and Legal Change: The Impact of a Decade," *Law and Human Behavior* 17 (1993): 371–98; C. Haney, "Infamous Punishment: The Psychological Effects of Isolation," *National Prison Project Journal* 8 (1993): 3–21; C. Haney, "The Social Context of Capital Murder: Social Histories and the Logic of Capital Mitigation," *Santa Clara Law Review* 35 (1995): 547–609; C. Haney, *Reforming Punishment: Psychological Limits to the Pain*

of Imprisonment (Washington, DC: American Psychological Association, 2006); C. Haney and P. G. Zimbardo, "The Past and Future of U.S. Prison Policy: Twenty-five Years After the Stanford Prison Experiment," *American Psychologist* 53 (1998): 709–27.

15. P. G. Zimbardo, C. Maslach, and C. Haney, "Reflections on the Stanford Prison Experiment: Genesis, Transformations, Consequences," in *Obedience to Authority: Current Perspectives on the Milgram Paradigm*, ed. T. Blass (Mahwah, NJ: Erlbaum, 1999), quote pp. 221, 225.

16. Ibid., p. 220.

17. C. Maslach, "Burned-out," *Human Behavior*, September 1976, pp. 16–22; C. Maslach, *Burnout: The Cost of Caring* (Englewood Cliffs, NJ: Prentice-Hall, 1982); C. Maslach, S. E. Jackson, and M. P. Leiter, *The Maslach Burnout Inventory*, (3rd ed.) (Palo Alto, CA: Consulting Psychologists Press, 1996); C. Maslach, and M. P. Leiter, *The Truth About Burnout* (San Francisco: Jossey-Bass, 1997).

18. C. Maslach, J. Stapp, and R. T. Santee, "Individuation: Conceptual Analysis and Assessment," *Journal of Personality and Social Psychology* 49 (1985): 729–38.

19. Curtis Banks went on to a distinguished career in academia, obtaining his Stanford Ph.D. in only three years and becoming the first African American to be a tenured professor in Princeton University's Psychology Department. He then moved on to teach at Howard University and also to perform valuable services at the Educational Testing Service and as founding editor of the *Journal of Black Psychology*. Sadly, he died prematurely in 1998 from cancer.

    David Jaffe likewise moved on from the SPE to a distinguished career in medicine, now serving as director of the Emergency Medicine Department at the St. Louis Children's Hospital and associate professor of pediatrics at Washington University, St. Louis, Missouri.

20. P. G. Zimbardo, "The Stanford Shyness Project," in *Shyness: Perspectives on Research and Treatment*, ed. W. H. Jones, J. M. Cheek, and S. R. Briggs, (New York: Plenum Press, 1986), pp. 17–25; P. G. Zimbardo, *Shyness: What It Is, What to Do About It* (Reading, MA: Addison-Wesley, 1977); P. G. Zimbardo and S. Radl, *The Shy Child* (New York: McGraw-Hill, 1986); P. G. Zimbardo, P. Pilkonis, and R. Norwood, "The Silent Prison of Shyness," *Psychology Today*, May 1975, pp. 69–70, 72; L. Henderson and P. G. Zimbardo, "Shyness as a Clinical Condition: The Stanford Model," In *International Handbook of Social Anxiety*, L. Alden and R. Crozier (eds.) (Sussex, UK: John Wiley & Sons), pp. 431–47.

21. *San Francisco Chronicle*, February 14, 1974.

22. A. Gonzalez and P. G. Zimbardo, "Time in Perspective: The Time Sense We Learn Early Affects How We Do Our Jobs and Enjoy Our Pleasures," *Psychology Today*, March 1985, pp. 21–26; P. G. Zimbardo and J. N. Boyd, "Putting Time in Perspective: A Valid, Reliable Individual-Differences Metric," *Journal of Personality and Social Psychology* 77 (1999): 1271–88.

23. G. Jackson, *Soledad Brother: The Prison Letters of George Jackson* (New York: Bantam Books, 1970), p. 111.

24. P. G. Zimbardo, S. Andersen, and L. G. Kabat, "Induced Hearing Deficit Generates Experimental Paranoia," *Science* 212 (1981): 1529–31; P. G. Zimbardo, S. LaBerge, and L. Butler, "Physiological Consequences of Unexplained Arousal: A Posthypnotic Suggestion Paradigm," *Journal of Abnormal Psychology* 102 (1993): 466–73.

25. P. G. Zimbardo, "A Passion for Psychology: Teaching It Charismatically, Integrating Teaching and Research Synergistically, and Writing About It Engagingly," in *Teaching Introductory Psychology: Survival Tips from the Experts*, ed. R. J. Sternberg (Washington, DC: American Psychological Association, 1997), pp. 7–34.

26. P. G. Zimbardo, "The Power and Pathology of Imprisonment," *Congressional Record*, serial no. 15, October 25, 1971, Hearings Before Subcommittee No. 3 of the Committee on the Judiciary, House of Representatives, Ninety-Second Congress, First Session on Corrections,

Part II; Prisons, Prison Reform and Prisoner's Rights: California (Washington, DC: U.S. Government Printing Office, 1971).

27. P. G. Zimbardo, "The Detention and Jailing of Juveniles," (Hearings Before U.S. Senate Committee on the Judiciary Subcommittee to Investigate Juvenile Delinquency, September 10, 11, and 17, 1973) (Washington, DC: U.S. Government Printing Office, 1974), pp. 141–61.

28. P. G. Zimbardo, "Transforming Experimental Research into Advocacy for Social Change," in *Applications of Social Psychology*, eds. M. Deutsch and H. A. Hornstein (Hillsdale, NJ: Erlbaum, 1983).

29. P. G. Zimbardo (consultant and on-screen performer), Larry Goldstein (producer), and Garrick Utley (correspondent); "Prisoner 819 Did a Bad Thing: The Stanford Prison Experiment," *Chronolog*, NBC-TV, November 26, 1971.

30. P. G. Zimbardo (on-screen performer), Jay Kernis (producer), and Lesley Stahl (correspondent), "Experimental Prison: The Zimbardo Effect," *60 Minutes*, NBC-TV, August 30, 1998; P. G. Zimbardo (on-screen performer), "The Stanford Prison Experiment Living Dangerously" series, National Geographic TV, May 2004.

31. Alex Gibney, writer-director, "The Human Behavior Experiments," Jigsaw Productions, June 1, 2006, Sundance channel.

32. J. Newton, and P. G. Zimbardo, "Corrections: Perspectives on Research, Policy, and Impact," unpublished report, Stanford University, ONR Technical Report Z-13, February 1975. (Also published in *Adolescence* 23 (76) [Winter 1984]: 911.)

33. C. Pogash, "Life Behind Bars Turns Sour Quickly for a Few Well-Meaning Napa Citizens," *San Francisco Examiner*, March 25, 1976, pp. 10–11.

34   Personal e-mail communication from Glenn Adams, May 4, 2004 (reprinted with permission).

35. S. H. Lovibond, X. Mithiran, and W. G. Adams, "The Effects of Three Experimental Prison Environments on the Behaviour of Non-Convict Volunteer Subjects," *Australian Psychologist* (1979): 273–87.

36. A. Banuazizi and S. Movahedi, "Interpersonal Dynamics in a Simulated Prison: A Methodological Analysis," *American Psychologist* 17 (1975): 152–60.

37. N. J. Orlando, "The Mock Ward: A Study in Simulation," in *Behavior Disorders: Perspectives and Trends*, O. Milton and R. G. Wahlers, eds. (3rd ed., Philadelphia: Lippincott, 1973), pp. 162–70.

38. D. Derbyshire, "When They Played Guards and Prisoners in the US, It Got Nasty. In Britain, They Became Friends," *The Daily Telegraph*, May 3, 2002, p. 3.

39. M. G. Bloche and J. H. Marks, "Doing unto Others as They Did to Us," *The New York Times*, November 4, 2005.

40. J. Mayer, "The Experiment," *The New Yorker*, July 11 and 18, 2005, pp. 60–71.

41. Gerald Gray and Alessandra Zielinski, "Psychology and U.S. Psychologists in Torture and War in the Middle East," *Torture* 16 (2006): 128–33, quotes on pp. 130–31.

42. "The Schlesinger Report," in *The Torture Papers*, eds. K. Greenberg and J. Dratel (UK: Cambridge University Press, 2005), pp. 970–71. We will have much more to say about the findings of this independent investigation in chapter 15.

43. Richard Alvarez, review of Stanford Prison Experiment, *Cover*, September 1995, p. 34.

44. Philip French, review of "Das Experiment," *The Observer*, online, March 24, 2002.

45. Peter Bradshaw, review of "Das Experiment," *The Guardian*, online, March 22, 2002.

46. Roger Ebert, review of "Das Experiment," *Chicago Sun-Times*, online, October 25, 2002.

47. Blake Gopnik, "A Cell with the Power to Transform," *The Washington Post*, June 16, 2005, pp. C1, C5.

48. W. Mares, *The Marine Machine: The Making of the United States Marine* (New York: Doubleday, 1971).

CHAPTER TWELVE: Investigating Social Dynamics: Power, Conformity, and Obedience

1. C. S. Lewis (1898–1963), professor of medieval and Renaissance English at Cambridge University, was also a novelist, a writer of children's books, and a popular speaker on moral and religious issues. In his best-known book, *The Screwtape Letters* (1944), he impersonated a veteran devil in Hell that writes letters encouraging the efforts of a novice devil hard at work on Earth. "The Inner Ring" was the Memorial Lecture at King's College, University of London, delivered to the students in 1944.

2. R. F. Baumeister and M. R. Leary, "The Need to Belong: Desire for Interpersonal Attachments as a Fundamental Human Motivation," *Psychological Bulletin* 117 (1995): 427–529.

3. R. B. Cialdini, M. R. Trost, and J. T. Newsome, "Preference for Consistency: The Development of a Valid Measure and the Discovery of Surprising Behavioral Implications," *Journal of Personality and Social Psychology* 69 (1995): 318–28; Also see L. Festinger, *A Theory of Cognitive Dissonance* (Stanford, CA: Stanford University Press, 1957).

4. P. G. Zimbardo and S. A. Andersen, "Understanding Mind Control: Exotic and Mundane Mental Manipulations," in *Recovery from Cults*, ed. M. Langone, (New York: W. W. Norton, 1993); see also A. W. Scheflin and E. M. Opton, Jr., *The Mind Manipulators: A Non-Fiction Account* (New York: Paddington Press, 1978).

5. In addition to normative, social pressures to go along with others' views, there are rational forces at work because people can serve to provide valuable information and wisdom. M. Deutsch and H. B. Gerard, "A Study of Normative and Informational Social Influence upon Individual Judgement," *Journal of Abnormal and Social Psychology* 51 (1955): 629–36.

6. Associated Press (July 26, 2005), " 'Cool Mom' Guilty of Sex with Schoolboys: She Said She Felt Like 'One of the Group.' " The report is of her sex and drug parties from October 2003 to October 2004 in the rural town of Golden, Colorado.

7. Self-serving, egocentric, and above-average biases have been investigated extensively. For a summary of the main effects across many different domains of application, see D. Myers, *Social Psychology*, 8th ed. (New York: McGraw-Hill, 2005), pp. 66–77.

8. E. Pronin, J. Kruger, K. Savitsky, and L. Ross, "You Don't Know Me, but I Know You: The Illusion of Asymmetric Insight," *Journal of Personality and Social Psychology* 81 (2001): 639–56.

9. M. Sherif, "A Study of Some Social Factors in Perception," *Archives of Psychology* 27 (1935): pp. 210–11.

10. S. E. Asch, "Studies of Independence and Conformity: A Minority of One Against a Unanimous Majority," *Psychological Monographs* 70 (1951): whole no. 416; S. E. Asch, "Opinions and Social Pressure," *Scientific American*, November 1955, pp. 31–35.

11. M. Deutsch and H. B. Gerard (1955).

12. G. S. Berns, J. Chappelow, C. F. Zin, G. Pagnoni, M. E. Martin-Skurski, and J. Richards, "Neurobiological Correlates of Social Conformity and Independence During Mental Rotation," *Biological Psychiatry* 58 (August 1, 2005): 245–53; Sandra Blakeslee, "What Other People Say May Change What You See," *New York Times*, online: www.nytimes.com/2005/06/28/science/28brai.html, June 28, 2005.

13. S. Moscovici and C. Faucheux, "Social Influence, Conformity Bias, and the Study of Active Minorities," in *Advances in Experimental Social Psychology*, vol. 6, ed. L. Berkowitz (New York: Academic Press, 1978), pp. 149–202.

14. E. Langer, *Mindfulness*. (Reading, MA: Addison-Wesley, 1989).

15. C. J. Nemeth, "Differential Contributions to Majority and Minority Influence," *Psychological Review* 93 (1986): 23–32.

16. S. Moscovici, "Social Influence and Conformity," in *The Handbook of Social Psychology*, 3rd. ed., eds. G. Lindzey and E. Aronson (New York: Random House, 1985), pp. 347–412.

17. T. Blass, *Obedience to Authority: Current Perspectives on the Miligram Paradigm* (Mahwah, NJ: Erlbaum, 1999), p. 62.

18. In 1949, seated next to me in senior class at James Monroe High School in the Bronx, New York, was my classmate Stanley Milgram. We were both skinny kids full of ambition and a desire to make something of ourselves so that we might escape from life in the confines of our ghetto. Stanley was the little smart one whom we went to for authoritative answers. I was the tall popular one, the smiling guy other kids would go to for social advice. Even then we were budding situationists. I had just returned to Monroe High from a horrible year at North Hollywood High School, where I had been shunned and friendless (because, as I later learned, there was a rumor circulating that I was from a New York Sicilian Mafia family), to be chosen "Jimmy Monroe," the most popular boy in Monroe High School's senior class. Stanley and I discussed once how that transformation could have happened. We agreed that I had not changed but the situation was what had mattered. When we met years later, at Yale University in 1960, as beginning assistant professors, him starting out at Yale and me at NYU, it turned out that Stanley really wanted to be popular and I really wanted to be smart. So much for unfulfilled desires.

    I should also mention a recent discovery I made about another commonality that I shared with Stanley. I was the one who initially constructed a basement laboratory that was later modified to be the site in which Milgram's Yale obedience experiments were conducted (after he could no longer use the elegant interaction laboratory of sociologist O. K. Moore). I had done so a few years earlier for a study I did with Irving Sarnoff to test Freudian predictions about the differences between fear and anxiety in their effects on social affiliation. I fabricated a little lab in the basement of the building where we taught Introductory Psychology courses. It had the delightfully British name Linsly-Chittenden Hall. It is also interesting that both his experiments and the SPE were conducted in basements.

19. T. Blass, *The Man Who Shocked the World* (New York: Basic Books, 2004), p. 116.

20. See R. Cialdini, *Influence.* (New York: McGraw-Hill, 2001).

21. J. L. Freedman and S. C. Fraser, "Compliance Without Pressure: The Foot-in-the-Door Technique," *Journal of Personality and Social Psychology* 4 (1966): 195–202; also see S. J. Gilbert, "Another Look at the Milgram Obedience Studies: The Role of the Graduated Series of Shocks," *Personality and Social Psychology Bulletin* 4 (1981): 690–95.

22. E. Fromm, *Escape from Freedom* (New York: Holt, Rinehart and Winston, 1941). In the United States, the fear of threats to national security posed by terrorists, amplified by government officials, has led many citizens, the Pentagon, and national leaders to accept the torture of prisoners as a necessary method of eliciting information that could prevent further attacks. That reasoning, I will argue in chapter 15, contributed to the abuses by American guards at Abu Ghraib prison.

23. H. C. Kelman and V. L. Hamilton, *Crimes of Obedience: Toward a Social Psychology of Authority and Responsibility* (New Haven, CT: Yale University Press, 1989).

24. Blass, *The Man Who Shocked the World*, Appendix C, "The Stability of Obedience Across Time and Place."

25. C. L. Sheridan and R. G. King, "Obedience to Authority with an Authentic Victim," *Proceedings of the Annual Convention of the American Psychological Association*, vol. 7 (Part 1), 1972, pp. 165–66.

26. M. T. Orne and C. H. Holland, "On the Ecological Validity of Laboratory Deceptions," *International Journal of Psychiatry* 6 (1968) 282–93.

27. C. K. Hofling, E. Brotzman, S. Dalrymple, N. Graves, and C. M. Pierce, "An Experimental Study in Nurse-Physician Relationships," *Journal of Nervous and Mental Disease* 143 (1966): 171–80.

28. A. Krackow and T. Blass, "When Nurses Obey or Defy Inappropriate Physician Orders: Attributional Differences," *Journal of Social Behavior and Personality* 10 (1995): 585–94.

29. E. Tarnow, "Self-Destructive Obedience in the Airplane Cockpit and the Concept of Obedience Optimization," in *Obedience to Authority*, ed. T. Blass, pp. 111–23.

30. W. Meeus and Q. A. W. Raaijmakers, "Obedience in Modern Society: The Utrecht Studies," *Journal of Social Issues* 51 (1995): 155–76.

31. From *The Human Behavior Experiments*, transcript: Sundance Lock, May 9, 2006, Jig Saw Productions, p. 20. Transcript available on www.prisonexp.org/pdf/HBE-transcript .pdf.

32. These quotes and information about the strip-search hoaxes come from an informative article by Andrew Wolfson, "A Hoax Most Cruel," in *The Courier-Journal*, October 9, 2004, available online at: www.courier-journal.com/apps/pbcs.dll/article?AID=/20051009 /NEWS01/510090392/1008Hoax.

33. Quoted from a 1979 television interview in Robert V. Levine, "Milgram's Progress," *American Scientist Online*, July–August 2004. Originally in Blass, *Obedience to Authority*, pp. 35–36.

34. R. Jones, "The Third Wave," in *Experiencing Social Psychology*, ed. A. Pines and C. Maslach (New York: Knopf, 1978), pp. 144–52; also see the article that Ron Jones wrote about his Third Wave class exercise, available at: www.vaniercollege.qc.ca/Auxilliary/Psychology/ Frank/Thirdwave.html.

35. "The Wave," television docudrama, directed by Alexander Grasshoff, 1981.

36. W. Peters, *A Class Divided Then and Now* (expanded ed.) (New Haven, CT: Yale University Press, 1985 [1971]). Peters was involved in the filming of both prizewinning documentaries, the ABC News documentary "The Eye of the Storm" (available from Guidance Associates, New York) and the follow-up PBS Frontline documentary "A Class Divided" (available online at www.pbs.org/wgbh/pages/frontline/shows/divided/etc/view.html).

37. H. H. Mansson, "Justifying the Final Solution," *Omega: The Journal of Death and Dying* 3 (1972): 79–87.

38. J. Carlson, "Extending the Final Solution to One's Family," unpublished report, University of Hawaii, Manoa, 1974.

39. C. R. Browning, *Ordinary Men: Reserve Police Battalion 101 and the Final Solution in Poland* (New York: HarperCollins, 1993), p. xvi.

40. E. Staub, *The Roots of Evil: The Origins of Genocide and Other Group Violence* (New York: Cambridge University Press, 1989), pp. 126, 127.

41. J. M. Steiner, "The SS Yesterday and Today: A Sociopsychological View," in *Survivors, Victims, and Perpetrators: Essays on the Nazi Holocaust*, ed. J. E. Dinsdale (Washington, DC: Hemisphere Publishing Corporation, 1980), pp. 405–56; quotes on p. 433. Also see A. G. Miller, *The Obedience Experiments: A Case Study of Controversy in Social Science* (New York: Praeger, 1986).

42. D. J. Goldhagen, *Hitler's Willing Executioners* (New York: Knopf, 1999). Also see the review by Christopher Reed, "Ordinary German Killers," in *Harvard Magazine*, March–April 1999, p. 23.

43. H. Arendt, *Eichmann in Jerusalem: A Report on the Banality of Evil*, revised and enlarged edition (New York: Penguin Books, 1994), pp. 25, 26, 252, 276. Following quotes are from this source.

44. M. Huggins, M. Haritos-Fatouros, and P. G. Zimbardo, *Violence Workers: Police Torturers and Murders Reconstruct Brazilian Atrocities* (Berkeley: University of Califrornia Press, 2002).

45. M. Haritos-Fatouros, *The Psychological Origins of Institutionalized Torture* (London: Routledge, 2003).

46. Archdiocese of São Paulo, *Torture in Brazil* (New York: Vintage, 1998).

47. Official site for School of the Americas is www.ciponline.org/facts/soa.htm/; also see a critical site: www.soaw.org/new/.

48. F. Morales, "The Militarization of the Police," *Covert Action Quarterly* 67 (Spring–Summer 1999): 67.

49. See the body of literature on suicide bombers; among the sources recommended are: Ariel Merari, "Suicide Terrorism in the Context of the Israeli-Palestinian Conflict," Institute of Justice Conference, Washington, DC, October 2004; Ariel Merari, "Israel Facing Terrorism," *Israel Affairs* 11 (2005): 223–37; Ariel Merari, "Suicidal Terrorism," in *Assessment, Treatment and Prevention of Suicidal Behavior,* eds. R. I. Yufit and D. Lester (New York: Wiley, 2005).

50. M. Sageman, "Understanding Terrorist Networks," November 1, 2004, available at www.fpri.org/enotes/20041101.middleeast.sageman.understandingterrornetworks .html. Also see M. Shermer, "Murdercide: Science Unravels the Myth of Suicide Bombers," *Scientific American,* January 2006, p. 33; A. B. Krueger, "Poverty Doesn't Create Terrorists," *The New York Times,* May 29, 2003.

51. T. Joiner, *Why People Die by Suicide.* Cambridge, MA: Harvard University Press, 2006; Scott Atran, "Genesis of Suicide Terrorism," *Science* 299 (2003): 1534–39; Mia M. Bloom, "Palestinian Suicide Bombing: Public Support, Market Share and Outbidding," *Political Science Quarterly* 119, no. 1 (2004): 61–88; Mia Bloom, *Dying to Kill: The Allure of Suicide Terrorism* (New York: Columbia University Press, 2005); Dipak K. Gupta and Kusum Mundra, "Suicide Bombing as a Strategic Weapon: An Empirical Investigation of Hamas and Islamic Jihad," *Terrorism and Political Violence* 17 (2005): 573–98; Shaul Kimi and Shemuel Even, "Who Are the Palestinian Suicide Bombers?" *Terrorism and Political Violence* 16 (2005): 814–40; Ami Pedhahzur, "Toward an Analytical Model of Suicide Terrorism—A Comment," *Terrorism and Political Violence* 16 (2004): 841–44. Robert A. Pape, "The Strategic Logic of Suicide Terrorism," *American Political Science Review* 97 (2003): 343–61; Christopher Reuter, *My Life as a Weapon: A Modern History of Suicide Bombing* (Princeton, NJ: Princeton University Press, 2004); Andrew Silke, "The Role of Suicide in Politics, Conflict, and Terrorism," *Terrorism and Political Violence* 18 (2006): 35–46; Jeff Victoroff, "The Mind of the Terrorist: A Review and Critique of Psychological Approaches," *Journal of Conflict Resolution* 49, no. 1 (2005): 3–42.

52. A. Merari, "Psychological Aspects of Suicide Terrorism," in *Psychology of Terrorism,* eds. B. Bongar, L. M. Brown, L. Beutler, and P. G. Zimbardo (New York: Oxford University Press, 2006).

53. Jonathan Curiel, "The Mind of a Suicide Bomber," *San Francisco Chronicle* (October 22, 2006): p. E1, 6; quote on p. E6.

54. T. McDermott, *Perfect Soldiers: The Hijackers: Who They Were, Why They Did It* (New York: HarperCollins, 2005).

55. M. Kakutani, "Ordinary but for the Evil They Wrought," *The New York Times,* May 20, 2005, p. B32.

56. Z. Coile, " 'Ordinary British Lads,' " *San Francisco Chronicle,* July 14, 2005, pp. A1, A10.

57. A. Silke, "Analysis: Ultimate Outrage," *The Times* (London), May 5, 2003.

58. I became connected to this experience through my acquaintance with the brother of one of the few people who had escaped the massacre, his sister, Diane Louie, and her boyfriend, Richard Clark. I offered them counseling when they returned to San Francisco and learned much from their firsthand horror accounts. Later, I became an expert witness for Larry Layton, accused of conspiracy to murder Congressman Ryan, and through him I became friends with his sister, Debbie Layton, another heroic resistor of Jim Jones's domination. We will learn more about them in our final chapter, where their heroism is discussed.

59. The transcript of Jones's last-hour speech on November 18, 1978, is known as the "Death Tape" (FBI no. Q042), and is available online free, courtesy of the Jonestown Institute in Oakland, California, as transcribed by Mary McCormick Maaga: http://jonestown.sdsu. edu/Aboutjonestown/Tapes/Tapes/Deathtape/Q042.maaga.html.

60. M. Banaji, "Ordinary Prejudice," *Psychological Science Agenda* 8 (2001): 8–16; quote on p. 15.

CHAPTER THIRTEEN: Investigating Social Dynamics: Deindividuation, Dehumanization, and the Evil of Inaction

1. Jonathan Swift, *Gulliver's Travels and Other Works* (London: Routledge, 1906 [1727]). Swift's condemnation of his fellow human beings comes indirectly by verbal attacks to his alter ego, Lemuel Gulliver, from various notables whom Gulliver encounters on his travels to Brobdingnag and elsewhere. We human Yahoos are described as "deformed creatures at their most base." We also learn that our inadequacies are beyond remedial redemption, since "there is not enough time to correct the vices and follies to which Yahoos are subject, even if their natures had been capable of the least disposition toward virtue and wisdom."

2. R. Weiss, "Skin Cells Converted to Stem Cells," *The Washington Post*, August 22, 2005, p. A01.

3. W. Golding, *Lord of the Flies* (New York: Capricorn Books, 1954), pp. 58, 63.

4. P. G. Zimbardo, "The Human Choice: Individuation, Reason, and Order Versus Deindividuation, Impulse, and Chaos," in *1969 Nebraska Symposium on Motivation*, eds. W. J. Arnold and D. Levine (Lincoln: University of Nebraska Press, 1970).

5. M. H. Bond and D. G. Dutton, "The Effect of Interaction Anticipation and Experience as a Victim on Aggressive Behavior," *Journal of Personality* 43 (1975): 515–27.

6. R. J. Kiernan and R. M. Kaplan, "Deindividuation, Anonymity, and Pilfering," paper presented at the Western Psychological Association Convention, San Francisco, April 1971.

7. S. C. Fraser, "Deindividuation: Effects of Anonymity on Aggression in Children," unpublished report, University of Southern California, 1974, reported in P. G. Zimbardo, *Psychology and Life*, 10th ed. (Glenview IL: Scott, Foresman, 1974). Unfortunately, this fine study was never published because the data set and procedural materials were destroyed in the fire that swept through many homes in California's Malibu Hills (October 1996), where these materials were being temporarily stored.

8. E. Diener, S. C. Fraser, A. L. Beaman, and R. T. Kelem, "Effects of Deindividuation Variables on Stealing Among Halloween Trick-or-Treaters," *Journal of Personality and Social Psychology* 33 (1976): 178–83.

9. R. J. Watson, Jr., "Investigation into Deindividuation Using a Cross-Cultural Survey Technique," *Journal of Personality and Social Psychology* 25 (1973): 342–45.

10. Some relevant references on deindividuation include: E. Diener, "Deindividuation: Causes and Consequences," *Social Behavior and Personality* 5 (1977): 143–56; E. Diener, "Deindividuation: The Absence of Self-Awareness and Self-Regulation in Group Members, in *Psychology of Group Influence*, ed. P. B. Paulus (Hillsdale, NJ: Erlbaum, 1980), pp. 209–42; L. Festinger, A. Pepitone, and T. Newcomb, "Some Consequences of De-individuation in a Group," *Journal of Abnormal and Social Psychology* 47 (1952): 382–89; G. Le Bon, *The Crowd: A Study of the Popular Mind* (London: Transaction, 1995 [1895]); T. Postmes and R. Spears, "Deindividuation and Antinormative Behavior: A Meta-analysis," *Psychological Bulletin* 123 (1998): 238–59; S. Prentice-Dunn and R. W. Rogers, "Deindividuation in Aggression," in *Aggression: Theoretical and Empirical Reviews*, eds. R. G. Geen and E. I. Donnerstein (New York: Academic Press, 1983), pp. 155–72; S. Reicher and M. Levine, "On the Consequences of Deindividuation Manipulations for the Strategic Communication of Self: Identifiability and the Presentation of Social Identity," *European Journal of Social Psychology* 24 (1994): 511–24; J. E. Singer, C. E. Brush and S. C. Lublin, "Some Aspects of Deindividuation: Identification and Conformity," *Journal of Experimental Social Psychology* 1 (1965): 356–78; C. B. Spivey and S. Prentice-Dunn, "Assessing the Directionality of Deindividuated Behavior: Effects of Deindividuation, Modeling, and Private Self-Consciousness on Aggressive and Prosocial Responses," *Basic and Applied Social Psychology* 4 (1990): 387–403.

11. E. Goffman, *Stigma: Notes on the Management of Spoiled Identity* (Englewood Cliffs, NJ: Prentice-Hall, 1963).

12. See C. Maslach and P. G. Zimbardo, "Dehumanization in Institutional Settings: 'Detached Concern' in Health and Social Service Professions; The Dehumanization of Imprisonment," paper presented at the American Psychological Association Convention, Montreal, Canada, August 30, 1973.

13. R. Ginzburg, *100 Years of Lynching* (Baltimore: Black Classic Press, 1988). Also see the photographs of lynchings that were distributed on postcards in J. Allen, H. Als, J. Lewis, and L. F. Litwack, *Without Sanctuary: Lynching Photography in America* (Santa Fe, NM: Twin Palms Publishers, 2004).

14. See H. C. Kelman, "Violence Without Moral Restraint: Reflections on the Dehumanization of Victims and Victimizers," *Journal of Social Issues* 29 (1973): 25–61.

15. B. Herbert, " 'Gooks' to 'Hajis.' " *The New York Times*, May 21, 2004.

16. A. Bandura, B. Underwood, and M. E. Fromson, "Disinhibition of Aggression Through Diffusion of Responsibility and Dehumanization of Victims," *Journal of Research in Personality* 9 (1975): 253–69.

17. See the extensive writings of Albert Bandura on moral disengagement, among them: A. Bandura, *Social Foundations of Thought and Action: A Social Cognitive Theory* (Englewood Cliffs, NJ: Prentice-Hall, 1986); A. Bandura, "Mechanisms of Moral Disengagement," in *Origins of Terrorism: Psychologies, Ideologies, Theologies, States of Mind*, ed. W. Reich (Cambridge, UK: Cambridge University Press, 1990) pp. 161–91; A. Bandura, "Moral Disengagement in the Perpetration of Inhumanities," *Personality and Social Psychology Review* (Special Issue on Evil and Violence) 3 (1999): 193–209; A. Bandura. "The Role of Selective Moral Disengagement in Terrorism," in *Psychosocial Aspects of Terrorism: Issues, Concepts and Directions*, ed. F. M. Mogahaddam and A. J. Marsella (Washington, DC: American Psychological Association Press, 2004), pp. 121–50; A. Bandura, C. Barbaranelli, G. V. Caprara, and C. Pastorelli, "Mechanisms of Moral Disengagement in the Exercise of Moral Agency," *Journal of Personality and Social Psychology* 71 (1996): 364–74; M. Osofsky, A. Bandura, and P. G. Zimbardo, "The Role of Moral Disengagement in the Execution Process," *Law and Human Behavior* 29 (2005): 371–93.

18. J. P. Leyens et al., "The Emotional Side of Prejudice: The Attribution of Secondary Emotions to In-groups and Out-groups," *Personality and Social Psychology Review* 4 (2000): 186–97.

19. N. Haslam, P. Bain, L. Douge, M. Lee, and B. Bastian, "More Human Than You: Attributing Humanness to Self and Others," *Journal of Personality and Social Psychology* 89 (2005): 937–50; quote, p. 950.

20. In one account from Reuters news service, a thirty-five-year-old Hutu mother named Mukankwaya said that she and other Hutu women had rounded up the children of their Tutsi neighbors whom they had come to perceive as their "enemies." With gruesome resolve, they bludgeoned the stunned youngsters to death with their large sticks. "They didn't cry because they knew us," she reported. "They just made big eyes. We killed too many to count." Her moral disengagement involved believing that she and the other women murderers were "doing the children a favor": it was better that they die now because they would be orphans, given that their fathers had been butchered with the machetes the government had given to Hutu men, and their mothers had been raped and killed by them. The children would have had a difficult life ahead, she and other Hutu mothers reasoned, so they beat them to death so they would avoid that bleak future.

21. See S. Keen, *Faces of the Enemy: Reflections on the Hostile Imagination* (San Francisco, CA: HarperSanFrancisco, 2004 [1991]). Also well worth watching is his companion DVD (2004).

22. From Harry Bruinius, *Better for All the World: The Secret History of Forced Sterilization and America's Quest for Racial Purity* (New York: Knopf, 2006).

23. See: F. Galton, *Hereditary Genius: An Inquiry into Its Laws and Consequences*, 2nd ed. (London: Macmillan, 1892; Watts and Co. 1950); R. A. Soloway, *Democracy and Denigration: Eugenics and the Declining Birthrate in England, 1877–1930* (Chapel Hill: University of North

Carolina Press, 1990); Race Betterment Foundation, *Proceedings of the Third Race Better-ment Conference* (Battle Creek, MI: Race Betterment Foundation, 1928); E. Black, *War Against the Weak: Eugenics and America's Campaign to Create a Master Race* (New York: Four Walls Eight Windows, 2003); E. Black, *IBM and the Holocaust: The Strategic Alliance Between Nazi Germany and America's Most Powerful Corporation* (New York: Crown, 2001).

24. M. L. King, Jr., *Strength to Love* (Philadelphia: Fortress Press, 1963), p. 18.

25. B. Latané and J. M. Darley, *The Unresponsive Bystander: Why Doesn't He Help?* (New York: Appleton-Century-Crofts, 1970).

26. J. M. Darley and B. Latané, "Bystander Intervention in Emergencies: Diffusion of Responsi-bilities," *Journal of Personality and Social Psychology* 8 (1968): 377–83.

27. T. Moriarity, "Crime, Commitment, and the Responsive Bystander: Two Field Experiments," *Journal of Personality and Social Psychology* 31 (1975): 370–76.

28. D. A. Schroeder, L. A. Penner, J. F. Dovidio, and J. A. Pilliavan, *The Psychology of Helping and Altruism: Problems and Puzzles* (New York: McGraw-Hill, 1995). Also see C. D. Batson, "Prosocial Motivation: Why Do We Help Others?" in *Advanced Social Psychology*, ed. A. Tesser (New York: McGraw-Hill, 1995), pp. 333–81; E. Straub, "Helping a Distressed Per-son: Social, Personality, and Stimulus Determinants," *Advances in Experimental Social Psy-chology*, vol. 7, ed. L. Berkowitz (New York: Academic Press, 1974), pp. 293–341.

29. J. M. Darley and C. D. Batson, "From Jerusalem to Jericho: A Study of Situational Variables in Helping Behavior," *Journal of Personality and Social Psychology* 27 (1973): 100–8.

30. C. D. Batson et al. "Failure to Help in a Hurry: Callousness or Conflict?," *Personality and So-cial Psychology Bulletin* 4 (1978): 97–101.

31. "Abuse Scandal to Cost Catholic Church at Least $2 Billion, Predicts Lay Leader," Associ-ated Press, July 10, 2005. See also the documentary film *Deliver Us from Evil*, which is about father Oliver O'Grady, convicted of serial child molestation of young boys and girls over a period of two decades in Northern California. Cardinal Roger Mahoney, who knew of the many complaints against him, did not remove O'Grady, but instead periodically relo-cated this sex addict to other parishes, where he would continue to pry on fresh crops of child victims. (The film was directed by Amy Berg; distributed by Lionsgate Films, October 2006).

32. D. Baum, "Letter from New Orleans: The Lost Year," *The New Yorker*, August 21, 2006: 44–59; D. Wiegand, "When the Levees Broke: Review of Spike Lee's Documentary" (*When the Levees Broke: A Requiem in Four Acts*, HBO-TV, August 21, 22, 2006), *San Francisco Chronicle*, August 21, 2006, pp. F1–F4.

33. J. Lipman-Blumen, *The Allure of Toxic Leaders: Why We Follow Destructive Bosses and Corrupt Politicians—and How We Can Survive Them* (New York: Oxford University Press, 2005). Quote p. ix.

34. L. Ross and R. E. Nisbett, *The Person and the Situation* (Philadelphia: Temple University Press, 1991).

35. A. Bandura, *Self-Efficacy: The Exercise of Control* (New York: Freeman, 1997).

36. R. Kueter, *The State of Human Nature* (New York: iUniverse, 2005). For a review of culture's psychological effects, see R. Brislin, *Understanding Culture's Influence on Behavior* (Orlando, FL: Harcourt Brace Jovanovich, 1993). Also see H. Markus and S. Kitayama, "Culture and the Self: Implications for Cognition, Emotion and Motivation," *Psychological Review* 98 (1991): 224–53.

37. L. Ross and D. Shestowsky, "Contemporary Psychology's Challenges to Legal Theory and Practice," *Northwestern University Law Review* 97 (2003): 1081–1114; quote p. 1114. It is also valuable to read the extensive review and analysis of the place of the situation in law and economics by two legal scholars, Jon Hanson and David Yosifon, "The Situation: An Introduction to the Situational Character, Critical Realism, Power Economics, and Deep Capture," *University of Pennsylvania Law Review* 129 (2003): 152–346. In addition, my re-search collaborator Craig Haney has written extensively on the need for greater inclusion

of contextual factors in legal justice; see, e. g., C. Haney, "Making Law Modern: Toward a Contextual Model of Justice," *Psychology, Public Policy and Law* 8 (2002): 3–63.

38. M. Snyder, "When Belief Creates Reality," in *Advances in Experimental Social Psychology*, vol. 18, ed. L. Berkowitz (New York: Academic Press, 1984), pp. 247–305.

39. D. L. Rosenhan, "On Being Sane in Insane Places," *Science* 179 (1973): 250–58.

40. F. D. Richard, D. F. Bond, Jr., and J. J. Stokes-Zoota, "One Hundred Years of Social Psychology Quantitatively Described," *Review of General Psychology* 7 (2003): 331–63.

41. S. T. Fiske, L. T. Harris, and A.J.C. Cudy, "Why Ordinary People Torture Enemy Prisoners," *Science (Policy Forum)* 306 (2004): 1482–83; quote, p. 1482. Also see Susan Fiske's analyses in *Social Beings* (New York: Wiley, 2003).

CHAPTER FOURTEEN: Abu Ghraib's Abuses and Tortures: Understanding and Personalizing Its Horrors

1. Final Report of the Independent Panel to Review DoD Detention Operations. The full report is available on the Stanford Prison Experiment website at www.prisonexp.org/pdf /SchlesingerReport.pdf/. It was issued on November 8, 2004.

2. Report on CBS's *60 Minutes II* website at www.cbsnews.com/stories/2004/04/27/60II /main614063.shtml.

3. Evidence exists that General Myers personally called Dan Rather eight days before the Abu Ghraib abuse report was scheduled to air on *60 Minutes II* to request that CBS delay broadcasting the segment. His justification for this delay was to avoid danger to "our troops" and to the "war effort." CBS complied with Myers's request and put off showing the piece for two weeks. It finally decided to air it only when the network discovered that *The New Yorker* magazine was preparing to publish a detailed report by the investigative journalist Seymour Hersh. The request showed that the military brass was well aware of the "image problems" that would be created by the upcoming media revelations.

4. Congressional Testimony: Donald Rumsfeld, Federal Document Clearing House, 2004, available at www.highbeam.com/library/wordDoc.doc?docid=1P1:94441824; Testimony of Secretary of Defense Donald H. Rumsfeld Before the Senate and House Armed Services Committees, May 7, 2004; available at www.defenselink.mil/speeches/2004/sp20040507-secdef1042.html.

5. Quoted in Adam Hochschild, "What's in a Word? Torture," *The New York Times*, May 23, 2004. Susan Sontag offered an elegant challenge to the notion that these deeds were merely "abuse" and not "torture" in her essay "Regarding the Torture of Others," *The New York Times Magazine*, May 23, 2004, pp. 25 ff.

6. The foreign minister of the Vatican, Archbishop Giovanni Lajolo, had a different perspective: "The torture? A more serious blow to the United States than September 11. Except that the blow was not inflicted by terrorists but by Americans against themselves." The editor of the London-based Arabic-language newspaper *Al Quds Al Arabi*, proclaimed, "The liberators are worse than the dictators. This is the straw that broke the camel's back for America."

7. "It's Not About Us; This Is War!" *The Rush Limbaugh Show*, May 4, 2004. See www.source watch.org/index.php?title=Rush_Limbaugh.

8. Senator James Inhofe's remarks come from the transcript of a Senate Armed Services Committee Hearing, May 11, 2004, in which Major General Taguba addressed the committee on the issue of Iraqi prisoner abuse, his first publicly delivered testimony to the committee, based on his six-thousand-page investigation (which took one month to conduct in nine volumes). The entire transcript (five Internet pages) is online at *The Washington Post* website at www.washingtonpost.com/wp-dyn/articles/A17812-2004May11.html.

9. Joseph Darby gave his first interview about his role in exposing the abuses to Wil S. Hylton,

in *GQ* magazine, September 2006, entitled "Prisoner of Conscience." (Darby quotes are from this source.) Available online at http://men.style.com/gq/features/landing?id= content_4785/.

10. There is an interesting parallel here with another soldier, Ronald Ridenhour, who blew the whistle on the 1968 My Lai massacre in Vietnam. He too was a bit of an outsider who came on the scene the day after some of his buddies had brutally slaughtered hundreds of Vietnamese civilians. Distressed both by their cavalier account of the atrocity and its violation of what he considered the fundamental principles of morality that America stood for, Ridenhour decided to go public. His repeated requests to superior officers, to President Nixon, and congressmen that this massacre be investigated were ignored or suppressed for more than a year. Finally, Ridenhour's persistence paid off. A young investigative reporter, Seymour Hersh, became involved and broke the story in his 1970 book, *My Lai 4: A Report on the Massacre and its Aftermath*. It was perhaps no accident that the same, now older, Seymour Hersh broke the story of the Abu Ghraib abuses in his *New Yorker* article (April 2004) and his book *Chain of Command: The Road from 9/11 to Abu Ghraib* (2004).

The sad aftermath of Darby's daring deed was that he had to be placed in protective custody for several years because many people wanted to kill him for humiliating the military. His wife and mother also had to go into hiding with him because of threats to their lives as well.

11. I wanted to start a Joe Darby Hero Fund, to collect donations nationwide that would be given to Darby once he was out of protective custody. A reporter for *USA Today*, Marilyn Elias, said her paper would run a story about this "hero in hiding" and mention the Hero Fund if I could provide a source where people could send donations. For months, I tried in vain to convince various organizations to be the public conduit for such funds, including Amnesty International, Darby's hometown bank, my Union Bank in Palo Alto, and a torture victims' association. Each gave various reasons that seemed spurious. I was able to encourage the then-president of the American Psychological Association, Diane Halperin, to give Darby a Presidential Citation at APA's annual convention, but against much opposition by members of its Board of Directors. It was all too political for too many people.

12. Quoted from "A Question of Torture," *PBS News Frontline*, October 18, 2005.

13. CBS, *60 Minutes II*, April 28, 2004.

14. An Army criminal investigative officer, Marci Drewry, was my informant about the conditions that existed at Abu Ghraib from the time the military took it over through the time of the investigations of abuse in Tier 1A. In a series of e-mails (September 16, 18, and 20, 2005) and a phone interview (September 8, 2005) she offered firsthand accounts of the "deplorable, miserable conditions facing the MPs as well as the prisoners. She served as assistant operations officer for the CID (Criminal Investigation Division) investigating crimes by U.S. soldiers in theater of war. Chief Warrant Officer Drewry was one of the first to see the images on the CD that Darby turned in. Her unit started the first internal investigation and completed it by February 2004. She told me that she wants the truth to come out about the conditions in the prison that might have influenced the MPs to behave as they did.

15. "80 Acres of Hell," History Channel program about Camp Douglas, June 3, 2006.

16. Reported in "Iraq Prison Abuse Stains Entire Brigade," *The Washington Times* (www.washingtontimes.com), May 10, 2004.

17. Janis Karpinski with Steven Strasser, *One Woman's Army: The Commanding General at Abu Ghraib Tells Her Story* (New York: Miramax Press, 2005).

18. BBC Radio 4 interview with Brigadier General Janis Karpinski, June 15, 2004. She also repeated these accusations in a conference held at Stanford University, which I introduced, on May 4, 2006.

19. The psychological assessment consisted of an interview with the military psychologist, Dr. Alvin Jones, on August 31 and September 2, 2004, followed by a battery of psychological tests. They included the Minnesota Multiphasic Inventory, Second Edition (MMPI-2); the Millon Clinical Multiaxial Inventory-111; and the Wechsler Abbreviated Intelligence Scale (WASI). The official psychology consultation report and the test data were sent to me on September 21 and forwarded to Dr. Larry Beutler, head of the Ph.D. training program at the Pacific Graduate School of Psychology in Palo Alto. He provided an independent test interpretation blind to the status and name of the test client. I administered the Maslach Burnout Inventory (MBI) at my home during my interview with Chip, and it was sent for interpretation to an expert on job stress, Dr. Michael Leiter, Center for Organizational Development in Wolfville, Canada. His formal evaluation was received on October 3, 2004. He was also blind to the background of the test client.

20. Psychology consultation report, August 31, 2004.

21. See my trade book for a general summary of this and related shyness research: P. G. Zimbardo, *Shyness: What It Is. What to Do About It* (Reading, MA: Perseus Books, 1977).

22. Personal letter, June 12, 2005.

23. Mimi Frederick, e-mail correspondence September 21, 2005. (Permission given to quote.)

24. The 372nd Military Police Company was a unit of reservists based in Cresaptown, Maryland. Most members of this company were from small, low-income towns in Appalachia, where military recruitment advertisements appear frequently in the local media. People there often join the military as teenagers in order to earn money or see the world, or just because it's a way to leave the town where they grew up. The members of the 372nd reported being a tight-knit group. See *Time* magazine, *Special Report*, May 17, 2004.

25. My interview with Chip, September 30, 2004, and personal letter, June 12, 2005.

26. Summary of Dr. Alvin Jones's report of his interview and battery of psychological tests with Frederick (August 31–September 2, 2004).

27. Dr. Jones's summary of all test results.

28. These and other quotations are from the "Test Interpretation of Client" on September 22, 2004, by Dr. Larry Beutler in a written report to me.

29. Dr. Leiter's evaluation was provided to me on October 3, 2004, based on the raw data submitted to him of Chip's responses on the MBI-General Survey. See C. Maslach and M. P. Leiter, *The Truth About Burnout* (San Francisco: Jossey-Bass, 1997). Also see M. P. Leiter and C. Maslach, *Preventing Burnout and Building Engagement: A Complete Package for Organizational Renewal* (San Francisco: Jossey-Bass, 2000).

30. There is a large psychological literature on cognitive overload and cognitive resource load. A few references are: D. Kirsh, "A Few Thoughts on Cognitive Overload," *Intellectica* 30 (2000): 19–51; R. Hester and H. Garavan, "Working Memory and Executive Function: The Influence of Content and Load on the Control of Attention," *Memory & Cognition* 33 (2005): 221–33; F. Pass, A. Renkl, and J. Swelle, "Cognitive Load Theory: Instructional Implications of the Interaction Between Information Structures and Cognitive Architecture," *Instructional Science* 32 (2004): 1–8.

31. Notes about the saga of Private Jessica Lynch are from a BBC 2 TV documentary indicating that the U.S. military faked and distorted virtually everything about her "heroic" narrative. The same military creation of a pseudohero occurred with the former NFL Arizona Cardinals football star Pat Tillman, who was killed by his own men's "friendly fire"—which was covered up until his family forced the truth to come out. The BBC exposé of Jessica Lynch was "War Spin: The Truth About Jessica," May 18, 2003 (reporter, John Kampfner). The transcript of the program can be accessed at: http://news.bbc.co.uk/2/hi/programmes/correspondent/3028585.stm. The case of Pat Tillman was covered in a two-part series in *The Washington Post*: S. Coll, "Barrage of Bullets Drowned Out Cries of Comrades: Communication Breakdown, Split Platoon Among Factors of 'Friendly Fire,' " *The Washington Post*, December 4, 2004, p A01; S. Coll, "Army Spun Tale Around Ill-Fated Mission," *The Wash-*

ington Post, December 6, 2004, p A01; The two articles are available online at www
.washingtonpost.com/wp-dyn/articles/A35717–2004Dec4.html and www.washington
post.com/wp-dyn/articles/A37679-2004Dec5.html. Pat Tillman's father, Patrick, a
lawyer, continues to investigate his son's death. A recent *New York Times* article offers new
details of the case: M. Davey and S. Eric "Two Years After Soldier's Death, Family's Battle
is with Army," *The New York Times*, March 21, 2006), p A01. See also the eloquent and
powerful statement by Pat's brother, Kevin, who joined the Army with Pat in 2002,
and served with him in Iraq and Afghanistan; titled "After Pat's Birthday." Online:
www.truthdig.com/report/item/200601019_after-pats-birthday/.

32. All interview questions and answers are from the September 30, 2004, interview at my
home, tape-recorded and then transcribed by my assistant Matt Estrada.

33. R. J. Smith and J. White, "General Granted Latitude at Prison: Abu Ghraib Used Aggressive
Tactics," *The Washington Post*, June 12, 2004, p. A01, available at www.washingtonpost
.com/wp-dyn/articles/A35612-2004Jun11.html.

34. A veteran military interrogator shared his view with me on the issue of interrogators manipulating Military Police personnel to assist them in getting the information they were
after: "THIS is where the rub lies. Unscrupulous interrogators (of the kind, in descending
order, of: junior military interrogators, contracted personnel, CIA personnel) willing to
play into preconceived notions on the part of folks willing to believe in them. I have had the
experience of personnel charged with the detention of others (in this case it was a company of infantry soldiers that were given the mission of running the prison) applying every
stereotype of an "interrogator" in the range of American culture; however, when I took the
time to explain not only that I did not engage in the behavior they suspected me of, but also
why I didn't do so, they not only understood my perspective on it, they agreed and *willingly
modified their operations to support it*. The control of one human being over another is an
awesome responsibility that must be taught, trained and understood, not *ordered*." Received August 3, 2006; source prefers to remain anonymous.

35. Chip Frederick, interview with me, September 30, 2004.

36. Ken Davis's statement was included in a documentary, "The Human Behavior Experiments," that aired on the Sundance Channel, June 1, 2006.

37. I. Janis, "Groupthink," *Psychology Today*, November 1971, pp. 43–46. The Senate
Intelligence Committee conclusions are available at http://intelligence.senate.gov/
conclusions.pdf.

38. S. T. Fiske, L. T. Harris, and A. J. Cuddy, "Why Ordinary People Torture Enemy Prisoners,"
Science 306 (2004): 1482–83; quote, p. 1483.

39. Personal communication by e-mail, August 30, 2006, with permission to reprint. Writer is
now working in the Security Office of the Department of Commerce.

40. General Taguba's report was presented to Congress on May 11, 2004.

41. We will have more to say in the next chapter about Major General Fay's report, which he
co-authored with Lieutenant General Jones. Part of the Fay/Jones Report is presented in
Steven Strasser, ed., *The Abu Ghraib Investigations: The Official Reports of the Independent
Panel and the Pentagon on the Shocking Prisoner Abuse in Iraq.* (New York: Public Affairs,
2004).

     The full report is available at http://news.findlaw.com/hdocs/docs/dod/fay82504
rpt.pdf.

42. *Fifth Estate*, "A Few Bad Apples: The Night of October 25, 2003," Canadian Broadcast
Company Television News, November 16, 2005, available at http://cbc.ca/fifth/bad
apples/resource.html.

43. M. A. Fuoco, E. Blazina, and C. Lash, "Suspect in Prisoner Abuse Has a History of Troubles," *Pittsburgh Post-Gazette*, May 8, 2004.

44. Testimony by a military intelligence analyst at Graner's pretrial hearing.

45. Stipulation of Fact, Case of *United States v. Frederick*, August 5, 2004.

46. Personal written communication from Chip Frederick to me from Fort Leavenworth, June 12, 2005.

47. Guard "Hellmann" on "The Human Behavior Experiments," June 1, 2006.

48.

DEVELOPMENTAL COUNSELING FORM

For use of this form, see FM 22-100; the proponent agency is TRADOC

DATA REQUIRED BY THE PRIVACY ACT OF 1974

AUTHORITY:	5 USC 301, Departmental Regulations; 10 USC 3013, Secretary of the Army and E.O. 9397 (SSN)
PRINCIPAL PURPOSE:	To assist leaders in conducting and recording counseling data pertaining to subordinates.
ROUTINE USES:	For subordinate leader development IAW FM 22-100. Leaders should use this form as necessary.
DISCLOSURE:	Disclosure is voluntary.

PART I - ADMINISTRATIVE DATA

Name (Last, First, MI) Graner, Charles	Rank/Grade CPL/E-4	Social Security No.	Date of Counseling 16 NOV 03
Organization 372nd Military Police Company		Name and Title of Counselor CPT ▇▇▇ / Platoon Leader	

PART II - BACKGROUND INFORMATION

Purpose of Counseling: *(Leader states the reason for the counseling, e.g., performance-professional growth or event-oriented counseling, and includes the leader's facts and observations prior to the counseling.)*
Performance
o Performance in Tier 1 at BCF

PART III - SUMMARY OF COUNSELING
Complete this section during or immediately subsequent to counseling.

Key Points of Discussion:
CPL Graner, you are doing a fine job in Tier 1 of the BCF. As the NCOIC of the "MI Hold" area, you have received many accolades from the MI units here and specifically from LTC ▇▇▇. Continue to perform at this level and it will help us succeed at our overall mission.

I am concerned about two matters related to your performance. First, SFC ▇▇▇ has spoken to you about your appearance while on duty. I require all soldiers to maintain the Army's uniform and appearance standards at all times and encourage them to exceed them when possible. I want to reinforce this issue with you now.

Second, due to the higher level of stress associated with working in tier 1, I am concerned that it does not affect your performance. Many times you have to deal with security detainees that are of the highest intelligence value. These detainees often try to incite our soldiers to aggressive acts by taunting them or not responding to commands. In addition, tier 1 houses the isolations cells for the hard site prison. These cells are filled with detainees whose noncompliant and/or aggressive behavior has placed them in isolation. Also, tier 1 holds detainees with mental health issues. These detainees add to the stress of working in tier 1.

There was an incident on 14 NOV 03 involving a security detainee whose actions in your words required you to use force to regain control of the situation. The detainee received abrasions and cuts on his face from the incident. Let me state first and foremost, you have an inherent right to self-defense that cannot be taken away from you. I 100 percent support your decision when you believe you must defend yourself. You stated that you escalated your actions through the approved levels of force. You stated you used the appropriate level of force up through the continuum of the use of force to contain the situation. Then you stated that you ceased all use of force and sought medical attention for the detainee. Statements from other MP working that evening do not shed any light on the incident. Unless other evidence presents itself, I accept your version of events.

OTHER INSTRUCTIONS
This form will be destroyed upon: reassignment *(other than rehabilitative transfers)*, separation at ETS, or upon retirement. For separation requirements and notification of loss of benefits/consequences see local directives and AR 635-200.

DA FORM 4856, JUN 1999   EDITION OF JUN 85 IS OBSOLETE   USAPA V1.00

49. Ibid. MP Ken Davis's report on "The Human Behavior Experiments."

50. See www.supportmpscapegoats.com.

51. Sontag, "Regarding the Torture of Others," May 23, 2004.

52. "Now That's Fucked Up": www.nowthatsfuckedup.com/bbs/index.php (see especially www.nowthatsfuckedup.com/bbs/ftopic41640.html.)

53. Allen et al., *Without Sanctuary: Lynching Photography in America.*

54. Browning, *Ordinary Men* (1993).

55. Janina Struk, *Photographing the Holocaust: Interpretations of the Evidence* (New York: Palgrave, 2004).

56. www.armenocide.am.

57. For more on Teddy Roosevelt's trophy photos with his son Kermit, see "On Safari with Theodore Roosevelt, 1909," available at www.eyewitnesstohistory.com/tr/htm. Interest-

ingly, although the expedition was billed as "collecting" a variety of animal species, it was actually a hunt-and-kill safari in which 512 animals were slain, among them 17 lions, 11 elephants, and 20 rhinoceros. Ironically, Theodore Roosevelt's grandson Kermit Jr. was head of the CIA's Operation Ajax in Iran, the agency's first successful coup d'état, which removed from power the (democratically elected) Prime Minister Mohammed Mossadegh in 1953. The CIA's rationale for this first coup was the Communist threat posed by allowing Mossadegh to remain in power. According to Stephen Kinzer, a veteran *New York Times* journalist, this operation set a pattern for the next half century, during which the United States and CIA successfully removed (or supported the removal of) heads of state in Guatemala (1954), then in Cuba, Chile, the Congo, Vietnam, and, most relevant to our story here, all the way to Saddam Hussein in Iraq (2003). Kinzer also notes that the environments in these countries after the coups d'état were often marked by instability, civil strife, and countless amounts of violence. These operations have had profound effects that reverberate to this day. The immense misery and suffering they created has turned whole regions of the world bitterly against the United States. To come full circle all the way from Operation Ajax and recently from the war zone of Iraq, the United States has embarked on another mission of counterintelligence and perhaps even made plans for war against Iran. Seymour Hersh, our familiar friend and journalist from *The New Yorker* who investigated My Lai and Abu Ghraib, exposed this revelation; www.newyorker.com/fact/content /?050124fa_fact; S. Kinzer, *All the Shah's Men: An American Coup and the Roots of Middle East Terror* (Hoboken, NJ: Wiley, 2003); S. Kinzer, *Overthrow: America's Century of Regime Change from Hawaii to Iraq* (New York: Times Books, 2006).

58. The quote is from my notes recorded during the panel (which I introduced), in which Janis Karpinski spoke as part of a session on "Crimes Against Humanity Committed by the Bush Administration," May 4, 2006. A veteran military interrogator casts doubt on this version of the top-down permission to MPs from interrogators to take the photos: "I do not believe that 'permission' to have come from the interrogators, if it came from anyone at all. . . . In my over two decades of being an interrogator and a supervisor of interrogation operations, I have heard just about every 'approach' there is, and it does not seem credible to me that an interrogator would not only willingly engage in an unlawful act that is of dubious value to the process of interrogation, but that he would conspire with others and depend on their trust." Received August 3, 2006; source prefers anonymity.

59. Judith Butler, "Torture, Sexual Politics, and the Ethics of Photography." Lecture presented at Stanford University symposium *Thinking Humanity After Abu Ghraib* (October 20, 2006).

60. This CBS report of abuses at Camp Bucca is available online at www.cbsnews/stories /2004/05/11/60II/main616849.shtml.

61. These accounts and much more are available in the Human Rights Watch report "Leadership Failure: Firsthand Accounts of Torture of Iraqi Detainees by U.S. Army's 82nd Airborne Division," September 24, 2005, available at http://hrw.org/reports/2005/us0905.

62. Chip Frederick's eight-year sentence was reduced by six months by order of the Commanding General, and by another eighteen months by the Army Clemency and Parole Board (August 2006), based on a variety of appeals and justifications for leniency in my statements and those of many others.

63. The kind of stress that Chip experienced nightly on Tier 1A, and later during his imprisonment, can have a major enduring impact on brain functioning, and in turn on mood, thinking, and behavior; see Robert M. Sapolsky, "Why Stress Is Bad for Your Brain," *Science* 273 (1996): 749–50.

64. Personal communication, June 12, 2005.

65. E. Aronson and J. Mills, "The Effect of Severity of Initiation on Liking for a Group," *Journal of Abnormal and Social Psychology* 59 (1959): 177–81.

66. Personal communication, February 25, 2005.
67. Personal communication, June 15, 2005.
68. Darius M. Rejali, *Torture and Modernity: Self, Society, and State in Modern Iran* (Boulder, CO: Westview Press, 1994). Also see his online essays available at http://archive .salon.com/opinion/feature/2004/06/18/torture_methods/index.html and http://archive.salon .com/opinion/feature/2004/06/18/torture_1/index.html.
69. A military officer reported to me, "I have myself used the term 'going Stanford' when describing uncharacteristic sadistic behavior on the part of persons in charge of others."
70. Hensley is a Board Certified Expert in Traumatic Stress (BC ETS) and diplomate with the American Academy of Experts in Traumatic Stress, who is now a psychological operations (PSYOP) and antiterrorism adviser to the federal government. Hensley, a doctoral learner at Capella University with a specialization in PTSD, has studied the abuses at Abu Ghraib extensively. Hensley also notes, "The reliability of the assertions expressed in this paper may be established by similar analysis of a representative selection of the defendants' unit. A positive correlation of similar data might indicate the validity of the Zimbardo Effect at the Abu Ghraib Detention Facility, thus explaining the deviant behavior" (p. 51). A. L. Hensley, "Why Good People Go Bad: A Psychoanalytic and Behavioral Assessment of the Abu Ghraib Detention Facility Staff." A strategic courts-martial defense strategy presented to the Area Defense Council in Washington, D.C., on December 10, 2004.
71. R. Norland, "Good Intentions Gone Bad," *Newsweek*, June 13, 2005, p. 40.

CHAPTER FIFTEEN: Putting the System on Trial: Command Complicity

1. Closing statement, October 21, 2004, by Major Michael Holley, Court-martial trial of Sergeant Ivan Frederick, Baghdad, October 20 and 21, 2005, pp. 353–54.
2. My closing spontaneous statement, October 21, 2004, p. 329.
3. "Administrative evil" functions by having agency operatives focus on developing the correct procedures, the right steps in a process that is the most efficient means to an end. These administrators do so without recognizing that the means to that end are immoral, illegal, and unethical. They are conveniently blinded from the realities of the substance of the abuses—and the horrendous consequences—that are generated by their policies and practices. Those guilty of administrative evil may be corporations, police and corrections departments, or military and government centers, as well as radical revolutionary groups.

    As we saw some forty years ago in the calculated approach of Robert McNamara to the war in Vietnam, reliance on a scientific-analytic mind-set along with a technical-rational-legalistic approach to social and political problems enables an organization and its members to engage in evil that is masked and ethically hidden. In one of its manifestations, the State sanctions its agents' engagement in actions ordinarily considered immoral, illegal, and evil by recasting them as necessary for the defense of national security. Just as the Holocaust and the internment of Japanese-American citizens during World War II were examples of administrative evil, so too, I argue, is the torture program of the Bush administration as part of its "war on terror."

    This profound concept of "administrative evil" has been developed by Guy B. Adams and Danny L. Balfour in their provocative book *Unmasking Administrative Evil*, re. ed. (New York: M. E. Sharpe, 2004).
4. A good single source on the Abu Ghraib chronology and the investigative reports can be found at www.globalsecurity.org/intell/world/iraq/abu-ghurayb-chronology.htm.
5. The investigative journalist Seymour M. Hersh broke the story of abuses and torture at Abu Ghraib in "Torture at Abu Ghraib. American Soldiers Brutalize Iraqis: How Far Up Does the Responsibility Go?," *The New Yorker*, May 5, 2004, p. 42, available at www.notin ourname.net/war/torture-5may04.htm.
6. Available at http://news.findlaw.com/nytimes/docs/iraq/tagubarpt.html#ThR1.14.
7. Part of the Fay/Jones Report is presented in Steven Strasser and Craig R. Whitney eds., *The

Abu Ghraib Investigations: The Official Reports of the Independent Panel and the Pentagon on the Shocking Prisoner Abuse in Iraq (New York: PublicAffairs, 2004). The full report is available at http://news.findlaw.com/hdocs/docs/dod/fay82504rpt.pdf. Also see Strasser and Whitney *The 9/11 Investigations: Staff Reports of the 9/11 Commission: Excerpts from the House-Senate Joint Inquiry Report on 9/11: Testimony from Fourteen Key Witnesses* (New York: Public Affairs, 2004).

8. It is reported that CENTCOM Commander General John Abizaid requested that an officer of higher rank than Major General Fay lead the investigation so that he would be able to interview senior officers, which Army regulations prevented Major General Fay from doing but allowed Lieutenant General Jones to do so.

9. Steven H. Miles, *Oath Betrayed: Torture, Medical Complicity, and the War on Terror* (New York: Random House, 2006).

10. Captain Wood's case was described in detail in "A Few Bad Apples," CBC News, *The Fifth Estate*, November 16, 2005.

11. Eric Schmitt, "Abuses at Prison Tied to Officers in Military Intelligence," *The New York Times*, August 26, 2004.

12. The members of the Independent Panel to Review DoD [Department of Defense] Detention Operations briefed Secretary of Defense Donald H. Rumsfeld as they delivered their final report on August 24, 2004. The four members of the panel included former secretary of defense Harold Brown; former representative Tillie Fowler (R–Fla.); General Charles A. Horner, USAF (Retired); and former secretary of defense James R. Schlesinger, Panel Chair. The full report, including Appendix G, can be found at www.prisonexp.org/pdf/SchlesingerReport.pdf.

13. See www.hrw.org. Another valuable resource to review is that provided in the report by the Canadian Broadcast Company's *Fifth Estate* program "A Few Bad Apples," which aired on November 16, 2005. It focused on the events in Tier 1A on the night of October 25, 2003, when several soldiers tortured Iraqi prisoners while others looked on. It is the incident reported in chapter 14, that was started by the rumor these prisoners had raped a boy, which turned out to be false. The CBC site is a source for a chronology of events leading up to this abuse, Seymour Hersh's articles on Abu Ghraib, and memos by Bush, Rumsfeld, and Sanchez; available at www.cbc.ca/fifth/badapples/resource.html.

14. See www.whitehouse.gov/news/releases/2004/05/20040506-9.html.

15. "Abu Ghraib Only the 'Tip of the Iceberg,' " *Human Rights Watch Report*, April 27, 2005.

16. E. Schmitt, "Few Punished in Abuse Cases," *The New York Times*, April 27, 2006, p. A24. This summary is based upon a full report prepared by New York University's Center for Human Rights and Global Justice in association with Human Rights Watch and Human Rights First. Their researchers compiled the statistics from about 100,000 documents obtained under the Freedom of Information Act. They note that about two thirds of all the abuses occurred in Iraq.

17. "Abu Ghraib Dog Handler Gets 6 Months," *CBS News Video Report*, May 22, 2006. Available at www.cbsnews.com/stories/2006/03/22/iraq/main1430842.shtml.

18. The full report is available at http://humanrightsfirst.info/PDF/06425-etn-by-the-numbers.PDF.

19. The full HRW report, including the quotations that I have extracted from it, is available at www.hrw.org/reports/2005/us0405/1.htm (for Executive Summary); see also /2.htm up to /6.htm for additional sections of this lengthy report.

20. Congressional Testimony of Secretary of Defense Donald Rumsfeld, Hearing of the Senate Armed Services Committee on Mistreatment of Iraqi Prisoners, Federal News Service, May 7, 2004.

21. See www.genevaconventions.org/.

22. "Report of the International Committee of the Red Cross (ICRC) on the Treatment by the Coalition Forces of Prisoners of War and Other Protected Persons by the Geneva Conven-

tions in Iraq During Arrest, Internment and Interrogation," February 2004. See http://download.repubblica.it/pdf/rapporto_crocerossa.pdf.

23. Amnesty International, "Beyond Abu Ghraib: Detention and Torture in Iraq," 2006, available at http://web.amnesty.org/library/print/ENGMDE140012006/.

24. Quote from "A Question of Torture," PBS *Frontline*, October 18, 2005.

25. J. White, "Some Abu Ghraib Prisoners 'Ghosted.' " *The Washington Post*, March 11, 2005.

26. A. W. McCoy, *A Question of Torture: CIA Interrogation from the Cold War to the War on Terror* (New York: Henry Holt, 2006), pp. 5, 6.

27. Testimony of Lieutenant General Ricardo Sanchez, Senate Armed Services Committee, Hearing on Iraq Prisoner Abuse, May 19, 2004.

28. Mark Danner, *Torture and Truth: America, Abu Ghraib and the War on Terrorism* (New York: The New York Review of Books, 2004), p. 33.

29. Janis Karpinski, interview on "A Question of Torture," PBS *Frontline*, October 18, 2005.

30. From Lt. Ricardo Sanchez to Commander Central Command, memorandum, Interrogation and Counter-Resistance Policy, September 14, 2003, available at www.aclu.org/Safeand Free/SafeandFree.cfm?ID=17851&c=206.

31. Joseph Darby interview, *GQ* magazine, September 2006.

32. *The New Yorker's* Jane Mayer, quoted on "A Question of Torture," PBS *Frontline*, October 18, 2005.

33. More recently (June 2006), nearly ninety detainees at Gitmo went on extended hunger strikes to protest their false imprisonment. A Navy commander dismissed this action as nothing more than an "attention-getting" tactic. To prevent them from dying, officials had to begin daily forced feeding through nose tubes of at least six of them administered by medics. That itself resembles a new kind of torture, though officials claim it is "safe and humane." See Ben Fox, "Hunger Strike Widens at Guantanamo," Associated Press, May 30, 2006, and Andrew Selsky, "More Detainees Join Hunger Strike at Guantanamo," Associated Press, June 2, 2006.

    In an earlier chapter, I noted the role of hunger strikes by political prisoners in Ireland and elsewhere to draw a parallel with the tactic used by our Prisoner Clay-416. One of the most celebrated of the Irish hunger strikers, who died for the cause, was Bobby Sands. It is remarkable that the organizer of the hunger strikes at Gitmo, Binyam Mohammed al-Habashi, has proclaimed that he and the other hunger strikers will either have their requests respected or die like Bobby Sands, who "had the courage of his convictions and starved himself to death. Nobody should believe for one moment that my brothers here have less courage." See Kate McCabe, "Political Prisoners' Resistance from Ireland to GITMO: 'No Less Courage,' " www.CounterPunch.com, May 5, 2006.

34. "GITMO Suicides Comment Condemned. U.S. Officials' "Publicity Stunt" Remark Draws International Backlash," Associated Press, June 12, 2006. The government official was Colleen Graffy, deputy assistant, U.S. Secretary of State for Public Diplomacy. The naval officer was Henry Harris.

35. Janis Karpinski, interview on "A Question of Torture," PBS *Frontline*, October 18, 2005. Also reported in "Iraq Abuse 'Ordered from the Top,' " BBC, June 15, 2004, available at http://news.bbc.co.uk/1/hi/world/americas/3806713.stm. When Miller arrived at Abu Ghraib, he said, "It's my opinion that you're treating the prisoners too well. At Guantánamo, the prisoners know that we are in charge, and they know that from the very beginning." He said, "You have to treat the prisoners like dogs, and if you think or feel differently, you've lost control." Available at www.truthout.org/docs_2006/012406Z.shtml.

36. Scott Wilson and Sewell Chan, "As Insurgency Grew, So Did Prison Abuse," *The Washington Post*, May 9, 2004. Also see Janis Karpinski, *One Woman's Army* (New York: Hyperion, 2005), pp. 196–205.

37. Jeffrey R. Smith, "General Is Said to Have Urged Use of Dogs," *The Washington Post*, May 26, 2004.

38. General Kern in "A Question of Torture," PBS *Frontline*, October 18, 2005.

39. Major General Geoffrey Miller retired from the military on July 31, 2006. He elected to retire without seeking a promotion or his third star because his legacy has been tarnished by allegations of his direct role in torture and abuse in Abu Ghraib and Gitmo prisons, according to military and congressional sources.

40. General Myers's statement about his continuing to blame only the MP "bad apples" for all the Abu Ghraib abuses, while ignoring or dismissing all the evidence from the many independent investigations that reveal extensive complicity by senior officers and many systemic failures indicates either his rigid perseverance or ignorance. Available at www.pbs.org/wgbh/pages/frontline/torture/etc/script.html.

41. More than 100,000 pages of government documents have been released detailing the abuses and torture of detainees, which can be searched via the ACLU's search engine for public access to these documents at: www.aclu.org/torturefoiasearch. The story about the April 2004 Army Information Paper is available at www.rawstory.com/news/2006/New_Army_documents_reveal_US_knew_0502.html.

42. Eric Schmitt, "Outmoded Interrogation Tactics Cited," *The New York Times*, June, 17, 2006, p. A11.

43. The *Toledo Blade* newspaper in Ohio and its reporters won a Pulitzer Prize for the investigation of atrocities committed by the "Tiger Force" in Vietnam, which, over a seven-month period, left a trail of civilian murders and mayhem that have been concealed by the military for three decades. This commando unit of the 101st Airborne Division was one of the most highly decorated units in Vietnam. The Army investigated allegations of their war crimes, mutilations, torture, murder, and indiscriminate attacks on civilians and found probable cause to indict eighteen soldiers but did not file any charges against them. See "Buried Secrets, Brutal Truths,' " www.toledoblade.com. Experts agree that an earlier probe of the Tiger Force rampage could have averted the My Lai carnage six months later.

44. An American reporter, Nir Rosen, who has been living in Iraq for three years and speaks Arabic, even its Iraqi dialect, reports that "The occupation has become one vast extended crime against the Iraqi people, and most of it has occurred unnoticed by the American people and the media"; see Nir Rosen, "The Occupation of Iraqi Hearts and Minds," June 27, 2006, available at http://truthdig.com/dig/item/20060627_occupation_iraq_hearts_minds/. See also the related commentary by the reporter Haifer Zangana, "All Iraq is Abu Ghraib. Our Streets Are Prison Corridors and Our Homes Cells as the Occupiers Go About Their Strategic Humiliation and Intimidation," *The Guardian*, July 5, 2006.

45. Anna Badkhen, "Atrocities Are a Fact of All Wars, Even Ours: It's Not Just Evil Empires Whose Soldiers Go Amok," *San Francisco Chronicle*, August 13, 2006, pp. E1, E6. Quote by John Pike, director of GlobalSecurity.org, on p. E1.

46. Dave Grossman, *On Killing: The Psychological Cost of Learning to Kill in War and Society* (Boston: Little, Brown, 1995). Grossman's website is www.killology.com.

47. Vicki Haddock, "The Science of Creating Killers: Human Reluctance to Take a Life Can Be Reversed Through Training in the Method Known as Killology," *San Francisco Chronicle*, August 13, 2006, pp. E1, E6. Quote by former Army private Steven Green, p. E1.

48. David S. Cloud, "Marines May Have Excised Evidence on 24 Iraqi Deaths," *The New York Times*, August 18, 2006; Richard A. Oppel, Jr., "Iraqi Leader Lambasts U.S. Military: He Says There Are Daily Attacks on Civilians by Troops," *The New York Times*, June 2, 2006.

49. D. S. Cloud and E. Schmitt, "Role of Commanders Probed in Death of Civilians," *The New York Times*, June 3, 2006; L. Kaplow, "Iraqi's Video Launched Massacre Investigation," Cox News Service, June 4, 2006.

50. MSNBC.COM, "Peers Vowed to Kill Him if He Talked, Soldier Says," Associated Press report, August 2, 2006, available at www.msnbc.com/id/14150285.

51. T. Whitmore, "Ex-Soldier Charged with Rape of Iraqi Woman, Killing of Family," June 3, 2006, available at http://news.findlaw.com/ap/0/51/07–04–2006/d493003212d3/a9c.html; Julie Rawe and Aparisim Ghosh, "A Soldier's Shame," *Time*, July 17, 2006, pp. 38–39.

52. "Blair Promises Iraq 'Abuse' Probe," BBC News, February 12, 2006; the story and the video images of this abuse are available at http://news.bbc.co.uk/1/hi/UK/4705482.STM.

53. Roger Brokaw and Anthony Lagouranis, on "A Question of Torture," PBS *Frontline*, October 18, 2005, available at www.pbs.org/wgbh/pages/frontline/torture/interviews.html.

54. "To take the gloves off" is generally taken to mean to fight an opponent with one's bare knuckles, removing the protection of the softer prizefighting gloves that are usually worn in such fights. Colloquially, it means to fight hard and tough, without constraints of the usual rules governing such combat between adversaries.

55. T. R. Reid, "Military Court Hears Abu Ghraib Testimony: Witness in Graner Case Says Higher-ups Condoned Abuse," *The Washington Post*, January 11, 2005, page A03. "Frederick, a staff sergeant who was demoted to private after pleading guilty to abuse at Abu Ghraib, said he had consulted with six senior officers, ranging from captains to lieutenant colonels, about the guards' actions but was never told to stop. Frederick also said that a CIA official, whom he identified as 'Agent Romero,' told him to 'soften up' one suspected insurgent for questioning. The agent told him he did not care what the soldiers did, 'just don't kill him,' Frederick testified." Available at www.washingtonpost.com/wp-dyn/articles/A62597-2005Jan10.html.

56. A. Zagorin, and M. Duffy, "*Time* Exclusive: Inside the Wire at Gitmo," *Time*, available at www.time.com/time/magazine/article/0,9171,1071284,00.html.

57. Quoted in Jane Mayer, "The Memo," *The New Yorker*, February 27, 2006, p. 35.

58. Details of the interviews with Captain Fishback and the two sergeants are posted on Human Rights Watch's report "Leadership Failure: Firsthand Accounts of Torture of Iraqi Detainees by the Army's 82nd Airborne Division," September 2005, vol. 17, no. 3(G), available at hrw.org/reports/2005/us0905/1.htm. Fishback's full letter to Senator McCain was published in *The Washington Post* on September 18, 2005; available at www.washingtonpost.com/wpdyn/content/article/2005/09/27/AR2005092701527.html.

59. Erik Saar and Viveca Novak, *Inside the Wire: A Military Intelligence Soldier's Eyewitness Account of Life at Guantanamo* (New York: Penguin Press, 2005).

60. Eric Saar, radio interview with Amy Goodman, "Democracy Now," Pacifica Radio, May 4, 2005, available at www.democracynow.org/article.pl?sid=05/05/04/1342253/.

61. Maureen Dowd, "Torture Chicks Gone Wild," *The New York Times*, January 30, 2005.

62. These quotes by Saar and Interrogator "Brooke" are in *Inside the Wire*, pp. 220–228.

63. See a fascinating story, A. C. Thompson and Trevor Paglen, "The CIA's Torture Taxi," San Francisco *Bay Guardian*, December 14, 2005, pp. 15 and 18. This investigation revealed a Boeing jet, no. N313P, owned by a private company, that had unprecedented clearance to land at any Army base in the world; its use was traced to the kidnapping of a German citizen of Lebanese descent, Khaled El-Masri. It is alleged to be one of twenty-six planes in the CIA fleet used for such renditions, according to one ACLU human rights expert, Steven Watt.

64. See Human Rights Watch, "The Road to Abu Ghraib," June 2004, available at www.hrw.org/reports/2004/usa0604/. See also John Barry, Michael Hirsh, and Michael Isikoff, "The Roots of Torture," *Newsweek*, May 24, 2004, available at http://msnbc.msn.com/id/4989422/site/newsweek/: "According to knowledgeable sources, the president's directive authorized the CIA to set up a series of secret detention facilities outside the United States, and to question those held in them with unprecedented harshness."

65. *Frontline*, "The Torture Question," transcript, p. 5.

66. Ibid.

67. Jan Silva, "Europe Prison Inquiry Seeks Data on 31 Flights: Romania, Poland Focus of Investigation into Alleged CIA Jails," Associated Press, Nov. 23, 2005.

68. "21 Inmates Held Are Killed, ACLU Says," Associated Press, October 24, 2005; full report by ACLU, "Operative Killed Detainees During Interrogations in Afghanistan and Iraq," October 24, 2005, available at www.aclu.org/news/NewsPrint.cfm?ID=19298&c=36.

69. See M. Huggins, M. Haritos-Fatouros, and P. G. Zimbardo, *Violence Workers: Police Torturers and Murderers Reconstruct Brazilian Atrocities* (Berkeley: University of California Press, 2002).

70. White House, President Bush Outlines Iraqi Threat: Remarks by the President on Iraq (October 7, 2002). Available at www.whitehouse.gov/news/releases/2002/10/20021007=8.html.

71. "Iraq on the Record: The Bush Administration's Public Statements on Iraq," prepared by the House of Representatives Committee on Government Reform—Minority Staff's Special Investigations Division, March 16, 2004, available at www.reform.house.gov/min/.

72. Ron Suskind, *"The One Percent Doctrine: Deep Inside America's Pursuit of Its Enemies Since 9/11"* (New York: Simon & Schuster, 2006), p. 10.

73. Adam Gopnik, "Read It and Weep," *The New Yorker,* August 28, 2006, pp. 21–22.

74. Philip Zimbardo with Bruce Kluger. "Phantom Menace: Is Washington Terrorizing Us More than Al Qaeda?" *Psychology Today,* 2003, 34–36; Rose McDermott and Philip Zimbardo elaborate on this theme in the chapter "The Politics of Fear: The Psychology of Terror Alerts," in *Psychology and Terrorism,* eds. B. Bonger, L. M. Brown, L. Beutler, J. Breckenridge, and Philip Zimbardo (New York: Oxford University Press, 2006), pp. 357–70.

75. *The Washington Post,* October 26, 2005, p. A18.

76. Letter to Senator John McCain by thirteen retired military commanders and ambassador Douglas Peterson, July 23, 2005. (Ultimately signed by twenty-eight retired military commanders.) Available at www.humanrightsfirst.org/us_law/etn/pdf/mccain-100305.pdf. McCain's comments about it on the Senate floor available at http://mccain.senate.gov/index.cfm?fuseaction=Newscenter.ViewPressRelease&Content_id=1611>&Content_id=1611.

77. John McCain, "The Truth About Torture," *Newsweek,* November 21, 2005, p. 35.

78. Cheney's remarks about the "dark side," made on *Meet the Press with Tim Russert,* September 16, 2001, at Camp David, Maryland, can be found in full at www.whitehouse.gov/vicepresident/news-speeches/speeches/vp20010916.html.

79. Quoted in Maureen Dowd, "System on Trial," *The New York Times,* November 7, 2005.

80. James Risen, *State of War: The Secret History of the C.I.A. and the Bush Administration* (New York: Free Press, 2006).

81. Anthony Lewis, "Making Torture Legal," *The Washington Post,* June 17, 2004, available at www.washingtonpost.com/wp-srv/nation/documents/dojinterrogationmemo20020801.pdf. The DOD memo of March 6, 2003, advising Rumsfeld on interrogation tactics is also online at www.news.findlaw.com/wp/docs/toture/30603wgrpt/.

82. K. J. Greenberg. and J. L. Dratel, eds., *The Torture Papers: The Road to Abu Ghraib* (New York: Cambridge University Press, 2005). Some of this material is available at www.Thinking Piece.com/pages/books.html.

83. Quote by Anthony Lewis, in Introduction to *The Torture Papers,* p. xiii. It should also be mentioned that a small coterie of Justice Department lawyers, all appointed by the Bush administration, rebelled against the legal rationales being proposed to give the president virtually unlimited powers for spying on citizens and torturing suspected enemies. *Newsweek* reporters revealed this "Palace Revolt" (February 2006) as "a quietly dramatic profile in courage." Some of them have paid a high price for defending the principle of a nation of laws and not men—being ostracized, denied promotions, and encouraged to leave the service.

84. Joshua Dratel, "The Legal Narrative," in *The Torture Papers*, p. xxi.

85. B. Minutaglio, *The President's Counselor: The Rise to Power of Alberto Gonzales* (New York: HarperCollins, 2006).

86. R. J. Gonzalez, Review of Minutaglio's *The President's Counselor, San Francisco Chronicle*, July 2, 2006, pp. M1 and M2.

87. Online: "Gitmo Interrogations Spark Battle Over Tactics: The Inside Story of Criminal Investigators Who Tried to Stop the Abuse," MSNBC.COM, October 23, 2006. www.msnbc.com/msn.com/id/15361458.

88. "FBI Fed Thousands of Spy Tips. Report: Eavesdropping by NSA Flooded FBI, Led to Dead Ends," *The New York Times*, January 17, 2006.

89. Eric Lichtblau and James Risen, "Spy Agency Mined Vast Data Trove, Officials Report." *The New York Times*, December 23, 2005. Also Adam Liptak and Eric Lichtblau, "Judge Finds Wiretap Actions Violate the Law," *The New York Times*, August 18, 2006.

90. Bob Herbert, "The Nixon Syndrome," *The New York Times*, January 9, 2006.

91. C. Savage, "Bush Challenges Hundreds of Laws." *The Boston Globe*, April 30, 2006.

92. L. Greenhouse, "Justices, 5–3, Broadly Reject Bush Plan to Try Detainees," *The New York Times*, June 30, 2006. A Navy lawyer who represented an assigned client detainee at Gitmo, was denied promotion by the Bush administration for taking his duty seriously and honestly. Lt. Cmdr. Charles Swift did not get his Yemeni citizen client to plead guilty before a military tribunal, as he had been urged to do. Rather, he concluded that such commissions were unconstitutional, and provided support for the Supreme Court's decision to reject them in *Hamdan v. Rumseld*. Denial of his promotion spelled the end of his twenty-year distinguished military career. According to a *New York Times* editorial, "With his defense of Mr. Hamdan and his testimony before Congress starting in July 2003, Commander Swift did as much as any single individual to expose the awful wrongs of Guantánamo Bay and Mr. Bush's lawless military commissions." "The Cost of Doing Your Duty," *New York Times*, October 11, 2006, p. A26.

93. Guy B. Adams and Danny L. Balfour, *Unmasking Administrative Evil* (New York: M. E. Sharpe, 2004). Similarly important background reading to understand the extent of the disaster visited on Iraq by the Bush administration's flawed policies and the Pentagon's denial of battlefield realities is found in Thomas Ricks, *Fiasco: The American Military Adventure in Iraq* (New York: Penguin Books, 2006).

94. The original story of this stealth attempt to gut the War Crimes Act was written by R. Jeffrey Smith, "War Crimes Act Changes Would Reduce Threat of Prosecution," *The Washington Post*, August 9, 2006, p. A1. It is more fully reported and developed by Jeremy Brecher and Brendan Smith in "Bush Aims to Kill War Crimes Act," *The Nation* online, September 5, 2006. Available at www.thenation.com/doc2006918brecher.

95. Lieutenant Colonel Jordan, who supervised the interrogation task force at Abu Ghraib, was charged with seven offenses and found guilty of criminal abuse by Army investigators—several years after those abuses came to light. He is reported to have dealt with the abuses by building a plywood wall so that he could not see them in action (according to a report on Salon.com, April 29, 2006). Jordan was charged with seven offenses from the articles of the Uniform Code of Military Justice on April 26, 2006, but no decision has been reached as of September 6, 2006. Available at cbsnews.com/stories/2006/04/26/iraq/main 1547777.shtml. Colonel Pappas was granted immunity from prosecution in a plea bargain to testify into Jordan's alleged offenses. Major General Geoffrey Miller invoked his constitutional right against self-incrimination when called to testify in related cases involving the use of dogs to threaten detainees. Story in Richard A. Serrano and Mark Mazzetti, "Abu Ghraib Officer Could Face Charges: Criminal Action Would Be First in Army's Higher Ranks," *Los Angeles Times*, January 13, 2006.

96. In January 2006, a tribunal was held in New York City by The International Commission of Inquiry on Crimes Against Humanity Committed by the Bush Administration of the

United States. Among other charges this tribunal leveled at the Bush administration were the following six counts that are in accordance with the command complicity charges I have brought against Rumsfeld, Tenet, Cheney, and Bush.

Torture. Count 1: The Bush administration authorized the use of torture and abuse in violation of international humanitarian and human rights law and domestic constitutional and statutory law.

Rendition. Count 2: The Bush administration authorized the transfer ("rendition") of persons held in U.S. custody to foreign countries where torture is known to be practiced.

Illegal Dentention. Count 3: The Bush administration authorized the indefinite detention of persons seized in foreign combat zones and in other countries far from any combat zone and denied them the protections of the Geneva Conventions on the treatment of prisoners of war and the protections of the U.S. Constitution; Count 4: The Bush administration authorized the roundup and detention in the United States of tens of thousands of immigrants on pretextual grounds and held them without charge or trial in violation of international human rights law and domestic constitutional and civil rights law; Count 5: The Bush administration used military forces to seize and detain indefinitely without charges U.S. citizens, denying them the right to challenge their detention in U.S. courts.

Murder. Count 6: The Bush administration committed murder by authorizing the CIA to kill those that the president designates, either U.S. citizens or noncitizens, anywhere in the world.

For more information about this tribunal and its conclusions, see www.bush commissionindictments_files/bushcommissionindictments.htm. Three videos of the testimonies from the Bush Crimes Commission are available for viewing, see details at: www.BushCommission.org.

97. Personal communication in interview with Colonel Larry James, Honolulu, April 25, 2005. James has reviewed and approved the accuracy of this section.

98. The horrors of Abu Ghraib are not over for Iraqis still detained there since the Americans have abandoned it—they are worse. A recent report indicates that their new captors, Iraqi guards and Iraqi authorities, are torturing them, nearly starving them on diets of rice and water, forcing them to live in filth, oppressive heat, and crammed into small cells almost twenty-four hours a day. On September 6, 2006, the first mass executions since the days of Saddam Hussein were carried out against twenty-seven men imprisoned in that hellhole. Some prisoners report wishing that the Americans were back in charge. Story available online at www.theage.com.au/articles/2006/09/10/1157826813724.html.

99. Reported in Vanora McWalters, "Britain's Top Legal Adviser: Close Guantanamo, Symbol of Injustice," *Los Angeles Times*, May 11, 2006.

100. E. Sciolino, "Spanish Magistrate Calls on U.S. to Close Prison at Guantanamo," *The New York Times*, June 4, 2006.

CHAPTER SIXTEEN: Resisting Situational Influences and Celebrating Heroism

1. These and related data are found in an important resource book published by the American Association of Retired People (AARP), based on extensive research by the social psychologist Anthony Pratkanis of hundreds of audiotapes recorded of con men and swindlers pitching their wares to potential victims. See his important book filled with specific advice about how to detect hoaxes and not be taken in by them: Anthony Pratkanis and Doug Shadel, *Weapons of Fraud: A Source Book for Fraud Fighters* (Seattle: AARP Press, 2005).

2. Andrew Wolfson, "A Hoax Most Cruel," *The Courier-Journal*, October 9, 2005.

3. Quote by former assistant manager Donna Summers in "The Human Behavior Experiments," Jigsaw productions, Sundance TV, June 1, 2006.

4. *Zorba the Greek* is Niko Kazantzakis's classic novel, written in 1952. Alexis Zorba was

portrayed by Anthony Quinn in the 1964 movie of the same name, directed by Michael Ca-coyannis, and co-starring Alan Bates as the shy, intellectual boss who is the foil to Zorba's boundless extroversion and devotion to living life with unbridled passion.

5. B. J. Sagarin, R. B. Cialdini, W. E. Rice, and S. B. Serna, "Dispelling the Illusion of Invulner-ability: The Motivations and Mechanisms of Resistance to Persuasion," *Journal of Personality and Social Psychology* 83 (2002): 526–41.

6. The MKULTRA program, secretly sponsored by the CIA in the 1950s and '60s, is well presented in John D. Marks, *The Search for the Manchurian Candidate: The CIA and Mind Control* (New York: Times Books, 1979). A more detailed scholarly presentation is found in Alan W. Scheflin and Edward Opton, Jr., *The Mind Manipulators* (New York: Grosset and Dunlap, 1978). See Alex Constantine's *Virtual Government: CIA Mind Control Operations in America* (Los Angeles: Feral House, 1997) for a fuller exposition of many other CIA-sponsored programs, such as Operation Mockingbird, designed to influence the American press and program public opinion.

7. A sample of my work in these diverse domains of social influence can be found in these publications: R. P. Abelson and P. G. Zimbardo, *Canvassing for Peace: A Manual for Volunteers* (Ann Arbor, MI: Society for the Psychological Study of Social Issues, 1970); P. G. Zimbardo, "Coercion and Compliance: The Psychology of Police Confessions," in *The Triple Revolution Emerging*, eds. R. Perruci and M. Pilisuk, (Boston: Little, Brown, 1971), pp. 492–508; P. G. Zimbardo, E. B. Ebbesen, and C. Maslach, *Influencing Attitudes and Changing Behavior*, 2nd ed. (Reading, MA: Addison-Wesley, 1977); P. G. Zimbardo and C. E. Hartley, "Cults Go to High School: A Theoretical and Empirical Analysis of the Initial Stage in the Recruitment Process," *Cultic Studies Journal* 2 (Spring–Summer 1985): 91–147; P. G. Zimbardo and S. A. Andersen, "Understanding Mind Control: Exotic and Mundane Mental Manipulations," *Recovery from Cults*, ed. M. Langone (New York: Norton Press, 1993), pp. 104–25; P. G. Zimbardo and M. Leippe, *The Psychology of Attitude Change and Social Influence* (New York: McGraw-Hill, 1991).

8. To learn more about basic social influence principles, see R. B. Cialdini, *Influence*, 4th ed. (Boston: Allyn & Bacon, 2001); A. R. Pratkanis, "Social Influence Analysis: An Index of Tactics," in *The Science of Social Influence: Advances and Future Progress*, ed. A. R. Pratkanis (Philadelphia: Psychology Press, 2007, in press); A. R. Pratkanis and E. Aronson, *Age of Propaganda: The Everyday Use and Abuse of Persuasion* (New York: W. H. Freeman, 2001); Robert Levine, *The Power to Persuade: How We're Bought and Sold* (New York: Wiley, 2003); Daryl Bem, *Beliefs, Attitudes, and Human Affairs* (Belmont, CA: Brooks/Cole, 1970); Richard Petty and John Cacioppo, *Communication and Persuasion: Central and Peripheral Routes to Attitude Change* (New York: Springer-Verlag, 1986); Steven Hassan, *Combatting Cult Mind Control* (Rochester, VT: Park Street Press, 1988); Brad Sagarin and Sarah Wood, "Resistance to Influence" in *The Science of Social Influence: Advances and Future Progress*, ed. A. R. Pratkanis (Philadelphia: Psychology Press, in press, 2007).

9. J. M. Burger, "The Foot-in-the-Door Compliance Procedure: A Multiple-Process Analysis and Review," *Personality and Social Psychology Review* 3 (1999): 303–25.

10. J. Freedman and S. Fraser, "Compliance Without Pressure: The Foot-in-the-Door Technique," *Journal of Personality and Social Psychology* 4 (1966): 195–202.

11. For some references to prosocial applications of the foot-in-the-door tactic, see J. Schwarzwald, A. Bizman, and M. Raz, "The Foot-in-the-Door Paradigm: Effects of Second Request Size on Donation Probability and Donor Generosity," *Personality and Social Psychology Bulletin* 9 (1983): 443–50; B. J. Carducci and P. S. Deuser, "The Foot-in-the-Door Technique: Initial Request and Organ Donation," *Basic and Applied Social Psychology* 5 (1984): 75–81; B. J. Carducci, P. S. Deuser, A. Bauer, M. Large, and M. Ramaekers, "An Application of the Foot in the Door Technique to Organ Donation," *Journal of Business and Psychology* 4 (1989): 245–49; R. D. Katzev and T. R. Johnson, "Comparing the Effects of Monetary Incentives and Foot-in-the-Door Strategies in Promoting Residential Electricity

Conservation," *Journal of Applied Social Psychology* 14 (1984): 12–27; T. H. Wang and R. D. Katsev, "Group Commitment and Resource Conservation: Two Field Experiments on Promoting Recycling," *Journal of Applied Social Psychology* 20 (1990): 265–75; R. Katzev and T. Wang, "Can Commitment Change Behavior? A Case Study of Environmental Actions," *Journal of Social Behavior and Personality* 9 (1994): 13–26.

12. M. Goldman, C. R. Creason, and C. G. McCall, "Compliance Employing a Two-Feet-in-the-Door Procedure," *Journal of Social Psychology* 114 (1981): 259–65.

13. For references on the prosocial effects of positive models, see J. H. Bryan and M. A. Test, "Models and Helping: Naturalistic Studies in Aiding Behavior," *Journal of Personality and Social Psychology* 6 (1967): 400–7; C. A. Kallgren, R. R. Reno, and R. B. Cialdini, "A Focus Theory of Normative Conduct: When Norms Do and Do Not Affect Behavior," *Personality and Social Psychology Bulletin* 26 (2000): 1002–12; R. A. Baron and C. R. Kepner, "Model's Behavior and Attraction Toward the Model as Determinants of Adult Aggressive Behavior," *Journal of Personality and Social Psychology* 14 (1970): 335–44; M. E. Rice and J. E. Grusec, "Saying and Doing: Effects on Observer Performance," *Journal of Personality and Social Psychology* 32 (1975): 584–93.

14. J. H. Bryan, J. Redfield, and S. Mader, "Words and Deeds About Altruism and the Subsequent Reinforcement Power of the Model," *Child Development* 42 (1971): 1501–8; J. H. Bryan and N. H. Walbek, "Preaching and Practicing Generosity: Children's Actions and Reactions," *Child Development* 41 (1970): 329–53.

15. For references on social identity labeling, also known as "altercasting," see R. E. Kraut, "Effects of Social Labeling on Giving to Charity," *Journal of Experimental Social Psychology* 9 (1973): 551–62; A. Strenta and W. DeJong, "The Effect of a Prosocial Label on Helping Behavior," *Social Psychology Quarterly* 44 (1981): 142–47; J. A. Piliavin and P. L. Callero, *Giving Blood* (Baltimore: Johns Hopkins University Press, 1991).

16. Robert S. McNamara et al., *Argument Without End: In Search of Answers to the Vietnam Tragedy* (New York: Perseus Books, 1999); R. S. McNamara and B. Van deMark, *In Retrospect: The Tragic Lessons of Vietnam* (New York: Vantage, 1996). Also see the DVD of Errol Morris's film *The Fog of War: Eleven Lessons from the Life of Robert S. McNamara*, 2004.

17. When a blaze broke out in 1979 in a Woolworth store in the British city of Manchester, most people escaped, but ten died in the fire when they could have readily fled to safety. The fire chief reported that they had died because they were following a "restaurant script" rather than a survival script. They had finished dinner and were waiting to pay their bill; one does not leave a restaurant until one's bill is paid. No one wanted to stand out from the others; no one wanted to be different. So they waited, and they all died.

This event is described in one of the vignettes in a British television production in which I was involved, called "The Human Zoo." It is available from Insight Media, New York.

18. E. J. Langer, *Mindfulness* (Reading, MA: Addison-Wesley, 1989).

19. D. F. Halpern, *Thought and Knowledge: An Introduction to Critical Thinking*, 4th ed. (Mahwah, NJ: Erlbaum, 2003).

20. C. Poche, P. Yoder, and R. Miltenberger, "Teaching Self-Protection to Children Using Television Techniques," *Journal of Applied Behavior Analysis*, vol. 21 (1988): pp. 253–61.

21. D. Kahneman and A. Tversky, "Prospect Theory: An Analysis of Decision Under Risk," *Econometrica* 47 (1979): 262–91. A. Tversky and D. Kahneman, "Loss Aversion in Riskless Choice: A Reference-Dependent Model," *Quarterly Journal of Economics* 106 (1991): 1039–61.

22. G. Lakoff, *Don't Think of an Elephant: Know Your Values and Frame the Debate* (White River Junction, VT: Chelsea Green, 2004). G. Lakoff and M. Johnson, *Metaphors We Live By*, 2nd ed. (Chicago: University of Chicago Press, 2003).

23. P. G. Zimbardo and J. N. Boyd, "Putting Time in Perspective: A Valid, Reliable Individual Differences Metric," *Journal of Personality and Social Psychology* 77 (1999): 1271–88.

24. Andre Stein, *Quiet Heroes: True Stories of the Rescue of Jews by Christians in Nazi-Occupied Holland* (New York: New York University Press, 1991).

25. This passage is from pp. 216–20 of Christina Maslach's reflections on the meaning of the Stanford Prison Experiment in the chapter written jointly with Craig Haney and me: P. G. Zimbardo, C. Maslach, and C. Haney, "Reflections on the Stanford Prison Experiment: Genesis, Transformations, Consequences," in *Obedience to Authority: Current Perspectives on the Milgram Paradigm*, ed. T. Blass (Mahwah, NJ: Erlbaum, 2000).

26. The alternative meanings of suicide terrorism can be found in a new book by the psychologist Fathali Moghaddam, *From the Terrorists' Point of View: What They Experience and Why They Come to Destroy Us* (New York: Praeger, 2006).

27. For full details, see Michael Wood's fascinating account of his attempt to follow the journey that Alexander took in his conquests: *In the Footsteps of Alexander The Great: A Journey from Greece to Asia* (Berkeley: University of California Press, 1997). There is also a remarkable BBC documentary of Wood's journey, produced by Maya Vision (1997).

28. Many of the ideas presented in this section were developed in collaboration with Zeno Franco and offered in greater detail in our co-authored article "Celebrating Heroism: a Conceptual Exploration," 2006 (submitted for publication). I am also engaged in new research that tries to understand the decision matrix at the time an individual resists social pressures to obey authority. My first study, in collaboration with Piero Bocchario, was recently completed at the University of Palermo, Sicily. "Inquiry into Heroic Acts: The Decision to Resist Obeying Authority." In preparation.

29. M. Seligman, T. Steen, N. Park, and C. Peterson, "Positive Psychology Progress," *American Psychologist* 60 (2005): 410–21. Also see D. Strumpfer, "Standing on the Shoulders of Giants: Notes on Early Positive Psychology (Psychofortology)," *South African Journal of Psychology* 35 (2005): 21–45.

30. *ARTFL Project: 1913 Webster's Revised Unabridged Dictionary*, http://humanities.uchicago.edu/orgs/ARTFL/forms_unrest/webster.form.html.

31. Adapted from definition footnotes pp. 334 and 689.

32. A. Eagly and S. Becker, "Comparing the Heroism of Women and Men," *American Psychologist* 60 (2005): 343–44.

33. Lucy Hughes-Hallett, *Heroes* (London: HarperCollins, 2004).

34. Ibid., p. 17. We should also remember that after Achilles has died and is a shade, he tells Odysseus that he would rather be the live servant of a peasant than a dead hero. Homer does not define heroism as battle skill and daring, but more socially as the establishment and maintenance of bonds of fidelity and mutual service among men. A swineherd can be as heroic as Achilles (and is so in Homer's *Odyssey*, where one protects Odysseus) if he upholds the rules of courtesy and mutual respect. "If ever my father, Odysseus, has served you by work done or promise kept, help me," Telemachus says as he visits the surviving heroes of the Trojan War in search of his father. Homer's take on heroism is thus far different from that of Hughes-Hallet.

35. Ibid., pp. 5–6. This is Aristotle's definition of a "tragic" hero. Macbeth is a hero in this sense, evil though he is and is known to be. The tragic hero must fall because he thinks he "is the law," as is seen in the character of Creon in *Antigone*.

36. "Medal of Honor Citations," available at www.army.mil/cmh-pg/moh1.htm.

37. U.S. Code, Subtitle B—Army, Part II—Personnel, Chapter 357—Decorations and Awards.

38. "Victoria Cross," available at http://en.wikipedia.org/wiki/Victoria_cross.

39. M. Hebblethwaite and T. Hissey, "George Cross Database," available at www.gc-database.co.uk/index.htm.

40. Governor-General, "Australian Bravery Decorations," available at www.itsanhonour.gov.au/honours_announcments.html.

41. S. Becker and A. Eagly, "The Heroism of Women and Men," *American Psychologist* 59 (2004): 163–78; quote, p. 164.

42. Peter Martens, "Definitions and Omissions of Heroism," *American Psychologist* 60 (2005): 342–43.

43. J. McCain and M. Salter, *Why Courage Matters* (New York: Random House, 2004), 14.

44. D. J. Boorstin, *The Image: A Guide to Pseudo-Events in America.* New York: Vantage Books, 1992 [1961], pp. 45, 76.

45. D. Denenberg and L. Roscoe, *50 American Heroes Every Kid Should Meet* (Brookfield, CT: Millbrook Press, 2001).

46. Pseudoheroism at its worst comes from the example of the shameless exploitation by the U.S. military of the American soldier Private Jessica Lynch. By exaggeration and false-hoods, Lynch was converted from an ordinary wounded, unconscious, captured young sol-dier into a Medal of Honor hero who had allegedly fought off her brutal captors singlehandedly. A totally fabricated scenario was constructed because the Army needed a hero at a time when there was little good news to send home from the war in Iraq. A BBC documentary exposed the many lies and deceptions that were involved in creating this fraudulent heroine. Nevertheless, Private Lynch's story was just too good not to be told by an NBC docudrama, headlined in major magazines, and retold in her book, which earned a million-dollar advance. See "Saving Pvt. Jessica Lynch," BBC America documentary, July 18, 2003; Rick Bragg, *I Am a Soldier, Too: The Jessica Lynch Story* (New York: Vintage, 2003).

47. A. Brink, "Leaders and Revolutionaries: Nelson Mandela," available at www.time.com/time/time100/leaders/profile/mandela.html.

48. D. Soccio, *Archetypes of Wisdom*, 2nd ed. (Belmont, CA: Wadsworth, 1995).

49. W. F. Cascio and R. Kellerman, *Leadership Lessons from Robben Island: A Manifesto for the Moral High Ground* (manuscript submitted for publication).

50. G. A. Kimble, M. Wertheimer, and C. L. White, *Portraits of Pioneers in Psychology* (Washing-ton, DC: American Psychological Association, 1991).

51. V. Navasky, "I. F. Stone," available at www.thenation.com/doc/20030721/navasky.

52. I had the good fortune to spend several days with Václav Havel on the occasion of my being awarded the Havel Foundation Vision 97 Award for my research and writings in October 2005. I recommend his collection of letters sent to his wife, Olga, from prison, and the po-litical background provided in their introduction by Paul Wilson: Václav Havel, *Letters to Olga: June 1979–September 1982* (New York: Knopf, 1988).

53. D. Soccio, *Archetypes of Wisdom* (Belmont, CA: Wadsworth, 1995).

54. S. Hersh, *My Lai 4: A Report on the Massacre and Its Aftermath* (New York: Random House, 1970). One of the most thorough accounts of the My Lai massacre, including personnel involved, photographs, and the events that led up to the trial of Lieutenant William Calley, Jr., is provided by Doug Linder in his "Introduction to the My Lai Courts-Martial," available online at www.law.umkc.edu/faculty/projects/ftirals/mylai/MY1_intro.htm/.

    The photographs of the My Lai massacre of dead women, children, babies, and el-derly Vietnamese were taken by the Army photographer assigned to Charlie Company, Ronald Haeberle, using his private camera, on March 16, 1968. He recorded no such atrocities on his second official Army camera. His photos exposed the military cover-up al-leging that those killed were insurgents rather than innocent, unarmed civilians murdered in cold blood. However, unlike Abu Ghraib, none of his photos included U.S. soldiers posing during acts of atrocity.

55. T. Angers, *The Forgotten Hero of My Lai: The Hugh Thompson Story* (Lafayette, LA: Acadian House Publishing, 1999).

56. The lyrics of the ode to Lieutenant Calley ran "Sir, I followed all my orders and did the best I could. / It's hard to judge the enemy and hard to tell the good. / Yet there's not a man among us who would not have understood."

57. Ron Ridenhour, letter of March 29, 1969, reproduced in David L. Anderson, ed., *Facing My Lai: Moving Beyond the Massacre* (Lawrence: University of Kansas Press; quote, pp. 201–6.

58. M. Bilton and K. Sim, *Four Hours in My Lai* (New York: Penguin, 1993).

59. Joe Darby spoke out publicly for the first time since exposing the Abu Ghraib atrocities in an interview with Wil S. Hylton in *GQ* magazine, September 2006, entitled "Prisoner of Conscience." (Darby quotes are from this source.) Available online at http://men.style.com/gq/features/landing?id=content_4785/.

60. K. Zernike, "Only a Few Spoke Up on Abuse as Many Soldiers Stayed Silent," *The New York Times*, May 22, 2004, p. 1.

61. E. Williamson, "One Soldier's Unlikely Act: Family Fears for Man Who Reported Iraqi Prisoner Abuse," *The Washington Post*, May 6, 2004, p. A16.

62. Colonel Larry James, personal communication, April 24, 2005.

63. H. Rosin, "When Joseph Comes Marching Home: In a Western Mountain Town Ambivalence About the Son Who Blew the Whistle at Abu Ghraib," *The Washington Post*, May 17, 2004, p. C01.

64. S. Pulliam and D. Solomon, "How Three Unlikely Sleuths Exposed Fraud at WorldCom," *The Wall Street Journal*, October 30, 2002, p. 1.

65. M. Swartz and S. Watkins, *Power Failure: The Inside Story of the Collapse of Enron* (New York: Random House, 2003).

66. R. Lacayo and A. Ripley, "Persons of the Year 2002: Cynthia Cooper, Colleen Rowley and Sherron Watkins," *Time*.

67. Jim Jones's final speech, November 1978, available at http://jonestown.sdsu.edu/AboutJonestown/Tapes/Tapes/DeathTape/death.html.

68. D. Layton, *Seductive Poison: A Jonestown Survivor's Story of Life and Death in the People's Temple* (New York: Doubleday, 2003). Also see her website, www.deborahlayton.com.

69. My ideas relating the mind control tactics of Jim Jones and those in Orwell's *1984*, along with a dose of the CIA's mind control program, MKULTRA, can be found in my chapter P. G. Zimbardo, "Mind Control in Orwell's *1984*: Fictional Concepts Become Operational Realities in Jim Jones' Jungle Experiment," in *1984: Orwell and Our Future*, eds. M. Nussbaum, J. Goldsmith, and A. Gleason (Princeton, NJ: Princeton University Press, 2005). A detailed account of Jonestown as a CIA supported experiment is given in the thesis of Michael Meires, *Was Jonestown a CIA Medical Experiment? A Review of the Evidence* (Lewiston, NY: E. Mellen Press, 1968). (Studies in American Religion Series, vol. 35).

70. See the story I co-wrote with the reporter Dan Sullivan about Richard Clark and Diane Louie: D. Sullivan and P. G. Zimbardo, "Jonestown Survivors Tell Their Story," *Los Angeles Times*, March 9, 1979, part 4, pp. 1, 10–12.

71. M. Grunwald, "A Tower of Courage," *The Washington Post*, October 28, 2001, p. 1.

72. United Airlines flight 93 was headed to San Francisco from New Jersey on the morning of September 11, 2001, when Saudi terrorists hijacked it. Evidence from the 9/11 Commission indicates that the pilot, flight attendants, and at least seven passengers fought back against the four hijackers. Their actions diverted the plane from its likely target of the Capitol building or the White House. All forty-four people aboard died when the plane nosedived into an empty field outside Shanksville, Pennsylvania. Its high-speed crash (nearly 600 mph) caused a crater 115 feet (35 meters) deep. A dramatic movie, *United Flight 93*, was made by Universal Studios in 2006.

73. Brink, "Leaders and Revolutionaries."

74. H. Arendt, *Eichmann in Jerusalem: A Report on the Banality of Evil* (rev. and enlarged edition) (New York: Penguin, 1994 [1963]) pp. 25–26.

75. Ibid., p. 276.

76. Ibid., p. 252.

77. C. R. Browning, *Ordinary Men: Reserve Police Battalion 101 and the Final Solution in Poland* (New York: HarperPerennial, 1992), p. xix.

78. E. Staub, *The Roots of Evil: The Origins of Genocide and Other Group Violence* (New York: Cambridge University Press, 1989), p. 126.

79. Z. Bauman, *Modernity and the Holocaust* (Ithaca, NY: Cornell University Press, 1989).

80. J. Conroy, *Unspeakable Acts, Ordinary People: The Dynamics of Torture* (New York: Knopf, 2000).

81. M. Haritos-Fatouros, *The Psychological Origins of Institutionalized Torture* (London: Routledge, 2003).

82. M. Huggins, M. Haritos-Fatouros, and P. G. Zimbardo, *Violence Workers: Police Torturers and Murderers Reconstruct Brazilian Atrocities* (Berkeley: University of California Press, 2002).

83. This conception of the banality of heroism was first presented in an essay by Zimbardo on *Edge* Annual Question 2006, an annual event sponsored by John Brockman inviting a range of scholars to reply to a provocative question, which that year was "What is your dangerous idea?" See www.edge.org.

84. See Francois Rochat and Andre Modigliani, "Captain Paul Grueninger: The Chief of Police Who Saved Jewish Refugees by Refusing to Do His Duty," in *Obedience to Authority: Current Perspectives on the Milgram Paradigm*, ed. T. Blass (Mahwah, NJ: Erlbaum, 2000).

85. Stanley Milgram, *Obedience to Authority: An Experimental View* (New York: Harper & Row, 1974). Also see Philip Zimbardo, Craig Haney, William Curtis Banks, and David Jaffe, "The Mind Is a Formidable Jailer: A Pirandellian Prison," *The New York Times Magazine*, April 8, 1973, pp. 36 ff.

86. Research on the personality correlates that differentiate "obedients" from "defiants" points to only a few significant predictors. Those who are high scorers on a measure of authoritarian personality (F-Scale) were more likely to obey authority, while defiants had lower F-scores. See A. C. Elms and S. Milgram, "Personality Characteristics Associated with Obedience and Defiance Toward Authoritative Command," *Journal of Experimental Research in Personality* 1 (1966): 282–89.

    A second variable that may influence the tendency to obey or disobey is one's belief in external controlling influences on one's life versus internal control, with greater obedience among those who accept the notion of their behavior as being controlled by external forces. In a similar vein, among Christian research participants, obedience was greatest among those who believed in divine control of their lives while those who were low on measures of belief in external divine control tended to reject scientific as well as religious authority. See Tom Blass, "Understanding Behavior in the Milgram Obedience Experiment: The Role of Personality, Situations, and Their Interactions," *Journal of Personality and Social Psychology* 60 (1991): 398–413.

87. E. Midlarsky, S. F. Jones, and R. Corley, "Personality Correlates of Heroic Rescue During the Holocaust," *Journal of Personality* 73 (2005): 907–34.

88. Malcolm Gladwell, "Personality Plus: Employers Love Personality Tests. But What Do They Really Reveal?" *The New Yorker* (September 20, 2004): 42. Available online at www.gladwell.com/2004/2004_09_20_a_personality.html.

89. Carol S. DePino, "Heroism Is a Matter of Degree," *El Dorado Times*, available at www.eldoradotimes.com/articles/2006/01/17/news/news6.txt.

90. Boorstin, (THE IMAGE, 1992), quote, p. 76.

91. Aleksandr I. Solzhenistyn, *The Gulag Archipelago, 1918–1956* (New York: Harper & Row, 1973).

Index

About the Type

This book was set in Photina, a typeface designed by José Mendoza in 1971. It is a very elegant design with high legibility, and its close character fit has made it a popular choice for use in quality magazines and art gallery publications.

Also available from Rider

Beyond Terror

The Truth About the Real Threats to Our World

Chris Abbott, Paul Rogers & John Sloboda

Is international terrorism really the single greatest
threat to world security?

Since the 9/11 attacks, many Western governments assume terrorism to
be the greatest threat we face. In response, their dangerous policies
attempt to maintain control and keep the status quo by using
overwhelming military force. This important book shows why this
approach has been such a failure, and how it distracts us from other,
much greater threats of climate change, competition over resources,
marginalisation of the majority of the world and global militarisation.

Unless urgent, coordinated action is taken in the next 5-10 years on all
these issues it will be almost impossible to avoid the earth becoming a
highly unstable place by the middle years of this century. *Beyond Terror*
offers an alternative path for politicians, journalists and concerned
citizens alike.

Buy Rider Books

Order further Rider titles from your local bookshop, or have them delivered direct to your door by Bookpost.

Also by Rider:

☐ **Beyond Terror**	9781846040702	£4.99
☐ **Making Terrorism History**	9781846040474	£3.99
☐ **Iran Awakening**	9781846040146	£7.99

Free postage and packing
Overseas customers allow £2 per paperback

Phone: 01624 677237

Post: Random House Books
C/o Bookpost
PO Box 29
Douglas, Isle of Man
IM99 1BQ

By fax: 01624 670923

By email: bookshop@enterprise.net

Cheques (payable to Bookpost) and credit cards accepted

Prices and availability subject to change without notice.
Allow 28 days for delivery.
When placing your order, please state if you do not wish to receive any
additional information.

www.rbooks.co.uk